Essentials of Economics

A Companion Website accompanies
Essentials of Economics 3rd edition
by John Sloman

Visit the *Essentials of Economics* Companion Website at
www.booksites.net/sloman to find valuable teaching and learning material including:

For students:

■ Study material designed to help you improve your results
■ Learning objectives for each chapter
■ Multiple choice questions to help test your learning
■ Up-to-date case studies with questions for self study
■ Topical economic issues relating to material directly in the book
■ Economics news articles which features on topical stories, with analysis and links to
  the book
■ Hotlinks to over 200 relevant sites on the web

For lecturers:

■ A secure, password-protected site with teaching material
■ Complete, downloadable Instructor's Manual
■ PowerPoint slides that can be downloaded and used as OHTs comprising:
  – Figures and tables from the book
  – Key models as full-colour animated slide shows
■ Teaching and learning case studies discussing various aspects of economic principles
■ Customisable lecture plans with integrated animated diagrams
■ Workshops to accompany each chapter of the book
■ Answers to workshops and question material

Also: This regularly maintained and updated site has a syllabus manager, search
functions, and email results functions.

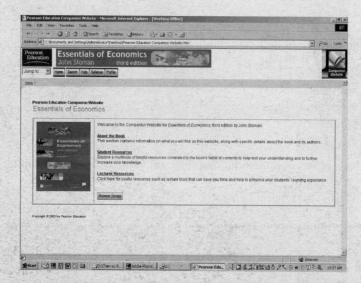

Essentials of Economics

John Sloman

third edition

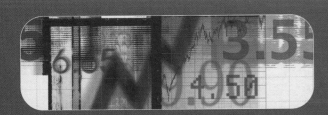

FT Prentice Hall

FINANCIAL TIMES

An imprint of **Pearson Education**

Harlow, England • London • New York • Boston • San Francisco • Toronto
Sydney • Tokyo • Singapore • Hong Kong • Seoul • Taipei • New Delhi
Cape Town • Madrid • Mexico City • Amsterdam • Munich • Paris • Milan

Pearson Education Limited
Edinburgh Gate
Harlow
Essex CM20 2JE
England

and Associated Companies throughout the world

Visit us on the World Wide Web at:
http://www.pearsoned.co.uk

First published 1998
Second edition 2001
Third edition 2004

© John Sloman 1998
© Pearson Education 2001, 2004

ISBN 0-273-68382-9

British Library Cataloguing-in-Publication Data
A catalogue record for this book is available from the British Library

10 9 8 7 6 5 4 3 2
09 08 07 06 05 04

Typeset by 35 in 9/12.5pt Stone Serif
Printed and bound by Mateu Cromo Artes Graficas, Madrid, Spain

The publisher's policy is to use paper manufactured from sustainable forests.

Contents

Detailed contents

Preface

To the student

Welcome to this introduction to economics. Whether you are planning to study economics beyond this level, or whether this will be your only exposure to this fascinating subject, I hope that you will find the book enjoyable and that it will give you some insight into the economy in which you live and the economic forces that shape all our lives.

Although you have probably never studied the subject before, you will almost certainly know quite a lot of economics already. After all, you make economic decisions virtually every day of your life. Every time you go shopping, you are acting as an 'economist': deciding what to buy with your limited amount of money. And it is not just with decisions about buying that we act as economists. How much to work (something that students are increasingly forced to do nowadays), how much to study, even how much time to devote to various activities during the course of the day, are all, in a way, *economic* choices.

To satisfy us as consumers, goods and services have to be produced. We will therefore study the behaviour of firms and what governs the decisions that they make. How will the decisions of big businesses differ from those of small firms? How will the degree of competition affect the extent to which we gain or lose from the activities of firms?

We will also look at some of the big economic issues that face us all as members of society in the twenty-first century. Despite huge advances in technology, and despite the comfortable lives led by many people in the industrialised world, we still suffer from unemployment, poverty and inequality, and in many countries (the UK included) the gap between rich and poor has grown wider; our environment is polluted; our economy still goes through periodic recessions; our growing affluence as consumers is increasingly bought at the expense of longer hours at work and growing levels of stress. So what can be done about these problems? This book seeks not only to analyse these problems but also to examine the sorts of policies that governments pursue in their attempt to address them.

The book is designed with one overriding aim: to make this exciting and highly relevant subject as clear to understand as possible. To this end, the book has a number of important features:

- A direct and straightforward written style; short paragraphs to aid rapid comprehension. The aim all the time is to provide maximum clarity.
- Key ideas highlighted and explained where they first appear (a new feature for this edition). These ideas are key elements in the economist's 'toolkit'. Whenever they recur later in the book, an icon appears in the margin and you are referred back to the page where they are defined and explained. All the key ideas are gathered together at the beginning of the Glossary.
- Clear chapter-opening pages, which set the scene for the chapter and provide a 'chapter map', giving page references of all the sections within the chapter.
- Summaries at the end of each section (rather than each chapter). This provides a very useful means of revising and checking your understanding.
- Definitions of all technical terms placed in the margin close to the position in the text where the term is used. The term itself is highlighted in the text.
- 'Pause for thought' questions integrated in the text (new for this edition). These are designed to help you reflect on what you have just read and to check on your understanding. Answers to all 'pause for thought' questions are given on the book's website.
- A comprehensive Index, including reference to all defined terms. This enables you to look up a definition as required and to see it used in context.
- An alphabetical Glossary at the end of the book. This gathers together all the defined terms.
- Plentiful use of up-to-date examples to illustrate the arguments. This helps to bring the subject alive and puts it in context.
- A careful use of colour to guide you through the text and make the structure easy to follow.
- Review questions at the end of each chapter for either individual or class use.
- Answers given at the end of the book to all odd-numbered questions. These questions will be helpful for self-testing, while the even-numbered ones can be used for class testing.
- Many boxes (typically four per chapter) providing case studies, news items, applications, or elaborations of the text. The boxes are of two types: Case Studies and Applications; and Exploring Economics.
- A comprehensive set of Web references at the end of each chapter (new for this edition). Each reference is numbered to match those in the Web Appendix at the end of the book. You can easily access any of these sites from this book's own website (at http://www.booksites.net/sloman). When you enter the site, click on **Hot Links**. You will find all the sites from the Web Appendix listed. Click on the one you want and the 'hot link' will take you straight to it.

Good luck with your studies, and have fun. Perhaps this will be just the beginning for you of a lifelong interest in economic issues and the economy.

To tutors

This third edition of *Essentials of Economics* is an abridged version of my *Economics* (fifth edition). Some passages have been directly transcribed, while others have been extensively rewritten in order to provide a consistent coverage of the 'essentials' of economics.

The book is designed specifically for one-semester courses in introductory economics. There are 12 chapters (6 micro, 4 macro and 2 international), each providing about a week's worth of reading. The book is also ideal for year-long courses that are designed for those not going on to specialise in economics, or where economics is only a subsidiary component at level 2.

Naturally, in a one-semester course, or in courses for non-specialists, tutors cannot hope to cover all the principles of economics. Thus some things have had to go. The book does not cover indifference curves or isoquants. The analysis of costs is developed with only an informal reference to production functions. Distribution theory is confined to the determination of wage rates. In macroeconomics, ISLM analysis has been left out, as have some of the more advanced debates in monetary and exchange rate theory. In addition, many passages have been simplified to reflect the nature of courses on which the book is likely to be used. The result is a book that is approximately half the length of *Economics* (fifth edition).

The book is also ideal for the new economics A-level syllabuses of the various boards and for courses, such as HND, where the economic environment component is part of a larger module.

While the coverage of this edition is similar to that of the second edition, the text has been thoroughly revised to take account of new events and new developments in the subject. Several passages have been extensively rewritten. For example, there is now more material on game theory. There are new sections on the environment (6.8) and on economic growth (10.7) and many new examples.

In addition to the new and revised material, the book now contains 'key ideas' and these are highlighted and explained when they first appear. There are 30 of these ideas, which are fundamental to the study of economics. Students can see them recurring throughout the book, and an icon appears in the margin to refer back to the page where the idea first appears. Showing how these ideas can be used in a variety of contexts helps students to 'think like an economist' and to relate the different parts of the subject to each other.

Another new feature is 'pause for thought'. These are questions integrated into the text, which are designed to make student learning more active and reflective. Students can access answers to all these questions on the website.

I hope that your students will find this an exciting and interesting text that is relevant to today's issues.

Supplements

Website

Visit the book's website at

http://www.booksites.net/sloman

This has an extensive range of materials for students and tutors.

For students

- Study materials designed to help you improve your results.
- Hot links to over 200 useful websites, listed in the Appendix at the back of this book, with relevant ones referred to at the end of each chapter.

- Economics News Articles, updated monthly: some 15 to 20 news items per month, with links to one or more newspaper articles per item. There are questions on each item and references to the relevant chapter(s) of the book.
- Several additional case studies per chapter, referred to at the end of each chapter.
- Self-test questions, organised chapter by chapter.
- Topical economic issues: these are written especially for the website and link to key concepts and pages in the book.
- Answers to all 'pause for thought' and box questions, to allow you to check your understanding as you progress.

For tutors

- All figures and tables from the book in PowerPoint®, animated and in full colour.
- Customisable full-colour lecture plans in PowerPoint with integrated animated diagrams.
- Key models as full-colour animated PowerPoint slide shows.
- Twelve workshops in Word.
- Teaching/learning case studies.
- Answers to even-numbered questions, questions in boxes and to all 12 workshops in a secure password-protected area of the site.

CD–ROM (new edition)

The tutor's CD has been thoroughly revised to take account of the changes in the third edition. It also contains various new features. It is available free of charge from Pearson Education to tutors using the book as a course text. It contains the following:

- Workshops in Word (one per chapter). These can be reproduced for use with large groups (up to 200 students). In A-level classes, they can be used as worksheets, either for use in class or for homework. Suggestions for use are given on the CD. Answers to all workshops are given in separate Word files.
- PowerPoint slide shows in full colour for use with a data projector in lectures and classes. These can also be made available to students by loading them on to a local network or virtual learning environment such as Blackboard® or WebCT®. All PowerPoint files are small enough to copy to a $3^1/_2$" disk (for portability) and are available in animated form in two versions: light text and lines on a dark background, and dark text and lines on a light background. They are also available in non-animated form for printing with dark text and lines on a clear background. The CD contains several types of these slide shows:
  - All figures from the book and most of the tables. Each figure is built up in a logical sequence, thereby allowing tutors to show them in lectures in an animated form.
  - A range of models. These show how the key models used in the book are developed. There are 26 of these models and each one builds up in around 20 to 50 screens.
  - Lecture plans. These are a series of bullet-point lecture plans. There is one for each chapter of the book. Each one can be easily edited, with points added,

deleted or moved, so as to suit particular lectures. A consistent use of colour is made to show how the points tie together. The lecture plans are also available in Word.

– Lecture plans with integrated diagrams. These lecture plans include animated diagrams and charts at the appropriate points.

■ Multiple-choice, short answer and true/false questions. This very large test bank is completely redesigned and contains many new questions.

■ Case studies. These are in Word and are also available in the Student section of the book's website. They can be reproduced and used for classroom exercises or for student assignments.

WinEcon: Sloman – Essentials of Economics version

The award-winning and widely used *WinEcon* software, produced and authored by the Economics Consortium of the Teaching and Learning Technology Programme (TLTP), is designed to support courses in introductory economics.

It is now available on CD in a version specially designed for *Essentials of Economics*. There is a separate chapter and section in this version of *WinEcon* to correspond with the relevant chapter and section in the book. The software is highly interactive and is attractive to use.

Acknowledgements

As with the second edition, my task of writing has been made much easier by the support I have had from many people. First and foremost, a massive thanks to my family and especially to my wife Alison, who has never complained about my long hours at the computer and has provided just the right balance of encouragement, humour and support.

Thanks to the team at Pearson Education, and especially to Catherine Yates, Stuart Hay and Karen Mclaren for all the work they have put in. Thanks too to the many users of the book who have given me feedback. I always value their comments. Finally, as always I owe a great debt to Mark Sutcliffe, my collaborator and co-author on other books. At times, it's great to talk and have a laugh.

Guided tour

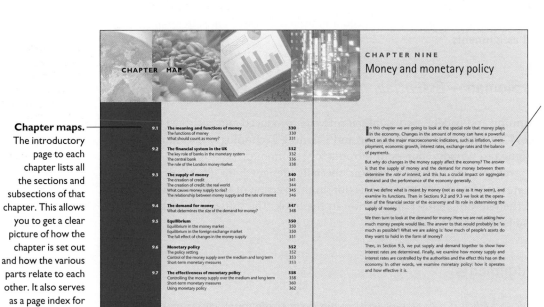

Chapter maps. The introductory page to each chapter lists all the sections and subsections of that chapter. This allows you to get a clear picture of how the chapter is set out and how the various parts relate to each other. It also serves as a page index for the chapter.

Chapter introductions. These give an overview of the topics to be covered in each chapter, and relate them to issues you are likely to hear about in the news or experience directly.

Key ideas. These are highlighted and explained where they first appear. They are key elements in the economist's toolkit and whenever they recur later in the book, an icon appears in the margin. These help students to 'think like an economist'.

Definitions. All key terms are highlighted in the text where they first appear and are defined in the margin. This is very useful for revision and allows you to see the terms used in context.

Boxes. There are two types of box: Case Studies and Applications; and Exploring Economics. They provide case studies, new items, applications, or elaborations of the text.

Pause for thought questions. These help you reflect on what you have just read and to check on your understanding.

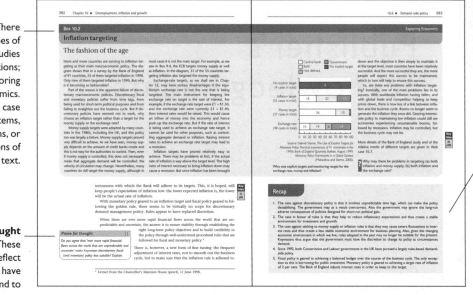

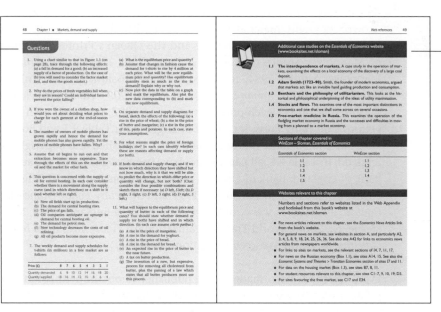

Recap sections. Summaries at the end of each section allow you to check up on your understanding at frequent intervals and provide an important revision tool.

Questions. These can be used for self-testing, or for class exercises or debate.

Web material. A comprehensive set of Web references at the end of each chapter provide additional case studies and Hot Links.

Publisher's acknowledgements

We are grateful to the following for permission to reproduce copyright material:

Organisation of the Petroleum Exporting Countries for Box 4.4 figure from *OPEC Annual Statistical Bulletin 2003*; National Statistics for Figures 5.1 and 5.2 from *Labour Market Trends*, Figures 5.9 and 5.10 from *Family Spending*, Figures 5.11 and 5.12 and Box 5.3 table from *New Earnings Survey*, Inland Revenue for Box 5.5, Figure 7.3 from Pocket Databank, Appendix 7.1 figures and tables from *UK National Income and Expenditure*, Table 8.1 from Series RURQ and YBHA, Box 10.3 figure from *Budget 2003, Economic and Fiscal Strategy Report*, Figure 10.6 from *Economic Trends Annual Supplement*, Table 12.1 from *UK Economic Accounts*, www.statistics.gov.uk Crown copyright material is reproduced with the permission of the Controller of Her Majesty's Stationery Office and the Queen's Printer for Scotland; Institute of Manpower Studies for Box 5.2 figure from *The Flexible Firm*, © Institute of Manpower Studies 1984, reprinted with permission; Oxford University Press for Box 7.4 table from *Human Development Report 2002 – Human Development Indicators*, © United Nations Development Programme 2002, reprinted with permission from Oxford University Press, Inc.; Bank of England for Table 9.1 and Box 9.2 tables from *Monetary and Financial Statistics (Bankstats)*, published and copyright of the Bank of England. In Table 9.1, all percentages have been calculated by the author and not the Bank of England; Bank of England and the authors for Box 10.2 figure from *Bank of England Quarterly Bulletin* August 1999 and *Monetary Policy Frameworks in a Global Context*, available at www.routledge.com (Bank of England, 1999; Mahadeva L. and Sterne, G., 2000); World Trade Organization for Figure 11.2 from *International Trade Statistics*, © World Trade Organization.

Every effort has been made by the publisher to obtain permission from the appropriate source to reproduce material which appears in this book. In some instances we have been unable to trace the owners of copyright material, and we would appreciate any information that would enable us to do so.

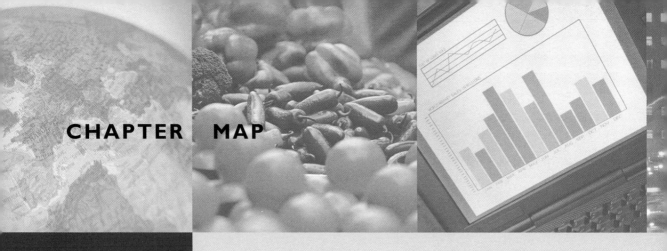

CHAPTER MAP

INTRODUCTION
Economic issues

Y ou may never have studied economics before, and yet when you open a newspaper what do you read? – a report from 'our economics correspondent'. Turn on the television news and what do you see? – an item on the state of the economy. Talk to friends and often the topic will turn to the price of this or that product, or whether you have got enough money to afford to do this or that.

The fact is that economics affects our daily lives. Continually we are being made aware of local, national and international economic issues: whether it be price increases, interest rate changes, fluctuations in exchange rates, unemployment, economic recessions or balance of payments problems.

We are also continually faced with economic problems and decisions of our own. What should I buy in the supermarket? Should I save up for a summer holiday, or spend more on day-to-day living? Should I go to university, or should I try to find a job now?

So just what is economics about? In this introduction we will attempt to answer this question and to give you some insights into the subject you will be studying by using this book.

We will also see how the subject is divided up, and in particular we will distinguish between the two major branches of economics: microeconomics and macroeconomics.

I.1 The economic problem

What is economics all about?

Production
The transformation of inputs into outputs by firms in order to earn profit (or meet some other objective).

Consumption
The act of using goods and services to satisfy wants. This will normally involve purchasing the goods and services.

Factors of production (or resources)
The inputs into the production of goods and services: labour, land and raw materials, and capital.

Labour
All forms of human input, both physical and mental, into current production.

Land (and raw materials)
Inputs into production that are provided by nature: e.g. unimproved land and mineral deposits in the ground.

Capital
All inputs into production that have themselves been produced: e.g. factories, machines and tools.

Many people think that economics is about *money*. Well, to some extent this is true. Economics has a lot to do with money: with how much money people are paid; how much they spend; what it costs to buy various items; how much money firms earn; how much money there is in total in the economy. But despite the large number of areas in which our lives are concerned with money, economics is more than just the study of money.

It is concerned with the following:

■ The production of goods and services: how much the economy produces; what particular combination of goods and services; how much each firm produces; what techniques of production it uses; how many people it employs.

■ The consumption of goods and services: how much the population as a whole spends (and how much it saves); what the pattern of consumption is in the economy; how much people buy of particular items; what particular individuals choose to buy; how people's consumption is affected by prices, advertising, fashion and other factors.

But we still have not quite got to the bottom of what economics is about. What is the crucial ingredient that makes a problem an *economic* one? The answer is that there is one central problem faced by all individuals and all societies. From this one problem stem all the other economic problems we shall be looking at throughout this book.

This central economic problem is the problem of *scarcity*. This applies not only in Ethiopia and the Sudan, but also in the UK, the USA, Japan, France and all other countries of the world. For an economist, scarcity has a very specific definition. Let us examine that definition.

The problem of scarcity

Ask people if they would like more money, and the vast majority would answer 'yes'. They want more money so that they can buy more goods and services; and this applies not only to poor people but also to most wealthy people too. The point is that human wants are virtually unlimited.

Yet the means of fulfilling human wants are limited. At any one time the world can produce only a limited amount of goods and services. This is because the world has only a limited amount of resources. These resources, or factors of production as they are often called, are of three broad types:

■ Human resources: labour. The labour force is limited both in number and in skills.

■ Natural resources: land and raw materials. The world's land area is limited, as are its raw materials.

■ Manufactured resources: capital. Capital consists of all those inputs that have themselves been produced in the first place. The world has a limited stock of capital: a limited supply of factories, machines, transportation and other equipment. The productivity of capital is limited by the state of technology.

So here is the reason for scarcity: human wants are virtually unlimited, whereas the resources available to satisfy these wants are limited. We can thus define scarcity as follows:

> **Scarcity** is the excess of human wants over what can actually be produced. Because of scarcity, various choices have to be made between alternatives.
>
> **Key Idea 1**

Definition

Scarcity
The excess of human wants over what can actually be produced to fulfil these wants.

Of course, we do not all face the problem of scarcity to the same degree. A poor person unable to afford enough to eat or a decent place to live will hardly see it as a 'problem' that a rich person cannot afford a second Ferrari. But economists do not claim that we all face an *equal* problem of scarcity. In fact this is one of the major issues economists study: how resources and products are *distributed*, whether between different individuals, different regions of a country or different countries of the world.

> *Pause for thought*
>
> If we would all like more money, why doesn't the government simply print a lot more?

But given that people, both rich and poor, want more than they can have, this makes them behave in certain ways. Economics studies that behaviour. It studies people at work, producing the goods that people want. It studies people as consumers buying the goods they themselves want. It studies governments influencing the level and pattern of production and consumption. In short, it studies anything to do with the process of satisfying human wants.

Demand and supply

We said that economics is concerned with consumption and production. Another way of looking at this is in terms of *demand* and *supply*. In fact, demand and supply and the relationship between them lie at the very centre of economics. But what do we mean by the terms, and what is their relationship with the problem of scarcity?

Demand is related to wants. If goods and services were free, people would simply demand whatever they wanted. Such wants are virtually boundless: perhaps limited only by people's imagination. *Supply*, on the other hand, is limited. It is related to resources. The amount firms can supply depends on the resources and technology available.

Given the problem of scarcity, given that human wants exceed what can actually be produced, *potential* demands will exceed *potential* supplies. Society therefore has to find some way of dealing with this problem. Somehow it has to try to match demand and supply. This applies at the level of the economy overall: *aggregate* demand will need to be balanced against *aggregate* supply. In other words, total spending in the economy must balance total production. It also applies at the level of individual goods and services. The demand and supply of cabbages must balance, and so must the demand and supply of DVD recorders, cars, houses and bus journeys.

But if potential demand exceeds potential supply, how are *actual* demand and supply to be made equal? Either demand has to be curtailed, or supply has to be increased, or a combination of the two. Economics studies this process. It studies how demand adjusts to available supplies, and how supply adjusts to consumer demands.

I.2 Dividing up the subject

What's meant by 'macroeconomics' and 'microeconomics'?

Economics is traditionally divided into two main branches – *macroeconomics* and *microeconomics*, where 'macro' means big, and 'micro' means small.

Macroeconomics is concerned with the economy as a whole. It is thus concerned with aggregate demand and aggregate supply. By 'aggregate demand' we mean the total amount of spending in the economy, whether by consumers, by customers outside the country for our exports, by the government, or by firms when they buy capital equipment or stock up on raw materials. By 'aggregate supply' we mean the total national output of goods and services.

Microeconomics is concerned with the individual parts of the economy. It is concerned with the demand and supply of *particular* goods and services and resources: cars, butter, clothes and haircuts; electricians, secretaries, blast furnaces, computers and oil.

Macroeconomics

Because things are scarce, societies are concerned that their resources should be used as *fully as possible*, and that over time their national output should *grow*.

The achievement of growth and the full use of resources is not easy, however, as demonstrated by the periods of high unemployment and stagnation that have occurred from time to time throughout the world (for example, in the 1930s, the early 1980s, the early 1990s and the early 2000s). Furthermore, attempts by government to stimulate growth and employment have often resulted in inflation and a large rise in imports. Even when societies do achieve growth, it can be short lived. Economies have often experienced cycles, where periods of growth alternate with periods of stagnation, such periods varying from a few months to a few years.

Macroeconomics, then, studies the determination of national output and its growth over time. It also studies the problems of recession, unemployment, inflation, the balance of international payments and cyclical instability, and the policies adopted by governments to deal with these problems.

Macroeconomic problems are closely related to the balance between aggregate demand and aggregate supply.

If aggregate demand is *too high* relative to aggregate supply, inflation and balance of trade deficits are likely to result.

▪ Inflation refers to a general rise in the level of prices throughout the economy. If aggregate demand rises substantially, firms are likely to respond by raising their prices. After all, if demand is high they can probably still sell as much as before (if not more) even at the higher prices, and thus make more profits. If firms in general put up their prices, inflation results.

Definitions

Macroeconomics
The branch of economics that studies economic aggregates (grand totals): e.g. the overall level of prices, output and employment in the economy.

Aggregate demand
The total level of spending in the economy.

Aggregate supply
The total amount of output in the economy.

Microeconomics
The branch of economics that studies individual units: e.g. households, firms and industries. It studies the interrelationships between these units in determining the pattern of production and distribution of goods and services.

Rate of inflation
The percentage increase in the level of prices over a 12-month period.

■ Balance of trade deficits are the excess of imports over exports. If aggregate demand rises, people are likely to buy more imports. In other words, part of the extra expenditure will go on Japanese DVD players, German cars, French wine, and so on. Also if inflation is high, home-produced goods will become uncompetitive with foreign goods. We are likely, therefore, to buy more foreign imports, and people abroad are likely to buy fewer of our exports.

If aggregate demand is *too low* relative to aggregate supply, unemployment and recession may well result.

■ Recession occurs when output in the economy declines: in other words, growth becomes negative. A recession is associated with a low level of consumer spending. If people spend less, shops are likely to find themselves with unsold stocks. As a result they will buy less from the manufacturers, which in turn will cut down on production.

■ Unemployment is likely to result from cutbacks in production. If firms are producing less, they will need to employ fewer people.

Macroeconomic *policy*, therefore, tends to focus on the balance of aggregate demand and aggregate supply. It can be demand-side policy, which seeks to influence the level of spending in the economy. This in turn will affect the level of production, prices and employment. Or it can be supply-side policy. This is designed to influence the level of production directly: for example, by trying to create more incentives for workers or businesspeople.

Microeconomics

Microeconomics and choice

Because resources are scarce, choices have to be made. There are three main categories of choice that must be made in any society.

■ *What* goods and services are going to be produced and in what quantities, given that there are not enough resources to produce all the things people desire? How many cars, how much wheat, how much insurance, how many rock concerts, etc. will be produced?

■ *How* are things going to be produced, given that there is normally more than one way of producing things? What resources are going to be used and in what quantities? What techniques of production are going to be adopted? Will cars be produced by robots or by assembly-line workers? Will electricity be produced from coal, oil, gas, nuclear fission, renewable resources or a mixture of these?

■ *For whom* are things going to be produced? In other words, how will the nation's income be distributed? After all, the higher your income, the more you can consume of the nation's output. What will be the wages of farm workers, printers, cleaners and accountants? How much will pensioners receive? How much of the nation's income will go to shareholders or landowners?

All societies have to make these choices, whether they be made by individuals, by groups or by the government. These choices can be seen as *micro*economic choices, since they are concerned not with the *total* amount of national output, but

<aside>
Definitions

Balance of trade
Exports of goods and services minus imports of goods and services. If exports exceed imports, there is a 'balance of trade surplus' (a positive figure). If imports exceed exports, there is a 'balance of trade deficit' (a negative figure).

Recession
A period where national output falls for two quarters or more.

Unemployment
The number of people who are actively looking for work but are currently without a job. (Note that there is much debate as to who should officially be counted as unemployed.)

Demand–side policy
Government policy designed to alter the level of aggregate demand, and thereby the level of output, employment and prices.

Supply–side policy
Government policy that attempts to alter the level of aggregate supply directly.
</aside>

with the *individual* goods and services that make it up: what they are, how they are made, and who gets the incomes to buy them.

Choice and opportunity cost

Choice involves sacrifice. The more food you choose to buy, the less money you will have to spend on other goods. The more food a nation produces, the less resources there will be for producing other goods. In other words, the production or consumption of one thing involves the sacrifice of alternatives. This sacrifice of alternatives in the production (or consumption) of a good is known as its opportunity cost.

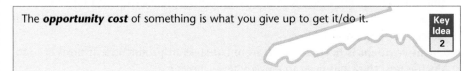

The **opportunity cost** of something is what you give up to get it/do it.

Key Idea 2

If the workers on a farm can produce either 1000 tonnes of wheat or 2000 tonnes of barley, then the opportunity cost of producing 1 tonne of wheat is the 2 tonnes of barley forgone. The opportunity cost of buying a textbook is the new pair of jeans you also wanted that you have had to go without. The opportunity cost of working overtime is the leisure you have sacrificed.

Rational choices

Economists often refer to rational choices. This simply means the weighing-up of the *costs* and *benefits* of any activity, whether it be firms choosing what and how much to produce, workers choosing whether to take a particular job or to work extra hours, or consumers choosing what to buy.

Imagine you are doing your shopping in a supermarket and you want to buy a bottle of wine. Do you spend a lot of money and buy a top-quality French wine, or do you buy a cheap eastern European one instead? To make a rational (i.e. sensible) decision, you will need to weigh up the costs and benefits of each alternative. The top-quality wine may give you a lot of enjoyment, but it has a high opportunity cost: because it is expensive, you will need to sacrifice quite a lot of consumption of other goods if you decide to buy it. If you buy the cheap bottle, however, although you will not enjoy it so much, you will have more money left over to buy other things: it has a lower opportunity cost.

Thus rational decision making, as far as consumers are concerned, involves choosing those items that give you the best value for money: i.e. the *greatest benefit relative to cost*.

The same principles apply to firms when deciding what to produce. For example, should a car manufacturer open up another production line? A rational decision will again involve weighing up the benefits and costs. The benefits are the revenues that the firm will earn from selling the extra cars. The costs will include the extra labour costs, raw material costs, costs of component parts, etc. It will be profitable to open up the new production line only if the revenues earned exceed the costs entailed: in other words, if it adds to profit.

Box I.1 Case Studies and Applications

The opportunity costs of studying economics

What are you sacrificing?

Key
Idea
2
p8

You may not have realised it, but you probably consider opportunity costs many times a day. The reason is that we are constantly making choices: what to buy, what to eat, what to wear, whether to go out, how much to study and so on. Each time we make such a choice, we are in effect rejecting some alternative. This alternative forgone is the opportunity cost of the action we chose.

Sometimes the opportunity costs of our actions are the direct monetary costs we incur. Sometimes it is more complicated.

Take the opportunity costs of your choices as a student of economics.

Buying a textbook costing £32.95

This does involve a direct money payment. What you have to consider is the alternatives you could have bought with the £32.95. You then have to weigh up the benefit from the best alternative against the benefit of the textbook.

1. What might prevent you from making the best decision?

Coming to classes

You may or may not be paying your own course fees. Even if you are, there is no extra (marginal) monetary cost in coming to classes once the fees have been paid. You will not get a refund by skipping classes!

So are the opportunity costs zero? No: by coming to classes you are *not* working in the library; you are *not* having an extra hour in bed; you are *not* sitting drinking coffee with friends, and so on. If you are making a rational decision to come to classes, then you will consider such possible alternatives.

2. If there are several other things you could have done, is the opportunity cost the sum of all of them?

Revising for an economics exam

Again, the opportunity cost is the best alternative to which you could have put your time. This might be revising for some *other* exam. You will probably want to divide your time sensibly between your subjects. A *sensible* decision is not to revise economics on any given occasion if you will gain a greater benefit from revising another subject. In such a case the (marginal) opportunity cost of revising economics exceeds the (marginal) benefit.

Choosing to study at university or college

What are the opportunity costs of being a student in higher education? At first it might seem that the costs would include the following:

- Tuition fees.
- Books, stationery, etc.
- Accommodation expenses.
- Transport.
- Food, entertainment and other living expenses.

But adding these up does *not* give the *opportunity* cost. The opportunity cost is the *sacrifice* entailed by going to university or college *rather* than doing something else. Let us assume that the alternative is to take a job that has been offered. The correct list of opportunity costs of higher education would include:

- Tuition fees paid by you (as opposed to your parents or anyone else).
- Books, stationery, etc.
- *Additional* accommodation and transport expenses over what would have been incurred by taking the job.
- Wages that would have been earned in the job *less* any student allowance or grant received.

3. Why is the cost of food not included?
4. Make a list of the benefits of higher education.
5. Is the opportunity cost to the individual of attending higher education different from the opportunity costs to society as a whole?

Marginal costs and benefits

In economics we argue that rational choices involve weighing up marginal costs and marginal benefits. These are the costs and benefits of doing a little bit more or a little bit less of a specific activity. They can be contrasted with the *total* costs and benefits of the activity.

Take a familiar example. What time will you set the alarm clock to go off tomorrow morning? Let us say that you have to leave home at 8.30. Perhaps you will set the alarm for 7.00. That will give you plenty of time to get up and get ready, but it will mean a relatively short night's sleep. Perhaps then you will decide to set it for 7.30 or even 8.00. That will give you a longer night's sleep, but much more of a rush in the morning to get ready.

So how do you make a rational decision about when the alarm should go off? What you have to do is to weigh up the costs and benefits of *additional* sleep. Each extra minute in bed gives you more sleep (the marginal benefit) but gives you more of a rush when you get up (the marginal cost). The decision is therefore based on the costs and benefits of *extra* sleep, not on the *total* costs and benefits of a whole night's sleep.

This same principle applies to rational decisions made by consumers, workers and firms. For example, the car firm we were considering just now will weigh up the marginal costs and benefits of producing cars: in other words, it will compare the costs and revenue of producing *additional* cars. If additional cars add more to the firm's revenue than to its costs, it will be profitable to produce them.

> ***Rational decision making*** involves weighing up the marginal benefit and marginal cost of any activity. If the marginal benefit exceeds the marginal cost, it is rational to do the activity (or to do more of it). If the marginal cost exceeds the marginal benefit, it is rational not to do it (or to do less of it).
>
> **Key Idea 3**

The social implications of choice

Microeconomics does not just study how choices are made. It also looks at their consequences. Under certain conditions the consequences may be an efficient use of the nation's resources.

However, a whole series of possible problems can arise from the choices that people make, whether they are made by individuals, by firms or by the government. These problems include such things as inefficiency, waste, inequality and pollution.

Take the case of pollution. It might be profitable for a firm to tip toxic waste into a river. But what is profitable for the firm will not necessarily be 'profitable' for society. There may be serious environmental consequences of the firm's actions.

Throughout the book we will be considering how well the economy meets various economic and social objectives: whether micro or macro. We will examine why problems occur and what can be done about them.

Illustrating economic issues

What sorts of diagram are used in economics?

Economics books and articles frequently contain diagrams. The reason is that diagrams are very useful for illustrating economic relationships. Ideas and arguments that might take a long time to explain in words can often be expressed clearly and simply in a diagram.

Two of the most common types of diagram used in economics are graphs and flow diagrams. In the next two sections we will look at one example of each. These examples are chosen to illustrate the distinction between microeconomic and macroeconomic issues.

The production possibility curve

We start by having a look at a production possibility curve. This diagram is a graph. Like many diagrams in economics it shows a simplified picture of reality – a picture stripped of all details that are unnecessary to illustrate the points being made. Of course, there are dangers in this. In the attempt to make a diagram simple enough to understand, we run the risk of oversimplifying. If this is the case, the diagram may be misleading.

A production possibility curve is shown in Figure I.1. The graph is based on the data shown in Table I.1.

Assume that some imaginary nation devotes all its resources – land, labour and capital – to producing just two goods, food and clothing. Various possible combinations that could be produced over a given period of time (e.g. a year) are shown in the table. Thus the country, by devoting all its resources to producing food, could produce 8 million units of food but no clothing. Alternatively, by producing, say, 7 million units of food it could release enough resources – land, labour and capital – to produce 2.2 million units of clothing. At the other extreme, it could produce 7 million units of clothing, with no resources at all being used to produce food.

The information in the table can be transferred to a graph (Figure I.1). We measure units of food on one axis (in this case the vertical axis) and units of clothing on the other. The curve shows all the combinations of the two goods that can be

Definition

Production possibility curve A curve showing all the possible combinations of two goods that a country can produce within a specified time period with all its resources fully and efficiently employed.

Units of food (millions)	Units of clothing (millions)
8.0	0.0
7.0	2.2
6.0	4.0
5.0	5.0
4.0	5.6
3.0	6.0
2.0	6.4
1.0	6.7
0.0	7.0

Table I.1
Maximum possible combinations of food and clothing that can be produced in a given time period

Figure I.1
A production
possibility curve

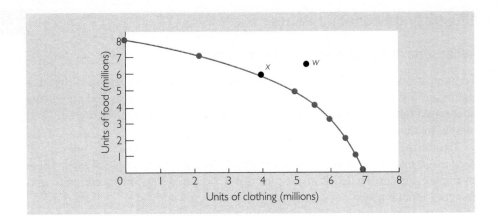

produced with all the nation's resources fully and efficiently employed. For example, production could take place at point *x*, with 6 million units of food and 4 million units of clothing being produced. Production cannot take place beyond the curve. For example, production is not possible at point *w*: the nation does not have enough resources to do this.

Note that there are two simplifying assumptions in this diagram. First, it is assumed that there are just two types of good that can be produced. It is necessary to make this assumption since we only have two axes on our graph. The other assumption is that there is only one type of food and one type of clothing. This is implied by measuring their output in particular units (e.g. tonnes). If food differed in type, there would be the possibility of producing a greater tonnage of food for a given amount of clothing simply by switching production from one foodstuff to another.

These two assumptions are obviously enormous simplifications when we consider the modern complex economies of the real world. But despite this, the diagram still allows important principles to be illustrated, and illustrated simply.

Microeconomics and the production possibility curve

A production possibility curve illustrates the microeconomic issues of *choice* and *opportunity cost*.

If the country chose to produce more clothing, it would have to sacrifice the production of some food. This sacrifice of food is the opportunity cost of the extra clothing.

The fact that to produce more of one good involves producing less of the other is illustrated by the downward-sloping nature of the curve. For example, the country could move from point *x* to point *y* in Figure I.2. In doing so it would be producing an extra 1 million units of clothing, but 1 million fewer units of food. Thus the opportunity cost of the 1 million extra units of clothing would be the 1 million units of food forgone.

It also illustrates the phenomenon of increasing opportunity costs. By this we mean that as a country produces more of one good it has to sacrifice ever-*increasing* amounts of the other. The reason for this is that different factors of production have different properties. People have different skills. Land differs in different parts

Definition

Increasing
opportunity costs
When additional
production of one good
involves ever-increasing
sacrifices of another.

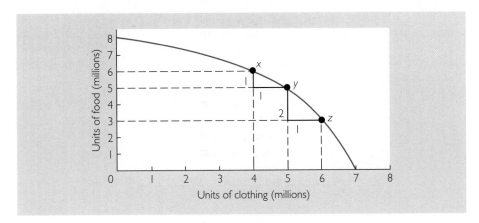

Figure I.2
Increasing
opportunity costs

of the country. Raw materials differ one from another; and so on. Thus as the nation concentrates more and more on the production of one good, it has to start using resources that are less and less suitable – resources that would have been bet-ter suited to producing other goods. In our example, then, the production of more and more clothing will involve a growing *marginal cost*: ever-increasing amounts of food have to be sacrificed for each additional unit of clothing produced.

It is because opportunity costs increase that the production possibility curve is bowed outward rather than being a straight line. Thus in Figure I.2 as production moves from point *x* to *y* to *z*, so the amount of food sacrificed rises for each addi-tional unit of clothing produced. The opportunity cost of the fifth million units of clothing is 1 million units of food. The opportunity cost of the sixth million units of clothing is 2 million units of food.

Macroeconomics and the production possibility curve

There is no guarantee that resources will be fully employed, or that they will be used in the most efficient way possible. The nation may thus be producing at a point inside the curve: for example, point *v* in Figure I.3.

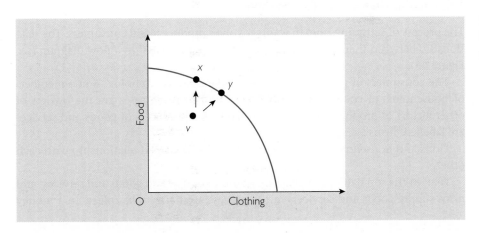

Figure I.3
Making a fuller use
of resources

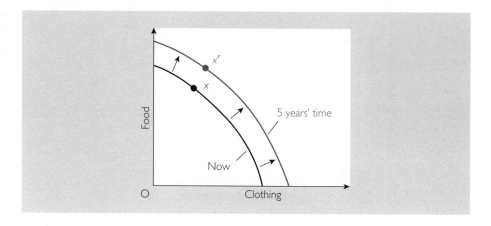

What we are saying here is that the economy is producing less of both goods than it could possibly produce, either because some resources are not being used (for example, workers may be unemployed), or because it is not using the most efficient methods of production possible, or a combination of the two. By using its resources to the full, however, the nation could move out on to the curve: to point *x* or *y*, for example. It could thus produce more clothing *and* more food.

Here we are not concerned with the combination of goods produced (a microeconomic issue), but with whether the total amount produced is as much as it could be (a macroeconomic issue).

Over time, the production possibilities of a nation are likely to increase. Investment in new plant and machinery will increase the stock of capital; new raw materials may be discovered; technological advances are likely to take place; through education and training, labour is likely to become more productive. This growth in potential output is illustrated by an outward shift in the production possibility curve. This will then allow actual output to increase: for example, from point *x* to point *x'* in Figure I.4.

Definition

Investment
The production of items that are not for immediate consumption.

Pause for thought

Will economic growth necessarily involve a parallel outward shift in the production possibility curve? Explain.

The circular flow of goods and incomes

The process of satisfying human wants involves producers and consumers. The relationship between them is two-sided and can be represented in a flow diagram (see Figure I.5).

The consumers of goods and services are labelled 'households'. Some members of households, of course, are also workers, and in some cases are the owners of other factors of production too, such as land. The producers of goods and services are labelled 'firms'.

Firms and households are in a twin 'demand and supply' relationship with each other.

First, in the top half of the diagram, households demand goods and services, and firms supply goods and services. In the process, exchange takes place. In a money

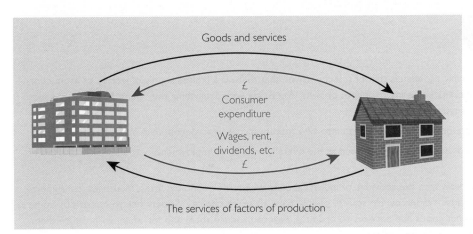

Figure I.5
Circular flow of
goods and incomes

economy (as opposed to a barter economy), firms exchange goods and services for money. In other words, money flows from households to firms in the form of consumer expenditure, while goods and services flow the other way – from firms to households.

This coming together of buyers and sellers is known as a market – whether it be a street market, a shop, the Internet, an auction, a mail-order system or whatever. Thus we talk about the market for apples, the market for oil, for cars, for houses, for televisions and so on.

Second, firms and households come together in the market for factors of production. This is illustrated in the bottom half of the diagram. This time the demand and supply roles are reversed. Firms demand the use of factors of production owned by households – labour, land and capital. Households supply them. Thus the services of labour and other factors flow from households to firms, and in exchange firms pay households money – namely, wages, rent, dividends and interest. Just as we referred to particular goods markets, so we can also refer to particular factor markets – the market for bricklayers, for secretaries, for hairdressers, for land, and so on.

There is thus a circular flow of incomes. Households earn incomes from firms, and firms earn incomes from households. The money circulates. There is also a circular flow of goods and services, but in the opposite direction. Households supply factor services to firms, which then use them to supply goods and services to households.

The flow diagram in Figure I.5, like the production possibility curve, can help us to distinguish between micro- and macroeconomics.

Microeconomics is concerned with the composition of the circular flow: *what* combinations of goods makes up the goods flow; *how* the various factors of production are combined to produce these goods; *for whom* the wages, dividends, rent and interest are paid out.

Macroeconomics is concerned with the total size of the flow and what causes it to expand and contract.

Recap

1. The central economic problem is that of scarcity. Given that there is a limited supply of factors of production (labour, land and capital), it is impossible to provide everybody with everything they want. Potential demands exceed potential supplies.

2. The subject of economics is usually divided into two main branches, macroeconomics and microeconomics.

3. Macroeconomics deals with aggregates such as the overall levels of unemployment, output, growth and prices in the economy.

4. Microeconomics deals with the activities of individual units within the economy: firms, industries, consumers, workers, etc. Because resources are scarce, people have to make choices. Society has to choose by some means or other *what* goods and services to produce, *how* to produce them and for *whom* to produce them. Microeconomics studies these choices.

5. Rational choices involve weighing up the marginal benefits of each activity against its marginal opportunity costs. If the marginal benefit exceeds the marginal cost, it is rational to choose to do more of that activity.

6. The production possibility curve shows the possible combinations of two goods that a country can produce in a given period of time. Assuming that the country is already producing on the curve, the production of more of one good will involve producing less of the other. This opportunity cost is illustrated by the slope of the curve. If the economy is producing within the curve as a result of idle resources or inefficiency, it can produce more of both goods by taking up this slack. In the longer term it can only produce more of both by shifting the curve outwards through investment, technological progress, etc.

7. The circular flow of goods and incomes shows the interrelationships between firms and households in a money economy. Firms and households come together in markets. In goods markets, firms supply goods and households demand goods. In the process, money flows from households to firms in return for the goods and services that the firms supply. In factor markets, firms demand factors of production and households supply them. In the process, money flows from firms to households in return for the services of the factors that households supply.

Questions

1. Imagine that you won millions of pounds on the National Lottery. Would your 'economic problem' be solved?

2. Would redistributing incomes from the rich to the poor reduce the overall problem of scarcity?

3. In what way does specialisation reduce the problem of scarcity?

4. Which of the following are macroeconomic issues, which are microeconomic ones and which could be either depending on the context?

   (a) Inflation.
   (b) Low wages in certain service industries.
   (c) The rate of exchange between the pound and the euro.
   (d) Why the price of cabbages fluctuates more than that of cars.
   (e) The rate of economic growth this year compared with last year.
   (f) The decline of traditional manufacturing industries.

5. Assume that in a household one parent currently works full time and the other stays at home to look after the family. How would you set about identifying and calculating the opportunity costs of the second parent now taking a full-time job? How would such calculations be relevant in deciding whether it is worth taking that job?

6. When you made the decision to study Economics, was it a 'rational' decision (albeit based on the limited information you had available at the time)? What additional information would you like to have had in order to ensure that your decision was the right one?

7. Assume you are looking for a job and are offered two. One is more unpleasant to do, but pays more. How would you make a rational choice of which of the two jobs to accept?

8. Imagine that a country can produce just two things: goods and services. Assume that over a given time period it could produce any of the following combinations:

Units of goods	0	10	20	30	40	50	60	70	80	90	100
Units of services	80	79	77	74	70	65	58	48	35	19	0

   (a) Draw the country's production possibility curve.
   (b) Assuming that the country is currently producing 40 units of goods and 70 units of services, what is the opportunity cost of producing another 10 units of goods?
   (c) Explain how the figures illustrate the principle of increasing opportunity cost.
   (d) Now assume that technical progress leads to a 10 per cent increase in the output of goods for any given amount of resources. Draw the new production possibility curve. How has the opportunity cost of producing extra units of services altered?

9. Under what circumstances would the production possibility curve be (a) a straight line, (b) bowed in towards the origin? Are these circumstances ever likely?

Additional case studies on the *Essentials of Economics* website
(www.booksites.net/sloman)

I.1 Scarcity and abundance. If scarcity is the central economic problem, is anything truly abundant?

I.2 Global economics. This examines how macroeconomics and microeconomics apply at the global level and identifies some key issues.

I.3 Buddhist economics. A different perspective on economic problems and economic activity.

Sections of Introduction covered in
WinEcon – Sloman, *Essentials of Economics*

Essentials of Economics section	*WinEcon* section
I.1	I.1
I.2	I.1
I.3	I.1

See also, *WinEcon* Chapter 13 on Basic Maths for Economics.

Websites relevant to this chapter

Numbers and sections refer to websites listed in the Web Appendix and hotlinked from this book's website at
www.booksites.net/sloman

■ For news articles relevant to this Introduction, see the *Economics News Articles* link from the book's website.

■ For a tutorial on finding the best economics websites see site C8 (*The Internet Economist*).

■ For general economics news sources, see websites in section A of the Web Appendix at the end of the book, and particularly A1–9, 24, 38, 39. See also A38 and 39 for links to newspapers worldwide; and A42 for links to economics news articles from newspapers worldwide.

■ For sources of economic data, see sites in section B and particularly B1–4, 33, 34.

■ For general sites for students of economics, see sites in section C and particularly C1–7.

■ For sites giving links to relevant economics websites, organised by topic, see sites I4, 7, 8, 11, 12, 17, 18.

Part A   Microeconomics

CHAPTER MAP

CHAPTER ONE
Markets, demand and supply

In this first half of the book we focus on microeconomics. Despite being 'small economics' – in other words, the economics of the individual parts of the economy, rather than the economy as a whole – it is still concerned with many of the big issues of today.

We will study why the pattern of production and consumption changes over time; why some people are rich and others poor; why our lives seem to be dominated by market forces beyond our control. We will look at the world of big business at one extreme and highly competitive markets at the other. We will look at many of the seemingly intractable problems we face: from the growing problem of pollution, to our limited power as consumers, to the widening inequality of incomes in society.

In this chapter, we examine how different economies of the world answer the key microeconomic questions of 'what to produce', 'how to produce' and 'for whom to produce'.

We start by looking at how economies would work if they were run totally by the government and did not rely on markets at all. We then look at the other extreme and consider economies that rely totally on the market. We will look at how markets work. We will examine what determines how much of any product gets produced and sold, and why some goods rise in price, whereas others fall. In the process we will be looking at one of the most important theories in the whole of economics: the theory of supply and demand.

1.1   Economic systems

Key
Idea

1
p5

Definitions

Centrally planned or command economy
An economy where all economic decisions are taken by the central authorities.

Free-market economy
An economy where all economic decisions are taken by individual households and firms, with no government intervention.

Mixed economy
An economy where economic decisions are made partly by the government and partly through the market.

Mixed market economy
A market economy where there is some government intervention.

Input–output analysis
This involves dividing the economy into sectors where each sector is a user of inputs from and a supplier of outputs to other sectors. The technique examines how these inputs and outputs can be matched to the total resources available in the economy.

How do countries differ in the way their economies are organised?

All societies are faced with the problem of scarcity. They differ considerably, however, in the way they tackle the problem. One important difference between societies is in the degree of government control of the economy.

At the one extreme lies the completely planned or command economy, where all the economic decisions are taken by the government.

At the other extreme lies the completely free-market economy. In this type of economy there is no government intervention at all. All decisions are taken by individuals and firms. Households decide how much labour and other factors to supply, and what goods to consume. Firms decide what goods to produce and what factors to employ. The pattern of production and consumption that results depends on the interactions of all these individual demand and supply decisions.

In practice, all economies are a mixture of the two. It is therefore the *degree* of government intervention that distinguishes different economic systems. Thus in the former communist countries of eastern Europe, the government played a large role, whereas in the United States, the government plays a much smaller role.

It is nevertheless useful to analyse the extremes in order to put the different mixed economies of the real world into perspective.

We start by having a brief look at the command economy. Then for the rest of this chapter we will see how a free-market economy operates. In subsequent chapters we will examine the various ways in which governments intervene in market economies: i.e. we will look at the various forms of mixed market economy.

The command economy

The command economy is usually associated with a socialist or communist economic system, where land and capital are collectively owned. The state plans the allocation of resources at three important levels:

■ It plans the allocation of resources between current consumption and investment for the future. By sacrificing some present consumption and diverting resources into investment, it could increase the economy's growth rate. The amount of resources it chooses to devote to investment will depend on its broad macroeconomic strategy: the importance it attaches to growth as opposed to current consumption.

■ At a microeconomic level it plans the output of each industry and firm, the techniques that will be used and the labour and other resources required by each industry and firm.

In order to ensure that the required inputs are available, the state would probably conduct some form of input–output analysis. All industries are seen as users of *inputs* from other industries and as producers of *output* for consumers or other industries. For example, the steel industry uses inputs from the coal and iron-ore industries and produces output for the vehicle and construction industries. Input–output analysis shows, for each industry, the sources of all its inputs and the destination of all its output. By its use the state attempts to match up the inputs and outputs of each industry so that the planned demand for each industry's product is equal to its planned supply.

■ It plans the distribution of output between consumers. This will depend on the government's aims. It may distribute goods according to its judgement of people's *needs*; or it may give more to those who produce more, thereby providing an *incentive* for people to work harder.

It may distribute goods and services directly (for example, by a system of rationing); or it may decide the distribution of money incomes and allow individuals to decide how to spend them. If it does the latter, it may still seek to influence the pattern of expenditure by setting appropriate prices: low prices to encourage consumption, and high prices to discourage consumption.

Assessment of the command economy

With central planning, the government could take an overall view of the economy. It could direct the nation's resources in accordance with specific national goals.

High growth rates could be achieved if the government directed large amounts of resources into investment. Unemployment could be largely avoided if the government carefully planned the allocation of labour in accordance with production requirements and labour skills. National income could be distributed more equally or in accordance with needs. The social repercussions of production and consumption (e.g. the effects on the environment) could be taken into account, provided the government was able to predict these effects and chose to take them into account.

In practice, a command economy could achieve these goals only at considerable social and economic cost. The reasons are as follows:

■ The larger and more complex the economy, the greater the task of collecting and analysing the information essential to planning, and the more complex the plan. Complicated plans are likely to be costly to administer and involve cumbersome bureaucracy.

■ If there is no system of prices, or if prices are set arbitrarily by the state, planning is likely to involve the inefficient use of resources. It is difficult to assess the relative efficiency of two alternative techniques that use different inputs, if there is no way in which the value of those inputs can be ascertained. For example, how can a rational decision be made between an oil-fired and a coal-fired furnace if the prices of oil and coal do not reflect their relative scarcity?

■ It is difficult to devise appropriate incentives to encourage workers and managers to be more productive without a reduction in quality. For example, if bonuses are given according to the quantity of output produced, a factory might produce shoddy goods, since it can probably produce a larger quantity of goods by cutting quality. To avoid this problem, a large number of officials may have to be employed to check quality.

■ Complete state control over resource allocation would involve a considerable loss of individual liberty. Workers would have no choice where to work; consumers would have no choice what to buy.

■ The government might enforce its plans even if they were unpopular.

■ If production is planned, but consumers are free to spend money incomes as they wish, then there will be a problem if the consumer wishes change. Shortages will occur if consumers decide to buy more, and surpluses will occur if they decide to buy less.

Pause for thought

Queues were a common feature of the former Soviet Union. Why do you think they were so commonplace? Is a system of queuing a fair way of allocating scarce goods and resources?

Most of these problems were experienced in the former USSR and the other Eastern bloc countries, and were part of the reason for the overthrow of their communist regimes (see Box 1.1).

Box 1.1

The rise and fall of planning in the former Soviet Union

Early years

The Bolsheviks under the leadership of Lenin came to power in Russia with the October revolution of 1917. The Bolsheviks, however, were opposed by the White Russians and civil war ensued.

During this period of *War Communism*, the market economy was abolished. Industry and shops were nationalised; workers were told what jobs to do; there were forced requisitions of food from peasants to feed the towns; the money economy collapsed as rampant inflation made money worthless; workers were allocated goods from distribution depots.

With the ending of the civil war in 1921, the economy was in bad shape. Lenin embarked on a *New Economic Policy*. This involved a return to the use of markets. Smaller businesses were returned to private hands, and peasants were able to sell their food rather than having it requisitioned. The economy began to recover.

Lenin died in 1924 and Stalin came to power.

The Stalinist system

The Soviet economy underwent a radical transformation from 1928 onwards. The key features of the Stalinist approach were collectivisation, industrialisation and central planning.

Collectivisation of agriculture

Peasant farms were abolished and replaced by large-scale collective farms where land was collectively owned and worked. Collectivisation initially caused massive disruption and famine, with peasants slaughtering their animals rather than giving them up to the collective. People died in their thousands. Despite an initial fall in output, more food was provided for the towns, and many workers left the land to work in the new industries.

In addition to the collective farms, state farms were established. These were owned by the state and were run by managers appointed by the state. Workers were paid a wage rather than having a share in farm income.

Both collective and state farms were given quotas of output that they were supposed to deliver for which the state would pay a fixed price.

Industry and central planning

A massive drive to industrialisation took place. To achieve this a vast planning apparatus was developed. At the top was *Gosplan,* the central planning agency. This prepared five-year plans and annual plans.

The five-year plans specified the general direction in which the economy was to move. The annual plans gave the details of just what was to be produced and with what resources for some 200 or so key products. Other products were planned at a lower level – by various industrial ministries or regional authorities.

The effect was that all factories were given targets that had to be achieved. It was the task of the planning authorities to ensure that the targets were realistic: that there were sufficient resources to meet the targets. The system operated without the aid of the price mechanism and the profit motive. The main incentive was the bonus: bonuses were paid to managers and workers if targets were achieved.

In the early years, very high growth rates were achieved; but this was at a cost of low efficiency. The poor flow of information from firms to the planners led to many inconsistencies in the plans. The targets were often totally unrealistic, and as a result there were frequent shortages and sometimes surpluses.

The free-market economy

Free decision making by individuals

The free-market economy is usually associated with a pure capitalist system, where land and capital are privately owned. All economic decisions are made by

With incentives purely geared to meeting targets, there was little product innovation and goods were frequently of poor quality and finish.

The limits of planning

Although most resources were allocated through planning, there were nevertheless some goods that were sold in markets. Any surpluses above their quota that were produced by collective farms could be sold in collective farm markets (street markets) in the towns. In addition, the workers on collective farms were allowed to own their own small private plots of land, and they too could sell their produce in the collective farm markets.

A large 'underground economy' flourished in which goods were sold on the black market and in which people did second 'unofficial' jobs (e.g. as plumbers, electricians or garment makers).

Gorbachev's reforms

Stalin died in 1953. The planning system, however, remained largely unchanged until the late 1980s.

During the 1970s growth had slowed down and by the time Mikhail Gorbachev came to power in 1985 many people were pressing for fundamental economic reforms. Gorbachev responded with his policy of *perestroika* (economic reconstruction), which among other things included the following:

■ Making managers more involved in preparing their own plans rather than merely being given instructions.

■ Insisting that firms cover their costs of production. If they could not, the state might refuse to bale them out and they could be declared bankrupt.

The aim of this was to encourage firms to be more efficient.

■ Improving the incentive system by making bonuses more related to genuine productivity. Workers had come to expect bonuses no matter how much or how little was produced.

■ Organising workers into small teams or 'brigades' (typically of around 10–15 workers). Bonuses were then awarded to the whole brigade according to its productivity. The idea was to encourage people to work more effectively together.

■ Stringent checks on quality by state officials and the rejection of substandard goods.

■ Allowing one-person businesses and co-operatives (owned by the workers) to be set up.

■ A greater willingness by the state to raise prices if there were substantial shortages.

These reforms, however, did not halt the economic decline. What is more, there was now an unhappy mix of planning and the market, with people unclear as to what to expect from the state. Many managers resented the extra responsibilities they were now expected to shoulder and many officials saw their jobs threatened. Queues lengthened in the shops and people became increasingly disillusioned with *perestroika*.

Following a failed coup in 1991, in which hard-line communists had attempted to reimpose greater state control, and with the consequent strengthening of the position of Boris Yeltsin, the Russian president and the main advocate of more radical reforms, both the Soviet Union and the system of central planning came to an end.

Russia embarked upon a radical programme of market reforms in which competition and enterprise were intended to replace state central planning (see Web case 1.5).

households and firms, which are assumed to act in their own self-interest. The following assumptions are usually made:

■ Firms seek to maximise profits.
■ Consumers seek to get the best value for money from their purchases.
■ Workers seek to maximise their wages relative to the human cost of working in a particular job.

It is also assumed that individuals are free to make their own economic choices; consumers are free to decide what to buy with their incomes; workers are free to choose where and how much to work; firms are free to choose what to sell and what production methods to use.

The resulting supply and demand decisions of firms and households are transmitted to each other through their effect on *prices*.

The price mechanism

> **Definition**
>
> **The price mechanism**
> The system in a market economy whereby price changes that occur in response to changes in demand and supply have the effect of making demand equal to supply.

The price mechanism works as follows. Prices respond to *shortages* and *surpluses*. Shortages cause prices to rise. Surpluses cause prices to fall.

If consumers decide they want more of a good (or if producers decide to cut back supply), demand will exceed supply. The resulting shortage will cause the price of the good to rise. This will act as an incentive to producers to supply more, since production will now be more profitable. It will discourage consumers from buying so much. *Price will continue rising until the shortage has thereby been eliminated.*

If, on the other hand, consumers decide they want less of a good (or if producers decide to produce more), supply will exceed demand. The resulting surplus will cause the price of the good to *fall*. This will act as a disincentive to producers, who will supply less, since production will now be less profitable. It will encourage consumers to buy more. *Price will continue falling until the surplus has thereby been eliminated.*

The same analysis can be applied to factor markets. If the demand for a particular type of labour exceeded its supply, the resulting shortage would drive up the wage rate (i.e. the price of labour), thus reducing firms' demand for that type of labour and encouraging more workers to take up that type of job. Wages would continue rising until demand equalled supply: until the shortage was eliminated.

Likewise if there were a surplus of a particular type of labour, the wage would fall until demand equalled supply.

The response of demand and supply to changes in price illustrates a very important feature of how economies work:

> **People respond to incentives**. It is important, therefore, that incentives are appropriate and have the desired effect.
>
> **Key Idea 4**

The effect of changes in demand and supply

How will the price mechanism respond to changes in consumer demand or producer supply? After all, the pattern of consumer demand changes. For example, people may decide they want more mountain bikes and fewer racers. Likewise the pattern of supply also changes. For example, changes in technology may allow the mass production of microchips at lower cost, while the production of hand-built furniture becomes relatively expensive.

In all cases of changes in demand and supply, the resulting changes in *price* act as both *signals* and *incentives*.

A change in demand.   A rise in demand is signalled by a rise in price. This then acts as an incentive for firms to produce more of the good: the quantity supplied rises. What in effect is happening is that the high price of these goods relative to their costs of production is signalling that consumers are willing to see resources diverted from other uses. But this is just what firms do. They divert resources from goods with lower prices relative to costs (and hence lower profits) to those goods that are more profitable.

A fall in demand is signalled by a fall in price. This then acts as an incentive for firms to produce less: such goods are now less profitable to produce. Thus the quantity supplied falls.

A change in supply.   A rise in supply is signalled by a fall in price. This then acts as an incentive for consumers to buy more: the quantity demanded rises. A fall in supply is signalled by a rise in price. This then acts as an incentive for consumers to buy less: the quantity demanded falls.

> **Changes in demand or supply cause markets to adjust**. Whenever such changes occur, the resulting 'disequilibrium' will bring an automatic change in prices, thereby restoring equilibrium (i.e. a balance of demand and supply).   **Key Idea 5**

The interdependence of markets

Key Idea 4 p26

The interdependence of goods and factor markets.   A rise in demand for a good will raise its price and profitability. Firms will respond by supplying more. But to do this they will need more inputs. Thus the demand for the inputs will rise, which in turn will raise the price of the inputs. The suppliers of inputs will respond to this incentive by supplying more. This can be summarised as follows:

1. Goods market
   - Demand for the good rises.
   - This creates a shortage.
   - This causes the price of the good to rise.
   - This eliminates the shortage by choking off some of the demand and encouraging firms to produce more.

2. Factor market
   - The increased supply of the good causes an increase in the demand for factors of production (i.e. inputs) used in making it.
   - This causes a shortage of those inputs.
   - This causes their prices to rise.
   - This eliminates their shortage by choking off some of the demand and encouraging the suppliers of inputs to supply more.

Key Idea 5 p27

Goods markets thus affect factor markets.

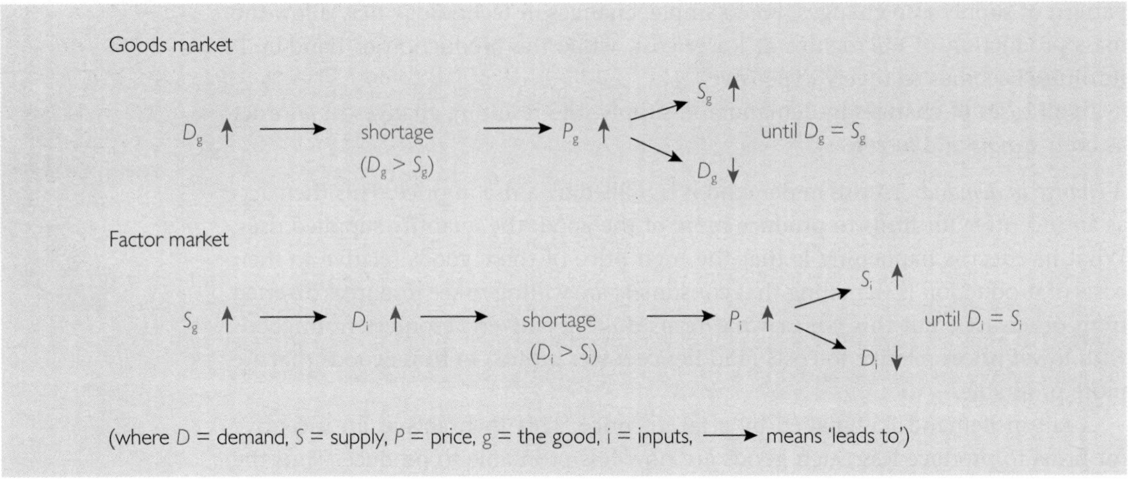

Goods market

D_g ↑ ⟶ shortage ⟶ P_g ↑ ⟨ S_g ↑ until $D_g = S_g$
        $(D_g > S_g)$ D_g ↓

Factor market

S_g ↑ ⟶ D_i ↑ ⟶ shortage ⟶ P_i ↑ ⟨ S_i ↑ until $D_i = S_i$
                $(D_i > S_i)$ D_i ↓

(where D = demand, S = supply, P = price, g = the good, i = inputs, ⟶ means 'leads to')

Figure 1.1
The price mechanism: the effect of a rise in demand

It is common in economics to summarise an argument like this by using symbols. It is a form of shorthand. Figure 1.1 summarises this particular sequence of events.

Interdependence exists in the other direction too: factor markets affect goods markets. For example, the discovery of raw materials will lower their price. This will lower the production costs of firms using these raw materials and increase the supply of the finished goods. The resulting surplus will lower the price of the good, which will encourage consumers to buy more.

> **Pause for thought**
>
> Summarise this last paragraph using symbols like those in Figure 1.1.

The interdependence of different goods markets. A rise in the price of one good will encourage consumers to buy alternatives. This will drive up the price of alternatives. This in turn will encourage producers to supply more of the alternatives.

Interdependence and the public interest. Even though all individuals are merely looking to their own self-interest in the free-market economy, they are in fact being encouraged to respond to the wishes of others through the incentive of the price mechanism. For example, if consumers want more of a product, firms will supply more – not out of the goodness of their hearts, but because it is profitable to do so. It is often claimed that this is a major advantage of a free-market economy. We will be examining this claim in subsequent chapters.

Key Idea
4
p26

Definition

Perfect competition (preliminary definition)
A situation where the consumers and producers of a product are price takers. (There are other features of a perfectly competitive market; these are examined in Chapter 4.)

Competitive markets

For the rest of this chapter we will examine the working of the price mechanism in more detail. We will look first at demand, then at supply, and then we will put the two together to look at the determination of price.

The markets we will be examining are highly competitive markets, with many firms competing against each other. In economics we call this perfect competition. This is where consumers and producers are too numerous to have any control over prices: they are price takers.

In the case of consumers, this means that they have to accept the prices as given for the things that they buy. On most occasions this is true. For example, when you get to the supermarket checkout you cannot start haggling with the checkout operator over the price of a can of beans or a tub of margarine.

In the case of firms, perfect competition means that producers are too small and face too much competition from other firms to be able to raise prices. Take the case of farmers selling wheat. They have to sell it at the current market price. If individually they try to sell at a higher price, no one will buy, since purchasers of wheat (e.g. flour millers) can get all the wheat they want at the market price.

Of course, many firms *do* have the power to choose their prices. This does not mean that they can simply charge whatever they like. They will still have to take account of overall consumer demand and their competitors' prices. Ford, when setting the price of its Focus cars, will have to ensure that they remain competitive with Astras, Golfs, 307s, etc. Nevertheless, most firms have some flexibility in setting their prices: they have a degree of 'market power'.

If this is the case, then why do we study *perfect* markets, where firms are price takers? One reason is that they provide a useful approximation to the real world and give us many insights into how a market economy works. Many markets do function very similarly to the markets we shall be describing.

Another is that perfect markets provide an ideal against which to compare the real world. It is often argued that perfect markets benefit the consumer, whereas markets dominated by big business may operate against the consumer's interests. For example, the consumer may end up paying higher prices in a market dominated by just a few firms than in one operating under perfect competition.

Definition

Price taker
A person or firm with no power to be able to influence the market price.

Recap

1. The economic systems of different countries vary according to the extent to which they rely on the market or the government to allocate resources.

2. At the one extreme, in a command economy, the state makes all the economic decisions. It plans how many resources to allocate for present consumption and how many for investment for future output. It plans the output of each industry, the methods of production it will use and the amount of resources it will be allocated. It plans the distribution of output between consumers.

3. A command economy has the advantage of being able to address directly various national economic goals, such as rapid growth and the avoidance of unemployment and inequality. A command economy, however, is likely to be inefficient: a large bureaucracy will be needed to collect and process information; prices and the choice of production methods are likely to be arbitrary; incentives may be inappropriate; shortages and surpluses may result.

4. At the other extreme is the free-market economy. In this economy, decisions are made by the interaction of demand and supply. Price changes act as the mechanism whereby demand and supply are balanced. If there is a shortage of a product, its price will rise until the shortage is eliminated. If there is a surplus, its price will fall until that is eliminated.

5. For the rest of this chapter we will be studying perfect markets. These are markets where both producers and consumers are price takers.

1.2   Demand

How much will people buy of any item?

The relationship between demand and price

The headlines announce, 'Major crop failures in Brazil and East Africa: coffee prices soar.' Shortly afterwards you find that coffee prices have doubled in the shops. What do you do? Presumably you will cut back on the amount of coffee you drink. Perhaps you will reduce it from, say, six cups per day to two. Perhaps you will give up drinking coffee altogether.

This is simply an illustration of the general relationship between price and consumption: *when the price of a good rises, the quantity demanded will fall*. This relationship is known as the law of demand. There are two reasons for this law:

- People will feel poorer. They will not be able to afford to buy so much of the good with their money. The purchasing power of their income (their *real income*)[1] has fallen. This is called the income effect of a price rise.
- The good will now be dearer relative to other goods. People will thus switch to alternative or 'substitute' goods. This is called the substitution effect of a price rise.

Similarly, when the price of a good falls, the quantity demanded will rise. People can afford to buy more (the income effect), and they will switch away from consuming alternative goods (the substitution effect).

Therefore, returning to our example of the increase in the price of coffee, we will not be able to afford to buy as much as before, and we will probably drink more tea, cocoa, fruit juices or even water instead.

A word of warning: be careful about the meaning of the words quantity demanded. They refer to the amount consumers are willing and able to purchase at a given price over a given period (e.g. a week, or a month, or a year). They do *not* refer to what people would simply *like* to consume. You might like to own a luxury yacht, but your demand for luxury yachts will almost certainly be zero at the current price.

The demand curve

Consider the hypothetical data in Table 1.1. The table shows how many kilos of potatoes per month would be purchased at various prices.

Columns (2) and (3) show the demand schedules for two individuals, Tracey and Darren. Column (4), by contrast, shows the total market demand schedule. This is the total demand by all consumers. To obtain the market demand schedule for potatoes, we simply add up the quantities demanded at each price by *all* consumers: i.e. Tracey, Darren and everyone else who demands potatoes. Notice that

---

[1] 'Real income' is income measured in terms of its purchasing power: i.e. after taking price changes into account. Thus if prices doubled and your money income stayed the same, your real income would have halved. In other words, you would only be able to buy half as much as before with your income.

Definitions

The law of demand
The quantity of a good demanded per period of time will fall as price rises and will rise as price falls, other things being equal.

Income effect
The effect of a change in price on quantity demanded arising from the consumer becoming better or worse off as a result of the price change.

Substitution effect
The effect of a change in price on quantity demanded arising from the consumer switching to or from alternative (substitute) products.

Quantity demanded
The amount of a good that a consumer is willing and able to buy at a given price over a given period of time.

Demand schedule for an individual
A table showing the different quantities of a good that a person is willing and able to buy at various prices over a given period of time.

	Price (pence per kg) (1)	Tracey's demand (kg) (2)	Darren's demand (kg) (3)	Total market demand (tonnes: 000s) (4)
A	20	28	16	700
B	40	15	11	500
C	60	5	9	350
D	80	1	7	200
E	100	0	6	100

Table 1.1
The demand for potatoes (monthly)

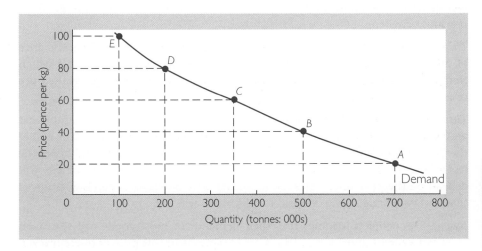

Figure 1.2
Market demand curve for potatoes (monthly)

we are talking about demand *over a period of time* (not at a *point* in time). Thus we would talk about daily demand, or weekly demand, or annual demand or whatever.

The demand schedule can be represented graphically as a demand curve. Figure 1.2 shows the market demand curve for potatoes corresponding to the schedule in Table 1.1. The price of potatoes is plotted on the vertical axis. The quantity demanded is plotted on the horizontal axis.

Point *E* shows that at a price of 100p per kilo, 100 000 tonnes of potatoes are demanded each month. When the price falls to 80p we move down the curve to point *D*. This shows that the quantity demanded has now risen to 200 000 tonnes per month. Similarly, if the price falls to 60p we move down the curve again to point *C*: 350 000 tonnes are now demanded. The five points on the graph (*A–E*) correspond to the figures in columns (1) and (4) of Table 1.1. The graph also enables us to read off the likely quantities demanded at prices other than those in the table.

A demand curve could also be drawn for an individual consumer. Like market demand curves, individuals' demand curves generally slope downwards from left to right: the lower the price of a product, the more is a person likely to buy.

Two points should be noted at this stage:

■ In textbooks, demand curves (and other curves too) are only occasionally used to plot specific data. More frequently they are used to illustrate general theoretical arguments. In such cases, the axes will simply be price and quantity, with the units unspecified.

- The term demand 'curve' is used even when the graph is a straight line! In fact, when using demand curves to illustrate arguments we frequently draw them as straight lines – it's easier.

Other determinants of demand

Price is not the only factor that determines how much of a good people will buy. Demand is also affected by the following:

Tastes. The more desirable people find the good, the more they will demand. Tastes are affected by advertising, by fashion, by observing other consumers, by considerations of health and by the experiences from consuming the good on previous occasions.

The number and price of substitute goods (i.e. competitive goods). The higher the price of substitute goods, the higher will be the demand for this good as people switch from the substitutes. For example, the demand for coffee will depend on the price of tea. If tea goes up in price, the demand for coffee will rise.

The number and price of complementary goods. Complementary goods are those that are consumed together: cars and petrol, shoes and polish, fish and chips. The higher the price of complementary goods, the fewer of them will be bought and hence the less will be the demand for this good. For example, the demand for electricity will depend on the price of electrical goods. If the price of electrical goods goes up, so that fewer are bought, the demand for electricity will fall.

Income. As people's incomes rise, their demand for most goods will rise. Such goods are called normal goods. There are exceptions to this general rule, however. As people get richer, they spend less on inferior goods such as cheap margarine, and switch to better-quality goods.

Distribution of income. If national income were redistributed from the poor to the rich, the demand for *luxury* goods would rise. At the same time, as the poor got poorer they might have to turn to buying inferior goods, whose demand would thus rise too.

Expectations of future price changes. If people think that prices are going to rise in the future, they are likely to buy more now before the price does go up.

To illustrate these six determinants, let us look at the demand for butter:

- Tastes: if it is heavily advertised, demand is likely to rise. If, on the other hand, there is a cholesterol scare, people may demand less for health reasons.
- Substitutes: if the price of margarine goes up, the demand for butter is likely to rise as people switch from one to the other.
- Complements: if the price of bread goes up, people will buy less bread and hence less butter to spread it on.
- Income: if people's incomes rise, they may well turn to consuming butter rather than margarine, or feel that they can afford to spread butter more thickly on their bread.
- Income distribution: if income is redistributed away from the poor, they may have to give up consuming butter and buy cheaper margarine instead, or simply buy less butter and use it more sparingly.

Definitions

Substitute goods
A pair of goods which are considered by consumers to be alternatives to each other. As the price of one goes up, the demand for the other rises.

Complementary goods
A pair of goods consumed together. As the price of one goes up, the demand for both goods will fall.

Normal good
A good whose demand rises as people's incomes rise.

Inferior good
A good whose demand falls as people's incomes rise.

Ceteris paribus
Latin for 'other things being equal'. This assumption has to be made when making deductions from theories.

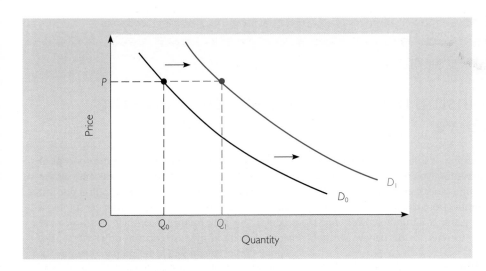

Figure 1.3
An increase in demand

■ Expectations: if it is announced in the news that butter prices are expected to rise in the near future, people are likely to buy more now and stock up their freezers while current prices last.

Movements along and shifts in the demand curve

A demand curve is constructed on the assumption that 'other things remain equal' (sometimes known by the Latin term ceteris paribus). In other words, it is assumed that none of the determinants of demand, other than price, changes.[2] The effect of a change in price is then simply illustrated by a movement along the demand curve: for example, from point B to point D in Figure 1.2 when the price of potatoes rises from 40p to 80p per kilo.

What happens, then, when one of these other determinants does change? The answer is that we have to construct a whole new demand curve: the curve shifts. If a change in one of the other determinants causes demand to rise – say, income rises – the whole curve will shift to the right. This shows that at each price, more will be demanded than before. Thus in Figure 1.3 at a price of P, a quantity of Q_0 was originally demanded. But now, after the increase in demand, Q_1 is demanded. (Note that D_1 is not necessarily parallel to D_0.)

If a change in a determinant other than price causes demand to fall, the whole curve will shift to the left.

To distinguish between shifts in and movements along demand curves, it is usual to distinguish between a change in *demand* and a change in the *quantity demanded*. A shift in demand is referred to as a change in demand, whereas a movement along the demand curve as a result of a change in price is referred to as a change in the quantity demanded.

> **Pause for thought**   ▮▮
>
> The price of cinema tickets rises and yet it is observed that cinema attendance increases. Does this means that the demand curve for cinema tickets is upward sloping?

---

[2] We make this assumption to keep the analysis simple at the outset. We can then drop the assumption by changing things one at a time and seeing what happens.

Box 1.2 Exploring Economics

Getting satisfaction

The relationship between marginal utility and the demand curve

When you buy something, it's normally because you want it. You want it because you expect to get pleasure, satisfaction or some other sort of benefit from it. This applies to everything from chocolate bars, to bus journeys, to CDs, to jeans, to insurance. Economists use the term 'utility' to refer to the benefit we get from consumption.

Clearly, the nature and amount of utility that people get varies from one product to another, and from one person to another. But there is a simple rule that applies to virtually all people and all products. *As you consume more of a product, and thus become more satisfied, so your desire for additional units of it will decline.*

Economists call this rule the principle of diminishing marginal utility.

> ***The principle of diminishing marginal utility.*** The more of a product a person consumes over a given period of time, the less will be the additional utility gained from one more unit.
>
> **Key Idea 6**

For example, the second cup of tea in the morning gives you less additional satisfaction than the first cup. The third cup gives less still. We call the additional utility you get from consuming an extra unit of a product the marginal utility (*MU*). So the rule says that the marginal utility will fall as we consume more of a product over a given period of time.

There is a problem, however, with the concept of marginal utility. How can it be measured? After all, we cannot get inside each other's heads to find out just how much pleasure we are getting from consuming a product! One way round the problem is to measure marginal utility in money terms: in other words, the amount that a person would be prepared to pay for one more unit of a product. Thus if you were prepared to pay 30p for an extra packet of crisps per week, then we would say that your marginal utility from consuming it is 30p. As long as you are prepared to pay more or the same as the actual price, you will buy an extra packet. If you are not prepared to pay that price, you will not.

We can now see how this relates to a downward-sloping demand curve. As the price of a good falls, it will be worth buying extra units. You will buy more because the price will now be below the amount you are prepared to pay: i.e. price is less than your marginal utility. But as you buy more, your marginal utility from consuming each extra unit will get less and less. How many extra units do you buy? You will stop when the marginal utility has fallen to the new lower price of the good: when $MU = P$.

?
1. How will your marginal utility from the consumption of electricity be affected by the number of electrical appliances you own?
2. How will your marginal utility from the consumption of butter depend on the amount of margarine you consume?
3. If a good were free, what would your marginal utility be from consuming it?

Definitions

Principle of diminishing marginal utility
As more units of a good are consumed, additional units will provide less additional satisfaction than previous units.

Marginal utility (*MU*)
The extra satisfaction gained from consuming one extra unit of a good within a given time period.

Recap

1. When the price of a good rises, the quantity demanded per period of time will fall. This is known as the 'law of demand'. It applies both to individuals' demand and to the whole market demand.

2. The law of demand is explained by the income and substitution effects of a price change.

3. The relationship between price and quantity demanded per period of time can be shown in a table (or 'schedule') or as a graph. On the graph, price is plotted on the vertical axis and quantity demanded per period of time on the horizontal axis. The resulting demand curve is downward sloping (negatively sloped).

4. Other determinants of demand include tastes, the number and price of substitute goods, the number and price of complementary goods, income, the distribution of income and expectations of future price changes.

5. If price changes, the effect is shown by a movement along the demand curve. We call this effect 'a change in the quantity demanded'.

6. If any other determinant of demand changes, the whole curve will shift. We call this effect 'a change in demand'. A rightward shift represents an increase in demand; a leftward shift represents a decrease in demand.

Supply   1.3

How much of any item will firms want to produce?

Supply and price

Imagine you are a farmer deciding what to do with your land. Part of your land is in a fertile valley. Part is on a hillside where the soil is poor. Perhaps, then, you will consider growing vegetables in the valley and keeping sheep on the hillside.

Your decision will depend to a large extent on the price that various vegetables will fetch in the market and likewise the price you can expect to get from sheep and wool. As far as the valley is concerned, you will plant the vegetables that give the best return. If, for example, the price of potatoes is high, you will probably use a lot of the valley for growing potatoes. If the price gets higher, you may well use the whole of the valley, perhaps being prepared to run the risk of potato disease. If the price is very high indeed, you may even consider growing potatoes on the hillside, even though the yield per hectare is much lower there.

In other words, the higher the price of a particular crop, the more you are likely to grow in preference to other crops. This illustrates the general relationship between supply and price: *when the price of a good rises, the quantity supplied will also rise*. There are three reasons for this:

■ As firms supply more, they are likely to find that beyond a certain level of output costs rise more and more rapidly.

In the case of the farm we have just considered, once potatoes have to be grown on the hillside, the costs of producing them will increase. Also, if the land has to be used more intensively, say by the use of more and more fertilisers, again the costs of producing extra potatoes are likely to rise quite rapidly. It is the same for manufacturers. Beyond a certain level of output, costs are likely

Table 1.2

The supply of potatoes (monthly)

	Price of potatoes (pence per kg)	Farmer X's supply (tonnes)	Total market supply (tonnes: 000s)
a	20	50	100
b	40	70	200
c	60	100	350
d	80	120	530
e	100	130	700

to rise rapidly as workers have to be paid overtime and as machines approach capacity working. If higher output involves higher costs of production, producers will need to get a higher price if they are to be persuaded to produce extra output.

■ The higher the price of the good, the more profitable it becomes to produce. Firms will thus be encouraged to produce more of it by switching from the production of less profitable goods.

■ Given time, if the price of a good remains high, new producers will be encouraged to set up in production. Total market supply thus rises.

The first two determinants affect supply in the short run. The third affects supply in the long run. We distinguish between short-run and long-run supply in Chapter 2 (page 64).

The supply curve

The amount that producers would like to supply at various prices can be shown in a supply schedule. Table 1.2 shows a monthly supply schedule for potatoes, both for an individual farmer (farmer X) and for all farmers together (the whole market).

The supply schedule can be represented graphically as a supply curve. A supply curve may be an individual firm's supply curve or a market curve (i.e. that of the whole industry).

Figure 1.4 shows the *market* supply curve of potatoes. As with demand curves, price is plotted on the vertical axis and quantity on the horizontal axis. Each of the points *a–e* corresponds to a figure in Table 1.2. For example, a price rise from 60p per kilo to 80p per kilo will cause a movement along the supply curve from point *c* to point *d*: total market supply will rise from 350 000 tonnes per month to 530 000 tonnes per month.

Not all supply curves will be upward sloping (positively sloped). Sometimes they will be vertical, or horizontal, or even downward sloping. This will depend largely on the time period over which firms' response to price changes is considered. This question is examined in Chapter 2 in the section on the elasticity of supply (Section 2.3) and in more detail in Chapters 3 and 4.

Other determinants of supply

Like demand, supply is not simply determined by price. The other determinants of supply are as follows:

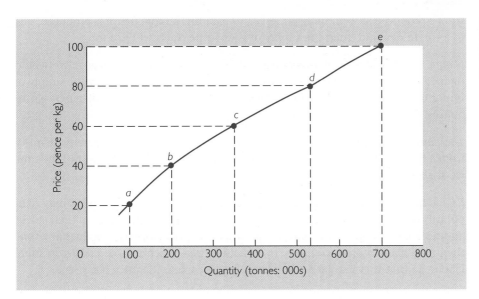

Figure 1.4
Market supply curve of potatoes (monthly)

The costs of production. The higher the costs of production, the less profit will be made at any price. As costs rise, firms will cut back on production, probably switching to alternative products whose costs have not risen so much.

The main reasons for a change in costs are:

■ Change in input prices: costs of production will rise if wages, raw material prices, rents, interest rates or any other input prices rise.
■ Change in technology: technological advances can fundamentally alter the costs of production. Consider, for example, how the microchip revolution has changed production methods and information handling in virtually every industry in the world.
■ Organisational changes: various cost savings can be made in many firms by re-organising production.
■ Government policy: costs will be lowered by government subsidies and raised by various taxes.

The profitability of alternative products (substitutes in supply). If some alternative product (a substitute in supply) becomes more profitable to supply than before, producers are likely to switch from the first good to this alternative. Supply of the first good falls. Other goods are likely to become more profitable if:

■ their prices rise;
■ their costs of production fall.

For example, if the price of carrots goes up, or the cost of producing carrots comes down, farmers may decide to produce more carrots. The supply of potatoes is therefore likely to fall.

The profitability of goods in joint supply. Sometimes when one good is produced, another good is also produced at the same time. These are said to be goods in joint supply. An example is the refining of crude oil to produce petrol. Other grade fuels

---

Definitions

Substitutes in supply
These are two goods where an increased production of one means diverting resources away from producing the other.

Goods in joint supply
These are two goods where the production of more of one leads to the production of more of the other.

will be produced as well, such as diesel and paraffin. If more petrol is produced, due to a rise in demand, then the supply of these other fuels will rise too.

Nature, 'random shocks' and other unpredictable events.   In this category we would include the weather and diseases affecting farm output, wars affecting the supply of imported raw materials, the breakdown of machinery, industrial disputes, earthquakes, floods and fire, and so on.

The aims of producers.   A profit-maximising firm will supply a different quantity from a firm that has a different aim, such as maximising sales. For most of the time we shall assume that firms are profit maximisers.

Expectations of future price changes.   If price is expected to rise, producers may temporarily reduce the amount they sell. Instead they are likely to build up their stocks and release them on to the market only when the price does rise. At the same time they may plan to produce more, by installing new machines, or taking on more labour, so that they can be ready to supply more when the price has risen.

To illustrate some of these determinants, let us return to the example of butter. What would cause the supply of butter to rise?

■ A reduction in the costs of producing butter. This could be caused, say, by a reduction in the price of nitrogen fertiliser. This would encourage farmers to use more fertiliser, which would increase grass yields, which in turn would increase milk yields per hectare. Alternatively, new technology may allow more efficient churning of butter. Or again, the government may decide to give subsidies to farmers to produce more butter.
■ A reduction in the profitability of producing cream or cheese. If these products become less profitable, due say to a reduction in their price, due in turn to a reduction in consumer demand, more butter is likely to be produced instead.
■ An increase in the profitability of skimmed milk. If consumers buy more skimmed milk, then an increased supply of skimmed milk is likely to lead to an increase in the supply of butter and other cream products, since they are jointly produced with skimmed milk.
■ If weather conditions are favourable, grass yields and hence milk yields are likely to be high. This will increase the supply of butter and other milk products.
■ If butter producers expect butter prices to rise in the future, they may well decide to release less on to the market now and put more into frozen storage until the price does rise.

Movements along and shifts in the supply curve

The principle here is the same as with demand curves. The effect of a change in price is illustrated by a movement along the supply curve: for example, from point *d* to point *e* in Figure 1.4 when price rises from 80p to 100p. Quantity supplied rises from 530 000 to 700 000 tonnes per month.

If any other determinant of supply changes, the whole supply curve will shift. A rightward shift illustrates an increase in supply. A leftward shift illustrates a

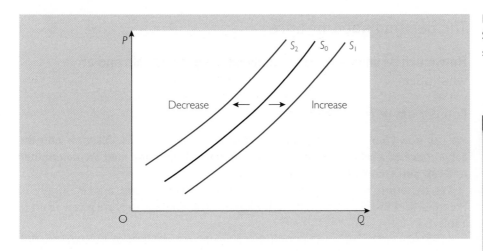

Figure 1.5
Shifts in the
supply curve

decrease in supply. Thus in Figure 1.5, if the original curve is S_0, the curve S_1 represents an increase in supply (more is supplied at each price), whereas the curve S_2 represents a decrease in supply (less is supplied at each price).

A movement along a supply curve is often referred to as a change in the quantity supplied, whereas a shift in the supply curve is simply referred to as a change in supply.

Recap

1. When the price of a good rises, the quantity supplied per period of time will usually also rise. This applies both to individual producers' supply and to the whole market supply.

2. There are two reasons in the short run why a higher price encourages producers to supply more: (a) they are now willing to incur higher costs per unit associated with producing more; (b) they will switch to producing this product instead of now less profitable ones. In the long run there is a third reason: new producers will be attracted into the market.

3. The relationship between price and quantity supplied per period of time can be shown in a table (or schedule) or as a graph. As with a demand curve, price is plotted on the vertical axis and quantity per period of time on the horizontal axis. The resulting supply curve is upward sloping (positively sloped).

4. Other determinants of supply include the costs of production, the profitability of alternative products, the profitability of goods in joint supply, random shocks and expectations of future price changes.

5. If price changes, the effect is shown by a movement along the supply curve. We call this effect 'a change in the quantity supplied'.

6. If any determinant *other* than price changes, the effect is shown by a shift in the whole supply curve. We call this effect 'a change in supply'. A rightward shift represents an increase in supply; a leftward shift represents a decrease in supply.

1.4   The determination of price

How much of any item will actually be bought and sold and at what price?

Equilibrium price and output

We can now combine our analysis of demand and supply. This will show how the actual price of a product and the actual quantity bought and sold are determined in a free and competitive market.

Let us return to the example of the market demand and market supply of potatoes, and use the data from Tables 1.1 and 1.2. These figures are given again in Table 1.3.

What will be the price and output that actually prevail? If the price started at 20p per kilogram, demand would exceed supply by 600 000 tonnes $(A - a)$. Consumers would be unable to obtain all they wanted and would thus be willing to pay a higher price. Producers, unable or unwilling to supply enough to meet the demand, will be only too happy to accept a higher price. The effect of the shortage, then, will be to drive up the price. The same would happen at a price of 40p per kilogram. There would still be a shortage; price would still rise. But as the price rises, the quantity demanded falls and the quantity supplied rises. The shortage is progressively eliminated.

What would happen if the price started at a much higher level: say at 100p per kilogram? In this case supply would exceed demand by 600 000 tonnes $(e - E)$. The effect of this surplus would be to drive the price down as farmers competed against each other to sell their excess supplies. The same would happen at a price of 80p per kilogram. There would still be a surplus; price would still fall.

In fact, only one price is sustainable. This is the price where demand equals supply: namely 60p per kilogram, where both demand and supply are 350 000 tonnes. When supply matches demand the market is said to clear. There is no shortage and no surplus.

This price, where demand equals supply, is called the equilibrium price. By equilibrium we mean a point of balance or a point of rest: in other words, a point towards which there is a tendency to move. In Table 1.3, if the price starts at other than 60p per kilogram, there will be a tendency for it to move towards 60p. The equilibrium price is the only price at which producers' and consumers' wishes are mutually reconciled: where the producers' plans to supply exactly match the consumers' plans to buy.

Definitions

Market clearing
A market clears when supply matches demand, leaving no shortage or surplus.

Equilibrium price
The price where the quantity demanded equals the quantity supplied: the price where there is no shortage or surplus.

Equilibrium
A position of balance. A position from which there is no inherent tendency to move away.

Table 1.3
The market demand and supply of potatoes (monthly)

Price of potatoes (pence per kg)	Total market demand (tonnes: 000s)	Total market supply (tonnes: 000s)
20	700 (A)	100 (a)
40	500 (B)	200 (b)
60	350 (C)	350 (c)
80	200 (D)	530 (d)
100	100 (E)	700 (e)

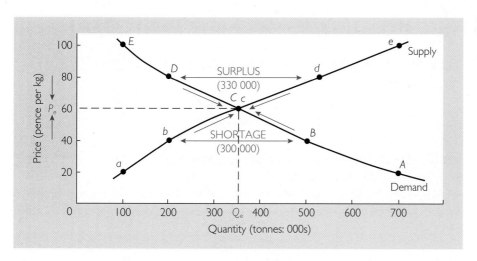

Figure 1.6

The determination of market equilibrium (potatoes: monthly)

> ***Equilibrium is the point where conflicting interests are balanced.*** Only at this point is the amount that demanders are willing to purchase the same as the amount that suppliers are willing to supply. It is a point which will be automatically reached in a free market through the operation of the price mechanism.
>
> **Key Idea 7**

Demand and supply curves

The determination of equilibrium price and output can be shown using demand and supply curves. Equilibrium is where the two curves intersect.

Figure 1.6 shows the demand and supply curves of potatoes corresponding to the data in Table 1.3. Equilibrium price is P_e (60p) and equilibrium quantity is Q_e (350 000 tonnes).

At any price above 60p, there would be a surplus. Thus at 80p there is a surplus of 330 000 tonnes ($d - D$). More is supplied than consumers are willing and able to purchase at that price. Thus a price of 80p fails to clear the market. Price will fall to the equilibrium price of 60p. As it does so, there will be a movement along the demand curve from point D to point C, and a movement along the supply curve from point d to point c.

At any price below 60p, there would be a shortage. Thus at 40p there is a shortage of 300 000 tonnes ($B - b$). Price will rise to 60p. This will cause a movement along the supply curve from point b to point c and along the demand curve from point B to point C.

Point Cc is the equilibrium: where demand equals supply.

Movement to a new equilibrium

The equilibrium price will remain unchanged only so long as the demand and supply curves remain unchanged. If either of the curves shifts, a new equilibrium will be formed.

Figure 1.7

Effect of a shift in the demand curve

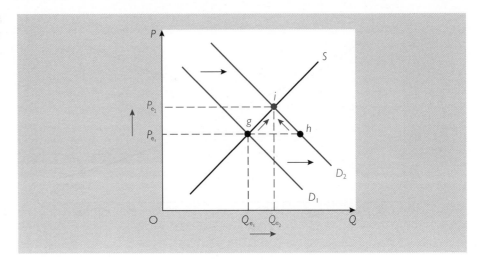

A change in demand

If one of the determinants of demand changes (other than price), the whole demand curve will shift. This will lead to a movement along the supply curve to the new intersection point.

For example, in Figure 1.7, if a rise in consumer incomes led to the demand curve shifting to D_2, there would be a shortage of $h - g$ at the original price P_{e_1}. This would cause price to rise to the new equilibrium P_{e_2}. As it did so, there would be a movement along the supply curve from point g to point i, and along the new demand curve (D_2) from point h to point i. Equilibrium quantity would rise from Q_{e_1} to Q_{e_2}.

The effect of the shift in demand, therefore, has been a movement along the supply curve from the old equilibrium to the new: from point g to point i.

A change in supply

Likewise, if one of the determinants of supply changes (other than price), the whole supply curve will shift. This will lead to a movement *along* the *demand* curve to the new intersection point.

For example, in Figure 1.8, if costs of production rose, the supply curve would shift to the left: to S_2. There would be a shortage of $g - j$ at the old price of P_{e_1}. Price would rise from P_{e_1} to P_{e_3}. Quantity would fall from Q_{e_1} to Q_{e_3}. In other words, there would be a movement along the demand curve from point g to point k, and along the new supply curve (S_2) from point j to point k.

> ### Pause for thought
>
> Is the following statement true? 'An increase in demand will cause an increase in price. This increase in price will cause a reduction in demand, until demand is reduced back to its original level.' Explain your answer and try using a demand and supply diagram to illustrate what is going on.

To summarise: a shift in one curve leads to a movement along the other curve to the new intersection point.

Sometimes a number of determinants might change. This may lead to a shift in *both* curves. When this happens, equilibrium simply moves from the point where the old curves intersected to the point where the new ones intersect.

Key Idea 7 p41

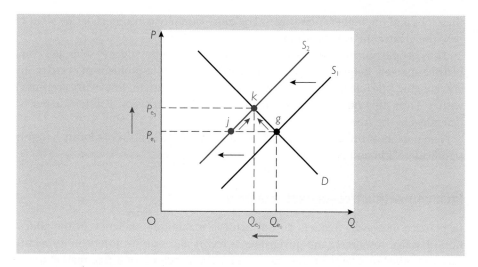

Figure 1.8
Effect of a shift in the supply curve

Recap

1. If the demand for a good exceeds the supply, there will be a shortage. This will lead to a rise in the price of the good.

2. If the supply of a good exceeds the demand, there will be a surplus. This will lead to a fall in the price.

3. Price will settle at the equilibrium. The equilibrium price is the one that clears the market: the price where demand equals supply.

4. If the demand or supply curve shifts, this will lead either to a shortage or to a surplus. Price will therefore either rise or fall until a new equilibrium is reached at the position where the supply and demand curves now intersect.

The free-market economy   1.5

How well does it serve us?

Advantages of a free-market economy

The fact that a free-market economy functions automatically is one of its major advantages. There is no need for costly and complex bureaucracies to co-ordinate economic decisions. The economy can respond quickly to changing demand and supply conditions.

When markets are highly competitive, no one has great power. Competition between firms keeps prices down and acts as an incentive to firms to become more efficient. The more firms there are competing, the more responsive they will be to consumer wishes.

The more efficiently firms can combine their factors of production, the more profit they will make. The more efficiently workers work, the more secure will be their jobs and the higher their wages. The more carefully consumers decide what to buy, the greater the value for money they will receive.

Thus people pursuing their own self-interest through buying and selling in competitive markets helps to minimise the central economic problem of scarcity, by encouraging the efficient use of the nation's resources in line with consumer wishes. From this type of argument, the following conclusion is often drawn by defenders of the free market:

'The pursuit of private gain results in the social good.' This is obviously a highly significant claim and has profound moral implications.

Key Idea 1 p5

Problems with a free-market economy

In practice, however, markets do not achieve maximum efficiency in the allocation of scarce resources, and governments feel it necessary to intervene to rectify this and other problems of the free market. The problems of a free market are as follows:

- Competition between firms is often limited. A few giant firms may dominate an industry. In these cases they may charge high prices and make large profits. Rather than merely responding to consumer wishes, they may attempt to persuade consumers by advertising. Consumers are particularly susceptible to advertisements for products that are unfamiliar to them.

Key Idea 4 p26

- Lack of competition and high profits may remove the incentive for firms to be efficient.
- Power and property may be unequally distributed. Those who have power and/or property (e.g. big business, unions, landlords) will gain at the expense of those without power and property.
- The practices of some firms may be socially undesirable or have adverse environmental consequences. For example, a chemical works may pollute the environment.
- Some socially desirable goods would simply not be produced by private enterprise. What firm would build and operate a lighthouse, unless it were paid for by the government?
- A free-market economy may lead to macroeconomic instability. There may be periods of recession with high unemployment and falling output, and other periods of rising prices.
- Finally, there is the ethical objection that a free-market economy, by rewarding self-interested behaviour, may encourage selfishness, greed, materialism and the acquisition or pursuit of power.

Key Idea 4 p26

We shall be examining these various problems in more detail in later chapters.

The mixed economy

Because of the problems of both free-market and command economies, all real-world economies are a mixture of the two systems. The economies of the former communist bloc all used the market mechanism to some extent. All market economies involve some degree of government intervention.

> **Government intervention may be able to rectify various failings of the market.** Government intervention in the market can be used to achieve various economic objectives that may not be best achieved by the market. Governments are not perfect, however, and their actions may bring adverse as well as beneficial consequences.
>
> **Key Idea 8**

In mixed market economies, the government may control the following:

- Relative prices of goods and inputs, by taxing or subsidising them or by direct price controls.
- Relative incomes, by the use of income taxes, welfare payments or direct controls over wages, profits, rents, etc.
- The pattern of production and consumption, by the use of legislation (e.g. making it illegal to produce unsafe goods), by direct provision of goods and services (e.g. education and defence), by taxes and subsidies or by nationalisation.
- The macroeconomic problems of unemployment, inflation, lack of growth, balance of trade deficits and exchange rate fluctuations, by the use of taxes and government expenditure, the control of bank lending and interest rates, the direct control of prices, and the control of the foreign exchange rate.

> **Definition**
>
> **Relative price**
> The price of one good compared with another (e.g. good X is twice the price of good Y).

Just how the government intervenes, and what the effects of the various forms of intervention are, will be examined in detail in later chapters.

The relative merits of alternative mixtures of government and the market depend on the weight attached to various political and economic goals: goals such as liberty, equality, efficiency in production, the fulfilling of consumer wishes, economic growth and full employment. No one type of mixed market economy is likely to be superior in all respects.

> **Pause for thought**
>
> Why do governments on the political right tend to intervene less in markets than governments on the political left? Does this mean that whether something is an economic 'problem' depends on your perspective?

Box 1.3 Case Studies and Applications

The UK housing market

The home-buyer's big dipper

If you are thinking of buying a house sometime in the future, then you may well follow the fortunes of the housing market with some trepidation. In the late 1980s there was a housing price explosion in the UK: in fact, between 1984 and 1989 house prices *doubled*. After several years of falling or gently rising house prices in the early and mid-1990s, there was another boom from 1996 to 2003, with house prices rising by 26 per cent per year at the peak (in the 12 months to January 2003). For many, owning a home of their own was becoming a mere dream.

House prices since the early 1980s

The diagram shows what happened to house prices in the period 1983 to 2003. The height of each bar measures the percentage by which average house prices rose in that particular year. You can see that house price inflation was very high in the late 1980s, reaching a peak of 23.3 per cent in 1988.

In their rush to buy a house before prices rose any further, many people in this period borrowed as much as they were able. Building societies and banks at that time had plenty of money to lend and were

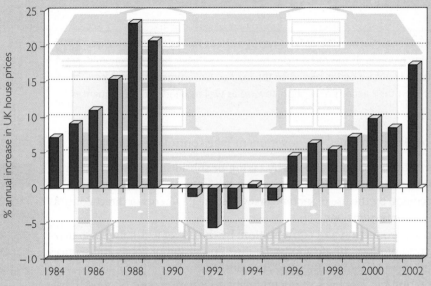

UK house price inflation (all houses, all buyers)

only too willing to do so. Many people, therefore, took out very large mortgages. In 1983 the average new mortgage was 2.08 times average annual earnings. By 1989 this figure had risen to 3.44.

After 1989 there followed a period of *falling* prices. From 1990 to 1995, house prices fell by 12.2 per cent. Many people now found themselves in a position of *negative equity*. This is the situation where the size of mortgage is greater than the value of the house. In other words, if they sold their house, they would end up still owing money! For this reason many people found that they could not move house.

Then in 1996, house prices began to recover and for the next three years rose moderately – by around 5 per cent per annum. But then they started rising rapidly again, and by 2002, house price inflation had returned to rates similar to those in the 1980s. Was this good news or bad news? For those who had been trapped in negative equity, it was good news. It was also good news for old people who wished to move into a retirement home and who had a house to sell. It was bad news for the first-time buyer, however! As

we shall see in many parts of this book, what is good news for one person is often bad news for another.

The determinants of house prices

House prices are determined by demand and supply. If demand rises (i.e. shifts to the right) or if supply falls (i.e. shifts to the left), the equilibrium price of houses will rise. Similarly, if demand falls or supply rises, the equilibrium price will fall.

So why did house prices rise so rapidly in the 1980s, only to fall in the early 1990s and then rise rapidly again in the late 1990s and early 2000s? The answer lies primarily in changes in the *demand* for housing. Let us examine the various factors that affected the demand for houses.

Incomes (actual and anticipated). The second half of the 1980s was a period of rapidly rising incomes. The economy was experiencing an economic 'boom'. Many people wanted to spend their extra incomes on housing: either buying a house for the first time, or moving to a better one. What is more, many people

Recap

1. A free-market economy functions automatically, and if there is plenty of competition between producers, this can help to protect consumers' interests.

2. In practice, however, competition may be limited; there may be great inequality; there may be adverse social and environmental consequences; there may be macroeconomic instability.

thought that their incomes would continue to grow, and were thus prepared to stretch themselves financially in the short term by buying an expensive house, confident that their mortgage payments would become more and more affordable over time.

The early 1990s, by contrast, was a period of recession, with rising unemployment and much more slowly growing incomes. People had much less confidence about their ability to afford large mortgages. The mid-1990s onwards saw incomes rising again.

The desire for home ownership. Mrs Thatcher (Prime Minister from 1979 to 1991) put great emphasis on the virtues of home ownership: a home-owning democracy. Certainly, the mood of the age was that it was very desirable to own one's own home. This fuelled the growth in demand in the 1980s.

The cost of mortgages. During the second half of the 1980s, mortgage interest rates were generally falling. This meant that people could afford larger mortgages, and thus afford to buy more expensive houses. In 1989, however, this trend was reversed. Mortgage interest rates were now rising. Many people found it difficult to maintain existing payments, let alone to take on a larger mortgage. From 1996 to 2003 mortgage rates were generally reduced again, once more fuelling the demand for houses.

The availability of mortgages. In the late 1980s, mortgages were readily available. Banks and building societies were prepared to accept smaller deposits on houses, and to grant mortgages of $3\frac{1}{2}$ times a person's annual income, compared with $2\frac{1}{2}$ times in the early 1980s. In the early 1990s, however, banks and building societies were more cautious about granting mortgages. They were aware that, with falling house prices, rising unemployment and the growing problem of negative equity, there was an increased danger that borrowers would default on payments. With the recovery of the economy in the mid-1990s, however, and with a growing number of mortgage lenders, mortgages became more readily available and for greater amounts relative to people's income.

Speculation. In the 1980s, people generally believed that house prices would continue rising. This encouraged people to buy as soon as possible, and to take out the biggest mortgage possible, before prices went up any further. There was also an effect on supply. Those with houses to sell held back until the last possible moment in the hope of getting a higher price. The net effect was for a rightward shift in the demand curve for houses and a leftward shift in the supply curve. The effect of this speculation, therefore, was to help bring about the very effect that people were predicting (see Section 2.5).

In the early 1990s, the opposite occurred. People thinking of buying houses held back, hoping to buy at a lower price. People with houses to sell tried to sell as quickly as possible before prices fell any further. Again the effect of this speculation was to aggravate the change in prices – this time a fall in prices.

Then, in the late 1990s, the return of rapidly rising prices encouraged people to buy more rapidly again, once more adding fuel to house price inflation. The speculation was compounded by worries about falling stock market prices. Many investors turned to buying property instead of shares.

What of the future?

By early 2003, the boom in house prices seemed to be coming to an end. With growing economic uncertainty, people were becoming increasingly worried about taking on large mortgage debt. And with house price inflation slowing down, speculation could go into reverse. It seemed unlikely that there would be a house price crash, however, with interest rates edging lower.

1. Draw supply and demand diagrams to illustrate what was happening to house prices (a) in the second half of the 1980s and the late 1990s and early 2000s; (b) in the early 1990s.
2. Are there any factors on the *supply* side that influence house prices?

---

3. All real-world economies are some mixture of the market and government intervention. Governments intervene in market economies in various ways in order to correct the failings of the free market. The degree and form of government intervention depend on the aims of governments and the nature of the problems they are attempting to tackle.

Questions

1. Using a chart similar to that in Figure 1.1 (on page 28), trace through the following effects: (a) a fall in demand for a good; (b) an increased supply of a factor of production. (In the case of (b) you will need to consider the factor market first, and then the goods market.)

2. Why do the prices of fresh vegetables fall when they are in season? Could an individual farmer prevent the price falling?

3. If you were the owner of a clothes shop, how would you set about deciding what prices to charge for each garment at the end-of-season sale?

4. The number of owners of mobile phones has grown rapidly and hence the demand for mobile phones has also grown rapidly. Yet the prices of mobile phones have fallen. Why?

5. Assume that oil begins to run out and that extraction becomes more expensive. Trace through the effects of this on the market for oil and the market for other fuels.

6. This question is concerned with the supply of oil for central heating. In each case consider whether there is a movement along the supply curve (and in which direction) or a shift in it (and whether left or right).

   (a) New oil fields start up in production.
   (b) The demand for central heating rises.
   (c) The price of gas falls.
   (d) Oil companies anticipate an upsurge in demand for central heating oil.
   (e) The demand for petrol rises.
   (f) New technology decreases the costs of oil refining.
   (g) All oil products become more expensive.

7. The weekly demand and supply schedules for t-shirts (in millions) in a free market are as follows:

Price (£)	8	7	6	5	4	3	2	1
Quantity demanded	6	8	10	12	14	16	18	20
Quantity supplied	18	16	14	12	10	8	6	4

   (a) What is the equilibrium price and quantity?
   (b) Assume that changes in fashion cause the demand for t-shirts to rise by 4 million at each price. What will be the new equilibrium price and quantity? Has equilibrium quantity risen as much as the rise in demand? Explain why or why not.
   (c) Now plot the data in the table on a graph and mark the equilibrium. Also plot the new data corresponding to (b) and mark the new equilibrium.

8. On separate demand and supply diagrams for bread, sketch the effects of the following: (a) a rise in the price of wheat; (b) a rise in the price of butter and margarine; (c) a rise in the price of rice, pasta and potatoes. In each case, state your assumptions.

9. For what reasons might the price of foreign holidays rise? In each case identify whether these are reasons affecting demand or supply (or both).

10. If both demand and supply change, and if we know in which direction they have shifted but not how much, why is it that we will be able to predict the direction in which *either* price *or* quantity will change, but not both? (Clue: consider the four possible combinations and sketch them if necessary: (a) *D* left, *S* left; (b) *D* right, *S* right; (c) *D* left, *S* right; (d) *D* right, *S* left.)

11. What will happen to the equilibrium price and quantity of butter in each of the following cases? You should state whether demand or supply (or both) have shifted and in which direction. (In each case assume *ceteris paribus*.)

   (a) A rise in the price of margarine.
   (b) A rise in the demand for yoghurt.
   (c) A rise in the price of bread.
   (d) A rise in the demand for bread.
   (e) An expected rise in the price of butter in the near future.
   (f) A tax on butter production.
   (g) The invention of a new, but expensive, process for removing all cholesterol from butter, plus the passing of a law which states that all butter producers must use this process.

Additional case studies on the *Essentials of Economics* website
(www.booksites.net/sloman)

1.1 **The interdependence of markets.** A case study in the operation of markets, examining the effects on a local economy of the discovery of a large coal deposit.

1.2 **Adam Smith (1723–90).** Smith, the founder of modern economics, argued that markets act like an invisible hand guiding production and consumption.

1.3 **Bentham and the philosophy of utilitarianism.** This looks at the historical and philosophical underpinning of the ideas of utility maximisation.

1.4 **Stocks and flows.** This examines one of the most important distinctions in economics and one that we shall come across on several occasions.

1.5 **Free-market medicine in Russia.** This examines the operation of the fledgling market economy in Russia and the successes and difficulties in moving from a planned to a market economy.

Sections of chapter covered in
WinEcon – Sloman, *Essentials of Economics*

Essentials of Economics section	*WinEcon* section
1.1	1.1
1.2	1.2
1.3	1.3
1.4	1.4
1.5	–

Websites relevant to this chapter

Numbers and sections refer to websites listed in the Web Appendix and hotlinked from this book's website at
www.booksites.net/sloman

■ For news articles relevant to this chapter, see the *Economics News Articles* link from the book's website.

■ For general news on markets, see websites in section A, and particularly A2, 3, 4, 5, 8, 9, 18, 24, 25, 26, 36. See also site A42 for links to economics news articles from newspapers worldwide.

■ For links to sites on markets, see the relevant sections of I4, 7, 11, 17.

■ For news on the Russian economy (Box 1.1), see sites A14, 15. See also the *Economic Systems and Theories > Transition Economies* section of sites I7 and 11.

■ For data on the housing market (Box 1.3), see sites B7, 8, 11.

■ For student resources relevant to this chapter, see sites C1–7, 9, 10, 19; D3.

■ For sites favouring the free market, see C17 and E34.

CHAPTER MAP

CHAPTER TWO
Markets in action

In this chapter we explore the working of markets in more detail. We start by examining one of the most important concepts in the whole of economics – that of elasticity (Sections 2.1–2.4).

A bumper harvest may seem like good news for farmers: after all, they will be able to sell more. But is it good news? Although they will sell more, the effect of the increased supply will be to drive down the price – and that's bad news for farmers! So will the increased sales (the good news) be enough to compensate for the reduction in price (the bad news)? Will farmers end up earning more or less from their bumper harvest? It all depends on just how much the price falls, and this depends on the *price elasticity of demand* for their produce. This is a measure of how *responsive* demand is to a change in price.

It is not just the responsiveness of *demand* that is important in determining the functioning of markets. It is also the responsiveness of *supply*. Why, do you think, do some firms respond to a rise in price by producing a lot more, whereas others only produce a little more? Is it simply because of different technologies? We will discover just what influences the price elasticity of supply in Section 2.3.

The chapter closes by looking at what happens if governments set about *controlling* prices. Why will shortages occur if the government sets the price too low, or surpluses if it sets it too high? When might governments feel that it is a good idea to fix prices?

2.1   Price elasticity of demand

How responsive is demand to a change in price?

When the price of a good rises, the quantity demanded will fall. That much is fairly obvious. But in most cases we will want to know more than this. We will want to know just *how much* the quantity demanded will fall. In other words, we will want to know how *responsive* demand is to a rise in price.

Take the case of two products: oil and cauliflowers. In the case of oil, a rise in price is likely to result in only a slight fall in the quantity demanded. If people want to continue driving, they have to pay the higher prices for fuel. A few may turn to riding bicycles, and some people may try to make fewer journeys, but for most people, a rise in the price of petrol and diesel will make little difference to how much they use their cars.

In the case of cauliflowers, however, a rise in price may lead to a substantial fall in the quantity demanded. The reason is that there are alternative vegetables that people can buy. Many people, when buying vegetables, are very conscious of their prices and will buy whatever is reasonably priced.

We call the responsiveness of demand to a change in price the price elasticity of demand. If we know the price elasticity of demand for a product, we can predict the effect on price and quantity of a shift in the *supply* curve for that product. For example, we can predict the effect of the bumper harvest that we considered at the beginning of the chapter.

Figure 2.1 shows the effect of a shift in supply with two quite different demand curves (D and D′). Curve D′ is more elastic than curve D. In other words, for any given change in price, there will be a larger change in quantity demanded along curve D′ than along curve D.

Assume that initially the supply curve is S_1, and that it intersects with both demand curves at point *a*, at a price of P_1 and a quantity of Q_1. Now supply shifts

Figure 2.1
Market supply and demand

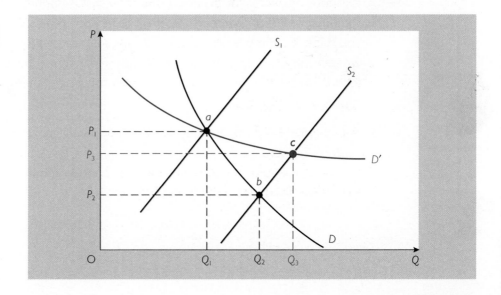

to S_2. What will happen to price and quantity? In the case of the less elastic demand curve D, there is a relatively large fall in price (to P_2) and a relatively small rise in quantity (to Q_2): equilibrium is at point b. In the case of the more elastic demand curve D', however, there is only a relatively small fall in price (to P_3) but a relatively large rise in quantity (to Q_3): equilibrium is at point c.

Measuring the price elasticity of demand

What we want to compare is the size of the change in quantity demanded with the size of the change in price. But since price and quantity are measured in different units, the only sensible way we can do this is to use percentage or proportionate changes. This gives us the following formula for the price elasticity of demand ($P\varepsilon_D$) for a product: percentage (or proportionate) change in quantity demanded divided by the percentage (or proportionate) change in price. Putting this in symbols gives:

$$P\varepsilon_D = \frac{\%\Delta Q_D}{\%\Delta P}$$

where ε (the Greek epsilon) is the symbol we use for elasticity, and Δ (the capital Greek delta) is the symbol we use for a 'change in'.

Thus if a 40 per cent rise in the price of oil caused the quantity demanded to fall by a mere 10 per cent, the price elasticity of oil over this range would be:

$$-10\%/40\% = -0.25$$

On the other hand, if a 5 per cent fall in the price of cauliflowers caused a 15 per cent rise in the quantity demanded, the price elasticity of demand for cauliflowers over this range would be:

$$15\%/-5\% = -3$$

Cauliflowers have a more elastic demand than oil, and this is shown by the figures. But just what do these two figures show? What is the significance of minus 0.25 and minus 3?

Interpreting the figure for elasticity

The use of proportionate or percentage measures

Elasticity is measured in proportionate or percentage terms for the following reasons:

- It allows comparison of changes in two qualitatively different things, and thus which are measured in two different types of unit: i.e. it allows comparison of *quantity* changes with *monetary* changes.
- It is the only sensible way of deciding *how big* a change in price or quantity is. Take a simple example. An item goes up in price by £1. Is this a big increase or a small increase? We can answer this only if we know what the original price was. If a can of beans goes up in price by £1, that is a huge price increase. If,

Definitions

Elastic demand
Where quantity demanded changes by a larger percentage than price. Ignoring the negative sign, it will have a value greater than 1.

Inelastic demand
Where quantity demanded changes by a smaller percentage than price. Ignoring the negative sign, it will have a value less than 1.

Unit elastic demand
Where quantity demanded changes by the same percentage as price. Ignoring the negative sign, it will have a value equal to 1.

however, the price of a house goes up by £1, that is a tiny price increase. In other words, it is the percentage or proportionate increase in price that we look at in deciding how big a price rise it is.

The sign (positive or negative)

Demand curves are generally downward sloping. This means that price and quantity change in opposite directions. A *rise* in price (a positive figure) will cause a *fall* in the quantity demanded (a negative figure). Similarly a *fall* in price will cause a *rise* in the quantity demanded. Thus when working out price elasticity of demand we either divide a negative figure by a positive figure, or a positive figure by a negative. Either way, we end up with a negative figure.

The value (greater or less than 1)

If we now ignore the negative sign and just concentrate on the value of the figure, this tells us whether demand is elastic or inelastic.

■ Elastic demand (ε > 1). This is where a change in price causes a proportionately larger change in the quantity demanded. In this case the value of elasticity will be greater than 1, since we are dividing a larger figure by a smaller figure.
■ Inelastic demand (ε < 1). This is where a change in price causes a proportionately smaller change in the quantity demanded. In this case elasticity will be less than 1, since we are dividing a smaller figure by a larger figure.
■ Unit elastic demand (ε = 1). This is where price and quantity demanded change by the same proportion. This will give an elasticity equal to 1, since we are dividing a figure by itself.

Determinants of price elasticity of demand

The price elasticity of demand varies enormously from one product to another. Table 2.1 gives some examples. But why do some products have a highly elastic demand, whereas others have a highly *in*elastic demand? What determines price elasticity of demand?

The number and closeness of substitute goods.   This is the most important determinant. The more substitutes there are for a good, and the closer they are, the more will people switch to these alternatives when the price of the good rises: the greater, therefore, will be the price elasticity of demand.

Returning to our examples of oil and cauliflowers, there is no close substitute for oil and thus demand is relatively inelastic. There are plenty of alternatives to cauliflowers, however, and thus demand is relatively elastic. Of course, the closeness is very often in the mind of the consumer. Some people may have a particular fondness for cauliflowers. For them demand will be less elastic than for people who are not fussy whether they eat cauliflowers, cabbages, broccoli or any other vegetable.

> *Pause for thought*
>
> Why will the price elasticity of demand for a particular brand of a product (e.g. Texaco) be greater than that for the product in general (e.g. petrol)? Is this difference the result of a difference in the size of the income effect or the substitution effect?

Product	Price elasticity of demand	Income elasticity of demand
Food	−0.21	+0.28
Medical services	−0.22	+0.22
Housing		
Rental	−0.18	+1.00
Owner occupied	−1.20	+1.20
Electricity	−1.14	+0.61
Cars	−1.20	+3.00
Beer	−0.26	+0.38
Wine	−0.88	+0.97
Cigarettes	−0.35	+0.50
Transatlantic air travel	−1.30	+1.40
Imports	−0.58	+2.73

Table 2.1

Estimates of price and income elasticity of demand for the USA

Source: W. Nicholson, *Intermediate Microeconomics*, 9th edition (South-Western, 2004).

The proportion of income spent on the good.   The higher the proportion of our income we spend on a good, the more we will be forced to cut consumption when its price rises: the bigger will be the income effect and the more elastic will be the demand.

Thus salt has a very low price elasticity of demand. We spend such a tiny fraction of our income on salt, that we would find little difficulty in paying a relatively large percentage increase in its price: the income effect of a price rise would be very small. By contrast, there will be a much bigger income effect when a major item of expenditure rises in price. For example, if mortgage interest rates rise (the 'price' of loans for house purchase), people may have to cut down substantially on their demand for housing, being forced to buy somewhere smaller and cheaper, or to live in rented accommodation.

The time period.   When price rises, people may take time to adjust their consumption patterns and find alternatives. The longer the time period after a price change, then, the more elastic is the demand likely to be.

To illustrate this, let us return to our example of oil. Between December 1973 and June 1974 the price of crude oil quadrupled, which led to similar increases in the prices of petrol and other oil products (such as central heating oil). Over the next few months, there was only a very small fall in the consumption of oil products. Demand was highly inelastic. The reason was that people still wanted to drive their cars and heat their houses.

Over time, however, as the higher oil prices persisted, new fuel-efficient cars were developed and many people switched to smaller cars or moved closer to their work. Similarly, people switched to gas or solid fuel central heating, and spent more money insulating their houses to save on fuel bills. Demand was thus much more elastic in the long run.

Recap

1. Price elasticity of demand is a measure of the responsiveness of demand to a change in price.

2. It is defined as the proportionate (or percentage) change in quantity demanded divided by the proportionate (or percentage) change in price. Given that demand curves are downward sloping, price elasticity of demand will have a negative value.

3. If quantity changes proportionately more than price, the figure for elasticity will be greater than 1 (ignoring the sign): demand is elastic. If the quantity changes proportionately less than price, the figure for elasticity will be less than 1 (again, ignoring the sign): demand is inelastic. If quantity and price change by the same proportion, the elasticity has a value of (minus) 1: demand is unit elastic.

4. Demand will be more elastic the greater the number and closeness of substitute goods, the higher the proportion of income spent on the good and the longer the time period that elapses after the change in price.

2.2   Price elasticity of demand and consumer expenditure

How much do we spend on a good at a given price?

One of the most important applications of price elasticity of demand concerns its relationship with the total amount of money that consumers spend on a product. Total consumer expenditure (*TE*) is simply price times quantity purchased.

$$TE = P \times Q$$

For example, if consumers buy 3 million units (*Q*) at a price of £2 per unit (*P*), they will spend a total of £6 million (*TE*). This is shown graphically in Figure 2.2 as the area of the shaded rectangle. But why? The area of a rectangle is simply its height multiplied by its length. But *TE* is simply price (the height of the shaded rectangle) multiplied by quantity (the length of the rectangle). Total consumer expenditure will be the same as the total revenue (*TR*) received by firms from the sale of the product (before any taxes or other deductions).

What will happen to consumer expenditure (and hence firms' revenue) if there is a change in price? The answer depends on the price elasticity of demand.

Definition

Total consumer expenditure on a product (*TE*) (per period of time)
The price of the product multiplied by the quantity purchased:
$TE = P \times Q$

Figure 2.2
Total expenditure

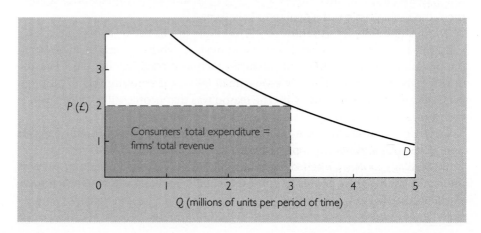

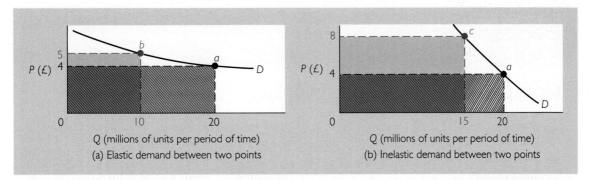

Figure 2.3
Price elasticity of demand and total expenditure

Elastic demand

As price rises so quantity demanded falls, and vice versa. When demand is elastic, quantity demanded changes proportionately more than price. Thus the change in quantity has a bigger effect on total consumer expenditure than does the change in price. For example, when the price rises, there will be such a large fall in consumer demand that less will be spent than before. This can be summarised as follows:

- *P* rises; *Q* falls proportionately more; therefore *TE* falls.
- *P* falls: *Q* rises proportionately more; therefore *TE* rises.

In other words, total expenditure changes in the same direction as *quantity*.

This is illustrated in Figure 2.3(a). Demand is elastic between points *a* and *b*. A rise in price from £4 to £5 causes a proportionately larger fall in quantity demanded: from 20 million to 10 million. Total expenditure *falls* from £80 million (the striped area) to £50 million (the pink shaded area).

When demand is elastic, then, a rise in price will cause a fall in total consumer expenditure and thus a fall in the total revenue that firms selling the product receive. A reduction in price, however, will result in consumers spending more, and hence firms earning more.

Inelastic demand

When demand is inelastic, it is the other way around. Price changes proportionately more than quantity. Thus the change in price has a bigger effect on total consumer expenditure than does the change in quantity. To summarise the effects:

- *P* rises; *Q* falls proportionately less; therefore *TE* rises.
- *P* falls; *Q* rises proportionately less; therefore *TE* falls.

In other words, total consumer expenditure changes in the same direction as *price*.

This is illustrated in Figure 2.3(b). Demand is inelastic between points *a* and *c*. A rise in price from £4 to £8 causes a proportionately smaller fall in quantity demanded: from 20 million to 15 million. Total expenditure *rises* from £80 million (the striped area) to £120 million (the pink shaded area).

In this case, firms' revenue will increase if there is a rise in price, and fall if there is a fall in price.

> **Definition**
>
> **Total revenue (*TR*) (per period)** The total amount received by firms from the sale of a product, before the deduction of taxes or any other costs. The price multiplied by the quantity sold. $TR = P \times Q$.

> **Pause for thought**   ▌▌
>
> If a firm faces an elastic demand curve, why will it not necessarily be in the firm's interests to produce more? (Clue: you will need to distinguish between revenue and profit. We will explore this relationship in the next chapter.)

Box 2.1 Exploring Economics

Shall we put up our price?

Competition, price and revenue

When you buy a can of drink on a train, or an ice-cream in the cinema, or a bottle of wine in a restaurant, you may well be horrified by its price. How can they get away with it?

The answer is that these firms are *not* price takers. They can choose what price to charge. We will be examining the behaviour of such firms in Chapter 4, but here it is useful to see how price elasticity of demand can help to explain their behaviour.

Take the case of the can of drink on the train. If you are thirsty, and if you haven't brought a drink with you, then you will have to get one from the train's bar, or go without. There is no substitute. What we are saying here is that the demand for drink on the train is inelastic at the normal shop price. This means that the train operator can put up the price of its drinks, and food too, and earn *more* revenue.

Generally, the less the competition a firm faces, the lower will be the elasticity of demand for its products, since there will be fewer substitutes (competitors) to which consumers can turn. The lower the

price elasticity of demand, the higher is likely to be the price that the firm charges.

When there is plenty of competition, it is quite a different story. Petrol stations in the same area may compete fiercely in terms of price. One station may hope that by reducing its price by 1p, or even 0.1p, per litre below that of its competitors, it can attract customers away from them. With a highly elastic demand, a small reduction in price may lead to a substantial increase in their revenue. The problem is, of course, that when they *all* reduce prices, no firm wins. No one attracts customers away from the others! In this case it is the customer who wins.

> **?** 1. Why may a restaurant charge very high prices for wine and bottled water and yet quite reasonable prices for food?
>
> 2. Why are clothes with designer labels so much more expensive than 'own brand' clothes from a chain store, even though they may cost a similar amount to produce?

Special cases

Figure 2.4 shows three special cases: (a) a totally inelastic demand ($P\varepsilon_D = 0$); (b) an infinitely elastic demand ($P\varepsilon_D = -\infty$); and (c) a unit elastic demand ($P\varepsilon_D = -1$).

Totally inelastic demand.   This is shown by a vertical straight line. No matter what happens to price, quantity demanded remains the same. It is obvious that the more the price rises, the bigger will be the level of consumer expenditure. Thus in Figure 2.4(a) consumer expenditure will be higher at P_2 than at P_1.

Infinitely elastic demand.   This is shown by a horizontal straight line. At any price above P_1 in Figure 2.4(b) demand is zero. But at P_1 (or any price below) demand is 'infinitely' large.

This seemingly unlikely demand curve is in fact relatively common for an *individual producer*. In a perfect market, as we have seen, firms are small relative to the whole market (like the small-scale grain farmer). They have to accept the price as given by supply and demand in the *whole market*, but at that price they can sell as much as they produce. (Demand is not *literally* infinite, but as far as the firm is concerned it is.) In this case, the more the individual farmer produces, the more revenue will be earned. In Figure 2.4(b), more revenue is earned at Q_2 than at Q_1.

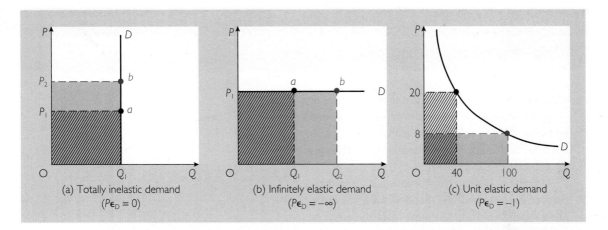

Figure 2.4
Elasticity of demand: special cases

Unit elastic demand. This occurs where price and quantity change in exactly the same proportion. Any rise in price will be exactly offset by a fall in quantity, leaving total revenue unchanged. In Figure 2.4(c) the striped area is exactly equal to the blue shaded area: in both cases total expenditure is £800.

You might have thought that a demand curve with unit elasticity would be a straight line at 45° to the axes. Instead it is a curve. The reason for its particular shape is that the proportionate *rise* in quantity must equal the proportionate *fall* in price (and vice versa). As we move down the demand curve, in order for the *proportionate* change in both price and quantity to remain constant there must be a bigger and bigger *absolute* rise in quantity and a smaller and smaller absolute fall in price. For example, a rise in quantity from 200 to 400 is the same proportionate change as a rise from 100 to 200, but its absolute size is double. A fall in price from £5 to £2.50 is the same percentage as a fall from £10 to £5, but its absolute size is only half.

> **Pause for thought**
>
> Two customers go to the fish counter at a supermarket to buy some cod. Neither looks at the price. Customer A orders 1 kilo of cod. Customer B orders £3 worth of cod. What is the price elasticity of demand of each of the two customers?

Recap

1. The total expenditure on a product is found by multiplying the quantity sold by the price of the product.

2. When demand is price elastic, a rise in price will lead to a reduction in total expenditure on the good and hence a reduction in the total revenue of producers.

3. When demand is price inelastic, a rise in price will lead to an increase in total expenditure on the good and hence an increase in the total revenue of producers.

Box 2.2

The measurement of elasticity

We have defined price elasticity as the percentage or proportionate change in quantity demanded divided by the percentage or proportionate change in price. But how, in practice, do we measure these changes for a specific demand curve?

A common mistake that students make is to think that you can talk about the elasticity of a whole *curve*. The mistake here is that in most cases the elasticity will vary along the length of the curve.

Take the case of the demand curve illustrated in Figure (a). Between points *a* and *b*, total expenditure rises ($P_2Q_2 > P_1Q_1$): demand is thus elastic between these two points. Between points *b* and *c*, however, total revenue falls ($P_3Q_3 < P_2Q_2$). Demand here is inelastic.

Normally, then, we can refer to the elasticity only of a *portion* of the demand curve, not of the *whole* curve.

There is, however, an exception to this rule. This is when the elasticity just so happens to be the same all the way along a curve, as in the three special cases illustrated in Figure 2.4.

Although we cannot normally talk about the elasticity of a whole curve, we can nevertheless talk about the elasticity between any two points on it. Remember the formula we used was:

$$\frac{\% \text{ or proportionate } \Delta Q}{\% \text{ or proportionate } \Delta P} \quad \text{(where } \Delta \text{ means 'change in')}$$

The way we measure a *proportionate* change in quantity is to divide that change by the level of *Q*: i.e. $\Delta Q/Q$. Similarly, we measure a proportionate change

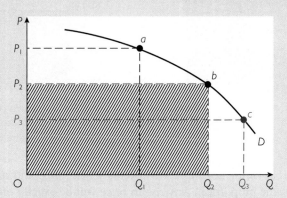

(a) Different elasticities along different portions of a demand curve

in price by dividing that change by the level of *P*: i.e. $\Delta P/Q$. Price elasticity of demand can thus now be rewritten as:

$$\frac{\Delta Q}{Q} \div \frac{\Delta P}{P}$$

But just what value do we give to *P* and *Q*? Consider the demand schedule given in the table and graphed in Figure (b). What is the elasticity of demand between points *m* and *n*? To answer this we need to identify ΔQ and *Q*, and ΔP and *P*. Let us start with the two quantity terms.

P(£)	Q(000s)
8	10
6	20
4	30
2	40

2.3   Price elasticity of supply ($P\varepsilon_S$)

How responsive is supply to a change in price?

When price changes, there will be not only a change in the quantity demanded, but also a change in the quantity *supplied*. Frequently we will want to know just how responsive quantity supplied is to a change in price. The measure we use is the price elasticity of supply.

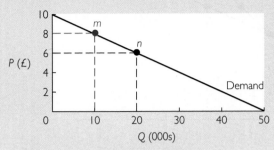

(b) Measuring elasticity using the arc method

Quantity

The difference in quantity (ΔQ) between 10 (point m) and 20 (point n) is 10.

$$\Delta Q = 10$$

But what is the *proportionate* change in Q ($\Delta Q/Q$)? Is it 10/10, taking $Q = 10$ (point m) as the base from which to measure the change in Q? Or is it 10/20, taking $Q = 20$ (point n)? To avoid this problem the average of the two quantities is used: in other words, the mid-point between them.

$$Q = 15 \text{ i.e. } \frac{(10 + 20)}{2}$$

$$\therefore \frac{\Delta Q}{Q} = \frac{10}{15}$$

Price

The difference in price between 8 (point m) and 6 (point n) is 2.

$$\Delta P = -2$$

The *proportionate* change in P is found in the same way as the proportionate change in Q. The base price is taken as the mid-point between the two prices:

$$P = 7 \text{ i.e. } \frac{(8 + 6)}{2}$$

$$\therefore \frac{\Delta P}{P} = \frac{-2}{7}$$

Elasticity

Now we have worked out figures for ΔQ, Q, ΔP and P, we can proceed to work out elasticity. Using the *average (or 'mid-point') formula*, price elasticity of demand is given by:

$$\frac{\Delta Q}{\text{average } Q} \div \frac{\Delta P}{\text{average } P}$$

In our example this would give the following elasticity between m and n:

$$10/15 \div -2/7 = -2.33$$

Since 2.33 is greater than 1, demand is elastic between m and n.

> **?** Referring to the same table, what is the price elasticity of demand between a price of (a) £6 and £4; (b) £4 and £2? What do you conclude about the elasticity of a straight-line demand curve as you move down it?

Figure 2.5 shows two supply curves. Curve S_2 is more elastic between any two prices than curve S_1. Thus, when price rises from P_1 to P_2 there is a larger increase in quantity supplied with S_2 (namely, Q_1 to Q_3) than there is with S_1 (namely, Q_1 to Q_2). For any shift in the demand curve there will be a larger change in quantity supplied and a smaller change in price with curve S_2 than with curve S_1. Thus the effect on price and quantity of a shift in the demand curve will depend on the price elasticity of supply.

Figure 2.5

Two supply curves of different elasticity

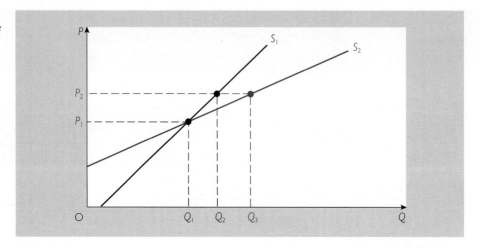

The formula for the price elasticity of supply ($P\varepsilon_S$) is: the percentage (or proportionate) change in quantity supplied divided by the percentage (or proportionate) change in price. Putting this in symbols gives:

$$P\varepsilon_S = \frac{\%\Delta Q_S}{\%\Delta P}$$

In other words, the formula is identical to that for the price elasticity of demand, except that quantity in this case is quantity *supplied*. Thus if a 10 per cent rise in price caused a 25 per cent rise in the quantity supplied, the price elasticity of supply would be:

$$25\%/10\% = 2.5$$

and if a 10 per cent rise in price caused only a 5 per cent rise in the quantity, the price elasticity of supply would be:

$$5\%/10\% = 0.5$$

In the first case, supply is elastic ($P\varepsilon_S > 1$); in the second it is inelastic ($P\varepsilon_S < 1$). Notice that, unlike the price elasticity of demand, the figure is positive (assuming that the supply curve is upward sloping). This is because price and quantity supplied change in the *same* direction.

The determinants of price elasticity of supply

The amount that costs rise as output rises.   The less the additional costs of producing additional output, the more will firms be encouraged to produce for a given price rise: the more elastic will supply be.

Supply is thus likely to be elastic if firms have plenty of spare capacity, if they can readily get extra supplies of raw materials, if they can easily switch away from producing alternative products and if they can avoid having to introduce overtime working (at higher rates of pay). If all these conditions hold, costs will be little affected by a rise in output and supply will be relatively elastic. The less these conditions apply, the less elastic will supply be.

Time period

■ Immediate time period. Firms are unlikely to be able to increase supply by much immediately. Supply is virtually fixed, or can vary only according to available stocks. Supply is highly inelastic.

Box 2.3 Case Studies and Applications

Advertising and its effect on the demand curve

How to increase sales and price

When we are told that brand X will make us more beautiful, enrich our lives, wash our clothes whiter, give us get-up-and-go, give us a new taste sensation or make us the envy of our friends, just what are the advertisers up to? 'Trying to sell the product', you may reply. In fact there is a bit more to it than this. Advertisers are trying to do two things:

■ Shift the product's demand curve to the right.
■ Make it less price elastic.

This is illustrated in the diagram.

D_1 shows the original demand curve with price at P_1 and sales at Q_1. D_2 shows the curve after an advertising campaign. The rightward shift allows an increased quantity (Q_2) to be sold at the original price. If the demand is also made highly inelastic, the firm can also raise its price and still have a substantial increase in sales. Thus in the diagram, price can be raised to P_2 and sales will be Q_3 – still substantially above Q_1. The total gain in revenue is shown by the shaded area.

How can advertising bring about this new demand curve?

Shifting the demand curve to the right

This will occur if the advertising brings the product to more people's attention and if it increases people's desire for the product.

Making the demand curve less elastic

This will occur if the advertising creates greater brand loyalty. People must be led to believe (rightly or wrongly) that competitors' brands are inferior. This will allow the firm to raise its price above that of its rivals with no significant fall in sales. There will only be a small substitution effect because consumers have been led to believe that there are no close substitutes.

? 1. Think of some advertisements that deliberately seek to make demand less elastic.
2. Imagine that 'Sunshine' sunflower margarine, a well-known brand, is advertised with the slogan, 'It helps you live longer'. What do you think would happen to the demand curve for a supermarket's *own* brand of sunflower margarine? Consider both the direction of shift and the effect on elasticity. Will the elasticity differ markedly at different prices? How will this affect the pricing policy and sales of the supermarket's own brand?

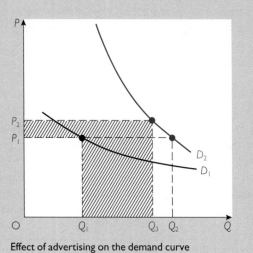

Effect of advertising on the demand curve

- Short run. If a slightly longer time period is allowed to elapse, some inputs can be increased (e.g. raw materials) while others will remain fixed (e.g. heavy machinery). Supply can increase somewhat.
- Long run. In the long run, there will be sufficient time for all inputs to be increased and for new firms to enter the industry. Supply, therefore, is likely to be highly elastic. In some circumstances the long-run supply curve may even slope downwards (see Section 3.2).

Recap

1. Price elasticity of supply measures the responsiveness of supply to a change in price. It has a positive value.

2. Supply will be more elastic the less costs per unit rise as output rises and the longer the time period.

2.4   Other elasticities

How does demand respond to changes in income and to changes in the price of other goods?

Income elasticity of demand

So far we have looked at the responsiveness of demand and supply to a change in price. But price is just one of the determinants of demand and supply. In theory, we could look at the responsiveness of demand or supply to a change in *any* one of their determinants. We could have a whole range of different types of elasticity of demand and supply.

> **Elasticity.** The responsiveness of one variable (e.g. demand) to a change in another (e.g. price). This concept is fundamental to understanding how markets work. The more elastic variables are, the more responsive is the market to changing circumstances.
>
> **Key Idea 9**

In practice there are just two other elasticities that are particularly useful to us, and both are demand elasticities.

The first is the income elasticity of demand ($Y\varepsilon_D$). This measures the responsiveness of demand to a change in consumer incomes (Y).[1] It enables us to predict how much the demand curve will shift for a given change in income. The formula for income elasticity of demand is: the percentage (or proportionate) change in demand divided by the percentage (or proportionate) change in income. Putting this in symbols gives:

---

[1] Note that we use the letter Y rather than the letter I to stand for 'income'. This is normal practice in economics. The reason is that the letter I is used for 'investment'.

$$Y\varepsilon_D = \frac{\%\Delta Q_D}{\%\Delta Y}$$

In other words, the formula is identical to that for the price elasticity of demand, except that we are dividing the change in demand by the change in *income* that caused it rather than by a change in price. Thus if a 2 per cent rise in income caused an 8 per cent rise in a product's demand, then its income elasticity of demand would be:

$$8\%/2\% = 4$$

The major determinant of income elasticity of demand is the degree of 'necessity' of the good. In a developed country, the demand for luxury goods expands rapidly as people's incomes rise, whereas the demand for basic goods, such as bread, rises only a little. Thus items such as cars and holidays abroad have a high income elasticity of demand, whereas items such as potatoes and bus journeys have a low income elasticity of demand (see Table 2.1 on page 55).

The demand for some goods actually decreases as income rises. These are *inferior goods* such as cheap margarine. As people earn more, so they switch to butter or better-quality margarine. Unlike normal goods, which have a positive income elasticity of demand, inferior goods have a negative income elasticity of demand.

Income elasticity of demand is an important concept to firms considering the future size of the market for their product. If the product has a high income elasticity of demand, sales are likely to expand rapidly as national income rises, but may also fall significantly if the economy moves into recession. (See Case 2.5, *Income elasticity of demand and the balance of payments*, on the book's website. This shows how the concept of income elasticity of demand can help us understand why so many developing countries suffer from chronic balance of trade problems.)

Cross-price elasticity of demand $(C\varepsilon_{D_{ab}})$

This is often known by its less cumbersome title of cross elasticity of demand. It is a measure of the responsiveness of demand for one product to a change in the price of another (either a substitute or a complement). It enables us to predict how much the demand curve for the first product will shift when the price of the second product changes. For example, knowledge of the cross elasticity of demand for Coca-Cola to the price of Pepsi would allow Coca-Cola to predict the effect on its own sales if the price of Pepsi were to change.

The formula for the cross-price elasticity of demand $(C\varepsilon_{D_{ab}})$ is: the percentage (or proportionate) change in demand for good a divided by the percentage (or proportionate) change in price of good b. Putting this in symbols gives:

$$C\varepsilon_{D_{ab}} = \frac{\%\Delta Q_{D_a}}{\%\Delta P_b}$$

If good b is a *substitute* for good a, a's demand will *rise* as b's price rises. In this case, cross elasticity will be a positive figure. For example, if the demand for butter rose by 2 per cent when the price of margarine (a substitute) rose by 8 per cent, then the cross elasticity of demand for butter with respect to margarine would be:

Pause for thought

Assume that you decide to spend a quarter of your income on clothes. What is (a) your income elasticity of demand; (b) your price elasticity of demand?

Definitions

Normal goods
Goods whose demand increases as consumer incomes increase. They have a positive income elasticity of demand. Luxury goods will have a higher income elasticity of demand than more basic goods.

Inferior goods
Goods whose demand *decreases* as consumer incomes increase. Such goods have a negative income elasticity of demand.

Cross-price elasticity of demand
The responsiveness of demand for one good to a change in the price of another.

Formula for cross-price elasticity of demand $(C\varepsilon_{D_{ab}})$
The percentage (or proportionate) change in demand for good a divided by the percentage (or proportionate) change in price of good b: $\%\Delta Q_{D_a} \div \%\Delta P_b$

$$2\%/8\% = 0.25$$

If good b is *complementary* to good a, however, a's demand will *fall* as b's price rises and thus as the quantity of b demanded falls. In this case, cross elasticity of demand will be a negative figure. For example, if a 4 per cent rise in the price of bread led to a 3 per cent fall in demand for butter, the cross elasticity of demand for butter with respect to bread would be:

$$-3\%/4\% = -0.75$$

The major determinant of cross elasticity of demand is the closeness of the substitute or complement. The closer it is, the bigger will be the effect on the first good of a change in the price of the substitute or complement, and hence the greater the cross elasticity – either positive or negative.

Firms will wish to know the cross elasticity of demand for their product when considering the effect on the demand for their product of a change in the price of a rival's product or of a complementary product. These are vital pieces of information for firms when making their production plans.

Another example of the usefulness of the concept of cross elasticity of demand is in the field of international trade and the balance of payments. A government will wish to know how a change in domestic prices will affect the demand for imports. If there is a high cross elasticity of demand for imports (because they are close substitutes for home-produced goods), and if prices at home rise due to inflation, the demand for imports will rise substantially, thus worsening the balance of trade.

Recap

1. Income elasticity of demand measures the responsiveness of demand to a change in income. For normal goods it has a positive value; for inferior goods it has a negative value.

2. Demand will be more income elastic the more luxurious the good and the less rapidly demand is satisfied as consumption increases.

3. Cross-price elasticity of demand measures the responsiveness of demand for one good to a change in the price of another. For substitute goods the value will be positive; for complements it will be negative.

4. The cross-price elasticity will be more elastic the closer the two goods are as substitutes or complements.

2.5   Markets and adjustment over time

How do markets respond over the longer term to a change in demand or supply?

The full adjustment of price, demand and supply to a situation of disequilibrium will not be instantaneous. It is necessary, therefore, to analyse the time path which supply takes in responding to changes in demand, and which demand takes in responding to changes in supply.

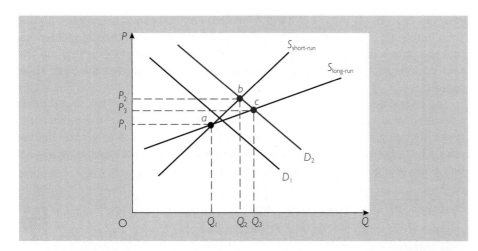

Figure 2.6
Response of supply
to an increase in
demand

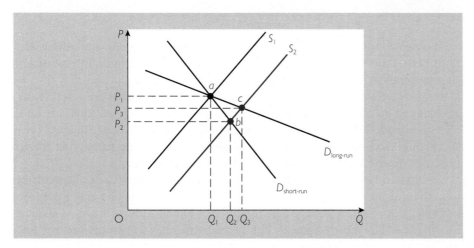

Figure 2.7
Response of demand
to an increase in
supply

Short-run and long-run adjustment

As we have already seen, the price elasticities of demand and supply vary with the time period under consideration. The reason is that producers and consumers take time to respond to a change in price. The longer the time period, the bigger the response, and thus the greater the elasticity of demand and supply.

This is illustrated in Figures 2.6 and 2.7. In both cases, as equilibrium moves from points *a* to *b* to *c*, there is a large short-run price change (P_1 to P_2) and a small short-run quantity change (Q_1 to Q_2), but a small long-run price change (P_1 to P_3) and a large long-run quantity change (Q_1 to Q_3).

Price expectations and speculation

In a world of shifting demand and supply curves, prices do not stay the same. Sometimes they go up; sometimes they come down. If prices are likely to change in the foreseeable future, this will affect the behaviour of buyers and sellers *now*. If, for example, it is now December and you are thinking of buying a new winter coat, you might decide to wait until the January sales, and in the meantime make do with your old coat. If, on the other hand, when January comes you see a new summer dress in the sales, you might well buy it now and not wait until the summer for fear that the price will have gone up by then. Thus a belief that prices will go up will cause people to buy now; a belief that prices will come down will cause them to wait.

The reverse applies to sellers. If you are thinking of selling your house and prices are falling, you will want to sell it as quickly as possible. If, on the other hand, prices are rising sharply, you will wait as long as possible so as to get the highest price. Thus a belief that prices will come down will cause people to sell now; a belief that prices will go up will cause them to wait.

People's actions are influenced by their expectations. People respond not just to what is happening now (such as a change in price), but to what they anticipate will happen in the future.

Key Idea 10

This behaviour of looking into the future and making buying and selling decisions based on your predictions is called speculation. Speculation is often based on current trends in price behaviour. If prices are currently rising, people may then try to decide whether they are about to peak and go back down again, or whether they are likely to go on rising. Having made their prediction, they will then act on it. This speculation will thus affect demand and supply, which in turn will affect price. Speculation is commonplace in many markets: the stock exchange, the foreign exchange market and the housing market are three examples.

Speculation tends to be self-fulfilling. In other words, the actions of speculators tend to bring about the very effect on prices that speculators had anticipated. For example, if speculators believe that the price of British Airways shares is about to rise, they will buy more BA shares. But by doing this they will ensure that the price *will* rise. The prophecy has become self-fulfilling.

Speculation can either help to reduce price fluctuations or aggravate them: it can be stabilising or destabilising.

Stabilising speculation

Speculation will tend to have a stabilising effect on price fluctuations when suppliers and/or demanders believe that a change in price is only *temporary*.

An initial fall in price. In Figure 2.8(a) demand has shifted from D_1 to D_2; equilibrium has moved from point a to point b, and price has fallen to P_2. How do people react to this fall in price?

Given that they believe this fall in price to be only temporary, suppliers *hold back*, expecting prices to rise again: supply shifts from S_1 to S_2. After all, why supply now when, by waiting, they could get a higher price?

Buyers *increase* their purchases, to take advantage of the temporary fall in price. Demand shifts from D_2 to D_3.

The equilibrium moves to point c, with price rising back towards P_1.

An initial rise in price. In Figure 2.8(b) demand has shifted from D_1 to D_2. Price has risen from P_1 to P_2.

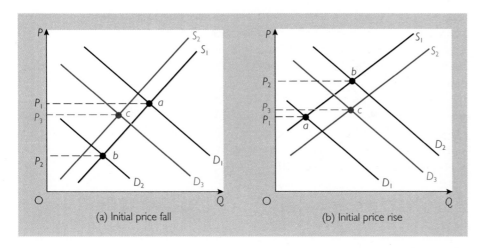

Figure 2.8
Stabilising speculation

(a) Initial price fall

(b) Initial price rise

Suppliers bring their goods to market now, before price falls again. Supply shifts from S_1 to S_2. Demanders, however, hold back until price falls. Demand shifts from D_2 to D_3. The equilibrium moves to point c, with price falling back towards P_1.

A good example of stabilising speculation occurs in agricultural commodity markets. Take the case of wheat. When it is harvested in the autumn there will be a plentiful supply. If all this wheat were to be put on the market, the price would fall to a very low level. Later in the year, when most of the wheat would have been sold, the price would then rise to a very high level. This is all easily predictable.

So what do farmers do? The answer is that they speculate. When the wheat is harvested they know the price will tend to fall, and so instead of bringing it all to market they put a lot of it into store. The more the price falls, the more they will put into store *anticipating that the price will later rise*. But this holding back of supplies prevents prices from falling. In other words, it stabilises prices.

Later in the year, when the price begins to rise, they will gradually release grain on to the market from the stores. The more the price rises, the more they will release on to the market *anticipating that the price will fall again by the time of the next harvest*. But this releasing of supplies will again stabilise prices by preventing them rising so much.

Rather than the farmers doing the speculation, it could be done by grain merchants. When there is a glut of wheat in the autumn, and prices are relatively low, they buy wheat on the grain market and put it into store. When there is a shortage in the spring and summer they sell wheat from their stores. In this way they stabilise prices just as the farmers did when they were the ones that operated the stores.

Destabilising speculation

Speculation will tend to have a destabilising effect on price fluctuations when suppliers and/or buyers believe that a change in price heralds similar changes to come.

An initial fall in price. In Figure 2.9(a) demand has shifted from D_1 to D_2 and price has fallen from P_1 to P_2. This time, believing that the fall in price heralds further falls in price to come, suppliers sell now before the price does fall. Supply shifts

Definition

Destabilising speculation Where the actions of speculators tend to make price movements larger.

Figure 2.9
Destabilising
speculation

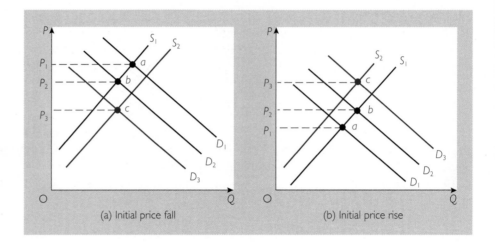

(a) Initial price fall   (b) Initial price rise

from S_1 to S_2. And demanders wait: they wait until price does fall further. Demand shifts from D_2 to D_3.

Their actions ensure that the price does fall further: to P_3.

An initial rise in price. In Figure 2.9(b) a price rise from P_1 to P_2 is caused by a rise in demand from D_1 to D_2. Suppliers wait until the price rises further. Supply shifts from S_1 to S_2. Demanders buy now before any further rise in price. Demand shifts from D_2 to D_3. As a result, the price continues to rise: to P_3.

Box 1.3 examined the housing market. In this market, speculation is frequently destabilising. Assume that people see house prices beginning to move upwards. This might be the result of increased demand brought about by a cut in mortgage interest rates or by growth in the economy. People may well believe that the rise in house prices signals a boom in the housing market: that prices will go on rising. Potential buyers will thus try to buy as soon as possible before prices rise any further. This increased demand (as in Figure 2.9(b)) will thus lead to even bigger price rises. This is precisely what happened in the UK housing market in 1999–2003.

Conclusion

In some circumstances, then, the action of speculators can help keep price fluctuations to a minimum (stabilising speculation). This is most likely when markets are relatively stable in the first place, with only moderate underlying shifts in demand and supply.

In other circumstances, however, speculation can make price fluctuations much worse. This is most likely in times of uncertainty, when there are significant changes in the determinants of demand and supply. Given this uncertainty, people may see price changes as signifying some trend. They then 'jump on the bandwagon' and do what the rest are doing, further fuelling the rise or fall in price.

Dealing with uncertainty and risk

When price changes are likely to occur, buyers and sellers will try to anticipate them. Unfortunately on many occasions no one can be certain just what these price changes will be. Take the case of stocks and shares. If you anticipate that the price of, say, Toyota shares is likely to go up substantially in the near future, you may well decide to buy some now and then sell them later after the price has risen. But you cannot be certain that they will go up in price: they may fall instead. If you buy the shares, therefore, you will be taking a gamble.

Now gambles can be of two types. The first is where you know the odds. Let us take the simplest case of a gamble on the toss of a coin. Heads you win; tails you lose. You know that the odds of winning are precisely 50 per cent. If you bet on the toss of a coin, you are said to be operating under conditions of risk. *Risk is when the probability of an outcome is known.* Risk itself is a measure of the *variability* of an outcome. For example, if you bet £1 on the toss of a coin, such that heads you win £1 and tails you lose £1, then the variability is –£1 to +£1.

The second form of gamble is the more usual. This is where the odds are not known or are known only roughly. Gambling on the stock exchange is like this. You may have a good idea that a share will go up in price, but is it a 90 per cent chance, an 80 per cent chance or what? You are not certain. Gambling under these sort of conditions is known as operating under uncertainty. *This is when the probability of an outcome is not known.*

You may well disapprove of gambling and want to dismiss people who engage in it as foolish or morally wrong. But 'gambling' is not just confined to horses, cards, roulette and the like. Risk and uncertainty pervade the whole of economic life and decisions are constantly having to be made whose outcome cannot be known for certain. Even the most morally upright person will still have to decide which career to go into, whether and when to buy a house, or even something as trivial as whether or not to take an umbrella when going out. Each of these decisions and thousands of others are made under conditions of uncertainty (or occasionally risk).

People's actions are influenced by their attitudes towards risk. Many decisions are taken under conditions of risk or uncertainty. Generally, the lower the probability of (or the more uncertain) the desired outcome of an action, the less likely will people be to undertake the action.

Key Idea 11

Stock holding as a way of reducing the problem of uncertainty

A simple way that suppliers can reduce the problem of uncertainty is by holding stocks. Take the case of the wheat farmers we saw in the previous section. At the time when they are planting the wheat in the spring, they are uncertain as to what the price of wheat will be when they bring it to market. If they keep no stores of wheat, they will just have to accept whatever the market price happens to be at harvest time. If, however, they have storage facilities, they can put the wheat into store if the price is low and then wait until it goes up. Alternatively, if the price of wheat is high at harvest time, they can sell it straight away. In other words, they can wait until the price is right.

Pause for thought

The demand for pears is more price elastic than the demand for bread and yet the price of pears fluctuates more than that of bread. Why should this be so? If pears could be stored as long and as cheaply as flour, would this affect the relative price fluctuations? If so, how?

A market in information

One way of reducing uncertainty is to buy information. For example, you might take advice on shares from a stockbroker, or buy a copy of a consumer magazine, such as *Which?* The buying and selling of information in this way helps substantially to reduce uncertainty.

Better information can also, under certain circumstances, help to make any speculation more stabilising. With poor information, people are much more likely to be guided by rumour or fear, which could well make speculation destabilising as people 'jump on the bandwagon'. If people generally are better informed, however, this is likely to make prices go more directly to a long-run stable equilibrium.

Recap

1. A complete understanding of markets must take into account the time dimension.

2. Given that producers and consumers take a time to respond fully to price changes, we can identify different equilibria after the elapse of different lengths of time. Generally, short-run supply and demand tend to be less price elastic than long-run supply and demand. As a result, any shifts in *D* or *S* curves tend to have a relatively bigger effect on price in the short run and a relatively bigger effect on quantity in the long run.

3. People often anticipate price changes and this will affect the amount they demand or supply. This speculation will tend to stabilise price fluctuations if people believe that the price changes are only temporary. However, speculation will tend to destabilise these fluctuations (i.e. make them more severe) if people believe that prices are likely to continue to move in the same direction as at present (at least for some time).

4. Many economic decisions are taken under conditions of risk or uncertainty. Uncertainty over future prices can be tackled by holding stocks. When prices are low, the stocks can be built up. When they are high, stocks can be sold. Uncertainty can be reduced by buying information.

2.6 Markets where prices are controlled

What happens if the government fixes prices?

At the equilibrium price, there will be no shortage or surplus. The equilibrium price, however, may not be the most *desirable* price. The government, therefore, may prefer to keep prices above or below the equilibrium price.

Key Idea 8 p45

Setting a minimum (high) price

If the government sets a minimum price above the equilibrium (a price floor), there will be a surplus: $Q_s - Q_d$ in Figure 2.10. Price will not be allowed to fall to eliminate this surplus. The government may do this for various reasons:

■ To protect producers' incomes. If the industry is subject to supply fluctuations (e.g. crops, due to fluctuations in weather) and if industry demand is price inelastic, prices are likely to fluctuate severely. Minimum prices will prevent the fall in producers' incomes that would accompany periods of low prices.

Key Idea 9 p64

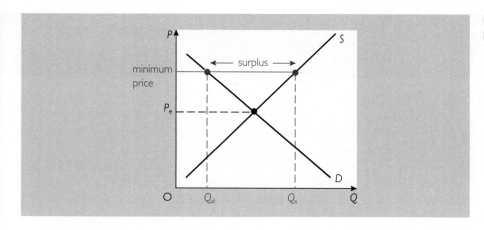

Figure 2.10
Minimum price:
price floor

■ To create a surplus (e.g. of grains), particularly in periods of plenty, which can be stored in preparation for possible future shortages.
■ In the case of wages (the price of labour), minimum wages legislation can be used to prevent workers' wage rates from falling below a certain level (see Box 5.4).

There are various methods the government can use to deal with the surpluses associated with minimum prices.

■ The government could buy the surplus and store it, destroy it or sell it abroad in other markets.
■ Supply could be artificially lowered by restricting producers to particular quotas. In Figure 2.10, supply could therefore be reduced to Q_d.
■ Demand could be raised by advertising, by finding alternative uses for the good, or by reducing consumption of substitute goods (e.g. by imposing taxes or quotas on substitutes, such as imports).

One of the problems with minimum prices is that firms with surplus on their hands may try to evade the price control and cut their prices.

Another problem is that high prices may cushion inefficiency. Firms may feel less need to find more efficient methods of production and cut their costs if their profits are being protected by the high price. Also the high price may discourage firms from producing alternative goods which they could produce more efficiently or which are in higher demand, but which nevertheless have a lower (free-market) price.

One of the best-known examples of governments fixing high minimum prices is the Common Agricultural Policy (CAP) of the European Union. This is examined in Box 2.4.

> **Pause for thought**   ▍▊▍
>
> *Draw a supply and demand diagram with the price of labour (the wage rate) on the vertical axis and the quantity of labour (the number of workers) on the horizontal axis. What will happen to employment if the government raises wages from the equilibrium to some minimum wage above the equilibrium?*

> **Definition**
>
> **Maximum price**
> A price ceiling set by the government or some other agency. The price is not allowed to rise above this level (although it is allowed to fall below it).

Setting a maximum (low) price

If the government sets a maximum price below the equilibrium (a price ceiling), there will be a shortage: $Q_d - Q_s$ in Figure 2.11. Price will not be allowed to rise to

Box 2.4

Agriculture and minimum prices

A problem of surpluses

Governments in many countries intervene in agricultural markets. The problems of fluctuating prices, dependency on foreign food imports, and the maintenance of farmers' and farm workers' incomes are but a few of the reasons for such intervention. The form that government intervention takes varies, from a series of subsidies or tax reliefs for farmers, to the more formal fixing of high minimum prices.

The fixing of high minimum prices has been the main policy used by the European Union in its Common Agricultural Policy (CAP). Here the Intervention Boards of the EU buy up any surpluses that result at a given 'intervention' price, usually set above the equilibrium.

The effects of this system are illustrated in the diagram, which shows the demand and supply of a particular agricultural product. Assume that the EU demand is D_{EU} and that EU supply is S_{EU}. Assume also that the world price is P_w. This will be the equilibrium price, since any shortage at P_w (i.e. $b - a$) will be imported at that price. Thus before intervention, EU demand is Q_{d_1} and EU supply is Q_{s_1} and imports are $Q_{d_1} - Q_{s_1}$.

Now assume that the EU sets an intervention price of P_i. At this high price, there will now be a surplus of $d - e$ (i.e. $Q_{s_2} - Q_{d_2}$). This will be bought by the appropriate Intervention Board. The cost to the EU of buying this surplus is shown by the total shaded area ($edQ_{s_2}Q_{d_2}$: i.e. the surplus multiplied by the intervention price). Unless the food is thrown away or otherwise disposed of, there will obviously then be the additional costs of storing this food: costs that have

been very high in some years as wine 'lakes' and grain and dairy 'mountains' have built up.

An alternative to storing the food is for the Board to sell the surpluses on the world market at the world price (P_w). In this case, the net cost to the Intervention Board would only be the area $edcf$: in other words, the amount purchased by the Board ($d - e$) multiplied by the difference in price paid by the Board and the price it receives on the world market ($P_i - P_w$). Alternatively, export subsidies could be paid to farmers who sell on world markets to bring the amount they receive up to the intervention price.

The justifications for such a policy are that: it assures food supplies (i.e. it encourages countries to be self-sufficient in food); it stabilises prices; and, by increasing farmers' incomes, it encourages them to

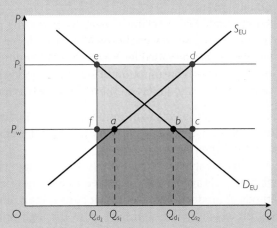

The EU system of high minimum prices in agricultural products

eliminate this shortage. The government may set maximum prices to prevent them rising above a certain level. This will normally be done for reasons of fairness. In wartime, or times of famine, the government may set maximum prices for basic goods so that poor people can afford to buy them.

The resulting shortages, however, create further problems. If the government merely sets prices and does not intervene further, the shortages will lead to the following:

invest in agriculture, which, in turn, results in a growth in agricultural productivity.

The CAP has been criticised on a number of counts:

■ Food surpluses are a costly waste of scarce resources. 'Guarantee' expenditure, as it is called, accounts for around half of the total EU budget (in the past it has been as high as three-quarters). This amounts each year to around €120 (approximately £80) per head of the EU population.

■ Although food prices are kept high generally, some are kept much higher above free-market prices than others. The effect is to give a very uneven amount of protection.

■ It has increased inequalities within agriculture. The bigger the farm, the bigger its output, and therefore the bigger the benefit the farmer receives from high prices. Similarly, richer agricultural regions of the EU receive more support than poorer ones.

■ By raising food prices it penalises the poor, who spend a larger proportion of their income on food than do the rich.

■ It has had harmful effects on the environment. By encouraging increased output, the CAP has encouraged the destruction of hedgerows and wildlife, and the increased use of chemical fertilisers and pesticides. Many of these chemicals have caused pollution.

■ EU food surpluses 'dumped' on to world markets have had a doubly damaging effect on agriculture in developing countries: (a) exporters of foodstuffs find it very difficult to compete with subsidised EU exports; (b) farmers in developing countries who are producing for their domestic market find that they cannot compete with cheap imports of food from the EU.

Agriculture in the developing world thus declines. Farmers' incomes are too low to invest in the land. Many migrate to the overcrowded cities and become slum dwellers in shanty towns, with little or no paid employment. The neglect of agriculture can then lead to famines if there is poor rainfall in any year. Calls are then made for European (and North American) food surpluses to be used for emergency aid: the same food surpluses that contributed to the problem in the first place!

As a result of these problems, various reforms to the CAP have been or are being implemented. These include: reducing supply by requiring farmers to 'set aside' (i.e. take out of use) a certain percentage of their land; cutting the level of intervention prices; providing grants or other incentives for farmers to farm less intensively or to diversify into alternative rural industries (such as tourism and forestry). However, intervention prices are still above free-market levels for many products, and surpluses remain.

?
One of the reforms to the CAP has been to reduce intervention prices and to compensate farmers for the resulting lost income by paying them grants ('income support') unrelated to current output. What, do you think, are the merits of this reform?

■ Allocation on a 'first come, first served' basis. This is likely to lead to queues developing, or firms adopting waiting lists. Queues were a common feature of life in the former communist eastern European countries where governments kept prices below the level necessary to equate demand and supply. In recent years, as part of their economic reforms, they have allowed prices to rise. This has had the obvious benefit of reducing or eliminating queues, but at the same time it has made life very hard for those on low incomes.

Figure 2.11
Maximum price:
price ceiling

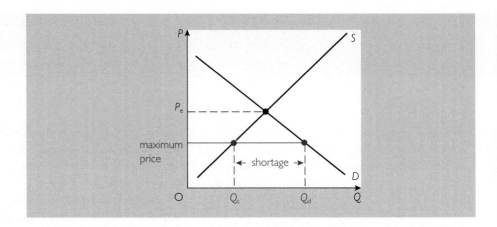

■ Firms deciding which customers should be allowed to buy: for example, giving preference to regular customers.

Neither of the above may be considered to be fair. Certain needy people may be forced to go without. Therefore, the government may adopt a system of rationing. People could be issued with a set number of coupons for each item rationed.

A major problem with maximum prices is likely to be the emergence of black markets, where customers, unable to buy enough in legal markets, may well be prepared to pay very high prices: prices above P_e in Figure 2.11.

Another problem is that the maximum prices reduce the quantity produced of an already scarce commodity. For example, artificially low prices in a famine are likely to reduce food supplies: if not immediately, then at the next harvest, because of less being sown. In many developing countries, governments control the price of basic foodstuffs in order to help the urban poor. The effect, however, is to reduce incomes for farmers, who are then encouraged to leave the land and flock into the ever-growing towns and cities.

To minimise these types of problem the government may attempt to reduce the shortage by encouraging supply: by drawing on stores, by direct government production, or by giving subsidies or tax relief to firms. Alternatively, it may attempt to reduce demand: by the production of more alternative goods (e.g. home-grown vegetables in times of war) or by controlling people's incomes.

One example of a maximum price is considered in Box 2.5. The 'price' in this case is the rent paid by tenants for private rented accommodation. Should the government set a rent ceiling in order to guarantee affordable accommodation? Would there be any problems with such a policy?

Definitions

Rationing
Where the government restricts the amount of a good that people are allowed to buy.

Black markets
Where people ignore the government's price and/or quantity controls and sell illegally at whatever price equates illegal demand and supply.

Key
Idea
8
p45

Box 2.5 Case Studies and Applications

Rent control

Cheap housing for all?

The purpose of rent control is to protect tenants from paying high rent, as well as to provide cheap housing for the very poor. However, many economists argue that in practice such rent controls only succeed in making a larger part of the population worse off. How is this so?

Referring to the diagram, assume that the rent for a particular type of accommodation is initially at the equilibrium level, R_0, where $D = S$. Now assume that legislation is passed that sets a rent ceiling of R_1. Despite this reduction in rent, the supply of rental accommodation will fall only slightly in the short run, as landlords cannot quickly transfer their accommodation to other uses. In the diagram this is shown by a movement from point a to point b on the relatively inelastic supply curve S.

With the rent set below equilibrium, there will be a shortage of rented property. In the short run, however, this will be relatively small (i.e. $Q_2 - Q_1$), and hence only a relatively small number of people will be unable to find accommodation. The remainder will benefit from the lower rents.

In the long run, however, many landlords will respond to the lower rent by putting their accommodation to other uses. The supply curve will become more elastic (curve S') and the supply of rented property will fall to Q_3 (point c). Shortages now increase (to $Q_2 - Q_3$) as less rental housing is available. More people become homeless – more, perhaps, than in an unregulated market.

Rent controls may have further adverse effects. First, on equity grounds it is somewhat arbitrary as to who gets and who does not get housing at the lower rent. Second, in the long run, those landlords who still keep their property available for rent may cut maintenance costs and let their property fall into disrepair.

Those in favour of rent controls counter these arguments by claiming that the demand and supply curves of rented accommodation are very inelastic. Take the case of the demand curve. People have got to live somewhere. If rent control is abolished, people will just have to pay the higher rent, or become homeless; and given that people will only sacrifice their home as a last resort, demand remains inelastic, and rents could rise to a very high level.

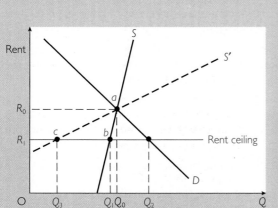

Effect of rent control

? 1. How could housing supplied by the public sector be made to rectify some of the problems we have identified above? (What would it do to the supply curve?)
2. If the government gives poor people rent allowances (i.e. grants), how will this affect the level of rents in an uncontrolled market? What determines the size of the effect?
3. The case for and against rent controls depends to a large extent on the long-run elasticity of supply. Do you think it will be relatively elastic or inelastic? Give reasons.

Key idea 8 p45

Recap

1. The government may fix minimum or maximum prices. If a minimum price is set above the equilibrium price, a surplus will result. If a maximum price is set below the equilibrium price, a shortage will result.

2. Minimum prices are set as a means of protecting the incomes of suppliers or creating a surplus for storage in case of future reductions in supply. If the government is not deliberately trying to create a surplus, it must decide what to do with it.

3. Maximum prices are set as a means of keeping prices down for the consumer. The resulting shortage will cause queues, waiting lists or the restriction of sales by firms to favoured customers. Alternatively, the government could introduce a system of rationing. If it does, then black markets are likely to arise. This is where goods are sold illegally above the maximum price.

Questions

1. Draw a diagram with two supply curves, one steeply sloping and one gently sloping. Ensure that the two curves cross. Draw a demand curve through the point where they cross and mark the equilibrium price and quantity. Now assume that the demand curve shifts to the right. Show how the shape of the supply curve will determine just what happens to price and quantity.

2. Which of the following will have positive signs and which will have negative ones? (a) price elasticity of demand; (b) income elasticity of demand (normal good); (c) income elasticity of demand (inferior good); (d) cross elasticity of demand (with respect to changes in price of a substitute good); (e) cross elasticity of demand (with respect to changes in price of a complementary good); (f) price elasticity of supply.

3. Demand for oil might be relatively elastic over the longer term, and yet it could still be observed that over time people consume more oil (or only very slightly less) despite rising oil prices. How can this apparent contradiction be explained?

4. How might a firm set about making the demand for its brand less elastic?

5. Assuming that a firm faces an inelastic demand and wants to increase its total revenue, in what direction should it change its price? Is there any limit to how far it should go in changing its price in this direction?

6. Why are both the price elasticity of demand and the price elasticity of supply likely to be greater in the long run?

7. Which are likely to have the highest cross elasticity of demand: two brands of coffee, or coffee and tea? Explain.

8. Redraw each of Figures 2.8 and 2.9, only this time assume that it was an initial shift in supply that caused price to change in the first place.

9. What are the advantages and disadvantages of speculation from the point of view of (a) the consumer; (b) firms?

10. Give some examples of decisions you have taken recently that were made under conditions of uncertainty. With hindsight do you think you made the right decisions?

11. Assume that the (weekly) market demand and supply of tomatoes are given by the figures shown at the bottom of this page:

Price (£ per kilo)	4.00	3.50	3.00	2.50	2.00	1.50	1.00
Q_d (000 kilos)	30	35	40	45	50	55	60
Q_s (000 kilos)	80	68	62	55	50	45	38

(a) What are the equilibrium price and quantity?

(b) What will be the effect of the government fixing a minimum price of (i) £3.00 per kilo; (ii) £1.50 per kilo?

(c) Suppose that the government paid tomato producers a subsidy of £1.00 per kilo. (i) Give the new supply schedule. (ii) What will be the new equilibrium price? (iii) How much will this cost the government?

(d) Alternatively, suppose that the government guaranteed tomato producers a price of £2.50 per kilo. (i) How many tomatoes would it have to buy in order to ensure that all the tomatoes produced were sold? (ii) How much would this cost the government?

(e) Alternatively, suppose it bought all the tomatoes produced at £2.50. (i) At what single price would it have to sell them in order to dispose of the lot? (ii) What would be the net cost of this course of action?

12. Think of two things that are provided free. In each case, identify when and in what form a shortage might occur. In what ways are/could these shortages be dealt with? Are they the best solution to the shortages?

13. Think of some examples where the price of a good or service is kept below the equilibrium. In each case consider the advantages and disadvantages of the policy.

Additional case studies on the *Essentials of Economics* website (www.booksites.net/sloman)

2.1 Rationing. A case study in the use of rationing as an alternative to the price mechanism. In particular, it looks at the use of rationing in the UK during the Second World War.

2.2 Adjusting to oil price shocks. A case study showing how demand and supply analysis can be used to examine the price changes in the oil market since 1973.

2.3 Advertising and its effects on the demand curve. How advertising a product can both shift the demand curve and change its elasticity.

2.4 Any more fares? Pricing on the buses: an illustration of the relationship between price and total revenue.

2.5 Income elasticity of demand and the balance of payments. This examines how a low income elasticity of demand for the exports of many developing countries can help to explain their chronic balance of payments problems.

2.6 Black markets. How black markets can develop when prices are fixed below the equilibrium.

2.7 Elasticities of demand for various foodstuffs. An examination of the evidence about price and income elasticities of demand for food in the UK.

2.8 The role of the speculator. This assesses whether the activities of speculators are beneficial or harmful to the rest of society.

2.9 The CAP and the environment. This case shows how the system of high intervention prices had damaging environmental effects. It also examines the more recent measures that the EU has adopted to reverse the effects.

2.10 The fallacy of composition. An illustration of how something that applies to an individual may not apply to a larger group. The example is taken from agriculture.

2.11 Dealing in futures markets. How buying and selling in futures markets can reduce uncertainty.

Sections of chapter covered in
WinEcon – Sloman, *Essentials of Economics*

Essentials of Economics section	*WinEcon* section
2.1	2.1
2.2	2.2
2.3	2.3
2.4	2.4
2.5	2.5
2.6	2.6

Websites relevant to this chapter

Numbers and sections refer to websites listed in the Web Appendix and hotlinked from this book's website at www.booksites.net/sloman

- For news articles relevant to this chapter, see the *Economics News Articles* link from the book's website.
- For general news on markets and market intervention, see websites in section A, and particularly A1–5, 7–9, 18, 24, 25, 26, 33, 36. See also A38 and 39 for links to newspapers worldwide; and A42 for links to economics news articles from newspapers worldwide.
- For information on advertising (Box 2.3), see site E37.
- For information on agriculture and the Common Agricultural Policy (Box 2.4), see sites E14 and G9.
- For student resources relevant to this chapter, see sites C1–7, 9, 10, 19; D3.
- For sites favouring the free market, see C17 and E34.

CHAPTER MAP

CHAPTER THREE

The supply decision

So far we have assumed that supply curves are generally upward sloping: that a higher price will encourage firms to supply more. But just how much will firms choose to supply at each price? It depends largely on the amount of profit they will make. If a firm can increase its profits by producing more, it will normally do so.

Profit is made by firms earning more from the sale of goods than they cost to produce. A firm's total profit is thus the difference between its total sales revenue (*TR*) and its total costs of production (*TC*). In order then to discover how a firm can maximise its profit or even get a sufficient level of profit, we must first consider what determines costs and revenue.

In Sections 3.1 and 3.2 we examine short-run and long-run costs respectively. Over the short run a firm will be limited in what inputs it can expand. For example, a manufacturing company might be able to use more raw materials, or possibly more labour, but it will not have time to open up another factory. Over the long run, however, a firm will have much more flexibility. It can, if it chooses, expand the whole scale of its operations.

In Section 3.3 we turn to the revenue side and see how a firm's revenue varies with output. Finally, Section 3.4 puts revenue and cost together to see how profit is determined. In particular, we shall see how profit varies with output and how the point of maximum profit is found.

3.1   Short-run costs

How do a firm's costs vary with output over the short term?

The cost of producing any level of output will depend on the amount of inputs used and the price the firm must pay for them. Let us first focus on the quantity of inputs used.

> ***Output depends on the amount of resources and how they are used.*** Different amounts and combinations of inputs will lead to different amounts of output. If output is to be produced efficiently, inputs should be combined in the optimum proportions.
>
> Key Idea 12

Short-run and long-run changes in production

If a firm wants to increase production, it will take time to acquire a greater quantity of certain inputs. For example, a manufacturer can use more electricity by turning on switches, but it might take a long time to obtain and install more machines, and longer still to build a second or third factory.

If, then, the firm wants to increase output in a hurry, it will only be able to increase the quantity of certain inputs. It can use more raw materials, more fuel, more tools and possibly more labour (by hiring extra workers or offering overtime to its existing workforce). But it will have to make do with its existing buildings and most of its machinery.

The distinction we are making here is between fixed factors and variable factors. A *fixed* factor is an input that cannot be increased within a given time period (e.g. buildings). A *variable* factor is one that can.

The distinction between fixed and variable factors allows us to distinguish between the short run and the long run.

The short run.   The short run is a time period during which at least one factor of production is fixed. In the short run, then, output can be increased by only using more variable factors. For example, if a shipping line wanted to carry more passengers in response to a rise in demand, it could possibly accommodate more passengers on existing sailings if there were space. It could possibly increase the number of sailings with its existing fleet, by hiring more crew and using more fuel. But in the short run it could not buy more ships: there would not be time for them to be built.

The long run.   The long run is a time period long enough for all inputs to be varied. Given long enough, a firm can build a second factory and install new machines.

The actual length of the short run will differ from firm to firm. It is not a fixed period of time. Thus if it takes a farmer a year to obtain new land, buildings and equipment, the short run is any time period up to a year and the long run is any time period longer than a year. On the other hand, if it takes a shipping company three years to obtain an extra ship, the short run is any period up to three years and the long run is any period longer than three years.

For the remainder of this section we will concentrate on *short-run* production and costs. We will look at the long run in Section 3.2.

Definitions

Fixed factor
An input that cannot be increased in supply within a given time period.

Variable factor
An input that *can* be increased in supply within a given time period.

Short run
The period of time over which at least one factor is fixed.

Long run
The period of time long enough for *all* factors to be varied.

Production in the short run: the law of diminishing returns

Production in the short run is subject to *diminishing returns*. You may well have heard of 'the law of diminishing returns': it is one of the most famous of all 'laws' of economics. To illustrate how this law underlies short-run production let us take the simplest possible case where there are just two factors: one fixed and one variable.

Take the case of a farm. Assume that the fixed factor is land and the variable factor is labour. Since the land is fixed in supply, output per period of time can be increased only by increasing the amount of workers employed. But imagine what would happen as more and more workers crowded on to a fixed area of land. The land cannot go on yielding more and more output indefinitely. After a point the additions to output from each extra worker will begin to diminish.

We can now state the law of diminishing (marginal) returns.

> **The law of diminishing marginal returns.** When increasing amounts of a variable factor are used with a given amount of a fixed factor, there will come a point when each extra unit of the variable factor will produce less extra output than the previous unit.
>
> **Key Idea 13**

Box 3.1 is a case study illustrating the law of diminishing returns. Box 3.2 shows that the law has potentially dire implications for us and the future inhabitants of our planet.

Box 3.1 Case Studies and Applications

Diminishing returns in the bread shop

Is the baker using his loaf?

Just up the road from where I live is a bread shop. Like many others, I buy my bread there on a Saturday morning. Not surprisingly, Saturday morning is the busiest time of the week for the shop and as a result it takes on extra assistants.

During the week only one assistant serves the customers, but on a Saturday morning there used to be five serving. But could they serve five times as many customers? No, they could not. There were diminishing returns to labour.

The trouble is that certain factors of production in the shop are fixed:

■ The shop is a fixed size. It gets very crowded on Saturday morning. Assistants sometimes have to wait while customers squeeze past each other to get to the counter, and with five serving, the assistants themselves used to get in each other's way.

■ There is only one cash till. Assistants frequently had to wait while other assistants used it.

■ There is only one pile of tissue paper for wrapping the bread. Again the assistants often had to wait.

The fifth and maybe even the fourth assistant ended up serving very few extra customers.

I am still going to the same bread shop and they still have only one till and one pile of tissue paper. But now only three assistants are employed on a Saturday! The shop, however, is just as busy.

? How would you advise the baker as to whether he should (a) employ four assistants on a Saturday; (b) extend his shop, thereby allowing more customers to be served on a Saturday morning?

Key Idea 13 p85

Box 3.2

Malthus and the dismal science of economics

Population growth + diminishing returns = starvation

Key
Idea
13
p85

The law of diminishing returns has potentially cataclysmic implications for the future populations of the world.

If the population of the world grows rapidly, then food output may not keep pace with it. There will be diminishing returns to labour as more and more people crowd on to the limited amount of land available.

This is already a problem in some of the poorest countries of the world, especially in sub-Saharan Africa. The land is barely able to support current population levels. Only one or two bad harvests are needed to cause mass starvation – witness the appalling famines in recent years in Ethiopia and the Sudan.

The relationship between population and food output was analysed as long ago as 1798 by the Reverend Thomas Robert Malthus (1766–1834) in his *Essay on the Principle of Population*. This book was a bestseller and made Robert Malthus perhaps the best known of all social scientists of his day.

Malthus argued as follows:

I say that the power of population is indefinitely greater than the power in the earth to produce subsistence for man.

Population when unchecked, increases in a geometrical ratio. Subsistence increases only in an arithmetical ratio. A slight acquaintance with numbers will show the immensity of the first power in comparison with the second.[1]

What Malthus was saying is that world population tends to double about every 25 years or so if unchecked. It grows geometrically, like the series: 1, 2, 4, 8, 16, 32, 64, etc. But food output, because of diminishing returns, cannot keep pace with this. It is likely to grow at only an arithmetical rate, like the series: 1, 2, 3, 4, 5, 6, 7, etc. It is clear that population, if unchecked, will soon outstrip food supply.

So what is the check on population growth? According to Malthus, it is starvation. As population grows, so food output per head will fall until, with more and more people starving, the death rate will rise. Only then will population growth stabilise at the rate of growth of food output.

Have Malthus' gloomy predictions been borne out by events? Two factors have mitigated the forces that Malthus described:

■ The rate of population growth tends to slow down as countries become more developed. Although improved health prolongs life, this tends to be more than offset by a decline in the birth rate as people choose to have smaller families.

[1] T. R. Malthus, *First Essay on Population* (Macmillan, 1926), pp. 13–14.

Measuring costs of production

Definition

Opportunity cost
Cost measured in terms of the best alternative forgone.

We are now ready to look at short-run costs. First of all, we will need to define just what we mean by costs. The term is used differently by economists and accountants.

When measuring costs, economists always use the concept of opportunity cost. Remember from the Introduction how we defined opportunity cost. It is the cost of any activity measured in terms of the *sacrifice* made in doing it: in other words, the cost measured in terms of the opportunities forgone.

Key
Idea
2
p8

World population levels and growth: actual and projected

Year	World population (billions)	Average annual rate of increase (%)		
		World	More developed regions	Less developed regions
1950	2.5			
		1.7	1.2	2.1
1960	3.0			
		2.0	1.0	2.4
1970	3.7			
		1.8	0.7	2.2
1980	4.5			
		1.7	0.6	2.1
1990	5.3			
		1.4	0.3	1.8
2000	6.1			
		1.2	0.2	1.5
2010	6.8			
		1.0	0.2	1.2
2020	7.5			
		0.8	0.1	1.1
2030	8.1			

Source: Various.

■ Technological improvements in farming have greatly increased food output per hectare.

The growth in food output has thus exceeded the rate of population growth in advanced countries.

The picture is much more gloomy, however, in developing countries. There *have* been advances in agriculture. The 'green revolution', whereby new high-yielding crop varieties have been developed (especially in the cases of wheat and rice), has led to food output growth outstripping population growth in many developing countries. India, for example, now exports grain.

Nevertheless, the Malthusian spectre is very real for some of the poorest developing countries, which are simply unable to feed their populations satisfactorily. It is these poorest countries of the world which have some of the highest rates of population growth. Many African countries have population growth rates of around 3 per cent per annum.

? The figures in the table above are based on the assumption that birth rates will fall faster than death rates. Under what circumstances might these forecasts underestimate the rate of growth of world population?

How do we apply this principle of opportunity cost to a firm? First we must discover what factors of production it is using. Then we must measure the sacrifice involved. To do this it is necessary to put factors into two categories.

Factors not owned by the firm: explicit costs

The opportunity cost of those factors not already owned by the firm is simply the price that the firm has to pay for them. Thus if the firm uses £100 worth of electricity, the opportunity cost is £100. The firm has sacrificed £100 that could have been spent on something else.

These costs are called explicit costs because they involve direct payment of money by firms.

Factors already owned by the firm: implicit costs

When the firm already owns factors (e.g. machinery), it does not as a rule have to pay out money to use them. Their opportunity costs are thus implicit costs. They are equal to what the factors could earn for the firm in some alternative use, either within the firm or hired out to some other firm.

Here are some examples of implicit costs:

- A firm owns some buildings. The opportunity cost of using them is the rent it could have received by letting them out to another firm.
- A firm draws £100 000 from the bank out of its savings in order to invest in new plant and equipment. The opportunity cost of this investment is not just the £100 000 (an explicit cost), but also the interest it thereby forgoes (an implicit cost).
- The owner of the firm could have earned £15 000 per annum by working for someone else. This £15 000, then, is the opportunity cost of the owner's time.

If there is no alternative use for a factor of production, as in the case of a machine designed to make a specific product, and if it has no scrap value, the opportunity cost of using it is *zero*. In such a case, if the output from the machine is worth more than the cost of all the *other* inputs involved, the firm might as well use the machine rather than let it stand idle.

What the firm paid for the machine – its historic cost – is irrelevant. Not using the machine will not bring that money back. It has been spent. These are sometimes referred to as 'sunk costs'.

Costs and inputs

A firm's costs of production will depend on the factors of production it uses. The more factors it uses, the greater its costs will be. More precisely, this relationship depends on two elements:

- The productivity of the factors. The greater their productivity, the smaller will be the quantity of them that is needed to produce a given level of output, and hence the lower will be the cost of that output.
- The price of the factors. The higher their price, the higher will be the costs of production.

In the short run, some factors used by the firm are fixed in supply. Their total costs, therefore, are fixed, in the sense that they do not vary with output. Rent on land is a fixed cost. It is the same whether the firm produces a lot or a little.

Pause for thought

Assume that a farmer decides to grow wheat on land that could be used for growing barley. Barley sells for £100 per tonne. Wheat sells for £150 per tonne. Seed, fertiliser, labour and other costs of growing crops are £80 per tonne for both wheat and barley. What are the farmer's costs and profit per tonne of growing wheat?

Definitions

Explicit costs
The payments to outside suppliers of inputs.

Implicit costs
Costs that do not involve a direct payment of money to a third party, but which nevertheless involve a sacrifice of some alternative.

Historic costs
The original amount the firm paid for factors it now owns.

Fixed costs
Total costs that do not vary with the amount of output produced.

Output (Q)	TFC (£)	TVC (£)	TC (£)
0	12	0	12
1	12	10	22
2	12	16	28
3	12	21	33
4	12	28	40
5	12	40	52
6	12	60	72
7	12	91	103

Table 3.1
Total costs for firm X

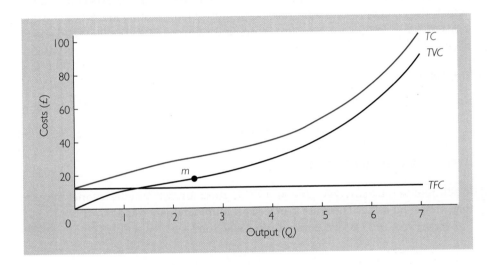

Figure 3.1
Total costs for firm X

The total cost of variable factors, however, does vary with output. The cost of raw materials is a variable cost. The more that is produced, the more raw materials are used and therefore the higher is their total cost.

Total cost

The total cost (*TC*) of production is the sum of the *total variable costs* (*TVC*) and the *total fixed costs* (*TFC*) of production.

$$TC = TVC + TFC$$

Consider Table 3.1 and Figure 3.1. They show the total costs for an imaginary firm for producing different levels of output (*Q*). Let us examine each of the three cost curves in turn.

Total fixed cost (TFC)

In our example, total fixed cost is assumed to be £12. Since this does not vary with output, it is shown by a horizontal straight line.

> **Definitions**
>
> **Variable costs**
> Total costs that do vary with the amount of output produced.
>
> **Total cost**
> The sum of total fixed costs and total variable costs:
> $TC = TFC + TVC$

Total variable cost (TVC)

With a zero output, no variable factors will be used. Thus $TVC = 0$. The TVC curve, therefore, starts from the origin (the bottom left-hand corner of the diagram).

The shape of the TVC curve follows from the law of diminishing returns. Initially, *before* diminishing returns set in, TVC rises less and less rapidly as more variable factors are added. For example, in the case of a factory with a fixed supply of machinery, initially as more workers are taken on, the workers can do increasingly specialist tasks and make a fuller use of the capital equipment. With this increasing productivity, so TVC will rise less and less quickly.

As output is increased beyond point m in Figure 3.1, diminishing returns set in. Given that extra workers (the extra variable factors) are producing less and less extra output, the extra units of output they do produce will be costing more and more in terms of wage costs. Thus TVC rises more and more rapidly. The TVC curve gets steeper.

Key Idea 13 p85

Total cost (TC)

Since $TC = TVC + TFC$, the TC curve is simply the TVC curve shifted vertically upwards by £12.

Average and marginal cost

In addition to total costs (TC, TFC and TVC), there are two other categories of costs that we will be using. These are average cost and marginal cost.

Average cost (AC) is cost per unit of production.

$$AC = TC/Q$$

Thus if it costs a firm £2000 to produce 100 units of a product, the average cost would be £20 for each unit (£2000/100).

Like total cost, average cost can be divided into the two components, fixed and variable. In other words, average cost equals average fixed cost ($AFC = TFC/Q$) plus average variable cost ($AVC = TVC/Q$).

$$AC = AFC + AVC$$

Marginal cost (MC) is the *extra* cost of producing *one more unit*: that is, the rise in total cost per one unit rise in output.

$$MC = \frac{\Delta TC}{\Delta Q}$$

where Δ means 'a rise in'.

For example, assume that a firm is currently producing 1 000 000 boxes of matches a month. It now increases output by 1000 boxes (another batch): $\Delta Q = 1000$. Assume that, as a result, total costs rise by £40: $\Delta TC = £40$. What is the cost of producing one more box of matches? It is:

$$MC = \frac{\Delta TC}{\Delta Q} = \frac{£40}{1000} = 4\text{p}$$

Definitions

Average (total) cost
Total cost (fixed plus variable) per unit of output:
$AC = TC/Q = AFC + AVC$

Average fixed cost
Total fixed cost per unit of output:
$AFC = TFC/Q$

Average variable cost
Total variable cost per unit of output:
$AVC = TVC/Q$

Marginal cost
The cost of producing one more unit of output:
$MC = \Delta TC/\Delta Q$

Output (Q) (units)	TFC (£)	AFC (TFC/Q) (£)	TVC (£)	AVC (TVC/Q) (£)	TC (TFC+TVC) (£)	AC (TC/Q) (£)	MC (ΔTC/ΔQ) (£)
0	12	–	0	–	12	–	
							10
1	12	12	10	10	22	22	
							6
2	12	6	16	8	28	14	
							5
3	12	4	21	7	33	11	
							7
4	12	3	28	7	40	10	
							12
5	12	2.4	40	8	52	10.4	
							20
6	12	2	60	10	72	12	
							31
7	12	1.7	91	13	103	14.7	

Table 3.2

Total, average and marginal costs for firm X

(Note that all marginal costs are variable, since, by definition, there can be no extra fixed costs as output rises.)

Given the *TFC*, *TVC* and *TC* for each output, it is possible to derive the *AFC*, *AVC*, *AC* and *MC* for each output using the above definitions. For example, using the data of Table 3.1, Table 3.2 can be constructed. Have a look at each of the columns in turn and try checking out how the figures are calculated. (Note that marginal cost is entered in the spaces between the lines. The reason is that marginal cost represents the rise in costs when going from one output to another.)

What will be the shapes of the *MC*, *AFC*, *AVC* and *AC* curves? These are illustrated in Figure 3.2. Let us consider each of these four curves in turn.

Key Idea
13
p85

Marginal cost (MC). The shape of the *MC* curve follows directly from the law of diminishing returns. Initially, in Figure 3.2, as more of the variable factor is used, extra units of output cost less than previous units. *MC* falls. This corresponds to the portion of the *TVC* curve in Figure 3.1 to the left of point *m*.

Beyond a certain level of output, diminishing returns set in. This is shown as point *x* in Figure 3.2 and corresponds to point *m* in Figure 3.1. Thereafter *MC* rises.

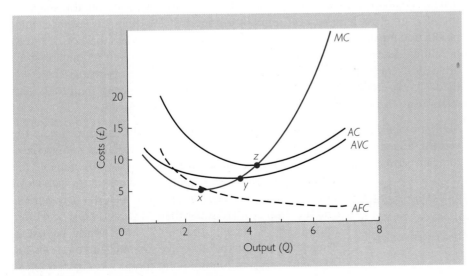

Figure 3.2

Average and marginal costs

Box 3.3 Exploring Economics

The relationship between averages and marginals

In this chapter we have just examined the concepts of *average* and *marginal* cost. We shall be coming across several other average and marginal concepts later on. It is useful at this stage to examine the general relationship between averages and marginals. In all cases there are three simple rules that relate them.

To illustrate these rules, consider the following example.

Imagine a room with ten people in it. Assume that the *average* age of those present is 20.

Now if a 20-year-old enters the room (the *marginal* age), this will not affect the average age. It will remain at 20. If a 56-year-old now comes in, the average age will rise: not to 56, of course, but to 23. This is found by dividing the sum of everyone's ages (276) by the number of people (12). If then a child of 10 were to enter the room, this would pull the average age down.

From this example we can derive the three universal rules about averages and marginals:

■ If the marginal equals the average, the average will not change.

■ If the marginal is above the average, the average will rise.

■ If the marginal is below the average, the average will fall.

? A cricketer scores the following number of runs in five successive innings:

Innings:	1	2	3	4	5
Runs:	20	20	50	10	0

These can be seen as the marginal number of runs from each innings. Calculate the total and average number of runs after each innings. Show how the average and marginal scores illustrate the three rules above.

Additional units of output cost more and more to produce, since they require ever-increasing amounts of the variable factor.

Average fixed cost (AFC). This falls continuously as output rises, since total fixed costs are being spread over a greater and greater output.

Average (total) cost (AC). The shape of the *AC* curve depends on the shape of the *MC* curve. As long as new units of output cost less than the average, their production must pull the average cost down. That is, if *MC* is less than *AC*, *AC* must be falling. Likewise, if new units cost more than the average, their production must drive the average up. That is, if *MC* is greater than *AC*, *AC* must be rising. Therefore, the *MC* curve crosses the *AC* curve at its minimum point (point *z* in Figure 3.2). This relationship between averages and marginals is explored in Box 3.3.

Average variable cost (AVC). Since *AVC* = *AC* – *AFC*, the *AVC* curve is simply the vertical difference between the *AC* and the *AFC* curves. Note that as *AFC* gets less, the gap between *AVC* and *AC* narrows. Since all marginal costs are variable (by definition, there are no marginal fixed costs), the same relationship holds between *MC* and *AVC* as it did between *MC* and *AC*. That is, if *MC* is less than *AVC*, *AVC* must be falling, and if *MC* is greater than *AVC*, *AVC* must be rising. Therefore, as with the *AC* curve, the *MC* curve crosses the *AVC* curve at its minimum point (point *y* in Figure 3.2).

Pause for thought

Why is the minimum point of the AVC curve at a lower level of output than the minimum point of the AC curve?

Recap

1. Production in the short run is subject to diminishing returns. As greater quantities of the variable factor(s) are used, so each additional unit of the variable factor will add less to output than previous units: i.e. output will rise less and less rapidly.

2. With some factors fixed in supply in the short run, their total cost will be fixed with respect to output. In the case of variable factors, their total cost will increase as more output is produced and hence as more of them are used.

3. Total cost can be divided into total fixed and total variable cost. Total variable cost will tend to increase less rapidly at first as more is produced, but then, when diminishing returns set in, it will increase more and more rapidly.

4. Marginal cost is the cost of producing one more unit of output. It will probably fall at first (corresponding to the part of the *TVC* curve where the slope is getting shallower), but will start to rise as soon as diminishing returns set in.

5. Average cost, like total cost, can be divided into fixed and variable costs. Average fixed cost will decline as more output is produced. The reason is that the total fixed cost is being spread over a greater and greater number of units of output. Average variable cost will tend to decline at first, but once the marginal cost has risen above it, it must then rise. The same applies to average cost.

Long-run costs   3.2

How do a firm's costs vary with output over the longer term?

Production in the long run: the scale of production

In the long run, *all* factors of production are variable. There is time for the firm to build a new factory (maybe in a different part of the country), to install new machines, to use different techniques of production, and in general to combine its inputs in whatever proportion and in whatever quantities it chooses.

If a firm were to double all of its inputs – something it could do in the long run – would it double its output? Or would output more than double or less than double? We can distinguish three possible situations:

Constant returns to scale.   This is where a given percentage increase in inputs will lead to the same percentage increase in output.

Increasing returns to scale.   This is where a given percentage increase in inputs will lead to a *larger* percentage increase in output.

Decreasing returns to scale.   This is where a given percentage increase in inputs will lead to a *smaller* percentage increase in output.

Notice the terminology here. The words 'to scale' mean that *all* inputs increase by the same proportion. Decreasing returns to *scale* are therefore quite different from

Table 3.3
Short-run and
long-run increases
in output

	Short run			Long run	
Input 1	Input 2	Output	Input 1	Input 2	Output
3	1	25	1	1	15
3	2	45	2	2	35
3	3	60	3	3	60
3	4	70	4	4	90
3	5	75	5	5	125

diminishing *marginal* returns (where only the *variable* factor increases). The differences between marginal returns to a variable factor and returns to scale are illustrated in Table 3.3.

In the short run, input 1 is assumed to be fixed in supply (at 3 units). Output can be increased only by using more of the variable factor (input 2). In the long run, however, both input 1 and input 2 are variable.

In the short-run situation, diminishing returns can be seen from the fact that output increases at a decreasing rate (25 to 45 to 60 to 70 to 75) as input 2 is increased. In the long-run situation, the table illustrates increasing returns to scale. Output increases at an *increasing* rate (15 to 35 to 60 to 90 to 125) as both inputs are increased.

Economies of scale

The concept of increasing returns to scale is closely linked to that of economies of scale. A firm experiences economies of scale if costs per unit of output fall as the scale of production increases. Clearly, if a firm is getting increasing returns to scale from its factors of production, then as it produces more it will be using smaller and smaller amounts of factors per unit of output. Other things being equal, this means that it will be producing at a lower average cost.

There are a number of reasons why firms are likely to experience economies of scale. Some are due to increasing returns to scale; some are not.

Specialisation and division of labour.   In large-scale plants, workers can do more simple, repetitive jobs. With this specialisation and division of labour less training is needed; workers can become highly efficient in their particular job, especially with long production runs; there is less time lost by workers switching from one operation to another; and supervision is easier. Workers and managers can be employed who have specific skills in specific areas.

Indivisibilities.   Some inputs are of a minimum size: they are indivisible. The most obvious example is machinery. Take the case of a combine harvester. A small-scale farmer could not make full use of one. They only become economical to use, therefore, on farms above a certain size. The problem of indivisibilities is made worse when different machines, each of which is part of the production process, are of a different size. For example, if there are two types of machine, one producing 6 units a day, the other packaging 4 units a day, a minimum of 12 units per day will have to be produced, involving two production machines and three packaging machines, if all machines are to be fully utilised.

Definitions

Economies of scale
Where increasing the scale of production leads to a lower cost per unit of output.

Specialisation and division of labour
Where production is broken down into a number of simpler, more specialised tasks, thus allowing workers to acquire a high degree of efficiency.

Indivisibilities
The impossibility of dividing a factor into smaller units.

Key
Idea
12
p84

The 'container principle'.   Any capital equipment that contains things (e.g. blast furnaces, oil tankers, pipes, vats) tends to cost less per unit of output the larger its size. The reason has to do with the relationship between a container's volume and its surface area. A container's cost depends largely on the materials used to build it and hence roughly on its *surface area*. Its output depends largely on its *volume*. Large containers have a bigger volume relative to surface area than do small containers. For example, a container with a bottom, top and four sides, with each side measuring 1 metre, has a volume of 1 cubic metre and a surface area of 6 square metres (6 surfaces of 1 square metre each). If each side was doubled in length to 2 metres, the volume would be 8 cubic metres and the surface area 24 square metres (6 surfaces of 4 square metres each). Thus an eightfold increase in capacity has been gained at only a fourfold increase in the container's surface area, and hence an approximate fourfold increase in cost.

Greater efficiency of large machines.   Large machines may be more efficient in the sense that more output can be gained for a given amount of inputs. For example, only one worker may be required to operate a machine, whether it be large or small. Also, a large machine may make more efficient use of raw materials.

By-products.   With production on a large scale, there may be sufficient waste products to make some by-product.

Multi-stage production.   A large factory may be able to take a product through several stages in its manufacture. This saves time and cost moving the semi-finished product from one firm or factory to another. For example, a large cardboard-manufacturing firm may be able to convert trees or waste paper into cardboard and then into cardboard boxes in a continuous sequence.

All the above are examples of plant economies of scale. They are due to an individual factory or workplace or machine being large. There are other economies of scale that are associated with the *firm* being large – perhaps with many factories.

Organisational economies.   With a large firm, individual plants can specialise in particular functions. There can also be centralised administration of the firms. Often, after a merger between two firms, savings can be made by rationalising their activities in this way.

Spreading overheads.   There are some expenditures that are only economic when the *firm* is large, such as research and development: only a large firm can afford to set up a research laboratory. This is another example of indivisibilities, only this time at the level of the firm rather than the plant. The greater the firm's output, the more these overhead costs are spread.

Financial economies.   Large firms may be able to obtain finance at lower interest rates than small firms. They may be able to obtain certain inputs cheaper by buying in bulk. (These are examples of economies of scale which are not the result of increasing returns to scale.)

Economies of scope.   Often a firm is large because it produces a range of products. This can result in each individual product being produced more cheaply than if it was produced in a single-product firm. The reason for these economies of scope is that various overhead costs and financial and organisational economies can be shared among the products. For example, a firm that produces a whole range of CD players, cassette recorders, amplifiers and tuners can benefit from shared marketing and distribution costs and the bulk purchase of electronic components.

Diseconomies of scale

When firms get beyond a certain size, costs per unit of output may start to increase. There are several reasons for such diseconomies of scale:

■ Management problems of co-ordination may increase as the firm becomes larger and more complex, and as lines of communication get longer. There may be a lack of personal involvement by management.
■ Workers may feel 'alienated' if their jobs are boring and repetitive, and if they feel an insignificantly small part of a large organisation. Poor motivation may lead to shoddy work.
■ Industrial relations may deteriorate as a result of these factors and also as a result of the more complex interrelationships between different categories of worker.
■ Production-line processes and the complex interdependencies of mass production can lead to great disruption if there are hold-ups in any one part of the firm.

Whether firms experience economies or diseconomies of scale depends on the conditions applying in each individual firm.

The size of the whole industry

As an *industry* grows in size, this can lead to external economies of scale for its member firms. This is where a firm, whatever its own individual size, benefits from the *whole industry* being large. For example, the firm may benefit from having access to specialist raw material or component suppliers, labour with specific skills, firms that specialise in marketing the finished product, and banks and other financial institutions with experience of the industry's requirements. What we are referring to here is the industry's infrastructure: the facilities, support services, skills and experience that can be shared by its members.

The member firms of a particular industry might, however, experience external diseconomies of scale. For example, as an industry grows larger, this may create a growing shortage of specific raw materials or skilled labour. This will push up their prices, and hence the firms' costs.

Long-run average cost

We turn now to *long-run* cost curves. Since there are no fixed factors in the long run, there are no long-run fixed costs. For example, the firm may rent more land in order to expand its operations. Its rent bill therefore goes up as it expands its output. All costs, then, in the long run are variable costs.

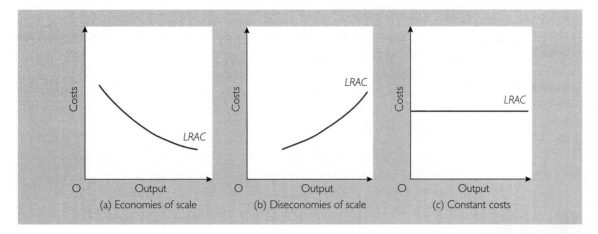

Figure 3.3
Alternative long-run average cost curves

Although it is possible to draw long-run total, marginal and average cost curves, we will concentrate on long-run average cost (*LRAC*) curves. These can take various shapes. If the firm experiences economies of scale, its *LRAC* curve will fall as the scale of production increases (diagram (a) in Figure 3.3). This, after all, is how we define economies of scale: namely, a reduction in average costs as the scale of production increases. If diseconomies of scale predominate, the *LRAC* curve will rise (diagram (b)). Alternatively, if the firm experiences neither economies nor diseconomies of scale, the *LRAC* curve will be horizontal (diagram (c)).

It is often assumed that as a firm expands, it will initially experience economies of scale and thus face a downward-sloping *LRAC* curve. After a point, however, all such economies will have been achieved and thus the curve will flatten out. Then, possibly after a period of constant *LRAC*, the firm will get so large that it will start experiencing diseconomies of scale and thus a rising *LRAC*. At this stage, production and financial economies begin to be offset by the managerial problems of running a giant organisation.

The effect of this is to give a saucer-shaped curve, as in Figure 3.4.

Definition

Long–run average cost curve
A curve that shows how average cost varies with output on the assumption that *all* factors are variable. (It is assumed that the least-cost method of production will be chosen for each output.)

Figure 3.4
A typical long-run avarage cost curve

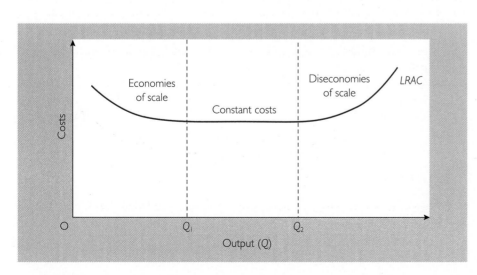

Assumptions behind the long-run average cost curve

There are three key assumptions that we make when constructing long-run average cost curves:

Factor prices are given.   At each level of output it is assumed that a firm will be faced with a given set of factor prices. If factor prices *change*, therefore, both short- and long-run cost curves will shift. Thus an increase in nationally negotiated wage rates would shift the curves upwards.

However, factor prices might be different at *different* levels of output. For example, one of the economies of scale that many firms enjoy is the ability to obtain bulk discount on raw materials and other supplies. In such cases the curve does *not* shift. The different factor prices are merely experienced at different points along the curve, and are reflected in the shape of the curve. Factor prices are still given for any particular level of output.

The state of technology and factor quality are given.   These are assumed to change only in the *very* long run (see next page). If a firm gains economies of scale, it is because it is being able to exploit *existing* technologies and make better use of the existing availability of factors of production.

Firms choose the least-cost combination of factors for each output.   The assumption here is that firms operate efficiently: that they choose the cheapest possible way of producing any level of output.

The relationship between long-run and short-run average cost curves

Take the case of a firm that has just one factory and faces a short-run average cost curve illustrated by $SRAC_1$ in Figure 3.5.

In the long run, it can build more factories. If it thereby experiences economies of scale (due, say, to savings on administration), each successive factory will allow it to produce with a new lower *SRAC* curve. Thus with two factories it will face curve $SRAC_2$; with three factories curve $SRAC_3$, and so on. Each *SRAC* curve corresponds to a particular amount of the factor that is fixed in the short run: in this case, the factory. (Many more *SRAC* curves could be drawn between the ones shown, since factories of different sizes could be built or existing ones could be expanded.)

Figure 3.5
Constructing long-run average cost curves from short-run average cost curves

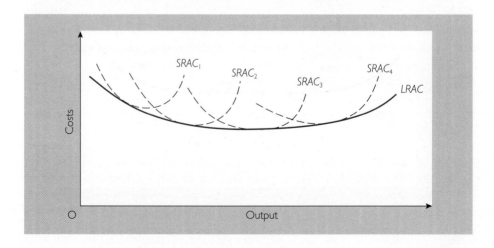

From this succession of short-run average cost curves we can construct a long-run average cost curve. This is shown in Figure 3.5. This is known as the envelope curve, since it envelops the short-run curves.

Long-run cost curves in practice

Firms do experience economies of scale. Some experience continuously falling *LRAC* curves, as in Figure 3.3(a). Others experience economies of scale up to a certain output and thereafter constant returns to scale.

Evidence is inconclusive on the question of diseconomies of scale. There is little evidence to suggest the existence of *technical* diseconomies, but the possibility of diseconomies due to managerial and industrial relations problems cannot be ruled out.

Some evidence on economies of scale in the UK is considered in Box 3.4.

Postscript: Decision making in different time periods

We have distinguished between the short run and the long run. Let us introduce two more time periods to complete the picture. The complete list then reads as follows.

Very short run (immediate run). All factors are fixed. Output is fixed. The supply curve is vertical. On a day-to-day basis a firm may not be able to vary output at all. For example, a flower seller, once the day's flowers have been purchased from the wholesaler, cannot alter the amount of flowers available for sale on that day. In the very short run, all that may remain for a producer to do is to sell an already produced good.

Short run. At least one factor is fixed in supply. More can be produced, but the firm will come up against the law of diminishing returns as it tries to do so.

Long run. All factors are variable. The firm may experience constant, increasing or decreasing returns to scale. But although all factors can be increased or decreased, they are of a fixed *quality*.

Very long run. All factors are variable, *and* their quality and hence productivity can change. Labour productivity can increase as a result of education, training, experience and social factors. The productivity of capital can increase as a result of new inventions (new discoveries) and innovation (putting inventions into practice).

Improvements in factor quality will reduce costs and thus shift the short- and long-run cost curves downwards.

Just how long the 'very long run' is will vary from firm to firm. It will depend on how long it takes to develop new techniques, new skills or new work practices.

It is important to realise that decisions *for* all four time periods can be made *at* the same time. Firms do not make short-run decisions *in* the short run and long-run decisions *in* the long run. They can make both short-run and long-run decisions today. For example, assume that a firm experiences an increase in consumer demand and anticipates that it will continue into the foreseeable future. It thus wants to increase output. Consequently, it makes the following four decisions *today*.

Box 3.4

Minimum efficient scale

The extent of economies of scale in practice

One of the most important studies of economies of scale was made in the late 1980s by C. F. Pratten.[1] Pratten found strong evidence that many firms, especially in manufacturing, experienced substantial economies of scale.

In a few cases long-run average costs fell continuously as output increased. For most firms, however, they fell up to a certain level of output and then remained constant.

Two methods are commonly used to measure the extent of economies of scale. The first involves identifying a *minimum efficient scale (MES)*. The *MES* is the size beyond which no significant additional economies of scale can be achieved: in other words, the point where the *LRAC* curve flattens off. In Pratten's studies he defined this level as the minimum scale above which any possible doubling in scale would reduce average costs by less than 5 per cent (i.e. virtually the bottom of the *LRAC* curve). In the diagram *MES* is shown at point *a*.

The *MES* can be expressed in terms either of an individual factory or of the whole firm. Where it refers to the minimum efficient scale of an individual factory, the *MES* is known as the *minimum efficient plant size (MEPS)*.

The *MES* can then be expressed as a percentage of the total size of the market or of total domestic production. The table shows *MES* for various plants and firms. The first column shows *MES* as a percentage of total UK production. The second column shows *MES* as a percentage of total EU production.

Expressing *MES* as a percentage of total output gives an indication of how competitive the industry

could be. In some industries (such as shoes and tufted carpets), economies of scale were exhausted (i.e. *MES* was reached) with plants or firms that were still small relative to total UK production and even smaller relative to total EU production. In such industries there would be room for many firms and thus scope for considerable competition.

In other industries, however, even if a single plant or firm were large enough to produce the whole output of the industry in the UK, it would still not be large enough to experience the full potential economies of scale: the *MES* is greater than 100 per cent. Examples include factories producing cellulose fibres, and car manufacturers. In such industries there is no possibility of competition. In fact, as long as the *MES* exceeds 50 per cent there will not be room for more than one firm large enough to gain full economies of scale. In this case the industry is said to be a *natural monopoly*. As we shall see in Chapters 4 and 6, when competition is lacking, consumers may suffer by firms charging prices considerably above costs.

The second way of measuring the extent of economies of scale is to see how much costs would increase if production were reduced to a certain fraction of *MES*. The normal fractions used are $^1/_2$ or $^1/_3$

[1] C. F. Pratten, 'A survey of the economies of scale', in *Research on the 'Costs of Non-Europe'*, vol. 2 (Office for Official Publications of the European Communities, 1988).

Product	MES as % of production		% additional cost at $^1/_2$ MES
	UK	EU	
Individual plants			
Cellulose fibres	125	16	3
Rolled aluminium semi-manufactures	114	15	15
Refrigerators	85	11	4
Steel	72	10	6
Electric motors	60	6	15
TV sets	40	9	9
Cigarettes	24	6	1.4
Ball-bearings	20	2	6
Beer	12	3	7
Nylon	4	1	12
Bricks	1	0.2	25
Tufted carpets	0.3	0.04	10
Shoes	0.3	0.03	1
Firms			
Cars	200	20	9
Lorries	104	21	7.5
Mainframe computers	>100	n.a.	5
Aircraft	100	n.a.	5
Tractors	98	19	6

Source: C. F. Pratten, 'A survey of the economics of scale', in *Research on the 'Costs of Non-Europe'*, vol. 2 (Office for Official Publications of the European Communities, 1988).

MES. This is illustrated in the diagram. Point *b* corresponds to $^1/_2$ *MES*; point *c* to $^1/_3$ *MES*. The greater the percentage by which *LRAC* at point *b* or *c* is higher than at point *a*, the greater will be the economies of scale to be gained by producing at *MES* rather than at $^1/_2$ *MES* or $^1/_3$ *MES*. For example, the table shows that greater economies of scale can be gained by moving from $^1/_2$ *MES* to *MES* in the production of electric motors than of cigarettes.

The main purpose of Pratten's study was to determine whether the creation of a large internal EU market with no trade barriers by the end of 1992 would significantly reduce costs and increase competition.

The table suggests that in all cases, other things being equal, the EU market is large enough for firms to gain the full economies of scale *and* for there to be enough firms for the market to be competitive.

1. Why might a firm operating with one plant achieve *MEPS* and yet not be large enough to achieve *MES*? (Clue: are all economies of scale achieved at plant level?)
2. Why might a firm producing bricks have an *MES* that is only 0.2 per cent of total EU production and yet face little effective competition from other EU countries?

- (*Very short run*) It accepts that for a few days it will not be able to increase output. It informs its customers that they will have to wait. It may temporarily raise prices to choke off some of the demand.
- (*Short run*) It negotiates with labour to introduce overtime working as soon as possible, to tide it over the next few weeks. It orders extra raw materials from its suppliers. It launches a recruitment drive for new labour so as to avoid paying overtime longer than is necessary.
- (*Long run*) It starts proceedings to build a new factory. The first step may be to discuss requirements with a firm of consultants.
- (*Very long run*) It institutes a programme of research and development and/or training in an attempt to increase productivity.

Although we distinguish these four time periods, it is the middle two we are primarily concerned with. The reason for this is that there is very little the firm can do in the *very* short run. And in the *very* long run, although the firm will obviously want to increase the productivity of its inputs, it will not be in the position to make precise calculations of how to do it. It will not know precisely what inventions will be made, or just what will be the results of its own research and development.

Recap

1. In the long run, a firm is able to vary the quantity it uses of all factors of production. There are no fixed factors and hence no long-run fixed costs.

2. If it increases all factors by the same proportion, it may experience constant, increasing or decreasing returns to scale.

3. Economies of scale occur when costs per unit of output fall as the scale of production increases. This can be the result of a number of factors, some of which are directly due to increasing (physical) returns to scale. These include the benefits of specialisation and division of labour, the use of larger and more efficient machines, and the ability to have a more integrated system of production. Other economies of scale arise from the financial and administrative benefits of large-scale organisations.

4. When constructing long-run cost curves it is assumed that factor prices are given, that the state of technology is given and that firms will choose the least-cost method of production for each given output.

5. The *LRAC* curve can be downward sloping, upward sloping or horizontal, depending in turn on whether there are economies of scale, diseconomies of scale or neither. Typically *LRAC* curves are drawn as saucer-shaped (or as I-shaped). As output expands, initially there are economies of scale. When these are exhausted the curve will become flat. When the firm becomes very large it may begin to experience diseconomies of scale. If this happens, the *LRAC* curve will begin to slope upwards again.

6. An envelope curve can be drawn which shows the relationship between short-run and long-run average cost curves. The *LRAC* curve envelops the short-run *AC* curves: it is 'tangential' to them (i.e. just touches them).

7. Four distinct time periods can be distinguished. In addition to the short- and long-run periods, we can also distinguish the very-short- and very-long-run periods. The very short run is when all factors are fixed. The very long run is where not only the quantity of factors but also their quality is variable (as a result of changing technology, etc.).

Revenue   3.3

How does a firm's revenue vary with its level of sales?

Throughout this chapter we are building up a theory of profit maximisation. We are attempting to find the output and price at which a firm maximises its profits, and how much profit it can make at that level. Remember that we defined a firm's total profit $(T\Pi)$ as its total revenue minus its total costs of production. (Note that we use Π, the Greek capital pi, to stand for profit.)

$$T\Pi = TR - TC$$

In the last two sections we have looked at costs in some detail. We must now turn to the revenue side of the equation. As with costs, we distinguish between three revenue concepts: total revenue (TR), average revenue (AR) and marginal revenue (MR).

Total, average and marginal revenue

Total revenue (TR)

Total revenue is the firm's total earnings per period of time from the sale of a particular amount of output (Q).

For example, if a firm sells 1000 units (Q) per month at a price of £5 each (P), then its monthly total revenue will be £5000: in other words, £5 × 1000 $(P \times Q)$. Thus:

$$TR = P \times Q$$

Average revenue (AR)

Average revenue is the amount that the firm earns per unit sold. Thus:

$$AR = TR/Q$$

So if the firm earns £5000 (TR) from selling 1000 units (Q), it will earn £5 per unit. But this is simply the price! Thus:

$$AR = P$$

(The only exception to this is when the firm is selling its products at different prices to different consumers. In this case AR is simply the (weighted) average price.)

Marginal revenue (MR)

Marginal revenue is the extra total revenue gained by selling one more unit (per time period). So if a firm sells an extra 20 units this month compared with what it expected to sell, and in the process earns an extra £100, then it is getting an extra £5 for each extra unit sold: $MR = £5$. Thus:

$$MR = \Delta TR/\Delta Q$$

We now need to see how each of these three revenue concepts $(TR, AR$ and $MR)$ varies with output. We can show this relationship graphically in the same way as we did with costs.

Definitions

Total revenue
A firm's total earnings from a specified level of sales within a specified period: $TR = P \times Q$

Average revenue
Total revenue per unit of output. When all output is sold at the same price, average revenue will be the same as price: $AR = TR/Q = P$

Marginal revenue
The extra revenue gained by selling one more unit per period of time: $MR = \Delta TR/\Delta Q$

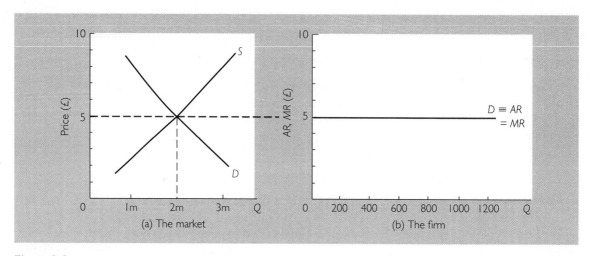

Figure 3.6
Deriving a firm's
AR and MR:
price-taking firm

The relationship will depend on the market conditions under which a firm operates. A firm that is too small to be able to affect market price will have different-looking revenue curves from a firm that is able to choose the price it charges. Let us examine each of these two situations in turn.

Revenue curves when price is not affected by the firm's output

Average revenue

If a firm is very small relative to the whole market, it is likely to be a price taker. That is, it has to accept the price given by the intersection of demand and supply in the whole market. But, being so small, it can sell as much as it is capable of producing at that price. This is illustrated in Figure 3.6.

Diagram (a) shows market demand and supply. Equilibrium price is £5. Diagram (b) looks at the demand for an individual firm that is tiny relative to the whole market. (Look at the difference in the scale of the horizontal axes in the two diagrams.)

Being so small, any change in its output will be too insignificant to affect the market price. It thus faces a horizontal demand 'curve' at this price. It can sell 200 units, 600 units, 1200 units or whatever without affecting this £5 price.

Average revenue is thus constant at £5. The firm's average revenue curve must therefore lie along exactly the same line as its demand curve.

Marginal revenue

In the case of a horizontal demand curve, the marginal revenue curve will be the same as the average revenue curve, since selling one more unit at a constant price (*AR*) merely adds that amount to total revenue. If an extra unit is sold at a constant price of £5, an extra £5 is earned.

Total revenue

Table 3.4 shows the effect on total revenue of different levels of sales with a constant price of £5 per unit.

As price is constant, total revenue will rise at a constant rate as more is sold. The *TR* 'curve' will therefore be a straight line through the origin, as in Figure 3.7.

Quantity (units)	Price ≡ AR = MR(£)	TR (£)
0	5	0
200	5	1000
400	5	2000
600	5	3000
800	5	4000
1000	5	5000
1200	5	6000

Table 3.4
Deriving total revenue: the firm is a price taker

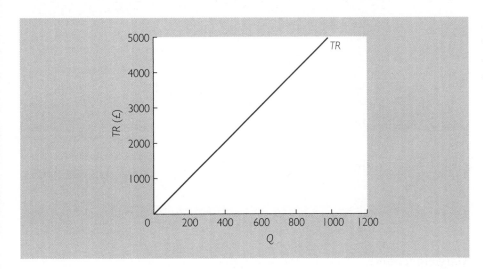

Figure 3.7
Total revenue curve for a price-taking firm

Revenue curves when price varies with output

The three curves (*TR, AR* and *MR*) will look quite different when price does vary with the firm's output.

If a firm has a relatively large share of the market, it will face a downward-sloping demand curve. This means that if it is to sell more, it must lower the price. But it could also choose to raise its price. If it does so, however, it will have to accept a fall in sales.

Average revenue

Remember that average revenue equals price. If, therefore, the price has to be reduced to sell more output, average revenue will fall as output increases.

Table 3.5 gives an example of a firm facing a downward-sloping demand curve. The demand curve (which shows how much is sold at each price) is given by the first two columns.

Note that, as in the case of a price-taking firm, the demand curve and the *AR* curve lie along exactly the same line (see Figure 3.8). The reason for this is simple: *AR = P*, and thus the curve relating price to quantity (the demand curve) must be the same as that relating average revenue to quantity (the *AR* curve).

Table 3.5

Revenues for a firm facing a downward-sloping demand curve

Q (units)	P = AR (£)	TR (£)	MR (£)
1	8	8	
2	7	14	6
3	6	18	4
4	5	20	2
5	4	20	0
6	3	18	−2
7	2	14	−4
.	.	.	.

Figure 3.8

AR and MR curves for a firm facing a downward-sloping demand curve

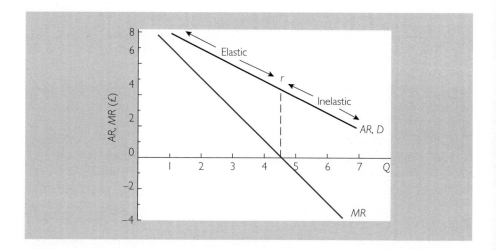

Marginal revenue

When a firm faces a downward-sloping demand curve, marginal revenue will be less than average revenue, and may even be negative. But why?

If a firm is to sell more per time period, it must lower its price (assuming it does not advertise). This will mean lowering the price not just for the extra units it hopes to sell, but also for those units it would have sold had it not lowered the price.

Thus the marginal revenue is the price at which it sells the last unit, *minus* the loss in revenue it has incurred by reducing the price on those units it could otherwise have sold at the higher price. This can be illustrated with Table 3.5.

Assume that price is currently £7. Two units are thus sold. The firm now wishes to sell an extra unit. It lowers the price to £6. It thus gains £6 from the sale of the third unit, but loses £2 by having to reduce the price by £1 on the two units it could otherwise have sold at £7. Its net gain is therefore £6 − £2 = £4. This is the marginal revenue: it is the extra revenue gained by the firm from selling one more unit. Try using this method to check out the remaining figures for *MR* in Table 3.5. (Note that in the table the figures for *MR* are entered in the spaces between the figures for the other three columns.)

There is a simple relationship between marginal revenue and *price elasticity of demand*. Remember from Chapter 2 (page 57) that if demand is price elastic, a *decrease* in price will lead to a proportionately larger increase in the quantity demanded and hence to an *increase* in revenue. Marginal revenue will thus be positive. If, however,

Ke
Ide

9
p6

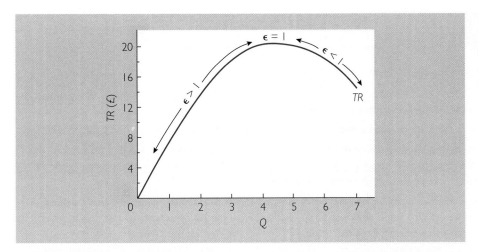

Figure 3.9
Total revenue for a firm facing a downward-sloping demand curve

demand is inelastic, a decrease in price will lead to a proportionately smaller increase in sales. In this case the price reduction will more than offset the increase in sales and as a result revenue will fall. Marginal revenue will be negative.

If, then, marginal revenue is a positive figure (i.e. if sales per time period are 4 units or less in Figure 3.8), the demand curve will be elastic at that quantity, since a rise in quantity sold (as a result of a reduction in price) would lead to a rise in total revenue. If, on the other hand, marginal revenue is negative (i.e. at a level of sales of 5 or more units in Figure 3.8), the demand curve will be inelastic at that quantity, since a rise in quantity sold would lead to a *fall* in total revenue.

Thus the demand (*AR*) curve of Figure 3.8 is elastic to the left of point *r* and inelastic to the right.

Total revenue

Total revenue equals price times quantity. This is illustrated in Table 3.5. The *TR* column from Table 3.5 is plotted in Figure 3.9.

Unlike the case of a price-taking firm, the *TR* curve is not a straight line. It is a curve that rises at first and then falls. But why? As long as marginal revenue is positive (and hence demand is price elastic), a rise in output will raise total revenue. However, once marginal revenue becomes negative (and hence demand is inelastic), total revenue will fall. The peak of the *TR* curve will be where $MR = 0$. At this point the price elasticity of demand will be equal to -1.

Shifts in revenue curves

We saw in Chapter 1 that a change in *price* will cause a movement along a demand curve. It is similar with revenue curves, except that here the causal connection is in the other direction. Here we ask what happens to revenue when there is a change in the firm's *output*. Again the effect is shown by a movement along the curves.

A change in any *other* determinant of demand, such as tastes, income or the price of other goods, will shift the demand curve. As this change affects the price at which each level of output can be sold, there will be a shift in all three revenue curves. An increase in revenue is shown by a vertical shift upwards; a decrease by a shift downwards.

Recap

1. Total revenue (*TR*) is the total amount a firm earns from its sales in a given time period. It is simply price times quantity: $TR = P \times Q$.

2. Average revenue (*AR*) is total revenue per unit: $AR = TR/Q$. In other words, $AR = P$.

3. Marginal revenue is the extra revenue earned from the sale of one more unit per time period: $MR = \Delta TR/\Delta Q$.

4. The *AR* curve will be the same as the demand curve for the firm's product. In the case of a price taker, the demand curve and hence the *AR* curve will be a horizontal straight line and will also be the same as the *MR* curve. The *TR* curve is an upward-sloping straight line from the origin.

5. A firm that faces a downward-sloping demand curve must obviously also face the same downward-sloping *AR* curve. The *MR* curve will also slope downwards, but will be below the *AR* curve and steeper than it. The *TR* curve will be an arch shape starting from the origin.

6. When demand is price elastic, marginal revenue will be positive and the *TR* curve will be upward sloping. When demand is price inelastic, marginal revenue will be negative and the *TR* curve will be downward sloping.

7. A change in output is represented by a movement along the revenue curves. A change in any other determinant of revenue will shift the curves up or down.

3.4   Profit maximisation

How much output should a firm produce if it wants to maximise its profit?

We are now in a position to put costs and revenue together to find the output at which profit is maximised, and also to find out how much that profit will be.

There are two ways of doing this. The first and simpler method is to use total cost and total revenue curves. The second method is to use marginal and average cost and marginal and average revenue curves. Although this method is a little more complicated (but only a little!), it is more useful when we come to compare profit maximising under different market conditions (see Chapter 4).

We will look at each method in turn. In both cases we will concentrate on the short run: namely, that period in which one or more factors are fixed in supply. In both cases we take the case of a firm facing a downward-sloping demand curve.

Short-run profit maximisation: using total curves

Table 3.6 shows the total revenue figures from Table 3.5. It also shows figures for total cost. These figures have been chosen so as to produce a *TC* curve of a typical shape.

Total profit (*TΠ*) is found by subtracting *TC* from *TR*. Check this out by examining the table. Where *TΠ* is negative, the firm is making a loss. Total profit is maximised at an output of 3 units: namely, where there is the greatest gap between total revenue and total costs. At this output, total profit is £4 (£18 − £14).

The *TR*, *TC* and *TΠ* curves are plotted in Figure 3.10. The size of the maximum profit is shown by the arrows.

Q (units)	TR (£)	TC (£)	TΠ (£)
0	0	6	−6
1	8	10	−2
2	14	12	2
3	18	14	4
4	20	18	2
5	20	25	−5
6	18	36	−18
7	14	56	−42
.	.	.	.

Table 3.6
Total revenue, total cost and total profit

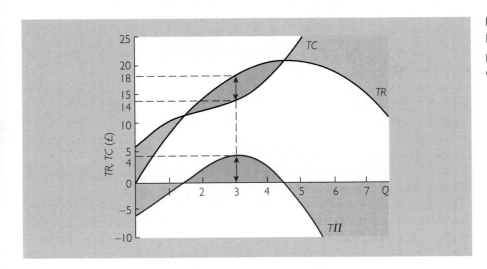

Figure 3.10
Finding maximum profit using totals curve

Short-run profit maximisation: using average and marginal curves

Table 3.7 is based on the figures in Table 3.6.

Finding the maximum profit that a firm can make is a two-stage process. The first stage is to find the profit-maximising output. To do this we use the *MC* and *MR*

Q (units)	P = AR (£)	TR (£)	MR (£)	TC (£)	AC (£)	MC (£)	TΠ (£)	AΠ (£)
0	9	0		6	–		−6	–
			8			4		
1	8	8		10	10		−2	−2
			6			2		
2	7	14		12	6		2	1
			4			2		
3	6	18		14	4²/₃		4	1¹/₃
			2			4		
4	5	20		18	4¹/₂		2	¹/₂
			0			7		
5	4	20		25	5		−5	−1
			−2			11		
6	3	18		36	6		−18	−3
			−4			20		
7	2	14		56	8		−42	−6
.	.	.		.	.		.	.

Table 3.7
Revenue, cost and profit

Figure 3.11

Finding the profit-maximising output using marginal curves

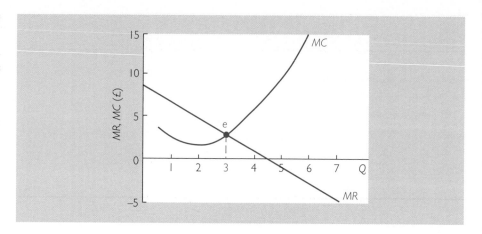

curves. The second stage is to find out just how much profit is at this output. To do this we use the *AR* and *AC* curves.

Stage 1: Using marginal curves to arrive at the profit-maximising output

Definition

Profit–maximising rule
Profit is maximised where marginal revenue equals marginal cost.

There is a very simple profit-maximising rule: if profits are to be maximised, *MR must equal MC*. From Table 3.7 it can be seen that *MR* = *MC* at an output of 3. This is shown as point *e* in Figure 3.11.

But why are profits maximised when *MR* = *MC*? The simplest way of answering this is to see what the position would be if *MR* did not equal *MC*.

Referring to Figure 3.11, at a level of output below 3, *MR* exceeds *MC*. This means that by producing more units there will be a bigger addition to revenue (*MR*) than to cost (*MC*). Total profit will *increase. As long as MR exceeds MC, profit can be increased by increasing production.*

At a level of output above 3, *MC* exceeds *MR*. All levels of output above 3 thus add more to cost than to revenue and hence *reduce* profit. *As long as MC exceeds MR, profit can be increased by cutting back on production.*

Profits are thus maximised where *MC* = *MR*: at an output of 3. This can be confirmed by reference to the *TΠ* column in Table 3.7.

Students worry sometimes about the argument that profits are maximised when *MR* = *MC*. Surely, they say, if the last unit is making no profit, how can profit be at a *maximum*? The answer is very simple. If you cannot add anything more to a total, the total must be at the maximum. Take the simple analogy of going up a hill. When you cannot go any higher, you must be at the top.

Stage 2: Using average curves to measure the size of the profit

Once the profit-maximising output has been discovered, we now use the average curves to measure the *amount* of profit at the maximum. Both marginal and average curves corresponding to the data in Table 3.7 are plotted in Figure 3.12.

First, average profit (*AΠ*) is found. This is simply *AR* − *AC*. At the profit-maximising output of 3, this gives a figure for *AΠ* of £6 − £4^2/$_3$ = £1^1/$_3$. Then total profit is obtained by multiplying average profit by output:

$$TΠ = AΠ \times Q$$

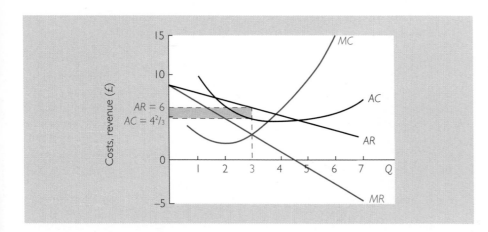

Figure 3.12

Measuring the maximum profit using average curves

This is shown as the shaded area. It equals £1$^1/_3$ × 3 = £4. This can again be confirmed by reference to the $T\Pi$ column in Table 3.7.

Pause for thought |||

What will be the effect on a firm's profit-maximising output of a rise in fixed costs?

Some qualifications

Long-run profit maximisation

Assuming that the AR and MR curves are the same in the long run as in the short run, long-run profits will be maximised at the output where MR equals the *long-run MC*. The reasoning is the same as with the short-run case.

The meaning of 'profit'

One element of cost is the opportunity cost to the owners of the firm incurred by being in business. This is the minimum return that the owners must make on their capital in order to prevent them from eventually deciding to close down and perhaps move into some alternative business. It is a *cost* since, just as with wages, rent, etc., it has to be covered if the firm is to continue producing. This opportunity cost to the owners is sometimes known as normal profit, and is *included in the cost curves*.

What determines this normal rate of profit? It has two components. First, someone setting up in business invests capital in it. There is thus an opportunity cost. This is the interest that could have been earned by lending it in some riskless form (e.g. by putting it in a savings account in a bank). Nobody would set up a business unless they expected to earn at least this rate of profit. Running a business is far from riskless, however, and hence a second element is a return to compensate for risk. Thus:

Normal profit (%) = Rate of interest on a riskless loan + A risk premium

The risk premium varies according to the line of business. In those businesses with fairly predictable patterns, such as food retailing, it is relatively low. Where outcomes are very uncertain, as in mineral exploration or the manufacture of fashion garments, it is relatively high.

Key Idea
2
p8

Definition

Normal profit
The opportunity cost of being in business. It consists of the interest that could be earned on a riskless asset, plus a return for risk taking. It is counted as a cost of production.

Figure 3.13
Loss-minimising
output

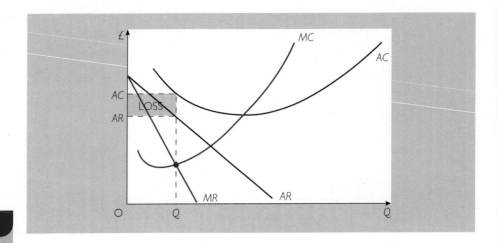

Thus if owners of a business earn normal profit, they will (just) be content to remain in that industry. If they earn more than normal profit, they will also (obviously) prefer to stay in this business. If they earn less than normal profit, then after a time they will consider leaving and using their capital for some other purpose.

Given that normal profits are included in costs, any profit that is shown diagrammatically (e.g. the shaded area in Figure 3.12) must therefore be over and above normal profit. It is known by several alternative names: supernormal profit, pure profit, economic profit, abnormal profit, producer's surplus (or sometimes simply profit). They all mean the same thing: the excess of total profit over normal profit.

Loss minimising

Sometimes there is no output at which the firm can make a profit. Such a situation is illustrated in Figure 3.13: the *AC* curve is above the *AR* curve at all levels of output.

In this case, the output where *MR* = *MC* will be the loss-minimising output. The amount of loss at the point where *MR* = *MC* is shown by the shaded area in Figure 3.13.

Whether or not to produce at all

The short run.   Fixed costs have to be paid even if the firm is producing nothing at all. Rent has to be paid, business rates have to be paid, and so forth. Providing, therefore, that the firm is more than covering its *variable* costs, it can go some way to paying off these fixed costs and therefore will continue to produce.

It will shut down if it cannot cover its variable costs: that is, if the *AVC* curve is above, or the *AR* curve is below, that illustrated in Figure 3.14. This situation is known as the short-run shut-down point.

The long run.   All costs are variable in the long run. If, therefore, the firm cannot cover its long-run average costs (which include normal profit), it will close down. The long-run shut-down point will be where the *AR* curve is tangential to (i.e. just touches) the *LRAC* curve.

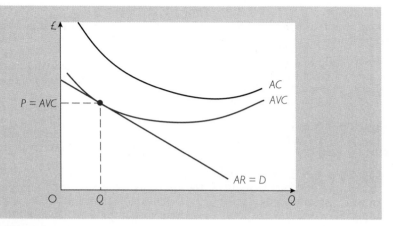

Figure 3.14
The short-run shut-down point

Recap

1. Total profit equals total revenue minus total cost. By definition, then, a firm's profits will be maximised at the point where there is the greatest gap between total revenue and total cost.

2. Another way of finding the maximum-profit point is to find the output where marginal revenue equals marginal cost. Having found this output, the level of maximum profit can be found by finding the average profit (AR − AC) and then multiplying it by the level of output.

3. Normal profit is the minimum profit that must be made to persuade a firm to stay in business in the long run. It is counted as part of the firm's costs. Supernormal profit is any profit over and above normal profit.

4. For a firm that cannot make a profit at any level of output, the point where MR = MC represents the loss-minimising output.

5. In the short run, a firm will close down if it cannot cover its variable costs. In the long run, it will close down if it cannot make normal profits.

Questions

1. Up to roughly how long is the short run in the following cases?

   (a) A mobile disco firm.
   (b) Electricity power generation.
   (c) A small grocery retailing business.
   (d) 'Superstore Hypermarkets plc'.

   In each case specify your assumptions.

2. Given that there is a fixed supply of land in the world, what implications can you draw from the law of diminishing returns about the effects of an increase in world population on food output per head?

3. The following are some costs incurred by a shoe manufacturer. Decide whether each one is a fixed cost or a variable cost or has some element of both.

   (a) The cost of leather.
   (b) The fee paid to an advertising agency.
   (c) Wear and tear on machinery.
   (d) Business rates on the factory.
   (e) Electricity for heating and lighting.
   (f) Electricity for running the machines.
   (g) Basic minimum wages agreed with the union.
   (h) Overtime pay.
   (i) Depreciation of machines as a result purely of their age (irrespective of their condition).

4. What economies of scale is a large department store likely to experience?

5. Why are many firms likely to experience economies of scale up to a certain size and then diseconomies of scale after some point beyond that?

6. Name some industries where external economies of scale are gained. What are the specific external economies in each case?

7. Examine Figure 3.3 (on page 97). What would (i) the firm's long-run total cost curve, and (ii) its long-run marginal cost curve look like in each of these three cases?

8. Under what circumstances is a firm likely to experience a flat-bottomed *LRAC* curve?

9. Draw a downward-sloping demand curve. Now choose scales for both axes. Read off various points on the demand curve and use them to construct a table showing price and quantity. Use this table to work out the figures for a marginal revenue column. Now use these figures to draw an *MR* curve.

10. Copy Figures 3.8 and 3.9 (which are based on Table 3.5). Now assume that incomes have risen and that, as a result, two more units per time period can be sold at each price. Construct a new table and plot the resulting new *AR*, *MR* and *TR* curves on your diagrams. Are the new curves parallel to the old ones? Explain.

11. What can we say about the slope of the *TR* and *TC* curves at the maximum-profit point? What does this tell us about marginal revenue and marginal cost?

12. From the information given in the following table, construct a table like Table 3.7.

Q	0	1	2	3	4	5	6	7
P	12	11	10	9	8	7	6	5
TC	2	6	9	12	16	21	28	38

Use your table to draw diagrams like Figures 3.10 and 3.12. Use these two diagrams to show the profit-maximising output and the level of maximum profit. Confirm your findings by reference to the table you have constructed.

13. Normal profits are regarded as a cost (and are included in the cost curves). Explain why.

14. What determines the size of normal profit? Will it vary with the general state of the economy?

15. A firm will continue producing in the short run even if it is making a loss, providing it can cover its variable costs. Explain why. Just how long will it be willing to continue making such a loss?

16. The price of pocket calculators and digital watches fell significantly in the years after they were first introduced, and at the same time demand for them increased substantially. Use cost and revenue diagrams to illustrate these events. Explain the reasoning behind the diagram(s) you have drawn.

17. The table at the bottom of this page shows the average cost and average revenue (price) for a firm at each level of output.

   (a) Construct a table to show *TC*, *MC*, *TR* and *MR* at each level of output (put the figures for *MC* and *MR* midway between the output figures).
   (b) Using *MC* and *MR* figures, find the profit-maximising output.
   (c) Using *TC* and *TR* figures, check your answer to (b).
   (d) Plot the *AC*, *MC*, *AR* and *MR* figures on a graph.
   (e) Mark the profit-maximising output and the *AR* and *AC* at this output.
   (f) Shade in an area to represent the level of profits at this output.

18. In February 2000, Unilever, the giant consumer products company, announced that it was to cut 25 000 jobs, close 100 plants and rely more on the Internet to purchase its supplies. It would use part of the money saved to increase promotion of its leading brands, such as Dove skin-care products, Lipton tea, Omo detergents and Calvin Klein cosmetics. The hope was to boost sales and increase profits. If it meets these targets, what is likely to have happened to its total costs, total revenue, average costs and average revenue? Give reasons for your answer.

Output	1	2	3	4	5	6	7	8	9	10
AC (£)	7.00	5.00	4.00	3.30	3.00	3.10	3.50	4.20	5.00	6.00
AR (£)	10.00	9.50	9.00	8.50	8.00	7.50	7.00	6.50	6.00	5.50

Additional case studies on the *Essentials of Economics* website (www.booksites.net/sloman)

3.1   The legal and organisational structure of firms. This case looks at the distinction between sole proprietorships, partnerships, private limited companies and public limited companies. It also distinguishes between U-form, M-form and H-form organisations.

3.2   Division of labour in a pin factory. This is the famous example of division of labour given by Adam Smith in his *Wealth of Nations* (1776).

3.3   Diminishing returns to nitrogen fertiliser. This case study provides a good illustration of diminishing returns in practice by showing the effects on grass yields of the application of increasing amounts of nitrogen fertiliser.

3.4   The fallacy of using historic costs. This looks at the example of the pricing of Christmas trees.

3.5   Followers of fashion. This case study examines the effects of costs on prices of fashion-sensitive goods.

3.6   Cost curves in practice. What do cost curves look like when fixed factors are divisible?

Sections of chapter covered in
WinEcon – Sloman, *Essentials of Economics*

Essentials of Economics section	*WinEcon* section
3.1	3.1
3.2	3.2
3.3	Covered in 3.4
3.4	3.4

Websites relevant to this chapter

Numbers and sections refer to websites listed in the Web Appendix and hotlinked from this book's website at www.booksites.net/sloman

■ For news articles relevant to this chapter, see the *Economics News Articles* link from the book's website.

■ For student resources relevant to this chapter, see sites C1–7, 9, 10, 14, 19, 20.

■ For a case study examining costs, see site D2.

■ For sites that look at companies, their scale of operation and market share, see B2 (third link); E4, 10; G7, 8.

■ For links to sites on various aspects of production and costs, see section *Microeconomics > Production* in sites I7 and 11.

CHAPTER MAP

CHAPTER FOUR
Market structures

As we saw in Section 3.4, a firm's profits are maximised where its marginal cost equals its marginal revenue: $MC = MR$. But we will want to know more than this.

What determines the *amount* of profit that a firm will make? Will its profits be large, or just enough for it to survive, or so low that it will be forced out of business? Will the price charged to the consumer be high or low? And, more generally, will the consumer benefit from the decisions a firm makes?

The answers to these questions depend on the amount of competition that a firm faces. A firm in a highly competitive environment will behave quite differently from a firm facing little or no competition. In particular, a firm facing competition from many other firms will be forced to keep its prices down and be as efficient as possible, simply to survive.

Even if a firm faces only one or two rivals, competition might be quite intense. Firms might put a lot of effort into producing more efficiently or into developing new or better products in order to gain a larger share of the market. They may, however, collude with each other to keep prices up.

When firms face little or no competition (like the local water company or a major pharmaceutical company), they may have considerable power over prices and we may end up paying a lot more.

In this chapter we look at different types of market and how well they serve the consumer.

4.1   The degree of competition

How much competition does a firm face?

It is traditional to divide industries into categories according to the degree of competition that exists between the firms within the industry. There are four such categories.

At one extreme is perfect competition where there are very many firms competing. Each firm is so small relative to the whole industry that it has no power to influence price. It is a price taker. At the other extreme is monopoly, where there is just one firm in the industry, and hence no competition from *within* the industry. In the middle come monopolistic competition, which involves quite a lot of firms competing and where there is freedom for new firms to enter the industry, and oligopoly, where there are only a few firms and where entry of new firms is restricted.

To distinguish more precisely between these four categories, the following must be considered:

- How freely can firms enter the industry: is entry free or restricted? If it is restricted, just how great are the barriers to the entry of new firms?
- The nature of the product. Do all firms produce an identical product, or do firms produce their own particular brand or model or variety?
- The degree of control the firm has over price. Is the firm a price taker or can it choose its price, and if so, how will changing its price affect its profits? What we are talking about here is the nature of the demand curve it faces. How elastic is it? If the firm puts up its price, will it lose (a) all its sales (a horizontal demand curve), or (b) a large proportion of its sales (a relatively elastic demand curve), or (c) just a small proportion of its sales (a relatively inelastic demand curve)?

> **Key Idea**
> 9
> p64

> **Market power benefits the powerful at the expense of others.** When firms have market power over prices, they can use this to raise prices and profits above the perfectly competitive level. Other things being equal, the firm will gain at the expense of the consumer. Similarly, if consumers or workers have market power they can use this to their own benefit.
>
> **Key Idea**
> 14

Table 4.1 shows the differences between the four categories.

The market structure under which a firm operates will determine its behaviour. Firms under perfect competition behave quite differently from firms that are monopolists, which behave differently again from firms under oligopoly or monopolistic competition.

This behaviour (or 'conduct') in turn affects the firm's performance: its prices, profits, efficiency, etc. In many cases it also affects other firms' performance: *their* prices, profits, efficiency, etc. The collective conduct of all the firms in the industry affects the whole industry's performance.

Definitions

Perfect competition
A market structure where there are many firms; where there is freedom of entry into the industry; where all firms produce an identical product; and where all firms are price takers.

Monopoly
A market structure where there is only one firm in the industry.

Monopolistic competition
A market structure where, like perfect competition, there are many firms and freedom of entry into the industry, but where each firm produces a differentiated product and thus has some control over its price.

Oligopoly
A market structure where there are few enough firms to enable barriers to be erected against the entry of new firms.

Table 4.1 Features of the four market structures

Type of market	Number of firms	Freedom of entry	Nature of product	Examples	Implication for demand curve for firm
Perfect competition	Very many	Unrestricted	Homogeneous (undifferentiated)	Cabbages, carrots (these approximate to perfect competition)	Horizontal. The firm is a price taker
Monopolistic competition	Many/several	Unrestricted	Differentiated	Builders, restaurants	Downward sloping, but relatively elastic. The firm has some control over price
Oligopoly	Few	Restricted	1. Undifferentiated or 2. Differentiated	1. Cement 2. Cars, electrical appliances	Downward sloping, relatively inelastic but depends on reactions of rivals to a price change
Monopoly	One	Restricted or completely blocked	Unique	Many prescription drugs, local water company	Downward sloping, more inelastic than oligopoly. The firm has considerable control over price

Economists thus see a causal chain running from market structure to the performance of that industry.

Structure → Conduct → Performance

First we look at the two extreme market structures: perfect competition and monopoly (Sections 4.2 and 4.3). Then we turn to look at the two intermediate cases of monopolistic competition and oligopoly (Sections 4.4 and 4.5).

These two intermediate cases are sometimes referred to collectively as imperfect competition. The vast majority of firms in the real world operate under imperfect competition. It is still worth studying the two extreme cases, however, because they provide a framework within which to understand the real world. Some industries tend more to the competitive extreme, and thus their performance corresponds to some extent to perfect competition. Other industries tend more to the other extreme: for example, when there is one dominant firm and a few much smaller firms. In such cases their performance corresponds more to monopoly.

> **Definition**
>
> **Imperfect competition** The collective name for monopolistic competition and oligopoly.

> **Pause for thought**
>
> Give one more example in each of the four market categories in Table 4.1.

Recap

1. There are four alternative market structures under which firms operate. In ascending order of firms' market power, they are: perfect competition, monopolistic competition, oligopoly and monopoly.
2. The market structure under which a firm operates affects its conduct, which in turn affects its performance.

4.2   Perfect competition

What happens when there are very many firms all competing against each other? Is this good for us as consumers?

The theory of perfect competition illustrates an extreme form of capitalism. In it, firms are entirely subject to market forces. They have no power whatsoever to affect the price of the product. The price they face is determined by the interaction of demand and supply in the whole *market*.

Assumptions

The model of perfect competition is built on four assumptions:

- Firms are *price takers*. There are so many firms in the industry that each one produces an insignificantly small proportion of total industry supply, and therefore has *no power whatsoever* to affect the price of the product. It faces a horizontal demand 'curve' at the market price: the price determined by the interaction of demand and supply in the whole market.
- There is complete *freedom of entry* into the industry for new firms. Existing firms are unable to stop new firms setting up in business. Setting up a business takes time, however. Freedom of entry, therefore, applies in the long run.
- All firms produce an *identical product*. (The product is 'homogeneous'.) There is therefore no branding or advertising.
- Producers and consumers have *perfect knowledge* of the market. That is, producers are fully aware of prices, costs and market opportunities. Consumers are fully aware of price, quality and availability of the product.

These assumptions are very strict. Few, if any, industries in the real world meet these conditions. Certain agricultural markets are perhaps closest to perfect competition. The market for certain fresh vegetables, such as potatoes, is an example. A potato grower is likely to face competition from so many others that he or she cannot affect the market price of any given variety of potatoes; there is freedom for farmers to set up in business growing potatoes; for any variety and grade of potatoes, each farmer produces a virtually identical product (potatoes are not branded by grower); knowledge of the market by both producers and consumers is very good.

The short-run equilibrium of the firm

Definition

The short run under perfect competition
The period during which there is too little time for new firms to enter the industry.

The determination of price, output and profit in the short run under perfect competition can best be shown in a diagram.

Figure 4.1 shows a short-run equilibrium for both industry and a firm under perfect competition. Both parts of the diagram have the same scale for the vertical axis. The horizontal axes have totally different scales, however. For example, if the horizontal axis for the firm were measured in, say, thousands of units, the horizontal axis for the whole industry might be measured in millions or tens of millions of units, depending on the number of firms in the industry.

Let us examine the determination of price, output and profit in turn.

Key
Idea

7
p41

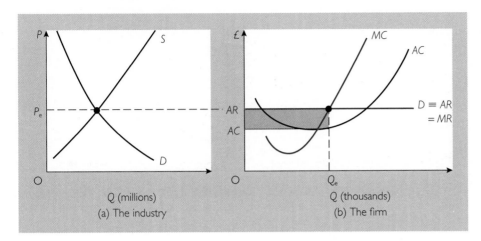

Figure 4.1
Short-run
equilibrium of
industry and firm
under perfect
competition

Price

The price is determined in the industry by the intersection of demand and supply. Being a price taker, the firm faces a horizontal demand (or average revenue) 'curve' at this price. It can sell all it can produce at the market price (P_e), but nothing at a price above P_e.

Output

The firm will maximise profit where marginal cost equals marginal revenue ($MR = MC$), at an output of Q_e. Note that, since the price is not affected by the firm's output, marginal revenue will equal price (see page 104 and Figure 3.6).

Profit

If the average cost (AC) curve (which includes normal profit) dips below the average revenue (AR) 'curve', the firm will earn supernormal profit. Supernormal profit per unit at Q_e is the vertical difference between AR and AC at Q_e. Total supernormal profit is the shaded rectangle in Figure 4.1 (i.e. profit per unit times quantity sold).

The short–run supply curve

The *firm's* short-run supply curve will be its (short-run) marginal cost curve. But why? A supply curve shows how much will be supplied at each price: it relates quantity to price. The marginal cost curve relates quantity to marginal cost. But, under perfect competition, given that $P = MR$, and $MR = MC$, P must equal MC. Thus the supply curve and the MC curve will follow the same line.

For example, in Figure 4.2(b), if price were P_1, profits would be maximised at Q_1 where $P_1 = MC$. Thus point a is one point on the supply curve. At a price of P_2, Q_2 would be produced. Thus point b is another point on the supply curve, and so on.

So, under perfect competition, the firm's supply curve depends entirely on production costs. This demonstrates why the firm's supply curve is upward sloping. Since marginal costs rise as output rises (due to diminishing marginal returns), a higher price will be necessary to induce the firm to increase its output.

Figure 4.2

Deriving the short-run supply curve

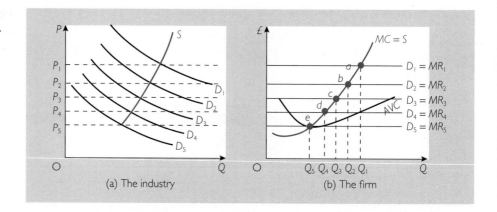

(a) The industry

(b) The firm

Note that the firm will not produce at a price below *AVC* (see page 112 above). Thus the supply curve is only that portion of the *MC* curve above point *e*.

What will be the short-run supply curve of the whole industry? This is simply the sum of the short-run supply curves (and hence *MC* curves) of all the firms in the industry. Graphically this will be a *horizontal* sum, since it is *quantities* that are being added.

> **Pause for thought**
>
> Will the industry supply be zero below a price of P_5 in Figure 4.2?

> **Definition**
>
> The long run under perfect competition
>
> The period of time which is long enough for new firms to enter the industry.

The long-run equilibrium of the firm

In the long run, if typical firms are making supernormal profits, new firms will be attracted into the industry. Likewise, if existing firms can make supernormal profits by increasing the scale of their operations, they will do so, since all factors of production are variable in the long run.

The effect of the entry of new firms and/or the expansion of existing firms is to increase industry supply. This is illustrated in Figure 4.3. At a price of P_1 supernormal profits are earned. The industry supply curve will thus shift to the right as

> **Key Idea**
> 7
> p41

> **Key Idea**
> 5
> p27

Figure 4.3

Long-run equilibrium under perfect competition

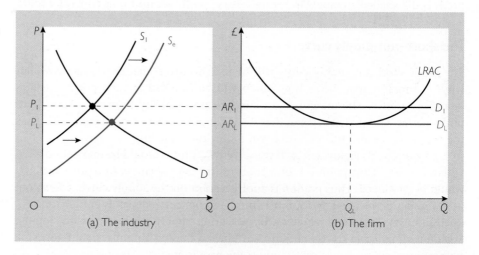

(a) The industry

(b) The firm

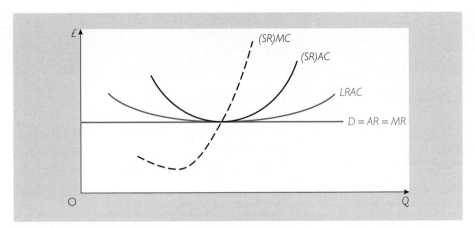

Figure 4.4
Long-run equilibrium
of the firm under
perfect competition

new firms enter. This in turn leads to a fall in price. Supply will go on increasing, and price falling, until firms are making only normal profits. This will be when price has fallen to the point where the demand 'curve' for the firm just touches the bottom of its long-run average cost curve. Q_L is thus the long-run equilibrium output of the firm, with P_L the long-run equilibrium price.

Since the *LRAC* curve is tangential to (i.e. just touching) all possible short-run *AC* curves (see Section 3.2), the full long-run equilibrium will be as shown in Figure 4.4 where:

$$LRAC = AC = MC = MR = AR$$

The incompatibility of perfect competition and substantial economies of scale

Why is perfect competition so rare in the real world – if it even exists at all? One important reason for this has to do with economies of scale.

In many industries, firms may have to be quite large if they are to experience the full potential economies of scale. But perfect competition requires there to be *many* firms. Firms must therefore be small under perfect competition: too small in most cases for economies of scale.

Once a firm expands sufficiently to achieve economies of scale, it will usually gain market power. It will be able to undercut the prices of smaller firms, which will thus be driven out of business. Perfect competition is destroyed.

Perfect competition could exist in any industry, therefore, only if there were no (or virtually no) economies of scale.

Is perfect competition good for consumers?

Generally it is argued that perfect competition is a 'good thing', and that the more perfect an industry becomes the better. We explore the arguments in Section 4.3 (page 129) after we have looked at monopoly, but at this stage the main points in favour of perfect competition can be identified.

Box 4.1

E-commerce

A modern form of perfect competition?

Anyone who fails to become an e-business will become an ex-business.

Phil Lawler, managing director of Hewlett-Packard

In five years' time, all companies will be Internet companies, or they won't be companies at all.

Andy Grove, chairman of Intel[1]

The massive growth in companies selling over the Internet has raised many questions. Will all companies become Internet companies? Is this the beginning of the end of shops as we know them? Will we all be caught up in a web, where big companies swallow up little ones, and where we, as consumers, end up with no power at all?

In practice, e-commerce could have large benefits for consumers. These include not only the obvious benefits of being able to do your shopping from your own home, but also of having a wider choice of products and at more reasonable prices. But why should prices be more reasonable? The answer is that e-commerce has the potential to make markets more competitive: in fact, in many cases, pretty close to *perfectly* competitive.

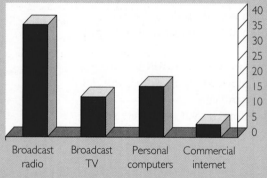

Source: US Commerce Dept.

Years to achieve 50 million users

[1] Quotes from 'The net imperative', *The Economist* (26 June 1999).

Moving markets back towards perfect competition?

To see the extent to which e-commerce is making markets more competitive, let's look at the assumptions of perfect competition.

Large number of firms. The growth of e-commerce has led to many new firms starting up in business. It's not just large firms like Amazon.com that are providing increased competition for established firms, but the thousands of small online companies that are being established every day. Many of these firms are selling directly to us as consumers. This is known as 'B2C' e-commerce (business-to-consumers). But many more are selling to other firms ('B2B'). More and more companies, from the biggest to the smallest, are transferring their purchasing to the web and are keen to get value for money.

The reach of the web is global. This means that firms, whether conventional or web-based, are having to keep an eye on the prices and products of competitors in the rest of the world, not just in the local neighbourhood. Firms' demand curves are thus becoming very price elastic. This is especially so for goods that are cheap to transport, or for services such as insurance and banking.

Perfect knowledge. If you go shopping to buy a new household item and want to get the best deal, then it can take you some time going from shop to shop comparing prices. If, however, you go online to buy the same item, you can very rapidly compare prices. Search engines can quickly locate a list of alternative suppliers. Or you can use an online shopping mall, such as ShoppingTrolley.net or Kelkoo.com. Better still, you can use a 'shopping bot', such as DealTime.com, mySimon.com or BottomDollar.com. These websites automatically inform you of the best available prices. And improved information is not confined to prices. 'Shopping agents', such as Frictionless.com give additional information on quality and service.

The competition through increased information over the Internet extends beyond e-commerce: it spills over to shops. As people increasingly compare prices in shops with prices online, so shops are having to be more and more competitive with their online counterparts.

Freedom of entry. Internet companies often have lower start-up costs than their conventional rivals. Their premises are generally much smaller, with no 'shop-front' costs and lower levels of stock holding. Marketing costs can also be relatively low, especially given the ease with which companies can be located with search engines and shopping bots. Internet companies are often smaller and more specialist, relying on Internet 'outsourcing' (buying parts, equipment and other supplies through the Internet), rather than making everything themselves. They are also more likely to use delivery firms rather than having their own transport fleet.

All this makes it relatively cheap for new firms to set up and begin trading over the Internet. Also, if the set-up costs are relatively low, there is less to lose if the company fails. This makes it more tempting for small firms to 'have a go'. It is also relatively easy for large firms to 'diversify' across into new businesses, especially if they are already trading on the Internet.

Identical products. With the use of shopping agents, customers can compare the prices of different firms for supplying identical products. This makes price competition very intense.

Not only do these factors make markets more price competitive, they also bring other benefits. Costs are driven down, as firms economise on stock holding, rely more on outsourcing and develop more efficient relationships with suppliers. The competition also encourages innovation, which improves quality and the range of products.

Is there a limit to e-commerce?

In 20 years, will we be doing all our shopping on the net? Will the only shopping malls be virtual ones?

Although e-commerce is revolutionising some markets, it is unlikely that things will go anything like that far.

For a start, going out shopping is itself an enjoyable experience. Many people like wandering round the shops, meeting friends, seeing what takes their fancy, trying on clothes, browsing through CDs and so on. 'Retail therapy' for many is an important means of 'de-stressing'. Also, with 'real shopping' you can see the goods and assess how much you like them. Then, of course, if you buy something, you can take it home with you straight away, rather than waiting for it to be delivered.

With online shopping, you have to rely on the web. Access may be slow and frustrating. 'Surfing' may instead become 'wading'. Then if you do buy something, you may not know how long you will have to wait for it to be delivered, or whether it will even arrive!

The Internet may reduce the costs of producing some items, but not all. With heavy or bulky items, or items where special deliveries have to be made, the extra distribution costs may outweigh cost savings elsewhere.

Finally there is the role of big companies. They do not like to see their powerful position in the market threatened and are likely to try to dominate Internet sales, thereby reducing the market's competitiveness. Amazon.com may have gained a foothold in the market, but large established booksellers are retaliating. Waterstones and Blackwells are now heavily promoting their Internet sales. Amazon.com may survive, but it will be difficult for new general booksellers to break into the market. As in any market, large powerful firms will try to erect barriers to the entry of new firms. The movement towards perfect competition is likely to be strongly resisted!

?
1. Why may the Internet work better for replacement buys than for new purchases?
2. Give three examples of products that are particularly suitable for selling over the Internet and three that are not. Explain your answer.

- Price equals marginal cost. Why is this desirable? To answer this, consider what would happen if they were not equal. If price were greater than marginal cost, this would mean that consumers were putting a higher value (P) on the production of extra units than they cost to produce (MC). Therefore more ought to be produced. If price were less than marginal cost, consumers would be putting a lower value on extra units than they cost to produce. Therefore less ought to be produced. When they are equal, therefore, production levels are just right. But, as we shall see later, it is only under perfect competition that $MC = P$.
- The combination of (long-run) production being at minimum average cost and the firm making only normal profit keeps prices at a minimum.
- Perfect competition is a case of 'survival of the fittest'. Inefficient firms will be driven out of business, since they will not be able to make even normal profits. This encourages firms to be as efficient as possible and, where possible, to invest in new improved technology.

In general, it can be argued that perfectly competitive markets result in economic efficiency.

> **Economic efficiency** is achieved when each good is produced at the minimum cost and where consumers get maximum benefit from their income.
>
> Key Idea 15

Recap

1. The assumptions of perfect competition are: a very large number of firms, complete freedom of entry, a homogeneous product and perfect knowledge of the good and its market by both producers and consumers.

2. In the short run, there is not time for new firms to enter the market, and thus supernormal profits can persist. In the long run, however, any supernormal profits will be competed away by the entry of new firms.

3. The short-run equilibrium for the firm will be where the price, as determined by demand and supply in the market, is equal to marginal cost. At this output the firm will be maximising profit.

4. The long-run equilibrium will be where the market price is just equal to firms' long-run average cost.

5. There can be no substantial economies of scale to be gained in a perfectly competitive industry. If there were, the industry would cease to be perfectly competitive as the large, low-cost firms drove the small, high-cost ones out of business.

Monopoly 4.3

What happens when there is only one firm in the market? Do we as consumers suffer?

What is a monopoly?

This may seem a strange question because the answer appears obvious. A monopoly exists when there is only one firm in the industry.

But whether an industry can be classed as a monopoly is not always clear. It depends how narrowly the industry is defined. For example, a textile company may have a monopoly on certain types of fabric, but it does not have a monopoly on fabrics in general. The consumer can buy fabrics other than those supplied by the company. A rail company may have a monopoly over rail services between two cities, but it does not have a monopoly over public transport between these two cities. People can travel by coach or air. They could also use private transport.

To some extent, the boundaries of an industry are arbitrary. What is more important for a firm is the amount of monopoly *power* it has, and that depends on the closeness of substitutes produced by rival industries. The Post Office has a monopoly over the delivery of letters, but it faces competition in communications from telephone, faxes and e-mail.

Barriers to entry

For a firm to maintain its monopoly position, there must be barriers to the entry of new firms. As we shall see, barriers also exist under oligopoly, but in the case of monopoly they must be high enough to block the entry of new firms. Barriers can take various forms.

Economies of scale. If the monopolist's costs go on falling significantly up to the output that satisfies the whole market, the industry may not be able to support more than one producer. This case is known as natural monopoly. It is particularly likely if the market is small. For example, two bus companies might find it unprofitable to serve the same routes, each running with perhaps only half-full buses, whereas one company with a monopoly of the routes could make a profit. Electricity transmission via a national grid is another example of a natural monopoly.

Even if a market could support more than one firm, a new entrant is unlikely to be able to start up on a very large scale. Thus the monopolist that is already experiencing economies of scale can charge a price below the cost of the new entrant and drive it out of business. If, however, the new entrant is a firm already established in another industry, it may be able to survive this competition.

Economies of scope. A firm that produces a range of products is also likely to experience a lower average cost of production. For example, a large pharmaceutical company producing a range of drugs and toiletries can use shared research, marketing, storage and transport facilities across its range of products. These lower costs make it difficult for a new single-product entrant to the market, since the large firm will be able to undercut its price and drive it out of the market.

> **Definition**
>
> **Natural monopoly** A situation where long-run average costs would be lower if an industry were under monopoly than if it were shared between two or more competitors.

Product differentiation and brand loyalty. If a firm produces a clearly differentiated product, where the consumer associates the product with the brand, it will be very difficult for a new firm to break into that market. Rank Xerox invented, and patented, the plain paper photocopier. After this legal monopoly (see below) ran out, people still associated photocopiers with Rank Xerox. It is still not unusual to hear someone say that they are going to 'Xerox the article' or, for that matter, 'Hoover their carpet'. Other examples of strong brand image include Guinness, Kellogg's Cornflakes, Coca-Cola, Nescafé and Sellotape. This barrier can occur even though the market is potentially big enough for two firms each gaining all the available economies of scale. In other words, the problem for the new firm is not in being able to produce at low enough costs, but in being able to produce a product sufficiently attractive to consumers who are loyal to the familiar brand.

Lower costs for an established firm. An established monopoly is likely to have developed specialised production and marketing skills. It is more likely to be aware of the most efficient techniques and the most reliable and/or cheapest suppliers. It is likely to have access to cheaper finance. It is thus operating on a lower cost curve. New firms would therefore find it hard to compete and would be likely to lose any price war.

Ownership of, or control over, key factors of production. If a firm governs the supply of vital inputs (say, by owning the sole supplier of some component part), it can deny access to these inputs to potential rivals. On a world scale, the de Beers company has a monopoly in fine diamonds because all diamond producers market their diamonds through de Beers.

Ownership of, or control over, wholesale or retail outlets. Similarly, if a firm controls the outlets through which the product must be sold, it can prevent potential rivals from gaining access to consumers. For example, Birds Eye Wall's used to supply freezers free to shops on the condition that they stocked only Wall's ice-cream in them.

Legal protection. The firm's monopoly position may be protected by patents on essential processes, by copyright, by various forms of licensing (allowing, say, only one firm to operate in a particular area) and by tariffs (i.e. customs duties) and other trade restrictions to keep out foreign competitors. Examples of monopolies protected by patents include most new medicines developed by pharmaceutical companies (e.g. anti-AIDS drugs), Microsoft's Windows operating systems, and agro-chemical companies, such as Monsanto, with various genetically modified plant varieties and pesticides.

Mergers and takeovers. The monopolist can put in a takeover bid for any new entrant. The sheer threat of takeovers may discourage new entrants.

Aggressive tactics. An established monopolist can probably sustain losses for longer than a new entrant. Thus it could start a price war, mount massive advertising campaigns, offer attractive after-sales service, introduce new brands to compete with new entrants, and so on.

Intimidation. The monopolist may resort to various forms of harassment, legal or illegal, to drive a new entrant out of business.

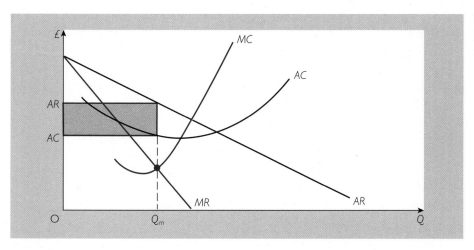

Figure 4.5
Profit maximising
under monopoly

Equilibrium price and output

Since there is, by definition, only one firm in the industry, the firm's demand curve is also the industry demand curve.

Compared with other market structures, demand under monopoly tends to be less elastic at each price. The monopolist can raise its price and consumers have no alternative firm to turn to within the industry. They either pay the higher price, or go without the good altogether.

Unlike the firm under perfect competition, the monopoly firm is thus a 'price maker'. It can choose what price to charge. Nevertheless, it is still constrained by its demand curve. A rise in price will reduce the quantity demanded.

As with firms in other market structures, a monopolist will maximise profit where $MR = MC$. In Figure 4.5 profit is maximised at Q_m. The supernormal profit obtained is shown by the shaded area.

These profits will tend to be larger the less elastic is the demand curve (and hence the steeper is the MR curve), and thus the bigger is the gap between MR and price (AR). The actual elasticity will depend on whether reasonably close substitutes are available in *other* industries. The demand for a rail service will be much less elastic (and the potential for profit greater) if there is no bus service to the same destination.

Since there are barriers to the entry of new firms, a monopolist's supernormal profits will not be competed away in the long run. The only difference, therefore, between short-run and long-run equilibrium is that in the long run the firm will produce where $MR = long$-$run \ MC$.

Monopoly versus perfect competition: which best serves the public interest?

Because it faces a different type of market environment, the monopolist will produce a quite different output and at a quite different price from a perfectly competitive industry.

Figure 4.6

Equilibrium of the industry under perfect competition and monopoly: with the same *MC* curve

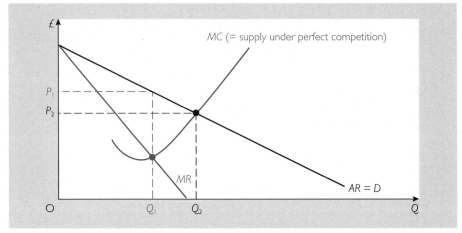

Let us compare the two.

Short-run price and output. Figure 4.6 compares the profit-maximising position for an industry under monopoly with that under perfect competition. Note that we are comparing the monopoly with the whole *industry* under perfect competition. That way we can assume, for sake of comparison, that they both face the same demand curve. We also assume for the moment that they both face the same cost curves.

The monopolist will produce Q_1 at a price of P_1. This is where $MC = MR$. If the same industry were under perfect competition, however, it would produce at Q_2 and P_2 – a higher output and a lower price. But why? The reason is that for each of the firms in the industry – and it is at this level that the decisions are made – marginal revenue is the same as price. Remember that the *firm* under perfect competition faces a perfectly elastic demand (*AR*) curve, which also equals *MR* (see Figure 4.1). Thus producing where $MC = MR$ also means producing where $MC = P$. When *all* firms under perfect competition do this, price and quantity in the *industry* will be given by P_2 and Q_2 in Figure 4.6.

In the short run, therefore, it would seem (other things being equal) that perfect competition better serves the consumer's interest than does monopoly.

Long-run price and output. Under perfect competition, freedom of entry eliminates supernormal profit and forces firms to produce at the bottom of their *LRAC* curve. The effect, therefore, is to keep long-run prices down. Under monopoly, however, barriers to entry allow profits to remain supernormal in the long run. The monopolist is not forced to operate at the bottom of the *AC* curve. Thus, other things being equal, long-run prices will tend to be higher, and hence output lower, under monopoly.

Thus, again, it would *seem* that perfect competition better serves the consumer's interests. But this assumes that the cost curves are the *same* under both perfect competition and monopoly. Let us, therefore, turn to costs.

> **Pause for thought**
>
> If the shares in a monopoly (such as a water company) were very widely distributed among the population, would the shareholders necessarily want the firm to use its monopoly power to make larger profits?

Key Idea 14 p118

Costs under monopoly.   The sheer survival of a firm in the long run under perfect competition requires that it uses the most efficient known technique, and develops new techniques wherever possible. The monopolist, however, sheltered by barriers to entry, can still make large profits even if it is not using the most efficient technique. It has less incentive, therefore, to be efficient. For this reason, costs may be *higher* under monopoly (another criticism of monopoly).

On the other hand, the monopoly may be able to achieve substantial economies of scale due to larger plant, centralised administration and the avoidance of unnecessary duplication (e.g. a monopoly water company would eliminate the need for several sets of rival water mains under each street). If this results in an *MC* curve substantially below that of the same industry under perfect competition, the monopoly may even produce a *higher* output at a *lower* price.

Another reason why a monopolist may operate with lower costs is that it can use part of its supernormal profits for research and development and investment. It may not have the same *incentive* to become efficient as the perfectly competitive firm which is fighting for survival, but it may have a much greater *ability* to become efficient than has the small firm with limited funds.

Although a monopoly faces no competition in the goods market, it may face an alternative form of competition in financial markets. A monopoly, with potentially low costs, which is currently run inefficiently, is likely to be subject to a takeover bid from another company. This competition for corporate control, as it is called, may thus force the monopoly to be efficient in order to prevent being taken over.

<table>
<tr><td>

Key Idea

4
p26

Key Idea

11
p71

</td></tr>
</table>

Innovation and new products.   The promise of supernormal profits, protected perhaps by patents, may encourage the development of new (monopoly) industries producing new products. It is this chance of making monopoly profits that encourages many people to take the risks of going into business.

> **Definition**
>
> **Competition for corporate control**
> The competition for the control of companies through takeovers.

Potential competition or potential monopoly? The theory of contestable markets

Potential competition

In recent years, economists have developed the theory of contestable markets. This theory argues that what is crucial in determining price and output is not whether an industry is *actually* a monopoly or competitive, but whether there is the real *threat* of competition.

If a monopoly is protected by high barriers to entry – say, it owns all the raw materials – then it will be able to make supernormal profits with no fear of competition.

If, however, another firm *could* take over from it with little difficulty, it will behave much more like a competitive firm. The threat of competition has a similar effect to actual competition.

As an example, consider a catering company that is given permission by a factory to run its canteen. The catering company has a monopoly over the supply of food to the workers in that factory. If, however, it starts charging high prices or providing a poor service, the factory could offer the running of the canteen to an

Box 4.2 Case Studies and Applications

Competition in the pipeline?

Monopoly in the supply of gas

Some of the best examples of monopoly in the UK are the privatised utilities such as telecommunications, water and gas. The government, recognising the dangers of high prices and high profits under monopoly, has attempted to introduce competition in various parts of these industries. But in other parts there is no competition: they remain monopolies.

This mixture of competition and monopoly is well illustrated in the UK market for gas. There are three parts to this market: production; storage and transportation; and supply to customers. In production there is considerable competition, with several companies operating in the North Sea. In storage and transportation, however, there is a monopoly. TransCo owns the expensive gas pipelines and storage facilities. TransCo was formed in 1997 when British Gas (BG) was split into two parts. Following a merger with National Grid (owner of the electricity transmission network) TransCo is now part of National Grid TransCo, the UK's largest utility. The other part of the former British Gas is British Gas Trading (BGT). BGT is involved in supply to the customer. It is part of Centrica, which also includes One.Tel, the AA and Goldfish. In supply, the market has been gradually opened up to competition.

First, in 1990, large industrial consumers of gas were allowed to choose their suppliers. This choice was extended to small industrial consumers in 1992. By 1993, BG's share of the industrial gas market had fallen to 41 per cent (from virtually 100 per cent in 1990). Gas competition has encouraged over 60 gas suppliers to join the market, and between 1995 and 2000 average prices to industrial and commercial users fell by 53 per cent (after taking inflation into account).

The market for domestic consumers in Great Britain was opened up to competition between 1996 and 1998. By 2003, there were 29 suppliers in this market and 37 per cent of households had switched to other suppliers. BGT's share of this market had fallen to 63 per cent. Competition had reduced gas prices to consumers by over 20 per cent (after taking inflation and increased wholesale gas prices into account).

But how do gas suppliers compete, given that TransCo has a monopoly of the pipelines? The answer is that TransCo is required to allow companies to use its pipelines. It charges them a rent for this service. Producers' supply is metered in; the gas used by companies supplying consumers is metered out. This enables the producing companies to charge the customer-supplying companies, and enables TransCo to work out the amount of rent to charge. This accounts for 30 to 40 per cent of the average household bill, depending on the wholesale price of gas from the North Sea.

One reason for splitting BG was the worry that it would charge very high rents to its competitors, thereby giving itself an unfair advantage. In other words, it would use its monopoly in one part of the industry to prevent fair competition in another part.

One solution to this monopoly problem would be for the government to regulate the size of the rent and to insist that BG charged itself the same rent as its competitors. This was the policy in the early 1990s. Ofgas, the regulatory agency set up by the government at the time of privatisation in 1986, attempted to get BG to charge all customers, including itself, the same rent. After the split, TransCo remains regulated (by Ofgem, the successor to Ofgas). This is to prevent it using its monopoly power to charge excessive rents or to discriminate unfairly between users of its pipelines.

What about regulation on the supply side? BGT was initially regulated, but as competition was introduced, so regulation was removed. By 2002, all regulation in supply had disappeared.

With TransCo's rental charges firmly and fairly regulated, many of the new entrants into the gas supply industry have offered prices to customers some 10 to 20 per cent below that of BGT. Not surprisingly, BGT has responded by reducing its own prices.

?

1. What possible *advantages* to the consumer could there be in (a) TransCo having a monopoly over gas pipelines; (b) BGT remaining a monopoly in the supply of gas to domestic households?
2. What are the arguments for and against Ofgem regulating the price of gas supplied to domestic households?

For more information on pricing and regulation in the gas industry, see the following websites:
www.ofgem.gov.uk
www.transco.uk.com
www.centrica.co.uk

Key Idea 8 p45

alternative catering company. This threat may force the original catering company to charge 'reasonable' prices and offer a good service.

Perfectly contestable markets

A market is perfectly contestable when the costs of entry and exit by potential rivals are zero, and when such entry can be made very rapidly. In such cases, the moment the possibility of earning supernormal profits occurs, new firms will enter, thus driving profits down to a normal level. The sheer threat of this happening, so the theory goes, will ensure that the firm already in the market will (a) keep its prices down, so that it just makes normal profits, and (b) produce as efficiently as possible, taking advantage of any economies of scale and any new technology. If the existing firm did not do this, entry would take place, and potential competition would become actual competition.

Contestable markets and natural monopolies

So why in such cases are the markets not *actually* perfectly competitive? Why do they remain monopolies?

The most likely reason has to do with economies of scale and the size of the market. To operate on a minimum efficient scale, the firm may have to be so large relative to the market that there is only room for one such firm in the industry. If a new firm does come into the market, then one or other of the two firms will not survive the competition. The market is simply not big enough for both of them.

If, however, there are no entry or exit costs, new firms will be perfectly willing to enter even though there is only room for one firm, provided they believe that they are more efficient than the existing firm. The existing firm, knowing this, will be forced to produce as efficiently as possible and with only normal profit.

The importance of costless exit

Setting up in a new business usually involves large expenditures on plant and machinery. Once this money has been committed, it becomes fixed costs. If these fixed costs are no higher than those of the existing firm, then the new firm could win the battle. But, of course, there is always the risk that it might lose.

But does losing the battle really matter? Can the firm not simply move to another market?

It does matter if there are substantial costs of exit. This will be the case if the capital equipment cannot be transferred to other uses – for example, a new blast furnace constructed by a new rival steel company. In this case, these fixed costs are known as sunk costs. The losing firm is left with capital equipment it cannot use. The firm may therefore be put off entering in the first place. The market is not perfectly contestable, and the established firm can make supernormal profit.

If, however, the capital equipment can be transferred, the exit costs will be zero (or at least very low), and new firms will be more willing to take the risks of entry. For example, a rival coach company may open up a service on a route previously operated by only one company, and where there is still only room for one operator. If the new firm loses the resulting battle, it can still use the coaches it has

Box 4.3

Windows cleaning

Microsoft, the Internet and the US Justice Department

On 18 May 1998, the US government initiated its biggest competition case for 20 years: it sued Microsoft, the world's largest software company. It accused Microsoft of abusing its market power and seeking to crush its rivals.

The case against Microsoft had been building for many years, but it was with the release of *Windows 98* that the US government decided to act. Windows, owned by Microsoft, is the operating system installed on more than 90 per cent of the world's personal computers. With *Windows 98*, Microsoft integrated its own Internet browser, *Internet Explorer*, into the Windows system. But it is in this area of Internet browsers that Microsoft faces stiff competition from Netscape Communications, which at the time controlled over 60 per cent of the market. US anti-trust officials argued that the integration of Microsoft's Internet browser with its operating system would stifle competition in Internet software. In other words, by controlling the operating software, Microsoft could force its Internet browser on to consumers and computer manufacturers.

The US Justice Department alleged that Microsoft had committed the following anti-competitive actions:

■ Back in May 1995, Microsoft attempted to collude with Netscape Communications to divide the Internet browser market. Netscape Communications refused.

■ Microsoft had forced personal computer manufacturers to install *Internet Explorer* in order to obtain a *Windows 95* operating licence.

■ Microsoft insisted that PC manufacturers conformed to a Microsoft front screen for Windows. This included specified icons, one of which was Microsoft's *Internet Explorer*.

■ It had set up reciprocal advertising arrangements with America's largest Internet service providers, such as America Online. Here Microsoft would promote America Online via Windows. In return, America Online would not promote Netscape's browsers.

In the face of these alleged abuses of its monopoly position, the US Justice Department argued that Microsoft should be required to do the following:

■ Remove the integrated browser from its *Windows 98* package, or include access to rival products.

■ End its practice of forcing PC manufacturers to install its Internet browser in order to gain a Windows licence.

■ Allow PC manufacturers to determine the opening screen when using the Windows system.

■ End agreements with Internet service providers that solely promoted Microsoft products.

Microsoft, in its defence, argued that the integration of its own browser into the Windows system was a natural part of the process of product innovation and development. Microsoft officials claimed that accusations of unfair trading practices were not founded: it was simply attempting to improve the quality of its product. If Microsoft was to do nothing with its Windows product, it would, over time, lose its dominant market position, and be replaced by a more innovative and superior product manufactured by a rival software producer. Bill Gates, the founder of Microsoft, reiterated this point. He argued:

> This suit is all about Microsoft's right to innovate on behalf of consumers, the right to integrate new technologies into the operating system as they develop.[1]

In this respect, Microsoft could be seen to be operating in the consumer's interest. The argument is that, in an environment where technology is changing rapidly, Microsoft's control over standards gives the user a measure of stability, knowing that any new products and applications will be compatible with existing ones. In other words, new software can be incorporated into existing systems.

[1] *Financial Times*, 21 May 1998.

Network effects

The key issue in respect of Microsoft then, was not so much the browser war, but far more fundamentally to do with the operating system, and how Microsoft used its ownership of this system to extend its leverage into other related high-technology markets.

> An operating system attracts software developed around that operating system, thereby discouraging new competition since any alternative faces not only the challenge of creating a better operating system but competing against a whole array of already existing software applications. Businesses train employees in one technology and are reluctant to abandon that investment in training, while the existence of a pool of people trained in that technology encourages other businesses to adopt that technology. And as desktop software has to be able to work with client–server networks and an array of other technologies, it becomes nearly impossible to abandon an established set of technology standards that tie those different parts together. These so-called 'network effects' give an incredible anti-competitive edge to companies like Microsoft that control so many different parts of the network.[2]

Network effects arise when consumers of a product benefit from it being used by *other* consumers. The more people who use it, the greater the benefit to each individual user. The problem for the consumer in such a scenario is that these network effects can lead to the establishment of a monopoly producer and hence to higher prices. There is also the problem of whether the best product is being produced by the monopolist. In such an instance, the consumer may be 'locked in' to using an inferior product or technology with limited opportunity (if any) to change.

Microsoft had been able to use consumer lock-in to drive competitors from the market. Where choice

did exist, for example in Internet browsers, Microsoft was using its operating system dominance to rectify its inferior market position.

Court findings

A verdict was reached on 7 June 2000, when Federal Judge Thomas Penfield Jackson ruled that Microsoft be split in two to prevent it operating as a monopoly. One company would produce and market the Windows operating system; the other would produce and market the applications software, such as *Microsoft Office* and the Web browser, *Internet Explorer*.

Microsoft appealed against the judgment to the US Federal Appeals Court, and in June 2001 the Court overturned the ruling and referred the case to a different judge for reconsideration. Judge Colleen Kollar-Kotelly urged both sides (Microsoft and the US Justice Department) to try to reach a settlement, and in November 2001 they did just that. They agreed that Microsoft would provide technical information about Windows to other companies to enable them to write software that would compete with Microsoft's own software. Also Microsoft would not be allowed to retaliate against computer manufacturers that installed rival products or removed icons for Microsoft applications.

Nine states, however, refused to sign up to the agreement and a further year went past before Judge Kollar-Kotelly gave her final ruling. Whilst she agreed with many of Judge Jackson's original findings, she did not require that Microsoft be split into two companies. Instead, she upheld the November 2001 agreement.

1. In what respects might Microsoft's behaviour be deemed to have been: (a) against the public interest; (b) in the public interest?
2. Being locked in to a product or technology is only a problem if such a product can be clearly shown to be inferior to an alternative. What difficulties might there be in establishing such a case?

Key Idea
14
p118

---

[2] N. Newman, *From Microsoft Word to Microsoft World: How Microsoft is building a global monopoly* (1997) www.netaction.org/msoft/world

purchased. It simply uses them for a different route. The cost of the coaches is not a sunk cost.

Costless exit, therefore, encourages firms to enter an industry, knowing that, if unsuccessful, they can always transfer their capital elsewhere.

The lower the exit costs, the more contestable the market. This implies that firms already established in other similar markets may provide more effective competition against monopolists, since they can simply transfer capital from one market to another. For example, studies of airlines in the USA show that entry to a particular route may be much easier for an established airline, which can simply transfer planes from one route to another.

Contestability and the consumer's interests

The more contestable the market, the more will a monopoly be forced to act like a firm under perfect competition. If, therefore, a monopoly operates in a perfectly contestable market, it might bring the 'best of both worlds' for the consumer. Not only will it be able to achieve low costs through economies of scale, but also the potential competition will keep profits and hence prices down.

> **Pause for thought**
>
> *Think of two examples of highly contestable monopolies (or oligopolies). How well is the consumer's interest served?*

Recap

1. A monopoly is where there is only one firm in an industry. In practice it is difficult to determine where a monopoly exists because it depends on how narrowly an industry is defined.

2. Barriers to the entry of new firms will normally be necessary to protect a monopoly from competition. Such barriers include economies of scale (making the firm a natural monopoly or at least giving it a cost advantage over new (small) competitors), control over supplies of inputs or over outlets, patents or copyright, and tactics to eliminate competition (such as takeovers or aggressive advertising).

3. Profits for the monopolist will be maximised (as for other firms) where $MC = MR$.

4. If demand and cost curves are the same in a monopoly and a perfectly competitive industry, the monopoly will produce a lower output and at a higher price than the perfectly competitive industry.

5. On the other hand, any economies of scale will, in part, be passed on to consumers in lower prices, and the monopolist's high profits may be used for research and development and investment, which in turn may lead to better products at possibly lower prices.

6. Potential competition may be as important as actual competition in determining a firm's price and output strategy.

7. The threat of this competition is greater the lower are the entry and exit costs to and from the industry. If the entry and exit costs are zero, the market is said to be perfectly contestable. Under such circumstances an existing monopolist will be forced to keep its profits down to the normal level if it is to resist entry of new firms. Exit costs will be lower, the lower are the sunk costs of the firm.

Monopolistic competition   4.4

What happens if there are quite a lot of firms competing, but each firm tries to attract us to its particular product or service?

Very few markets in practice can be classified as perfectly competitive or as a pure monopoly. The vast majority of firms do compete with other firms, often quite aggressively, and yet they are not price takers: they do have some degree of market power. Most markets, therefore, lie between the two extremes of monopoly and perfect competition, in the realm of 'imperfect competition'. As we saw in Section 4.1, there are two types of imperfect competition: namely, monopolistic competition and oligopoly.

Monopolistic competition is nearer to the competitive end of the spectrum. It can best be understood as a situation where there are a lot of firms competing but where each firm does nevertheless have some degree of market power (hence the term 'monopolistic' competition): each firm has some discretion as to what price to charge for its products.

Assumptions

■ There are *quite a large number of firms*. As a result each firm has only a small share of the market, and therefore its actions are unlikely to affect its rivals to any great extent. What this means is that each firm in making its decisions does not have to worry how its rivals will react. It assumes that what its rivals choose to do will *not* be influenced by what it does.

This is known as the assumption of independence. (As we shall see later, this is not the case under oligopoly. There we assume that firms believe that their decisions *do* affect their rivals, and that their rivals' decisions will affect them. Under oligopoly we assume that firms are *inter*dependent.)

■ There is *freedom of entry* of new firms into the industry. If any firm wants to set up in business in this market, it is free to do so.

In these two respects, therefore, monopolistic competition is like perfect competition.

■ Unlike perfect competition, however, each firm produces a product or provides a service in some way different from its rivals. As a result it can raise its price without losing all its customers. Thus its demand curve is downward sloping, albeit relatively elastic given the large number of competitors to which customers can turn. This is known as the assumption of product differentiation.

Petrol stations, restaurants, hairdressers and builders are all examples of monopolistic competition.

A typical feature of monopolistic competition is that, although there are many firms in the industry, there is only one firm in a particular location. This applies particularly in retailing. There may be many newsagents in a town, but only one in a particular street. In a sense, therefore, it has a local monopoly. People may be prepared to pay higher prices there to avoid having to go elsewhere.

Key idea
9
p64

Definitions

Independence (of firms in a market) Where the decisions of one firm in a market will not have any significant effect on the demand curves of its rivals.

Product differentiation Where one firm's product is sufficiently different from its rivals' to allow it to raise the price of the product without customers all switching to the rivals' products. A situation where a firm faces a downward-sloping demand curve.

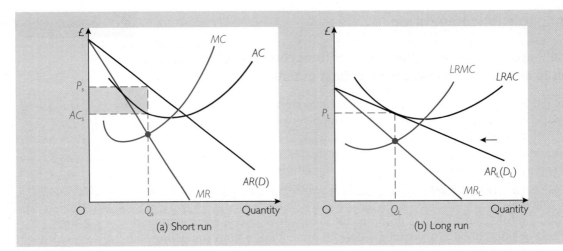

Figure 4.7
Equilibrium of
the firm under
monopolistic
competition

Equilibrium of the firm

Short run

As with other market structures, profits are maximised at the output where $MC =$ MR. The diagram is the same as for the monopolist, except that the AR and MR curves are more elastic. This is illustrated in Figure 4.7(a). As with perfect competition, it is possible for the monopolistically competitive firm to make supernormal profit in the short run. This is shown as the shaded area.

Just how much profit the firm will make in the short run depends on the strength of demand: the position and elasticity of the demand curve. The further to the right the demand curve is relative to the average cost curve, and the less elastic the demand curve is, the greater will be the firm's short-run profit. Thus a firm whose product is considerably differentiated from its rivals may be able to earn considerable short-run profits.

> **Pause for thought**
>
> *Which of these two items is a petrol station more likely to sell at a discount: (a) oil; (b) sweets? Why?*

Long run

If typical firms are earning supernormal profit, new firms will enter the industry in the long run. As new firms enter, they will take some of the customers away from the established firms. The demand for the established firms' product will therefore fall. Their demand (AR) curve will shift to the left, and will continue doing so as long as supernormal profits remain and thus new firms continue entering.

Long-run equilibrium will be reached when only normal profits remain: when there is no further incentive for new firms to enter. This is illustrated in Figure 4.7(b). The firm's demand curve settles at D_L, where it just touches the firm's $LRAC$ curve. Output will be Q_L: where $AR_L = LRAC$. (At any other output, $LRAC$ is greater than AR and thus less than normal profit would be made.)

Key Idea 7 p41

Key Idea 3 p10

Key Idea 9 p64

Key Idea 5 p25

Non-price competition

One of the biggest problems with the simple model in Figure 4.7 is that it concentrates on price and output decisions. In practice, the profit-maximising firm under monopolistic competition will also need to decide the exact variety of product to produce and how much to spend on advertising it. This will lead the firm to take part in non-price competition.

Non-price competition involves two major elements: product development and advertising.

The major aims of *product development* are to produce a product that will sell well (i.e. one in high or potentially high demand) and one that is different from rivals' products (i.e. has an inelastic demand due to lack of close substitutes). For shops or other firms providing a service, 'product development' takes the form of attempting to provide a service which is better than, or at least different from, that of rivals: personal service, late opening, certain lines stocked, and so on.

The major aim of *advertising* is to sell the product. This can be achieved not only by informing people of the product's existence and availability, but also by trying to persuade them to purchase it. Like product development, successful advertising will both increase demand and also make the firm's demand curve less elastic, since it stresses the specific qualities of this firm's product over its rivals' (see Box 2.3).

Product development and advertising not only increase a firm's demand and hence revenue, they also involve increased costs. So how much should a firm advertise, say to maximise profits?

For any given price and product, the optimal amount of advertising is where the revenue from *additional* advertising (MR_A) is equal to its cost (MC_A). As long as $MR_A > MC_A$, additional advertising will add to profit. But extra amounts spent on advertising are likely to lead to smaller and smaller increases in sales. Thus MR_A falls, until $MR_A = MC_A$. At that point no further profit can be made. It is at a maximum.

Two problems arise with this analysis:

- The effect of product development and advertising on demand will be difficult for a firm to forecast.
- Product development and advertising are likely to have different effects at different prices. Profit maximisation, therefore, will involve the more complex choice of the optimum combination of price, type of product, and level and variety of advertising.

> **Key Idea 9** p64

> **Definition**
>
> **Non-price competition** Competition in terms of product promotion (advertising, packaging, etc.) or product development.

> **Pause for thought** ||||
>
> Why will additional advertising lead to smaller and smaller increases in sales?

Monopolistic competition and the public interest

Comparison with perfect competition

> **Key Idea 15** p126

It is often argued that monopolistic competition leads to a less efficient allocation of resources than perfect competition.

Figure 4.8 compares the long-run equilibrium positions for two firms. One firm is under perfect competition and thus faces a horizontal demand curve. It will produce an output of Q_1 at a price of P_1. The other is under monopolistic competition

Figure 4.8
Long-run equilibrium of the firm under perfect and monopolistic competition

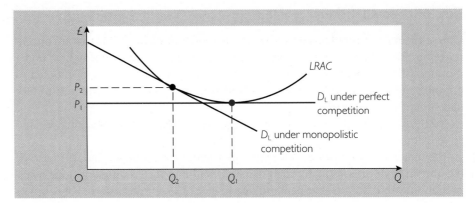

and thus faces a downward-sloping demand curve. It will produce the lower output of Q_2 at the higher price of P_2. A crucial assumption here is that a firm would have the *same* long-run average cost (*LRAC*) curve in both cases. Given this assumption, monopolistic competition has the following disadvantages:

■ Less will be sold and at a higher price.
■ Firms will not be producing at the least-cost point.

By producing more, firms would move to a lower point on their *LRAC* curve. Thus firms under monopolistic competition are said to have excess capacity. In Figure 4.8 this excess capacity is shown as $Q_1 - Q_2$. In other words, monopolistic competition is typified by quite a large number of firms (e.g. petrol stations), all operating at less than optimum output, and thus being forced to charge a price above that which they could charge if they had a bigger turnover. How often have you been to a petrol station and had to queue for the pumps?

So how does this affect the consumer? Although the firm under monopolistic competition may charge a higher price than under perfect competition, the difference may be very small. Although the firm's demand curve is downward sloping, it is still likely to be highly elastic due to the large number of substitutes. Furthermore, the consumer may benefit from monopolistic competition by having a greater variety of products to choose from. Each firm may satisfy some particular requirement of particular consumers.

Comparison with monopoly

The arguments are very similar here to those when comparing perfect competition and monopoly.

On the one hand, freedom of entry for new firms and hence the lack of long-run supernormal profits under monopolistic competition are likely to help keep prices down for the consumer and encourage cost saving. On the other hand, monopolies are likely to achieve greater economies of scale and have more funds for investment and research and development.

Recap

1. Monopolistic competition occurs where there is free entry to the industry and quite a large number of firms operating independently of each other, but where each firm has some market power as a result of producing differentiated products or services.

2. In the short run, firms can make supernormal profits. In the long run, however, freedom of entry will drive profits down to the normal level. The long-run equilibrium of the firm is where the (downward-sloping) demand curve just touches the long-run average cost curve.

3. The long-run equilibrium is one of excess capacity. Given that the demand curve is downward sloping, the point where it just touches the *LRAC* curve will not be at the bottom of the *LRAC* curve. Increased production would thus be possible at *lower* average cost.

4. Firms under monopolistic competition may engage in non-price competition, in the forms of product development and advertising, in order to maintain an advantage over their rivals.

5. Monopolistically competitive firms, because of excess capacity, may have higher costs, and thus higher prices, than perfectly competitive firms, but consumers may gain from a greater diversity of products.

6. Monopolistically competitive firms may have fewer economies of scale than monopolies and conduct less research and development, but the competition may keep prices lower than under monopoly. Whether there will be more or less choice for the consumer is debatable.

Oligopoly   4.5

What happens if there are just a few firms that dominate the market? Will there be fierce competition between them, or will there be a 'cosy' relationship where we as consumers end up paying higher prices?

Oligopoly occurs when just a few firms between them share a large proportion of the industry.

There are, however, significant differences in the structure of industries under oligopoly and similarly significant differences in the behaviour of firms. The firms may produce a virtually identical product (e.g. metals, chemicals, sugar, petrol). Most oligopolists, however, produce differentiated products (e.g. cars, soap powder, soft drinks, electrical appliances). Much of the competition between such oligopolists is in terms of the marketing of their particular brand. Marketing practices may differ considerably from one industry to another.

The two key features of oligopoly

Despite the differences between oligopolies, there are two crucial features that distinguish oligopoly from other market structures.

Barriers to entry

Unlike firms under monopolistic competition, there are various barriers to the entry of new firms. These are similar to those under monopoly (see pages 127–8). The size of the barriers, however, will vary from industry to industry. In some cases entry is relatively easy, whereas in others it is virtually impossible.

Interdependence of the firms

Because there are only a few firms under oligopoly, each firm has to take account of the others. This means that they are mutually dependent: they are interdependent. Each firm is affected by its rivals' actions. If a firm changes the price or specification of its product, for example, or the amount of its advertising, the sales of its rivals will be affected. The rivals may then respond by changing their price, specification or advertising. No firm can therefore afford to ignore the actions and reactions of other firms in the industry.

> **People often think and behave strategically.** How you think others will respond to your actions is likely to influence your own behaviour. Firms, for example, when considering a price or product change will often take into account the likely reactions of their rivals.

It is impossible, therefore, to predict the effect on a firm's sales of, say, a change in the price of its product without first making some assumption about the reactions of other firms. Different assumptions will yield different predictions. For this reason there is no single generally accepted theory of oligopoly. Firms may react differently and unpredictably.

Competition and collusion

Oligopolists are pulled in two different directions:

■ The interdependence of firms may make them wish to *collude* with each other. If they can club together and act as if they were a monopoly, they could jointly maximise industry profits.
■ On the other hand, they will be tempted to *compete* with their rivals to gain a bigger share of industry profits for themselves.

These two policies are incompatible. The more fiercely firms compete to gain a bigger share of industry profits, the smaller these industry profits will become! For example, price competition drives down the average industry price, while competition through advertising raises industry costs. Either way, industry profits fall.

Sometimes firms will collude. Sometimes they will not. The following sections examine first collusive oligopoly (both open and tacit), and then non-collusive oligopoly.

Equilibrium of industry under collusive oligopoly

When firms under oligopoly engage in collusion, they may agree on prices, market share, advertising expenditure, etc. Such collusion reduces the uncertainty they

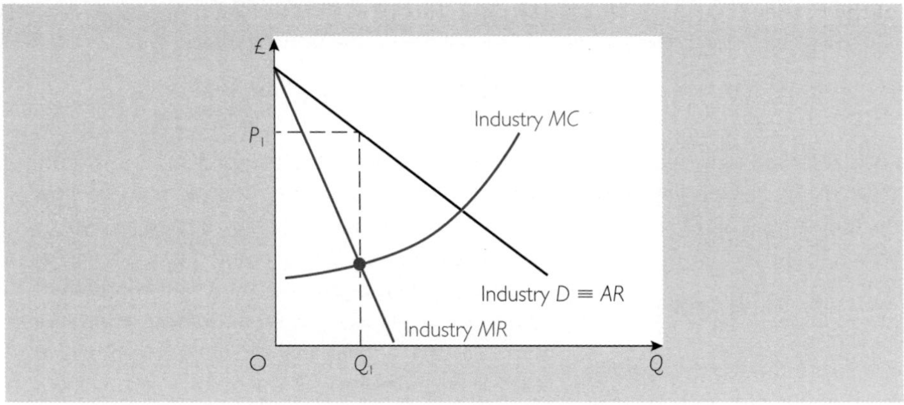

Figure 4.9
Profit-maximising
cartel

Definitions

Cartel
A formal collusive agreement.

Quota (set by a cartel)
The output that a given member of a cartel is allowed to produce (production quota) or sell (sales quota).

Tacit collusion
Where oligopolists take care not to engage in price cutting, excessive advertising or other forms of competition. There may be unwritten 'rules' of collusive behaviour, such as price leadership.

face. It reduces the fear of engaging in competitive price cutting or retaliatory advertising, both of which could reduce total industry profits.

A formal collusive agreement is called a cartel. The cartel will maximise profits if it acts like a monopoly: if the members behave as if they were a single firm. This is illustrated in Figure 4.9.

The total market demand curve is shown with the corresponding market MR curve. The cartel's MC curve is the *horizontal* sum of the MC curves of its members (since we are adding the *output* of each of the cartel members at each level of marginal cost). Profits are maximised at Q_1 where $MC = MR$. The cartel must therefore set a price of P_1 (at which Q_1 will be demanded).

Having agreed on the cartel price, the members may then compete against each other using *non-price competition*, to gain as big a share of resulting sales (Q_1) as they can.

Alternatively, the cartel members may somehow agree to divide the market between them. Each member would be given a quota. The sum of all the quotas must add up to Q_1. If the quotas exceeded Q_1, either there would be output unsold if price remained fixed at P_1, or the price would fall.

But if quotas are to be set by the cartel, how will it decide the level of each individual member's quota? The most likely method is for the cartel to divide the market between the members according to their current market share. That is the solution most likely to be accepted as 'fair'.

In many countries, including the UK, cartels are illegal. They are seen by the government as a means of driving up prices and profits, and thereby as being against the public interest. Where open collusion is illegal, firms may simply break the law, or get round it. Alternatively, firms may stay within the law, but still *tacitly* collude by watching each other's prices and keeping theirs similar. Firms may tacitly 'agree' to avoid price wars or aggressive advertising campaigns.

> **Pause for thought**
>
> If this 'fair' solution were adopted, what effect would it have on the industry MC curve in Figure 4.9?

Tacit collusion

One form of tacit collusion is where firms keep to the price that is set by an established leader. The leader may be the largest firm: the firm that dominates the

Box 4.4

OPEC – the rise and fall and rise again of a cartel

The history of the world's most famous cartel

OPEC is probably the best known of all cartels. It was set up in 1960 by the five major oil-exporting countries: Saudi Arabia, Iran, Iraq, Kuwait and Venezuela. Its stated objectives were as follows:

- The co-ordination and unification of the petroleum policies of member countries.
- The organisation of means to ensure the stabilisation of prices, eliminating harmful and unnecessary fluctuations.

The years leading up to 1960 had seen the oil-producing countries increasingly in conflict with the international oil companies, which extracted oil under 'concessionary agreement'. Under this scheme, oil companies were given the right to extract oil in return for royalties. This meant that the oil-producing countries had little say over output and price levels.

Despite the formation of OPEC in 1960, it was not until 1973 that control of oil production was effect-ively transferred from the oil companies to the oil countries, with OPEC making the decisions on how much oil to produce and thereby determining its oil revenue. By this time OPEC consisted of 13 members.

OPEC's pricing policy over the 1970s consisted of setting a market price for Saudi Arabian crude (the market leader), and leaving other OPEC members to set their prices in line with this: a form of 'dominant firm' price leadership.

As long as demand remained buoyant, and was price inelastic, this policy allowed large price increases with consequent large revenue increases. In 1973/4, after the Arab–Israeli war, OPEC raised the price of oil from around \$3 per barrel to over \$12. The price was kept at roughly this level until 1979. And yet the sales of oil did not fall significantly.

After 1979, however, following a further increase in the price of oil from around \$15 to \$40 per barrel, demand did fall. This was largely due to the recession

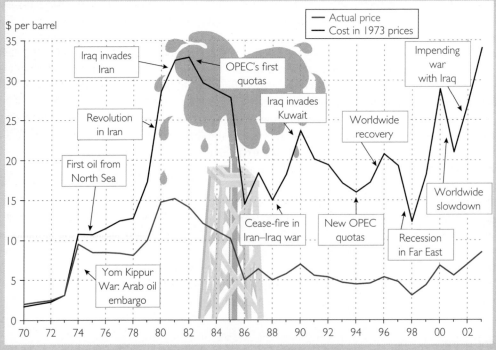

Oil prices and the effects of OPEC quotas, wars and the ups and downs of the world economy

Source: *OPEC Annual Statistical Bulletin 2003.*

of the early 1980s (although this recession was in turn largely caused by governments' responses to the oil price increases).

Faced by declining demand, OPEC after 1982 agreed to limit output and allocate production quotas in an attempt to keep the price up. A production ceiling of 16 million barrels per day was agreed in 1984.

The cartel was beginning to break down, however, due to the following:

■ The world recession and the resulting fall in the demand for oil.
■ Growing output from non-OPEC members.
■ 'Cheating' by some OPEC members which exceeded their quota limits.

With a glut of oil, OPEC could no longer maintain the price. The 'spot' price of oil (the day-to-day price at which oil was trading on the open market) was falling, as the graph shows.

The trend of lower oil prices was reversed in the late 1980s. With the world economy booming, the demand for oil rose and along with it the price. Then in 1990 Iraq invaded Kuwait and the Gulf War ensued. With the cutting off of supplies from Kuwait and Iraq, the supply of oil fell and there was a sharp rise in its price.

But with the ending of the war and the recession of the early 1990s, the price rapidly fell again and only slowly recovered as the world economy started expanding once more. On the demand side, the development of energy-saving technology plus increases in fuel taxes led to a relatively slow growth in consumption. On the supply side, the growing proportion of output supplied by non-OPEC members, plus the adoption in 1994 of a relatively high OPEC production ceiling of $24\frac{1}{2}$ million barrels per day, meant that supply kept pace with demand.

The situation for OPEC deteriorated further in the late 1990s, following a recession in the Far East. Oil demand fell by some 2 million barrels per day. By early 1999, the price had fallen to around $10 per barrel – a mere $2.70 in 1973 prices! In response, OPEC members agreed to cut production by 4.3 million barrels per day. The objective was to push the

price back up to around $18–$20 per barrel. But, with the Asian economy recovering and the world generally experiencing more rapid economic growth, the price rose rapidly and soon overshot the $20 mark. By mid-2000 it had reached $30: a tripling in price in just 12 months. With the world economy then slowing down, however, the price rapidly fell back, reaching $18 in November 2001.

In late 2001 the relationship between OPEC and non-OPEC oil producers changed. The ten members of the OPEC cartel decided to cut production by 1.5 million barrels a day. This followed an agreement with five of the major oil producers *outside* of the cartel to reduce their output too, the aim being to push oil prices upwards and then stabilise them at around $25. The alliance between OPEC and non-OPEC oil producers was the first such instance of its kind in the oil industry. As a result, it seemed that OPEC might now once again be able to control the market for oil.

But how successfully could this arrangement cope with crisis? With worries over an impending war with Iraq and a strike in Venezuela, the price rose again in late 2002, passing the $30 mark in early 2003. OPEC claimed that it could maintain supply and prevent prices from surging even with an Iraq war, but with prices rising rapidly above $30, many doubted that it could.

This illustrates the difficulty of using supply quotas to achieve a particular price. With demand being price inelastic but income elastic (responsive to changes in world income), and with considerable speculative movements in demand, the equilibrium price for a given supply quota can fluctuate wildly.

?

1. What conditions facilitate the formation of a cartel? Which of these conditions were to be found in the oil market in (a) the early 1970s; (b) the mid-1980s; (c) 2000?
2. Could OPEC have done anything to prevent the long-term decline in real oil prices since 1981?
3. Many oil analysts are predicting a rapid decline in world oil output in 10 to 20 years as world reserves are depleted. What effect is this likely to have on OPEC's behaviour?

Figure 4.10

A price leader aiming to maximise profits for a given market share

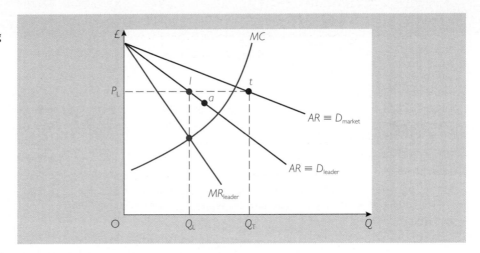

Dominant firm price leadership
Where firms (the followers) choose the same price as that set by a dominant firm in the industry (the leader).

Barometric firm price leadership
Where the price leader is the one whose prices are believed to reflect market conditions in the most satisfactory way.

industry. This is known as dominant firm price leadership. Alternatively, the price leader may simply be the one that has proved to be the most reliable to follow: the one that is the best barometer of market conditions. This is known as barometric firm price leadership.

Dominant firm price leadership. How does the leader set the price? This depends on the assumptions it makes about its rivals' reactions to its price changes. If it assumes that rivals will simply follow it by making exactly the same percentage price changes up or down, then a simple model can be constructed. This is illustrated in Figure 4.10. The leader assumes that it will maintain a constant market share (say, 50 per cent).

The leader will maximise profits where its marginal revenue is equal to its marginal cost. It knows its current position on its demand curve (say, point *a*). It then estimates how responsive its demand will be to industry-wide price changes and thus constructs its demand and MR curves on that basis. It then chooses to produce Q_L at a price of P_L: at point *l* on its demand curve (where $MC = MR$). Other firms then follow that price. Total market demand will be Q_T, with followers supplying that portion of the market not supplied by the leader: namely, $Q_T - Q_L$.

There is one problem with this model. That is the assumption that the followers will want to maintain a constant market share. It is possible that if the leader raises its price, the followers may want to supply more at this new price. On the other hand, the followers may decide merely to maintain their market share for fear of invoking retaliation from the leader, in the form of price cuts or an aggressive advertising campaign.

Barometric firm price leadership. A similar exercise can be conducted by a barometric firm. Although the firm is not dominating the industry, its price will be followed by the others. It merely tries to estimate its demand and MR curves – assuming, again, a constant market share – and then produces where $MR = MC$ and sets price accordingly.

In practice, which firm is taken as the barometer may frequently change. Whether we are talking about oil companies, car producers or banks, any firm may take the initiative in raising prices. If the other firms are merely waiting for someone to take the lead – say, because costs have risen – they will all quickly follow suit. For example, if one of the bigger building societies or banks raises its mortgage rates by 1 per cent, this is likely to stimulate the others to follow suit.

Other forms of tacit collusion

An alternative to having an established leader is for there to be an established set of simple 'rules of thumb' that everyone follows. One such example is average cost pricing. Here producers, instead of equating *MC* and *MR*, simply add a certain percentage for profit on top of average costs. Thus, if average costs rise by 10 per cent, prices will automatically be raised by 10 per cent. This is a particularly useful rule of thumb in times of inflation, when all firms will be experiencing similar cost increases.

> **Pause for thought**
>
> *If a firm has a typically shaped average cost curve and sets prices 10 per cent above average cost, what will its supply curve look like?*

Another rule of thumb is to have certain price benchmarks. Thus clothes may sell for £9.95, £14.95, £19.95, etc. (but not £12.31, £16.42 or £20.04). If costs rise, then firms simply raise their price to the next benchmark, knowing that other firms will do the same.

Rules of thumb can also be applied to advertising (e.g. you do not criticise other firms' products, only praise your own); or to the design of the product (e.g. lighting manufacturers tacitly agreeing not to bring out an everlasting light bulb).

Factors favouring collusion

Collusion between firms, whether formal or tacit, is more likely when firms can clearly identify with each other or some leader and when they trust each other not to break agreements. It is easier for firms to collude if the following conditions apply:

- There are only very few firms, all well known to each other.
- They are open with each other about costs and production methods.
- They have similar production methods and average costs, and are thus likely to want to change prices at the same time and by the same percentage.
- They produce similar products and can thus more easily reach agreements on price.
- There is a dominant firm.
- There are significant barriers to entry and thus there is little fear of disruption by new firms.
- The market is stable. If industry demand or production costs fluctuate wildly, it will be difficult to make agreements, partly due to difficulties in predicting and partly because agreements may frequently have to be amended. There is a particular problem in a declining market where firms may be tempted to undercut each other's price in order to maintain their sales.
- There are no government measures to curb collusion.

Non-collusive oligopoly: the breakdown of collusion

In some oligopolies, there may be only a few (if any) factors favouring collusion. In such cases, the likelihood of price competition is greater.

Key Idea

10
p68

Definitions

Average cost pricing
Where a firm sets its price by adding a certain percentage for (average) profit on top of average cost.

Price benchmark
A price that is typically used. Firms, when raising a price, will usually raise it from one benchmark to another.

Box 4.5

Rip-off Britain

Evidence of oligopolistic collusion?

In recent years there have been repeated allegations that British consumers are paying much higher prices than their European counterparts on a wide range of goods. The car industry, the large supermarket chains and the banks have all been charged with 'ripping off' the consumer. Such has been the level of concern that all three industries have been referred to the Competition Commission (see Section 6.5).

Key Idea

8
p45

Car industry

The clearest evidence of anti-competitive pricing behaviour in the UK car industry came with the admission by Volvo in July 1999 that it had entered secret agreements to keep British car prices high. This appeared to be just the tip of an iceberg, with car manufacturers fixing prices through the system of selective and exclusive distribution (SED). In other words, manufacturers would only supply through 'official' dealers who would sell at the list price (or at small agreed 'discounts').

When we consider the difference in price between identical models in the UK and mainland Europe the discrepancies are huge. The Competition Commission report, published in April 2000, found that car buyers in the UK were paying on average some 10 to 12 per cent more than those in France, Germany and Italy for the same models. For 58 of the 71 models analysed by the Commission, the UK price was at least 20 per cent higher than in the cheapest country. The Commission concluded that British car buyers were paying around 10 per cent too much for new cars, or some £1100 for an average car.

The price discrepancies between the UK and Europe were maintained by car manufacturers blocking cheaper European cars coming into the UK.

Manufacturers have been accused of adopting a number of anti-competitive practices. These include threatening mainland European car dealers with losing their dealership if they sell to British buyers, and delaying the delivery date of right-hand drive models to mainland European dealers in the hope that British buyers change their minds and go back to a British dealership.

Supermarkets

The Competition Commission inquiry into supermarkets, which began in April 1999, followed a nine-month investigation by the Office of Fair Trading into the major supermarket chains' business activities. The OFT identified three major areas of concern: the use of barriers to entry, the lack of effective price competition, and the relationship between the large supermarket chains and their suppliers.

The main issue concerns the major supermarket chains' huge buying and selling power. They have been able to drive costs down by forcing suppliers to offer discounts. Many suppliers, such as growers, have found their profit margins cut to the bone. However, these cost savings have not been passed on from supplier to shopper. The supermarket chains have adopted a system of 'shadow pricing', a form of tacit collusion whereby they all observe each other's prices and ensure that they remain at similar levels: often similarly high levels rather than similarly low levels! This has limited the extent of true price competition, and the resulting high prices have seen profits grow as costs have been driven ever downwards.

Since the OFT referral, the £6.7 billion takeover of Asda by Wal-Mart, the world's largest retailer, with a reputation of being a ruthless price cutter, promised to change the whole issue of pricing in the super-market sector. Of the supermarket chains, Asda has always been one of the cheapest. With the Wal-Mart takeover, the drive to cut prices gained fresh momentum. Asda planned to slash prices on hundreds of products, with most seeing some price reduction.

Tesco in response, striving to maintain its position as the UK's number one supermarket retailer, launched its own price-cutting campaign. It was determined not to get left behind in the price-cutting war.

Despite these apparent price wars, the Competition Commission was still concerned that competition was being restricted. It sought to answer a number of questions. Is price competition limited to a relatively small number of frequently purchased items, and at stores that face the most local competition? Are cost reductions 'being rapidly and fully passed through to consumers'? Is 'the pattern of prices and margins across different types of product, including branded and own label products, related to costs to the extent that would be expected in a fully competitive market? This would include products persistently sold at a loss, which may benefit consumers in the short term but which may distort competition and consumer choice, and may adversely affect the supply or availability of such products in the longer term.'[1]

One solution suggested by the Competition Commission would be to force supermarkets to publish their prices on the Internet, thereby allowing consumers or consumers' organisations to make easy comparisons of the prices charged by different supermarkets.

Banks

According to a Treasury report, chaired by Don Cruickshank,[2] UK banks are making excessive profits of some £3 billion to £5 billion per year, with bank customers paying up to £400 a year too much in charges and interest rates. The report found that current accounts were the least competitive product. They pay little or no interest to customers in credit and charge exorbitant amounts if you go overdrawn. But it was not just current accounts: mortgages, savings accounts, credit cards and personal loans were all identified as often being poor products.

Banks have tight control over cheque clearing, money transmission systems and cash machines. This makes it difficult for new competitors to enter the market. For example, a new bank without an extensive network of cash machines would find it difficult to attract customers, given the hefty charges for using other banks' machines. In addition, bank customers are often unwilling to consider changing accounts, fearing that this will involve a lot of time and expense.

Small businesses were found to be facing even more excessive charges. The government thus asked the Competition Commission to inquire into this particular aspect of the provision of banking services.

1. Identify the main barriers to entry in the supermarket and banking sectors.
2. In what forms of tacit collusion are firms in the three industries described likely to engage?

[1] *Supply of Groceries from Multiple Stores Monopoly Inquiry: Annex 2 To Issues Letter* (Competition Commission, 2000).

[2] *Competition in UK Banking: A Report to the Chancellor of the Exchequer* (TSO, 2000).

Even if there is collusion, there will always be the temptation for individual oligopolists to 'cheat', by cutting prices or by selling more than their allotted quota. The danger, of course, is that this would invite retaliation from the other members of the cartel, with a resulting price war. Price would then fall and the cartel could well break up in disarray.

When considering whether to break a collusive agreement, even if only a tacit one, a firm will ask: (1) 'How much can we get away with without inviting retaliation?' and (2) 'If a price war does result, will we be the winners? Will we succeed in driving some or all of our rivals out of business and yet survive ourselves, and thereby gain greater market power?'

The position of rival firms, therefore, is rather like that of generals of opposing armies or the players in a game. It is a question of choosing the appropriate *strategy*: the strategy that will best succeed in outwitting your opponents. The strategy a firm adopts will, of course, be concerned not just with price but also with advertising and product development.

The firm's choice of strategy will depend on (a) how it thinks its rivals will react to any price changes or other changes it makes; (b) its willingness to take a gamble. Economists have developed game theory, which examines the best strategy a firm can adopt for each assumption about its rivals' behaviour.

Key Idea
16
p142

Definitions

Game theory (or the theory of games)
The study of alternative strategies that oligopolists may choose to adopt, depending on their assumptions about their rivals' behaviour.

Maximin
The strategy of choosing the policy whose worst possible outcome is the least bad.

Non–collusive oligopoly: game theory

The simplest case is where there are just two firms with identical costs, products and demand. They are both considering which of two alternative prices to charge. Table 4.2 shows typical profits they could each make.

Let us assume that at present both firms (X and Y) are charging a price of £2 and that they are each making a profit of £10 million, giving a total industry profit of £20 million. This is shown in the top left-hand box (A).

Now assume they are both (independently) considering reducing their price to £1.80. In making this decision they will need to take into account what their rival might do, and how this will affect them. Let us consider X's position. In our simple example there are just two things that its rival, firm Y, might do. Either Y could cut its price to £1.80, or it could leave its price at £2. What should X do?

One alternative is to go for the *cautious* approach and think of the worst thing that its rival could do. If X kept its price at £2, the worst thing for X would be if its rival Y cut its price. This is shown by box C: X's profit falls to £5 million. If,

Table 4.2
Profits for firms X and Y at different prices

		X's price	
		£2	£1.80
Y's price	£2	**A** £10m each	**B** £5m for Y £12m for X
	£1.80	**C** £12m for Y £5m for X	**D** £8m each

however, X cut its price to £1.80, the worst outcome would again be for Y to cut its price, but this time X's profit only falls to £8 million. In this case, then, if X is cautious, it will *cut its price to £1.80*. Note that Y will argue along similar lines, and if it is cautious, it too will cut its price to £1.80. This policy of adopting the safer strategy is known as maximin. Following a maximin strategy, the firm will opt for the alternative that will maximise its minimum possible profit.

An alternative strategy is to go for the *optimistic* approach and assume that your rivals react in the way most favourable to you. Here the firm goes for the strategy that yields the highest possible profit. In X's case this again means cutting price, only this time on the optimistic assumption that firm Y will leave its price unchanged. If firm X is correct in its assumption, it will move to box B and achieve the maximum possible profit of £12 million. This strategy of going for the maximum possible profit is known as maximax. Note that again the same argument applies to Y. Its maximax strategy will be to cut price and hopefully end up in box C.

Given that in this 'game' *both* approaches, maximin and maximax, lead to the *same* strategy (namely, cutting price), this is known as a dominant strategy game. The result is that the firms will end up in box D, earning a lower profit (£8 million each) than if they had charged the higher price (£10 million each in box A).

The equilibrium outcome of a game where there is no collusion between the players (box D in this game) is known as a Nash equilibrium, after John Nash, a US mathematician (and the subject of the film *A Beautiful Mind*) who introduced the concept in 1951.

In our example, collusion rather than a price war would have benefited both firms. Yet, even if they did collude, both would be tempted to cheat and cut prices. This is known as the prisoners' dilemma. An example is given in Box 4.6.

More complex games with no dominant strategy

More complex 'games' can be devised with more than two firms, many alternative prices, differentiated products and various forms of non-price competition (e.g. advertising). In such cases, the cautious (maximin) strategy may suggest a different policy (e.g. do nothing) from the high-risk (maximax) strategy (e.g. cut prices substantially).

In complex and changing situations, firms may alter their tactics in the light of new circumstances. Thus in some cases firms may compete hard for a time (in price or non-price terms) and then realise that maybe no one is winning. Firms may then jointly raise prices and reduce advertising. Later, after a period of tacit collusion, competition may break out again. This may be sparked off by the entry of a new firm, by the development of a new product design, by a change in market demand, or simply by one or more firms no longer being able to resist the temptation to 'cheat'. In short, the behaviour of particular oligopolists may change quite radically over time.

The importance of threats and promises

In many situations, an oligopolist will make a threat or promise that it will act in a certain way. As long as the threat or promise is credible (i.e. its competitors believe it), the firm can gain and it will influence its rivals' behaviour.

Key Idea
10
p68

Definitions

Maximax
The strategy of choosing the policy that has the best possible outcome.

Dominant strategy game
Where the *same* policy is suggested by different strategies.

Nash equilibrium
The position resulting from everyone making their optimal decision based on their assumptions about their rivals' decisions. Without collusion, there is no incentive for any firm to move from this position.

Prisoners' dilemma
Where two or more firms (or people), by attempting independently to choose the best strategy for whatever the other(s) are likely to do, end up in a worse position than if they had co-operated in the first place.

Credible threat (or promise)
One that is believable to rivals because it is in the threatener's interests to carry it out.

Box 4.6 Case Studies and Applications

The prisoners' dilemma

Game theory is relevant not just to economics. A famous non-economic example is the prisoners' dilemma.

Nigel and Amanda have been arrested for a joint crime of serious fraud. Each is interviewed separately and given the following alternatives:

■ First, if they say nothing, the court has enough evidence to sentence both to a year's imprisonment.

■ Second, if either Nigel or Amanda *alone* confesses, he or she is likely to get only a three-month sentence but the partner could get up to ten years.

■ Third, if both confess, they are likely to get three years each.

What should Nigel and Amanda do?

Let us consider Nigel's dilemma. Should he confess in order to get the short sentence (the maximax strategy)? This is better than the year he would get for not confessing. There is, however, an even better reason for confessing. Suppose Nigel doesn't confess but, unknown to him, Amanda does confess. Then Nigel ends up with the long sentence. Better than this is to confess and to get no more than three years: this is the safest (maximin) strategy.

Amanda is in the same dilemma. The result is simple. When both prisoners act selfishly by confessing, they both end up in position D with relatively long prison terms. Only when they collude will they end up in position A with relatively short prison terms, the best combined solution.

Of course the police know this and will do their best to prevent any collusion. They will keep Nigel and Amanda in separate cells and try to persuade each of them that the other is bound to confess.

Thus the choice of strategy depends on:

■ Nigel's and Amanda's risk attitudes: i.e. are they 'risk lovers' or 'risk averse'?

■ Nigel's and Amanda's estimates of how likely the other is to own up.

? 1. Why is this a dominant strategy 'game'?
  2. How would Nigel's choice of strategy be affected if he had instead been involved in a joint crime with Jeremy, Pauline, Diana and Dave, and they had all been caught?

Let us now look at two real-world examples of the prisoners' dilemma.

Standing at concerts

When people go to some public event, such as a concert or a match, they often stand in order to get a better view. But once people start standing, everyone is likely to do so: after all, if they stayed sitting, they would not see at all. In this Nash equilibrium, most people are worse off, since, except for tall people, their view is likely to be worse and they lose the comfort of sitting down.

Too much advertising

Why do firms spend so much on advertising? If they are aggressive, they do so to get ahead of their rivals (the maximax approach). If they are cautious, they do so in case their rivals increase their advertising (the maximin approach). Although in both cases it may be in the individual firm's best interests to increase advertising, the resulting Nash equilibrium is likely to be one of excessive advertising: the total spent on advertising (by all firms) is not recouped in additional sales.

? Give one or two other examples (economic or non-economic) of the prisoners' dilemma.

	Amanda's alternatives	
	Not confess	Confess
Nigel's alternatives — Not confess	**A** Each gets 1 year	**C** Nigel gets 10 years / Amanda gets 3 months
Nigel's alternatives — Confess	**B** Nigel gets 3 months / Amanda gets 10 years	**D** Each gets 3 years

Alternatives for Nigel and Amanda

Take the simple situation where a large oil company, such as Esso, states that it will match the price charged by any competitor within a given radius. Assume that competitors believe this 'price promise' but also that Esso will not try to *undercut* their price. In the simple situation where there is only one other filling station in the area, what price should it charge? Clearly it should charge the price that would maximise its profits, assuming that Esso will charge the *same* price. In the absence of other filling stations in the area, this is likely to be a relatively high price.

Now assume that there are several filling stations in the area. What should the company do now? Its best bet is probably to charge the same price as Esso and hope that no other company charges a lower price and forces Esso to cut its price. Assuming that Esso's threat is credible, other companies are likely to reason in a similar way.

The importance of timing

Most decisions by oligopolists are made by one firm at a time rather than simultaneously by all firms. Sometimes a firm will take the initiative. At other times it will respond to decisions taken by other firms.

Take the case of a new generation of large passenger aircraft that can fly further without refuelling. Assume that there is a market for a 500-seater version of this type of aircraft and a 400-seater version, but that the market for each size of aircraft is not big enough for the two manufacturers, Boeing and Airbus, to share it profitably. Let us also assume that the 400-seater market would give an annual profit of £50 million to a single manufacturer and that the 500-seater would give an annual profit of £30 million, but that if both manufacturers produced the same version, they would each make an annual loss of £10 million.

Assume that Boeing announces that it is building the 400-seater plane. What should Airbus do? The choice is illustrated in Figure 4.11. This diagram is called a decision tree and shows the sequence of events. The small square at the left of the

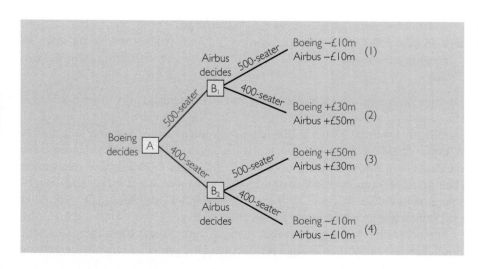

Figure 4.11
A decision tree

Definitions

First-mover advantage
When a firm gains from being the first to take action.

Kinked demand theory
The theory that oligopolists face a demand curve that is kinked at the current price: demand being significantly more elastic above the current price than below. The effect of this is to create a situation of price stability.

diagram is Boeing's decision point (point A). If it had decided to build the 500-seater plane, we would move up the top branch. Airbus would now have to make a decision (point B_1). If it too built the 500-seater plane, we would move to outcome 1: a loss of £10m for both manufacturers. Clearly, with Boeing building a 500-seater plane, Airbus would choose the 400-seater plane: we would move to outcome 2, with Boeing making a profit of £30m and Airbus a profit £50m. Airbus would be very pleased!

Boeing's best strategy at point A, however, would be to build the 400-seater plane. We would then move to Airbus's decision point B_2. In this case, it is in Airbus's interests to build the 500-seater plane. Its profit would be only £30m (outcome 3), but this is better than the £10m loss if it too built the 400-seater plane (outcome 4). With Boeing deciding first, the Nash equilibrium will thus be outcome 3.

There is clearly a first-mover advantage here. Once Boeing has decided to build the more profitable version of the plane, Airbus is forced to build the less profitable one. Naturally, Airbus would like to build the more profitable one and be the first mover. Which company succeeds in going first depends on how advanced they are in their research and development and in their production capacity.

More complex decision trees. The aircraft example is the simplest version of a decision tree, with just two companies and each one making only one key decision. In many business situations, much more complex trees could be constructed. The 'game' would be more like chess, with many moves and several options on each move. If there were more than two companies, the decision tree would be more complex still.

Pause for thought

Give an example of decisions that two firms could make in sequence, each one affecting the other's next decision.

Non-collusive oligopoly: the kinked demand curve

Even when there is no collusion, prices under oligopoly can often remain stable, with little apparent price competition. One explanation for this is that oligopolists often face a kinked demand curve. This occurs when two conditions hold:

- If an oligopolist cuts its price, its rivals will feel forced to follow suit and cut theirs, to prevent losing customers to the first firm.
- If an oligopolist raises its price, however, its rivals will *not* follow suit since, by keeping their prices the same, they will thereby gain customers from the first firm.

On these assumptions, each oligopolist will face a demand curve that is *kinked* at the current price and output (see Figure 4.12). A rise in price will lead to a large fall in sales as customers switch to the now lower-priced rivals. The firm will thus be reluctant to raise its price. Demand is relatively elastic above the kink. On the other hand, a fall in price will bring only a modest increase in sales, since rivals lower their prices too and therefore customers do not switch. The firm will thus also be reluctant to reduce its price. Demand is relatively inelastic below the kink. Thus oligopolists will be reluctant to change prices at all.

The possibility of having a kinked demand curve is not the only reason why firms may be reluctant to change prices. Changing prices will involve modifying

Key Idea 9 p64

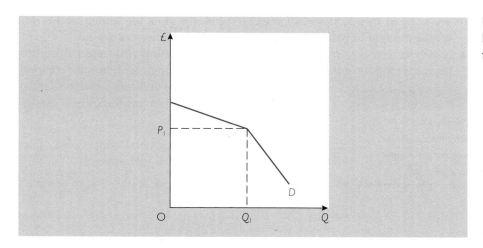

Figure 4.12
Kinked demand for a firm under oligopoly

price lists, working out new revenue predictions and revaluing stocks of finished goods; it may also upset customers.

Oligopoly and the consumer

When oligopolists act collusively and jointly maximise industry profits, they are in effect acting together as a monopoly. In such cases, prices may be very high. This is clearly not in the best interests of consumers.

Furthermore, in two respects, oligopoly may be more disadvantageous than monopoly:

■ Depending on the size of the individual oligopolists, there may be less scope for economies of scale to mitigate the effects of market power.
■ Oligopolists are likely to engage in much more extensive advertising than a monopolist.

These problems will be less severe, however, if oligopolists do not collude, if there is some degree of price competition and if barriers to entry are weak.

Also the power of oligopolists in certain markets may to some extent be offset if they sell their product to other powerful firms. Thus oligopolistic producers of baked beans or soap powder sell a large proportion of their output to giant supermarket chains, which can use their market power to keep down the price at which they purchase these products. This phenomenon is known as countervailing power.

In some respects, oligopoly has *advantages* to society over other market structures:

■ Oligopolists, like monopolists, can use part of their supernormal profit for research and development. Unlike monopolists, however, oligopolists will have a considerable *incentive* to do so. If the product design is improved, this may allow the firm to capture a larger share of the market, and it may be some time before rivals can respond with a similarly improved product. If, in addition, costs are reduced by technological improvement, the resulting higher profits will enable the firm to withstand better a price war should one break out.

■ Non-price competition through product differentiation may result in greater choice for the consumer. Take the case of stereo equipment. Non-price competition has led to a huge range of different products of many different specifications, each meeting the specific requirements of different consumers.

It is difficult to draw any general conclusions, since oligopolies differ so much in their performance.

> **Pause for thought**
>
> Assume that two brewers announce that they are about to merge. What information would you need to help you decide whether the merger would be in the consumer's interests?

Recap

1. An oligopoly is where there are just a few firms in the industry with barriers to the entry of new firms. Firms recognise their mutual dependence.

2. Oligopolists want to maximise their joint profits. This tends to make them collude to keep prices high. On the other hand, they want the biggest share of industry profits for themselves. This tends to make them compete.

3. Whether they compete or collude depends on the conditions in the industry. They are more likely to collude if there are few of them; if they are open with each other; if they have similar products and cost structures; if there is a dominant firm; if there are significant entry barriers; if the market is stable; and if there is no government legislation to prevent collusion.

4. Collusion can be open or tacit.

5. A formal collusive agreement is called a 'cartel'. A cartel aims to act as a monopoly. It can set price and leave the members to compete for market share, or it can assign quotas. There is always a temptation for cartel members to 'cheat' by undercutting the cartel price if they think they can get away with it and not trigger a price war.

6. Tacit collusion can take the form of price leadership. This is where firms follow the price set by either a dominant firm in the industry or one seen as a reliable 'barometer' of market conditions. Alternatively, tacit collusion can simply involve following various rules of thumb such as average cost pricing and benchmark pricing.

7. Non-collusive oligopolists will have to work out a price strategy. This will depend on their attitudes towards risk and on the assumptions they make about the behaviour of their rivals. Game theory examines various strategies that firms can adopt when the outcome of each is not certain. They can adopt a low-risk 'maximin' strategy of choosing the policy that has the least-bad worst outcome, or a high-risk 'maximax' strategy of choosing the policy with the best possible outcome, or some compromise. Either way, a 'Nash' equilibrium is likely to be reached which is not in the best interests of the firms collectively. It will entail a lower level of profit than if they had colluded.

8. Because firms are likely to face a kinked demand curve, they are likely to keep their prices stable unless there is a large shift in costs or demand.

9. Whether consumers benefit from oligopoly depends on the particular oligopoly and how competitive it is; whether there is any countervailing power; whether the firms engage in extensive advertising and of what type; whether product differentiation results in a wide range of choice for the consumer; and how much of the profits are ploughed back into research and development. Since these conditions vary substantially from oligopoly to oligopoly, it is impossible to state just how well or how badly oligopoly in general serves the consumer's interest.

Price discrimination

In what situations will firms be able to charge different prices to different consumers? How will we as consumers benefit or lose from the process?

Up to now we have assumed that a firm will sell its output at a single price. Sometimes, however, firms may practise price discrimination. This is where consumers are grouped into two or more independent markets and a separate price is charged in each market. Examples include different-priced seats on buses for adults and children, different prices for the same seats on aircraft (depending on when they are booked), and different prices charged for the same product in different countries or different parts of the same country. (There are other forms of price discrimination, but this – known as 'third-degree price discrimination' – is the most common.)

> **Definition**
>
> **Price discrimination**
> Where a firm sells the same product at different prices.

Conditions necessary for price discrimination to operate

As we shall see, a firm will be able to increase its profits if it can engage in price discrimination. But under what circumstances will it be able to charge discriminatory prices? There are three conditions that must be met:

- The firm must be able to set its price. Thus price discrimination will be impossible under perfect competition, where firms are price takers.
- The markets must be separate. Consumers in the low-priced market must not be able to resell the product in the high-priced market. For example, children must not be able to resell a half-priced child's cinema ticket for use by an adult.
- Demand elasticity must differ in each market. The firm will charge the higher price in the market where demand is less elastic, and thus less sensitive to a price rise.

Key Idea
9
p64

Advantages to the firm

Price discrimination allows the firm to earn a higher revenue from any given level of sales. Figure 4.13 represents a firm's demand curve. If it is to sell 200 units without price discrimination, it must charge a price of P_1. The total revenue it earns is shown by the grey area. If, however, it can practise price discrimination by selling 150 of those 200 units at the higher price of P_2, it will gain the pink area in addition to the grey area.

Another advantage the firm gains by price discrimination is that it may be able to use it to drive competitors out of business. If a firm has a monopoly in one market (e.g. the home market), it may be able to charge a high price due to its relatively inelastic demand, and thus make high profits. If it is under oligopoly in another market (e.g. the export market), it may use the high profits in the first market to subsidise a very low price in the oligopolistic market, thus forcing its competitors out of business.

Figure 4.13
Third-degree price discrimination

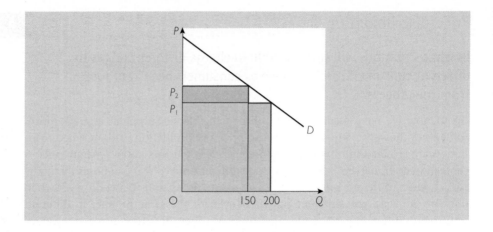

Large bus companies in the UK have been accused of doing this. They use the profits made from the high fares on routes where they face no competition to subsidise fares on routes where they do face competition, often from a small rival attempting to break into the market. The aim is to drive the small company out of business. Sometimes on these routes, the large company charges fares that are below cost (thereby making a temporary loss on these routes). This practice is known as predatory pricing.

> **Definition**
>
> **Predatory pricing** Selling at a price below average variable cost in order to drive competitors from the market.

Price discrimination and the consumer

No clear-cut decision can be made over the desirability of price discrimination from the point of view of the consumer. Some people will benefit from it; others will lose. Those paying the higher price will probably feel that price discrimination is unfair to them. On the other hand, those charged the lower price may thereby be able to obtain a good or service they could otherwise not afford: e.g. concessionary bus fares for senior citizens.

Competition. As explained above, a firm may use price discrimination to drive competitors out of business. On the other hand, it might use its profits from its high-priced market to break into another market and withstand a possible price war. Competition is thereby increased.

Profits. Price discrimination raises a firm's profits. This could be seen to be against the interests of the consumer, especially if the average price of the product is raised. On the other hand, the higher profits may be reinvested and lead to lower costs in the future.

Key Idea
14
p118

Box 4.7 Exploring Economics

Profit-maximising prices and output

Identifying different prices in different markets

Assuming that a firm wishes to maximise profits, what discriminatory prices should it charge and how much should it produce?

Assume that the firm sells an identical product in two separate markets X and Y with demand and MR curves as shown in the diagrams.

Diagram (c) shows the MC and MR curves for the firm as a whole. This MR curve is found by adding the amounts sold in the two markets at each level of MR (in other words, the horizontal addition of the two MR curves). Thus, for example, with output of 1000 units in market X and 2000 in market Y, making 3000 in total, revenue would increase by £5 if one extra unit were sold, whether in market X or Y.

Total profit is maximised where MC = MR: i.e. at an output of 3000 units in total. This output must then be divided between the two markets so that MC is equal to MR in each market: i.e. MC = MR = £5 in each market. MR must be the same in both markets, otherwise revenue could be increased by switching output to the market with the higher MR.

The profit-maximising price in each market will be given by the relevant demand curve. Thus, in market X, 1000 units will be sold at £9 each, and in market Y, 2000 units will be sold at £7 each.

? 1. Why is the higher price charged in the market with the less elastic demand curve?

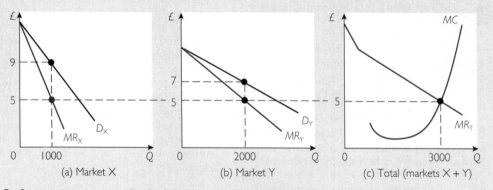

Profit-maximising output under third-degree price discrimination

Recap

1. Price discrimination is where a firm sells the same product at different prices in different markets.

2. Price discrimination allows the firm to earn a higher revenue from a given level of sales.

3. Some people will gain from price discrimination; others will lose. It is likely to be particularly harmful when it is used as a means of driving competitors from the market (predatory pricing).

Questions

1. A perfectly competitive firm faces a price of £14 per unit. It has the short-run cost schedule shown at the bottom of this page.

   (a) Copy the table and put in additional rows for average cost and marginal cost at each level of output. (Enter the figures for marginal cost in the space between each column.)
   (b) Plot AC, MC and MR on a diagram.
   (c) Mark the profit-maximising output.
   (d) How much (supernormal) profit is made at this output?
   (e) What would happen to the price in the long run if this firm were typical of others in the industry? Why would we need to know information about long-run average cost in order to give a precise answer to this question?

2. If the industry under perfect competition faces a downward-sloping demand curve, why does an individual firm face a horizontal demand curve?

3. On a diagram similar to Figure 4.3, show the long-run equilibrium for both firm and industry under perfect competition. Now assume that the demand for the product falls. Show the short-run and long-run effects.

4. If supernormal profits are competed away under perfect competition, why will firms have an incentive to become more efficient?

5. Is it a valid criticism of perfect competition to argue that it is incompatible with economies of scale?

6. As an illustration of the difficulty in identifying monopolies, try and decide which of the following are monopolies: British Telecom; your local evening newspaper; a water company; the village post office; the Royal Mail; Interflora; the London Underground; ice-creams in the cinema; Guinness; food sold in a train buffet car; Tipp-Ex; the board game 'Monopoly'.

7. Try this brain teaser. A monopoly would be expected to face an inelastic demand. After all, there are no direct substitutes. And yet, if it produces where $MR = MC$, MR must be positive, and demand must therefore be elastic. Therefore the monopolist must face an elastic demand! Can you solve this conundrum?

8. For what reasons would you expect a monopoly to charge (a) a higher price, and (b) a lower price than if the industry were operating under perfect competition?

9. In which of the following industries are exit costs likely to be low: (a) steel production; (b) market gardening; (c) nuclear power generation; (d) specialist financial advisory services; (e) production of fashion dolls; (f) production of a new drug; (g) contract catering; (h) mobile discos; (i) car ferry operators? Are these exit costs dependent on how narrowly the industry is defined?

10. Think of three examples of monopolies (local or national) and consider how contestable their markets are.

11. Think of ten different products or services and estimate roughly how many firms there are in the market. You will need to decide whether 'the market' is a local one, a national one or an international one. In what ways do the firms compete in each of the cases you have identified?

12. Assume that a monopolistically competitive industry is in long-run equilibrium. On a diagram like Figure 4.7, show the effect of a fall in demand on a firm's price and profit in (a) the short run and (b) the long run.

13. Imagine there are two types of potential customer for jam sold by a small food shop. The one is the person who has just run out and wants some now. The other is the person who looks in the cupboard, sees that the pot of jam is less than half full and thinks, 'I will soon

Output	0		1		2		3		4		5		6		7		8
TC (£)	10		18		24		30		38		50		66		91		120

need some more.' How will the price elasticity of demand differ between these two customers?

14. Why may a food shop charge higher prices than supermarkets for 'essential items' and yet very similar prices for delicatessen items?

15. Firms under monopolistic competition generally have spare capacity. Does this imply that if, say, half of the petrol stations were closed down, the consumer would benefit? Explain.

16. Will competition between oligopolists always reduce total industry profits?

17. In which of the following industries is collusion likely to occur: bricks, beer, margarine, cement, crisps, washing powder, blank audio or video cassettes, carpets?

18. Devise a box diagram like that in Table 4.2 (on page 150), only this time assume that there are three firms each considering the two strategies of keeping price the same or reducing it by a set amount. Is the game still a 'dominant strategy game'?

19. Which of the following are examples of effective countervailing power?

(a) Power stations buying coal from a large mining company.
(b) A large office hiring a photocopier from Rank Xerox.
(c) Marks and Spencer buying clothes from a garment manufacturer.
(d) A small village store (but the only one for miles around) buying food from a wholesaler.

Is it the size of the purchasing firm that is important in determining its power to keep down the prices charged by its suppliers?

20. If a cinema could sell all its seats to adults in the evenings at the end of the week, but only a few on Mondays and Tuesdays, what price discrimination policy would you recommend to the cinema in order for it to maximise its weekly revenue?

21. Think of two examples of price discrimination. In what ways do the consumers gain or lose? What information would you need to be certain in your answer?

Additional case studies on the *Essentials of Economics* website (www.booksites.net/sloman)

4.1 Is perfect best? An examination of the meaning of the word 'perfect' in perfect competition.

4.2 B2B electronic marketplaces. This case study examines the growth of firms trading with each other over the Internet (business to business or 'B2B') and considers the effects on competition.

4.3 Measuring monopoly power. An examination of how the degree of monopoly power possessed by a firm can be measured.

4.4 Concentration ratios. One way of measuring the degree of market power in an industry.

4.5 X-inefficiency. A type of inefficiency suffered by many large firms, resulting in a wasteful use of resources.

4.6 Airline deregulation in the USA and Europe. Whether the deregulation of various routes has led to more competition and lower prices.

4.7 Edward Chamberlin (1899–1967). The birth of the monopolistic competition model.

4.8 The motor vehicle repair and servicing industry. A case study of monopolistic competition.

4.9 Curry wars. Monopolistic competition in the take-away food market.

4.10 Bakeries: oligopoly or monopolistic competition? A case study on the bread industry, showing that small-scale local bakeries can exist alongside giant national bakeries.

4.11 Oligopoly in the brewing industry. A case study showing how the UK brewing industry is becoming more concentrated.

4.12 The global vitamin cartel. A case study showing oligopolistic collusion in the production and sale of vitamins.

4.13 Cartels set in concrete, steel and cardboard. This examines some of the best-known Europe-wide cartels of recent years.

4.14 Merger activity. This examines mergers in Europe: their causes and consequences.

4.15 A product's life cycle. How market conditions vary at different stages in a product's life.

4.16 Peak load pricing. An example of price discrimination.

4.17 How do UK companies set prices? A summary of the findings of a Bank of England survey on how firms set prices in practice.

Sections of chapter covered in
WinEcon – Sloman, *Essentials of Economics*

Essentials of Economics section	*WinEcon* section
4.1	4.1
4.2	4.2
4.3	4.3
4.4	4.4
4.5	4.5
4.6	4.6

Websites relevant to this chapter

Numbers and sections refer to websites listed in the Web Appendix and hotlinked from this book's website at www.booksites.net/sloman

- For news articles relevant to this chapter, see the *Economics News Articles* link from the book's website.
- For general news on companies and markets, see websites in section A, and particularly A2, 3, 4, 5, 8, 9, 18, 24, 25, 26, 36. See also A38 and 39 for links to newspapers worldwide; and A42 for links to economics news articles from newspapers worldwide.
- For sites that looks at competition and market power, see B2 (third link); E4, 10, 18; G7, 8. See also links in I7, 11, 14 and 17.
- For regulation of the gas industry (Box 4.2), see E16.
- For a site on game theory, see A40 including its home page. See also D4; C20; I17 and 4 (in the EconDirectory section).

CHAPTER MAP

CHAPTER FIVE

Wages and the distribution of income

Why do pop stars, footballers and stockbrokers earn such large incomes? Why, on the other hand, do cleaners, hospital porters and workers in clothing factories earn very low incomes?

The explanation for differences in wages lies in the working of labour markets. In the first part of the chapter we will consider how labour markets operate. In particular, we will focus on the determination of wage rates in different types of market: ones where employers are wage takers, ones where they can choose the wage rate, and ones where wage rates are determined by a process of collective bargaining.

In Section 5.4 we ask the more general question of why some people are rich and others poor, and consider the degree of inequality in our society: a society that includes the super-rich, with their luxury yachts and their villas abroad, and people living in slum conditions, with not enough to feed and clothe themselves or their children properly; a society where people begging in the streets are an all too familiar sight.

The chapter closes with a consideration of what can be done to reduce inequality. Is the solution to tax the rich very heavily so that the money can be redistributed to the poor? Or might this discourage people from working so hard? Would it be better, then, to focus on benefits and increase the support for the poor?

5.1   Labour market trends

How has the pattern of employment changed in recent years?

The labour market has undergone great change in recent years. Advances in technology, changes in the pattern of output, a need to be competitive in international markets and various social changes have all contributed to changes in work practices and in the structure and composition of the workforce.

Major changes include the following:

■ A shift from agricultural and manufacturing to service-sector employment. Figure 5.1 reveals that employment in agriculture has been falling over a long historical period. The fall in manufacturing employment, however, has been more recent, starting in the 1960s and gathering pace through the 1970s, 1980s and 1990s. By contrast, employment in the service industries has grown steadily since 1946. In fact since 1979, it has expanded by over 5 million jobs.

■ A rise in part-time employment, and a fall in full-time employment (see Figure 5.2). In 1971 approximately one in six workers in the UK was part time; by 2003 this had risen to one worker in four. In the EU as a whole, the figure is one in six. The fall in the proportion of full-time employees closely mirrors the decline in manufacturing, where jobs were more likely to be on a full-time basis. At the same time, the growth in part-time work reflects the growth in the service sector, where many jobs are part time. Since 1979 part-time employment has risen by over 2.2 million.

Figure 5.1

Employment in different sectors of the UK economy

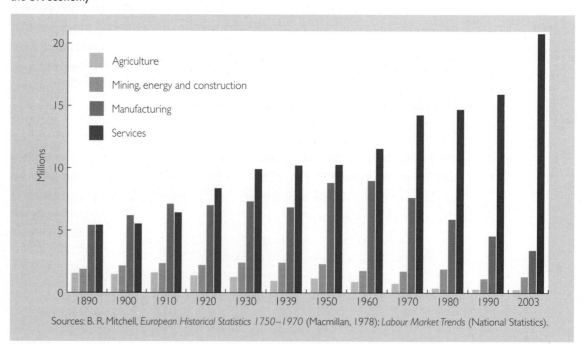

Sources: B. R. Mitchell, *European Historical Statistics 1750–1970* (Macmillan, 1978); *Labour Market Trends* (National Statistics).

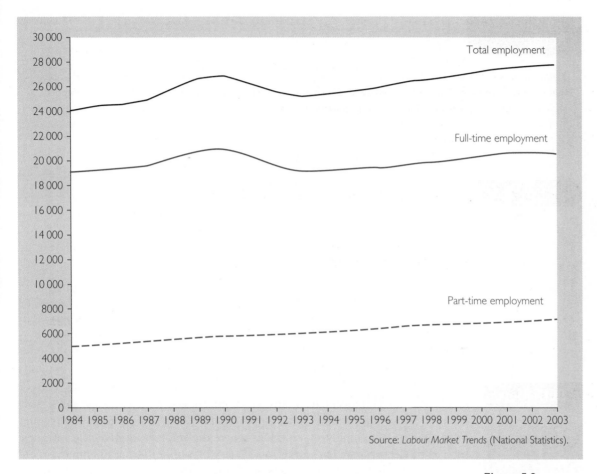

Source: *Labour Market Trends* (National Statistics).

Figure 5.2
The growth of part-time employment (employees)

- A rise in female participation rates. Women now constitute approximately half of the paid labour force. The rise in participation rates is strongly associated with the growth in the service sector and the creation of part-time positions. Nearly half of all female workers, about 6.3 million, are in part-time work.
- A rise in the proportion of workers employed on fixed-term contracts, or on a temporary or casual basis. Many firms nowadays prefer to employ only their core workers/managers on a permanent ('continuing') basis. They feel that it gives them more flexibility in responding to changing market conditions to have the remainder of their workers employed on a short-term basis, and, perhaps, to make use of agency staff or to contract out work.
- Downsizing. It has become very fashionable in recent years for companies to try to 'trim' the numbers of their employees in order to reduce costs. There is now, however, a growing consensus that the process may have gone too far. The cost of reducing its workforce may be that a company loses revenue: if it cuts back on people who had been employed in marketing its products, or in developing new products or in ensuring that quality is maintained, then it is likely to lose market share. It might reduce unit costs, but total profits could nevertheless fall, not rise.

Definition

Downsizing
Where firms reduce the size of their workforce in order to reduce costs and thereby increase profits.

Recap

Major changes in the UK labour market over recent years include: a movement towards service-sector employment; a rise in part-time working; a growth in female employment levels; a rise in the proportion of temporary, short-term contracts and casual employment; downsizing.

5.2   Wage determination in a perfect market

Why are some people paid higher wage rates than others?

Perfect labour markets

When looking at the market for labour, it is useful to make a similar distinction to that made in goods markets: the distinction between perfect and imperfect markets. That way we can gain a clearer understanding of the effects of power, or lack of it, in the labour market. Although in practice few labour markets are totally perfect, many do at least approximate to it.

The assumptions of perfect labour markets are similar to those of perfect goods markets. The main one is that everyone is a wage taker. In other words, neither employers nor employees have any economic power to affect wage rates. This situation is not uncommon. Small employers are likely to have to pay the 'going wage rate' to their employees, especially where the employee is of a clear category, such as an electrician, a bar worker, a secretary or a porter. As far as employees are concerned, being a wage taker means not being a member of a union and therefore not being able to use collective bargaining to push up the wage rate.

The other assumptions of a perfect labour market are as follows:

> ### Definition
>
> **Wage taker**
> An employer (or employee) who is unable to influence the wage rate.

- Freedom of entry. There are no restrictions on the movement of labour. For example, workers are free to move to alternative jobs or to areas of the country where wage rates are higher. There are no barriers erected by, say, unions, professional associations or the government. Of course, it takes time for workers to change jobs and maybe to retrain. This assumption therefore applies only in the long run.
- Perfect knowledge. Workers are fully aware of what jobs are available at what wage rates and with what conditions of employment. Likewise employers know what labour is available and how productive that labour is.
- Homogeneous labour. It is usually assumed that, in perfect markets, workers of a given category are identical in terms of productivity. For example, it would be assumed that all bricklayers are equally skilled and motivated.

Wage rates and employment under perfect competition are determined by the interaction of the market demand and supply of labour. This is illustrated in Figure 5.3. It shows, for each wage rate in a particular labour market, the number of hours that workers would supply and the number of hours of labour that firms would demand.

Ke
Ide.
7
p41

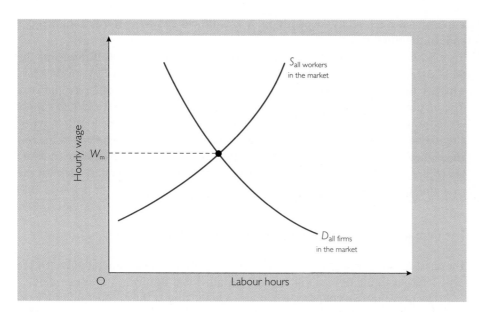

Figure 5.3
A perfectly competitive labour market

Generally it would be expected that the supply and demand curves slope the same way as in goods markets. The higher the wage rate paid for a certain type of job, the more workers will want to do that job. This gives an upward-sloping supply curve of labour. On the other hand, the higher the wage rate that employers have to pay, the less labour they will want to employ. Either they will simply produce less output, or they will substitute other factors of production, like machinery, for labour. Thus the demand curve for labour slopes downwards.

We now turn to look at the supply and demand for labour in more detail.

The supply of labour

The supply of labour in each market will typically be upward sloping. The higher the wage rate offered in a particular type of job, the more people will want to do that job.

The *position* of the market supply curve of labour will depend on the number of people willing and able to do the job at each given wage rate. This depends on three things:

- The number of qualified people.
- The non-wage benefits or costs of the job, such as the pleasantness or otherwise of the working environment, job satisfaction or dissatisfaction, status, power, the degree of job security, holidays, perks and other fringe benefits.
- The wages and non-wage benefits in alternative jobs.

A change in the wage rate will cause a movement along the supply curve. A change in any of these other three determinants will shift the whole curve: a rightward shift representing an increase in supply; a leftward shift, a decrease.

The elasticity of supply of labour

How *responsive* will the supply of labour be to a change in the wage rate? If the market wage rate goes up, will a lot more labour become available or only a little? This responsiveness (elasticity) depends on (a) the difficulties and costs of changing jobs and (b) the time period.

Another way of looking at the elasticity of supply of labour is in terms of the mobility of labour: the willingness and ability of labour to move to another job, whether in a different location (geographical mobility) or in a different industry (occupational mobility). The mobility of labour (and hence the elasticity of supply of labour) will be higher when there are alternative jobs in the same location, when alternative jobs require similar skills and when people have good information about these jobs. It is also much higher in the long run, when people have the time to acquire new skills and when the education system has had time to adapt to the changing demands of industry.

The demand for labour: the marginal productivity theory

The market demand curve for labour will typically be downward sloping. To see why, let us examine how many workers an individual firm will want to employ.

In the previous two chapters, when we were looking at the production of goods, we assumed that firms aim to maximise profits. The theory of labour demand is based on the same assumption. This theory is generally known as the marginal productivity theory.

The profit-maximising approach

How many workers should a firm employ in order to maximise profits? The firm will answer this question by weighing up the costs of employing extra labour against the benefits. It will use exactly the same principles as in deciding how much output to produce.

In the goods market, the firm will maximise profits where the marginal cost of producing an extra unit of a *good* equals the marginal revenue from selling it: $MC = MR$.

In the labour market, the firm will maximise profits where the marginal cost of employing an extra *worker* equals the marginal revenue that the worker's output earns for the firm: MC of labour = MR of labour. The reasoning is simple. If an extra worker adds more to a firm's revenue than to its costs, the firm's profits will increase. It will be worth employing that worker. But as more workers are employed, diminishing returns to labour will set in (see page 85). Each extra worker will produce less than the previous one, and thus earn less revenue for the firm. Eventually the marginal revenue from extra workers will fall to the level of their marginal cost. At that point, the firm will stop employing extra workers. There are no additional profits to be gained. Profits are at a maximum.

Measuring the marginal cost and revenue of labour

Marginal cost of labour (MC_L).   This is the extra cost of employing one more worker. Under perfect competition the firm is too small to affect the market wage. It faces a horizontal supply curve. In other words, it can employ as many workers as it chooses at the market wage rate. Thus the additional cost of employing one more person will simply be the wage rate: $MC_L = W$.

Key
Ide
12
p84

Key
Ide
3
p10

Key
Ide
13
p85

Marginal revenue of labour (MRP$_L$).   The marginal revenue that the firm gains from employing one more worker is called the marginal revenue product of labour (MRP$_L$). The MRP$_L$ is found by multiplying two elements – the *marginal physical product* of labour (MPP$_L$) and the marginal revenue gained by selling one more unit of output (MR).

$$MRP_L = MPP_L \times MR$$

The MPP$_L$ is the extra output produced by the last worker. Thus if the last worker produces 100 tonnes of output per week (MPP$_L$), and if the firm earns an extra £2 for each additional tonne sold (MR), then the worker's MRP is £200. This extra worker is adding £200 to the firm's revenue.

Definition

Marginal revenue product (of a factor)
The extra revenue a firm earns from employing one more unit of a variable factor: $MRP_{factor} = MPP_{factor} \times MR_{good}$

The profit-maximising level of employment for a firm

The MPP$_L$ curve is illustrated in Figure 5.4(a). As more workers are employed, there will come a point when diminishing returns set in (point *x*). The MPP$_L$ curve thus slopes down after this point. The MRP$_L$ curve will be of a similar shape to the MPP$_L$ curve, since it is merely being multiplied by a constant figure, MR. (Under perfect competition MR = P and does not vary with output.) The MRP$_L$ curve is illustrated in Figure 5.4(b), along with the MC$_L$ 'curve'.

Profits are maximised at an employment level of Q$_e$, where MC$_L$ (i.e. the wage rate, W) = MRP$_L$. Why? At levels of employment less than Q$_e$, MRP$_L$ exceeds MC$_L$. The firm will increase profits by employing more labour. At levels of employment greater than Q$_e$, MC$_L$ exceeds MRP$_L$. In this case the firm will increase profits by reducing employment.

Derivation of the firm's demand curve for labour

No matter what the wage rate, the quantity of labour demanded will be found from the intersection of W and MRP$_L$ (see Figure 5.5). At a wage rate of W$_1$, Q$_1$ labour is demanded (point *a*); at W$_2$, Q$_2$ is demanded (point *b*); at W$_3$, Q$_3$ is demanded (point *c*). Thus the MRP$_L$ curve shows the quantity of labour employed at each wage rate. But this is just what the demand curve for labour shows. Thus the MRP$_L$ curve is the demand curve for labour.

Figure 5.4
Diminishing returns and employment

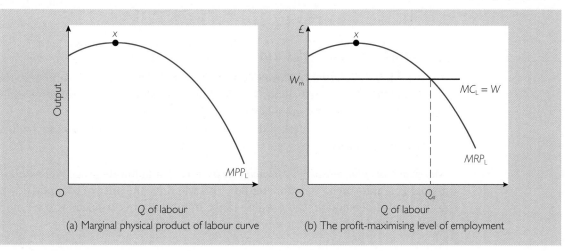

(a) Marginal physical product of labour curve

(b) The profit-maximising level of employment

Figure 5.5

Deriving the firm's demand curve for labour

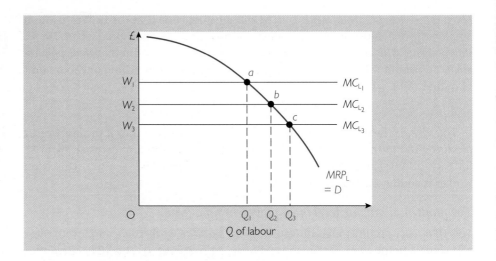

There are three determinants of the demand for labour by a firm:

Definition

Derived demand
The demand for a factor of production depends on the demand for the good which uses it.

- The wage rate. This determines the position *on* the demand curve. (Strictly speaking we would refer here to the wage determining the 'quantity demanded' rather than the 'demand'.)
- The productivity of labour (MPP_L). This determines the position *of* the demand curve.
- The demand for the good. The higher the market demand for the good, the higher will be its market price, and hence the higher will be the *MR*, and thus the MRP_L. This too determines the position of the demand curve. It shows how the demand for labour (and other factors) is a derived demand: i.e. one derived from the demand for the good. For example, the higher the demand for houses, and hence the higher their price, the higher will be the demand for bricklayers.

Pause for thought

If the productivity of a group of workers rises by 10 per cent, will the wage rate they are paid also rise by 10 per cent? Explain why or why not.

A change in the wage rate is represented by a movement along the demand curve for labour. A change in the productivity of labour or in the demand for the good *shifts* the curve.

Market demand and its elasticity

For the same reason that the firm's demand for labour is downward sloping, so the whole market demand for labour will be downward sloping. At lower wage rates, firms in total will employ more labour.

The *elasticity* of this market demand for labour depends on various factors. Elasticity will be greater:

The greater the price elasticity of demand for the good. A fall in the wage rate will lead to higher employment and more output. This will drive the price of the good down. If the market demand for the good is elastic, this fall in price will lead to a lot more being sold and hence to a lot more people being employed.

Key Idea
9
p64

The easier it is to substitute labour for other factors and vice versa.   If labour can be readily substituted for other factors, then a reduction in the wage rate will lead to a large increase in labour used to replace these other factors.

The greater the wage cost as a proportion of total costs.   If wages are a large proportion of total costs and the wage rate falls, total costs will fall significantly; therefore production will increase significantly, and so too will the demand for labour.

The longer the time period.   Given sufficient time, firms can respond to a fall in wage rates by reorganising their production processes to make use of the now relatively cheap labour.

Wages and profits under perfect competition

The wage rate (W) is determined by the interaction of demand and supply in the labour market. This will be equal to the value of the output that the last person produces (MRP_L).

Profits to the individual firm arise from the fact that the MRP_L curve slopes downward (diminishing returns), with the last worker adding less to the revenue of firms than previous workers already employed.

If *all* workers in the firm receive a wage equal to the MRP of the last worker, everyone but the last worker will receive a wage *less* than their MRP. This excess of MRP_L over W of previous workers provides a surplus to the firm over its wages bill (see Figure 5.6). Part of this will be required for paying non-wage costs; part will be profits for the firm.

Perfect competition between firms will ensure that profits are kept down to *normal* profits. If the surplus over wages is such that *supernormal* profits are made, new firms will enter the industry. The price of the good (and hence MRP_L) will fall, and the wage rate will be bid up, until only normal profits remain.

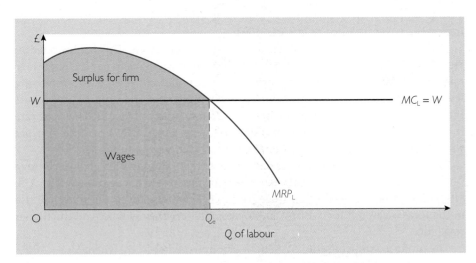

Figure 5.6
Wages and a firm's surplus over wages

Recap

1. Wage rates in a competitive labour market are determined by the interaction of demand and supply.

2. The market supply of labour curve will normally be upward sloping. Its elasticity will depend on the occupational and geographical mobility of labour. The more readily labour can transfer between jobs and regions, the more elastic will be the supply of labour.

3. The demand for labour depends on labour's productivity. A profit-maximising employer will continue taking on extra workers until MRP_L has fallen (due to diminishing returns) to equal MC_L (= W under perfect competition).

4. The firm's demand curve for labour is its MRP_L curve.

5. The elasticity of demand for labour depends on the elasticity of demand for the good, the ease of substituting labour for other factors and vice versa, wages as a proportion of total costs, and the time period involved.

6. If supernormal profits are made, new firms will enter the industry. The price of the good will fall, and the wage rate will be bid up, until only normal profits remain.

5.3 | Wage determination in imperfect markets

How are wage rates affected by big business and by unions?

In the real world, many firms have the power to influence wage rates: they are not wage takers. This is one of the major types of labour market 'imperfection'.

When a firm is the only employer of a particular type of labour, this situation is called a monopsony. The Post Office is a monopsony employer of postal workers. Another example is when a factory is the only employer of certain types of labour in that district. It therefore has local monopsony power. When there are just a few employers, this is called oligopsony.

Monopsonists (and oligopsonists too) are 'wage setters' not 'wage takers'. Thus a large employer in a small town may have considerable power to resist wage increases or even to force wage rates down.

Such firms face an upward-sloping supply curve of labour. This is illustrated in Figure 5.7. If the firm wants to take on more labour, it will have to pay a higher wage rate to attract workers away from other industries. But conversely, by employing less labour it can get away with paying a lower wage rate. The supply curve shows the wage rate that must be paid to attract a given quantity of labour. The wage rate it pays is the *average cost* to the firm of employing labour (AC_L): i.e. the cost per worker. The supply curve is also therefore the AC_L curve.

The *marginal* cost of employing one more worker (MC_L) will be above the wage (AC_L). The reason is that the wage rate has to be raised to attract extra workers. The MC_L will thus be the new higher wage paid to the new employee *plus* the small rise in the total wages bill for existing employees: after all, they will be paid the higher wage too.

The profit-maximising employment of labour would be at Q_1, where $MC_L = MRP_L$. The wage (found from the AC_L curve) would thus be W_1.

Definitions

Monopsony
A market with a single buyer or employer.

Oligopsony
A market with just a few buyers or employers.

Key Idea 14 p118

Figure 5.7

Monopsony

If this had been a perfectly competitive labour market, employment would have been at the higher level Q_2, with the wage rate at the higher level W_2, where $W = MRP_L$. What in effect the monopsonist is doing, therefore, is forcing the wage rate down by restricting the number of workers employed.

The role of trade unions

Unions and market power

How can unions influence the determination of wages, and what might be the consequences of their actions?

The extent to which unions will succeed in pushing up wage rates depends on their power and militancy. It also depends on the power of firms to resist and on their ability to pay higher wages. In particular, the scope for unions to gain a better deal for their members depends on the sort of market in which the employers are producing.

Unions facing competitive employers

If the employers are producing under perfect or monopolistic competition, unions can raise wage rates only at the expense of employment. Firms are only earning normal profit. Thus if unions force up the wage rate, the marginal firms will go bankrupt and leave the industry. Fewer workers will be employed. The fall in output will lead to higher prices. This will enable the remaining firms to pay a higher wage rate.

Figure 5.8 illustrates these effects. If unions force the wage rate up from W_1 to W_2, employment will fall from Q_1 to Q_2. There will be a surplus of people ($Q_3 - Q_2$) wishing to work in this industry for whom no jobs are available.

The union is in a doubly weak position. Not only will jobs be lost as a result of forcing up the wage rate, but also there is a danger that these unemployed people will undercut the union wage, unless the union can prevent firms from employing non-unionised labour.

In a competitive market, then, the union is faced with the choice between wages and jobs. Its actions will thus depend on its objectives.

Figure 5.8

Monopoly union
facing producers
under perfect
competition

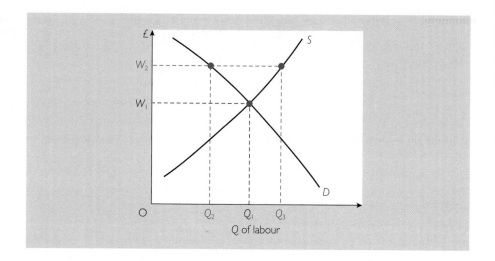

*At what wage rate in Figure 5.8 would
employment be maximised: (a)* W$_1$; *(b) a wage
rate above* W$_1$; *(c) a wage rate below* W$_1$?
Explain.

Wage rates can be increased without a reduction in the
level of employment only if, as part of the bargain, the productivity of labour is increased. This is called a productivity
deal. The *MRP* curve, and hence the *D* curve in Figure 5.8,
shifts to the right.

Bilateral monopoly

Definition

Productivity deal
Where, in return for a
wage increase, a union
agrees to changes in
working practices that
will increase output
per worker.

What happens when a union monopoly faces a monopsony employer? What will
the wage rate be? What will the level of employment be? Unfortunately, economic
theory cannot give a precise answer to these questions. There is no 'equilibrium'
level as such (see Box 5.1). Ultimately the wage rate and level of employment will
depend on the relative bargaining strengths and skills of unions and management.

Strange as it may seem, unions may be in a stronger position to make substantial gains for their members when they are facing a powerful employer. There is
often considerable scope for them to increase wage rates *without* this leading to a
reduction in employment, or even for them to increase both the wage rate *and*
employment. The reason is that if firms have power in the *goods* market too, and
are making supernormal profit, then there is scope for a powerful union to redistribute some of these profits to wages.

The actual wage rate under bilateral monopoly is usually determined through a
process of negotiation or 'collective bargaining'. The outcome of this bargaining
will depend on a wide range of factors, which vary substantially from one industry
or firm to another.

Collective bargaining

Sometimes when unions and management negotiate, *both* sides can gain from the
resulting agreement. For example, the introduction of new technology may allow
higher wages, improved working conditions and higher profits. Usually, however,
one side's gain is the other's loss. Higher wages mean lower profits. Either way, both
sides will want to gain the maximum for themselves.

Wages under bilateral monopoly

All to play for?

There is no single equilibrium wage rate under bilateral monopoly. This box shows why.

Assume first that there is no union. The diagram shows that a monopsonist employer will maximise profits by employing Q_1 workers at a wage rate of W_1. (Q_1 is where $MRP_L = MC_L$).

What happens when a union is introduced into this situation? Wages will now be set by negotiation between unions and management. Once the wage rate has been agreed, the employer can no longer drive the wage rate down by employing fewer workers. If it tried to pay less than the agreed wage, it could well be faced by a strike, and thus have a zero supply of labour!

Similarly, if the employer decided to take on *more* workers, it would not have to *increase* the wage rate as long as the negotiated wage were above the free-market wage: as long as the wage rate were above that given by the supply curve S_1.

The effect of this is to give a new supply curve that is horizontal up to the point where it meets the original supply curve. For example, let us assume that the union succeeds in negotiating a wage rate of W_2. The supply curve will be horizontal at this level to the left of point x. To the right of this point it will follow the original supply curve S_1, since to acquire more than Q_3 workers it would have to raise the wage rate above W_2.

If the supply curve is horizontal to the left of point x at a level of W_2, so too will be the MC_L curve. The reason is simply that the extra cost to the employer of taking on an extra worker (up to Q_3) is merely the negotiated wage rate: no rise has to be given to existing employees. If MC_L is equal to the wage, the profit-maximising employment ($MC_L = MRP_L$) will now be where $W = MRP_L$. At a negotiated wage rate of W_2, the firm will therefore choose to employ Q_1 workers.

What this means, therefore, is that the union can push the wage right up from W_1 to W_2 and the firm will still *want* to employ Q_1. In other words, a wage rise can be obtained *without* a reduction in employment.

The union could go further still. By threatening industrial action, it may be able to push the wage rate above W_2 and still insist that Q_1 workers are employed (i.e. no redundancies). The firm may be prepared to see profits drop right down to normal level rather than face a strike and risk losses. The absolute upper limit to the wage rate will be that at which the firm is forced to close down.

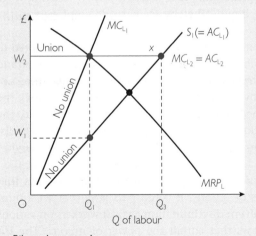

Bilateral monopoly

? 1. If the negotiated wage rate were somewhere between W_1 and W_2, how would the resulting level of employment compare with that at W_1?
2. What in practice will determine just how much the agreed wage rate is above W_1?

The outcome of the negotiations will depend on the relative bargaining strengths of both sides. In bargaining there are various threats or promises that either side can make. For these to be effective, of course, the other side must believe that they will be carried out.

Union *threats* might include strike action, picketing, working to rule or refusing to co-operate with management – for example, in the introduction of new technology. Alternatively, in return for higher wages or better working conditions, unions might *offer* no-strike agreements (or an informal promise not to take industrial action), increased productivity, reductions in the workforce, or long-term deals over pay.

In turn, employers might threaten employees with plant closure, lock-outs, redundancies or the employment of non-union labour. Alternatively, in return for lower wage increases, they might offer various 'perks' such as productivity bonuses, profit-sharing schemes, better working conditions, more overtime, better holidays or security of employment.

Strikes, lock-outs and other forms of industrial action impose costs on both unions and firms. Unions lose pay. Firms lose revenue. It is usually in both sides' interests, therefore, to settle by negotiation. Nevertheless to gain the maximum advantage, each side must persuade the other that it will carry out its threats if pushed.

The approach described so far has essentially been one of confrontation. The alternative is for both sides to concentrate on increasing the total net income of the firm by co-operating on ways to increase efficiency or the quality of the product. This approach is more likely when unions and management have built up an atmosphere of trust over time.

The role of government in collective bargaining

The government can influence the outcome of collective bargaining in a number of ways. One is to try to set an example. It may take a tough line in resisting wage demands by public-sector workers, hoping thereby to persuade employers in the private sector to do likewise.

Alternatively, it could act as an arbitrator. Past governments have attempted to mediate in pay disputes that they felt were damaging to the economy. 'Beer and sandwiches at No. 10 Downing Street' for the two sides in a dispute were not uncommon during the Labour government of the 1960s. More formally, the government can set up arbitration or conciliation machinery. For example, the Advisory, Conciliation and Arbitration Service (ACAS) conciliates in over 1000 disputes each year. It also provides, on request by both sides, an arbitration service, where its findings will be binding.

Another approach is to use legislation. The government could pass laws that restrict the behaviour of employers or unions. It could pass laws that set a minimum wage rate (see Box 5.4), or prevent discrimination against workers on various grounds. Similarly, it could pass laws that curtail the power of unions. The UK Conservative governments between 1979 and 1997 put considerable emphasis on reducing the power of trade unions and making labour markets more 'flexible'. Several Acts of Parliament were passed. These included the following measures:

■ Employees were given the right to join any union or not to join a union at all. This effectively ended closed-shop agreements.

Definitions

Picketing
Where people on strike gather at the entrance to the firm and attempt to dissuade workers or delivery vehicles from entering.

Working to rule
Where union members are instructed to stick to the letter of their job description and to refuse to take on any extra duties.

Lock-out
Where workers are (temporarily) laid off until they are prepared to agree to the firm's conditions.

Closed shop
Where a firm agrees to employ only members of a recognised union.

Ke
Ide
8
p4

- Secret postal ballots of the union membership were made mandatory for the operation of a political fund, the election of senior union officials, and strikes and other official industrial action.
- Political strikes, sympathy action and action against other non-unionised companies were made illegal.
- Lawful action was confined to that against workers' own direct employers, even to their own particular place of work. All secondary action was made unlawful.
- It was made unlawful for employers to penalise workers for choosing to join or refusing to join a trade union. It was also made unlawful for employers to deny employment on the grounds that an applicant does not belong to a union.

The effect of these measures was considerably to weaken the power of trade unions in the UK.

The efficiency wage hypothesis

We have seen that a union may be able to force an employer to pay a wage above the market-clearing rate. But it may well be in employers' interests to do so, even in non-unionised sectors.

One explanation for this phenomenon is the efficiency wage hypothesis. This states that the productivity of workers rises as the wage rate rises. As a result, employers are frequently prepared to offer wage rates above the market-clearing level, attempting to balance increased wage costs against gains in productivity. But why may higher wage rates lead to higher productivity? Several explanations have been advanced.

Less 'shirking'.   In many jobs it is difficult to monitor the effort that individuals put into their work. Workers may thus get away with shirking or careless behaviour. The business could attempt to reduce shirking by imposing a series of sanctions, the most serious of which would be dismissal. The greater the wage rate currently received, the greater will be the cost to the individual of dismissal, and the less likely it is, therefore, that workers will shirk. The business will benefit not only from the additional output, but also from a reduction in the costs of having to monitor workers' performance. As a consequence, the efficiency wage rate for the business will lie above the market-determined wage rate.

Reduced labour turnover.   If workers receive on-the-job training or retraining, then to lose a worker once the training has been completed is a significant cost to the business. Labour turnover, and hence its associated costs, can be reduced by paying a wage above the market-clearing rate. By paying such a wage rate, the business is seeking a degree of loyalty from its employees.

Self-selection.   A high wage rate will tend to attract the most productive workers. As such, it acts as a form of selection device, reducing the costs to the business of employing workers of lower quality.

Morale.   A simple reason for offering wage rates above the market-clearing level is to motivate the workforce – to create the feeling that the firm is a 'good' employer that cares about its employees. As a consequence, workers might be more industrious and more willing to accept the introduction of new technology (with the re-organisation that it involves).

Definitions

Secondary action
Industrial action taken against a firm not directly involved in the dispute.

Efficiency wage hypothesis
The hypothesis that the productivity of workers is affected by the wage rate that they receive.

Efficiency wage rate
The profit-maximising wage rate for the firm after taking into account the effects of wage rates on worker motivation, turnover and recruitment.

Key Idea 15 p126

Key Idea 4 p26

Box 5.2

Flexible labour markets

New work practices for old?

The last two decades have seen sweeping changes in the ways that firms organise their workforces. Two world recessions combined with rapid changes in technology have led many firms to question the wisdom of appointing workers on a permanent basis to specific jobs. Instead, they want to have the greatest flexibility possible to respond to new situations. If demand falls, they want to be able to 'shed' labour without facing large redundancy costs. If demand rises, they want rapid access to additional labour supplies. If technology changes, say with the introduction of new computerised processes, they want to have the flexibility to move workers around, or to take on new workers in some areas and lose workers in others.

What many firms seek, therefore, is flexibility in employing and allocating labour. What countries are experiencing is an increasingly flexible labour market, as workers and employment agencies respond to the new 'flexible firm'.

There are three main types of flexibility in the use of labour:

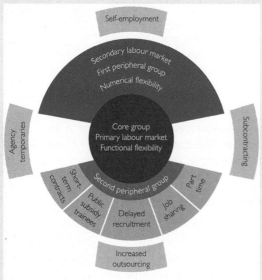

Source: Institute of Manpower Studies (1984).

The flexible firm

Functional flexibility. This is where an employer is able to transfer labour between different tasks within the production process. It contrasts with traditional forms of organisation where people were employed to do a specific job, and then stuck to it. A functionally flexible labour force will tend to be multi-skilled and relatively highly trained.

Numerical flexibility. This is where the firm is able to adjust the size and composition of its workforce according to changing market conditions. To achieve this, the firm is likely to employ a large proportion of its labour on a part-time or casual basis, or even subcontract out specialist requirements, rather than employing such labour skills itself.

Financial flexibility. This is where the firm has flexibility in its wage costs. In large part it is a result of functional and numerical flexibility. Financial flexibility can be achieved by rewarding individual effort and productivity rather than paying a given rate for a particular job. Such rates of pay are increasingly negotiated at the local level rather than being nationally set. The result is not only a widening of pay differentials between skilled and unskilled workers, but also growing differentials in pay between workers within the same industry but in different parts of the country.

The diagram shows how these three forms of flexibility are reflected in the organisation of a flexible firm, an organisation quite different from that of the traditional firm. The most significant difference is that the labour force is segmented. The core group, drawn from the *primary labour market*, will be composed of *functionally* flexible workers, who have relatively secure employment and are generally on full-time permanent contracts. Such workers will be relatively well paid and receive wages reflecting their scarce skills.

The periphery, drawn from the *secondary labour market*, is more fragmented than the core, and can be subdivided into a first and a second peripheral group.

The first peripheral group is composed of workers with a lower level of skill than those in the core – skills that tend to be general rather than firm specific. Thus workers in the first peripheral group can usually be drawn from the external labour market. Such workers may be employed on full-time contracts, but they will generally face less secure employment than those workers in the core.

The business gains a greater level of numerical flexibility by drawing labour from the second peripheral group. Here workers are employed on a variety of short-term, part-time contracts, often through a recruitment agency. Some of these workers may be working from home, or online from another country, such as India, where wage rates are much lower. Workers in the second peripheral group have little job security.

As well as being able to supplement the level of labour in the first peripheral group, the second periphery can also provide high-level specialist skills that supplement the core. In this instance the business can subcontract or hire self-employed labour, minimising its commitment to such workers. The business thereby gains both functional and numerical flexibility simultaneously.

The Japanese model

The application of new flexible working patterns is becoming more prevalent in businesses in the UK and elsewhere in Europe, and in North America. In Japan, the practice of flexibility has been part of the business way of life for many years and was crucial in shaping the country's economic success in the 1970s and 1980s. In fact we now talk of a Japanese model of business organisation, which many of its competitors seek to emulate.

The model is based around four principles:

■ Total quality management (TQM). This involves all employees working towards continuously improv-ing all aspects of quality, both of the finished product and of methods of production.

■ Elimination of waste. According to the 'just-in-time' (JIT) principle, businesses should take delivery of just sufficient quantities of raw materials and parts, at the right time and place. Stocks are kept to a minimum and hence the whole system of production runs with little, if any, slack. For example, supermarkets today have smaller storerooms relative to the total shopping area than they did in the past, and take more frequent deliveries.

■ A belief in the superiority of teamwork in the core group. Collective effort is a vital element in Japanese working practices. Teamwork is seen not only to enhance individual performance, but also to involve the individual in the running of the business and thus to create a sense of commitment.

■ The use of functional and numerical flexibility within Japanese business is widely practised. Both are seen as vital components in maintaining high levels of productivity.

The principles of this model are now widely accepted as being important in creating and maintaining a competitive business in a competitive marketplace.

Within the EU, the UK has been one of the most successful in cutting unemployment and creating jobs. Much of this success has been attributed to increased labour market flexibility. As a result, other EU countries, such as Italy and Germany, are seeking to emulate many of the measures the UK has adopted.

1. Is a flexible firm more likely or less likely to employ workers up to the point where their $MRP = MC_L$?
2. How is the advent of flexible firms likely to alter the gender balance of employment and unemployment?
3. What are the dangers of adopting a 'just-in-time' approach to managing production?

The paying of efficiency wages above the market-clearing wage will depend upon the type of work involved. Workers who occupy skilled positions, especially where the business has invested time in their training (thus making them costly to replace) are likely to receive efficiency wages considerably above the market wage. By contrast, workers in unskilled positions, where shirking can be easily monitored, where little training takes place and where workers can be easily replaced, are unlikely to command an 'efficiency wage premium'. In such situations, rather than keeping wage rates high, the business will probably try to pay as little as possible.

Recap

1. Where a firm has monopoly power in employing labour, it is known as a 'monopsonist'. Such a firm will employ workers to the point where $MRP_L = MC_L$. Since the wage is below MC_L, the monopsonist, other things being equal, will employ fewer workers at a lower wage than would be employed in a perfectly competitive labour market.

2. If a union has monopoly power, its power to raise wages will be limited if the employer operates under perfect or monopolistic competition in the goods market. A rise in wage rates will force the employer to cut back on employment, unless there is a corresponding rise in productivity.

3. In a situation of bilateral monopoly (where a monopoly union faces a monopsony employer) the union may have considerable scope to raise wage rates above the monopsony level. There is no unique equilibrium wage. The wage rate will depend on the outcome of a process of collective bargaining between union and management.

4. Collective bargaining is the process by which employers and unions negotiate wage levels and the terms and conditions of employment. Both sides can use threats and promises to determine the outcome of the negotiating process. The success of such threats and promises depends upon factors such as the power of the union or the employer; attitudes and the determination to win; scope for compromise; negotiating skills; information; and the role of government.

5. The efficiency wage hypothesis states that a firm might pay above the market-clearing wage rate so as to: reduce shirking; reduce labour turnover; improve the quality of labour recruited; and stimulate worker morale. The level of efficiency wage rates will largely be determined by the types of job workers do, and the level and scarcity of the skills they possess.

5.4   Causes of inequality

Why are some people rich and others poor?

Inequality in the UK

Figure 5.9 shows the distribution of income in the UK (from all sources). The population is placed into five equal-sized groups (or 'quintiles') of households, from the poorest 20 per cent of households up to the richest 20 per cent. The following points can be drawn from these statistics:

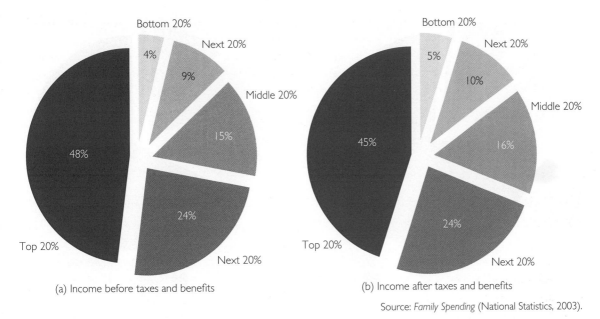

(a) Income before taxes and benefits

(b) Income after taxes and benefits

Source: *Family Spending* (National Statistics, 2003).

Figure 5.9
Size distribution of
UK income by
quintile group of
households: 2001/2

- In 2001/2, the richest 20 per cent of households earned 48 per cent of national income, and even after the deduction of taxes their share was still 45 per cent.
- The poorest 20 per cent, by contrast, earned a mere 4 per cent of national income, and even after the receipt of benefits, this had risen to only 5 per cent.

Inequality has grown dramatically in the UK and many other countries in recent years. Between 1977 and 2001/2, the post-tax-and-benefits share of UK national income of the poorest 40 per cent of households fell from 23 per cent to 15 per cent; while the share of the top 20 per cent grew from 37 per cent to 45 per cent.

Distribution of income by source

Figure 5.10 shows the sources of household incomes in the UK. Wages and salaries constitute by far the largest element. However, their share fell from 77 per cent to 69 per cent of national income between 1970 and 2001/2. Conversely, the share coming from social security benefits and pensions rose from 12 per cent to 18 per cent, reflecting the higher level of unemployment in 2002 compared with 1970 and the growing proportion of the population past retirement age.

In contrast to wages and salaries, investment income (dividends, interest and rent) accounts for a very small percentage of household income – a mere 4 per cent in 2001/2.

With the growth of small businesses and the increased numbers of people being 'employed' on a freelance basis, so the proportion of incomes coming from self-employment has grown. It rose from 6 per cent in 1980 to 9 per cent in 2001/2.

Distribution of wages and salaries by occupation

The major cause of differences in incomes between individuals in employment is the differences in wages and salaries between different occupations. Differences in full-time wages and salaries are illustrated in Figure 5.11. This shows the average

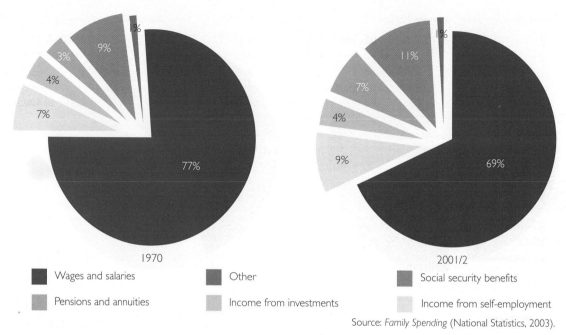

1970

2001/2

■ Wages and salaries   ■ Other   ■ Social security benefits

■ Pensions and annuities   ■ Income from investments   ☐ Income from self-employment

Source: *Family Spending* (National Statistics, 2003).

Figure 5.10

Sources of UK household income as a percentage of gross household income

gross weekly earnings of full-time adult male workers in selected occupations in 2002. As can be seen, there are considerable differences in earnings between different occupations.

About 6 per cent of the earnings in Figure 5.11 come from overtime (on average about $2^{1}/_{2}$ hours per week). The amount of overtime worked differs markedly, however, between occupations. Thus it is not just the basic hourly wage rate that explains differences in earnings from one occupation to another, but also the number of hours worked and the overtime rate.

Since the late 1970s, wage differentials have widened. Part of the explanation lies in a shift in the demand for labour. Many firms have adopted new techniques that require a more highly educated workforce. Wage rates in some of these skilled occupations have increased substantially.

At the same time there has been a decline in the number of unskilled jobs in industry, and along with it, a decline in the power of unions to represent such people. Where low-skilled jobs remain, there is intense pressure on employers to reduce wage costs if they are competing with companies based in developing countries, where wage rates are much lower.

As prospects for the unskilled decline in industry, so people with few qualifications increasingly compete for low-paid service-sector jobs (e.g. in supermarkets, fast-food outlets and call centres). The growth in people seeking part-time work has also kept wage rates down in this sector.

> **Pause for thought**
>
> If fringe benefits (such as long holidays, company cars, free clothing/uniforms, travel allowances and health insurance) were included, do you think the level of inequality would increase or decrease? Explain why.

Distribution of wages and salaries by sex

Box 5.3 looks at some of the aspects of income inequality between the sexes. Figure 5.12 gives examples of average gross weekly earnings of full-time adult female

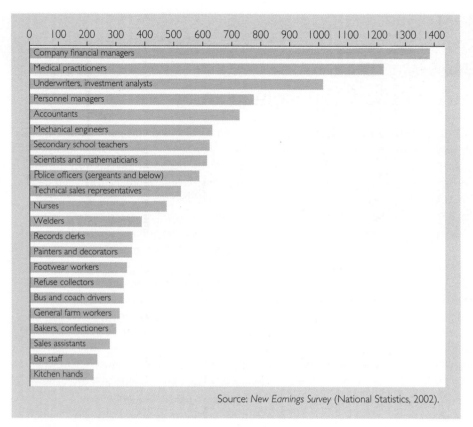

Figure 5.11
Average gross weekly earnings of UK full-time adult male employees (£): selected occupations: 2002

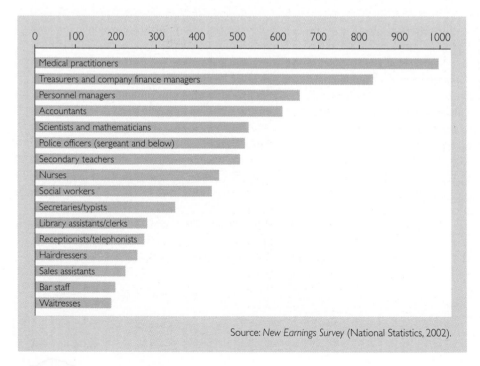

Figure 5.12
Average gross weekly earnings of full-time adult female employees (£): selected occupations: 2002

Box 5.3

Equal pay for equal work?

Wage inequalities between women and men

One of the key characteristics shown in Table (a) below is that female gross hourly earnings relative to male gross hourly earnings increased substantially during the early 1970s. Having peaked at around 74 per cent in the late 1970s, they remained at about that level for the next ten years. They then rose again to just above 80 per cent by the early 2000s.

The inequality between male and female earnings can in part be explained by the fact that men and women are occupationally segregated. As women pre-dominate in poorly paid occupations, the difference in earnings is somewhat to be expected. But if you consider Table (b), you can see that quite substantial earning differentials persist within particular occupations.

So why has this inequality persisted? There are a number of possible reasons:

■ The marginal productivity of labour in typically female occupations may be lower than in typically male occupations. This may in part be due to simple questions of physical strength. More often, however, it is due to the fact that women tend to work in more labour-intensive occupations. If there is less capital equipment per female worker than there is per male worker, then it would be expected that the marginal product of a woman would be less than that of a man.

■ Many women take career breaks to have children. For this reason, employers are sometimes more willing to invest money in training men (thereby increasing their marginal productivity), and more willing to promote men.

■ Women tend to be less geographically mobile than men. If social norms are such that the man's job is seen as somehow more 'important' than the woman's, then a couple will often move if that is necessary for the man to get promotion. The woman, however, will have to settle for whatever job she can get in the same locality as her partner.

■ A smaller proportion of women workers are members of unions than men. Even when they are members of unions, these are often in jobs where unions are weak (e.g. clothing industry workers, shop assistants and secretaries).

■ Part-time workers (mainly women) have less bargaining power, less influence and less chance of obtaining promotion.

■ Custom and practice. Despite equal pay legislation, many jobs done wholly or mainly by women continue to be low paid, irrespective of questions of productivity.

■ Prejudice. Some employers may prefer to give senior posts to men on grounds purely of sexual prejudice. This is very difficult to legislate against when the employer can simply claim that the 'better' person was given the job.

(a) Average gross hourly earnings, excluding the effects of overtime, for full-time UK employees, aged 18 and over: 1970–2002 (pence per hour)

	1970	1974	1978	1982	1986	1988	1990	1992	1994	1996	1998	2000	2002
Men	67	105	200	355	482	573	689	810	865	939	1026	1126	1259
Women	42	71	148	262	358	429	528	638	688	750	822	913	1022
Differential	25	34	52	93	124	144	161	172	177	189	204	213	237
Women's earnings as a % of men's	63.1	67.4	73.5	73.9	74.3	75.0	76.6	78.8	79.5	79.9	80.1	81.1	81.2

Source: *New Earnings Survey* (National Statistics, 2002).

(b) Average gross hourly earnings, excluding the effects of overtime, for selected occupations, full-time UK employees on adult rates: 2002

Occupation	Men	Women	Women's earnings as a % of men's
	(£ per hour)		
Nurses	12.13	11.89	98.0
Bar staff	5.40	5.07	93.9
Social workers	12.38	11.58	93.5
Police officers (sergeant and below)	14.74	13.30	90.2
Secondary school teachers	19.32	17.37	89.9
Laboratory technicians	10.64	9.46	88.9
Legal professionals	26.77	22.78	85.1
Sales assistants	6.69	5.67	84.8
Personnel managers	20.26	17.07	84.3
Chefs/cooks	7.34	6.13	83.5
Medical practitioners	29.39	23.76	80.8
Computer operators	10.01	7.58	75.7
Assemblers and lineworkers	8.46	6.35	75.1
All occupations	12.59	10.22	81.2
Average gross weekly pay	513.80	383.40	74.6
Average weekly hours worked (incl. overtime)	40.9	37.5	
Average weekly overtime	2.4	0.7	

Source: *New Earnings Survey* (National Statistics, 2002).

Which of the above reasons could be counted as economically 'irrational' (i.e. paying different wage rates to women and men for other than purely economic reasons)? Certainly the last two would classify. Paying different wage rates on these grounds would *not* be in the profit interests of the employer.

Some of the others, however, are more difficult to classify. The causes of the inequality in wage rates may be traced back beyond the workplace: perhaps to the educational system, or to a culture that discourages women from being so aggressive in seeking promotion or 'self-advertisement' or to the legal right to maternity but not paternity leave. Even if it is a manifestation of profit-maximising behaviour by employers that women in some circumstances are paid less than their male counterparts (and is thus not an example of 'irrationality'), the reason why it is more profitable for employers to pay men more than women may indeed reflect discrimination elsewhere or at some other point in time.

? 1. If we were to look at weekly rather than hourly pay and included the effects of overtime, what do you think would happen to the pay differentials in Table (a)?

2. In Table (b), which of the occupations have a largely female workforce?

3. If employers were forced to give genuinely equal pay for equal work, how would this affect the employment of women and men? What would determine the magnitude of these effects?

4. What measures could a government introduce to increase the number of women getting higher-paid jobs?

workers in 2002. The average for all occupations was £383. This compares with £514 for men. There are three important factors to note:

■ Women are paid less than men in the same occupations. You will see this if you compare some of the occupations in Figure 5.12 with the same ones in Figure 5.11.
■ Women tend to be employed in lower-paid occupations than men.
■ Women do much less overtime than men (on average 0.7 hours per week, compared with 2.4 for men).

Causes of inequality

We turn now to identify the major causes of inequality. The problem has many dimensions and there are many factors that determine the pattern and depth of inequality. It is thus wrong to try to look for a single cause, or even the major one. What follows then is a list of the possible determinants of inequality:

■ Differences in ability. People differ in strength, intelligence, dexterity, etc. Some of these differences are innate and some are acquired through the process of 'socialisation' – education, home environment, peer group, etc.
■ Differences in attitude. Some people are adventurous, willing to take risks, willing to move for better jobs, keen to push themselves forward. Others are much more cautious.
■ Differences in qualifications. These are reflections of a number of things: ability, attitudes towards study, access to educational establishments, the quality of tuition, attitudes and income of parents, etc.

The above three sets of factors will cause differences in people's marginal productivity and hence differences in wage rates. Wages will also reflect the following:

■ Differences in hours worked. Some people do a full-time job plus overtime, or a second job; others work only part time.
■ Differences in the pleasantness/unpleasantness of jobs. Other things being equal, unpleasant, arduous or dangerous jobs will need to pay higher wage rates.
■ Differences in power. Monopoly power in the supply of labour or goods, and monopsony power in the demand for labour, are unequally distributed in the economy.
■ Differences in the demand for goods. Workers employed in expanding industries will tend to have a higher marginal revenue product because their output has a higher market value.
■ Discrimination, whether by race, sex, age, social background, etc.

Inequality is not just the result of differences in wages. It is also caused by the following:

■ Differences in household composition. Other things being equal, the more dependants there are in a household, the lower the income will be *per member* of that household. Figure 5.13 gives an extreme example of this. It shows the

Key Idea 11 p71

Key Idea 14 p118

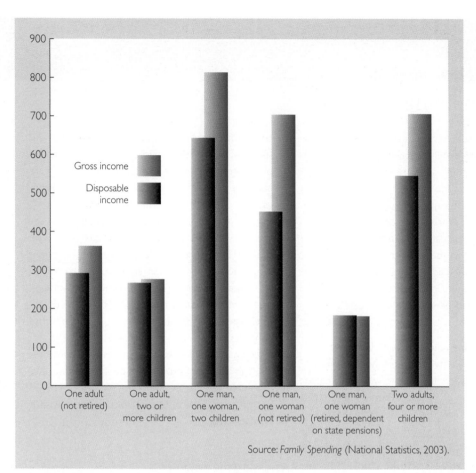

Figure 5.13
Weekly income for
different types of UK
household (£):
2001/2

Source: *Family Spending* (National Statistics, 2003).

average household income in the UK in 2001/2 of four different categories of household.

Households with two adults and four or more children had a lower average income than households with two adults and just two children. This means that they had a very much lower income *per member* of the household. There is a twin problem for many large households. Not only may there be relatively more children and old-age dependants, but also the total household income will be reduced if one of the adults stays at home to look after the family, or works only part time.

■ Inequality of wealth. People with wealth are able to obtain an income other than from their own labour (e.g. from rent or dividends on shares). The greater the inequality of wealth, the greater is the inequality of income likely to be.

■ Degree of government support. The greater the support for the poor, the less will be the level of inequality in the economy.

■ Unemployment. This has been one of the major causes of poverty and hence inequality in recent years.

Key
idea

8
p45

Pause for thought   ‖‖‖

Which of these causes of inequality are reflected in differences in the marginal revenue product of labour?

Box 5.4

Minimum wage legislation

A way of helping the poor?

It is a serious national evil that any class of His Majesty's subjects should receive less than a living wage in return for their utmost exertions. It was formerly supposed that the workings of the laws of supply and demand would naturally regulate or eliminate that evil, but whereas in what we call 'sweated trades' you have no parity of bargaining between employers and employed, when the good employer is continually undercut by the bad, and the bad again by the worse, there you have not a condition of progress, but of progressive degeneration.

Winston Churchill (1909)

Key Idea

8
p45

One way of helping to relieve poverty is for the government to institute a legal minimum hourly wage. A form of minimum-wage legislation was introduced in the UK as long ago as 1909 by Winston Churchill, who was at the time President of the Board of Trade in the Liberal government. This involved the setting up of wages councils. These were independent bodies representing workers in low-pay industries that were poorly unionised. The councils set legally enforceable minimum hourly rates of pay for their respective industries.

In 1993, the Conservative government of the day, following its philosophy of free-market economics, announced the abolition of the wages councils. As a result, the UK became one of the few industrial countries with no legally guaranteed minimum rates of pay. That was to change again, however, when the Labour government introduced a new national minimum wage in April 1999.

The call for a minimum wage had grown stronger as the number of low-paid workers within the UK had increased. There were many people working as cleaners, kitchen hands, garment workers, security guards and shop assistants, who were receiving pittance rates of pay, sometimes less than £2 per hour. There were several factors explaining the growth in the size of the low-pay sector.

■ *Unemployment.* Very high rates of unemployment since the early 1980s had shifted the balance of power from workers to employers. Employers were able to force many wage rates downwards, especially of unskilled and semi-skilled workers.

■ *Growth in part-time employment.* Changes in the structure of the UK economy, in particular the growth in the service sector and the growing proportion of women seeking work, had led to an increase in part-time employment, with many part-time workers not receiving the same rights, privileges and hourly pay as their full-time equivalents.

■ *Changes in labour laws.* The abolition of the wages councils and the introduction of various new laws to reduce the power of labour (see pages 178–9) had taken away what little protection there was for low-paid workers.

Assessing the arguments

The principal argument against imposing a national minimum wage concerns its impact on employment. Many fear that unemployment will rise as employers respond to higher wage costs by shedding labour. If you raise wage rates above the equilibrium level, there will be surplus labour: i.e. unemployment (see Figure 5.8 on page 176). However, the impact of a national minimum wage on employment is not so simple.

In the case of a firm operating in *competitive* labour and goods markets, the demand for low-skilled workers is relatively wage sensitive. Any rise in wages paid by this employer would lead to a large fall in its sales and hence in employment. But given that *all* firms face the minimum wage, individual employers are more able to pass on higher wages in higher prices, knowing that their competitors are doing the same.

When employers have a degree of *monopsony* power, however, it is not even certain that they would *want* to reduce employment. Remember what we argued in the diagram in Box 5.1 (on page 177) when we were examining the effects of unions driving up wages. The argument is the same with a minimum wage. The minimum wage can be as high as W_2 and the firm will still want to employ as many workers as at W_2. The point is that the firm can no longer drive down the wage rate by employing fewer workers, so the incentive to cut its workforce has been removed. Indeed, if the minimum wage rate were above W_1 but below W_2, the firm would now want to employ *more* workers (where the minimum wage rate (= MC_L) is equal to the MRP_L). What is effectively happening is that the minimum wage is redistributing the firm's income from profits to wages.

In the long run, the effect on unemployment will depend on the extent to which the higher wages are compensated by higher labour productivity. In several EU countries, where minimum wages have been in force for many years, unemployment has, until the mid-1990s, been no higher than in the UK, but investment and labour productivity are generally higher.

Modest rises in the minimum wage seem to have little if any effect on unemployment. The issue, then, seems to be how *high* can the minimum wage be set before unemployment begins to rise?

The minimum wage in the UK

The minimum wage was introduced in April 1999 at a rate of £3.60 per hour. There was a lower 'development rate' of £3.00 for those between 18 and 21. The government had sought advice from the Low Pay Commission, which argued that a £3.60 rate would 'offer real benefits to the low paid, while avoiding unnecessary risks to business and jobs'. The minimum wage has been raised in October each year: to £3.70

in 2000, £4.10 in 2001, £4.20 in 2002, £4.50 in 2003 and £4.85 in 2004, with equivalent rises in the development rate (£4.10 in 2004).

Some 1.3 million workers benefit from the minimum wage and there have been virtually no adverse effects on unemployment. The main beneficiaries have been women – the majority of whom work part time and many of whom are lone parents – and people from ethnic minorities. Even the Conservative Party, previously staunch opponents of a minimum wage, has dropped its opposition.

The biggest weakness of minimum wages as a means of relieving poverty is that they only affect the employed. One of the main causes of poverty is unemployment. Clearly the unemployed do not benefit from the minimum wage.

Another cause of poverty is a large number of dependants in a family. If there is only one income earner, he or she may be paid above the minimum wage and yet the family could be very poor. By contrast, many of those who have been helped by the minimum wages are second income earners in a family.

These are not arguments against minimum wages. They merely suggest that minimum wages cannot be the sole answer to poverty.

? 1. If an increase in wage rates for the low paid led to their being more motivated, how would this affect the marginal revenue product and the demand for such workers? What implications does your answer have for the effect on employment in such cases? (See page 179 on the efficiency wage hypothesis.)

2. If minimum wages encourage employers to substitute machines for workers, will this necessarily lead to higher long-term unemployment in (a) that industry and (b) the economy in general?

Recap

1. Wages and salaries constitute by far the largest source of income, and thus inequality can be explained mainly in terms of differences in wages and salaries. These differences reflect differences in the productivity of workers, consumer demand, power and discrimination.

2. Apart from differences in wages and salaries between occupations, other determinants of income inequality include differences in household composition, inequality of wealth, unemployment and the level of government benefits.

5.5   The redistribution of income

How can income be redistributed from rich to poor? What will be the effects of doing so?

In this section we will look at policies to redistribute incomes more equally, and in particular we will focus on the use of government social security benefits and taxation. In doing so, we will be focusing on the economic and social goal of 'equity'.

Ke Ide 8 p45

> **Equity** is where income is distributed in a way that is considered to be fair or just. Note that an equitable distribution is not the same as a totally equal distribution and that different people have different views on what is equitable.
>
> Key Idea 17

Definitions

Progressive tax
A tax whose average rate with respect to income rises as income rises.

Regressive tax
A tax whose average rate with respect to income falls as income rises.

Proportional tax
A tax whose average rate with respect to income stays the same as income rises.

Taxation

If taxes are to be used as a means of achieving greater equality, the rich must be taxed proportionately more than the poor. The degree of redistribution will depend on the degree of 'progressiveness' of the tax. In this context, taxes may be classified as follows:

■ Progressive tax. As people's income (Y) rises, the percentage of their income paid in the tax (T) rises. In other words, the average rate of tax (T/Y) rises. Income taxes are progressive (but much less progressive in the UK than they used to be).

■ Regressive tax. As people's income rises, the percentage of their income paid in the tax falls: T/Y falls. An extreme form of regressive tax is a lump-sum tax. This is levied at a fixed *amount* (not rate) irrespective of income. The 'poll tax', introduced in Scotland in 1989 and England in 1990 as the new form of local taxation, was an example of such a tax. But it proved massively unpopular with the electorate, and was replaced by the 'council tax' (based on property values) in 1993.

■ Proportional tax. As people's income rises, the percentage of their income paid in the tax stays the same: T/Y is constant.

The more progressive a tax, the more it will redistribute incomes away from the rich. Regressive taxes will have the opposite effect, since they tax the rich proportionately less than the poor.

Problems with using taxes to redistribute incomes

Assuming that it is desirable to redistribute incomes from rich to poor, how successfully can taxes accomplish this, and at what economic cost?

Taxation takes away income. It can thus reduce the incomes of the rich. But no taxes, however progressive, can *increase* the incomes of the poor. This will require subsidies (i.e. benefits).

But what about tax cuts? Can bigger tax cuts not be given to the poor? This is possible only if the poor are already paying taxes in the first place. Take the two cases of income tax and taxes on goods and services.

■ Income tax. If the government cuts income tax, then anyone currently paying it will benefit. A cut in tax *rates* will give proportionately more to the rich, since they have a larger proportion of taxable income relative to total income. An increase in personal *allowances*, on the other hand, will give the same *absolute* amount to everyone above the new tax threshold. This will therefore represent a smaller proportionate gain to the rich. In either case, however, there will be no gain at all to those people below the tax threshold. They paid no income tax in the first place. These poorest of all people therefore gain nothing at all from income tax cuts.

■ Taxes on goods and services. Since taxes such as VAT and excise duties on alcoholic drinks, tobacco, petrol and gambling are generally regressive, any cut in their rate will benefit the poor proportionately more than the rich. A more dramatic effect would be obtained by cutting the rate most on those goods consumed relatively more by the poor (e.g. on domestic fuel).

The government may not wish to cut the overall level of taxation, given its expenditure commitments. In this case, it can switch the burden of taxes from regressive to progressive taxes: it could cut taxes on certain goods and services and raise income taxes and taxes on company profits. That way, at least some benefit is gained by the very poor.

Taxation and incentives

One of the major justifications given by the Conservative governments after 1979 for *cutting* both the basic and higher rates of income tax was that it increased the incentive to work.

This whole question of incentives is highly charged politically. If the Conservatives are correct, then there is a trade-off between output and equity. High and progressive income taxes can lead to a more equal distribution of income, but a smaller national output. Alternatively, by cutting taxes there will be a bigger national output, but less equally divided. If many on the political left are correct, however, by raising income taxes we can have both a more equal society and a *bigger* national output: there is no trade-off.

The key to analysing these arguments is to distinguish between the *income effect* and the *substitution effect* of raising taxes. Raising income tax does two things.

Key
Idea

4
p26

Key
Idea

2
p8

Key
Idea

8
p45

Definitions

Income effect of a tax rise
Tax increases reduce people's incomes and thus encourage people to work more.

Substitution effect of a tax rise
Tax increases reduce the opportunity cost of leisure and thus encourage people to work less.

Means-tested benefits
Benefits whose amount depends on the recipient's income or assets.

Universal benefits
Benefits paid to everyone in a certain category irrespective of their income or assets.

■ It reduces disposable incomes. People therefore are encouraged to work *more* in an attempt to maintain their consumption of goods and services. This is called the income effect. 'I have to work more to make up for the higher taxes', a person might say.

■ It reduces the opportunity cost of leisure. Since higher income taxes reduce take-home pay, an extra hour taken in leisure now involves a smaller sacrifice in consumption. Thus people may substitute leisure for consumption, and work less. This is called the substitution effect. 'What is the point of doing overtime', another person might say, 'if so much of the overtime pay is going in taxes?'

The relative size of the income and substitution effects is likely to differ for different types of people. For example, the *income* effect is likely to dominate for those people with a substantial proportion of long-term commitments: for example, people with families, with mortgages and other debts. Such people may feel forced to work more to maintain their disposable income. Clearly for such people, higher taxes are *not* a disincentive to work. The income effect is also likely to be relatively large for people on higher incomes, for whom an increase in tax rates represents a substantial cut in income.

The *substitution* effect is likely to dominate for those with few commitments: those whose families have left home, the single, and second income earners in families where that second income is not relied on for 'essential' consumption.

Although high income earners may work more when there is a tax *rise*, they may still be discouraged by a steeply progressive tax *structure*. If they have to pay very high marginal rates of tax, it may simply not be worth their while seeking promotion or working harder.

One final point should be stressed. For many people there is no choice in the amount they work. The job they do dictates the number of hours worked, irrespective of changes in taxation.

Pause for thought

How will tax cuts affect the willingness of women with employed partners to return to paid work after having brought up a family? (Clue: think about the size of the income and substitution effects.)

Benefits

Benefits can be either cash benefits or benefits in kind.

Cash benefits

Means-tested benefits. Means-tested benefits are available only to those whose income (and savings in some instances) fall below a certain level. In order to obtain such benefits, therefore, people must apply for them and declare their personal circumstances to the authorities.

The benefits could be given as grants or merely as loans. They could be provided as general income support or for the meeting of specific needs, such as rents, fuel bills and household items.

Universal benefits. Universal benefits are those that everyone is entitled to, irrespective of their income, if they fall into a certain category. Examples include state pensions, and unemployment, sickness and invalidity benefits.

People who are working pay social security contributions (National Insurance Contributions in the UK), based on their earnings. When they retire, become unemployed or fall sick they are entitled to benefits (unemployment benefit is known as the jobseeker's allowance in the UK). In many countries, there is a time limit on unemployment benefits. After that, people have to accept whatever work is available or rely on a lower level of social security payments.

Benefits in kind

Individuals receive other forms of benefit from the state, not as direct monetary payments, but in the form of the provision of free or subsidised goods or services. These are known as benefits in kind. The two largest items in most countries are health care and education. They are very differently distributed, however. This difference can largely be explained on age grounds. Old people use a large proportion of health services, but virtually no education services.

Benefits in kind tend to be consumed roughly equally by the different income groups. Nevertheless they do have some equalising effect, since they represent a much larger proportion of poor people's income than rich people's. They still have a far smaller redistributive effect, however, than cash benefits.

Figure 5.14 shows the expenditure on social protection benefits in selected European countries. These include unemployment, sickness, invalidity, maternity, family, survivors' and housing benefits and state pensions. They are mainly cash benefits, but do include some benefits in kind. They exclude health and education. As you can see, the benefits vary significantly from one country to another. Part of the reason for this is that countries differ in their rates of unemployment and in the age structure of their population. Thus Ireland has the lowest percentage of people over 65 in the EU and the smallest share of benefits devoted to pensions. Despite this, however, the generosity and coverage of benefits varies considerably from country to country, reflecting, in part, the level of income per head.

Definition
Benefits in kind
Goods or services which the state provides directly to the recipient at no charge or at a subsidised price. Alternatively, the state can subsidise the private sector to provide them.

Benefits and the redistribution of income

Key idea

17
p192

It might seem that means-tested benefits are a much more efficient system of redistributing income from the rich to the poor: the money is directed to those most in need. With universal benefits, by contrast, many people may receive them who have little need for them. Do families with very high incomes need child benefit? Would it not be better for the government to redirect the money to those who are genuinely in need?

There are, however, serious problems in attempting to redistribute incomes by the use of means-tested benefits:

■ Not everyone entitled to means-tested benefits actually receives them. This may be due to a number of factors:
  – Ignorance of the benefits available. This in turn may be due to the complexities of the system.
  – Difficulties in applying for the benefits. People may give up rather than having to face difficult forms or long queues or harassed benefit office staff.
  – Reluctance to reveal personal circumstances.
  – The perception that the benefits are 'charity' and therefore demeaning.
  Thus some of the poorest families may receive no support.

Figure 5.14

Social protection benefits in various European countries

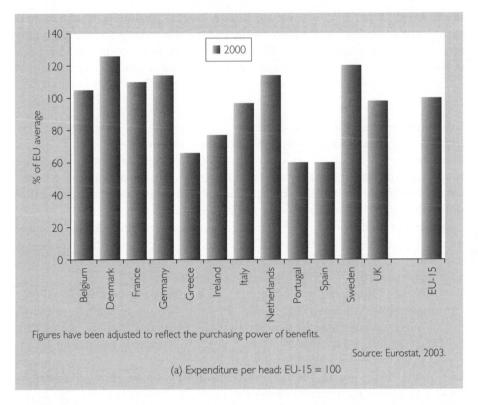

Figures have been adjusted to reflect the purchasing power of benefits.

Source: Eurostat, 2003.

(a) Expenditure per head: EU-15 = 100

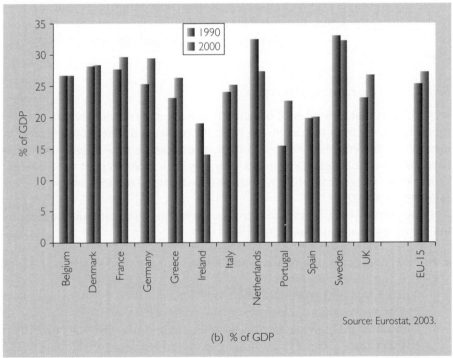

Source: Eurostat, 2003.

(b) % of GDP

- The levels of income above which people become ineligible for benefits may be set too low. Even if they were raised, there will always be some people just above these levels who will still find difficulties.
- Means tests based purely on *income* (or even universal benefits based on broad categories) ignore the very special needs of many poor people. A person earning £80 a week living in a small, well-appointed flat with a low rent will have less need of assistance than another person who also earns £80 per week but lives in a cold, draughty and damp house with large bills to meet. If means tests are to be fair, then *all* of a person's circumstances need to be taken into account.

The tax/benefit system and the problem of disincentives: the 'poverty trap'

When means-tested benefits are combined with a progressive income tax system, there can be a serious problem of disincentives. As poor people earn more money, so not only do they start paying income taxes and national insurance, but also they begin losing means-tested benefits. Theoretically, it is possible to have a marginal tax-plus-lost-benefit rate in excess of 100 per cent. In other words, for every extra £1 earned, taxes and lost benefits add up to more than £1. High marginal tax-plus-lost-benefit rates obviously act as a serious disincentive. What is the point of getting a job or trying to earn more money, if you end up earning little more or actually losing money?

This situation is known as the poverty trap. People are trapped on low incomes with no realistic means of bettering their position.

The problem of the poverty trap would be overcome by switching to a system of universal benefits unrelated to income. For example, *everyone* could receive a flat payment from the state fixed at a sufficiently high level to cover their basic needs. There would still be *some* disincentive, but this would be confined to an income effect: people would not have the same need to work if the state provided a basic income. But there would no longer be the disincentive to work caused by a result-ing *loss* of benefits (a substitution effect).

The big drawback with universal benefits, however, is their cost. If they were given to everyone and were large enough to help the poor, their cost would be enormous. Thus although the benefits themselves would not create much dis-incentive effect, the necessary taxation to fund them almost certainly would.

There is no ideal solution to this conundrum. On the one hand, the more narrowly benefits are targeted on the poor, the greater the problem of the poverty trap. On the other hand, the more widely they are spread, the greater the cost of providing any given level of support to individuals.

> **Definition**
>
> **Poverty trap**
> Where poor people are discouraged from working or getting a better job because any extra income they earn will be largely taken away in taxes and lost benefits.

> **Pause for thought**
>
> *Does the targeting of benefits to those in greatest need necessarily increase the poverty trap?*

Box 5.5 Case Studies and Applications

UK tax credits

An escape from the poverty trap?

Tax credits were introduced in the UK in 1999 in the form of working families tax credit, which was replaced in 2003 by working tax credit (WTC) and child tax credit (CTC). These credits are paid either as tax relief or as a cash benefit.

Working tax credit is designed for working people on low incomes. To be eligible for the basic amount (see the table), people without children must be aged 25 or over and work at least 30 hours per week. People with children must work at least 16 hours per week. Couples and lone parents receive an additional amount. There is a further addition for anyone with children who works at least 30 hours per week, or for couples who *jointly* work at least 30 hours per week. This is designed as an incentive for people to move from part-time to full-time work. Recipients of WTC also get paid 70 per cent of eligible childcare costs up to £135 for one child and £200 for two or more children. For each pound earned above a threshold amount, relief is reduced by 37p.

Child tax credit provides support to families with children, whether or not anyone in the family works. It is paid in addition to WTC and child benefit. There is a basic rate and an additional amount per child (see the table). Relief tapers off for incomes over a threshold amount.

Apart from targeting support at poorer families, these tax credits are intended to improve incentives to work, by reducing the poverty trap (see page 197). In other words, the aim is to reduce the financial penalties for parents working, by tapering off more slowly the rate at which benefits are lost. With a lost-benefit rate of 37 per cent, the combined marginal tax-plus-lost-benefit rate (the 'marginal deduction rate') is typically around 58 to 70 per cent, depending on a person's marginal rate of tax and other means-tested benefits received.

Although the introduction of these tax credits has reduced the typical marginal deduction rate for poor families, the rate is still very high. For many poor parents, therefore, the incentive to work is still relatively low.

There is another effect from reducing the rate at which benefit tapers off. Some benefit will now be available to slightly less poor families. Although this is good in terms of providing support for them, there is now more of a disincentive for parents in such families to work extra hours, or to take a better job, since the marginal deduction rate is now higher. In other words, although they are better off, they will take home less for each extra hour worked.

WTC and CTC illustrate the general problem of providing support to poor people which is affordable for taxpayers without creating disincentives to work. The more gently the support tapers off (and hence the less the disincentive to earn extra money), the more costly it is to finance.

? Economists sometimes refer to an 'unemployment trap'. People are discouraged from taking work in the first place. Explain how such a 'trap' arises. Does the working tax credit create an unemployment trap? What are the best ways of eliminating, or at least reducing, the unemployment trap?

WTC and CTC rates: 2003/4

Working tax credit (WTC)	Weekly amount (£)
Basic element	29.20
Addition for couples and lone parents	28.80
Addition for those working 30 hours or more	11.90
Income threshold (above which WTC is reduced)	97.00

Child tax credit (CTC)	Weekly amount (£)
Basic element	10.45
Additional amount per child	27.75
Income threshold (above which CTC is reduced)	253.76

Source: Inland Revenue.

1. Taxes can be categorised as progressive, regressive or proportional. Progressive taxes have the effect of reducing inequality. The more steeply progressive they are, the bigger the reduction in inequality.

2. Taxes on their own cannot increase the incomes of the poor. Cutting taxes, however, *can* help the poor if the cuts are carefully targeted.

3. Using taxes to redistribute incomes can cause disincentives. Raising taxes has two effects on the amount people wish to work. On the one hand, people will be encouraged to work more in order to maintain their incomes. This is the income effect. On the other hand, they will be encouraged to substitute leisure for income, since an hour's leisure now costs less in forgone income. This is the substitution effect. The relative size of the income and substitution effects will depend on the nature of the tax change. The substitution effect is more likely to outweigh the income effect for those with few commitments, for people just above the tax threshold of the newly raised tax and in cases where the highest rates of tax are increased.

4. Benefits can be cash benefits or benefits in kind. They can be universal or means tested. Universal benefits include child benefit, state pensions, unemployment benefits, and sickness and invalidity benefits. Benefits in kind include health care, education and free school meals.

5. Means-tested benefits can be specifically targeted to those in need and are thus more 'cost-effective'. However, there can be serious problems with such benefits, including: limited take-up, time-consuming procedures for claimants, some relatively needy people falling just outside the qualifying limit and inadequate account taken of *all* relevant circumstances affecting a person's needs.

6. The poverty trap occurs when the combination of increased taxes and reduced benefits removes the incentive for poor people to earn more. The more steeply progressive this combined system is at low incomes, the bigger the disincentive effect.

Questions

1. If a firm faces a shortage of workers with very specific skills, it may decide to undertake the necessary training itself. If, on the other hand, it faces a shortage of unskilled workers, it may well offer a small wage increase in order to obtain the extra labour. In the first case it is responding to an increase in demand for labour by attempting to shift the supply curve. In the second case it is merely allowing a movement along the supply curve. Use a demand and supply diagram to illustrate each case. Given that elasticity of supply is different in each case, do you think that these are the best policies for the firm to follow?

2. For what types of reason does the marginal revenue product differ between workers in different jobs?

3. Why, do you think, are some of the lowest-paid jobs the most unpleasant?

4. The wage rate a firm has to pay and the output it can produce vary with the number of workers as shown in the table below (all figures are hourly).
Assume that output sells at £2 per unit.
   (a) Copy the table and add additional rows for TC_L, MC_L, TRP_L and MRP_L. Put the figures for MC_L and MRP_L in the spaces between the columns.
   (b) How many workers will the firm employ in order to maximise profits?
   (c) What will be its hourly wage bill at this level of employment?
   (d) How much hourly revenue will it earn at this level of employment?

Number of workers	1	2	3	4	5	6	7	8
Wage rate (AC_L) (£)	3	4	5	6	7	8	9	10
Total output (TPP_L)	10	22	32	40	46	50	52	52

(e) Assuming that the firm faces other (fixed) costs of £30 per hour, how much hourly profit will it make?

(f) Assume that the workers now form a union and that the firm agrees to pay the negotiated wage rate to all employees. What is the maximum to which the hourly wage rate could rise without causing the firm to try to reduce employment below that in (b) above? (See the diagram in Box 5.1.)

(g) What would be the firm's hourly profit now?

5. The figures shown in the table below are for a monopsonist employer. Fill in the missing figures for columns (3) and (4). How many workers should the firm employ if it wishes to maximise profits?

6. To what extent can trade unions be seen to be (a) an advantage, (b) a disadvantage to (i) workers in unions, (ii) employers bargaining with unions, (iii) non-union members in firms where there is collective bargaining, (iv) workers in non-unionised jobs?

7. Identify four groups of workers, two with very high wages and two with very low wages. Explain why they get the wages they do.

8. Do any of the following contradict marginal productivity theory: (a) wage scales related to length of service (incremental scales); (b) nationally negotiated wage rates; (c) discrimination; (d) firms taking the lead from other firms in determining this year's pay increase?

9. For what reasons is the average gross weekly pay of women only 74 per cent of that of men in the UK?

10. Does the existence of overtime tend to increase or decrease inequality?

11. Distinguish between proportional, progressive and regressive taxation. Could a progressive tax have a constant marginal rate?

12. If a person earning £5000 per year pays £500 in a given tax and a person earning £10 000 per year pays £800, is the tax progressive or regressive? Explain.

13. A proportional tax will leave the distribution of income unaffected. Why should this be so, given that a rich person will pay a larger absolute amount than a poor person?

14. Under what circumstances would a rise in income tax act as (a) a disincentive and (b) an incentive to effort?

15. Who is likely to work harder as a result of a cut in income tax rates – a person on a high income or a person on a low income? Why? Would your answer be different if personal allowances were zero?

16. What tax changes (whether up or down) will both have a positive incentive effect and also redistribute incomes more equally?

17. What is meant by 'the poverty trap'? Would a system of universal benefits be the best solution to the problem of the poverty trap?

18. How would you go about deciding whether person A or person B gets more personal benefit from each of the following: (a) an electric fire; (b) a clothing allowance of £x; (c) draught-proofing materials; (c) child benefit? Do your answers help you in deciding how best to allocate benefits?

Number of workers (1)	Wage rate (£) (2)	Total cost of labour (£) (3)	Marginal cost of labour (£) (4)	Marginal revenue product (£) (5)
1	100	100		230
			110	
2	105	210		240
			120	
3	110	330		240
4	115			230
5	120			210
6	125			190
7	130			170
8	135			150
9	140			130
10	145			

Additional case studies on the *Essentials of Economics* website (www.booksites.net/sloman)

5.1 Labour as a factor of production. An examination of some of the ethical consequences of treating labour as an 'input' into production.

5.2 Telecommuters. This case study looks at the growth in the number of people working from home.

5.3 Life at the mill. Monopsony in Victorian times as reported by Friedrich Engels.

5.4 Poverty in the past. Extreme poverty in Victorian England.

5.5 The rise and decline of the labour movement. A brief history of trade unions in the UK.

5.6 How useful is marginal productivity theory? How accurately does the theory describe employment decisions by firms?

5.7 Profit sharing. An examination of the case for and against profit sharing as a means of rewarding workers.

5.8 Ethnic minorities in the UK labour market. This case study looks at differences in income and employment between different ethnic groups in the UK.

5.9 How can we define poverty? This examines different definitions of poverty and, in particular, distinguishes between absolute and relative measures of poverty.

5.10 How to reverse the UK's increased inequality. Recommendations of the Rowntree Foundation.

5.11 Adam Smith's maxims of taxation. This looks at the principles of a good tax system as identified by Adam Smith.

5.12 Taxation in the UK. This case study looks at the various types of tax in the UK. It gives the current tax rates and considers how progressive the system is.

5.13 The poll tax. This case charts the introduction of the infamous poll tax (or 'community charge') in the UK and its subsequent demise.

5.14 The Laffer curve. This curve suggests that raising tax rates beyond a certain level will *reduce* tax revenue. But will cutting tax rates increase revenue?

5.15 The system of benefits in the UK. A description of the various benefits used in the UK and their redistributive effects.

5.16 Negative income tax and redistribution. This case looks at the possible effects of introducing negative income taxes (tax credits).

Sections of chapter covered in
WinEcon – Sloman, *Essentials of Economics*

Essentials of Economics section	*WinEcon* section
5.1	–
5.2	5.2
5.3	5.3
5.4	5.4
5.5	5.5

Websites relevant to this chapter

Numbers and sections refer to websites listed in the Web Appendix and hotlinked from this book's website at www.booksites.net/sloman

■ For news articles relevant to this chapter, see the *Economics News Articles* link from the book's website.

■ For general news on labour markets, see websites in section A, and particularly A1, 2, 4, 5 and 7. See also A42 for links to economics news articles from newspapers worldwide.

■ For data on labour markets, see links in B1 or 2, especially to *Labour Market Trends* on the National Statistics site. See also B9 and links in B19; the labour topic in B33; and the *resources > statistics* links in H3.

■ For information on international labour standards and employment rights, see site H3.

■ Sites I7 and I11 contain links to *Labour economics, Labour force and markets* and *Labour unions* in the *Microeconomics* section and to *Distribution of income and wealth* in the *Macroeconomics* section. Site I4 has links in the *Directory* section to *Labour* and *Labour Economics*. Site I17 in the *Labour Economics* section has links to various topics, such as *Labour Unions, Minimum Wage, Poverty* and *Work*.

■ Links to the TUC and Confederation of British Industry sites can be found at E32 and 33.

■ For information on poverty and inequality, see sites B18; E9, 13.

■ For information on taxes, benefits and the redistribution of income, see E9, 30, 36; G5, 13. See also *The Virtual Economy* at D1.

■ For student resources relevant to this chapter, see sites C1–7, 9, 10, 19; D3.

CHAPTER MAP

CHAPTER SIX
Market failures and government policy

In recent years, governments throughout the world have tended to put more reliance on markets as the means of allocating resources. Policies of privatisation, deregulation, cutting government expenditure and taxes, and generally 'leaving things to the market' have been widely adopted, not only by conservative governments, but also by those of the centre and centre left.

But despite this increased reliance on markets, markets often fail. Despite our growing wealth and prosperity, our rivers are polluted, our streets are congested and often strewn with litter, our lives are dominated by the interests of big business and the quality of many of the goods we buy is very poor.

Governments are thus still expected to play a major role in the economy: from the construction and maintenance of roads, to the provision of key services such as education, health care and law and order, to social protection in the form of pensions and social security, to the regulation of businesses, to the passing of laws to protect the individual.

In this chapter we identify the various ways in which the market fails to look after society's interests (Sections 6.1–6.3). Then we look at how the government can set about putting right these failings (Sections 6.4–6.6). Then we look at some of the shortcomings of governments, and ask: should we have more or less intervention? In the final section we turn to problems of the environment as a case study in market failure and government intervention.

Definitions

Social efficiency
Production and consumption at the point where $MSB = MSC$.

Equity
A fair distribution of resources.

Externalities
Costs or benefits of production or consumption experienced by society but not by the producers or consumers themselves. Sometimes referred to as 'spillover' or 'third-party' costs or benefits.

In order to decide the optimum amount of government intervention, it is first necessary to identify the various social goals that intervention is designed to meet. Two of the major objectives of government intervention identified by economists are social efficiency and equity.

Equity. Most people would argue that the free market fails to lead to a *fair* distribution of resources, if it results in some people living in great affluence whilst others live in dire poverty. Clearly what constitutes 'fairness' is a highly contentious issue: those on the political right generally have a quite different view from those on the political left. Nevertheless, most people would argue that the government does have some duty to redistribute incomes from the rich to the poor through the tax and benefit system, and perhaps to provide various forms of legal protection for the poor (such as a minimum wage rate). We looked at the causes of inequality and policies of redistribution in Chapter 5. In this chapter, therefore, we focus on the second issue: that of social efficiency.

Social efficiency. If the marginal benefits to society – or 'marginal social benefits' (*MSB*) – of producing (or consuming) any given good or service exceed the marginal costs to society – or 'marginal social costs' (*MSC*) – then it is said to be socially efficient to produce (or consume) more. For example, if people's gains from having additional motorways exceed *all* the additional costs to society (both financial and non-financial), then it is socially efficient to construct more motorways.

If, however, the marginal social costs of producing (or consuming) any good or service exceed the marginal social benefits, then it is socially efficient to produce (or consume) less.

It follows that if the marginal social benefits of any activity are equal to the marginal social costs, then the current level is the optimum. To summarise: to achieve social efficiency in the production of any good or service, the following should occur:

$$MSB > MSC \rightarrow \text{produce more}$$

$$MSC > MSB \rightarrow \text{produce less}$$

$$MSB = MSC \rightarrow \text{keep production at its current level}$$

Similar rules apply to consumption. For example, if the marginal social benefits of consuming more of any good or service exceed the marginal social cost, then society would benefit from more of the good being consumed.

Social efficiency is an example of 'allocative efficiency': in other words, the best allocation of resources between alternative uses.

> *Allocative efficiency in any activity is achieved where any reallocation would lead to a decline in net benefit.* It is achieved where marginal benefit equals marginal cost. Private efficiency is achieved where marginal private benefit equals marginal private cost (*MB = MC*). Social efficiency is achieved where marginal social benefit equals marginal social cost (*MSB = MSC*).
>
> **Key Idea 18**

In the real world, the market rarely leads to social efficiency: the marginal social benefits of most goods and services do not equal the marginal social costs. Part of the problem is that many of our actions have spillover effects on other people

Key Idea 17 p19

Key Idea 15 p126

(these are known as 'externalities'), part is a lack of competition, part is a lack of knowledge by both producers and consumers, and part is the fact that markets may take a long time to adjust to any disequilibrium, given the often considerable short-run immobility of factors of production.

In this chapter we examine these various 'failings' of the free market and what the government can do to rectify the situation. We also examine why the government itself may fail to achieve social efficiency.

> *Markets generally fail to achieve social efficiency.* There are various types of market failure. Market failures provide one of the major justifications for government intervention in the economy.

 Key Idea 19

Market failures: externalities and public goods   6.1

What will happen if certain markets are 'missing'?

Externalities

The market will not lead to social efficiency if the actions of producers or consumers affect people *other than themselves*. These effects on other people are known as externalities: they are the side-effects, or 'third-party' effects, of production or consumption. Externalities can be either desirable or undesirable. Whenever other people are affected beneficially, there are said to be external benefits. Whenever other people are affected adversely, there are said to be external costs.

Definitions

External benefits
Benefits from production (or consumption) experienced by people *other* than the producer (or consumer).

> *Externalities are spillover costs or benefits.* Where these exist, even an otherwise perfect market will fail to achieve social efficiency.

 Key Idea 20

Thus the full cost to society (the social cost) of the production of any good or service is the private cost faced by firms plus any externalities of production (positive or negative). Likewise the full benefit to society (the social benefit) from the consumption of any good is the private benefit enjoyed by consumers plus any externalities of consumption (positive or negative).

There are four major types of externality.

External costs
Costs of production (or consumption) borne by people *other* than the producer (or consumer).

Social cost
Private cost plus externalities in production.

Social benefit
Private benefit plus externalities in consumption.

External costs of production (MSC > MC)

When a chemical firm dumps waste into a river or pollutes the air, the community bears costs additional to those borne by the firm. The marginal *social* cost (*MSC*) of chemical production exceeds the marginal private cost (*MC*). Diagrammatically, the *MSC* curve is above the *MC* curve. This is shown in Figure 6.1(a), which assumes that the firm in other respects is operating in a perfect market, and is therefore a price taker (i.e. faces a horizontal demand curve).

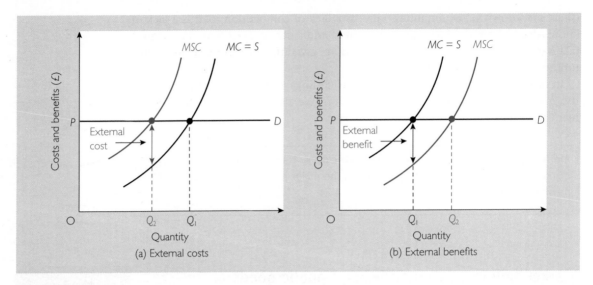

Figure 6.1
Externalities in production

(a) External costs

(b) External benefits

The firm maximises profits at Q_1: the output where marginal cost equals price (see Section 4.2). The price is what people buying the good are prepared to pay for one more unit (if it wasn't, they wouldn't buy it) and therefore reflects their marginal benefit. We assume no externalities from consumption, and therefore the marginal benefit to consumers is the same as the marginal *social* benefit (*MSB*). The *socially* optimum output would be Q_2, where P (i.e. *MSB*) = *MSC*. The firm, however, produces Q_1 which is more than the optimum. Thus external costs lead to over-production from society's point of view.

The problem of external costs arises in a free-market economy because no one has legal ownership of the air or rivers and no one, therefore, can prevent or charge for their use as a dump for waste. Such a 'market' is missing. Control must, therefore, be left to the government or local authorities.

Other examples include extensive farming that destroys hedgerows and wildlife, acid rain caused by smoke from coal-fired power stations, and nuclear waste from nuclear power stations.

External benefits of production (MSC < MC)

Imagine a bus company that spends money training its bus drivers. Each year some drivers leave to work for coach and haulage companies. These companies' costs are reduced as they do not have to train such drivers. Society has benefited from their training (including the bus drivers themselves, who have acquired marketable skills) even though the bus company has not. The marginal *social* cost of the bus service, therefore, is less than the marginal *private* cost to the company.

In Figure 6.1(b), the *MSC* curve is *below* the *MC* curve. The level of output (i.e. number of passenger miles) provided by the bus company is Q_1 where $P = MC$, a *lower* level than the social optimum, Q_2, where $P = MSC$.

Another example of external benefits in production is that of research and development. If other firms have access to the results of the research, then clearly the benefits extend beyond the firm that finances it. Since the firm only receives the private benefits, it will conduct a less than optimal amount of research. Another example is the beneficial effect on the atmosphere from a forestry company planting new woodlands.

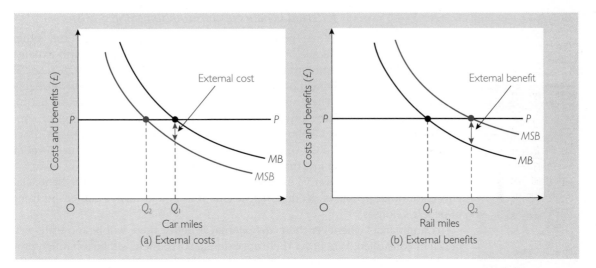

(a) External costs   (b) External benefits

Figure 6.2
Externalities in
consumption

External costs of consumption (MSB < MB)

Figure 6.2(a) shows the marginal benefit and price to a motorist (i.e. the consumer) of using a car. It is assumed that the marginal benefit declines as the motorist travels more miles.[1] The optimal distance travelled for this motorist will be Q_1 miles: i.e. where marginal benefit (MB) = price (P) (where price is the cost of petrol, oil, wear and tear, etc. per mile). The reasoning is as follows: if the marginal benefit from the consumption of any good or service, measured in terms of what you are prepared to pay for it, exceeds its price (i.e. the marginal cost to the consumer), the consumer will gain by consuming more of it. If, however, the marginal benefit is less than the price, the consumer will gain by consuming less. The optimum level of consumption from the motorist's point of view, therefore, will be where $MB = P$: i.e. Q_1 miles.

When people use their cars, however, other people suffer from their exhaust, the added congestion, the noise, etc. These 'negative externalities' make the marginal social benefit of using cars less than the marginal private benefit of the motorist. Thus the MSB curve is below the MB curve. Assuming that there are no externalities in *production*, and therefore that marginal social cost is given by the price, the *social* optimum will be where $MSB = P$: i.e. at Q_2. But this is less than the actual level of consumption, Q_1. Thus, when there are negative externalities in consumption, the actual level of consumption will be too great from society's point of view.

Other examples of negative externalities of consumption include the effects on other people of noisy radios in public places, the smoke from cigarettes, and litter.

---

[1] To understand this, consider your own position (assuming you had a car). If you had only a little money available for motoring, or if the price of petrol was very high, then you would only use your car for essential journeys: journeys with a high marginal private benefit (or 'marginal utility' as it is often referred to by economists). If your income increased, or if the price of petrol came down, you would use your car more (i.e. travel additional miles), but these additional journeys would be yielding you less additional benefit per mile than previous journeys, since they would be less essential to you. The more miles you travel, the less essential each *additional* mile: i.e. the marginal benefit diminishes. This is an example of the principle of diminishing marginal utility, which we saw in Box 1.2.

Key
Idea

6
p34

Definition

Principle of diminishing marginal utility
As more units of a good are consumed, additional units will provide less additional satisfaction than previous units.

Pause for thought

Is it likely that the MSB curve will be parallel to the MB curve in each of the diagrams of Figure 6.2?

Definitions

Public good
A good or service that has the features of non-rivalry and non-excludability and as a result would not be provided by the free market.

Non-rivalry
Where the consumption of a good or service by one person will not prevent others from enjoying it.

Non-excludability
Where it is not possible to provide a good or service to one person without it thereby being available to others to enjoy.

Free-rider problem
Where it is not possible to exclude other people from consuming a good that someone has bought.

Pause for thought

Which of the following have the property of non-rivalry: (a) a can of drink; (b) public transport; (c) a commercial radio broadcast; (d) the sight of flowers in a public park?

External benefits of consumption (MSB > MB)

When people travel by train rather than by car, other people benefit by there being less congestion and exhaust and fewer accidents on the roads. Thus the marginal social benefit of rail travel is *greater* than the marginal private benefit to the rail passenger. There are external benefits from rail travel. In Figure 6.2(b), the *MSB* curve is *above* the private *MB* curve. The socially optimal level of consumption (Q_2) will thus be above the actual level of consumption (Q_1). In other words, when there are 'positive externalities' in consumption, the actual level of consumption will be too low from society's point of view.

Other examples of positive externalities of consumption include the beneficial effects for other people of deodorants, vaccinations and attractive gardens in front of people's houses.

To summarise: whenever there are external benefits, there will be too little produced or consumed. Whenever there are external costs, there will be too much produced or consumed. The market will not equate *MSB* and *MSC*.

The above arguments have been developed in the context of perfect competition, with prices given to the producer or consumer by the market. Externalities also occur in all other types of market.

Public goods

There is a category of goods where the positive externalities are so great that the free market, whether perfect or imperfect, may not produce at all. They are called public goods. Examples include lighthouses, pavements, flood-control dams, public drainage, public services such as the police and even government itself.

Public goods have two important characteristics: *non-rivalry* and *non-excludability*.

■ If I consume a bar of chocolate, it cannot then be consumed by someone else. If, however, I enjoy the benefits of street lighting, it does not prevent you or anyone else doing the same. There is thus what we call non-rivalry in the consumption of such goods. These goods tend to have large external benefits relative to private benefits. This makes them socially desirable, but privately unprofitable. No single individual would pay to have a pavement built along his or her street. The private benefit would be too small relative to the cost. And yet the social benefit to all the other people using the pavement may far outweigh the cost.

■ If I spend money erecting a flood-control dam to protect my house, my neighbours will also be protected by the dam. I cannot prevent them enjoying the benefits of my expenditure. This feature of non-excludability means that they would get the benefits free, and would therefore have no incentive to pay themselves. This is known as the free-rider problem.

The free-rider problem. People are often unwilling to pay for things if they can make use of things other people have bought. This problem can lead to people not purchasing things that would be to the benefit of themselves and other members of society.

Key Idea 21

When goods have these two features, the free market will simply not provide them. Thus these public goods can only be provided by the government or by the government subsidising private firms. (Note that not all goods and services produced by the public sector come into the category of 'public goods and services': thus education and health are publicly provided, but they *can* be, and indeed are, privately provided as well.)

Recap

1. Social efficiency will be achieved where $MSC = MSB$ for each good and service. In practice, however, markets fail to achieve social efficiency. One reason for this is the existence of externalities.

2. Externalities are spillover costs or benefits. Whenever there are external costs, the market will (other things being equal) lead to a level of production and consumption *above* the socially efficient level. Whenever there are external benefits, the market will (other things being equal) lead to a level of production and consumption *below* the socially efficient level.

3. Public goods will not be provided by a free market. The problem is that they have large external benefits relative to private benefits and without government intervention it would not be possible to prevent people having a 'free ride' and thereby escaping contributing to their cost of production.

Market failures: monopoly power   6.2

What problems arise from big business?

Key Idea
19
p207

Whenever markets are imperfect, whether as pure monopoly or monopsony, or whether as some form of imperfect competition, the market will fail to equate MSB and MSC, even if there are no externalities.

Take the case of monopoly. A monopoly will produce less than the socially efficient output. This is illustrated in Figure 6.3. A monopoly faces a downward-sloping demand curve, and therefore marginal revenue is below average revenue ($= P = MSB$). Profits are maximised at an output of Q_1, where marginal revenue

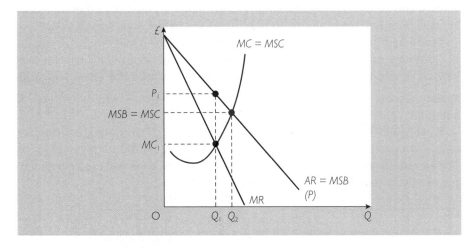

Figure 6.3
The monopolist producing less than the social optimum

Figure 6.4

Deadweight loss from a monopoly

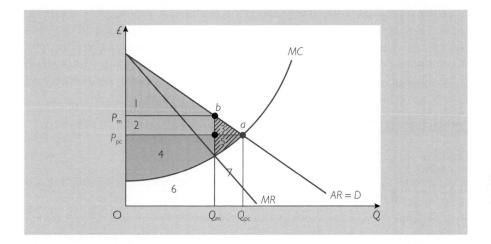

equals marginal cost (see Figure 4.5 on page 129). If there are no externalities, the socially efficient output will be at the higher level of Q_2, where $MSB = MSC$.

Deadweight loss under monopoly

Consumer and producer surplus

One way of analysing the welfare loss that occurs under monopoly is to use the concepts of *consumer* and *producer surplus*. Consumer surplus is the excess of consumers' total benefit (or 'utility') from consuming a good over their total expenditure on it. Producer surplus is just another name for profit. The two concepts are illustrated in Figure 6.4. The diagram shows an industry that is initially under perfect competition and then becomes a monopoly (but faces the same revenue and cost curves).

Let us start by examining consumer and producer surplus under *perfect competition*.

Consumer surplus.   Under perfect competition the industry will produce an output of Q_{pc} at a price of P_{pc}, where $MC = P (= AR)$: i.e. at point a (see pages 129–31).

Consumers' total benefit is given by the area under the demand curve (the sum of all the areas 1–7). The reason for this is that each point on the demand curve shows how much the last consumer is prepared to pay (i.e. the benefit to the marginal consumer). The area under the demand curve thus shows the total of all these marginal benefits from zero consumption to the current level: i.e. it gives total benefit.

Consumers' total expenditure is $P_{pc} \times Q_{pc}$ (areas $4 + 5 + 6 + 7$).

Consumer surplus is the difference between total benefit and total expenditure: in other words, the area between the price and the demand curve (areas $1 + 2 + 3$).

Producer surplus.   Producer surplus (profit) is the difference between total revenue and total cost.

Total cost is the area under the MC curve (areas $6 + 7$). The reason for this is that each point on the marginal cost curve shows what the last unit costs to produce. The area under the MC curve thus gives all the marginal costs starting from an output of zero to the current output: i.e. it gives total costs.[2]

---

[2] Strictly speaking, the sum of all marginal costs gives total *variable* costs. Producers' surplus is therefore total revenue minus total variable costs: i.e. total profit plus total fixed costs.

Total revenue is $P_{pc} \times Q_{pc}$ (areas 4 + 5 + 6 + 7).
Producer surplus is thus the area between the price and the MC curve (areas 4 + 5).

Total (private) surplus.   Total consumer plus producer surplus is therefore the area between the demand and MC curves. This is shown by the total shaded area (areas 1 + 2 + 3 + 4 + 5).

The effect of monopoly on total surplus

What happens when the industry is under *monopoly*? The firm will produce where $MC = MR$, at an output of Q_m and a price of P_m (at point *b* on the demand curve). Total revenue is $P_m \times Q_m$ (areas 2 + 4 + 6). Total cost is the area under the MC curve (area 6). Thus producer surplus is areas 2 + 4. This is clearly a *larger* surplus than under perfect competition (since area 2 is larger than area 5): monopoly profits are larger than profits under perfect competition.

Consumer surplus, however, will be much smaller. With consumption at Q_m, total benefit to consumers is given by areas 1 + 2 + 4 + 6, whereas consumer expenditure is given by areas 2 + 4 + 6. Consumer surplus, then, is simply area 1. (Note that area 2 has been transformed from consumer surplus to producer surplus.)

Total surplus under monopoly is therefore areas 1 + 2 + 4: a smaller surplus than under perfect competition. 'Monopolisation' of the industry has resulted in a loss of total surplus of areas 3 + 5. The producer's gain is less than consumers' loss. This net loss of total surplus is known as the deadweight welfare loss of monopoly.

Definition

Deadweight welfare loss The loss of consumer plus producer surplus in imperfect markets (when compared with perfect competition).

Conclusions

As was shown in Section 4.3, there are possible social *advantages* from powerful firms; advantages such as economies of scale and more research and development. These advantages may outweigh deadweight loss from monopoly power. It can be argued that an ideal situation would be where firms are large enough to gain economies of scale and yet were somehow persuaded or compelled to produce where $P = MC$ (assuming no externalities).

Pause for thought

Assume that a monopoly existed in an industry where there were negative externalities. Could the socially efficient output be Q_m in Figure 6.4? If so, would this make monopoly socially efficient?

Recap

1. Monopoly power will (other things being equal) lead to a level of output below the socially efficient level.

2. This will result in deadweight welfare loss, which is the loss in total producer and consumer surplus.

3. Consumer surplus is the excess of what consumers are prepared to pay (which is how we measure the benefit to consumers) over what they actually pay. Producer surplus is the excess of total revenue over total cost (i.e. total profit).

4. The effect of monopoly will be to give a higher producer surplus than under perfect competition, but a much lower consumer surplus. Thus total surplus is lower.

5. There are potential gains from monopoly, such as economies of scale and higher investment. Such gains have to be offset against the deadweight loss.

6.3   Other market failures

In what other ways may a market fail to make the best use of scarce resources?

Ignorance and uncertainty

Perfect competition assumes that consumers, firms and factor suppliers have perfect knowledge of costs and benefits. In the real world there is often a great deal of ignorance and uncertainty. Thus people are unable to equate marginal benefit with marginal cost.

Consumers purchase many goods only once or a few times in a lifetime. Cars, washing machines, televisions and other consumer durables fall into this category. Consumers may not be aware of the quality of such goods until they have purchased them, by which time it is too late. Advertising may contribute to people's ignorance by misleading them as to the benefits of a good.

Firms are often ignorant of market opportunities, prices, costs, the productivity of labour (especially white-collar workers), the activity of rivals, etc.

Many economic decisions are based on expected future conditions. Since the future can never be known for certain, many decisions will be taken which, in retrospect, will be seen to have been wrong.

In some cases it may be possible to obtain the information through the market. There may be an agency that will sell you the information, or a newspaper, magazine or website that contains the information. In such cases you will have to decide whether the cost to you of obtaining the information is worth the benefit it will provide you. A problem here is that you may not have sufficient information to judge how reliable the information is that you are obtaining!

Immobility of factors and time-lags in response

Even under conditions of perfect competition, factors may be very slow to respond to changes in demand or supply. Labour, for example, may be highly immobile both occupationally and geographically. This can lead to large price changes and hence to large supernormal profits and high wages for those in the sectors of rising demand or falling costs. The long run may be a very long time coming!

In the meantime, there will be further changes in the conditions of demand and supply. Thus the economy is in a constant state of disequilibrium and the long run never comes. As firms and consumers respond to market signals and move towards equilibrium, so the equilibrium position moves and the social optimum is never achieved.

> ***The problem of time lags.*** Many economic actions can take a long time to take effect. This can cause problems of instability and an inability of the economy to achieve social efficiency.
>
> **Key Idea 22**

Whenever monopoly/monopsony power exists, the problem is made worse as firms or unions put up barriers to the entry of new firms or factors of production.

Protecting people's interests

Dependants

People do not always make their own economic decisions. They are often dependent on decisions made by others. Parents make decisions on behalf of their children; partners on each other's behalf; younger adults on behalf of old people; managers on behalf of shareholders, etc.

A free market will respond to these decisions, however good or bad they may be; whether they be in the interest of the dependant or not. Thus the government may feel it necessary to protect dependants.

The principal–agent problem

The problem of dependants is an example of a wider issue, known as the principal–agent problem. One of the features of a complex modern economy is that people (principals) have to employ others (agents) to carry out their wishes. If you want to go on holiday, it is easier to go to a travel agent to sort out the arrangements than to do it all yourself. Likewise, if you want to buy a house, it is more convenient to go to an estate agent. The point is that these agents have specialist knowledge and can save you, the principal, a great deal of time and effort. This is merely an example of the benefits of specialisation and the division of labour.

It is the same with firms. They employ people with specialist knowledge and skills to carry out specific tasks. Companies frequently employ consultants to give them advice, or engage the services of specialist firms such as an advertising agency. It is the same with the employees of the company. They can be seen as 'agents' of their employer. In the case of workers, they can be seen as the agents of management. Junior managers are the agents of senior management. Senior managers are the agents of the directors, who are themselves agents of the shareholders. Thus in large firms there is often a complex chain of principal–agent relationships. Indeed, it is often claimed that in large companies there tends to be a 'divorce' between the owners of the firm (the shareholders), who are the principals, and the controllers of the firm (the managers), who are the shareholders' agents.

These relationships have an inherent danger for the principal: there is asymmetric information between the two sides. The agent knows more about the situation than the principal – in fact, this is part of the reason why the principal employs the agent in the first place. The danger is that the agent may well not act in the principal's best interests, and may be able to get away with it because of the principal's imperfect knowledge. The estate agent trying to sell you a house may not tell you about the noisy neighbours or that the vendor is prepared to accept a much lower price. A second-hand car dealer may 'neglect' to tell you about the rust on the underside of the car or that it has a history of unreliability.

> **Definitions**
>
> **Principal–agent problem**
> Where people (principals), as a result of lack of knowledge, cannot ensure that their best interests are served by their agents.
>
> **Asymmetric information**
> Where one party in an economic relationship (e.g. an agent) has more information than another (e.g. the principal).

> *The principal–agent problem.* Where people (principals), as a result of a lack of knowledge, cannot ensure that their best interests are served by their agents. Agents may take advantage of this situation to the disadvantage of the principals.
>
> **Key Idea 23**

So how can principals tackle the problem? There are two elements in the solution:

■ The principals must have some way of *monitoring* the performance of their agents. Thus a company might employ efficiency experts to examine the operation of its management.
■ There must be *incentives* for agents to behave in the principals' interests. Thus managers' salaries could be more closely linked to the firm's profitability.

In a competitive market, managers' and shareholders' interests are more likely to coincide. Managers have to ensure that the company remains efficient or it may not survive the competition and they might lose their jobs. In monopolies and oligopolies, however, where supernormal profits can often be relatively easily earned, the interests of shareholders and managers are likely to diverge. Here it will be in shareholders' interests to institute incentive mechanisms that ensure that their agents, the managers, are motivated to strive for profitability.

Poor economic decision making by individuals on their own behalf

The government may feel that people need protecting from poor economic decisions that they make on their *own* behalf. It may feel that in a free market people will consume too many harmful things. Thus if the government wants to discourage smoking and drinking, it can put taxes on tobacco and alcohol. In more extreme cases it could make various activities illegal: activities such as prostitution, certain types of gambling, and the sale and consumption of drugs.

On the other hand, the government may feel that people consume too little of things that are good for them: things such as education, health care and sports facilities. Such goods are known as merit goods. The government could either provide them free or subsidise their production.

> **Pause for thought**
>
> How do merit goods differ from public goods?

> **Definition**
>
> **Merit goods**
> Goods which the government feels that people should consume but tend to underconsume and which therefore ought to be subsidised or provided free.

Macroeconomic goals

The free market is unlikely to achieve simultaneously the *macroeconomic* objectives of rapid economic growth, full employment, stable prices and a balance of international payments. These problems and the methods of government intervention to deal with them are examined in the second part of this book.

How far can economists go in advising governments?

It is not within the scope of economics to make judgements as to the relative importance of social goals. Economics can only consider means to achieving stated goals. First, therefore, the goals have to be clearly stated by the policy makers. Second, they have to be quantifiable so that different policies can be compared as to their relative effectiveness in achieving the particular goal. Certain goals, such as growth in national income, changes in the distribution of income and greater efficiency, are relatively easy to quantify. Others, such as enlightenment or the sense of community wellbeing, are virtually impossible to quantify. For this reason, economics tends to concentrate on the means of achieving a relatively narrow range of goals. The danger is that by economists concentrating on a limited number of goals, they may well influence the policy makers – the government, local authorities, various pressure groups, etc. – into doing the same, and thus into neglecting other perhaps important social goals.

Different objectives are likely to conflict. For example, economic growth may conflict with greater equality. In the case of such 'trade-offs', all the economist can do is to demonstrate the effects of a given policy, and leave the policy makers to decide whether the benefits in terms of one goal outweigh the costs in terms of another goal.

Societies face trade-offs between economic objectives. For example, the goal of faster growth may conflict with that of greater equality; the goal of lower unemployment may conflict with that of lower inflation (at least in the short run). This is an example of opportunity cost: the cost of achieving more of one objective may be achieving less of another. The existence of trade-offs means that policy makers must make choices.

Key Idea 24

Where there are two or more alternative policies, economists can go further than this. They may be asked to consider the relative effectiveness of the various policies or even themselves to suggest alternative policies. In such cases it may be possible to say that policy A is preferable to policy B because its benefits are greater or its costs lower in terms of all stated goals. On the other hand, if policy A better achieves one goal and policy B better achieves another, once more all the economist can do is to point this out and leave the policy makers to decide.

Recap

1. Ignorance and uncertainty may prevent people from consuming or producing the levels they would otherwise choose. Information may sometimes be provided (at a price) by the market, but it may be imperfect and in some cases not available at all.

2. Markets may respond sluggishly to changes in demand and supply. The time lags in adjustment can lead to a permanent state of disequilibrium and to problems of instability.

3. In a free market there may be inadequate provision for dependants and an inadequate output of merit goods. Also, because of asymmetric information, agents may not always act in the best interests of their principals.

4. Although economists cannot make ultimate pronouncements on the rights and wrongs of the market – that involves making moral judgements (and economists here are no different from any other person) – they can point out the consequences of the market and of various government policies, and also the trade-offs that exist between different objectives.

Box 6.1

Should health-care provision be left to the market?

A case of multiple market failures

When you go shopping you may well pay a visit to the chemist and buy some paracetamol tablets, some sticking plasters or a tube of ointment. These health-care products are being sold through the market system in much the same way as other everyday goods and services such as food, household items and petrol.

But many health-care services and products are not allocated through the market in this way. In the UK, the National Health Service provides free hospital treatment, a free general practitioner service and free prescriptions for certain categories of people (such as pensioners and children). Their marginal cost to the patient is thus zero. Of course, these services use resources and they thus have to be paid for out of taxes. In this sense they are not free. (Have you heard the famous saying, 'There's no such thing as a free lunch'?)

But why are these services not sold directly to the patient, thereby saving the taxpayer money? There are, in fact, a number of reasons why the market would fail to provide the optimum amount of health care.

People may not be able to afford treatment

This is a problem connected with the distribution of income. Because income is unequally distributed, some people will be able to afford better treatment than others, and the poorest people may not be able to afford treatment at all. On grounds of equity, therefore, it is argued that health care should be provided free – at least for poor people.

The concept of equity that is usually applied to health care is that of treatment according to medical need rather than according to the ability to pay.

? 1. Does this argument also apply to food and other basic goods?

Difficulty for people in predicting their future medical needs

If you were suddenly taken ill and required a major operation, or maybe even several, it could be very expensive indeed for you if you had to pay. On the other hand, you may go through life requiring very little if any medical treatment. In other words, there is great uncertainty about your future medical needs. As a result it would be very difficult to plan your finances and budget for possible future medical expenses if you had to pay for treatment. Medical insurance is a possible solution to this problem, but there is still a problem of equity. Would the chronically sick or very old be able to obtain cover, and if so, would they be able to afford the premiums?

Externalities

Health care generates a number of benefits external to the patient. If you are cured of an infectious disease, for example, it is not just you who benefits but also others, since you will not infect them. In addition, your family and friends benefit from seeing you well; and if you have a job you will be able to get back to work, thus reducing the disruption there. These external benefits of health care could be quite large.

If the sick have to pay the cost of their treatment, they may decide not to be treated – especially if they are poor. They may not take into account the effect that their illness has on other people. The market, by equating *private* benefits and costs, would produce too little health care.

Key Idea 17 p192

Key Idea 11 p71

Key Idea 20 p207

Patient ignorance

Markets only function well to serve consumer wishes if the consumer has the information to make informed decisions. For many products that we buy, we have a pretty good idea how much we will like them. In the case of health care, however, 'consumers' (i.e. patients) may have very poor knowledge. If you have a pain in your chest, it may be simple muscular strain, or it may be a symptom of heart disease. You rely on the doctor (the *supplier* of the treatment) to give you the information: to diagnose your condition. Two problems could arise here with a market system of allocating health care.

The first is that unscrupulous doctors might advise more expensive treatment than is necessary, or drugs companies might try to persuade you to buy a more expensive branded product rather than an identical cheaper version. This is an example of the principal–agent problem and the problem of asymmetric information (see page 215).

The second is that patients suffering from the early stages of a serious disease might not consult their doctor until the symptoms become acute, by which time it might be too late to treat the disease, or very expensive to do so. With a free health service, however, a person is likely to receive an earlier diagnosis of serious conditions. On the other hand, some patients may consult their doctors over trivial complaints.

Oligopoly

If doctors and hospitals operated in the free market as profit maximisers, it is unlikely that competition would drive down their prices. Instead it is possible that they would collude to fix standard prices for treatment, so as to protect their incomes.

Even if doctors did compete openly, it is unlikely that consumers would have the information to enable them to 'shop around' for the best value. Doctor A may charge less than doctor B, but is the quality of service the same? Simple bedside manner – the thing that may most influence a patient's choice – may be a poor indicator of the doctor's skill and judgement.

To argue that the market system will fail to provide an optimal allocation of health-care resources does not in itself prove that free provision is the best alternative. In the USA there is much more reliance on *private medical insurance*. Only the very poor get free treatment. Alternatively, the government may simply *subsidise* the provision of health care, so as to make it cheaper rather than free. This is the case with prescriptions and dental treatment in the UK, where many people have to pay part of the cost of treatment. Also the government can *regulate* the behaviour of the providers of health care, so as to prevent exploitation of the patient. Thus only people with certain qualifications are allowed to operate as doctors, nurses, pharmacists, etc.

2. If health care is provided free, the demand is likely to be high. How is this high demand dealt with? Is this a good way of dealing with it?

3. Go through each of the market failings identified in this box. In each case consider what alternative policies are open to a government to tackle them. What are the advantages and disadvantages of these alternatives?

Key idea 23 p216

Key idea 14 p118

6.4   Government intervention: taxes and subsidies

Will taxing the bad and subsidising the good solve the problem of externalities?

Faced with all the problems of the free market, what is a government to do?

There are several policy instruments that the government can use. At one extreme it can totally replace the market by providing goods and services itself. At the other extreme it can merely seek to persuade producers, consumers or workers to act differently. Between the two extremes the government has a number of instruments it can use to change the way markets operate. These include taxes, subsidies, laws and regulatory bodies. In this and the next two sections we examine these different forms of government intervention.

The use of taxes and subsidies

A policy instrument particularly favoured by many economists is that of taxes and subsidies. They can be used for two main purposes: (a) to promote greater social efficiency by altering the composition of production and consumption, and (b) to redistribute incomes. We examined their use for the second purpose in the last chapter. Here we examine their use to achieve greater social efficiency.

When there are imperfections in the market, social efficiency will not be achieved. Marginal social benefit (*MSB*) will not equal marginal social cost (*MSC*). A different level of output would be more desirable. Taxes and subsidies can be used to correct these imperfections. Essentially the approach is to tax those goods or activities where the market produces too much, and subsidise those where the market produces too little.

Taxes and subsidies to correct externalities

The rule here is simple: the government should impose a tax equal to the marginal external cost (or grant a subsidy equal to the marginal external benefit).

Assume, for example, that a chemical works emits smoke from a chimney and thus pollutes the atmosphere. This creates external costs for the people who breathe in the smoke. The marginal social cost of producing the chemicals thus exceeds the marginal private cost to the firm: $MSC > MC$.

This is illustrated in Figure 6.5. The marginal pollution cost (the externality) is shown by the vertical distance between the MC and MSC curves. For simplicity, it is assumed that the firm is a price taker. It produces Q_1 where $P = MC$ (its profit-maximising output), but in doing so takes no account of the external pollution costs it imposes on society.

If the government now imposes a tax on production equal to the marginal pollution cost, it will effectively 'internalise' the externality. The firm will have to pay an amount in tax equal to the external cost it creates. It will therefore now maximise profits at Q_2, where $P = MC + \text{tax}$. But this is the socially optimum output where $MSB = MSC$.

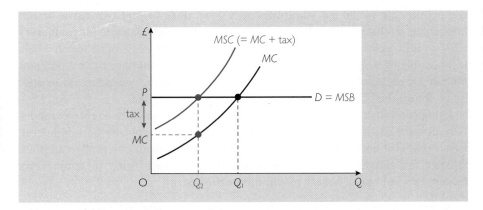

Figure 6.5
Using taxes to correct a distortion: the first-best world

Taxes and subsidies to correct for monopoly

If the problem of monopoly that the government wishes to tackle is that of *excessive profits*, it can impose a lump-sum tax on the monopolist: that is, a tax of a fixed absolute amount irrespective of how much the monopolist produces, or the price it charges. Since a lump-sum tax is an additional *fixed* cost to the firm, and hence will not affect the firm's marginal cost, it will not reduce the amount that the monopolist produces (which *would* be the case with a per-unit tax). The 'windfall tax' imposed in 1997 by the UK Labour government on the profits of various privatised utilities is an example of such a tax.

If the government is concerned that the monopolist produces less than the socially efficient output, it could give the monopolist a *per-unit subsidy* (which would encourage the monopolist to produce more). But would this not *increase* the monopolist's profit? The answer to this is to impose a harsh lump-sum tax in addition to the subsidy. The tax would not undo the subsidy's benefit of encouraging the monopolist to produce more, but it could be used to reduce the monopolist's profits below the original (i.e. pre-subsidy) level.

Advantages of taxes and subsidies

Many economists favour the tax/subsidy solution to market imperfections (especially the problem of externalities) because it still allows the market to operate. It forces firms to take on board the full social costs and benefits of their actions. It also has the flexibility of being adjustable according to the magnitude of the problem. For example, the bigger the external costs of a firm's actions, the bigger the tax can be.

What is more, when firms are taxed for *bad* practices, such as polluting, they are encouraged to find socially better ways of producing. The tax thus acts as an incentive over the longer term to reduce pollution: the more a firm can reduce its pollution, the more taxes it can save. Likewise, when *good* practices are subsidised, firms are given the incentive to adopt more good practices.

Key idea
4
p26

Disadvantages of taxes and subsidies

Infeasible to use different tax and subsidy rates. Each firm produces different levels and types of externalities and operates under different degrees of imperfect competition. It would be administratively very difficult and expensive, if not impossible, to charge every offending firm its own particular tax rate (or grant every relevant firm its own particular rate of subsidy). Even in the case of pollution where it is possible to measure a firm's emissions, there would still have to be a different tax rate for each pollutant and even for each environment, depending on its ability to absorb the pollutant and the number of people affected.

Using combinations of lump-sum taxes and per-unit subsidies to correct monopoly distortions to price, output and profit would also probably be impractical. Given that cost and revenue curves differ substantially from one firm to another, separate tax and subsidy rates would be needed for each firm. An army of tax inspectors would be necessary to administer the system!

Lack of knowledge. Even if a government did decide to charge a tax equal to each offending firm's marginal external costs, it would still have the problem of measuring those costs and apportioning blame. The damage to lakes and forests from acid rain has been a major concern since the beginning of the 1980s. But just how serious is that damage? What is its current monetary cost? How long lasting is the damage? Just what and who are to blame? These are questions that cannot be answered precisely. It is thus impossible to fix the 'correct' pollution tax on, say, a particular coal-fired power station.

> **Pause for thought**
>
> *Why is it easier to use taxes and subsidies to tackle the problem of car exhaust pollution than to tackle the problem of peak-time traffic congestion in cities?*

Despite these problems, it is nevertheless possible to charge firms by the amount of a particular emission. For example, firms could be charged for chimney smoke by so many parts per million of a given pollutant. Although it is difficult to 'fine-tune' such a system so that the charge reflects the precise number of people affected by the pollutant and by how much, it does go some way to internalising the externality. As Box 6.4 on page 238 shows, many countries in recent years have introduced 'green' taxes, seeing them as an effective means of protecting the environment.

Recap

1. Taxes and subsidies are one means of correcting market distortions.

2. Externalities can be corrected by imposing tax rates equal to the size of marginal external costs, and granting rates of subsidy equal to marginal external benefits.

3. Taxes and subsidies can also be used to affect monopoly price, output and profit. Subsidies can be used to persuade a monopolist to increase output (and reduce price) to the competitive level. Lump-sum taxes can then be used to reduce monopoly profits without affecting the new price or output.

4. Taxes and subsidies have the advantages of 'internalising' externalities and of providing incentives to reduce external costs. On the other hand, they may be impractical to use when different rates are required for each case, or when it is impossible to know the full effects of the activities that the taxes or subsidies are being used to correct.

Government intervention: laws and regulation   6.5

Should the government try to stop 'bad behaviour' by big business?

Laws prohibiting or regulating undesirable structures or behaviour

Laws are frequently used to correct market imperfections. Laws can be of three main types: those that prohibit or regulate behaviour that imposes external costs, those that prevent firms providing false or misleading information, and those that prevent or regulate monopolies and oligopolies. For example, in the UK, under the 2002 Enterprise Act, it is a criminal offence for two or more firms to engage in cartel agreements, such as price fixing, market sharing or supply restrictions (see page 144). Convicted offenders may receive a prison sentence of up to five years and/or an unlimited fine.

Advantages of legal restrictions

■ They are usually simple and clear to understand and are often relatively easy to administer. For example, various polluting activities could be banned or restricted.

■ When the danger is very great, or when the extent of the danger is not as yet known, it might be much safer to ban various practices altogether (e.g. the use of various toxic chemicals) rather than to rely on taxes.

■ When a decision needs to be taken quickly, it might be possible to invoke emergency action. For example, in a city like Athens it has been found to be simpler to ban or restrict the use of private cars during a chemical smog emergency than to tax their use.

■ Because consumers suffer from imperfect information, consumer protection laws can make it illegal for firms to sell shoddy or unsafe goods, or to make false or misleading claims about their products.

Disadvantages of legal restrictions

The main problem is that legal restrictions tend to be a rather blunt weapon. If, for example, a firm were required to reduce the effluent of a toxic chemical to 20 tonnes per week, there would be no incentive for the firm to reduce it further. With a tax on the effluent, however, the more the firm reduced the effluent, the less tax it would pay. Thus with a system of taxes there is a *continuing* incentive to cut pollution, to improve safety, or whatever.

Regulatory bodies

Rather than using the blunt weapon of general legislation to ban or restrict various activities, a more 'subtle' approach can be adopted. This involves the use of various regulatory bodies. Having identified possible cases where action might be required (e.g. potential cases of pollution, misleading information or the abuse of monopoly power), the regulatory body would probably conduct an investigation and then prepare a report containing its findings and recommendations. It might also have the power to enforce its decisions. In the UK there are regulatory bodies for each of the major privatised utilities (see Box 6.2).

Box 6.2

Regulating privatised industries

Is it the best way of dealing with their monopoly power?

From the early 1980s, the Thatcher and Major governments engaged in extensive programmes of 'privatisation', returning most of the nationalised industries to the private sector. Nationalised industries, they claimed, were bureaucratic, inefficient, unresponsive to consumer wishes and often a burden on the taxpayer.

Other countries have followed similar programmes of privatisation in what has become a worldwide phenomenon. Privatisation has been seen by many governments as a means of revitalising ailing industries and raising revenues to ease budgetary problems.

Key Idea 8 p45

However, privatisation has brought its own problems. Consumers have complained of poor service and high prices. The result is that governments have been increasingly concerned to *regulate* the behaviour of these industries, many of which have considerable market power.

The system of regulation in the UK

In each of the major privatised industries – gas and electricity, telecommunications, water and railways – there is a separate regulatory office. Their legal authority is contained in the Act of privatisation, but their real power lies in the terms of their licences and price-setting formulae.

The price-setting formulae are essentially of the '*RPI* minus *X*' variety. What this means is that the industries can raise their prices by the rate of increase in the retail price index (RPI) (i.e. by the rate of inflation) *minus* a certain percentage (*X*) to take account of expected increases in efficiency. The idea is that this will force the industry to pass such cost savings on to the consumer.

The licence also permits the regulator to monitor other aspects of the behaviour of the industry and to require it to take various measures. For example, the Strategic Rail Authority sets minimum standards for the punctuality and frequency of trains. Generally, however, the approach has been one of negotiation with the industry.

Assessing the system of regulation in the UK

The system that has evolved in the UK has various advantages.

- It is a *discretionary* system, with the regulator able to judge individual examples of the behaviour of the industry on their own merits. The regulator has a detailed knowledge of the industry, which would not be available to government ministers or other bodies such as the Office of Fair Trading. The regulator could thus be argued to be the best person to decide on whether the industry is acting in the public interest.
- The system is *flexible*, since it allows for the licence and price formula to be changed as circumstances change.
- The '*RPI* minus *X*' formula provides an *incentive* for the privatised firms to be as efficient as possible. If they can lower their costs by more than *X*, they will, in theory, be able to make larger profits and keep them. If, on the other hand, they do not succeed in reducing costs sufficiently, they will make a loss. There is thus a continuing pressure on them to cut costs.

There are, however, some inherent problems with the way in which regulation operates in the UK.

- The '*RPI* minus *X*' formula was designed to provide an incentive for the firms to cut costs. But if *X* is too low, the firm might make excessive profits. Frequently regulators have underestimated the scope for cost reductions resulting from new technology and reorganisation, and have thus initially set *X* too low. As a result, instead of *X* remaining constant for a number of years, as intended, new higher values for *X* have been set after only one or two years. Alternatively, one-off price cuts have been ordered, as happened when the water companies were required by OFWAT to cut prices by an average of 10 per cent in 2000. In either case the incentive for the industry to cut costs is reduced. What is the point of being more efficient if the regulator is merely going to take away the extra profits?

■ Regulation is becoming increasingly complex. This makes it difficult for the industries to plan and may lead to a growth of 'short-termism'. One of the claimed advantages of privatisation was to give greater independence to the industries from short-term government interference, and allow them to plan for the longer term. In practice, one type of interference may have been replaced by another.

■ There may also be the danger of regulatory capture. As regulators become more and more involved in their industry and get to know the senior managers at a personal level, so they are increasingly likely to see the managers' point of view and become less and less tough. Commentators do not believe that this has happened yet: the regulators are generally independently minded. But it is a danger for the future.

■ Alternatively, regulators could be captured by government. Instead of being totally independent, there to serve the interests of the consumer, they might bend to pressures from the government to do things which might help the government win the next election.

Increasing competition in the privatised industries

Where natural monopoly exists (see page 127), competition is impossible in a free market. Of course, the industry *could* be broken up by the government, with firms prohibited from owning more than a certain percentage of the industry. But this would lead to higher costs of production. Firms would be operating further back up a downward-sloping long-run average cost curve.

But many parts of the privatised industries are not natural monopolies. Generally it is only the *grid* that is a natural monopoly. In the case of gas and water, it is the pipelines. It would be wasteful to duplicate these. In the case of electricity it is the power lines: the national grid and the local power lines. In the case of

the railways it is the track. *Other* parts of these industries, however, have generally been opened up to competition (with the exception of water). Thus there are now many producers and sellers of electricity and gas. This is possible because they are given access, by law, to the national and local electricity grids and gas pipelines.

Even for the parts where there is a natural monopoly, they could be made contestable monopolies. One way of doing this is by granting operators a licence for a specific period of time. This is known as franchising, which has been the approach used for the railways. Once a company has been granted a franchise, it has the monopoly of passenger rail services over specific routes. But the awarding of the franchise can be highly competitive, with rival companies putting in competitive bids, in terms of both price (or, in the case of railways, the level of government subsidy required) and the quality of service.

Despite attempts to introduce competition into the privatised industries, they are still dominated by giant companies. Even if they are no longer strictly monopolies, they still have considerable market power. Competition is far from being perfect! The scope for price leadership or other forms of oligopolistic collusion is great. Thus although regulation through the price formula has been progressively abandoned as elements of competition have been introduced, the regulators have retained a role similar to that of the OFT: they can intervene to prevent cases of collusion and the abuse of monopoly power. The companies, however, do have the right of appeal to the Competition Commission.

?

1. Should regulators of utilities that have been privatised into several separate companies allow (a) mergers between these companies or similar companies from abroad; (b) mergers with firms in other industries?

2. If an industry regulator adopts an $RPI - X$ formula for price regulation, is it desirable that the value of X should be adjusted as soon as cost conditions change?

Definitions

Regulatory capture
Where the regulator is persuaded to operate in the industry's interests rather than those of the consumer.

Franchising
Where a firm is granted the licence to operate a given part of an industry for a specified length of time.

Another example concerns the prevention or regulation of the abuse of market power. The Office of Fair Trading (OFT) is the official body that investigates and reports on suspected cases of anti-competitive practices, such as the refusal by a manufacturer to supply retailers that discount its products, or a firm conducting 'predatory pricing' – deliberately selling at a loss in part of the market in order to undercut the price of a new entrant. The OFT can order such firms to cease or modify these practices. If they do not, the OFT can impose fines of up to 10 per cent of the firm's annual revenue. Alternatively the OFT can refer such firms to the Competition Commission (see Box 4.5, page 148). The Commission then conducts an investigation, and makes a ruling.

The advantage of this method is that a case-by-case approach can be used. All the various circumstances surrounding a particular case can be taken into account, with the result that the most appropriate solution can be adopted.

Pause for thought

What other forms of intervention are likely to be necessary to back up the work of regulatory bodies?

The problems with this approach, however, are that (a) investigations may be expensive and time consuming, (b) only a few cases may be examined and (c) offending firms may make various promises of good behaviour which, owing to a lack of follow-up by the regulatory body, may not in fact be carried out.

Recap

1. Laws can be used to regulate activities that impose external costs, to regulate monopolies and oligopolies, and to provide consumer protection. Legal controls are often simpler and easier to operate than taxes, and are safer when the danger is potentially great. Nevertheless, legal controls tend to be rather a blunt weapon, although discretion can sometimes be allowed in the administration of the law.

2. Regulatory bodies can be set up to monitor and control activities that might be against the public interest (e.g. anti-competitive behaviour of oligopolists). They can conduct investigations of specific cases and can be very thorough. The investigations, however, may be expensive and time consuming, and may not be acted on by the authorities.

Other forms of government intervention 6.6

What other means does the government have to correct market failures?

Changes in property rights

One cause of market failure is the limited nature of property rights. If someone dumps a load of rubble in your garden, the law should protect you. It is *your* garden, *your* property, and you can thus insist that it is removed. If, however, someone dumps a load of rubble in his or her *own* garden, but which is next door to yours, what can you do? You can still see it from your window. It is still an eyesore. But you have no property rights over the next-door garden.

Property rights define who owns property, to what uses it can be put, the rights other people have over it and how it may be transferred. By *extending* these rights, individuals may be able to prevent other people imposing costs on them, or charge them for doing so.

The trouble is that in many instances this type of solution is totally impractical. It is impractical when *many* people are *slightly* inconvenienced, especially if there are many culprits imposing the costs. For example, if I were disturbed by noisy lorries outside my home, it would not be practical to negotiate with every haulage company involved. What if I wanted to ban the lorries from the street but my next-door neighbour wanted to charge them 10p per journey? Who gets their way?

Where the extension of private property rights becomes a more practical solution is when the culprits are few in number, are easily identifiable and impose clearly defined costs. Thus a noise abatement Act could be passed which allowed me to prevent my neighbours playing noisy radios, having noisy parties or otherwise disturbing the peace in my home. The onus would be on me to report them. Or if I chose, I could agree not to report them if they paid me adequate compensation.

But even in cases where only a few people are involved, there may still be the problem of litigation. Justice may not be free, and there is thus a conflict with equity. The rich can afford 'better' justice. They can employ top lawyers. Thus even if I have a right to sue a large company for dumping toxic waste near me, I may not have the legal muscle to win.

Finally there is the broader question of *equity*. The extension of private property rights may favour the rich (who tend to have more property) at the expense of the poor. Ramblers may get great pleasure from strolling across a great country estate, along public rights of way. This may annoy the owner. If the owner's property rights are now extended to exclude the ramblers, is this a social gain?

Of course, equity considerations can also be dealt with by altering property rights, but in a different way. *Public* property like parks, open spaces, libraries and historic buildings could be extended. Also the property of the rich could be redistributed to the poor. Here it is less a question of the rights that ownership confers, and more a question of altering the ownership itself.

> **Pause for thought**
>
> *Would it be a good idea to extend countries' territorial waters in order to bring key open seas fishing grounds within countries' territory? Could this help to solve the problem of over-fishing?*

Provision of information

When ignorance is a reason for market failure, the direct provision of information by the government or one of its agencies may help to correct that failure. An example is the information on jobs provided by job centres to those looking for work. They thus help the labour market to work better and increase the elasticity of supply of labour. Another example is the provision of consumer information – for example, on the effects of smoking, or of eating certain foodstuffs. Another is the provision of government statistics on prices, costs, employment, sales trends, etc. This enables firms to plan with greater certainty.

The direct provision of goods and services

In the case of public goods and services, such as streets, pavements, seaside illumination and national defence, the market may completely fail to provide. In this case the government must take over the role of provision. Central government, local government or some other public agency could provide these goods and services directly. Alternatively, they could pay private firms to do so. The public would pay through central and local taxation.

But just what quantity of the public good should be provided? How can the level of public demand or public 'need' be identified? Should any charge at all be made to consumers for each unit consumed?

With a pure public good, once it is provided the marginal cost of supplying one more consumer is zero. Take the case of a lighthouse. Once it is constructed and in operation, there is no extra cost of providing the service to additional passing ships. Even if it were *possible* to charge ships each time they make use of it, it would not be socially desirable. Assuming no external costs, *MSC* is zero. Thus *MSB* = *MSC* at a price of zero. Zero is thus the socially efficient price.

But what about the construction of a new public good, like a new road or a new lighthouse? How can a rational decision be made by the government as to whether it should go ahead? This time the marginal cost is not zero: extra roads and lighthouses cost money to build. The solution is to identify all the costs and benefits to society from the project (private and external) and to weigh them up. This is known as cost–benefit analysis. If the social benefits of the project exceed the social costs, then it would be socially efficient to go ahead with it. Many proposed public projects are subjected to cost–benefit analysis in order to assess their desirability.

The government could also provide goods and services directly which are *not* public goods. Examples include health and education. There are four reasons why such things are provided free or at well below cost.

Social justice.   Society may feel that these things should not be provided according to ability to pay. Rather they should be provided as of right: an equal right based on need.

Large positive externalities.   People other than the consumer may benefit substantially. If a person decides to get treatment for an infectious disease, other people benefit by not being infected. A free health service thus helps to combat the spread of disease.

Definition

Cost–benefit analysis
The identification, measurement and weighing-up of the costs and benefits of a project in order to decide whether or not it should go ahead.

Dependants. If education were not free, and if the quality of education depended on the amount spent, and if parents could choose how much or little to buy, then the quality of children's education would depend not just on their parents' income, but also on how much they cared. A government may choose to provide such things free in order to protect children from 'bad' parents. A similar argument is used for providing free prescriptions and dental treatment for all children.

Ignorance. Consumers may not realise how much they will benefit. If they had to pay, they may choose (unwisely) to go without. Providing health care free may persuade people to consult their doctors before a complaint becomes serious.

Recap

1. An extension of property rights may allow individuals to prevent others imposing costs on them, or to charge them for so doing. This is not practical, however, when many people are affected to a small degree, or where several people are affected but differ in their attitudes towards what they want doing about the 'problem'.

2. The government may provide information in cases where the private sector fails to provide an adequate level.

3. The government may also provide goods and services directly. These could be in the category of public goods or other goods where the government feels that provision by the market is inadequate.

More or less intervention?   6.7

Can the government always put things right?

Government intervention in the market can itself lead to problems. The case for non-intervention (*laissez-faire*) or very limited intervention is not that the market is the *perfect* means of achieving given social goals, but rather that the problems created by intervention are greater than the problems overcome by that intervention.

Drawbacks of government intervention

Shortages and surpluses. If the government intervenes by fixing prices at levels other than the equilibrium, this will create either shortages or surpluses (see Section 2.6).

If the price is fixed *below* the equilibrium, there will be a shortage. For example, if the rent of council houses is fixed below the equilibrium in order to provide cheap housing for poor people, demand will exceed supply. In the case of such shortages the government will have to adopt a system of waiting lists, or rationing, or giving certain people preferential treatment. Alternatively it will have to allow allocation to be on a first-come, first-served basis or allow queues to develop. Black markets are likely to occur.

If the price is fixed *above* the equilibrium price, there will be a surplus. Such surpluses are obviously wasteful. (The problem of food surpluses in the European Union was examined in Box 2.4).

Poor information.   The government may not know the full costs and benefits of its policies. It may genuinely wish to pursue the interests of consumers or any other group and yet may be unaware of people's wishes or misinterpret their behaviour.

Bureaucracy and inefficiency.   Government intervention involves administrative costs. The more wide reaching and detailed the intervention, the greater the number of people and material resources that will be involved. These resources may be used wastefully.

Lack of market incentives.   If government intervention removes market forces or cushions their effect (by the use of subsidies, welfare provisions, guaranteed prices or wages, etc.), it may remove certain useful incentives. Subsidies may allow inefficient firms to survive. Welfare payments may discourage effort. The market may be imperfect, but it does tend to encourage efficiency by allowing the efficient to receive greater rewards.

Shifts in government policy.   The economic efficiency of industry may suffer if government intervention changes too frequently. It makes it difficult for firms to plan if they cannot predict tax rates, subsidies, price and wage controls, etc.

Lack of freedom for the individual.   Government intervention involves a loss of freedom for individuals to make economic choices. The argument is not just that the pursuit of individual gain is seen to lead to the social good, but that it is desirable in itself that individuals should be as free as possible to pursue their own interests with the minimum of government interference: that minimum being largely confined to the maintenance of laws consistent with the protection of life, liberty and property.

Advantages of the free market

Although markets in the real world are not perfect, even imperfect markets can be argued to have positive advantages over government provision or even government regulation. These might include the following:

Automatic adjustments.   Government intervention requires administration. A free-market economy, on the other hand, leads to automatic, albeit imperfect, adjustment to demand and supply changes.

Dynamic advantages of capitalism.   The chances of making high monopoly/oligopoly profits will encourage capitalists to invest in new products and new techniques. Prices may be high initially, but consumers will gain from the extra choice of products. Furthermore, if profits are high, new firms will sooner or later break into the market and competition will ensue.

> **Pause for thought**
>
> Are there any features of free-market capitalism that would discourage innovation?

A high degree of competition even under monopoly/oligopoly.   Even though an industry at first sight may seem to be highly monopolistic, competitive forces may still work as a result of the following:

- A fear that excessively high profits might encourage firms to attempt to break into the industry (assuming that the market is contestable).

- Competition from closely related industries (e.g. coach services for rail services, or electricity for gas).
- The threat of foreign competition.
- Countervailing powers. Large powerful producers often sell to large powerful buyers. For example, the power of detergent manufacturers to drive up the price of washing powder is countered by the power of supermarket chains to drive down the price at which they purchase it. Thus power is to some extent neutralised.
- The competition for corporate control (see page 131).

Should there be more or less intervention in the market?

No firm conclusions can be drawn in the debate between those who favour more and those who favour less government intervention, for the following reasons:

- Many moral, social and political issues are involved which cannot be settled by economic analysis. For example, it could be argued that freedom to set up in business and freedom from government regulation are desirable *for their own sake*. As a fundamental ethical point of view this can be disputed, but not disproved.
- In principle, the issue of whether a government ought to intervene in any situation could be settled by weighing up the costs and benefits of that intervention. However, such costs and benefits, even if they could be identified, are extremely difficult if not impossible to measure, especially when the costs are borne by different people from those who receive the benefits and when externalities are involved.
- Often the effect of more or less intervention simply cannot be predicted: there are too many uncertainties.

Nevertheless, economists can make a considerable contribution to analysing problems of the market and the effects of government intervention.

Recap

1. Government intervention in the market may lead to shortages or surpluses; it may be based on poor information; it may be costly in terms of administration; it may stifle incentives; it may be disruptive if government policies change too frequently; it may remove certain liberties.

2. By contrast, a free market leads to automatic adjustments to changes in economic conditions; the prospect of monopoly/oligopoly profits may stimulate risk taking and hence research and development and innovation; there may still be a high degree of actual or potential competition under monopoly and oligopoly.

3. It is impossible to draw firm conclusions about the 'optimum' level of government intervention. This is partly due to the moral/political nature of the question, partly due to the difficulties of measuring costs and benefits of intervention/non-intervention, and partly due to the difficulties of predicting the effects of government policies, especially over the longer term.

6.8   The environment: a case study in market failure

How can economists contribute to the environmental debate?

The environmental problem

Global warming, pollution of the land, rivers and seas, the depletion of fish stocks, the chopping down of rainforests, the reduction in biodiversity, the dirty and rubbish-strewn nature of many cities and the despoiling of the countryside have become major concerns around the world in recent years. And yet, in many cases the degradation of the environment is getting worse.

There are some grounds for optimism, however. Many newer industrial processes are cleaner and make a more efficient use of resources. This leads to less waste and a slowdown in the rate of extraction of various minerals and fossil fuels.

In addition, as resources become scarcer, so their prices rise. This encourages people to use less of them, either by using more efficient technology or by switching to renewable alternatives. Thus as fossil fuels gradually run out, so a rise in their price will encourage the switch to solar, wave and wind power.

Finally, public opinion can put important pressure on governments and firms. Many firms have found it to be in their commercial interests to have a 'green image'. Likewise, governments have generally found it in their interests to respond to pressures for a cleaner, greener environment.

Despite these developments, however, many aspects of environmental degradation continue to worsen:

- Since 1970, more than 30 per cent of natural species have been destroyed.
- Consumption of natural resources and carbon dioxide emissions have both doubled over the last 40 years and continue to grow at a similar rate.
- Over the same period, the consumption of marine fish has more than doubled, and the world's fish stocks are now seriously depleted.
- Over 80 per cent of the coral in the Indian Ocean is dead (as a result of global warming). Coral reefs provide many countries with fish and help prevent tidal waves and coastal erosion.
- Tropical countries are projected to lose another 10 per cent of their forests over the next 20 years.
- In developed countries, motor vehicle use is expected to increase by 40 per cent, energy use by 35 per cent and air passenger kilometres by 300 per cent over the same period.
- Toxic chemicals are widespread in the environment and up to 6 per cent of disease is caused by pollution.

Part of the problem is the growing pressure on the environment of a rapidly expanding world population (see Box 3.2). But a major cause of the problem is the failure of the market system.

Market failures

The market system will fail to provide an adequate protection for the environment for a number of reasons.

The environment as a common resource.   The air, the seas and many other parts of the environment are not privately owned. They are a global 'commons', and thus have the characteristic of 'non-excludability' (see page 210). Many of the 'services' provided by the environment do not have a price, so there is no economic incentive to economise on their use.

Yet most environmental resources are *scarce*: there is 'rivalry' in their use. This is where common resources differ from public goods. One person's use of a common resource diminishes the amount or quality available for others. At a zero price, these resources will be overused. This is why fish stocks in many parts of the world are severely depleted, why virgin forests are disappearing (cut down for timber or firewood), why many roads are so congested and why the atmosphere is becoming so polluted (being used as a common 'dump' for emissions). In each case, a resource that is freely available is overused. This is known as the 'tragedy of the commons'.

Externalities.   One of the major problems of the environment being a public good is that of externalities. When people pollute the environment, the costs are borne mainly by others. The greater these external costs, the lower will be the socially efficient level of output (Q_2 in Figure 6.1(a) on page 208). Because no one owns the environment, there is no one to enforce property rights over it. If a company pollutes the air that I breathe, I cannot stop it because the air does not belong to me.

Ignorance.   There have been many cases of people causing environmental damage without realising it, especially when the effects build up over a long time. Take the case of aerosols. It was not until the 1980s that scientists connected their use to ozone depletion. Even when the problems are known to scientists, consumers may not appreciate the full environmental costs of their actions. So even if people would like to be more 'environmentally friendly' in their activities, they might not have the knowledge to be so.

Inter-generational problems.   The environmentally harmful effects of many activities are long term, whereas the benefits are immediate. Thus consumers and firms are frequently prepared to continue with various practices and leave future generations to worry about their environmental consequences. The problem, then, is a reflection of the importance that people attach to the present relative to the future.

> **Pause for thought**   ‖‖‖
>
> Look through the categories of possible market failings in Sections 6.1 to 6.3. Are there any others, in addition to the four we have just identified, that will result in a socially inefficient use of the environment?

Policy alternatives

Charging for use of the environment (as a resource or a dump)

One way of 'pricing the environment' is for the government to impose environmental charges on consumers or firms. Thus *emissions charges* could be levied on firms discharging waste. Another example is the use of *user charges* to households for sewage disposal or rubbish collection. The socially efficient level of environmental use would be where the marginal social benefits and costs of that use were equal. This is illustrated in Figure 6.6, which shows the emission of toxic waste into a river by a chemical plant.

It is assumed that all the benefits from emitting the waste into the river accrue to the firm (i.e. there is no external benefit). Marginal private and marginal social benefits are thus the same (*MB = MSB*). The curve slopes downwards because, with a downward-sloping demand curve for the *good*, higher output will have a lower marginal benefit, and so too will the waste associated with it.

But what about the marginal costs? Without charges, the marginal private cost of using the river for emitting the waste is zero. The pollution of the river, however,

> **Definition**
>
> **Environmental charges**
> Charges for using natural resources (e.g. water or national parks), or for using the environment as a dump for waste (e.g. factory emissions or sewage).

Box 6.3

A deeper shade of green

How should we treat the environment?

How green are you? Do you see the environment as there for you to use as you choose, or do we all have responsibilities for looking after the environment – responsibilities towards each other, or to future generations, or to the animals and plants that share the planet with us, or even to the planet itself? In this box we examine some of the different approaches to looking after the environment, and ask what implications they have for sustainability.

The free-market approach.   At one extreme, we could regard the world as there purely for ourselves: a resource that belongs to individual property owners to do with as they choose; or a 'common asset', such as the air and seas, for individuals to use for their own benefit. In this view of the world, we are entitled simply to weigh up the marginal costs and benefits to ourselves of any activity. Sustainability is only achieved in this free-market world to the extent that resource prices rise as they become scarce and to the extent that environmentally-friendly technologies are in firms' (or consumers') private interests.

In terms of Figure 6.1(a) on page 208, assuming that there were external environmental costs (shown by the vertical difference between the *MSC* and *MC*

curves), no account would be taken of these, and production would remain at the free-market level of Q_1.

The social efficiency approach. A somewhat less extreme version of this view is one that takes the social costs and benefits of using the environment into account: i.e. not just the costs and benefits to the direct producer or consumer, but to people in general. Here we would apply the standard rules for social efficiency: that if marginal social benefit exceeds marginal social cost we should do more of the activity, and if marginal social cost exceeds marginal social benefit we should do less. In Figure 6.1(a), the social efficiency approach would give an optimum output of Q_2.

Even though this approach does take into account environmental externalities (such as pollution) these environmental costs are only costs to the extent that they adversely affect *human beings*.

Within this general approach, however, more explicit account can be taken of sustainability, by including in the external costs the costs of our use of the environment today to *future* generations. For example, we could take into account the effects of global warming not just on ourselves, but on our children and their descendants.

K(
Id

1
p2

Figure 6.6

An emissions charge

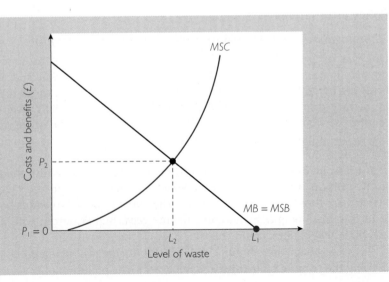

The conservationist approach. Many environment-alists argue that our responsibilities should not be limited to each other, or even to future generations, but should include the environment for its own sake. Such a view would involve downplaying the relative importance of material consumption and economic growth and putting greater emphasis on the mainten-ance of ecosystems. Growth in consumption would be ethically acceptable only if it led to no (or only very minor) environmental degradation. Maintenance of the environment is thus seen as an ethical constraint on human activity. In Figure 6.1(a) the optimum pro-duction would be below Q_2 as long as the *MSC* curve only included costs to *society* and not the broader costs to the environment for its own sake.

The Gaia approach. The strongest approach to sus-tainability involves a fundamentally different ethical standpoint. Here the Earth itself, and its various natural species of animals and plants have moral rights. According to this 'Gaia philosophy', people are seen as mere custodians of the planet: the planet does not belong to us, any more than a dog belongs to the fleas on its back! This view of the environ-ment is similar to that held by indigenous peoples living in marginal areas, such as the Aborigines in Australia and the Bushmen of the Kalahari, and to various other 'hunter-gatherer' peoples in developing countries. Their ethic is that the land they leave their descendants should be as good, if not better, than the land they inherited from their ancestors. Conservation is the 'prime directive'. This approach to the environ-ment has been dubbed the 'deep green' approach.

In this approach, Figure 6.1(a) is irrelevant. The question is not whether environmental degradation is a price worth paying for the benefits of consump-tion. Production should be avoided that involves *any* environmental degradation.

?
1. If, according to the deep green approach, we should not do anything that involves environ-mental degradation, does this imply that the cost of environmental damage is infinite?
2. If the adverse effects on the environment of a person's actions were confined to that person's own property (e.g. a farmer cutting down hedgerows on his or her own land), would this matter if we took a social efficiency approach towards sustainability? Would there be any *external* costs?

imposes an external cost on those living by the river or using it for fishing or water supply. The marginal external cost rises as the river becomes less and less able to cope with increased levels of emission. As there is no private cost, the marginal social cost is the same as the marginal external cost.

Without a charge, the firm will emit L_1, since this is where its private marginal cost (= 0) equals its private marginal benefit. The socially efficient level of emission is L_2 and the socially efficient level of emission charge, therefore, is P_2.

Environmental ('green') taxes and subsidies

A tax could be imposed on the output (or consumption) of a *good*, wherever exter-nal environmental costs are generated. These are known as green taxes. In this case, the good already has a price: the tax has the effect of increasing the price. To achieve a socially efficient output, the rate of tax should be equal to the marginal external cost (see Figure 6.5 on page 221). The alternative is to subsidise activities that reduce pollution (such as the installation of loft insulation). Here the rate of subsidy should be equal to the marginal external benefit.

| Definition |

Green tax
A tax on output designed to charge for the adverse effects of production on the environment. The socially efficient level of a green tax is equal to the marginal environmental cost of production.

Although green taxes and subsidies are theoretically a means of achieving social efficiency, they do have serious limitations (see Box 6.4).

Laws and regulations

The traditional way of tackling pollution has been to set maximum permitted levels of emission or resource use, or minimum acceptable levels of environmental quality, and then to fine firms contravening these limits. Clearly, there have to be inspectors to monitor the amount of pollution, and the fines have to be large enough to deter firms from exceeding the limit.

Virtually all countries have environmental regulations of one sort or another. For example, the EU has over 200 items of legislation covering areas such as air and water pollution, noise, the marketing and use of dangerous chemicals, waste management, the environmental impacts of new projects (such as power stations, roads and quarries), recycling, depletion of the ozone layer and global warming.

Given the uncertainty over the environmental impacts of pollutants, especially in the longer term, it is often better to play safe and set tough emissions or ambient standards. These could always be relaxed at a later stage if the effects turn out not to be so damaging, but it might be too late to reverse damage if the effects turn out to be more serious. Taxes may be a more sophisticated means of reaching a socially efficient output, but regulations are usually more straightforward to devise, easier to understand by firms and easier to implement.

Education

People's attitudes are very important in determining the environmental consequences of their actions. Fortunately for the environment, people are not always out simply to maximise their own self-interest. If they were, then why would people often buy more expensive 'green' products, such as environmentally friendly detergents? The answer is that many people like to do their own little bit, however small, towards protecting the environment.

This is where education can come in. If children, and adults for that matter, were made more aware of environmental issues and the consequences of their actions, then people's consumption habits could change and more pressure would be put on firms to improve their 'green credentials'.

Tradable permits

Definition

Tradable permits Each firm is given a permit to produce a given level of pollution. If less than the permitted amount is produced, the firm is given a credit. This can then be sold to another firm, allowing it to exceed its original limit.

A policy measure that has grown in popularity in recent years is that of tradable permits. This is a combination of regulations and market-based systems. A maximum permitted level of emission is set for a given pollutant for a given factory, and the firm is given a permit to emit up to this amount. If it emits less than this amount, it is given a credit for the difference, which it can then use in another of its factories, or sell to another firm, to enable it to go that amount *over* its permitted level. Thus the overall level of emissions is given by regulations, whereas their distribution is determined by the market.

Take the example of firms A and B, which are currently producing 12 units of a pollutant each. Now assume that a standard is set permitting them to produce only 10 units each. If firm A managed to reduce the pollutant to 8 units, it would be given a credit for 2 units. It could then sell this to firm B, enabling B to continue emitting 12 units. The effect would still be a total reduction of 4 units between the two firms. However, by allowing them to trade in pollution permits, pollution reduction can be concentrated in the firms where it can be achieved at lowest cost. In our example, if it cost firm B more to reduce its pollution than firm A, the permits could be sold from A to B at a price that was profitable to both (i.e. at a price above the cost of emission reduction to A, but below the cost of emission reduction to B). Given the resulting reduced cost of pollution control, it might be politically easier to impose tougher standards (i.e. impose lower permitted levels of emission).

The principle of tradable permits can be used as the basis of international agreements on pollution reduction. Each country could be required to achieve a certain percentage reduction in a pollutant (e.g. carbon dioxide – CO_2 – or sulphur dioxide – SO_2), but any country exceeding its reduction could sell its right to these emissions to other (presumably richer) countries.

A similar principle can be used for using natural resources. Thus fish quotas could be assigned to fishing boats or fleets or countries. Any parts of these quotas not used could then be sold.

The main advantage of tradable permits is that they combine the simplicity of regulations with the benefits of achieving pollution reduction in the most efficient way. The government can simply set the total amount of permitted discharge according to the ability of the environment to absorb the pollutants; and it can do this without any knowledge of the specific costs and benefits of individual firms. This is the main benefit of regulations over taxes and charges. Then it can let the market in tradable permits allocate the reduction in pollution to where it can be achieved at least cost (the same effect as with taxes).

There are, however, various problems with tradable permits. One is how to distribute the permissions in a way that all firms regard as fair. Another is the possibility that trade will lead to pollution being concentrated in certain geographical areas. Another is that it may reduce the pressure on dirtier factories (or countries) to cut their emissions. Finally, the system will only lead to significant cuts in pollution if the permitted levels are low. Once the system is in place, the government might then feel the pressure is off to reduce the permitted levels.

> **Pause for thought**
>
> To what extent will the introduction of tradable permits lead to a lower level of total pollution (as opposed to its redistribution)?

How much can we rely on governments?

If governments are to be relied upon to set the optimum green taxes or regulations, several conditions must be met.

First, they must have the will to protect the environment. But governments are accountable to their electorates and must often appease various pressure groups, such as representatives of big business. In the USA, for example, there has been great resistance to cuts in greenhouse gases from the automobile, power and various other industries, many of which have powerful representation in Congress. One of the problems is that many of the environmental effects of our actions today will be on future generations, but governments represent today's generation, and today's generation may not be prepared to make the necessary sacrifices. This brings us back to the importance of education.

Second, it must be possible to identify just what the optimum is. This requires a knowledge of just what the environmental effects are of various activities, such as the emission of CO_2 into the atmosphere, and that is something on which scientists disagree.

Finally, there is the problem that many environmental issues are global and not just local or national. Many require concerted action by governments around the world. The history of international agreements on environmental issues, however, is plagued with difficulties between countries, which seem concerned mainly with their own national interests.

Key Idea 16 142

Box 6.4

Green taxes

Their growing popularity in the industrialised world

Increasingly, countries are introducing 'green' taxes in order to discourage pollution as goods are produced, consumed or disposed of. The table below shows the range of green taxes used around the world and the chart shows green tax revenues as a percentage of GDP in various countries. As you can see, they are higher than average in Scandinavian countries, reflecting the strength of their environmental concerns. They are lowest in the USA. By far the largest green tax revenues come from fuel taxes. Fuel taxes are relatively high in the UK and so, therefore, are green tax revenues.

There are various problems, however, with using the tax weapon in the fight against pollution.

Identifying the socially efficient tax rate

It will be difficult to identify the appropriate amount of tax for each firm, given that each one is likely to produce different amounts of pollutants for any given level of output. Even if two firms produce exactly the same amount of pollutants, the environmental dam-

age might be quite different because the ability of the environment to cope with it will differ between the two locations. Also the number of people suffering will differ (a factor that is very important when considering the *human* impact of pollution). What is more, the harmful effects are likely to build up over time, and predicting these effects is fraught with difficulty.

Problems of demand inelasticity

The less elastic the demand for the product, the less effective will be a tax in cutting production and hence in cutting pollution. Thus taxes on petrol would have to be very high indeed to make significant reductions in the consumption of petrol and hence significant reductions in the exhaust gases that contribute to global warming and acid rain.

Problems with international trade

If a country imposes pollution taxes on its industries, its products will become less competitive in world trade. To compensate for this, it may be necessary to

Types of environmental taxes and charges

Motor fuels	**Other goods**	**Air transport**
Leaded/unleaded	Batteries	Noise charges
Diesel (quality differential)	Plastic carrier bags	Aviation fuels
Carbon/energy taxation	Glass containers	
Sulphur tax	Drink cans	**Water**
	Tyres	Water charges
Other energy products	CFCs/halons	Sewage charges
Carbon/energy tax	Disposable razors/cameras	Water effluent charges
Sulphur tax or charge	Lubricant oil charge	Manure charges
NO_2 charge	Oil pollutant charge	
Methane charge	Solvents	**Direct tax provisions**
		Tax relief on green investment
Agricultural inputs		Taxation on free company cars
Fertilisers	**Waste disposal**	Employer-paid commuting expenses taxable
Pesticides	Municipal waste charges	Employer-paid parking expenses taxable
Manure	Waste-disposal charges	Commuter use of public transport tax deductible
	Hazardous waste charges	
Vehicle-related taxation	Landfill tax or charges	
Sales tax depends on car size	Duties on waste water	
Road tax depends on car size		

Key Idea 18 p206

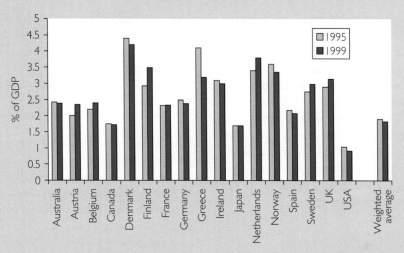

Source: *Environmentally Related Taxes Database* (OECD, 2002).

Green tax revenues as a percentage of GDP

give the industries tax rebates for exports. Also, taxes would have to be imposed on imports of competitors' products from countries where there is no equivalent green tax.

Effects on employment

Reduced output in the industries affected by green taxes will lead to a reduction in employment. If, however, the effect were to encourage investment in new cleaner technology, employment might not fall. Furthermore, employment opportunities could be generated elsewhere, if the extra revenues from the green taxes were spent on alternative products (e.g. buses and trains rather than cars).

Redistributive effects

The poor spend a higher proportion of their income on domestic fuel than the rich. A 'carbon tax' on such fuel will, therefore, have the effect of redistributing incomes away from the poor. The poor also spend a larger proportion of their income on food than do the rich. Taxes on agriculture, designed to reduce intensive use of fertilisers and pesticides, will again tend to hit the poor proportionately more than the rich.

Not all green taxes, however, are regressive. The rich spend a higher proportion of their income on motoring than the poor. Thus petrol and other motoring taxes could have a progressive effect. Also, other taxes, such as those on packaging, batteries and disposable items, are likely to be neutral in their impact, since their prime purpose is to encourage people to switch to non-polluting alternatives.

Despite these problems, such taxes can still move output closer to the socially efficient level. What is more, they have the major advantage of providing a continuing incentive to firms to find cleaner methods of production and thereby save more on their tax bills.

? Is it a good idea to use the revenues from green taxes to subsidise green alternatives (e.g. using petrol taxes for subsidising rail transport)?

Key
Idea
17
p192

Box 6.5

The problem of urban traffic congestion

Does Singapore have the answer?

It takes only one hour to drive from one end of Singapore to the other. Yet the average Singaporean driver travels an estimated 18 600 km per year, more than the average US driver, and over 50 per cent more than the average Japanese driver. In Singapore in 2003 there were a little over 400 000 cars, giving a vehicle density of 225 motor vehicles per km of road. This compares with a vehicle density in the USA of only 27 motor vehicles per km. It is hardly surprising that traffic congestion has become a major focus of public debate, particularly as the demand for cars is set to increase as consumer affluence grows.

The problem of traffic congestion

Traffic congestion is a classic example of the problem of externalities. When people use their cars, not only do they incur private costs (petrol, wear and tear on the vehicle, tolls, the time taken to travel, etc.), but also they impose costs on other people. These external costs include the following:

Congestion costs: time.   When a person uses a car on a congested road, it will add to the congestion. This will therefore slow down the traffic even more and increase the journey time of other car users.

Congestion costs: monetary.   Congestion increases fuel consumption, and the stopping and starting increases the costs of wear and tear. When a motorist adds to congestion, therefore, there will be additional monetary costs imposed on other motorists.

Environmental costs.   When motorists use a road they reduce the quality of the environment for others. Cars emit fumes and create noise. This is bad enough for pedestrians and other car users, but can be particularly distressing for people living along the road. Driving can cause accidents – a problem that increases as drivers become more impatient as a result of delays.

Exhaust gases cause long-term environmental damage and are one of the main causes of the green-

house effect and of the increased acidity of lakes and rivers and the poisoning of forests. They can also cause long-term health problems (e.g. for asthma sufferers).

The socially efficient level of road usage

These externalities mean that road usage will be above the social optimum. This is illustrated in the diagram. Costs and benefits are shown on the vertical axis and are measured in money terms. Thus any non-monetary costs or benefits (such as time costs) must be given a monetary value. The horizontal axis measures road usage in terms of cars per minute passing a specified point on the road.

For simplicity it is assumed that there are no external benefits from car use and that therefore marginal private and marginal social benefits are the same. The *MSB* curve is shown as downward sloping. The reason for this is that different road users put a different value on any given journey. If the marginal (private) cost of making the journey were high, only those for whom the journey had a high marginal benefit would travel along the road. If the marginal cost of making the journey fell, more people would make the journey: people choosing to make the journey as long as the marginal cost of the journey was less than the marginal benefit. Thus the greater the number of cars, the lower the marginal benefit.

The marginal (private) cost curve (*MC*) is likely to be constant up to the level of traffic flow at which congestion begins to occur. This is shown as point *a* in the diagram. Beyond this point, marginal cost is likely to rise as time costs increase (i.e. journey times lengthen) and as fuel consumption rises.

The marginal *social* cost curve (*MSC*) is drawn above the marginal private cost curve. The vertical difference between the two represents the external costs. Up to point *b*, external costs are simply the environmental costs. Beyond point *b*, there are also

Key Idea 18 p206

Key Idea 19 p207

Key Idea 20 p207

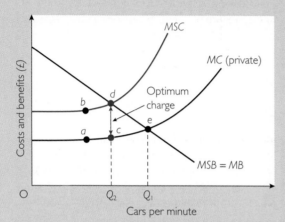

Actual and optimum road usage

external congestion costs, since additional road users slow down the journey of *other* road users. These external costs get progressively greater as traffic grinds to a halt.

The actual level of traffic flow will be at Q_1, where marginal private costs and benefits are equal (point *e*). The socially efficient level of traffic flow, however, will be at the lower level of Q_2 where marginal social costs and benefits are equal (point *d*). In other words, there will be an excessive level of road usage.

So what can governments do to 'internalise' these externalities?

The Singapore solution

In contrast to its neighbours, many of which are suffering more acute urban traffic congestion problems, Singapore has an integrated transport policy. This includes the following:

■ Restricting the number of new car licences, and allowing their price to rise to the corresponding equilibrium. This makes car licences in Singapore among the most expensive in the world.

■ A 111-kilometre-long mass rail transit (MRT) system with subsidised fares. Trains are comfortable, clean and frequent. Stations are air-conditioned.

■ A programme of building new estates near MRT stations.

■ Cheap, frequent buses, serving all parts of the island.

But it is in respect of road usage that the Singaporean authorities have been most innovative.

The first innovation came in 1975. The city centre was made a restricted zone. Motorists who wished to enter this zone had to buy a ticket (an 'area licence') at any one of 33 entry points. Police were stationed at these entry points to check that cars had paid and displayed.

Then in 1990 a quota system for new cars was established. The government decides the total number of cars the country should have, and issues just enough licences each month to maintain that total. These licences (or 'Certificates of Entitlement') are for ten years and are offered at auction. Their market price varies from around £10 000 to £30 000.

A problem with the licences is that they are a once-and-for-all payment, which does not vary with the amount people use their car. In other words, their marginal cost (for additional miles driven) is zero. Many people feel that, having paid such a high price for their licence, they ought to use their car as much as possible in order to get value for money!

With traffic congestion steadily worsening, it was recognised that something more had to be done. Either the area licensing scheme had to be widened, or some other form of charging had to be adopted. The decision was taken to introduce electronic road pricing (ERP). This alternative would not only save on police labour costs, but enable charge rates to be varied according to levels of congestion, times of the day, and locality. What, then, would be the optimum charge? If the objective is to reduce traffic from Q_1 to Q_2 in the diagram, then a charge of $d - c$ should be levied.

Since 1998 all vehicles in Singapore have been fitted with an in-vehicle unit (IU). Every journey made requires the driver to insert a smart card into the IU. On specified roads, overhead gantries read the IU and deduct the appropriate charge from the card. The charge varies with the time of day. If a car does not have sufficient funds on its smart card, the car's details are relayed to a control centre and a fine is imposed. The system has the benefit of operating on three-lane highways and does not require traffic to slow down. What is more, it is very flexible, with the possibility of adjusting the road price (i.e. the charge) to keep traffic at the desired level. The ERP system operates on Mondays to Fridays from 7.30 a.m. to 7.00 p.m. in the central area and from 7.30 a.m. to 9.30 a.m. on the expressways and outer ring roads.

The system was expensive to set up, however. Cheaper schemes have been adopted elsewhere, such as Norway and parts of the USA. These operate by funnelling traffic into a single lane in order to register the car, but this has the disadvantage of slowing the traffic down.

One message is clear from the Singapore solution. Road pricing alone is not enough. Unless there are fast, comfortable and affordable public transport alternatives, the demand for cars will be highly price inelastic. People have to get to work!

?
1. Referring to a town or city with which you are familiar, consider what would be the most appropriate mix of policies to deal with its traffic congestion problems.
2. Explain how, by varying the charge debited from the smart card according to the time of day or level of congestion, a socially optimal level of road use can be achieved.

Recap

1. The effects of population pressures and market failures have led to growing environmental degradation.

2. The market fails to achieve a socially efficient use of the environment because large parts of the environment are a common resource, because production or consumption often generates environmental externalities, because of ignorance of the environmental effects of our actions, and because of a lack of concern for future generations.

3. One approach to protecting the environment is to impose charges for using the environment or taxes per unit of output. The problem with these methods is in identifying the appropriate charges or tax rates, since these will vary according to the environmental impact.

4. Another approach is to use laws and regulations, such as making certain practices illegal or putting limits on discharges. This is a less sophisticated alternative to taxes or charges, but it is safer when the environmental costs of certain actions are unknown.

5. Education can help to change attitudes towards the environment and the behaviour of consumers and firms.

6. Tradable permits are a mix of regulations and market-based systems. Firms are given permits to emit a certain level of pollution and these can then be traded. A firm that can reduce its pollution relatively cheaply below its permitted level can sell this credit to another firm that finds it more costly to do so. The system is an efficient and administratively cheap way of limiting pollution to a designated level. It can, however, lead to pollution being concentrated in certain areas and can reduce the pressure on firms to find cleaner methods of production.

7. Although governments can make a major contribution to reducing pollution, government action is unlikely to lead to the optimum outcome (however defined). Governments may be more concerned with short-run political considerations and will not have perfect information.

Questions

1. The table at the bottom of the page gives the costs and benefits of an imaginary firm operating under perfect competition whose activities create a certain amount of pollution. (It is assumed that the costs of this pollution to society can be accurately measured.)

   (a) What is the profit-maximising level of output for this firm?
   (b) What is the socially efficient level of output?
   (c) Why might the marginal pollution costs increase in the way illustrated in this example?

2. In Figure 6.1 (page 208) the *MSC* curve is drawn parallel to the *MC* curve. Under what circumstances would it have a steeper slope than the MC curve?

3. Give additional examples of each of the four types of externality to those given on pages 207–10.

4. Give some examples of public goods (other than those given on page 210). Does the provider of these goods or services (the government or local authority) charge for their use? If so, is the method of charging based on the amount of the good people use? Is it a good method of charging? Could you suggest a better method?

5. Distinguish between publicly provided goods, public goods and merit goods.

6. Name some goods or services provided by the government or local authorities that are not public goods.

7. Some roads could be regarded as a public good, but some could be provided by the market. Which types of road could be provided by the market? Why? Would it be a good idea?

8. Assume that you have decided to buy a new video recorder. How do you set about ensuring that you make the right choice between the available makes?

9. Assume that you wanted the information given in (a)–(h) below. In which cases could you (i) buy perfect information; (ii) buy imperfect information; (iii) obtain information without paying for it; (iv) not obtain information?

   (a) Which washing machine is the more reliable?
   (b) Which of two jobs that are vacant is the more satisfying?
   (c) Which builder will repair my roof most cheaply?
   (d) Which builder will make the best job of repairing my roof?
   (e) Which builder is best value for money?
   (f) How big a mortgage would it be wise for me to take out?
   (g) What course of higher education should I follow?
   (h) What brand of washing powder washes whiter?

   In which cases are there non-monetary costs to you of finding out the information? How can you know whether the information you acquire is accurate or not?

Output (units)	Price per unit (MSB) (£)	Marginal (private) costs to the firm (MC)(£)	Marginal external (pollution) costs (MEC) (£)	Marginal social costs (MSC = MC + MEC) (£)
1	100	30	20	50
2	100	30	22	52
3	100	35	25	60
4	100	45	30	75
5	100	60	40	100
6	100	78	55	133
7	100	100	77	177
8	100	130	110	240

10. Make a list of pieces of information a firm might want to know and consider whether it could buy the information and how reliable that information might be.

11. Assume that a country had no state education at all. For what reasons might the private education system not provide the optimal allocation of resources to and within education?

12. Assume that a firm discharges waste into a river. As a result, the marginal social costs (MSC) are greater than the firm's marginal (private) costs (MC). The table at the bottom of this page shows how MC, MSC, AR and MR vary with output. Assume that the marginal private benefit (MB) is given by the price (AR). Assume also that there are no externalities on the consumption side, and that therefore MSB = MB.

(a) How much will the firm produce if it seeks to maximise profits?
(b) What is the socially efficient level of output (assuming no externalities on the demand side)?
(c) How much is the marginal external cost at this level of output?
(d) What size of tax would be necessary for the firm to reduce its output to the socially efficient level?
(e) Why is the tax less than the marginal externality?
(f) Why might it be equitable to impose a lump-sum tax on this firm?
(g) Why will a lump-sum tax not affect the firm's output (assuming that in the long run the firm can still make at least normal profit)?

13. On a diagram similar to Figure 6.5 (on page 221), demonstrate how a subsidy can correct for an external benefit.

14. Why might it be better to ban certain activities that cause environmental damage rather than to tax them?

15. To what extent could property rights (either public or private) be successfully extended and invoked to curb the problem of industrial pollution (a) of the atmosphere, (b) of rivers, (c) by the dumping of toxic waste, (d) by the erection of ugly buildings and (e) by the creation of high levels of noise?

16. What protection do private property rights in the real world give to sufferers of noise (a) from neighbours, (b) from traffic, (c) from transistor radios at the seaside?

17. How suitable are legal restrictions in the following cases?

(a) Ensuring adequate vehicle safety (e.g. that tyres have sufficient tread or that the vehicle is roadworthy).
(b) Reducing traffic congestion.
(c) Preventing the abuse of monopoly power.
(d) Ensuring that mergers are in the public interest.
(e) Ensuring that firms charge a price equal to marginal cost.

18. How would you evaluate the following?

(a) The external effects of building a reservoir in an area of outstanding natural beauty.
(b) The external effects of acid rain pollution from a power station.

19. Many economists have argued that a form of 'congestion tax' ought to be imposed on motorists who use their cars on busy roads, to take account of the external costs they impose on other road users and pedestrians. Compare the relative advantages and disadvantages of the following measures:

(a) Increasing the rate of duty on petrol.
(b) Increasing the annual road fund licence.
(c) Using a system such as that in Singapore (see Box 6.5), where charges are deducted from a pre-paid smart card inserted into a device in the car. Charges vary according

Output	1	2	3	4	5	6	7	8
MC	23	21	23	25	27	30	35	42
MSC	35	34	38	42	46	52	60	72
TR	60	102	138	168	195	219	238	252
AR	60	51	46	42	39	36.5	34	31.5
MR	60	42	36	30	27	24	19	14

to the time of day and/or the level of congestion.

(d) Installing cameras that record number plates of cars in a designated zone, and then fining their owners if a daily fixed fee for driving in the zone has not been paid (this system is used in London).

(e) Setting up toll booths to charge motorists for using certain stretches of road.

(f) The use of bus and cycle lanes at peak times.

(g) Subsidising public transport.

20. Give examples of how the government intervenes to protect the interests of dependants from bad economic decisions taken on their behalf.

21. What are the possible arguments in favour of fixing prices (a) below and (b) above the equilibrium? Are there any means of achieving the same social goals without fixing prices?

22. Make out a case for (a) increasing and (b) decreasing the role of the government in the allocation of resources.

Additional case studies on the *Essentials of Economics* website (www.booksites.net/sloman)

6.1 Corporate social responsibility. An examination of social responsibility as a goal of firms and its effect on business performance.

6.2 The police as a public service. The extent to which policing can be classified as a public good.

6.3 Deadweight loss from taxes on goods and services. This shows the welfare loss from the imposition of a tax, which must be weighed against the redistributive and other gains from the tax.

6.4 Libertarianism. The views of the 'neo Austrian' right that market capitalism has dynamic advantages in creating incentives to innovate and take risks.

6.5 Public choice theory. This examines how economists have attempted to extend their analysis of markets to the field of political decision making.

6.6 Perverse subsidies. An examination of the use of subsidies around the world that are harmful to the environment.

6.7 Selling the environment. This looks at the proposals made at international climate conferences to use market-based solutions to global warming.

6.8 Restricting car access to Athens. A case study that examines how the Greeks have attempted to reduce local atmospheric pollution from road traffic.

6.9 The right track for reform? How successful has rail privatisation been in the UK?

6.10 Can the market provide adequate protection for the environment? This explains why markets generally fail to take into account environmental externalities.

6.11 Environmental auditing. Are businesses becoming greener? A growing number of firms are subjecting themselves to an 'environmental audit' to judge just how 'green' they are.

Sections of chapter covered in
WinEcon – Sloman, *Essentials of Economics*

Essentials of Economics section	*WinEcon* section
6.1	6.1
6.2	6.2
6.3	6.3
6.4	6.4
6.5	6.5
6.6	–
6.7	–
6.8	Covered in 6.1

Websites relevant to this chapter

Numbers and sections refer to websites listed in the Web Appendix and hotlinked from this book's website at
www.booksites.net/sloman

- For news articles relevant to this chapter, see the *Economics News Articles* link from the book's website.
- For general news on market failures and government intervention, see websites in section A, and particularly A1–5, 18, 19, 24, 31. See also links to newspapers in A38 and 39; and see A42 for links to economics news articles from newspapers worldwide.
- Sites I7 and 11 contain links to *Competition and monopoly, Policy and regulation* and *Transport* in the *Microeconomics* section; they also have an *Industry and commerce* section. Site I4 has links to *Environmental* and *Environmental Economics* in the *EconDirectory* section. Site I17 has several sections of links in the *Issues in Society* section.
- UK and EU departments relevant to competition policy can be found at sites E10; G7, 8.
- UK regulatory bodies can be found at sites E4, 11, 16, 18, 19, 21, 22, 25, 29.
- For information on taxes and subsidies, see E30, 36; G13. For use of green taxes (Box 6.4), see H5; G11; E2, 14, 30.
- For information on health and the economics of health care (Box 6.1), see E8; H9. See also links in I8 and 17.
- For sites favouring the free market, see C17; D34. See also C18 for the development of ideas on the market and government intervention.
- For the economics of the environment, see links in I4, 7, 11, 17. For policy on the environment and transport, see E2, 7, 11, 14, 29; G10, 11. See also H11.
- For student resources relevant to this chapter, see sites C1–7, 9, 10, 19.

Part B Macroeconomics

CHAPTER MAP

CHAPTER SEVEN

Aggregate demand and supply, and macroeconomic problems

We turn now to *macroeconomics*. This will be the subject for this second part of the book. As we have already seen, microeconomics focuses on *individual* markets. In macroeconomics we take a much loftier view. We examine the economy as a whole. We still examine demand and supply, but now it is the *total* level of spending in the economy and the total level of production. In other words, we examine *aggregate demand* and *aggregate supply*.

In particular, we will be examining three key issues. The first is national output. What determines the size of national output? What causes it to grow? Why do growth rates fluctuate? Why do economies sometimes surge ahead and at other times languish in recession?

The second is employment and unemployment. What causes unemployment? If people who are unemployed want jobs, and if consumers want more goods and services, then why does our economy fail to provide a job for everyone who wants one?

Then there is the issue of inflation. Why is it that the general level of prices always seems to rise, and only rarely fall? Why is inflation a problem, and would it be a good thing or a bad thing if prices *did* fall? Why do countries' central banks, such as the Bank of England, set targets for the rate of inflation?

In this chapter, we take an overview of these issues and look at two simple models that help us to understand them. The first is the circular flow of income; the second is the aggregate demand and supply model.

7.1   Macroeconomic objectives

What are the major economic problems that economies as a whole suffer from?

Economic growth

Governments try to achieve high rates of economic growth over the long term: in other words, growth that is sustained over the years and is not just a temporary phenomenon. To this end, governments also try to achieve *stable* growth, avoiding both recessions and excessive short-term growth that cannot be sustained (governments are nevertheless sometimes happy to give the economy an excessive boost as an election draws near!).

> ***Economies suffer from inherent instability***. As a result, economic growth and other macroeconomic indicators tend to fluctuate.
>
> Key Idea 25

Table 7.1 shows the average annual growth in output between 1960 and 2002 for selected countries. As you can see, the differences between countries are quite substantial.

Table 7.1 Economic growth, unemployment and inflation

	France	Germany	Italy	Japan	UK	USA	EU (15)	OECD[1]	Brazil	Malaysia	Singapore
Growth (average % per annum)											
1960–9	7.5	4.4	5.3	10.9	2.9	4.3	3.5	4.6	5.4	6.5	8.8
1970–9	3.2	2.6	3.8	4.3	2.0	2.8	3.2	3.6	8.1	7.9	8.3
1980–9	2.2	1.8	2.4	4.0	2.4	2.5	2.2	2.6	3.0	5.8	6.1
1990–6	1.3	2.4	1.4	2.3	1.8	2.5	1.8	2.4	1.7	9.0	8.9
1997–2002	2.6	1.5	1.8	0.7	2.6	3.2	2.4	2.7	1.9	3.2	4.4
Unemployment (average %)											
1960–9	1.5	0.9	5.1	1.3	2.2	4.1	2.5	2.5	n.a.	n.a.	n.a.
1970–9	3.7	2.3	6.4	1.7	4.5	6.1	4.0	4.3	n.a.	n.a.	3.6
1980–9	9.0	5.9	9.5	2.5	10.0	7.2	9.3	7.3	n.a.	6.2	3.6
1990–6	10.9	7.0	10.2	2.6	9.0	6.3	9.8	7.2	5.2	3.5	2.5
1997–2002	10.1	8.5	10.7	4.6	5.9	4.7	8.5	6.8	6.8	3.2	3.3
Inflation (average % per annum)											
1960–9	4.2	3.2	4.4	4.9	4.1	2.8	3.7	3.1	46.1	−0.3	1.1
1970–9	9.4	5.0	13.9	9.0	13.0	6.8	10.3	9.2	30.6	7.3	5.9
1980–9	7.3	2.9	11.2	2.5	7.4	5.5	7.4	8.9	332.0	2.2	2.5
1990–6	2.4	3.1	5.1	1.4	4.4	3.4	4.0	5.4	1276.0	3.7	2.5
1997–2002	1.3	1.3	2.2	−0.1	2.4	2.3	1.8	3.0	6.3	2.6	0.8

[1] The Organisation for Economic Co-operation and Development: the 30 major industrialised countries (excluding Russia but including Turkey and Mexico).

Unemployment

Governments also aim to ensure that unemployment is as low as possible, not only for the sake of the unemployed themselves, but also because it represents a waste of human resources and because unemployment benefits are a drain on government revenues.

Unemployment in the 1980s and early 1990s was significantly higher than in the 1950s, 1960s and 1970s. Then, in the late 1990s and early 2000s, unemployment fell in many countries.

Inflation

By inflation we mean a general rise in prices throughout the economy. Government policy here is to keep inflation both low and stable. One of the most important reasons for this is that it will aid the process of economic decision making. For example, businesses will be able to set prices and wage rates, and make investment decisions with far more confidence.

Today we are used to inflation rates of around 2 or 3 per cent, but it was not long ago that inflation in most developed countries was in double figures. In 1975, UK inflation reached 24 per cent.

The balance of payments

A country's balance of payments account records all transactions between the residents of that country and the rest of the world. These transactions enter as either debit items or credit items. The debit items include all payments *to* other countries: these include the country's purchases of imports, the spending on investment it makes abroad and the interest and dividends paid to people abroad who have invested in the country. The credit items include all receipts *from* other countries: from the sales of exports, from inward investment expenditure and from interest and dividends earned from abroad.

The sale of exports and any other receipts earn foreign currency. The purchase of imports or any other payments abroad use up foreign currency. If we start to spend more foreign currency than we earn, one of two things must happen. Both are likely to be a problem.

The balance of payments will go into deficit.   In other words, there will be a shortfall of foreign currencies. The government will therefore have to borrow money from abroad, or draw on its foreign currency reserves to make up the shortfall. This is a problem because, if it goes on too long, overseas debts will mount, along with the interest that must be paid; and/or reserves will begin to run low.

The exchange rate will fall.   The exchange rate is the rate at which one currency exchanges for another. For example, the exchange rate of the pound into the dollar might be £1 = $1.60.

If the government does nothing to correct the balance of payments deficit, then the exchange rate must fall: for example, to $1.55 or $1.50, or lower. (We will show just why this is so in Chapter 12.) A falling exchange rate is a problem because it pushes up the price of imports and may fuel inflation. Also, if the exchange rate fluctuates, this can cause great uncertainty for traders and can damage international trade and economic growth.

Definitions

Rate of inflation
The percentage increase in prices over a 12-month period.

Balance of payments account
A record of the country's transactions with the rest of the world. It shows the country's payments to or deposits in other countries (debits) and its receipts or deposits from other countries (credits). It also shows the balance between these debits and credits under various headings.

Exchange rate
The rate at which one national currency exchanges for another. The rate is expressed as the amount of one currency that is necessary to purchase *one unit* of another currency (e.g. €1.55 = £1).

In order to achieve the goals of high and sustainable economic growth, low unemployment, low inflation, a satisfactory balance of payments and stable exchange rates, the government may seek to control several 'intermediate' variables. These include interest rates, the supply of money, taxes and government expenditure. We will be looking at the relationship between all these in the coming chapters.

Recap

1. Macroeconomics, like microeconomics, looks at issues such as output, employment and prices; but it looks at them in the context of the whole economy.

2. The four main macroeconomic goals that are generally of most concern to governments are economic growth, reducing unemployment, keeping inflation low and stable, and avoiding balance of payments and exchange rate problems.

7.2 The circular flow of income

Why does money go round and round from firms to consumers and back again?

Ke
Ide
24
p21

Unfortunately, the pursuit of any one of the four objectives that we have identified may make at least one of the others worse. For example, attempts to increase the rate of economic growth by giving tax cuts so as to boost consumer spending, and thereby encourage investment, may lead to higher inflation. It is thus important to understand the relationship between the four objectives.

One way in which the objectives are linked is through their relationship with aggregate demand (AD). This is the total spending on goods and services made within the country ('domestically produced goods and services'). This spending consists of four elements: consumer spending on domestically produced goods and services (C_d), investment expenditure by firms (I), government spending (G) and the expenditure by residents abroad on this country's exports (X). Thus:[1]

$$AD = C_d + I + G + X$$

To show how the four objectives are related to aggregate demand, we can use a simple model of the economy. This is the *circular flow of income*, and is shown in Figure 7.1. It is an extension of the model we looked at back in the Introduction (see Figure I.5 on page 15).

> ## Definition
>
> **Aggregate demand (AD)**
> Total spending on goods and services made in the economy. It consists of four elements, consumer spending (C), investment (I), government spending (G) and the expenditure on exports (X), less any expenditure on foreign goods and services (M):
> $AD = C + I + G + X - M$

---

[1] Investment, government expenditure and export expenditure are also only on domestically produced goods and services (and thus strictly speaking should also be written with a subscript 'd'). If, alternatively, we were also to include in C, I, G and X any component of expenditure going on imports, we would then have to subtract imports (M) again to get back to aggregate demand. Thus another way of writing aggregate demand is $AD = C + I + G + X - M$ (where each of C, I, G and X includes expenditure on both domestic *and* imported goods and services).

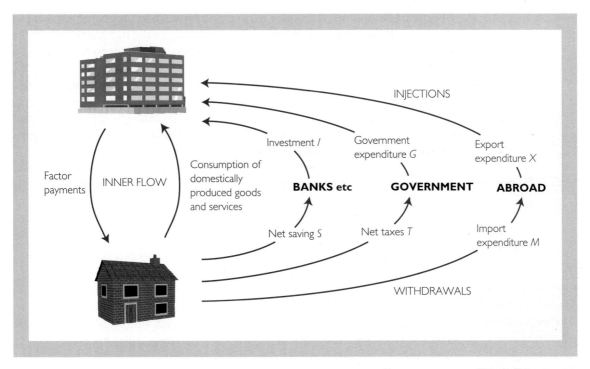

Figure 7.1
The circular flow
of income

In the diagram, the economy is divided into two major groups: *firms* and *households*. Each group has two roles. Firms are producers of goods and services; they are also the employers of labour and other factors of production. Households (which include all individuals) are the consumers of goods and services; they are also the suppliers of labour and various other factors of production. In the diagram there is an inner flow and various outer flows of incomes between these two groups.

Before we look at the various parts of the diagram, a word of warning. Do not confuse *money* and *income*. Money is a stock concept. At any given time, there is a certain quantity of money in the economy (e.g. £1 billion). But that does not tell us the level of national *income*. Income is a flow concept (as is expenditure). It is measured as so much *per period of time*. The relationship between money and income depends on how rapidly the money *circulates*: its 'velocity of circulation'. (We will examine this concept in detail later on.) If there is £1 billion of money in the economy and each £1 on average is paid out as income five times per year, then annual national income will be £5 billion.

The inner flow, withdrawals and injections

The inner flow

Firms pay money to households in the form of wages and salaries, dividends on shares, interest and rent. These payments are in return for the services of the factors of production – labour, capital and land – that are supplied by households. Thus on the left-hand side of Figure 7.1, money flows directly from firms to households as 'factor payments'.

Households, in turn, pay money to domestic firms when they consume domestically produced goods and services (C_d). This is shown on the right-hand side of the inner flow. There is thus a circular flow of payments from firms to households to firms and so on.

If households spend *all* their incomes on buying domestic goods and services, and if firms pay out *all* this income they receive from consumers as factor payments to domestic households, and if the velocity at which money circulates does not change, the flow will continue at the same level indefinitely. The money just goes round and round at the same speed and incomes remain unchanged.

In the real world, of course, it is not as simple as this. Not all income gets passed on round the inner flow; some is *withdrawn*. At the same time, incomes are injected into the flow from outside. Let us examine these withdrawals and injections.

Withdrawals (W)

Only part of the incomes received by households will be spent on the goods and services of domestic firms. The remainder will be withdrawn from the inner flow. Likewise, only part of the incomes generated by firms will be paid to domestic households. The remainder of this will also be withdrawn. There are three forms of withdrawals (or 'leakages' as they are sometimes called).

Net saving (S). Saving is income that households choose not to spend but to put aside for the future. Savings are normally deposited in financial institutions such as banks and building societies. This is shown in Figure 7.1. Money flows from households to 'banks, etc'. What we are seeking to measure here, however, is the *net* flow from households to the banking sector. We therefore have to subtract from saving any borrowing or drawing on past savings by households to arrive at the net saving flow. Of course, if household borrowing exceeded saving, the net flow would be in the other direction: it would be negative.

Net taxes (T). When people pay taxes (to either central or local government), this represents a withdrawal of money from the inner flow in much the same way as saving: only in this case people have no choice. Some taxes, such as income tax and employees' national insurance contributions, are paid out of household incomes. Others, such as VAT and excise duties, are paid out of consumer expenditure. Others, such as corporation tax, are paid out of firms' incomes before being received by households as dividends on shares. (For simplicity, however, we show taxes being withdrawn at just one point. It does not affect the argument.)

When, however, people receive *benefits* from the government, such as working tax credit, child benefit and pensions, the money flows the other way. Benefits are thus equivalent to a 'negative tax'. These benefits are known as transfer payments. They transfer money from one group of people (taxpayers) to others (the recipients).

In the model, 'net taxes' (T) represents the *net* flow to the government from households and firms. It consists of total taxes minus benefits.

Import expenditure (M). Not all consumption is of totally home-produced goods. Households spend some of their incomes on imported goods and services, or on goods and services using imported components. Although the money that consumers spend on such goods initially flows to domestic retailers, it will eventually find its way abroad, either when the retailers or wholesalers themselves import the goods, or when domestic manufacturers purchase imported inputs to make their products. This expenditure on imports constitutes the third withdrawal from the inner flow. This money flows abroad.

Total withdrawals are simply the sum of net saving, net taxes and the expenditure on imports:

$$W = S + T + M$$

Injections (J)

Only part of the demand for firms' output (i.e. aggregate demand) arises from consumers' expenditure. The remainder comes from other sources outside the inner flow. These additional components of aggregate demand are known as injections (J). There are three types of injection.

Investment (I).   This is the money that firms spend which they obtain from various financial institutions – either past savings or loans, or through a new issue of shares. They may invest in plant and equipment or may simply spend the money on building up stocks of inputs, semi-finished or finished goods.

Government expenditure (G).   When the government spends money on goods and services produced by firms, this counts as an injection. Examples of such government expenditure include spending on roads, hospitals and schools. (Note that government expenditure in this model does not include state benefits. These transfer payments, as we saw above, are the equivalent of negative taxes and have the effect of reducing the T component of withdrawals.)

Export expenditure (X).   Money flows into the circular flow from abroad when residents abroad buy our exports of goods and services.

Total injections are thus the sum of investment, government expenditure and exports:

$$J = I + G + X$$

> **Definition**
>
> **Injections (J)**
> Expenditure on the production of domestic firms coming from outside the inner flow of the circular flow of income. Injections equal investment (I) plus government expenditure (G) plus expenditure on exports (X).

The relationship between withdrawals and injections

There are indirect links between saving and investment, taxation and government expenditure, and imports and exports, via financial institutions, the government (central and local) and foreign countries respectively. If a greater proportion of income is saved, there will be more available for banks and other financial institutions to lend out. If tax receipts are higher, the government may be more keen to increase its expenditure. Finally, if imports increase, incomes of people abroad will increase, which will enable them to purchase more of our exports.

These links, however, do not guarantee that $S = I$ or $G = T$ or $M = X$. For a period of time, financial institutions can lend out (I) more or less than they receive from depositors (S); governments can spend (G) more or less than they receive in taxes (T); and exports (X) can exceed imports (M) or vice versa.

A major point here is that the decisions to save and invest are made by different people, and thus they plan to save and invest different amounts. Likewise the demand for imports may not equal the demand for exports. As far as the government is concerned, it may choose not to make $T = G$. It may choose not to spend all its tax revenues: to run a 'budget surplus' ($T > G$); or it may choose to spend more than it receives in taxes: to run a 'budget deficit' ($G > T$) – by borrowing or printing money to make up the difference.

Thus planned injections (J) may not equal planned withdrawals (W).

The circular flow of income and the four macroeconomic objectives

If planned injections are not equal to planned withdrawals, what will be the consequences? If injections exceed withdrawals, the level of expenditure will rise: there will be a rise in aggregate demand. This extra spending will increase firms' sales and thus encourage them to produce more. Total output in the economy will rise. Thus firms will pay out more in wages, salaries, profits, rent and interest. In other words, national income will rise.

The rise in aggregate demand will have the following effects upon the four macroeconomic objectives:

Key Idea 24 p217

- There will be economic growth. The greater the initial excess of injections over withdrawals, the bigger will be the rise in national income.
- Unemployment will fall as firms take on more workers to meet the extra demand for output.
- Inflation will tend to rise. The greater the rise in aggregate demand relative to the capacity of firms to produce, the more will firms find it difficult to meet the extra demand, and the more likely they will be to raise prices.

> **Pause for thought**   ‖‖
>
> What will be the effect on each of the four objectives if planned injections are less than planned withdrawals?

- The exports and imports part of the balance of payments will tend to deteriorate. The higher demand sucks more imports into the country, and higher domestic inflation makes exports less competitive and imports relatively cheaper compared with home-produced goods. Thus imports will tend to rise and exports will tend to fall.

Equilibrium in the circular flow

When injections do not equal withdrawals, a state of disequilibrium will exist. This will set in train a process to bring the economy back to a state of equilibrium where injections are equal to withdrawals.

To illustrate this, let us consider the situation again where injections exceed withdrawals. Perhaps there has been a rise in business confidence so that investment has risen. Or perhaps there has been a tax cut so that withdrawals have fallen. As we have seen, the excess of injections over withdrawals will lead to a rise in national income. But as national income rises, so households will not only spend more on domestic goods (C_d), but also save more (S), pay more taxes (T) and buy more imports (M). In other words, withdrawals will rise. This will continue until they have risen to equal injections. At that point, national income will stop rising, and so will withdrawals. Equilibrium has been reached.

Key Idea 7 p41

Recap

1. The circular flow of income model depicts the flows of money round the economy. The inner flow shows the direct flows between firms and households. Money flows from firms to households in the form of factor payments, and back again as consumer expenditure on domestically produced goods and services.

2. Not all incomes get passed on directly round the inner flow. Some is withdrawn in the form of saving, some is paid in taxes, and some goes abroad as expenditure on imports.

3. Likewise not all expenditure on domestic firms is by domestic consumers. Some is injected from outside the inner flow in the form of investment expenditure, government expenditure and expenditure on the country's exports.

4. Planned injections and withdrawals are unlikely to be the same.

5. If injections exceed withdrawals, national income will rise. As a result, unemployment will tend to fall, inflation will tend to rise, imports will tend to rise and exports fall. The reverse will happen if withdrawals exceed injections.

6. If injections exceed withdrawals, the rise in national income will lead to a rise in withdrawals. This will continue until $W = J$. At this point the circular flow will be in equilibrium.

Economic growth and the business cycle   7.3

Is a country's economic growth likely to be constant over time?

The distinction between actual and potential growth

Before examining the causes of economic growth, it is essential to distinguish between *actual* and *potential* economic growth.

Actual growth is the percentage annual increase in national output or 'GDP' (gross domestic product): in other words, the rate of growth in actual output produced. When statistics on GDP growth rates are published, it is actual growth they are referring to. (We examine the measurement of GDP in the appendix to this chapter.)

Potential growth is the speed at which the economy *could* grow. It is the percentage annual increase in the economy's *capacity* to produce: the rate of growth in potential output. Potential output represents a ceiling on a country's output and hence will limit the living standards that can be achieved by its residents.

> ***Living standards are limited by a country's ability to produce.*** Potential national output depends on the country's resources, technology and productivity. **Key Idea 26**

Two of the major factors contributing to potential economic growth are:

■ An increase in resources – natural resources, labour or capital.

■ An increase in the efficiency with which these resources can be used, through advances in technology, improved labour skills or improved organisation.

If the potential growth rate exceeds the actual growth rate, there will be an increase in spare capacity and an increase in unemployment: there will be a growing gap between potential and actual output. To close this gap, the actual growth rate

Definitions

Actual growth
The percentage annual increase in national output actually produced.

Potential growth
The percentage annual increase in the capacity of the economy to produce.

Potential output
The output that could be produced in the economy if there were full employment of resources (including labour).

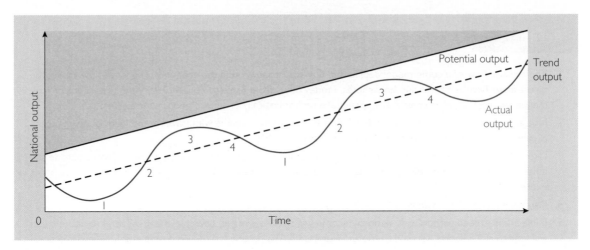

Figure 7.2
The business cycle

would temporarily have to exceed the potential growth rate. In the long run, however, the actual growth rate will be limited to the potential growth rate.

There are thus two major issues concerned with economic growth: the short-run issue of ensuring that actual growth is such as to keep actual output as close as possible to potential output; and the long-run issue of what determines the rate of potential economic growth.

Economic growth and the business cycle

Although growth in potential output varies to some extent over the years – depending on the rate of advance of technology, the level of investment and the discovery of new raw materials – it nevertheless tends to be much more steady than the growth in actual output.

Actual growth tends to fluctuate. In some years there is a high rate of economic growth: the country experiences a boom. In other years, economic growth is low or even negative: the country experiences a recession.[2] This cycle of booms and recessions is known as the business cycle or trade cycle.

There are four 'phases' of the business cycle. They are illustrated in Figure 7.2.

Key Idea 25 p250

> **Definition**
>
> **Business cycle or trade cycle**
> The periodic fluctuations of national output round its long-term trend.

1. *The upturn.* In this phase, a contracting or stagnant economy begins to recover, and growth in actual output resumes.
2. *The expansion.* During this phase there is rapid economic growth: the economy is booming. A fuller use is made of resources and the gap between actual and potential output narrows.
3. *The peaking out.* During this phase, growth slows down or even ceases.
4. *The slowdown, recession or slump.* During this phase there is little or no growth or even a decline in output. Increasing slack develops in the economy.

A word of caution: do not confuse a high *level* of output with a high *rate of growth* in output. The level of output is highest in phase 3. The rate of growth in output is highest in phase 2 (i.e. where the curve is steepest).

---

[2] In official statistics, a recession is defined as when an economy experiences falling national output (negative growth) for two or more quarters.

Long-term output trend.   A line can be drawn showing the trend of national output over time (i.e. ignoring the cyclical fluctuations around the trend). This is shown as the dashed line in Figure 7.2. If the average level of potential output that is unutilised stays constant from one cycle to another, the trend line will have the same slope as the potential output line. In other words, the trend rate of growth will be the same as the potential rate of growth. If, however, the level of unutilised potential changes from one cycle to another, then the trend line will have a different slope from the potential output line. For example, if unemployment and unused industrial capacity *rise* from one peak to another, or from one trough to another, the trend line will move further away from the potential output line (i.e. it will be less steep).

> **Pause for thought**   ‖‖
>
> *If the average percentage (as opposed to the average level) of potential output that was unutilised remained constant, would the trend line have the same slope as the potential output line?*

The business cycle in practice

The business cycle illustrated in Figure 7.2 is a 'stylised' cycle. It is nice and smooth and regular. Drawing it this way allows us to make a clear distinction between each of the four phases. In practice, however, business cycles are highly irregular. They are irregular in two ways.

The length of the phases.   Some booms are short lived, lasting only a few months or so. Others are much longer, lasting perhaps three or four years. Likewise some recessions are short while others are long.

The magnitude of the phases.   Sometimes in phase 2 there is a very high rate of economic growth, perhaps 5 per cent per annum or more. On other occasions in phase 2 growth is much gentler. Sometimes in phase 4 there is a recession, with an actual decline in output (e.g. in the early 1980s and early 1990s). On other occasions, phase 4 is merely a 'pause', with growth simply slowing down.

Nevertheless, despite the irregularity of the fluctuations, cycles are still clearly discernible, especially if we plot *growth* on the vertical axis rather than the *level* of output. This is done in Figure 7.3, which shows the business cycles in selected industrial countries from 1971 to 2003.

Causes of fluctuations in actual growth

The major determinants of variations in the rate of actual growth in the *short run* are variations in the growth of aggregate demand.

A rapid rise in aggregate demand will create shortages. This will tend to stimulate firms to increase output, thereby reducing slack in the economy. Likewise, a reduction in aggregate demand will leave firms with increased stocks of unsold goods. They will therefore tend to reduce output.

Aggregate demand and actual output, therefore, fluctuate together in the short run. A boom is associated with a rapid rise in aggregate demand: the faster the rise in aggregate demand, the higher the short-run rate of actual growth. A recession, by contrast, is associated with a reduction in aggregate demand.

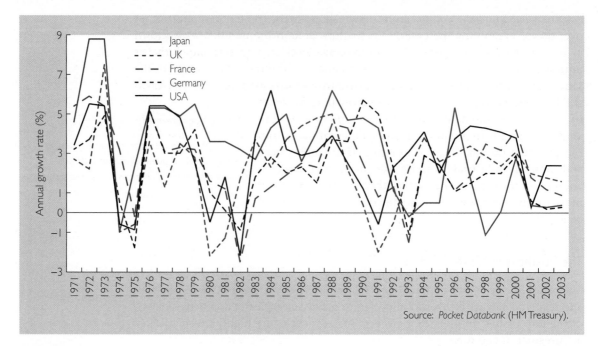

Source: *Pocket Databank* (HM Treasury).

Figure 7.3
Growth rates in selected industrial countries: 1971–2003

A rapid rise in aggregate demand, however, is not enough to ensure a continuing high level of growth over a *number* of years. Without an expansion of potential output too, rises in actual output must eventually come to an end. Once spare capacity has been used up, once there is full employment of labour and other resources, the rate of growth of actual output will be restricted to the rate of growth of potential output. This is illustrated in Figure 7.2. As long as actual output is below potential output, the actual output curve can slope upwards more steeply than the potential output curve. But once the gap between the two curves has been closed, the actual output curve can only slope as steeply as the potential output curve: the two curves cannot cross – actual output cannot be above potential output.

In the long run, therefore, there are two determinants of actual growth:

■ The growth in aggregate demand. This determines whether potential output will be realised.
■ The growth in potential output.

Causes of potential growth

We now turn to the *supply* question. Here we are concerned with the capacity of the economy to produce. There are two main determinants of potential output: (a) the amount of resources available and (b) their productivity.

Increases in the quantity of resources

Capital. The nation's output depends on its stock of capital (*K*). An increase in this stock will increase output. If we ignore the problem of machines wearing out or becoming obsolete and needing replacing, then the stock of capital will increase by the amount of investment. The rise in output that results will depend on the productivity of capital: how much extra capital you need to produce extra output.

The rate of growth in potential output depends on two things. The first is the marginal capital/output ratio (k). This is the amount of extra capital (ΔK) divided by the extra annual output that it produces (ΔY). Thus $k = \Delta K/\Delta Y$. The lower the value of k, the higher is the productivity of capital (i.e. the less extra capital you need to produce extra output). The second determinant of potential growth is the proportion of national income that is invested (i), which, assuming that all saving is invested, will equal the proportion of national income that is saved (s). The formula for growth becomes:

$$g = i/k \text{ (or } g = s/k)$$

Thus if 20 per cent of national income went in new investment (i = 20 per cent), and if each £1 of new investment yielded 25p of extra income per year (k = 4), then the growth rate would be 5 per cent. A simple example will demonstrate this. If national income is £100 billion, then £20 billion will be invested (i = 20%). This will lead to extra annual output of £5 billion (k = 4). Thus national income grows to £105 billion: a growth of 5 per cent.

But what determines the rate of investment? There are a number of determinants. These include the confidence of business people about the future demand for their products, the profitability of business, the tax regime, the rate of growth in the economy and the rate of interest.

Over the long term, if investment is to increase, then *saving* must increase in order to finance that investment. Put another way, people must be prepared to forgo a certain amount of consumption in order to allow resources to be diverted into producing more capital goods: factories, machines, etc.

Note that if investment is to increase, there may also need to be a steady increase in *aggregate demand*. In other words, if firms are to be encouraged to increase their capacity by installing new machines or building new factories, they may need first to see the *demand* for their products growing. Here a growth in *potential* output is the result of a growth in aggregate demand and hence *actual* output.

Labour.   If there is an increase in the working population, there will be an increase in potential output. This increase in working population may result from a larger 'participation rate': a larger proportion of the total population in work or seeking work. For example, if a greater proportion of women with children decide to join the labour market, the working population will rise.

Alternatively, a rise in the working population may be the result of an increase in total population. There is a problem here. If a rise in total population does not result in a greater *proportion* of the population working, output *per head of the population* may not rise at all. In practice, many developed countries are faced with a growing proportion of their population above retirement age, and thus a potential *fall* in output per head of the population.

Land and raw materials.   Land is virtually fixed in quantity. Land reclamation schemes and the opening up of marginal land can only add tiny amounts to national output. Even if new raw materials are discovered (e.g. oil), this will result

Box 7.1

The costs of economic growth

Is more necessarily better?

For many developing countries economic growth is a necessity if they are to remove mass poverty. When the majority of their population is underfed, poorly housed, with inadequate health care and little access to education, few would quarrel with the need for an increase in productive potential. The main query is whether the benefits of economic growth will flow to the mass of the population, or whether they will be confined to the few who are already relatively well off.

For developed countries the case for economic growth is less clear cut. Economic growth is usually measured in terms of the growth in national output valued in prices as given by the market. The problem is that there are many 'goods' and 'bads' that are not included when measuring national output. Economic growth, therefore, is not the same as growth in a nation's *welfare*. True, there can be major advantages of economic growth, and certainly, other things being equal, the majority of the population wants higher levels of production and consumption. But it is important to recognise the costs of economic growth. Indeed, some people regard these costs as so serious that they advocate a policy of *zero economic growth*.

So, what are the benefits and costs of economic growth?

The benefits of growth

Increased levels of consumption. Provided economic growth outstrips population growth, it will lead to higher real income per head. This can lead to higher levels of consumption of goods and services. If human welfare is related to the level of consumption, then growth provides an obvious gain to society.

It can help avoid other macroeconomic problems. People have aspirations of rising living standards. Without a growth in productive potential, people's demands for rising incomes are likely to lead to higher inflation, balance of payments crises (as more imports are purchased), industrial disputes, etc. Growth in productive potential helps to meet these aspirations and avoid macroeconomic crises.

It can make it easier to redistribute incomes to the poor. If incomes rise, the government can redistribute incomes from the rich to the poor *without the rich losing*. For example, as people's incomes rise, they automatically pay more taxes. These extra revenues for the government can be spent on programmes to alleviate poverty.

Without a continuing rise in national income the scope for helping the poor is much more limited.

Society may feel that it can afford to care more for the environment. As people grow richer, they may become less preoccupied with their own private consumption and more concerned to live in a clean environment. The regulation of pollution tends to be tougher in developed countries than in the developing world.

The costs of growth

In practice, more consumption may not make people happier; economies may be no less crisis riven; income may not be redistributed more equally; the environment may not be better protected. More than this, some people argue that growth may worsen these problems and create additional problems besides.

The current opportunity cost of growth. To achieve faster growth, firms will probably need to invest more. This will require financing. The finance can come from a higher saving rate or higher taxes. Either way, there must be a cut in consumption. In the short run, therefore, higher growth leads to *less* consumption, not more.

In the diagram, assume that consumption is currently at a level of C_1. Its growth over time is shown by the line out from C_1. Now assume that the government pursues a policy of higher growth. Consumption has to *fall* to finance the extra investment. Consumption falls to, say, C_2. The growth in consumption is now shown by the line out from C_2. Not until time t_1 is reached (which may be several years into the future) does consumption overtake the levels it would have reached with the previous lower growth rate.

Key
Idea
17
p19

Key
Idea
2
p8

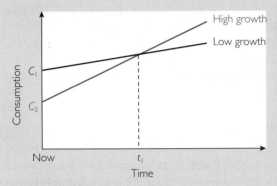

High and low growth paths

Growth may simply generate extra demands. 'The more people have, the more they want.' If this is so, more consumption may not increase people's happiness at all. It is often observed that rich people tend to be miserable!

Social effects. Many people claim that an excessive pursuit of material growth by a country can lead to a more greedy, more selfish and less caring society. As society becomes more industrialised, violence, crime, loneliness, stress-related diseases, suicides, divorce and other social problems are likely to rise.

Environmental costs. A richer society may be more concerned for the environment, but it is also likely to do more damage to it. The higher the level of consumption, the higher is likely to be the level of pollution and waste. What is more, many of the environmental costs are likely to be underestimated due to a lack of scientific knowledge. Acid rain and the depletion of the ozone layer have been two examples.

Non-renewable resources. If growth involves using a greater amount of resources, rather than using the same amount of resources more efficiently, certain non-renewable resources will run out more rapidly. Unless viable alternatives can be found for various minerals and fossil fuels, present growth may lead to shortages for future generations.

Key Idea
20
p207

Effects on the distribution of income. While some people may gain from a higher standard of living, others are likely to lose. If the means to higher growth are greater incentives (such as cuts in higher rates of income tax), then the rich might get richer, with little or no benefits 'trickling down' to the poor.

Key Idea
17
p192

Growth involves changes in production: both in terms of the goods produced and in terms of the techniques used and the skills required. The more rapid the rate of growth, the more rapid the rate of change. People may find that their skills are no longer relevant. Their jobs may be replaced by machines. People may thus find themselves unemployed, or forced to take low-paid, unskilled work.

Conclusion

So should countries pursue growth? The answer depends on (a) just what costs and benefits are involved, (b) what weighting people attach to them, and (c) how opposing views are to be reconciled. A problem is that the answer involves a judgement about what a 'desirable' society should look like and that depends on your point of view. Generally, however, the electorate seems to want economic growth. As long as that is so, governments will tend to pursue policies to achieve growth. That is why we need to study the causes of growth and the policies that governments can pursue.

One thing the government can do is to view the problem as one of *constrained optimisation*. It sets constraints: levels of environmental protection, minimum wages, maximum rates of depletion of non-renewable resources, etc. It then seeks policies that will maximise growth, while keeping within these constraints.

1. Is a constrained optimisation approach a *practical* solution to the possible costs of economic growth?
2. Are worries about the consequences of economic growth a 'luxury' that only rich countries can afford?

only in *short-term growth*: i.e. while the rate of extraction is building up. Once the rate of extraction is at a maximum, economic growth will cease. Output will simply remain at the new higher level, until eventually the raw materials will begin to run out. Output will then fall back again.

The problem of diminishing returns. If a single factor of production increases in supply while others remain fixed, diminishing returns will set in (see pages 85–7). For example, if the quantity of capital increases with no increase in other factors of production, then diminishing returns to capital will set in. The rate of return on capital will fall. Unless *all* factors of production increase, therefore, the rate of growth is likely to slow down.

The solution to the problem of diminishing returns is for there to be an increase in the *productivity* of resources.

> **Key Idea**
> **13**
> p85

Increases in the productivity of resources

Technological improvements can increase the productivity of capital. Much of the investment in new machines is not just in extra machines, but in superior machines producing a higher rate of return. Consider the microchip revolution of recent years. Modern computers can do the work of many people and have replaced many machines that were cumbersome and expensive to build. Improved methods of transport have reduced the costs of moving goods and materials. Improved communications (such as e-mail and the Internet) have reduced the costs of transmitting information.

> **Pause for thought**
>
> Will the rate of actual growth have any effect on the rate of potential growth?

As a result of technical progress, the productivity of capital has tended to increase over time. Similarly, as a result of new skills, improved education and training, and better health, the productivity of labour has also tended to increase over time.

Policies to achieve growth

How can governments increase a country's growth rate? Policies differ in two ways.

> **Key Idea**
> **8**
> p45

First, they may focus on the demand side or the supply side of the economy. In other words, they may attempt to create sufficient *aggregate demand* to ensure that firms wish to invest and that potential output is realised. Alternatively, they may seek to increase *aggregate supply* by concentrating on measures to increase potential output: measures to encourage research and development, innovation and training.

Second, they may be market-orientated or interventionist policies. Many economists and politicians, especially those on the political right, believe that the best environment for encouraging economic growth is one where private enterprise is allowed to flourish: where entrepreneurs are able to reap substantial rewards from investment in new techniques and new products. Such economists therefore advocate policies designed to free up the market. Others, however, argue that a free market will be subject to considerable cyclical fluctuations. The resulting uncertainty will discourage investment. Such economists, therefore, tend to advocate active intervention by the government to reduce these fluctuations.

Recap

1. Actual growth must be distinguished from potential growth. The actual growth rate is the percentage annual increase in the output that is actually produced, whereas potential growth is the percentage annual increase in the capacity of the economy to produce (whether or not it is actually produced).

2. Actual growth will fluctuate with the course of the business cycle. The cycle can be broken down into four phases: the upturn, the expansion, the peaking out, and the slowdown or recession. In practice, the length and magnitude of these phases vary: the cycle is thus irregular.

3. Actual growth is determined by potential growth and by the level of aggregate demand. If actual output is below potential output, actual growth can temporarily exceed potential growth, if aggregate demand is rising sufficiently. In the long term, however, actual output can grow only as fast as potential output will permit.

4. Potential growth is determined by the rate of increase in the *quantity* of resources: capital, labour, land and raw materials; and by the *productivity* of resources. The productivity of capital can be increased by technological improvements and the more efficient use of the capital stock; the productivity of labour can be increased by better education, training, motivation and organisation.

5. Whether governments can best achieve rapid growth through market-orientated or interventionist policies is highly controversial.

Unemployment   7.4

If people want to consume more goods, why are so many people out of work?

Unemployment fluctuates with the business cycle. In recessions, such as those experienced by most countries in the early 1980s, early 1990s and early 2000s, unemployment tends to rise. In boom years, such as the late 1980s and late 1990s, it tends to fall. Figure 7.4 shows these cyclical movements in unemployment for selected countries.

As well as experiencing fluctuations in unemployment, most countries have experienced long-term changes in average unemployment rates. This is illustrated in Table 7.2, which shows average unemployment in the UK, the EU and the OECD for four unemployment cycles (minimum to minimum). Average unemployment rates in the 1980s and 1990s were higher than in the 1970s, and average rates in the 1970s were, in turn, higher than in the 1950s and 1960s. In certain countries, however, such as the USA and the UK, the late 1990s and early 2000s have seen a long-term fall in unemployment.

Period	UK	EU	OECD
1964–73	3.0	2.7	3.0
1974–79	5.0	4.7	4.9
1980–90	9.4	8.7	7.2
1991–2001	8.0	9.3	7.1

Table 7.2

Average unemployment for given cycles (%)

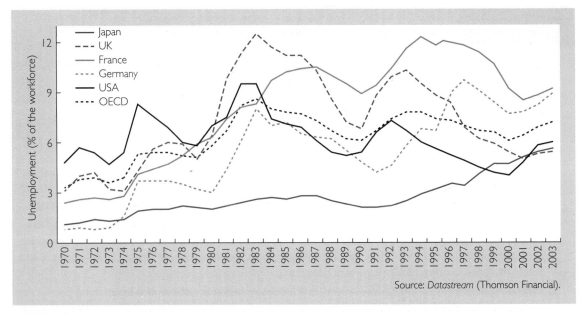

Source: *Datastream* (Thomson Financial).

Figure 7.4 Unemployment in selected industrial countries: 1970–2003

The meaning of 'unemployment'

Unemployment can be expressed either as a number (e.g. 1.5 million) or as a percentage (e.g. 5 per cent). But just who should be included in the statistics? Should it be everyone without a job? The answer is clearly no, since we would not want to include children and pensioners. We would probably also want to exclude those who were not looking for work, such as parents choosing to stay at home to look after children.

The most usual definition that economists use for the number unemployed is: *those of working age who are without work, but who are available for work at current wage rates*. If the figure is to be expressed as a percentage, then it is a percentage of the total labour force. The labour force is defined as: *those in employment (including the self-employed, those in the armed forces and those on government training schemes) plus those unemployed*. Thus if 22.5 million people were employed and 2.5 million people were unemployed, the unemployment rate would be:

$$\frac{2.5}{22.5 + 2.5} \times 100 = 10 \text{ per cent}$$

Official measures of unemployment

Claimant unemployment

Two common measures of unemployment are used in official statistics. The first is claimant unemployment. This is simply a measure of all those in receipt of unemployment-related benefits. In the UK claimants receive the 'job seeker's allowance'.

Country	Total (all ages)	Women (all ages)	Men (all ages)	Total under 25 years old	Women under 25 years old	Men under 25 years old
Belgium	7.3	8.2	6.6	18.2	17.7	18.5
France	8.7	9.9	7.8	20.0	22.2	18.3
Germany	8.6	8.3	8.7	9.7	7.9	11.3
Ireland	4.4	4.0	4.6	8.0	7.1	8.8
Japan	5.4	5.1	5.5	9.9	8.7	11.1
Netherlands	2.7	3.0	2.5	5.2	5.2	5.3
Spain	11.3	16.4	8.0	22.2	27.3	18.4
UK	5.1	4.5	5.6	12.1	10.2	13.7
USA	5.8	5.6	5.9	12.0	11.1	12.8
EU-15	7.7	8.7	6.9	15.1	15.5	14.8

Table 7.3
Standardised unemployment rates in different sections of the labour market: 2002

Source: *Eurostatistics* (Eurostat).

Claimant statistics have the advantage of being very easy to collect. However, they exclude all those of working age available for work at current wage rates, but who are *not* eligible for benefits. If the government changes the eligibility conditions so that fewer people are now eligible, this will reduce the number of claimants and hence the official number unemployed, even if there has been no change in the numbers with or without work. In the UK, there have been over 30 changes to eligibility conditions since 1979, all but one of which have had the effect of reducing the claimant figures!

Standardised unemployment rates

Recognising the weaknesses of the claimant statistics, the UK government since 1998 has used the standardised unemployment rate as the main measure of unemployment. This is the measure used by the International Labour Organisation (ILO) and the Organisation for Economic Co-operation and Development (OECD), two international organisations that publish unemployment statistics for many countries.

In this measure, the unemployed are defined as people of working age who are without work, available to start work within two weeks and *actively seeking employment* or waiting to take up an appointment. The figures are compiled from the results of national labour force surveys. In the UK the labour force survey is conducted quarterly.

But is the standardised unemployment rate likely to be higher or lower than the claimant unemployment rate? The standardised rate is likely to be higher to the extent that it includes people seeking work who are nevertheless not entitled to claim benefits, but lower to the extent that it excludes those who are claiming benefits and yet who are not actively seeking work. Clearly, the tougher the benefit regulations, the lower the claimant rate will be relative to the standardised rate.

Table 7.3 shows standardised unemployment rates for different countries by age and sex.

Unemployment and the labour market

We now turn to the causes of unemployment. These causes fall into two broad categories: *equilibrium* unemployment and *disequilibrium* unemployment. To make

Definition
Standardised unemployment rate The measure of the unemployment rate used by the ILO and OECD. The unemployed are defined as persons of working age who are without work, available for work and actively seeking employment.

Figure 7.5

Disequilibrium
unemployment

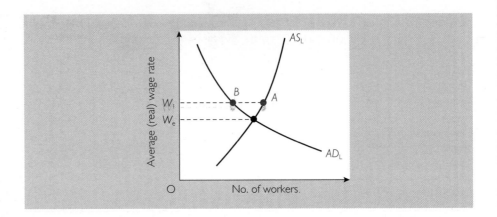

Figure 7.5

Disequilibrium
unemployment

Definitions

Aggregate supply of labour curve
A curve showing the total number of people willing and able to work at different average real wage rates.

Aggregate demand for labour curve
A curve showing the total demand for labour in the economy at different average real wage rates.

Disequilibrium unemployment
Unemployment resulting from real wages in the economy being above the equilibrium level.

Equilibrium ('natural') unemployment
The difference between those who would like employment at the current wage rate and those willing and able to take a job.

clear the distinction between the two, it is necessary to look at how the labour market works.

Figure 7.5 shows the aggregate demand for labour and the aggregate supply of labour: that is, the total demand and supply of labour in the whole economy. The *real* average wage rate is plotted on the vertical axis. This is the average wage rate expressed in terms of its purchasing power: in other words, after taking prices into account.

The aggregate supply of labour curve (AS_L) shows the number of workers *willing to accept jobs* at each wage rate. This curve is relatively inelastic, since the size of the workforce at any one time cannot change significantly. Nevertheless it is not totally inelastic because (a) a higher wage rate will encourage some people to enter the labour market (e.g. parents raising children), and (b) the unemployed will be more willing to accept job offers rather than continuing to search for a better-paid job.

The aggregate demand for labour curve (AD_L) slopes downwards. The higher the wage rate, the more will firms attempt to economise on labour and to substitute other factors of production for labour.

The labour market is in equilibrium at a wage of W_e, where the demand for labour equals the supply. If the wage rate were above W_e, the labour market would be in a state of disequilibrium. At a wage rate of W_1, there is an excess supply of labour of $A - B$. This is called disequilibrium unemployment.

For disequilibrium unemployment to occur, two conditions must hold:

- The aggregate supply of labour must exceed the aggregate demand.
- There must be a 'stickiness' in wages. In other words, the wage rate must not immediately fall to W_e.

Even when the labour market *is* in equilibrium, however, not everyone looking for work will be employed. Some people will hold out, hoping to find a better job. The curve N in Figure 7.6 shows the total number in the labour force. The horizontal difference between it and the aggregate supply of labour curve (AS_L) represents the excess of people looking for work over those actually willing to accept jobs. Q_e represents the equilibrium level of employment and the distance $D - E$ represents the equilibrium level of unemployment. This is sometimes known as the *natural level of unemployment*.

Key
Idea

7
p41

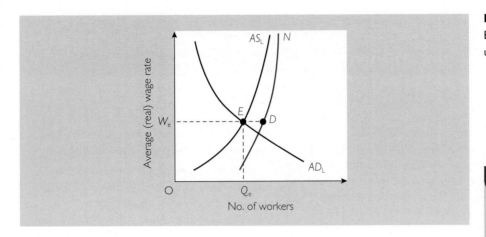

Figure 7.6
Equilibrium
unemployment

Types of disequilibrium unemployment

There are three possible causes of disequilibrium unemployment.

Real-wage unemployment

Real-wage unemployment is where trade unions use their monopoly power to drive wages above the market-clearing level. In Figure 7.5, the wage rate is driven up above W_e. Excessive real wage rates were blamed by the Thatcher and Major governments for the high unemployment of the 1980s and 1990s. The possibility of higher real-wage unemployment was also one of the reasons for their rejection of a national minimum wage.

The solution to real-wage unemployment would seem to be a reduction in real wage rates. It may be very difficult, however, to prevent unions pushing up wages. Even if the government did succeed in reducing the average real wage rate, there would then be a problem of reduced consumer expenditure and hence a reduced demand for labour, with the result that unemployment might not fall at all.

Demand-deficient or cyclical unemployment

Demand-deficient cyclical unemployment is associated with economic recessions. As the economy moves into recession, consumer demand falls. Firms find that they are unable to sell their current level of output. For a time they may be prepared to build up stocks of unsold goods, but sooner or later they will start to cut back on production and cut back on the amount of labour they employ. In Figure 7.5 the AD_L curve shifts to the left. The deeper the recession becomes and the longer it lasts, the higher will demand-deficient unemployment become.

As the economy recovers and begins to grow again, so demand-deficient unemployment will start to fall again. Because demand-deficient unemployment fluctuates with the business cycle, it is sometimes referred to as 'cyclical unemployment'. Figure 7.4 (on page 266) showed the fluctuations in unemployment in various industrial countries. If you compare this figure with Figure 7.3 (on page 260), you can see how unemployment tends to rise in recessions and fall in booms.

Definitions

Real-wage unemployment
Disequilibrium unemployment caused by real wages being driven up above the market-clearing level.

Demand-deficient or cyclical unemployment
Disequilibrium unemployment caused by a fall in aggregate demand with no corresponding fall in the real wage rate.

Pause for thought

If this analysis is correct, namely that a reduction in wages will reduce the aggregate demand for goods, what assumption must we make about the relative proportions of wages and profits that are spent (given that a reduction in real wage rates will lead to a corresponding increase in rates of profit)? Is this a realistic assumption?

Box 7.2 Case Studies and Applications

The costs of unemployment

Is it just the unemployed who suffer?

The most obvious cost of unemployment is to the *unemployed themselves*. There is the direct financial cost of the loss in their earnings, measured as the difference between their previous wage and their unemployment benefit. Then there are the personal costs of being unemployed. The longer people are unemployed, the more dispirited they may become. Their self-esteem is likely to fall, and they are more likely to succumb to stress-related illness.

Then there are the costs to the *family and friends* of the unemployed. Personal relations can become strained, and there may be an increase in domestic violence and the number of families splitting up.

Then there are the *broader costs to the economy*. Unemployment benefits are a cost borne by taxpayers. There may also have to be extra public spending on benefit offices, social services, health care and the police. What is more, unemployment represents a loss of output. In other words, actual output is below potential output. Apart from the lack of income to the unemployed themselves, this under-utilisation of resources leads to lower incomes for other people too:

■ The government loses tax revenues, since the unemployed pay no income tax and national insurance, and, given that the unemployed spend less, they pay less VAT and excise duties.
■ Firms lose the profits that could have been made, had there been full employment.

■ Other workers lose any additional wages they could have earned from the higher national output.

What is more, the longer people remain unemployed, the more deskilled they tend to become, thereby reducing *potential* as well as actual income.

Finally there is some evidence that higher unemployment leads to increased *crime and vandalism*. This obviously imposes a cost on the sufferers.

The costs of unemployment are to some extent offset by benefits. If workers voluntarily quit their jobs to look for a better one, then they must reckon that the benefits of a better job more than compensate for their temporary loss of income. From the nation's point of view, a workforce that is prepared to quit jobs and spend a short time unemployed will be a more adaptable, more mobile workforce – one that is responsive to changing economic circumstances. Such a workforce will lead to greater allocative efficiency in the short run and more rapid economic growth over the longer run.

Long-term involuntary unemployment is quite another matter. The costs clearly outweigh any benefits, both for the individuals concerned and for the economy as a whole. A demotivated, deskilled pool of long-term unemployed is a serious economic and social problem.

? How might an economist set about measuring the various costs of unemployment to family, friends and society at large?

Demand-deficient unemployment can also exist in the longer term if the economy is constantly run at below full capacity and labour markets continue not to be in equilibrium. Even at the peak of the business cycle, actual output may be considerably below potential output.

Growth in the labour supply

If labour supply rises with no corresponding increase in the demand for labour, the equilibrium real wage rate will fall. If the real wage rate is 'sticky' downwards, unemployment will occur. This tends not to be such a serious cause of unemployment as demand deficiency, since the supply of labour changes relatively slowly. Nevertheless there is a problem of providing jobs for school leavers each year with the sudden influx of new workers on to the labour market.

There is also a potential problem over the longer term if social trends lead more women with children to seek employment. In practice, however, with the rapid growth of part-time employment, and the lower average wage rate paid to women, this has not been a major cause of excess labour supply.

Equilibrium unemployment (or natural unemployment)

If you look at Figure 7.4, you can see how unemployment was higher in the 1980s and 1990s than in the 1970s. Part of the reason for this was the growth in equilibrium unemployment.

Although there may be overall *macro*economic equilibrium, with the *aggregate* demand for labour equal to the *aggregate* supply, and thus no disequilibrium unemployment, at a *micro*economic level supply and demand may not match. In other words, there may be vacancies in some parts of the economy, but an excess of labour (unemployment) in others. This is equilibrium unemployment. There are various types of equilibrium unemployment.

Frictional (search) unemployment

Frictional unemployment occurs when people leave their jobs, either voluntarily or because they are sacked or made redundant, and are then unemployed for a period of time while they are looking for a new job. They may not get the first job they apply for, despite a vacancy existing. The employer may continue searching, hoping to find a better-qualified person. Likewise, unemployed people may choose not to take the first job they are offered. Instead, they may continue searching, hoping that a better one will turn up.

The problem is that information is imperfect. Employers are not fully informed about what labour is available; workers are not fully informed about what jobs are available and what they entail. Both employers and workers, therefore, have to search: employers searching for the right labour and workers searching for the right jobs.

One obvious remedy for frictional unemployment is for there to be better job information. This could be provided by government job centres, by private employment agencies, or by local and national newspapers.

Structural unemployment

Structural unemployment is where the structure of the economy changes. Employment in some industries may expand while in others it contracts. There are two main reasons for this.

A change in the pattern of demand. Some industries experience declining demand. This may be due to a change in consumer tastes. Certain goods may go out of fashion. Or it may be due to competition from other industries. For example, consumer demand may shift away from coal and to other fuels. This will lead to structural unemployment in mining areas.

Key idea 7 p41

Key idea 22 p214

Definitions

Frictional (search) unemployment Unemployment that occurs as a result of imperfect information in the labour market. It often takes time for workers to find jobs (even though there *are* vacancies) and in the meantime they are unemployed.

Structural unemployment Unemployment that arises from changes in the pattern of demand or supply in the economy. People made redundant in one part of the economy cannot immediately take up jobs in other parts (even though there are vacancies).

A change in the methods of production (technological unemployment). New techniques of production often allow the same level of output to be produced with fewer workers. This is known as 'labour-saving technical progress'. Unless output expands sufficiently to absorb the surplus labour, people will be made redundant. This creates technological unemployment. An example is the job losses in the banking industry caused by the increase in the number of cash machines and by the development of telephone and Internet banking.

Structural unemployment often occurs in particular regions of the country. When it does, it is referred to as regional unemployment. This is most likely to occur when particular industries are concentrated in particular areas. For example, the decline in the South Wales coal mining industry led to high unemployment in the Welsh valleys.

The level of structural unemployment will depend on three factors:

■ The degree of regional concentration of industry. The more that industries are concentrated in particular regions, the greater will be the level of structural unemployment if particular industries decline.

■ The speed of change of demand and supply in the economy. The more rapid the rate of technological change or the shift in consumer tastes, the more rapid will be the rate of redundancies.

■ The immobility of labour. Where workers are less able or less willing to move to a new job, the higher will be the level of structural unemployment.

Seasonal unemployment

Seasonal unemployment occurs when the demand for certain types of labour fluctuates with the seasons of the year. This problem is particularly severe in holiday areas, such as Cornwall, where unemployment can reach very high levels in the winter months.

Definitions

Technological unemployment Structural unemployment that occurs as a result of the introduction of labour-saving technology.

Regional unemployment Structural unemployment occurring in specific regions of the country.

Seasonal unemployment Unemployment associated with industries or regions where the demand for labour is lower at certain times of the year.

Recap

1. The two most common measures of unemployment are claimant unemployment (those claiming unemployment-related benefits) and ILO/OECD standardised unemployment (those available for work and actively seeking work or waiting to take up an appointment).

2. Unemployment can be divided into disequilibrium and equilibrium unemployment.

3. Disequilibrium unemployment occurs when the average real wage rate is above the level that will equate the aggregate demand and supply of labour. It can be caused by unions or government pushing up wages (real-wage unemployment), by a fall in aggregate demand (demand-deficient unemployment), or by an increase in the supply of labour.

4. Equilibrium unemployment occurs when there are people unable or unwilling to fill job vacancies. This may be due to poor information in the labour market and hence a time lag before people find suitable jobs (frictional unemployment), to a changing pattern of demand or supply in the economy and hence a mismatching of labour with jobs (structural unemployment – specific types being technological and regional unemployment), or to seasonal fluctuations in the demand for labour.

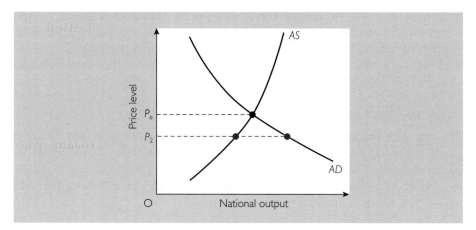

Figure 7.7
Aggregate demand
and aggregate supply

Aggregate demand and supply

7.5

What determines the level of output and the level of prices in an economy?

Before we examine the causes of inflation (the rate of increase in prices), we need to look at how the *level* of prices in the economy is determined. It is determined by the interaction of aggregate demand and aggregate supply. The analysis is similar to that of demand and supply in individual markets, but there are some crucial differences. Figure 7.7 shows an aggregate demand and an aggregate supply curve.

As with demand and supply curves for individual goods, we plot price on the vertical axis, except that now it is the *general* price level; and we plot quantity on the horizontal axis, except that now it is the *total quantity of national output* (GDP). Let us examine each curve in turn.

Aggregate demand curve

Remember what we said about aggregate demand earlier in the chapter. It is the total level of spending on the country's products and consists of four elements: consumer spending (C), private investment (I), government expenditure on goods and services (G) and expenditure on exports (X) less expenditure on imports (M). Thus:

$$AD = C + I + G + X - M$$

The aggregate demand curve shows how much national output (GDP) will be demanded at each level of prices. But why will the AD curve slope downwards: why will people demand fewer products as prices rise? There are three main reasons:

■ If prices rise, people will be encouraged to buy fewer of the country's products and more imports instead (which are now relatively cheaper); the country will also sell fewer exports. Thus aggregate demand will be lower.
■ As prices rise, people will need more money to pay for their purchases. With a given supply of money in the economy, this will have the effect of driving up

interest rates (we will explore this in Chapter 9). The effect of higher interest rates will be to discourage borrowing and encourage saving. Both will have the effect of reducing spending and hence reducing aggregate demand.

■ If prices rise, the value of people's savings will be eroded. They may thus save more (and spend less) to compensate.

Aggregate supply curve

The aggregate supply curve slopes upwards – at least in the short run. In other words, the higher the level of prices, the more will be produced. The reason is simple: provided that factor prices (and in particular, wage rates) do not rise as rapidly as product prices, firms' profitability at each level of output will be higher than before. This will encourage them to produce more.

Equilibrium

The equilibrium price level will be where aggregate demand equals aggregate supply. To demonstrate this, consider what would happen if aggregate demand exceeded aggregate supply: for example, at P_2 in Figure 7.7. The resulting shortages throughout the economy would drive up prices. This would cause a movement up *along* both the *AD* and *AS* curves until *AD* = *AS* (at P_e).

Shifts in the AD or AS curves

If there is a change in the price level there will be a movement *along* the *AD* and *AS* curves. If any other determinant of *AD* or *AS* changes, the respective curve will shift. The analysis here is very similar to shifts and movements along demand and supply curves in individual markets (see pages 33 and 38).

The aggregate demand curve will shift if there is a change in any of its components – consumption, investment, government expenditure, or exports minus imports. Thus if the government decides to spend more, or if customers spend more as a result of lower taxes, or if business confidence increases so that firms decide to invest more, the *AD* curve will shift to the right.

Similarly, the aggregate supply curve will shift to the right if there is a rise in labour productivity or in the stock of capital: in other words, if there is a rise in potential output.

> **Pause for thought**
>
> Give some examples of events that could shift (a) the AD curve to the left; (b) the AS curve to the left.

Effect of a shift in the aggregate demand curve

If there is an increase in aggregate demand, the *AD* curve will shift to the right. This will lead to a combination of higher prices and higher output, depending on the elasticity of the *AS* curve. The more elastic the *AS* curve, the more will output rise relative to prices. We will consider the shape of the *AS* curve in more detail in Chapter 10.

Recap

1. Equilibrium in the economy occurs where aggregate demand equals aggregate supply.

2. A diagram can be constructed to show aggregate demand and aggregate supply, with the price level on the vertical axis and national output (GDP) on the horizontal axis.

3. The AD curve is downward sloping, meaning that aggregate demand will be lower at a higher price level. The reason is that at higher prices: (a) there will be more imports and fewer exports; (b) interest rates will tend to be higher, resulting in reduced borrowing and increased saving; (c) people will be encouraged to save more to maintain the value of their savings.

4. The AS curve is upward sloping because the higher prices resulting from higher demand will encourage firms to produce more (assuming that costs do not rise as rapidly as prices).

5. A change in the price level will cause a movement along the AD and AS curves. A change in any other determinant of either AD or AS will cause a shift in the respective curve.

6. The amount that prices and output rise as a result of an increase in aggregate demand will depend on the shape of the AS curve.

Inflation   7.6

Why do prices have a tendency to rise?

Key Idea 27 p275

The rate of inflation measures the annual percentage *increase* in prices. The usual measure is that of *retail* prices. The government publishes an index of retail prices each month, and the rate of inflation is the percentage increase in that index over the previous 12 months. Figure 7.8 shows the rates of inflation for the USA, Japan, the UK, the EU and the OECD. As you can see, inflation was particularly severe between 1973 and 1983, and relatively low in the mid-1980s and in recent years.

It is also possible to give the rates of inflation for other prices. For example, indices are published for commodity prices, for food prices, for house prices (see Box 1.3), for import prices, for prices after taking taxes into account and so on. Their respective rates of inflation are simply their annual percentage increase. Likewise it is possible to give the rate of inflation of wage rates ('wage inflation').

When there is inflation, we have to be careful in assessing how much national output, consumption, wages, etc. are increasing. Take the case of GDP. GDP in year 2 may seem higher than in year 1, but this may be partly (or even wholly) the result of higher prices. Thus GDP in money terms may have risen by 5 per cent, but if inflation is 3 per cent, real growth in GDP will be only 2 per cent. In other words, the volume of output will be only 2 per cent higher.

> **Definition**
>
> **Real growth values**
> Values of the rate of growth of GDP or any other variable after taking inflation into account. The real value of the growth in a variable equals its growth in money (or 'nominal') value minus the rate of inflation.

The distinction between nominal and real figures. Nominal figures are those using current prices, interest rates, etc. Real figures are figures corrected for inflation. **Key Idea 27**

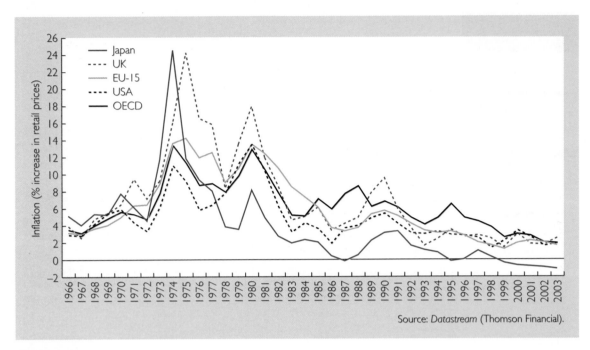

Source: *Datastream* (Thomson Financial).

Figure 7.8

Inflation rates in selected industrial countries and groups of countries: 1966–2003

Before we proceed, a word of caution: be careful not to confuse a rise or fall in *inflation* with a rise or fall in *prices*. A rise in inflation means a *faster* increase in prices. A fall in inflation means a *slower* increase in prices (but still an increase as long as inflation is positive).

Causes of inflation

Demand-pull inflation

Demand-pull inflation is caused by continuing rises in aggregate demand. In Figure 7.9, the *AD* curve shifts to the right (and continues doing so). Firms will respond to the rise in aggregate demand partly by raising prices and partly by increasing output (there is a move up along the *AS* curve). Just how much they raise prices depends on how much their costs rise as a result of increasing output. This in turn depends on how close actual output is to potential output. The less slack there is in the economy, the more will firms respond to a rise in demand by raising their prices (the steeper will be the *AS* curve).

Demand-pull inflation is typically associated with a booming economy. Many economists therefore argue that it is the counterpart of demand-deficient unemployment. When the economy is in recession, demand-deficient unemployment will be high, but demand-pull inflation will be low. When, on the other hand, the economy is near the peak of the business cycle, demand-pull inflation will be high, but demand-deficient unemployment will be low.

Cost-push inflation

Cost-push inflation is associated with continuing rises in costs and hence continuing leftward (upward) shifts in the AS curve. Such shifts occur when costs of production rise *independently* of aggregate demand. If firms face a rise in costs, they

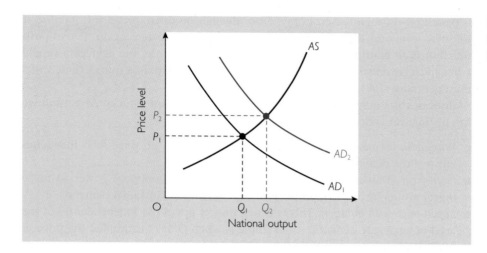

Figure 7.9
Demand-pull
inflation

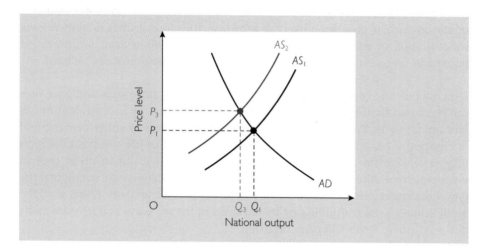

Figure 7.10
Cost-push inflation

will respond partly by raising prices and passing the costs on
to the consumer, and partly by cutting back on production.
This is illustrated in Figure 7.10. There is a leftward shift in
the aggregate supply curve: from AS_1 to AS_2. This causes the
price level to rise to P_3 and the level of output to *fall* to Q_3.

Just how much firms raise prices and cut back on pro-
duction depends on the shape of the aggregate demand curve. The less elastic the
AD curve, the less sales will fall as a result of any price rise, and hence the more will
firms be able to pass on the rise in their costs to consumers as higher prices.

Note that the effect on output and employment is the opposite of demand-pull
inflation. With demand-pull inflation, output and hence employment tend to rise.
With cost-push inflation, however, output and employment tend to fall.

It is important to distinguish between *single* shifts in the aggregate supply curve
(known as 'supply shocks') and *continuing* shifts. If there is a single leftward shift in
aggregate supply, there will be a single rise in the price level. For example, if the
government raises the excise duty on oil, there will be a single rise in oil prices and
hence in industry's fuel costs. This will cause *temporary* inflation while the price rise

> **Pause for thought**
>
> *If there is a general rise in costs of production
> across the country, does this necessarily mean
> that there is pure cost-push inflation?*

is passed on through the economy. Once this has occurred, prices will stabilise at the new level and the rate of inflation will fall back to zero again. If cost-push inflation is to continue over a number of years, therefore, the aggregate supply curve must *continually* shift to the left. If cost-push inflation is to *rise*, these shifts must get more rapid.

Rises in costs may originate from a number of different sources. As a result we can distinguish various types of cost-push inflation.

- *Wage-push inflation.* This is where trade unions push up wage rates independently of the demand for labour.
- *Profit-push inflation.* This is where firms use their monopoly power to make bigger profits by pushing up prices independently of consumer demand.
- *Import-price-push inflation.* This is where import prices rise independently of the level of aggregate demand. An example is when OPEC quadrupled the price of oil in 1973/4.

In all these cases, inflation occurs because one or more groups are exercising economic power. The problem is likely to get worse, therefore, if there is an increasing concentration of economic power over time (for example, if firms or unions get bigger and bigger, and more monopolistic) or if groups become more militant.

Demand-pull and cost-push inflation can occur together, since wage and price rises can be caused both by increases in aggregate demand and by independent causes pushing up costs. Even when an inflationary process *starts* as either demand-pull or cost-push, it is often difficult to separate the two. An initial cost-push inflation may encourage the government to expand aggregate demand to offset rises in unemployment. Alternatively, an initial demand-pull inflation may strengthen the power of certain groups, who then use this power to drive up costs. Either way, the result is likely to be continuing rightward shifts in the *AD* curve and leftward shifts in the *AS* curve. Prices will carry on rising.

Structural (demand-shift) inflation

When the *pattern* of demand (or supply) changes in the economy, certain industries will experience increased demand and others decreased demand. If prices and wage rates are inflexible downwards in the contracting industries, and prices and wage rates rise in the expanding industries, the overall price and wage level will rise. The problem will be made worse, the less elastic is supply to these shifts.

Thus a more rapid structural change in the economy can lead to both increased structural unemployment and increased structural inflation. An example of this problem was the so-called north–south divide in the UK during the second half of the 1980s. The north experienced high structural unemployment as old industries declined, while the south experienced excess demand. This excess demand in the south, among other things, led to rapid house price inflation, and rapid increases

Definition

Menu costs
The costs associated with having to adjust price lists or labels.

Box 7.3 Case Studies and Applications

The costs of inflation

Is inflation more than a mere inconvenience?

A lack of growth is obviously a problem if people want higher living standards. Unemployment is obviously a problem, both for the unemployed themselves and also for society, which suffers a loss in output and has to support the unemployed. But why is inflation a problem? If prices go up by 10 per cent, does it really matter? Provided your wages kept up with prices, you would have no cut in your living standards.

If people could correctly anticipate the rate of inflation and fully adjust prices and incomes to take account of it, then the costs of inflation would indeed be relatively small. For us as consumers, they would simply be the relatively minor inconvenience of having to adjust our notions of what a 'fair' price is for each item when we go shopping. For firms, they would again be the relatively minor costs of having to change price labels, or prices in catalogues or on menus, or to adjust slot machines. These are known as menu costs.

In reality, people frequently make mistakes when predicting the rate of inflation and are not able to adapt fully to it. This leads to the following problems, which are likely to be more serious the higher the rate of inflation becomes and the more the rate fluctuates.

Redistribution. Inflation redistributes income away from those on fixed incomes and those in a weak bargaining position, to those who can use their economic power to gain large pay, rent or profit increases. It redistributes wealth to those with assets (e.g. property) that rise in value particularly rapidly during periods of inflation, and away from those with savings that pay rates of interest below the rate of inflation and hence whose value is eroded by inflation. Pensioners may be particularly badly hit by rapid inflation.

Uncertainty and lack of investment. Inflation tends to cause uncertainty in the business community, especially when the rate of inflation fluctuates. (Generally, the higher the rate of inflation, the more it fluctuates.) If it is difficult for firms to predict their costs and revenues, they may be discouraged from investing. This will reduce the rate of economic growth. On the other hand, as will be explained in Chapter 10,

policies to reduce the rate of inflation may themselves reduce the rate of economic growth, especially in the short run. This may then provide the government with a policy dilemma.

Balance of payments. Inflation is likely to worsen the balance of payments. If a country suffers from relatively high inflation, its exports will become less competitive in world markets. At the same time, imports will become relatively cheaper than home-produced goods. Thus exports will fall and imports will rise. As a result the balance of payments will deteriorate and/or the exchange rate will fall, or interest rates will have to rise. Each of these effects can cause problems. This is examined in more detail in Chapter 12.

Resources. Extra resources are likely to be used to cope with the effects of inflation. Accountants and other financial experts may have to be employed by companies to help them cope with the uncertainties caused by inflation.

The costs of inflation may be relatively mild if inflation is kept to single figures. They can be very serious, however, if inflation gets out of hand. If inflation develops into 'hyperinflation', with prices rising perhaps by several hundred per cent or even thousands per cent per year, the whole basis of the market economy will be undermined. Firms constantly raise prices in an attempt to cover their rocketing costs. Workers demand huge pay increases in an attempt to stay ahead of the rocketing cost of living. Thus prices and wages chase each other in an ever-rising inflationary spiral. People will no longer want to save money. Instead they will spend it as quickly as possible before its value falls any further. People may even resort to barter in an attempt to avoid using money altogether (see Web case 7.7).

?
1. Do you personally gain or lose from inflation? Why?
2. Make a list of those who are most likely to gain and those who are most likely to lose from inflation. Explain.

Key Idea 27 p275

Key Idea 17 p192

Key Idea 11 p71

in incomes for various groups of workers and firms. With many prices and wage rates being set *nationally*, the inflation in the south then 'spilt over' into the north.

Expectations and inflation

Workers and firms take account of the *expected* rate of inflation when making decisions.

Key Idea 10 p68

Imagine that a union and an employer are negotiating a wage increase. Let us assume that both sides expect a rate of inflation of 5 per cent. The union will be happy to receive a wage rise somewhat above 5 per cent. That way, the members would be getting a *real* rise in incomes. The employers will be happy to pay a wage rise somewhat below 5 per cent. After all, they can put their price up by approximately 5 per cent, knowing that their rivals will do the same. The actual wage rise that the two sides agree on will thus be somewhere around 5 per cent.

Now let us assume that the expected rate of inflation is 10 per cent. Both sides will now negotiate around this benchmark, with the outcome being somewhere round about 10 per cent.

Thus the higher the expected rate of inflation, the higher will be the level of pay settlements and price rises, and hence the higher will be the resulting actual rate of inflation.

In recent years the importance of expectations in explaining the actual rate of inflation has been increasingly recognised by economists. We examine this in Chapter 10.

Recap

1. Demand-pull inflation occurs as a result of continuing increases in aggregate demand.

2. Cost-push inflation occurs when there are continuing increases in the costs of production independent of rises in aggregate demand. Cost-push inflation can be of a number of different varieties: wage-push, profit-push or import-price-push.

3. Inflation can also be caused by shifts in the pattern of demand in the economy, with prices rising in sectors of increasing demand but being reluctant to fall in sectors of declining demand.

4. Expectations play a crucial role in determining the level of inflation. The higher people expect inflation to be, the higher it will be.

Appendix   Measuring national income and output

Three routes: one destination

To assess how fast the economy has grown we must have a means of *measuring* the value of the nation's output. The measure we use is *gross domestic product* (GDP).

Key Idea 26 p257

GDP can be calculated in three different ways, which should all result in the same figure. These three methods are illustrated in the simplified circular flow of income shown in Figure 7.A1.

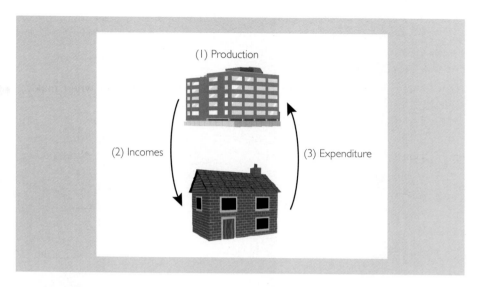

Figure 7.A1
The circular flow of national income and expenditure

(1) Production

(2) Incomes

(3) Expenditure

The product method

The first method of measuring GDP is to add up the value of all the goods and services produced in the country, industry by industry. In other words, we focus on firms and add up all their production. Thus method number one is known as the *product method*.

In the national accounts these figures are grouped together into broad categories such as manufacturing, construction and distribution. The figures for the UK economy for 2001 are shown in Figure 7.A2(a).

When we add up the output of various firms we must be careful to avoid *double counting*. For example, if a manufacturer sells a television to a retailer for £200 and the retailer sells it to the consumer for £300, how much has this television contributed to GDP? The answer is *not* £500. We do not add the £200 received by the manufacturer to the £300 received by the retailer: that would be double counting. Instead we either just count the final value (£300) or the value added at each stage (£200 by the manufacturer + £100 by the retailer).

The sum of all the values added by all the various industries in the economy is known as gross value added at basic prices (GVA).

How do we get from GVA to GDP? The answer has to do with taxes and subsidies on products. Taxes paid on goods and services (such as VAT and duties on petrol and alcohol) and any subsidies on products are *excluded* from gross value added (GVA), since they are not part of the value added in production. Nevertheless the way GDP is measured throughout the EU is at *market prices*: i.e. at the prices actually paid at each stage of production. Thus GDP at market prices (sometimes referred to simply as GDP) is GVA *plus* taxes on products *minus* subsidies on products.

The income method

The second approach is to focus on the incomes generated from the production of goods and services. A moment's reflection will show that this must be the same as the sum of all values added at each stage of production. Value added is simply the

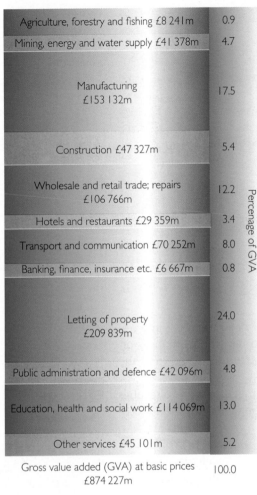

	Percentage of GVA
Agriculture, forestry and fishing £8 241m	0.9
Mining, energy and water supply £41 378m	4.7
Manufacturing £153 132m	17.5
Construction £47 327m	5.4
Wholesale and retail trade; repairs £106 766m	12.2
Hotels and restaurants £29 359m	3.4
Transport and communication £70 252m	8.0
Banking, finance, insurance etc. £6 667m	0.8
Letting of property £209 839m	24.0
Public administration and defence £42 096m	4.8
Education, health and social work £114 069m	13.0
Other services £45 101m	5.2
Gross value added (GVA) at basic prices £874 227m	100.0

plus Taxes on products	£120 499m
less Subsidies on products	£6 712m
GDP (at market prices)	**£988 014m**

(a) Product-based measure

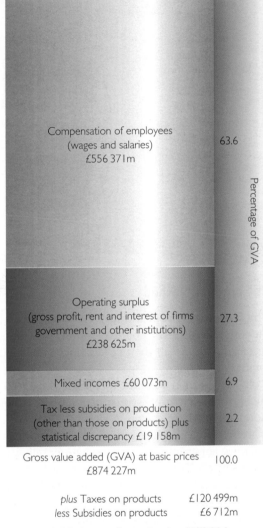

	Percentage of GVA
Compensation of employees (wages and salaries) £556 371m	63.6
Operating surplus (gross profit, rent and interest of firms government and other institutions) £238 625m	27.3
Mixed incomes £60 073m	6.9
Tax less subsidies on production (other than those on products) plus statistical discrepancy £19 158m	2.2
Gross value added (GVA) at basic prices £874 227m	100.0

plus Taxes on products	£120 499m
less Subsidies on products	£6 712m
GDP (at market prices)	**£988 014m**

(b) By category of income

Source: *UK National Income and Expenditure 2001* (National Statistics, 2002).

Figure 7.A2
UK GDP: 2001

difference between a firm's revenue from sales and the costs of its purchases from other firms. This difference is made up of wages and salaries, rent, interest and profit. In other words, it consists of the incomes earned by those involved in the production process.

Since GVA is the sum of all values added, it must also be the sum of all incomes generated: the sum of all wages and salaries, rent, interest and profit.

Figure 7.A2(b) shows how these incomes are grouped together in the official statistics. As you can see, the total is the same as that in Figure 7.A2(a), even though the components are quite different.

Note that we do not include *transfer payments* such as social security benefit and pensions. Since these are not payments for the production of goods and services, they are excluded from GVA. Conversely, part of people's gross income is paid in income taxes. Since it is this *gross* (pre-tax) income that arises from the production of goods and services, we count wages, profits, interest and rent *before* the deduction of income taxes.

As with the product approach, if we are working out GVA, we measure incomes before the payment of taxes on products or the receipt of subsidies on products, since it is these pre-tax-and-subsidy incomes that arise from the value added by production. When working out GDP, however, we add in these taxes and subtract these subsidies to arrive at a *market price* valuation.

The expenditure method

The final approach to calculating GDP is to add up all expenditure on final output (which will be at market prices). This will include the following:

- Consumer expenditure (C). This includes all expenditure on goods and services by households and by non-profit institutions serving households (NPISH) (e.g. clubs and societies).
- Government expenditure (G). This includes central and local government expenditure on final goods and services. Note that it includes non-marketed services (such as health and education), but excludes transfer payments, such as pensions and social security payments.
- Investment expenditure (I). This includes investment in capital, such as buildings and machinery. It also includes the value of any increase (+) or decrease (–) in inventories, whether of raw materials, semi-finished goods or finished goods.
- Exports of goods and services (X).
- Imports of goods and services (M). These have to be *subtracted* from the total in order to leave just the expenditure on *domestic* product. In other words, we subtract the part of consumer expenditure, government expenditure and investment that goes on imports. We also subtract the imported component (e.g. raw materials) from exports.

$$\text{GDP (at market prices)} = C + G + I + X - M$$

Table 7.A1 shows the calculation of UK GDP by the expenditure approach.

	£ million	% of GDP
Consumption expenditure of households and NPISH (C)	655 265	66.3
Government final consumption (G)	190 663	19.3
Gross capital formation (I)	164 048	16.6
Exports of goods and services (X)	268 451	27.2
Imports of goods and services (M)	−290 912	−29.5
Statistical discrepancy	499	0.1
GDP at market prices	**988 014**	**100.0**

Table 7.A1
UK GDP at market prices by category of expenditure: 2001

Source: *UK National Income and Expenditure* (National Statistics, 2002).

Box 7.4

The Human Development Index (HDI)

A measure of human welfare?

GDP is not a complete measure of a country's economic welfare: nor is it meant to be. So is there any alternative that takes other factors into account and gives a more complete picture of human wellbeing?

Since 1990, the United Nations Development Program (UNDP) has published an annual Human Development Index (HDI). This is an attempt to provide a more broadly-based measure of development than GDP. HDI is a score from 0 to 1 and is based on three sets of variables: (1) life expectancy at birth; (2) education (a weighted average of adult literacy (two-thirds) and average years of schooling (one-third)); and (3) real GDP per head.

The GDP element is measured in US dollars and is adjusted to take into account inflation and the purchasing power of each country's currency. In other words, a 'purchasing-power parity exchange rate' is used. This is the rate of exchange into the US dollar that would allow a given amount of the domestic currency to buy the same amount of goods in the USA as at home. The GDP figures are also adjusted to take into account the fact that the human value of an extra dollar is less to rich countries than to poor countries.

Countries are then placed in one of three groups according to their HDI: high human development (0.8 to 1.0), medium human development (0.5 to 0.799) and low human development (below 0.5).

The table below, based on the 2002 *Human Development Report*, gives the HDIs for selected countries and their rankings. It also gives rankings for GDP per capita. The final column shows the divergence between the two rankings. A positive number shows that a country has a higher ranking for HDI than GDP per capita. As can be seen, the rankings differ substantially in some cases between the two measures. For some countries, such as Australia, Sweden, Armenia and Tanzania, GDP understates their relative level of human development, whereas for others, such as Qatar, Saudi Arabia and South Africa, GDP per capita overstates their relative level of human development. Thus Angola's GDP per capita is over six times that of Tanzania and yet its HDI is lower.

The point is that countries with similar levels of national income may use that income quite differently.

Recently, work has been done to adjust HDI figures for various other factors, such as overall income distribution, gender inequalities and inequalities by region or ethnic group. Thus the overall HDI can be adjusted downwards to reflect greater degrees of inequality. Alternatively separate HDIs can be produced for separate regions, ethnic groups or women and men within a country.

? 1. For what reasons are HDI and per-capita GDP rankings likely to diverge?

2. Why do Qatar and Saudi Arabia have such a large negative figure in the final column of the table?

From GDP to national income

Gross national income. Some of the incomes earned in the country will go abroad. These include wages, interest, profit and rent earned in this country by foreign residents and remitted abroad, and taxes on production paid to foreign governments and institutions (e.g. the EU). On the other hand, some of the incomes earned by domestic residents will come from abroad. Again, these can be in the form of wages, interest, profit or rent, or in the form of subsidies received from governments or institutions abroad. Gross *domestic* product, however, is concerned with those

Human Development Index for selected countries

Country	HDI ranking	HDI	GDP per head (PPP$)	GDP (PPP$) ranking	GDP (PPP$) rank *minus* HDI rank
High human development					
Norway	1	0.939	28 433	3	2
Australia	2	0.936	24 574	12	10
Canada	3	0.936	26 251	6	3
Sweden	4	0.936	22 636	17	13
USA	6	0.934	31 872	3	−3
UK	14	0.923	22 093	19	5
Singapore	26	0.876	20 767	21	−5
Qatar	48	0.801	18 789	24	−24
Medium human development					
Russia	55	0.775	7 473	55	0
Saudi Arabia	68	0.754	10 815	42	−26
Brazil	69	0.750	7 037	57	−12
Armenia	72	0.745	2 215	116	44
China	87	0.718	3 617	94	7
South Africa	94	0.702	8 908	45	−49
India	115	0.571	2 248	115	0
Low human development					
Bangladesh	132	0.470	1 483	128	−4
Nigeria	136	0.455	853	147	11
Tanzania	140	0.436	501	161	21
Angola	146	0.422	3 179	102	−44
Malawi	151	0.397	586	159	8
Sierra Leone	162	0.258	448	162	0

Source: *Human Development Report, 2002 – Human Development Indicators* (United Nations Development Program) (http://www.undp.org/hdr2002/hdi.pdf).

incomes generated *within* the country, irrespective of ownership. If, then, we are to take 'net income from abroad' into account (i.e. these inflows minus outflows), we need a new measure. This is gross national income (GNY).[3] It is defined as follows:

GNY at market prices = GDP at market prices + Net income from abroad

> ### Definition
> **Gross national income (GNY)**
> GDP plus net income from abroad.

---

[3] In the official statistics, this is referred to as *GNI*. We use *Y* to stand for income, however, to avoid confusion with investment.

Table 7.A2
UK GDP, GNY and
NNY at market
prices: 2001

	£ million
Gross domestic product (GDP)	988 014
Plus net income from abroad	5 756
Gross national income (GNY)	993 770
Less capital consumption (depreciation)	−111 275
Net national income (NNY)	882 495

Source: *UK National Income and Expenditure* (National Statistics, 2002).

Thus GDP focuses on the value of domestic production, whereas GNY focuses on the value of incomes earned by domestic residents.

Net national income.   The measures we have used so far ignore the fact that each year some of the country's capital equipment will wear out or become obsolete: in other words, they ignore capital depreciation. If we subtract an allowance for depreciation (or 'capital consumption') we get net national income (NNY).

NNY at market prices = GNY at market prices – Depreciation

Table 7.A2 shows GDP, GNY and NNY figures for the UK.

Households' disposable income

Finally, we come to a term called households' disposable income. It measures the income people have available for spending (or saving): i.e. after any deductions for income tax, national insurance, etc. have been made. It is the best measure to use if we want to see how changes in household income affect consumption.

How do we get from GNY at market prices to households' disposable income? We start with the incomes that firms receive[4] from production (plus income from abroad) and then deduct that part of their income that is *not* distributed to households. This means that we must deduct taxes that firms pay – taxes on goods and services (such as VAT), taxes on profits (such as corporation tax) and any other taxes – and add in any subsidies they receive. We must then subtract allowances for depreciation and any undistributed profits. This gives us the gross income that households receive from firms in the form of wages, salaries, rent, interest and distributed profits.

To get from this what is available for households to spend, we must subtract the money that households pay in income taxes and national insurance contributions, but add all benefits to households such as pensions and child benefit.

Households' disposable income = GNY at market prices –
Taxes paid by firms + Subsidies received by firms –
Depreciation – Undistributed profits –
Personal taxes + Benefits

Definitions

Depreciation
The decline in value of capital equipment due to age or wear and tear.

Net national income (NNY)
GNY minus depreciation.

Households' disposable income
The income available for households to spend: i.e. personal incomes after deducting taxes on incomes and adding benefits.

Pause for thought

1. Should we include the sale of used items in the GDP statistics? For example, if you sell your car to a garage for £2000 and it then sells it to someone else for £2500, has this added £2500 to GDP, or nothing at all, or merely the value that the garage adds to the car: i.e. £500?
2. What items are excluded from national income statistics which would be important to take account of if we were to get a true indication of a country's standard of living?

---

[4] We also include income from any public sector production of goods or services (e.g. health and education) and production by non-profit institutions serving households.

Questions

1. The table at the bottom of the page shows index numbers for real GDP (national output) for various countries (1995 = 100).

    Using the formula $G = (Y_t - Y_{t-1})/Y_{t-1} \times 100$ (where G is the rate of growth, Y is the index number of output, t is any given years and $t - 1$ is the previous year):

    (a) Work out the growth rate for each country for each year from 1996 to 2003.
    (b) Plot the figures on a graph. Describe the pattern that emerges.

2. For simplicity, taxes are shown as being withdrawn from the inner flow of the circular flow of income (see Figure 7.1 on page 253) at just one point. In practice, different taxes are withdrawn at different points. At what point of the flow would the following be paid: (a) income taxes people pay on the dividends they receive on shares; (b) VAT; (c) business rates; (d) employees' national insurance contributions?

3. In terms of the UK circular flow of income, are the following net injections, net withdrawals or neither? If there is uncertainty, explain your assumptions.

    (a) Firms are forced to take a cut in profits in order to give a pay rise.
    (b) Firms spend money on research.
    (c) The government increases personal tax allowances.
    (d) The general public invests more money in building societies.
    (e) UK investors earn higher dividends on overseas investments.
    (f) The government purchases US military aircraft.

    (g) People draw on their savings to finance holidays abroad.
    (h) People draw on their savings to finance holidays in the UK.
    (i) The government runs a budget deficit (spends more than it receives in tax revenues) and finances it by borrowing from the general public.
    (j) The government runs a budget deficit and finances it by printing more money.

4. Will the rate of actual growth have any effect on the rate of potential growth?

5. Figure 7.2 on page 258 shows a decline in actual output in recessions. Redraw the diagram, only this time show a mere slowing down of growth in phase 4.

6. Why do cyclical swings seem much greater when we plot growth, rather than the level of output, on the vertical axis?

7. At what point of the business cycle is the country now? What do you predict will happen to growth over the next two years? On what basis do you make your prediction?

8. For what possible reasons may one country experience a persistently faster rate of economic growth than another?

9. Would it be desirable to have zero unemployment?

10. What major structural changes have taken place in the UK economy in the last ten years that have contributed to structural unemployment?

	1995	1996	1997	1998	1999	2000	2001	2002	2003
USA	100	103.6	108.1	112.8	117.1	121.6	121.9	124.9	126.9
Japan	100	103.5	105.4	104.2	104.4	107.3	107.8	108.1	108.3
Germany	100	100.8	102.2	104.3	106.3	109.6	110.3	110.6	110.7
France	100	101.1	103.0	106.6	110.0	114.6	116.7	118.1	119.2
UK	100	102.6	106.1	109.3	111.9	115.4	117.7	119.6	121.0

Note: 2003 figures are projected.
Sources: Various.

11. What are the causes of unemployment in the area where you live?

12. What would be the benefits and costs of increasing the rate of unemployment benefit?

13. Consider the most appropriate policy for tackling each of the different types of unemployment.

14. Do any groups of people gain from inflation?

15. If everyone's incomes rose in line with inflation, would it matter if inflation were 100 per cent or even 1000 per cent per annum?

16. Imagine that you had to determine whether a particular period of inflation was demand-pull, or cost-push, or a combination of the two. What information would you require in order to conduct your analysis?

Additional case studies on the *Essentials of Economics* website (www.booksites.net/sloman)

7.1 Introducing theories of economic growth. An overview of classical and more modern theories of growth (a more detailed account of economic growth is given in Section 10.7).

7.2 Technology and unemployment. Does technological progress destroy jobs?

7.3 Cost-push illusion. When rising costs are not a symptom of cost-push inflation.

7.4 Cost-push inflation and supply shocks. The distinction between one-off price rises caused by a supply shock, such as an oil price rise or a rise in tax rates, and cost-push inflation.

7.5 Is inflation dead? Just because we have low inflation, it does not mean that inflationary forces are dead!

7.6 Disinflation in Europe and Japan. What happens when there is negative inflation? Is it a case of survival of the fittest?

7.7 Hyperinflation in Germany (1923). The historical case study when inflation in Germany reached 7 trillion per cent!

7.8 Output gaps. A means of measuring excess or deficient demand.

7.9 The GDP deflator. An examination of how GDP figures are corrected to take inflation into account.

7.10 Simon Kuznets and the system of national income accounting. This looks at the work of Simon Kuznets, who devised the system of national income accounting that is used around the world. It describes some of the patterns of economic growth that he identified.

7.11 Comparing national income statistics. The importance of taking the purchasing power of local currencies into account.

7.12 Taking into account the redistributive effects of growth. This case shows how figures for economic growth can be adjusted to allow for the fact that poor people's income growth would otherwise count for far less than rich people's.

7.13 The use of ISEW. An alternative measure to GDP for estimating economic welfare.

Sections of chapter covered in WinEcon – Sloman, *Essentials of Economics*	
Essentials of Economics section	*WinEcon* section
7.1	7.1
7.2	7.2
7.3	7.3
7.4	7.5
7.5	7.6
7.6	7.6
Appendix	7.4

Websites relevant to this chapter

Numbers and sections refer to websites listed in the Web Appendix and hotlinked from this book's website at www.booksites.net/sloman

■ For news articles relevant to this chapter, see the *Economics News Articles* link from the book's website.

■ For general news on macroeconomic issues, both national and international, see websites in section A, and particularly A1–5. See also links to newspapers worldwide in A38 and 39, and the news search feature in Google at A41. See also A42 for links to economics news articles from newspapers worldwide.

■ For macroeconomic data, see links in B1 or 2; also see B4 and 12. For UK data, see B3 and 34. For EU data, see G1 > *The Statistical Annex*. For US data, see *Current economic indicators* in B5 and the *Data* section of B17. For international data, see B15, 21, 24, 31, 33. For links to data sets, see B28; I14.

■ For national income statistics for the UK (Appendix), see B1, *I. National Statistics* > the fourth link > *Economy* > *United Kingdom Economic Accounts* and *United Kingdom National Accounts – The Blue Book.*

■ For the Human Development Index (Box 7.4) see site H17.

■ For data on UK unemployment, see B1, *I. National Statistics* > the fourth link > *Labour Market* > *Labour Market Trends.* For international data on unemployment, see G1; H3 and 5.

■ For student resources relevant to this chapter, see sites C1–7, 9, 10, 19.

CHAPTER MAP

CHAPTER EIGHT

The determination of national income and the role of fiscal policy

In this chapter we look at the determination of national income, employment and inflation in the short run: i.e. over a period of up to two years.

The analysis is based on the theory developed by John Maynard Keynes in the 1930s (see Box 8.1), a theory that has had a profound influence on economics. Keynes argued that, without government intervention to steer the economy, countries could lurch from unsustainable growth to deep and prolonged recessions.

In Sections 8.1–8.4 we examine what determines the level of national output and why it tends to fluctuate (i.e. why there is a business cycle). As we shall see, Keynes placed particular emphasis on the role of aggregate demand (total spending) in determining economic activity. If aggregate demand is too low, there will be a recession with high unemployment. On the other hand, if aggregate demand is too high, there will be inflation.

Then in the remainder of the chapter (Sections 8.5 and 8.6), we look at the use of government policy to control aggregate demand so as to stabilise the level of output and keep the economy as close as possible to full employment. We focus on the use of fiscal policy. This involves altering taxes and/or government spending.

Keynesianism had its birth in the 1920s and 1930s. The UK, like most of the rest of the world, was suffering from a deep and prolonged recession (the Great Depression). Governments seemed powerless to deal with the problem. The solution was found by the Cambridge economist John Maynard Keynes (see Box 8.1). He argued that the cause of the problem was a lack of spending: a lack of aggregate demand. The economy was caught in a vicious circle. People's spending was low because their income was low. Their income was low because wages and employment were low. Wages and employment were low because production was low. Production was low because consumer spending was low: there was no point in firms producing any more if it could not be sold.

The answer, argued Keynes, was for the government to break the vicious circle. It should deliberately seek to expand aggregate demand, either by increasing its own expenditure (for example, on public works such as roads, hospitals and schools), or by cutting taxes, thereby encouraging consumers to spend more. Either way, firms would be encouraged to produce more and take on more workers.

In general, Keynesians argue that free markets will fail to meet the macroeconomic objectives of rapid economic growth and low unemployment with simultaneously low inflation and the avoidance of balance of payments problems. They thus argue that the government should intervene to manage the economy.

In this chapter we examine the Keynesian theory of the determination of national income. We consider what determines the level of national income and whether there will be full employment, or a recession with high unemployment. We also examine the use of government policy to manage aggregate demand: to ensure that it is high enough to avoid a recession, but not so high as to cause demand-pull inflation.

In later chapters, and especially Chapter 10, we shall look at alternative views to those of Keynesians, and especially at 'new classical' views. New classical economists argue that free markets generally work very well in achieving the various macroeconomic goals. By contrast, government intervention generally does more harm than good. The role of government should be not to *manage* the economy, but simply to create a sound financial environment in which the free-enterprise economy can flourish. Primarily this means keeping inflation in check by not allowing the money supply to expand too rapidly.

8.1 The equilibrium level of national income

What determines the level of a country's output in the short run?

The Keynesian analysis of output and employment can be explained most simply in terms of the circular flow of income diagram. Figure 8.1 shows a simplified version of the circular flow that we looked at in Section 7.2.

If injections (J) do not equal withdrawals (W), a state of disequilibrium exists. What will bring them back into equilibrium is a change in national income and employment.

Start with a state of equilibrium, where injections equal withdrawals. If there is now a rise in injections – say, firms decide to invest more – aggregate demand ($C_d + J$) will be higher. Firms will respond to this increased demand by using more

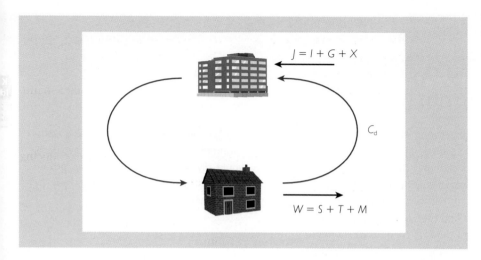

Figure 8.1
The circular flow
of income

labour and other resources, and thus paying out more incomes (Y) to households. Household consumption will rise and so firms will sell more.

Firms will respond by producing more, and thus using more labour and other resources. Household incomes will rise again. Consumption and hence production will rise again, and so on. There will thus be a multiplied rise in incomes and employment. This is known as the multiplier effect and is an example of the 'principle of cumulative causation'.

The principle of cumulative causation. An initial event can cause an ultimate effect that is much larger.

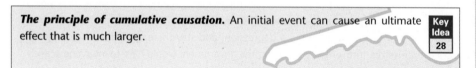

Key Idea 28

> **Definition**
>
> **Multiplier effect**
> An initial increase in aggregate demand of £xm leads to an eventual rise in national income that is greater than £xm.

The process, however, does not go on for ever. Each time household incomes rise, households save more, pay more taxes and buy more imports. In other words, withdrawals rise. When withdrawals have risen to match the increase in injections, equilibrium will be restored and national income and employment will stop rising. The process can be summarised as follows:

$$J > W \rightarrow Y\uparrow \rightarrow W\uparrow \text{ until } J = W$$

Similarly, an initial fall in injections (or rise in withdrawals) will lead to a multiplied fall in national income and employment:

$$J < W \rightarrow Y\downarrow \rightarrow W\downarrow \text{ until } J = W$$

Thus equilibrium in the circular flow of income can be at *any* level of output and employment.

Showing equilibrium with a Keynesian diagram

Equilibrium can be shown on a 'Keynesian' diagram. This plots various elements of the circular flow of income (such as consumption, withdrawals, injections and

Box 8.1

The Keynesian revolution

'In the long run we are all dead'

Up until the early 1920s, economists generally believed that there could be no such thing as mass unemployment. The reasoning of these 'classical' economists was simple: if there was unemployment in any given labour market, then all that was necessary was for a fall in real wage rates and the 'surplus' labour would disappear. In terms of Figure 7.5 (page 268), if unemployment is $A - B$, then a simple reduction in real wage rates from W_1 to W_e will eliminate the unemployment.

But in the early 1920s, the UK plunged into a deep recession that persisted until the outbreak of the Second World War in 1939. The UK was followed in 1929 by many other countries after the crash on the US stock exchange (the 'Wall Street crash'). The world experienced the 'Great Depression'.

How did the classical economists explain what had seemed impossible? They argued that, as a result of growing unionisation, wage rates were not sufficiently flexible downwards. What was needed was a willingness on the part of workers to accept wage cuts, so as to 'price themselves into employment'. What would also help would be an increase in saving, so as to provide a greater fund of money for businesses to borrow for investment: investment that would get the economy growing again.

What was *not* needed, they argued, was an increase in government spending (a problem, given the growing expenditure on unemployment benefits as the number of unemployed rose). Increased government expenditure would mean more government borrowing (if higher taxes were to be avoided), and this would divert funds away from the private sector. Private investment would be 'crowded out' by increased government spending.

Keynes' response

This analysis was criticised by John Maynard Keynes. In 1936 his *General Theory of Employment, Interest and Money* was published. Probably no other economist and no other book has ever had such a profound influence on the subject of economics and on the policies pursued by governments. Indeed, throughout the 1950s and 1960s, governments in the UK and the USA, and many other countries too, considered themselves to be 'Keynesian'.

Full employment, maintained Keynes, was not a natural state of affairs. The economy could slide into a depression, and stay there. To achieve full employment, the government would have to intervene actively in the economy to ensure a sufficient level of aggregate demand. With government intervention, however, a depression would become merely a *short-term* problem – a problem that the intervention could cure.

The classical economists seemed more concerned with the *long* term: with issues of efficiency, productivity and *potential* output. Keynes was not particularly interested in the long-run future of the world. 'Take

aggregate demand) against national income. There are two approaches to finding equilibrium: the withdrawals and injections approach; and the income and expenditure approach. Let us examine each in turn.

The withdrawals and injections approach

In Figure 8.2, national income (Y) is plotted on the horizontal axis. Withdrawals (W) and injections (J) are plotted on the vertical axis.

As national income rises, so withdrawals (saving, taxes and imports) will rise. Thus the withdrawals curve slopes upwards. But the amount that businesses plan care of the short run and the long run will look after itself' might have been Keynes' maxim. Keynes himself put it more succinctly: 'In the long run we are all dead'.

Keynes strongly criticised the classical economists' claim that the cause of the persistence of the Great Depression was a reluctance of real wage rates to fall. In Chapter 2 of the *General Theory*, he argues:

> ... the contention that the unemployment which characterizes a depression is due to a refusal by labour to accept a reduction of money wages is not clearly supported by the facts. It is not very plausible to assert that unemployment in the United States in 1932 was due either to labour obstinately refusing to accept a reduction of money wages or to its obstinately demanding a real wage beyond what the productivity of the economic machine was capable of furnishing. Wide variations are experienced in the volume of employment without any apparent change either in the minimum real demands of labour or in its productivity. Labour is not more truculent in the depression than in the boom – far from it. Nor is its physical productivity less. These facts from experience are a *prima facie* ground for questioning the classical analysis.

Keynes also criticised the classical economists' arguments that increased saving would help to bring the economy out of depression. In fact, argued Keynes, it would do the reverse. An increase in saving would mean a decrease in consumer spending. Firms would sell fewer goods. They would thus cut back on production and also on their workforce.

Keynes' solution to mass unemployment

Keynes argued that the solution to mass unemployment was for the government to spend *more*, not less. Rather than raising taxes, or increasing borrowing from the general public, it could pay for the extra spending by expanding the money supply. Extra spending would stimulate firms to produce more and to take on more workers.

As more people were employed, so they would spend more. This would encourage firms to produce even more, and to take on even more workers. There would be a 'multiplied' rise in income and employment.

After the Second World War, 'Keynesianism' became the new orthodoxy and remained so for more than 20 years. Governments of both parties accepted responsibility for ensuring that aggregate demand was kept at a sufficiently high level to maintain full, or near full, employment.

? How do you think a classical economist would reply to Keynes' arguments?

to invest, that the government plans to spend and that overseas residents plan to import from the UK (i.e. UK exports) are all only slightly affected by the current level of UK national income. Thus injections, for simplicity, are assumed to be independent of national income. The injections line, therefore, is drawn as a horizontal straight line. (This does not mean that injections are constant over time: merely that they are constant with respect to national income. If injections rise, the whole line will shift upwards.)

Withdrawals equal injections at point x in the diagram. Equilibrium national income is thus Y_e. If national income were below this level, say at Y_1, injections would exceed withdrawals (by an amount $a - b$). This additional net expenditure

Figure 8.2

Equilibrium national
income: withdrawals
equal injections

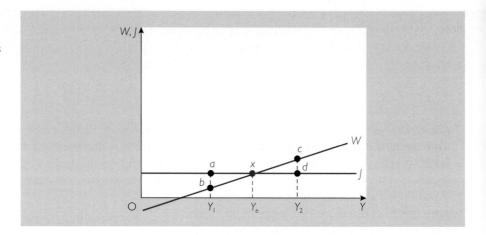

injected into the economy would encourage firms to produce more. This in turn
would cause national income to rise. But as people's incomes rose, so they would
save more, pay more taxes and buy more imports. In other words, withdrawals
would rise. There would be a movement up along the W curve. This process would
continue until $W = J$ at point x.

If, on the other hand, national income were initially at Y_2, withdrawals would
exceed injections (by an amount $c - d$). This deficiency of demand would cause production and hence national income to fall. As it did so, there would be a movement
down along the W curve until again point x was reached.

The income and expenditure approach

In Figure 8.3 two continuous lines are shown. The 45° line out from the origin
plots $C_d + W$ against Y. It is a 45° line because by definition $Y = C_d + W$. To understand this, consider what can happen to national income: either it must be spent

Figure 8.3

Equilibrium national
income: national
income equals
national expenditure

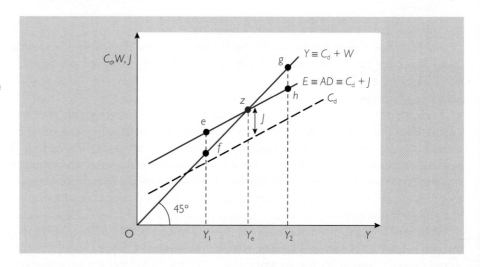

on domestically produced goods (C_d) or it must be withdrawn from the circular flow – there is nothing else that can happen to it. Thus if Y were £100 billion, then $C_d + W$ must also be £100 billion. If you draw a line such that whatever value is plotted on the horizontal axis (Y) is also plotted on the vertical axis ($C_d + W$), the line will be at 45 degrees (assuming that the axes are drawn to the same scale).

The other continuous line plots aggregate demand. In this diagram it is known as the *national (or aggregate) expenditure line* (E). It consists of $C_d + J$: in other words, the total spending on the product of domestic firms (see Figure 8.1).

To show how this line is constructed, consider the dashed line. This shows C_d. It is flatter than the 45° line. The reason is that for any given rise in national income, only *part* will be spent on domestic product, while the remainder will be withdrawn: i.e. C_d rises less quickly than Y. The E line consists of $C_d + J$. But we have assumed that J is constant with respect to changes in Y. Thus the E line is simply the C_d line shifted upwards by the amount of J.

If national expenditure exceeded national income, at say Y_1, there would be excess demand in the economy (of $e - f$). In other words, people would be buying more than was currently being produced. Firms would thus find their stocks dwindling and would therefore increase their level of production. In doing so, they would employ more factors of production. National income would thus rise. As it did so, C_d and hence E would rise. There would be a movement up along the E line. But because not all the extra income would be consumed (i.e. some would be withdrawn), expenditure would rise less quickly than income: the E line is flatter than the Y line. As income rises towards Y_e, the gap between Y and E gets smaller. Once point z is reached, $Y = E$. There is then no further tendency for income to rise.

If national income exceeded national expenditure, at say Y_2, there would be insufficient demand for the goods and services currently being produced. Firms would find their stocks of unsold goods building up. They would thus respond by producing less and employing fewer factors of production. National income would thus fall and go on falling until Y_e was reached.

Note that if Y and E, and W and J were plotted on the same diagram, point z (in Figure 8.3) would be vertically above point x (in Figure 8.2).

ey
ea
7
41

> **Pause for thought**
>
> (a) Why does a − b in Figure 8.2 equal e − f in Figure 8.3?
>
> (b) Why does c − d in Figure 8.2 equal g − h in Figure 8.3?

Recap

1. In the simple Keynesian model, equilibrium national income is where withdrawals equal injections, and where national income equals the total expenditure on domestic products: where $W = J$ and where $Y = E$.

2. The relationships between national income and the various components of the circular flow of income can be shown on a diagram, where national income is plotted on the horizontal axis and the various components of the circular flow are plotted on the vertical axis.

3. Equilibrium national income can be shown on this diagram either at the point where the W and J lines cross, or where the E line crosses the 45° line (Y).

8.2   The multiplier

What will be the effect on output of a rise in spending?

When injections rise (or withdrawals fall), this will cause national income to rise. But by how much? The answer is that there will be a *multiplied* rise in income: i.e. national income will rise by more than the rise in injections (or fall in withdrawals). The size of the multiplier is given by the letter k, where:

$$k = \Delta Y/\Delta J$$

Thus if injections rose by £10 million (ΔJ) and as a result national income rose by £30 million (ΔY), the multiplier would be 3.

But what determines the size of the rise in income (ΔY)? In other words, what determines the size of the multiplier? This can be shown graphically using either the withdrawals and injections approach or the income and expenditure approach. (You may omit one, if you choose.)

The withdrawals and injections approach

Assume that injections rise from J_1 to J_2 in Figure 8.4. Equilibrium will move from point a to point b. Income will thus rise from Y_{e_1} to Y_{e_2}. But this rise in income (ΔY) is bigger than the rise in injections (ΔJ) that caused it. This is the multiplier effect. It is given by $(c - a)/(b - c)$ (i.e. $\Delta Y/\Delta J$).

It can be seen that the size of the multiplier depends on the *slope of the W curve*. The flatter the curve, the bigger will be the multiplier: i.e. the bigger will be the rise in national income from any given rise in injections. The slope of the W curve is given by $\Delta W/\Delta Y$. This is the proportion of a rise in national income that is withdrawn, and is known as the marginal propensity to withdraw (*mpw*).

The point here is that the less is withdrawn each time money circulates, the more will be recirculated and hence the bigger will be the rise in national income. The size of the multiplier thus varies inversely with the size of the *mpw*. The bigger the *mpw*, the smaller the multiplier; the smaller the *mpw*, the bigger the multiplier. In fact the multiplier formula is simply the inverse of the *mpw*:

$$k = 1/mpw$$

Thus if the *mpw* were $1/4$, the multiplier would be 4. So if J increased by £10 million, Y would increase by £40 million. To understand why, consider what must happen to withdrawals. Injections have risen by £10 million, thus withdrawals must rise by

K
Id
28
p2

Definitions

Multiplier
The number of times by which a rise in national income (ΔY) exceeds the rise in injections (ΔJ) that caused it:
$k = \Delta Y/\Delta J$

Marginal propensity to withdraw
The proportion of an increase in national income that is withdrawn from the circular flow of income:
$mpw = \Delta W/\Delta Y$

Multiplier formula
The formula for the multirula is:
$k = 1/mpw$ or $1/(1 - mpc_d)$

Figure 8.4
The multiplier: a shift in injections

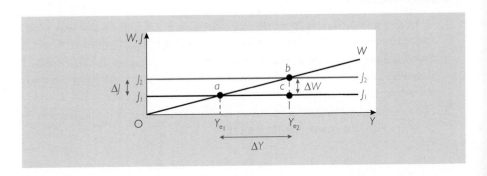

£10 million to restore equilibrium ($J = W$). But with an *mpw* of $^1/_4$, this £10 million rise in withdrawals must be one-quarter of the rise in national income that has resulted from the extra injections. Thus Y must rise by £40 million.

An alternative formula uses the concept of the marginal propensity to consume domestically produced goods (mpc_d). This is the proportion of a rise in national income that is spent on domestically produced goods, and thus is not withdrawn. Thus if a quarter of a rise in national income is withdrawn, the remaining three-quarters will recirculate as C_d. Thus:

$$mpw + mpc_d = 1$$

$$\text{and } mpw = 1 - mpc_d$$

Thus the alternative formula for the multiplier is:

$$k = 1/(1 - mpc_d)$$

But why is the multiplier given by the formula $1/mpw$? This can be illustrated by referring to Figure 8.4. The *mpw* is the slope of the W line. In the diagram this is given by the amount $(b - c)/(c - a)$. The multiplier is defined as $\Delta Y/\Delta J$. In the diagram this is the amount $(c - a)/(b - c)$. But this is merely the inverse of the *mpw*. Thus the multiplier equals $1/mpw$.[1]

The income and expenditure approach

Assume in Figure 8.5 that injections rise by £20 billion. The expenditure line thus shifts upward by £20 billion to E_2. The same effect would be achieved by

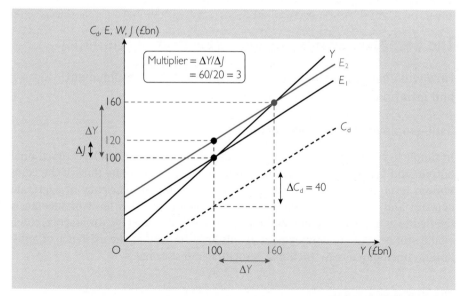

Figure 8.5
The multiplier: a shift in the expenditure function

---

[1] In some elementary textbooks, the formula for the multiplier is given as $1/mps$ (where *mps* is the marginal propensity to save: the proportion of a rise in income saved). The reason for this is that it is assumed (for simplicity) that there is only one withdrawal, namely saving, and only one injection, namely investment. As soon as this assumption is dropped, $1/mps$ becomes the wrong formula.

withdrawals falling by £20 billion, and hence consumption of domestically produced goods rising by £20 billion. Equilibrium national income rises by £60 billion, from £100 billion to £160 billion (where the E_2 line crosses the Y line).

What is the size of the multiplier? It is $\Delta Y / \Delta J$: in other words, £60bn/£20bn = 3. This can be derived from the multiplier formula:

$$k = \frac{1}{1 - mpc_d}$$

The mpc_d is given by $\Delta C_d / \Delta Y$ = £40bn/£60bn = $^2/_3$ (i.e. the slope of the C_d line). Thus:

$$k = \frac{1}{1 - {}^2/_3} = \frac{1}{{}^1/_3} = 3$$

Pause for thought

Think of two reasons why a country might have a steep E line, and hence a high value for the multiplier.

Recap

1. If injections rise (or withdrawals fall), there will be a multiplied rise in national income. The multiplier is defined as $\Delta Y / \Delta J$. Thus if a £10 million rise in injections led to a £50 million rise in national income, the multiplier would be 5.

2. The size of the multiplier depends on the marginal propensity to withdraw (*mpw*). The smaller the *mpw*, the less will be withdrawn each time incomes are generated round the circular flow, and thus the more will go round again as *additional* demand for domestic product. The multiplier formula is 1/*mpw* or 1/(1 − *mpc_d*).

8.3   The Keynesian analysis of unemployment and inflation

How will changes in the level of spending affect unemployment and inflation?

Definitions

Full-employment level of national income
The level of national income at which there is no deficiency of demand.

Deflationary gap
The shortfall of national expenditure below national income (and injections below withdrawals) at the full-employment level of national income.

'Full-employment' national income

In simple Keynesian theory, it is assumed that there is a maximum level of national output, and hence real income, that can be obtained at any one time. If the equilibrium level of income is at this level, there will be no deficiency of aggregate demand and hence no disequilibrium unemployment. This level of income is referred to as the full-employment level of national income (Y_F). (In practice, there would still be some unemployment at this level because of the existence of equilibrium unemployment – frictional, structural and seasonal.)

The deflationary gap

If the equilibrium level of national income (Y_e) is below the full-employment level (Y_F), there will be excess capacity in the economy and hence demand-deficient unemployment. There will be what is known as a deflationary gap. This situation is illustrated in Figure 8.6.

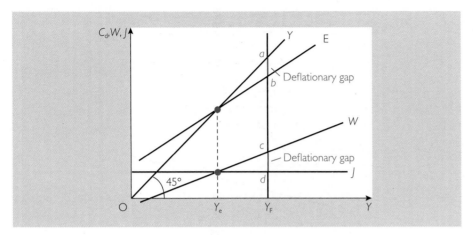

Figure 8.6
The deflationary gap

The full-employment level of national income (Y_F) is represented by the vertical line. The equilibrium level of national income is Y_e, where $W = J$ and $Y = E$. The deflationary gap is $a - b$: namely, the amount that the E line is below the 45° line at the full-employment level of national income (Y_F). It is also $c - d$: the amount that injections fall short of withdrawals at the full-employment level of income.

If national income is to be raised from Y_e to Y_F, injections will have to be raised and/or withdrawals lowered so as to close the deflationary gap.

Note that the size of the deflationary gap is *less* than the amount by which Y_e falls short of Y_F. This is another illustration of the multiplier. If injections are raised by $a - b$ (i.e. $c - d$), national income will rise by $Y_F - Y_e$. The multiplier is thus given by:

$$\frac{Y_F - Y_e}{a - b}$$

The inflationary gap

If at the full-employment level of income, national expenditure *exceeds* national income, there will be a problem of excess demand. Y_e will be above Y_F. The problem is that Y_F represents a real ceiling to output. In the short run, national income *cannot* expand beyond this point. Y_e cannot be reached. The result will therefore be demand-pull inflation.

This situation involves an inflationary gap. This is the amount by which expenditure exceeds income or injections exceed withdrawals at the full-employment level of national income. This is illustrated by the gaps $e - f$ and $g - h$ in Figure 8.7.

To eliminate this inflation, the inflationary gap must be closed, either by raising withdrawals or by lowering injections.

Definition

Inflationary gap
The excess of national expenditure over income (and injections over withdrawals) at the full-employment level of national income.

> **Pause for thought** ‖‖
>
> Assume that full-employment national income is £500 billion and that current national income is £450 billion. Assume also that the mpc_d is $^4/_5$.
> (a) Is there an inflationary or deflationary gap?
> (b) What is the size of this gap?

Policy implications

Keynesians advocate an active policy of demand management: raising aggregate demand (for example, by raising government expenditure or lowering taxes) to

Figure 8.7

The inflationary gap

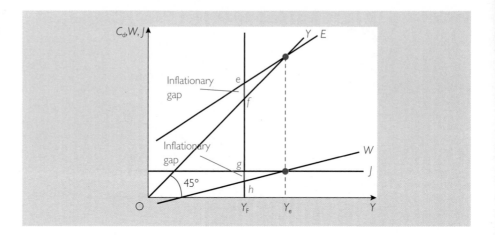

close a deflationary gap, and reducing aggregate demand to close an inflationary gap.

Unemployment and inflation at the same time

The simple analysis of deflationary and inflationary gaps implies that the aggregate supply curve looks like AS_1 in Figure 8.8. Up to Y_F, output and employment can rise with no rise in prices at all. The deflationary gap is being closed. At Y_F no further rises in output are possible. Any further rise in aggregate demand is entirely reflected in higher prices. An inflationary gap opens. In other words, this implies that either inflation *or* unemployment can occur, but not both simultaneously.

Two important qualifications need to be made to this analysis to explain the occurrence of both unemployment *and* inflation at the same time.

First, there are *other* types of inflation and unemployment not caused by an excess or deficiency of aggregate demand: for example, cost-push and expectations-generated inflation; frictional and structural unemployment.

Thus, even if a government could manipulate national income so as to get Y_e and Y_F to coincide, this would not eliminate all inflation and unemployment – only

Figure 8.8

Unemployment and inflation

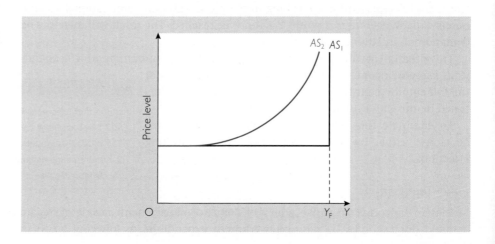

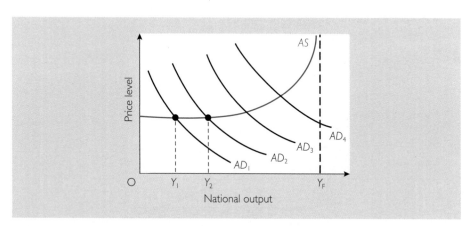

Figure 8.9
The effects of increases in aggregate demand on national output

demand-pull inflation and demand-deficient unemployment. Keynesians argue, therefore, that governments should use a whole package of policies, each tailored to the specific type of problem. But certainly one of the most important of these policies will be the management of aggregate demand.

Second, not all firms operate with the same degree of slack. A rise in aggregate demand can lead to *both* a reduction in unemployment *and* a rise in prices: some firms responding to the rise in demand by taking up slack and hence increasing output; other firms, having little or no slack, responding by raising prices; others doing both. Similarly, labour markets have different degrees of slack and therefore the rise in demand will lead to various mixes of higher wages and lower unemployment. Thus the *AS* curve will look like AS_2 in Figure 8.8.

In Figure 8.9 aggregate demand curves have been added. If aggregate demand were initially at AD_1, equilibrium would be at Y_1, considerably below the full-employment potential. A rise in aggregate demand to AD_2 would lead to a rise in national income (to Y_2), but given the high level of unemployment and spare capacity, there is likely to be little in the way of price rises: the *AS* curve is virtually flat. But as slack is taken up, the *AS* curve becomes steeper. Firms, finding it increasingly difficult to raise output in the short run, simply respond to a rise in demand by raising prices. As Y_F is approached, so the *AS* curve becomes vertical: it is impossible in the short run to raise output beyond the capacity of firms.

In the longer term, if increased demand leads to more investment and increased capacity (potential output), the level of national income at which there is full employment will rise: the Y_F line will shift to the right, and with it the short-run *AS* curve. A long-run *AS* curve, in this view, therefore, would be more elastic than the short-term one (a view that new classical economists strongly disagree with, as we shall see in Chapter 10).

The Phillips curve

The relationship between inflation and unemployment was examined in a famous article by A. W. Phillips back in 1958. He showed the statistical relationship between wage inflation and unemployment in the UK from 1861 to 1957. With wage inflation (W) on the vertical axis and the unemployment rate (U) on the horizontal axis, a scatter of points was obtained. Each point represented the observation for a

Figure 8.10

The Phillips curve

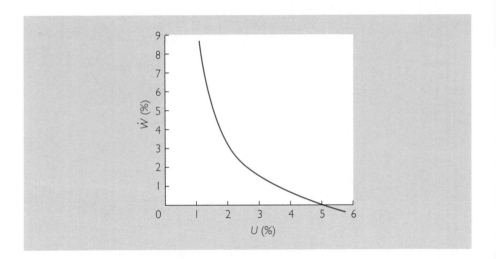

particular year. The curve that best fitted the scatter has become known as the Phillips curve. It is illustrated in Figure 8.10 and shows an inverse relationship between inflation and unemployment.

Given that wage increases over the period were approximately 2 per cent above price increases (made possible because of increases in labour productivity), a similar-shaped, but lower curve could be plotted showing the relationship between *price* inflation and unemployment.

The curve has often been used to illustrate the effects of changes in aggregate demand. When aggregate demand rose (relative to potential output), inflation rose and unemployment fell: there was a movement upwards along the curve. When aggregate demand fell, there was a movement downwards along the curve.

The Phillips curve was bowed in to the origin. The usual explanation for this is that as aggregate demand expanded, at first there would be plenty of surplus labour, which could be employed to meet the extra demand without the need to raise wage rates very much. But as labour became increasingly scarce, firms would find that they had to offer increasingly higher wage rates to obtain the labour they required, and the position of trade unions would be increasingly strengthened.

The *position* of the Phillips curve depended on *non*-demand factors causing inflation and unemployment: frictional and structural unemployment; and cost-push, structural and expectations-generated inflation. If any of these non-demand factors changed so as to raise inflation or unemployment, the curve would shift outwards to the right. The relative stability of the curve, over the 100 years or so observed by Phillips, suggested therefore that these non-demand factors had changed little.

The Phillips curve seemed to present governments with a simple policy choice. They could trade off inflation against unemployment. Lower unemployment could be bought at the cost of higher inflation, and vice versa. Unfortunately, the experience since the late 1960s has suggested that no such simple relationship exists beyond the short run.

From about 1966 the Phillips curve relationship seemed to break down. The UK, along with many other countries in the western world, began to experience growing unemployment *and* higher rates of inflation as well.

Definition

Phillips curve
A curve showing the relationship between (price) inflation and unemployment. The original Phillips curve plotted *wage* inflation against unemployment for the years 1861–1957.

Key Idea
24
p217

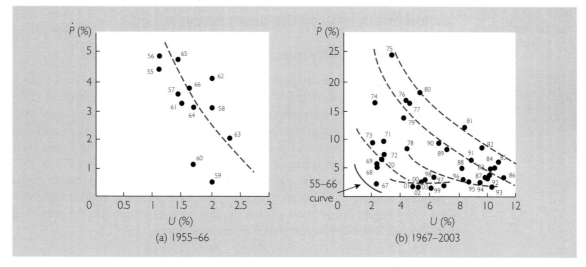

(a) 1955–66

(b) 1967–2003

Figure 8.11
The breakdown of
the Phillips curve

Figure 8.11 shows price inflation and unemployment in the UK from 1955 to 2003. From 1955 to 1966 a curve similar to the Phillips curve can be fitted through the data (diagram (a)). From 1967 to 2003, however, no simple picture emerges. Certainly the original Phillips curve can no longer fit the data; but whether the curve shifted to the right in the 1970s and 1980s, and then shifted back to the left somewhat, and more recently has become virtually horizontal with the success of the Bank of England in getting inflation to be near the target of 2.5 per cent (see the dashed lines); or whether the relationship has broken down completely, or whether there is some quite different relationship between inflation and unemployment, is not clear. There is much controversy among economists on this issue. We will examine the controversies in Chapter 10.

Recap

1. If equilibrium national income (Y_e) is below the full-employment level of national income (Y_F), there will be a deflationary gap. This gap is equal to $Y - E$ or $W - J$ at Y_F. This gap can be closed by increasing injections or reducing withdrawals. This will then cause a multiplied rise in national income (up to a level of Y_F) and will eliminate demand-deficient unemployment.

2. If equilibrium national income exceeds the full-employment level of income, the inability of output to expand to meet this excess demand will lead to demand-pull inflation. This excess demand gives an inflationary gap, which is equal to $E - Y$ or $J - W$ at Y_F. This gap can be closed by reducing injections or increasing withdrawals.

3. This simple analysis tends to imply that the AS curve will be horizontal up to Y_F and then vertical. If allowance is made for other types of inflation and unemployment, the AS curve will be upward sloping but getting steeper as full employment is approached and as bottlenecks increasingly occur.

4. The Phillips curve showed the trade-off between inflation and unemployment. There seemed to be a simple inverse relationship between the two. After 1966, however, the relationship broke down as inflation *and* unemployment rose.

5. Although economists recognise that the relationships between inflation and unemployment are more complex than was thought back in the 1950s, there is some disagreement as to precisely what these relationships are.

Keynesian analysis of the business cycle

Why do countries suffer from periodic booms and recessions?

Keynesians blame fluctuations in output and employment on fluctuations in aggregate demand. Theirs is therefore a 'demand-side' explanation of the business cycle. In the upturn (phase 1) aggregate demand starts to rise (see Figure 7.2 on page 258). It rises rapidly in the expansionary phase (phase 2). It then slows down and may start to fall in the peaking-out phase (phase 3). It then falls or remains relatively stagnant in the recession (phase 4).

Keynesians seek to explain why aggregate demand fluctuates, and then to devise appropriate stabilisation policies to iron out these fluctuations. A more stable economy, they argue, will provide a better climate for investment and the growth of both individual businesses and the economy as a whole.

Instability of investment: the accelerator

One of the major factors contributing to the ups and downs of the business cycle is the instability of investment.

In a recession, investment in new plant and equipment can all but disappear. After all, what is the point in investing in additional capacity if you cannot even sell what you are currently producing? When an economy begins to recover from a recession, however, and confidence returns, investment can rise very rapidly. In percentage terms, the rise in investment may be *several times that of the rise in income*. When the growth of the economy slows down, however, investment can fall dramatically.

The point is that investment depends not so much on the *level* of national income and consumer demand, as on their *rate of change*. The reason is that investment (except for replacement investment) is to provide *additional* capacity, and thus depends on how much demand has risen, not on its level. But growth rates change by much more than the level of output. For example, if economic growth is 1 per cent in 2004 and 2 per cent in 2005, then in 2005 output has gone up by 2 per cent, but growth has gone up by 100 per cent (i.e. it has doubled). Thus changes in investment tend to be much more dramatic than changes in national income. This is known as the accelerator theory. Box 8.2 gives an example of the accelerator effect.

These fluctuations in investment, being injections into the circular flow, will then have a multiplied effect on national income and will thus magnify the upswings and downswings of the business cycle.

Fluctuations in stocks

Firms hold stocks of finished goods. These stocks tend to fluctuate with the course of the business cycle, and these fluctuations in stocks themselves contribute to fluctuations in output.

Ke
Ide
2'
p2

Definition
Accelerator theory The *level* of investment depends on the *rate of change* of national income, and as a result tends to be subject to substantial fluctuations.

Pause for thought

Under what circumstances would you expect a rise in national income to cause a large accelerator effect?

Imagine an economy that is recovering from a recession. At first, firms may be cautious about increasing production: doing so may involve taking on more labour or making additional investment. Firms may not want to make these commitments if the recovery could soon peter out. They may, therefore, run down their stocks rather than increase output. Initially the recovery from recession will be slow.

If the recovery does continue, however, firms will start to gain more confidence and will increase their production. Also they will find that their stocks have got rather low and will need building up. This gives a further boost to production, and for a time the growth in output will exceed the growth in demand. This extra growth in output will then, via the multiplier, lead to a further increase in demand.

Once stocks have been built up again, the growth in output will slow down to match the growth in demand. This slowing down in output will, via the accelerator and multiplier, contribute to the ending of the expansionary phase of the business cycle.

As the economy slows down, firms may for a time be prepared to carry on producing and build up stocks. The increase in stocks thus cushions the effect of falling demand on output and employment.

If the recession continues, firms will be unwilling to go on building up stocks. But as firms attempt to reduce their stocks back to the desired level, production will fall *below* the level of sales, despite the fact that sales themselves are lower. This could therefore lead to a dramatic fall in output and, via the multiplier, to an even bigger fall in sales.

Eventually, once stocks have been run down to the minimum, production will have to rise again to match the level of sales. This will contribute to a recovery and the whole cycle will start again.

Determinants of the course of the business cycle

Keynesians seek to answer two key questions: why do booms and recessions last for several months or even years, and why do they eventually come to an end? Let us examine each in turn.

Why do booms and recessions persist for a period of time?

Time lags. It takes time for changes in injections and withdrawals to be fully reflected in changes in national income, output and employment. The multiplier process takes time. Moreover, consumers, firms and government may not all respond immediately to new situations. Their responses are spread out over a period of time.

'Bandwagon' effects. Once the economy starts expanding, expectations become buoyant. People think ahead and adjust their spending behaviour: they consume and invest more *now*. Likewise in a recession a mood of pessimism may set in. The effect is cumulative.

The multiplier and accelerator interact: they feed on each other. A rise in income causes a rise in investment (the accelerator). This, being an injection into the circular flow, causes a multiplied rise in income. This then causes a further accelerator effect, and a further multiplier effect, and so on.

Box 8.2

The accelerator: an example

Demonstrating the instability of investment

The following example illustrates some important features of the accelerator. It looks at the investment decisions made by a firm in response to change in the demand for its product. The firm is taken as representative of firms throughout the economy. The example is based on various strict assumptions. These help to keep the analysis simple.

■ The firm's machines last exactly 10 years and then need replacing.
■ At the start of the example, the firm has 10 machines in place, one 10 years old, one 9 years old, one 8 years old, one 7, one 6 and so on. Thus one machine needs replacing each year.
■ Machines produce exactly 100 units of output per year. This figure cannot be varied.
■ The firm always adjusts its output and its stock of machinery to match consumer demand.

The example shows what happens to the firm's investment over a six-year period when there is first a substantial rise in consumer demand, then a levelling off and then a slight fall. It illustrates the following features of the accelerator (see the table below):

Investment will rise when the growth of national income (and hence consumer demand) is rising ($\Delta Y_{t+1} > \Delta Y_t$). Years 1 to 2 illustrate this. The rise in consumer demand is zero in year 1 and 1000 units in year 2. Investment rises from 1 to 11 machines. The growth in investment may be considerably greater than the growth in consumer demand, giving a large accelerator effect. Between years 1 and 2, consumer demand doubles but investment goes up by a massive *eleven* times!

Investment will be constant even when national income is growing, if the increase in income this year is the same as last year ($\Delta Y_{t+1} = \Delta Y_t$). Years 2 to 3 illustrate this.

The accelerator effect

				Year			
	0	1	2	3	4	5	6
Quantity demanded by consumers (sales)	1000	1000	2000	3000	3500	3500	3400
Number of machines required	10	10	20	30	35	35	34
Induced investment (I_i) (extra machines)		0	10	10	5	0	0
Replacement investment (I_r)		1	1	1	1	1	0
Total investment ($I_i + I_r$)		1	11	11	6	1	0

Why do booms and recessions come to an end?
What determines the turning points?

Ceilings and floors. Actual output can go on growing more rapidly than potential output only as long as there is slack in the economy. As full employment is approached and as more and more firms reach full capacity, so a ceiling to output is reached.

At the other extreme, there is a basic minimum level of consumption that people tend to maintain. During a recession, people may not buy much in the way of luxury and durable goods, but they will still continue to buy food and other basic goods. There is thus a floor to consumption.

The industries supplying these basic goods will need to maintain their level of replacement investment. Also there will always be some minimum investment demand as firms, in order to survive competition, need to install the latest equipment. There is thus a floor to investment too.

Consumer demand continues to rise by 1000 units, but investment is constant at 11 machines.

Investment will fall even if national income is still growing, if the rate of growth is slowing down ($\Delta Y_{t+1} < \Delta Y_t$). Years 3 to 4 illustrate this. Consumer demand rises now by 500 units (rather than the 1000 units last year). Investment falls from 11 to 6 machines.

If national income is constant, investment will be confined to replacement investment only. Years 4 to 5 illustrate this. Investment falls to the one machine requiring replacement.

If national income falls, even if only slightly, investment can be wiped out altogether. Years 5 to 6 illustrate this. Even though demand has fallen by only $^1/_{35}$, investment will fall to zero. Not even the machine that is wearing out will be replaced.

In practice, the accelerator will not be as dramatic and clear cut as this. The effect will be extremely difficult to predict for the following reasons:

■ Many firms may have spare capacity and/or carry stocks. This will enable them to meet extra demand without having to invest.
■ The willingness of firms to invest will depend on their confidence of *future* demand. Just because demand has currently risen, firms are not going to

rush out and spend large amounts of money on machines that will last many years if it is quite likely that next year demand will fall back again.
■ Firms may make their investment plans a long time in advance and may be unable to change them quickly.
■ Even if firms do decide to invest more, the producer goods industries may not have the capacity to meet a sudden surge in demand for machines.
■ Machines do not as a rule suddenly wear out. A firm could thus delay replacing machines and keep the old ones for a bit longer if it was uncertain about its future level of demand.

All these points tend to reduce the magnitude of the accelerator and to make it very difficult to predict. Nevertheless the effect still exists. Firms still take note of changes in consumer demand when deciding how much to invest. Evidence shows that fluctuations in investment are far more severe than fluctuations in national income.

? If there is an initial change in injections or withdrawals, then theoretically this will set off a chain reaction between the multiplier and accelerator. Assuming that there is an initial rise in injections, trace through the multiplier and accelerator effects. Why is it unlikely that national income will go on rising more and more rapidly?

Echo effects.   Durable consumer goods and capital equipment may last several years, but eventually they will need replacing. The replacement of goods and capital purchased in a previous boom may help to bring a recession to an end.

The accelerator.   For investment to continue rising, consumer demand must rise at a *faster and faster* rate. If this does not happen, investment will fall back and the boom will break.

Random shocks.   National or international political, social or natural events can affect the mood and attitudes of firms, governments and consumers, and thus affect aggregate demand.

Changes in government policy.   In a boom, a government may become most worried by inflation and balance of payments deficits and thus pursue contractionary

Box 8.3

Business expectations and their effect on investment

Recent European experience

Investment is highly volatile. It is subject to far more violent swings than national income. This can be seen in Figure (a), which shows EU growth in GDP and growth in investment from 1985 to 2003. The maximum annual growth in GDP was 4.2 per cent and the maximum fall was 0.4 per cent. By contrast, the maximum annual growth in investment was 9.5 per cent and the maximum fall was 8.8 per cent. The differences were even greater for individual EU countries.

These figures are consistent with the accelerator theory, which argues that the *level* of investment depends on the *rate of change* of national income. A relatively small percentage change in national income can give a much bigger percentage change in investment.

Another factor affecting investment is the degree of business optimism. While this is partly determined by current rates of economic growth, there are many other factors that can affect the business climate. These include world political events (such as a war or a US election), national and international macroeconomic policies and shocks to the world economy (such as oil price changes). Of course, to the extent that these other factors affect confidence, which in turn affects investment, so they will affect economic growth.

In the boom years of the late 1980s, business optimism was widespread throughout Europe. Investment was correspondingly high, and with it there was a high rate of economic growth.

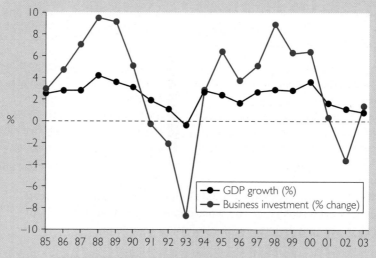

(a) EU-15 growth in GDP and business investment

Pause for thought

Why is it difficult to predict precisely when a recession will come to an end and the economy will start growing rapidly?

policies. In a recession, it may become most worried by unemployment and lack of growth and thus pursue expansionary policies. These government policies, if successful, will bring about a turning point in the cycle.

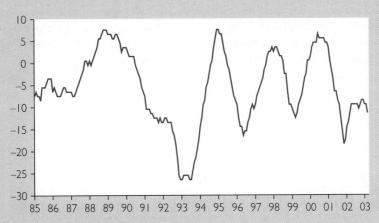

(b) EU-15 industry confidence indicator

Surveys of European business expectations in the early 1990s, however, told a very different story. Pessimism was rife. Europe was in the grip of a recession. Growth slowed right down and output actually fell in 1993. Along with this decline in growth and deteriorating levels of business and consumer confidence, there was a significant fall in investment.

The industrial confidence indicator for the EU as a whole is plotted in Figure (b). The indicator shows the percentage excess of confident over pessimistic replies to business questionnaires: a negative figure means that there was a higher percentage of pessimistic responses. You can see that the indicator was strongly negative in 1993. After 1993, pessimism began to decrease, and by the last quarter of 1994 the EU industrial confidence indicator became positive.

Between 1995 and 2000, the industrial confidence indicator swung between positive and negative values. These swings were similar in direction to those in the rate of economic growth. For example, both the rate of growth and the confidence indicator rose in 1997/8 and 2000 and fell in 1996.

Then, in 2001, with the world economy slowing down and the 11 September attack on the World Trade Center in New York, industrial confidence plummeted, and so did investment. As global uncertainties persisted and with impending and then actual war against Iraq, the confidence indicator remained low through 2002 and into 2003.

1. How is the existence of surveys of business confidence likely to affect firms' expectations and actions?
2. Why, if the growth in output slows down (but is still *positive*), is investment likely to *fall* (i.e. the growth in investment be *negative*)? If you look at Figure (a) you will see that this happened in 1991 and 1992 and in 2001 and 2002.

Keynesians argue that governments should attempt to reduce cyclical fluctuations by the use of active stabilisation policies. A more stable economy will provide a better climate for long-term investment, which will lead to faster growth in both potential and actual output. The policy traditionally favoured by Keynesians for stabilising the economy is *fiscal policy*. This is considered in the next section.

Recap

1. Keynesians explain cyclical fluctuations in the economy by examining the causes of fluctuations in the level of aggregate *demand*.

2. A major part of the Keynesian explanation of the business cycle is the instability of investment. The accelerator theory helps to explain this instability. It relates the level of investment to *changes* in national income and consumer demand. An initial increase in consumer demand can result in a very large percentage increase in investment; but as soon as the rise in consumer demand begins to level off, investment will fall; and even a slight fall in consumer demand can reduce investment to virtually zero.

3. Keynesians identify other causes of cyclical fluctuations, such as cycles in the holding of stocks, time lags, 'bandwagon' effects, the *interaction* of the multiplier and accelerator, ceilings and floors to output, echo effects, swings in government policy and random shocks.

8.5 The role of fiscal policy

How can government expenditure and taxation be used to affect the level of economic activity?

Definitions

Fiscal policy
Policy to affect aggregate demand by altering government expenditure and/or taxation.

Fine tuning
The use of demand management policy (fiscal or monetary) to smooth out cyclical fluctuations in the economy.

Budget deficit
The excess of central government's spending over its tax receipts.

Fiscal policy involves the government manipulating the level of government expenditure and/or rates of tax so as to affect the level of aggregate demand. An *expansionary* fiscal policy will involve raising government expenditure (an injection into the circular flow of income) or reducing taxes (a withdrawal from the circular flow). This will increase aggregate demand and lead to a *multiplied* rise in national income. A *deflationary* (i.e. a contractionary) fiscal policy will involve cutting government expenditure and/or raising taxes.

During the 1950s and 1960s, when fiscal policy was seen by both governments and economists as the major way of controlling the economy, it was used to perform two main functions.

■ To prevent the occurrence of *fundamental* disequilibria in the economy. In other words, expansionary fiscal policy could be used to prevent mass unemployment, such as that experienced in the Great Depression of the 1930s or in east and south-east Asia, Russia and Brazil in the late 1990s. Likewise deflationary fiscal policy could be used to prevent excessive inflation, such as that experienced in many countries in the early 1970s.

■ To smooth out the fluctuations in the economy associated with the business cycle. This would involve reducing government expenditure or raising taxes during the boom phase of the cycle. This would dampen down the expansion and prevent 'overheating' of the economy with its attendant rising inflation and deteriorating balance of payments. Conversely, during the recessionary phase, as unemployment grew and output declined, the government should cut taxes or raise government expenditure in order to boost the economy. If these stabilisation policies were successful, they would amount merely to fine tuning. Problems of excess or deficient demand would never be allowed to get severe.

Any movement of aggregate demand away from a steady growth path would be immediately 'nipped in the bud'.

Deficits and surpluses

Central government deficits and surpluses

Since an expansionary fiscal policy will involve raising government expenditure and/or lowering taxes, this will have the effect of either increasing the budget deficit or reducing the budget surplus. A budget deficit in any one year is where central government's expenditure exceeds its revenue from taxation. A budget surplus is where tax revenues exceed central government expenditure. With the exception of short periods (1969–70, 1987–90 and 1998–2001), governments in the UK, like most governments around the world, have run budget deficits.

Public-sector deficits and surpluses

To get a complete view of the overall stance of fiscal policy – just how expansionary or contractionary it is – we would need to look at the deficit or surplus of the entire public sector: namely, central government, local government and public corporations.

If the public sector spends more than it earns (through taxes and the revenues of public corporations, etc.) the amount of this deficit is known as the public-sector net cash requirement (PSNCR) (previously known as the public-sector borrowing requirement (PSBR)). The reason for the name 'public-sector net cash requirement' is simple. If the public sector runs a deficit in the current year of, say, £1 billion, then it will have to borrow £1 billion this year (require 'cash') in order to finance it (see Chapter 9 for methods of government borrowing). Table 8.1 shows UK PSNCR from 1986 to 2002.

If the public sector runs a surplus (a negative figure for the PSNCR), then this will be used to reduce the accumulated debts from the past. The accumulated debts of central and local government are known as the general government debt. Table 8.2 shows general government deficits and debt for various countries.

The use of fiscal policy

Automatic fiscal stabilisers

To some extent, government expenditure and taxation will have the effect of *automatically* stabilising the economy. For example, as national income rises, the amount of tax people pay automatically rises. This rise in withdrawals from the

Definitions

Budget surplus
The excess of central government's tax receipts over its spending.

Fiscal stance
How deflationary or reflationary the Budget is.

Public-sector net cash requirement (PSNCR) or public-sector borrowing requirement (PSBR)
The (annual) deficit of the public sector (central government, local government and public corporations), and thus the amount that the public sector must borrow.

General government debt
The accumulated central and local government deficits (less surpluses) over the years: i.e. the total amount owed by central and local government, to both domestic and overseas creditors.

Table 8.1 UK public-sector borrowing (public-sector net cash requirement, PSNCR)

	1986	1988	1990	1992	1994	1996	1997	1998	1999	2000	2001	2002
PSNCR (+ = deficit) (£bn)	+2.6	−11.5	−1.3	+28.6	+39.4	+24.8	+11.9	−6.6	−1.3	−37.6	−2.9	+17.1
PSNCR (% of GDP)	+0.7	−2.4	−0.2	+4.7	+5.8	+3.3	+1.5	−0.8	−0.1	−4.0	−0.3	+1.6

Source: www.statistics.gov.uk (National Statistics): Series RURQ and YBHA.

Table 8.2

General government deficits/surpluses as a percentage of GDP

Country	General government deficits (−) or surpluses (+)		General government debt	
	Average 1990–95	Average 1996–2002	Average 1990–95	Average 1996–2002
Belgium	−6.4	−1.8	128.9	117.3
France	−4.3	−2.4	48.5	64.3
Ireland	−2.6	+2.2	84.2	52.4
Italy	−10.2	−2.7	115.4	115.5
Japan	−0.8	−5.7	68.8	108.7
Netherlands	−4.2	0.0	75.8	64.2
Sweden	−6.1	+1.2	65.3	67.8
UK	−5.3	−0.4	52.1	57.4
USA	−4.5	+0.1	72.9	66.0
Euro area	−5.1	−1.9	66.8	75.7

circular flow of income helps to dampen down the rise in national income. This effect will be bigger if taxes are progressive (i.e. rise by a bigger percentage than national income). Some government expenditure will have a similar effect. For example, total government expenditure on unemployment benefits will fall, if rises in national income cause a fall in unemployment. This again will have the effect of dampening the rise in national income.

Discretionary fiscal policy

Key Idea

8
p45

Key Idea

28
p293

If there is a fundamental disequilibrium in the economy or substantial fluctuations in national income, these automatic stabilisers will not be enough. The government may thus choose to *alter* the level of government expenditure or the rates of taxation. This is known as discretionary fiscal policy.

If government expenditure on goods and services (roads, health care, education, etc.) is raised, this will create a full multiplied rise in national income. The reason is that all the money gets spent and thus all of it goes to boosting aggregate demand.

Cutting taxes (or increasing benefits), however, will have a smaller effect on national income than raising government expenditure on goods and services by the same amount. The reason is that cutting taxes increases people's *disposable* incomes, of which only *part* will be spent. Part will be withdrawn into extra saving, imports and other taxes. In other words, not all the tax cuts will be passed on round the circular flow of income as extra expenditure. Thus if one-fifth of a cut in taxes is withdrawn and only four-fifths is spent, the tax multiplier will only be four-fifths as big as the government expenditure multiplier.

> **Definition**
>
> **Discretionary fiscal policy**
> Deliberate changes in tax rates or the level of government expenditure in order to influence the level of aggregate demand.

> **Pause for thought**
>
> Why will the multiplier effect of government transfer payments, such as child benefit, pensions and social security, be less than the full multiplier effect from government expenditure on goods and services?

Recap

1. An expansionary fiscal policy involves raising government expenditure and/or reducing taxes. A contractionary fiscal policy involves the reverse.

2. The government's fiscal policy determines the size of the budget deficit or surplus and the size of the public-sector deficit (PSNCR) or surplus.

3. Automatic fiscal stabilisers are tax revenues that rise and government expenditures that fall as national income rises. They have the effect of reducing the size of the multiplier and thus reducing cyclical upswings and downswings.

4. Discretionary fiscal policy is where the government deliberately changes taxes or government expenditure in order to alter the level of aggregate demand. Changes in government expenditure on goods and services will have a full multiplier effect. Changes in taxes and benefits will have a smaller multiplier effect as some of the tax/benefit changes will merely affect other withdrawals and thus have a smaller net effect on consumption of domestic product.

The effectiveness of fiscal policy   8.6

Is fiscal policy a reliable means of controlling the economy?

How successful can fiscal policy be? Can it 'fine tune' demand? Can it achieve the level of national income the government would like it to achieve?

The effectiveness of fiscal policy depends on a number of factors, including the following:

- The accuracy of forecasting. Governments would obviously like to act as swiftly as possible to prevent a problem of excess or deficient demand. The more reliable the forecasts of what is likely to happen to aggregate demand, the more able will the government be to intervene quickly.
- The extent to which changes in government expenditure (G) and taxation (T) affect total injections and withdrawals. Will changes in G or T be partly offset by changes in *other* injections and withdrawals? If so, are these changes predictable?
- The extent to which changes in injections and withdrawals affect national income. Is it possible to predict the size of the multiplier and accelerator effects?

Key idea
22
p214

- The timing of the effects. It is no good simply being able to predict the *magnitude* of the effects of fiscal policy. It is also necessary to predict *how long* they will take. If there are long time lags with fiscal policy, it will be far less successful as a means of reducing fluctuations.
- The extent to which changes in aggregate demand have the desired effects on output, employment, inflation and the balance of payments.
- The extent to which fiscal policy has undesirable side-effects, such as higher taxes reducing incentives.

Box 8.4

Discretionary fiscal policy in Japan

Attempts to jumpstart the economy

1991–6

After experiencing an average annual economic growth rate of nearly 4 per cent from 1980 to 1991, it was a shock for the Japanese when their growth rate plummeted to less than 1 per cent in 1992, followed by a mere 0.4 per cent in 1993 and 1.1 per cent in 1994.

In response to the slowdown, the Japanese government injected into the economy a sequence of five public spending packages over the period 1992–6 totalling ¥59 500 billion (£330 billion): an average increase in government spending of 7 per cent a year in real terms. There were also substantial cuts in taxes. This, combined with the economic slowdown, moved the public-sector finances massively into deficit. A general government surplus of 3 per cent of GDP in 1991 was transformed into a deficit of nearly 5 per cent of GDP by 1996 (see the table below). Japan's general government debt rose from 61 per cent of GDP in 1991 to over 90 per cent by 1997.

In addition to this fiscal stimulus, the government reduced interest rates nine times, to a record low of 0.5 per cent by 1996. It also pursued a policy of business deregulation, especially within the service and financial sectors. Yet despite all these measures, it was not until 1996 that significant economic growth resumed (see the table).

Why did such an expansionary fiscal (and monetary) policy prove to be so ineffective? The answer can be found in the behaviour of the other components of aggregate demand.

In previous decades the prosperity of Japanese business was built upon an export-led growth strategy. If there was a lack of demand at home, surplus capacity in the economy could simply be exported. But this option was no longer so easy. Growing competition from other Asian exporters and sluggish demand in the USA and Europe meant that Japanese firms were finding it harder to export.

As far as investment was concerned, the slowdown in the economy and poor export sales, plus high levels of debt from the expansion of the late 1980s, reduced profits to near record lows and created a climate of business pessimism. After increases in investment averaging 10 per cent per year from 1987 to 1990, investment fell for three successive years after 1991.

Japanese macroeconomic indicators: 1980–2003

	1980–91	1992	1993	1994	1995	1996	1997	1998	1999	2000	2001	2002	2003[1]
% annual growth in real GDP	3.8	0.9	0.4	1.1	1.8	3.5	1.9	−1.1	0.2	2.8	0.4	0.3	1.0
General government budget balance as % of GDP	−1.1	0.8	−2.4	−2.8	−4.2	−4.9	−3.7	−5.5	−7.1	−7.4	−7.2	−7.9	−7.7
General government debt as % of GDP		63.5	69.0	73.9	80.4	86.5	92.0	103.0	115.8	123.4	132.6	142.7	151.0

[1] Forecast.
Source: *European Economy*.

Problems of magnitude

Before changing government expenditure or taxation, the government will need to calculate the effect of any such change on national income, employment and inflation. Predicting these effects, however, is often very unreliable for a number of reasons.

Consumers too were in a pessimistic mood. Even with a ¥5000 billion cut in taxation in 1994, consumer spending on domestic goods and services grew only marginally, whereas *saving* increased sharply, as did *imports*.

Although the total fiscal stimulus over the period was large, the incremental nature of the government's action failed on each occasion to stimulate business and consumer activity to any significant degree.

1997–

The recovery of 1996 was short lived. With other countries, such as Thailand and Indonesia, experiencing a large economic downturn in 1997, and with a growing mood of pessimism across the region, the Japanese economy plunged into recession. By 1998, amidst bank failures and speculative outflows of money from the country, the economy was in a state of crisis. The government's response was once more to resort to fiscal policy.

A ¥16 000 billion (£80 billion) expansionary fiscal package in April 1998 was followed six months later by another package worth ¥24 000 billion (£120 billion). This second package included over ¥8000 billion on public works projects and cuts in the maximum rate of income tax from 65 per cent to 50 per cent (worth ¥4200 billion) and substantial cuts in corporate taxes. One novel feature of the package was the distribution of shopping vouchers to 35 million citizens: the elderly and families with young children. These free vouchers were worth ¥700 billion (£3.5 billion).

One of the biggest problems in stimulating the economy was the very high marginal propensity to save. Given the continuing pessimism of workers about the security of their jobs, many people responded to tax cuts by saving more, especially given that prices were stable or falling and hence the value of money saved would not be eroded by inflation. Even the shopping voucher scheme had limited success, as people used them to replace existing expenditure and saved the money they no longer needed to use.

Another problem was the mood of businesses. With banks collapsing under the weight of bad debt, with loans to industry consequently cut, with Japanese companies eager to cut costs, and with business pessimism about consumer and export demand, investment was being cut back. Reductions in business taxes were not enough to reverse this.

A modest recovery was under way in 2000 (see the table), but in 2001, with the USA slipping into recession and with the European economy slowing down, Japanese exports began to fall and a mood of pessimism rapidly returned. The government had hoped that supply-side reforms would make the economy more competitive, but these are long-term policies and the problem was immediate.

So what could be done? The answer was very little. With interest rates of virtually zero, there was little scope for an expansionary monetary policy, and with a general government deficit of nearly 8 per cent of GDP and a debt of nearly 150 per cent of GDP and rising, there was now little scope for fiscal policy either. The Japanese hoped that world recovery would eventually come and allow a resumption of export-led growth.

?
If tax cuts are largely saved, should an expansionary fiscal policy be confined to increases in government spending?

Predicting the effect of changes in government expenditure

A rise in government expenditure of £x may lead to a rise in total injections (relative to withdrawals) that is smaller than £x. This will occur if the rise in government expenditure *replaces* a certain amount of private expenditure. For example, a rise in expenditure on state education may dissuade some parents from sending their children to private schools. Similarly, an improvement in the national health service may lead to fewer people paying for private treatment.

Crowding out.   Another reason for the total rise in injections being smaller than the rise in government expenditure is a phenomenon known as crowding out. If the government relies on pure fiscal policy – that is, if it does not finance an increase in the budget deficit by increasing the money supply (which would make the policy a combination of fiscal and monetary policy) – it will have to borrow the money from individuals and firms. It will thus be competing with the private sector for finance and will have to offer higher interest rates. This will force the private sector too to offer higher interest rates, which may discourage firms from investing and individuals from buying on credit. Thus government borrowing *crowds out* private borrowing. In the extreme case, the fall in consumption and investment may completely offset the rise in government expenditure, with the result that aggregate demand does not rise at all.

Predicting the effect of changes in taxes

A cut in taxes, by increasing people's real disposable income, increases not only the amount they spend but also the amount they save. The problem is that it is not easy to predict the relative size of these two increases. In part it will depend on whether people feel that the cut in tax is only temporary, in which case they may simply save the extra disposable income, or permanent, in which case they may adjust their consumption upwards.

Predicting the resulting multiplied effect on national income

Even if the government *could* predict the net *initial* effect on injections and withdrawals, the ultimate effect on national income will still be hard to predict for the following reasons:

Ke
Ide

28
p29

■ The size of the *multiplier* may be difficult to predict, since it is difficult to predict how much of any rise in income will be withdrawn. In other words, it is difficult to predict the size of the *mpw*. For example, the amount of a rise in income that households save or consume will depend on their expectations about future price and income changes.
■ Induced investment through the *accelerator* is also extremely difficult to predict. It may be that a relatively small fiscal stimulus will be all that is necessary to restore business confidence, and that induced investment will rise substantially. In such a case, fiscal policy can be seen as a 'pump primer'. It is used to *start* the process of recovery, and then the *continuation* of the recovery is left to the market. But for pump priming to work, business people must *believe* that it will work. If they are cautious and fear that the recovery will falter, they may hold back from investing. This lack of investment will probably mean that the recovery *will* falter and that, therefore, the effects of the fiscal expansion will be very modest. The problem is in predicting just how the business community will react. Business confidence can change very rapidly and in ways that could not have been foreseen a few months earlier.

Definitions

Crowding out
Where increased public expenditure diverts money or resources away from the private sector.

Pure fiscal policy
Fiscal policy that does not involve any change in money supply.

Random shocks

Forecasts cannot take into account the unpredictable, such as the attack on the World Trade Center in New York in September 2001. Unfortunately, unpredictable events do occur and may seriously undermine the government's fiscal policy.

The problem of timing

Fiscal policy can involve considerable time lags. If these are long enough, fiscal policy could even be *de*stabilising. Expansionary policies taken to cure a recession may not come into effect until the economy has *already* recovered and is experiencing a boom. Under these circumstances, expansionary policies are quite inappropriate: they simply worsen the problems of overheating. Similarly, contractionary policies taken to prevent excessive expansion may not take effect until the economy has already peaked and is plunging into recession. The contractionary policies only deepen the recession.

This problem is illustrated in Figure 8.12. Path (a) shows the course of the business cycle without government intervention. Ideally, with no time lags, the economy should be dampened in stage 2 and stimulated in stage 4. This would make the resulting course of the business cycle more like path (b), or even, if the policy were perfectly stabilising, a straight line. With time lags, however, contractionary policies taken in stage 2 may not come into effect until stage 4, and expansionary policies taken in stage 4 may not come into effect until stage 2. In this case the resulting course of the business cycle will be more like path (c). Quite obviously, in these circumstances 'stabilising' fiscal policy actually makes the economy *less* stable.

There are five possible lags associated with fiscal policy.

Time lag to recognition. Since the business cycle can be irregular and forecasting unreliable, governments may be unwilling to take action until they are convinced that the problem is serious.

Time lag between recognition and action. Most significant changes in government expenditure have to be planned well in advance. The government cannot increase spending on motorways overnight or suddenly start building new hospitals.

Figure 8.12
Fiscal policy: stabilising or destabilising?

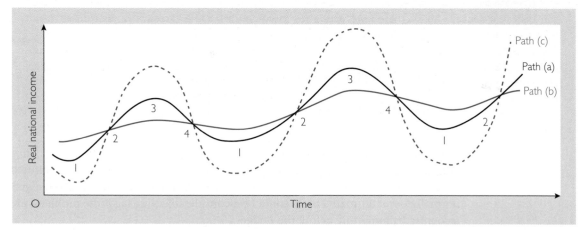

Box 8.5

Following the golden rule

Fiscal policy in a straitjacket?

If the government persistently runs a budget deficit, the national debt will rise. If it rises faster than GDP, it will account for a growing proportion of GDP. There is then likely to be an increasing problem of 'servicing' this debt: i.e. paying the interest on it. The government could find itself having to borrow more and more to meet the interest payments, and so the national debt could rise faster still. As the government borrows more and more, so it has to pay higher interest rates to attract finances. If it is successful in this, borrowing and hence investment by the private sector could be crowded out (see page 318).

Recognising these problems, many governments in recent years have attempted to reduce their debts.

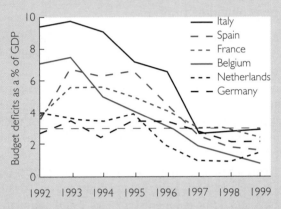

Getting budget deficits down

Preparing for EMU

In signing the Maastricht Treaty in 1992, the EU countries agreed that to be eligible to join the single currency, they should have sustainable deficits and debts. This was interpreted as follows: the general government deficit should be no more than 3 per cent of GDP and general government debt should be no more than 60 per cent of GDP, or should at least be falling towards that level at a satisfactory pace.

But in the mid-1990s, several of the countries that were subsequently to join the euro had deficits and debts substantially above these levels (see the figure). Getting them down proved a painful business. Government expenditure had to be cut and taxes increased. Fiscal policy, unfortunately, proved to be powerful! Unemployment rose and growth remained low.

The EU Stability and Growth Pact

In June 1997, at the European Council in Amsterdam, the EU countries agreed that governments adopting the euro should seek to balance their budgets (or even aim for a surplus) averaged over the course of the business cycle, and that deficits should not exceed 3 per cent of GDP in any one year. A country's deficit is permitted to exceed 3 per cent only if its GDP has declined by at least 2 per cent (or 0.75 per cent with special permission from the Council of Ministers). Otherwise, countries with deficits exceeding 3 per cent are required to make deposits of money with the European Central Bank. These then become fines if the excessive budget deficit is not eliminated within two years.

There are two main aims of targeting a zero budget deficit over the business cycle. The first is to allow automatic stabilisers to work without 'bumping into' the 3 per cent deficit ceiling in years when economies

Changes in taxes and benefits cannot be introduced overnight either. They normally have to wait to be announced in the Budget and will not be instituted until the new financial year or at some other point in the future. As Budgets normally occur annually, there could be a considerable time lag if the problems are recognised a long time before the Budget.

are slowing. The second is to allow a reduction in government debts as a proportion of GDP (assuming that GDP grows on average at around 2–3 per cent per year).

The main criticism of aiming for a zero deficit over the cycle has been that this would mean a further reduction in deficits, which by the start of the euro in 1999 were typically only just meeting the 3 per cent ceiling. In other words, meeting the zero deficit target would mean further deflationary fiscal policies: something that most political leaders in Europe felt to be inappropriate at a time when there were fears of a world recession.

Also there is the issue of whether the Pact is flexible enough. In 2002 and 2003, Germany was suffering from virtually zero growth with unemployment exceeding 11 per cent (4.7 million), a problem aggravated by the world recession. As a consequence of falling tax revenues and increased expenditure on unemployment benefits, its deficit breached the 3 per cent ceiling: it was 3.75 per cent of GDP in 2002. The German government had to make promises to rein in expenditure and raise taxes in order to escape censure by the European Commission – just at a time when the German economy needed a boost to aggregate demand. Critics accused the Pact of being too restrictive and of not taking into account world economic circumstances.

Labour's golden rule

The Labour government in the UK has adopted a similar approach to that of the Stability and Growth Pact. Under its 'golden rule', the government pledges that over the economic cycle, it will borrow only to invest (e.g. in roads, hospitals and schools) and not to fund current spending (e.g. on wages, administration and benefits). Investment is exempted from the zero borrowing rule because it contributes towards the growth of GDP. Indeed, in its 1998 'Comprehensive Spending Review', the government announced that government investment expenditure would double as a percentage of GDP. The government has also set itself the target of maintaining a stable public-sector debt/GDP ratio below 40 per cent.

To allow the golden rule to operate, government departments are set three-year spending limits and each has separate current and capital (investment) budgets.

As with the Stability and Growth Pact, the argument is that by using an averaging rule over the cycle, automatic stabilisers will be allowed to work. Deficits of receipts over current spending can occur when the economy is in recession or when growth is sluggish, helping to stimulate the economy. Surpluses can occur in boom periods, helping to dampen the economy.

As with the Stability and Growth Pact, however, a major concern is whether the policy provides too much of a straitjacket. Does it prevent the government using substantial discretionary boosts to the economy at times of serious economic slowdown? Probably, yes, but the golden rule does permit some degree of discretionary fiscal policy and, unlike the Stability and Growth Pact, does not impose a ceiling on cyclical deficits.

? What effects will government investment expenditure have on public-sector debt (a) in the short run; (b) in the long run?

Time lag between action and changes taking effect. A change in tax rates may not immediately affect tax payments, as some taxes are paid in arrears and new rates may take time to apply.

Time lag between changes in government expenditure and taxation and the resulting change in national income, prices and employment. The multiplier round takes time.

Accelerator effects take time. The multiplier and accelerator go on interacting. It all takes time.

Consumption may respond slowly to changes in taxation.   If taxes are cut, consumers may respond initially by saving the extra money. They may only later increase consumption.

If the fluctuations in aggregate demand can be forecast, and if the lengths of the time lags are known, then all is not lost. At least the fiscal measures can be taken early and their delayed effects can be taken into account.

Side-effects of fiscal policy

The purpose of fiscal policy is to control aggregate demand. In doing so, however, it may create certain undesirable side-effects. These include:

Cost inflation.   If the economy is overheating and inflation is rising, the government may raise taxes. Although this will lower aggregate demand, a rise in expenditure taxes and corporation taxes will usually be passed on in full or in part to the consumer in higher prices. This in turn could lead to higher wage claims, as could a rise in income tax.

Welfare and distributive justice.   The use of fiscal policy may conflict with various social programmes. The government may want to introduce cuts in public expenditure in order to reduce inflation. But where are the cuts to be made? Cuts will often fall on people who are relatively disadvantaged. After all, it is these people who are the most reliant on the welfare state and other public provision (such as state education).

Incentives.   Both automatic stabilisers, in the form of steeply progressive income taxes, and discretionary rises in taxes could be a disincentive to effort (see Section 5.5). People may substitute leisure for income – the substitution effect may outweigh the income effect. What is the point in working more or harder, they may say, if so much is going to be taken in taxes? It could work the other way, however: faced with higher tax bills, people may work more in order to maintain their living standards – the income effect may outweigh the substitution effect.

An alternative to using fiscal policy is to use monetary policy. This involves taking measures to control the money supply and interest rates. The role of money and monetary policy is the subject for the next chapter.

Steady as you go

Given the problems of pursuing active fiscal policy, many governments today take a much more passive approach. Instead of changing the policy as the economy changes, a rule is set for the level of public finances. This rule is then applied year after year, with taxes and government expenditure being planned to meet that rule. For example, a target could be set for the PSNCR, with government expenditure and taxes being adjusted to keep the PSNCR at or within its target level. Box 8.5 looks at some examples of fiscal targets.

Recap

1. The effectiveness of fiscal policy depends on the accuracy of forecasting and on the predictability of the direct and eventual effects of the fiscal measures.

2. There are problems in predicting the magnitude of the effects of discretionary fiscal policy. Expansionary fiscal policy can act as a pump primer and stimulate increased private expenditure, or it can crowd out private expenditure. The extent to which it acts as a pump primer depends crucially on business confidence – something that is very difficult to predict beyond a few weeks or months. The extent of crowding out depends on monetary conditions and the government's monetary policy.

3. There are five possible time lags involved with fiscal policy: the time lag before the problem is diagnosed, the lag between diagnosis and new measures being announced, the lag between announcement and implementation, the lag while the multiplier and accelerator work themselves out, and the lag before consumption responds fully to new economic circumstances.

4. Discretionary fiscal policy can involve side-effects, such as disincentives, higher costs and adverse effects on social programmes.

5. Today many governments prefer a more passive approach towards fiscal policy. Targets are set for one or more measures of the public-sector finances, and then taxes and government expenditure are adjusted so as to keep to the target.

Questions

1. An economy is currently in equilibrium. The following figures refer to elements in its national income accounts.

	£bn
Consumption (total)	60
Investment	5
Government expenditure	8
Imports	10
Exports	7

(a) What is the current equilibrium level of national income?
(b) What is the level of injections?
(c) What is the level of withdrawals?
(d) Assuming that tax revenues are £7 billion, how much is the level of saving?
(e) If national income now rises to £80 billion and, as a result, the consumption of domestically produced goods rises to £58 billion, what is the mpc_d?
(f) What is the value of the multiplier?
(g) Given an initial level of national income of £80 billion, now assume that spending on exports rises by £4 billion, spending on investment rises by £1 billion and government expenditure falls by £2 billion. By how much will national income change?

2. What is the relationship between the mpc_d and the mpw?

3. Assume that the multiplier has a value of 3. Now assume that the government decides to increase aggregate demand in an attempt to reduce unemployment. It raises government expenditure by £100 million with no increase in taxes. Firms, anticipating a rise in their sales, increase investment by £200 million, of which £50 million consists of purchases of foreign machinery. How much will national income rise? (Assume no other changes in injections.)

4. On a Keynesian diagram, draw three W lines of different slopes, all crossing the J line at the same point. Now draw a second J line above the first. Mark the original equilibrium and all the new ones corresponding to each of the W lines. Using this diagram, show how the size of the multiplier varies with the mpw.

5. Why does the slope of the *E* line in a Keynesian diagram equal the mpc_d? (Clue: draw an mpc_d line.)

6. On a Keynesian diagram, draw two *E* lines of different slopes, both crossing the *Y* line at the same point. Now draw another two *E* lines, parallel with the first two and crossing each other vertically above the point where the first two crossed. Using this diagram, show how the size of the multiplier varies with the mpc_d.

7. What factors could explain why some countries have a higher multiplier than others?

8. The present level of a country's exports is £12 billion; investment is £2 billion; government expenditure is £4 billion; *total* consumer spending (not C_d) is £36 billion; imports are £12 billion and expenditure taxes are £2 billion. The economy is currently in equilibrium. It is estimated that an income of £50 billion is necessary to generate full employment. The *mpw* is 0.25.

   (a) Is there an inflationary or deflationary gap in this situation?
   (b) What is the size of the gap? (Don't confuse this with the difference between Y_e and Y_F.)
   (c) What would be the appropriate government policies to close this gap?

9. The table below shows part of a country's national expenditure schedule (£bn).

   (a) What is the government expenditure multiplier?

   Assume that full employment is achieved at a level of national income of £200 billion.

   (b) Is there an inflationary or a deflationary gap, and what is its size?
   (c) By how much would government expenditure have to be changed in order to close

this gap (assuming no shift in other injections or withdrawals)?

10. In what way will the nature of aggregate supply influence the effect of a change in aggregate demand on prices and real national income?

11. Why does investment in construction and producer goods industries tend to fluctuate more than investment in retailing and the service industries?

12. How can the interaction of the multiplier and accelerator explain cyclical fluctuations in national income?

13. Why is it difficult to predict the size of the multiplier and accelerator?

14. Assume that there is a trade-off between unemployment and inflation, traced out by a 'Phillips curve'. What could cause a leftward shift in this curve?

15. How does the size of (a) the budget deficit and (b) the national debt vary with the course of the business cycle?

16. How would the withdrawals curve shift in each of the following cases? (a) A reduction in the basic rate of tax. (b) An increase in personal allowances.

17. Under what circumstances is a rise in taxes likely to have a disincentive effect?

18. What factors determine the effectiveness of discretionary fiscal policy?

19. Give some examples of changes in one injection or withdrawal that can affect others.

20. Why is it difficult to use fiscal policy to 'fine tune' the economy?

National income (Y)	100	120	140	160	180	200	220
National expenditure (E)	115	130	145	160	175	190	205

Additional case studies on the *Essentials of Economics* website (www.booksites.net/sloman)

8.1   Classical 'remedies' for unemployment. How the policies advocated by the classical economists to cure unemployment would, according to Keynes, make the problem worse.

8.2   The paradox of thrift. How saving more can make the country worse off.

8.3   John Maynard Keynes (1883–1946). Profile of the great economist.

8.4   Keynes' views on the consumption function. An analysis of how the assumptions made by Keynes affect the shape of the consumption function.

8.5   Deriving the multiplier formula. Using simple algebra to show how the multiplier formula is derived.

8.6   A. W. H. Phillips. A portrait of the shy economist and engineer who invented the famous Phillips curve and Phillips machine.

8.7   The multiplier/accelerator interaction. A numerical example showing how the interaction of the multiplier and accelerator can cause cycles in economic activity.

8.8   Has there been an accelerator effect since 1978? An examination of the evidence for an accelerator effect in the UK.

8.9   The national debt. This explores the question of whether it matters if a country has a high national debt.

8.10 Fine tuning in 1959 and 1960. This looks at two Budgets in the era of Keynesian 'fine tuning'.

8.11 Trends in public expenditure. This case examines attempts to control public expenditure in the UK and relates them to the crowding-out debate.

8.12 The crowding-out effect. The circumstances in which an increase in public expenditure can replace private expenditure.

8.13 Injections against the contagion. The use of discretionary fiscal policy in the late 1990s.

Sections of chapter covered in *WinEcon* – Sloman, *Essentials of Economics*

Essentials of Economics section	*WinEcon* section
8.1	8.1
8.2	8.2
8.3	8.3
8.4	8.4
8.5	—
8.6	8.6

Websites relevant to this chapter

Numbers and sections refer to websites listed in the Web Appendix and hotlinked from this book's website at www.booksites.net/sloman

■ For news articles relevant to this chapter, see the *Economics News Articles* link from the book's website.

■ For general news on national economies, the international economy and fiscal policy, see websites in section A, and particularly A1–5. See also links to newspapers worldwide in A38 and 39, and the news search feature in Google at A41. See also links to economics news in A42.

■ For data on economic growth, employment and the business cycle, see links in B1 or 2; also see B4 and 12. For UK data, see B3 and 34. For EU data, see G1 > *The Statistical Annex*. For US data, see *Current economic indicators* in B5 and the *Data* section of B17. For international data, see B15, 21, 24, 31, 33. For links to data sets, see B28; I14.

■ For information on the development of ideas, see C12, 18; see also links under *Methodology and History of Economic Thought* in C14; and links to economists in I4 and I7. See also sites I7 and I1 > *Economic Systems and Theories > History of Economic Thought.*

■ For a model of the economy (based on the Treasury model), see *The Virtual Economy* (site D1). In addition to the model, where you can devise your own Budget, there are worksheets and outlines of theories and the work of famous economists.

■ For information on UK fiscal policy and government borrowing, see sites E30, 36; F2. See also sites A1–8 at Budget time. For fiscal policy in the euro zone, see *Public Finances in EMU* in H1.

■ Sites I7 and I1 contain links to fiscal policy: go to *Macroeconomics > Macroeconomic Policy > Taxes and Taxation.*

■ For student resources relevant to this chapter, see sites C1–7, 9, 10, 19.

CHAPTER MAP

CHAPTER NINE

Money and monetary policy

In this chapter we are going to look at the special role that money plays in the economy. Changes in the amount of money can have a powerful effect on all the major macroeconomic indicators, such as inflation, unemployment, economic growth, interest rates, exchange rates and the balance of payments.

But why do changes in the money supply affect the economy? The answer is that the supply of money and the demand for money between them determine the *rate of interest*, and this has a crucial impact on aggregate demand and the performance of the economy generally.

First we define what is meant by money (not as easy as it may seem), and examine its functions. Then in Sections 9.2 and 9.3 we look at the operation of the financial sector of the economy and its role in determining the supply of money.

We then turn to look at the demand for money. Here we are not asking how much money people would like. The answer to that would probably be 'as much as possible'! What we are asking is: how much of people's assets do they want to hold in the form of money?

Then, in Section 9.5, we put supply and demand together to show how interest rates are determined. Finally, we examine how money supply and interest rates are controlled by the authorities and the effect this has on the economy. In other words, we examine monetary policy: how it operates and how effective it is.

9.1   The meaning and functions of money

What is this thing called 'money'?

Before going any further we must define precisely what we mean by 'money'. Money is more than just notes and coin. In fact, the main component of a country's money supply is not cash, but deposits in banks and other financial institutions. Only a very small proportion of these deposits are kept by the banks in their safes or tills in the form of cash. The bulk of the deposits appear merely as bookkeeping entries in the banks' accounts.

This may sound very worrying. Will a bank have enough cash to meet its customers' demands? The answer is yes. Only a small fraction of a bank's total deposits will be withdrawn at any one time, and banks always make sure that they have the ability to meet their customers' demands. The chances of banks running out of cash are practically nil. What is more, the bulk of all but very small transactions are not conducted in cash at all. With the use of cheques, credit cards and debit cards, most money is simply transferred from the purchaser's to the seller's bank account without the need for first withdrawing it in cash.

What items should be included in the definition of money? To answer this we need to identify the *functions* of money.

The functions of money

The main purpose of money is for buying and selling goods, services and assets: i.e. as a medium of exchange. It also has three other important functions. Let us examine each in turn.

A medium of exchange

In a subsistence economy where individuals make their own clothes, grow their own food, provide their own entertainments, etc., people do not need money. If people want to exchange any goods, they will do so by barter. In other words, they will do swaps with other people.

The complexities of a modern developed economy, however, make barter totally impractical for most purposes. Someone else may have something you want, but there is no guarantee that they will want what you have to offer them in return. What is more, under a system of capitalism, where people are employed by others to do a specialist task, it would be totally impractical for people to be paid in food, clothes, cars, electrical goods, etc. What is necessary is a medium of exchange that is generally acceptable as a means of payment for goods and services and as a means of payment for labour and other factor services. 'Money' is any such medium.

Money as a medium of exchange is in effect being used as a 'means of settling a debt'. When you buy a good or service, you thereby incur a debt. This must be settled with a money payment. The debt can be settled immediately (e.g. when you buy something in a shop with cash) or later (e.g. when you buy something on credit and make the payment, say, at the end of the month).

To be a suitable physical means of exchange, money must be light enough to carry around, must come in a number of denominations, large and small, and must not be easy to forge. Alternatively, money must be in a form that enables it to be

> **Definition**
>
> **Medium of exchange**
> Something that is acceptable in exchange for goods and services.

transferred *indirectly* through some acceptable mechanism. For example, money in the form of bookkeeping entries in bank accounts can be transferred from one account to another by the use of such mechanisms as cheques, debit cards, standing orders and direct debits.

A means of storing wealth

People need a means whereby the fruits of *today's* labour can be used to purchase goods and services in the *future*. People need to be able to store their wealth: they want a means of saving. Money is one such medium in which to hold wealth. It can be saved.

A means of evaluation

Money allows the value of goods, services and assets to be compared. The value of goods is expressed in terms of prices, and prices are expressed in money terms. Money also allows dissimilar things, such as a person's wealth or a company's assets, to be added up. Similarly, a country's GDP is expressed in money terms. Money thus serves as a 'unit of account'.

A means of establishing the value of future claims and payments

People often want to agree *today* the price of some *future* payment. For example, workers and managers will want to agree the wage rate for the coming year. Firms will want to sign contracts with their suppliers, specifying the price of raw materials and other supplies. The use of money prices is the most convenient means of measuring future claims.

What should count as money?

What items, then, should be included in the definition of money? Unfortunately, there is no sharp borderline between money and non-money.

Cash (notes and coin) obviously counts as money. It readily meets all the functions of money. Goods (fridges, cars and cabbages) do not count as money. But what about various financial assets such as bank accounts and stocks and shares? Do they count as money? The answer is: it depends on how narrowly money is defined.

Countries thus use several different measures of money supply. All include cash, but they vary according to what additional items are included. To understand their significance and the ways in which money supply can be controlled, it is first necessary to look at the various types of account in which money can be held and at the various financial institutions involved.

> **Pause for thought**
>
> Why are debit cards not counted as money?

Recap

1. Money's main function is as a medium of exchange. In addition, it is a means of storing wealth, a means of evaluation and a means of establishing the value of future claims and payments.

2. What counts as money depends on how narrowly it is defined. All definitions include cash, but they vary according to what other financial assets are included.

9.2   The financial system in the UK

Where do banks and other financial institutions fit in?

In order to understand the role of the financial sector in determining the supply of money, it is important to distinguish different types of financial institution. Each type has a distinct part to play in determining the size of the money supply.

The key role of banks in the monetary system

By far the largest element of money supply is bank deposits. It is not surprising then that banks play an absolutely crucial role in the monetary system.

The most important of the banks in the UK for the functioning of the economy and for the implementation of monetary policy are the retail banks. These are the familiar high street banks, such as Barclays, Lloyds TSB, HSBC and NatWest, and ex-building societies such as the Abbey National and HBOS (Halifax). They specialise in providing branch banking facilities to members of the general public, but they do also lend to business, albeit often on a short-term basis. Their business is in retail deposits and loans. These are deposits and loans made through their branch network at published rates of interest. The branches are like 'retail outlets' for banking services.

The other major category of banks are the wholesale banks. These include *investment banks* such as Morgan Stanley, Rothschild, SG Hambros and Goldman Sachs. They often act as 'brokers', arranging loans for companies from a number of different sources. They also offer financial advice to industry and provide assistance to firms in raising new capital through the issue of new shares. Many of these banks are overseas banks, especially Japanese and American; others include the wholesale arm of the retail banks. These have expanded their business enormously in recent years. Their major specialism is the finance of international trade and capital movements, and they deal extensively in the foreign exchange market. Most of their deposits are in foreign currencies. They are known as *wholesale* banks because they specialise in receiving large deposits from and making large loans to industry, to each other and to other financial institutions: these are known as wholesale deposits and loans.

Banks are in the business of deposit taking and lending. To understand this, we must distinguish between banks' liabilities and assets. The total liabilities and assets for the UK banks are set out in a balance sheet in Table 9.1.

Liabilities

Customers' deposits in banks (and other deposit-taking institutions such as building societies) are liabilities to these institutions. This means simply that the customers have the claim on these deposits and thus the institutions are liable to meet the claims.

There are four major types of deposit: sight deposits, time deposits, certificates of deposit and 'repos'.

Table 9.1 Balance sheet of UK banks: February 2003

Sterling liabilities	£bn	%	Sterling assets	£bn	%
Sight deposits		(36.2)	Notes and coin	7.2	(0.4)
UK banks, etc.	105.1		Balances with Bank of England	1.7	(0.1)
UK public sector	4.6		Market loans		(22.9)
UK private sector	459.7		UK banks	236.1	
Non-residents	59.3		CDs, etc.	77.5	
Time deposits		(34.8)	Non-residents	88.1	
UK banks, etc.	142.4		Bills of exchange		(1.7)
UK public sector	9.1		Treasury	12.3	
UK private sector	299.6		UK bank bills	6.8	
Non-residents	153.0		Other	11.0	
Certificates of deposit (CDs)	157.7	(9.1)	Reverse repos	92.0	(5.2)
Sale and repurchase agreements (repos)	104.2	(6.0)	Investments	128.6	(7.3)
Other	242.9	(13.9)	Advances	1034.8	(59.0)
			Miscellaneous	58.8	(3.4)
Total sterling liabilities	1737.6	(100.0)	**Total sterling assets**	1754.9	(100.0)
Liabilities in other currencies	2133.4		Assets in other currencies	2116.1	
Total liabilities	3871.0		Total assets	3871.0	

Source: *Monetary and Financial Statistics* (Bank of England).

Sight deposits.   Sight deposits are any deposits that can be withdrawn on demand by the depositor without penalty. In the past, sight accounts did not pay interest. Today, however, there are some sight accounts that do.

The most familiar form of sight deposits is current accounts at banks. Depositors are normally issued with cheque books and/or debit cards (e.g. Switch or Connect) which enable them to spend the money directly without first having to go to the bank and draw the money out in cash. In the case of debit cards, the person's account is electronically debited when the purchase is made and the card is 'swiped' across the machine. This process is known as EFTPOS (electronic funds transfer at point of sale).

An important feature of current accounts is that banks often allow customers to be overdrawn. That is, they can draw on their account and make payments to other people in excess of the amount of money they have deposited.

Time deposits.   Time deposits require notice of withdrawal. However, they normally pay a higher rate of interest than sight accounts. With some types of account a depositor can withdraw a certain amount of money on demand, but there will be a penalty of so many days' lost interest. They are not cheque-book or debit-card accounts. The most familiar forms of time deposits are the deposit and savings accounts in banks and the various savings accounts in building societies. No overdraft facilities exist with time deposits.

Certificates of deposit.   Certificates of deposit (CDs) are certificates issued by banks to customers (usually firms) for large deposits of a fixed term (e.g. £100 000 for 18 months). They can be sold by one customer to another, and thus provide a means

Definitions

Sight deposits
Deposits that can be withdrawn on demand without penalty.

Time deposits
Deposits that require notice of withdrawal or where a penalty is charged for withdrawals on demand.

Certificates of deposit (CDs)
Certificates issued by banks for fixed-term interest-bearing deposits. They can be resold by the owner to another party.

whereby the holders can get money quickly if they need it, without the banks that have issued the CD supplying the money. The use of CDs has grown rapidly in recent years. Their use by firms has meant that, at a wholesale level, sight accounts have become less popular.

Sale and repurchase agreements ('repos').   If banks have a temporary shortage of funds, they can sell some of their financial assets to other banks or to the Bank of England (see below), and later repurchase them on some agreed date, often about a fortnight later. These sale and repurchase agreements (repos) are in effect a form of loan, with the bank borrowing for a period of time using some of its financial assets as the security for the loan. The most usual assets to use in this way are government bonds, normally called 'gilt-edged securities' or simply 'gilts' (see below). Sale and repurchase agreements involving gilts are known as *gilt repos*. As we shall see, gilt repos play a vital role in the operation of monetary policy.

Assets

Banks' financial assets are its claims on others. There are three main categories of assets.

Cash and operational balances in the central bank (Bank of England in the UK, European Central Bank (ECB) in the euro zone).   Banks need to hold a certain amount of their assets as cash. This is largely to meet the day-to-day demands of customers for cash. They also keep 'operational balances' in the central bank. These are like the banks' own current accounts and are used for clearing purposes (i.e. for settling the day-to-day payments between the banks). They can be withdrawn in cash on demand. In the UK, banks are also required to deposit a small fraction of their assets as 'cash ratio deposits' with the Bank of England.

Cash and balances in the Bank of England, however, earn no interest for banks. The vast majority of banks' assets are therefore in the form of various types of loan – to individuals and firms, to other financial institutions and to the government. These are 'assets' because they represent claims that the banks have on other people. Loans can be grouped into two types: short and long term.

Short-term loans.   These are in the form of *market loans, bills of exchange* or *reverse repos*. The market for these various types of loan is known as the money market.

■ Market loans are made primarily to other banks or financial institutions ('inter-bank' loans). They consist of (a) money lent 'at call' (i.e. reclaimable on demand or at 24 hours' notice), (b) money lent 'at short notice' (i.e. money lent for a few days) and (c) CDs (i.e. certificates of deposit made in other banks or building societies).

■ Bills of exchange are loans either to companies (guaranteed by another bank and hence called 'bank bills') or to the government (Treasury bills). These are, in effect, an IOU, with the company issuing them (in the case of bank bills) or the Bank of England (in the case of Treasury bills) promising to pay the holder a specified sum on a particular date (typically three months later). Since bills do not pay interest, they are sold below their face value (at a 'discount') but redeemed on maturity at face value. This enables the purchaser, in this case the bank, to earn a return.

Definitions

Sale and repurchase agreements (repos)
An agreement between two financial institutions whereby one in effect borrows from another by selling its assets, agreeing to buy them back (repurchase them) at a fixed price and on a fixed date.

Assets
Possessions, or claims held on others.

Money market
The market for short-term loans and deposits.

Market loans
Short-term loans: e.g. money at call and short notice.

Bill of exchange
A certificate promising to repay a stated amount on a certain date, typically three months from the issue of the bill. Bills pay no interest as such, but are sold at a discount and redeemed at face value, thereby earning a rate of discount for the purchaser.

- Reverse repos. When a sale and repurchase agreement is made, the financial institution *purchasing* the assets (e.g. gilts) is, in effect, giving a short-term loan. The other party agrees to buy back the assets (i.e. pay back the loan) on a set date. The assets temporarily held by the bank making the loan are known as 'reverse repos'.

Longer-term loans. These consist primarily of loans to customers, both personal customers and businesses. These loans, also known as *advances*, are of four main types: fixed-term (repayable in instalments over a set number of years – typically six months to five years), overdrafts (often for an unspecified term), outstanding balances on credit-card accounts and mortgages (typically for 25 years).

Banks also make *investments*. These are partly in government bonds ('gilts') which are effectively loans to the government. The government sells bonds, which then pay a fixed sum each year in interest until the maturity date (perhaps 20 years in the future), when the loan will be repaid at face value by the government. Once issued, bonds can then be bought and sold on the stock exchange. Banks are normally only prepared to buy gilts that have less than five years to maturity. Banks also invest in various subsidiary financial institutions and in building societies.

Definitions

Reverse repos
When gilts or other assets are *purchased* under a sale and repurchase agreement. They become an asset to the purchaser.

Liquidity
The ease with which an asset can be converted into cash without loss.

Liquidity and profitability

As we have seen, banks keep a range of liabilities and assets. The balance of items in this range is influenced by two important considerations: profitability and liquidity.

Profitability. Profits are made by lending money out at a higher rate of interest than that paid to depositors.

Liquidity. The liquidity of an asset is the ease with which it can be converted into cash without loss. Cash itself, by definition, is perfectly liquid.

Some assets, such as money lent at call to other financial institutions, are highly liquid. Although not actually cash, these assets can be converted into cash on demand with no financial penalty. Other assets, however, are much less liquid. Personal loans to the general public or mortgages for house purchase can only be redeemed by the bank as each instalment is paid. Other advances for fixed periods are only repaid at the end of that period.

Banks must always be able to meet the demands of their customers for withdrawals of money. To do this, they must hold sufficient cash or other assets that can be readily turned into cash. In other words, banks must maintain sufficient liquidity.

Profitability is the major aim of banks and most other financial institutions. However, the aims of profitability and liquidity tend to conflict. In general, the more liquid an asset, the less profitable it is, and vice versa. Personal and business loans to customers are profitable to banks, but highly illiquid. Cash is totally liquid, but earns no profit.

Thus financial institutions like to hold a range of assets with varying degrees of liquidity and profitability.

Pause for thought

Why might a bank choose to reduce the proportion of liquid assets that it holds?

Box 9.1 Case Studies and Applications

Changes in the banking industry

Is bigger better?

There are considerable economies of scale in banking. These have resulted in a wave of mergers and take-overs. The process has been hastened by increasing deregulation in the banking industry, which has permitted banks to take on a whole range of functions.

The economies of scale arise in the process known as 'financial intermediation'. This involves providing a link between those who want to deposit money and those who want to borrow it. It involves matching the supply of funds to the demand for them.

If there were many small banks, much of their business would be in dealing with each other: in balancing inflows and outflows of funds between them. Even with computers, this would be a costly process and would involve the banks having to maintain substantial reserves in case outflows exceeded inflows. With fewer bigger banks, however, an increased proportion of the flow of funds would be between their *own* customers and thus would not involve dealing with other banks. Thus reserves could be smaller as a percentage of total assets.

Also, as banks get bigger and the number of customers increases, so *net* withdrawals (positive or negative) diminish as a proportion of total deposits held. This, again, means that banks need to hold a smaller proportion of reserves: they can operate with a lower liquidity ratio. This increases banks' profitability, since cash reserves earn banks no money, and money at call earns a low rate.

Banks also benefit from economies of scope (see page 95). This means that they gain economies by diversifying into different but related activities. Thus traditional retail banks, such as Barclays and NatWest, have diversified into wholesale banking, stockbroking, discounting bills, insurance, foreign exchange dealing and a whole range of financial services to the corporate sector. This diversification not only reduces average costs, since customers can receive more than one service from the same premises or through the same Internet site or telephone service, but also reduces risk. If one part of the business became less profitable, this could be offset by increased profits from another.

Today it makes more sense to talk of retail or wholesale banking *activity*, rather than retail or wholesale banks. After all, the same banks are involved in both types of activity – and many more.

1. Are there any circumstances where diversification could lead to increased risks?
2. To what extent are the lower costs associated with Internet banking attributable to economies of scale?

The ratio of an institution's liquid assets to total assets is known as its liquidity ratio. For example, if a bank had £100 million of assets, of which £10 million were liquid and £90 million were illiquid, the bank would have a 10 per cent liquidity ratio. If a financial institution's liquidity ratio is too high, it will make too little profit. If the ratio is too low, there will be the risk that customers' demands may not be able to be met: this would cause a crisis of confidence and possible closure. Institutions thus have to make a judgement as to what liquidity ratio is best – one that is neither too high nor too low.

The central bank

The Bank of England is the UK's central bank. The European Central Bank (ECB) is the central bank for the countries using the euro. The Federal Reserve Bank of

America (the Fed) is the USA's central bank. All countries have a central bank and they fulfil two vital roles in the economy.

The first is to oversee the whole monetary system and ensure that banks and other financial institutions operate as stably and as efficiently as possible.

The second is to act as the government's agent, both as its banker and in carrying out monetary policy. The Bank of England traditionally worked in very close liaison with the Treasury, and there used to be regular meetings between the Governor of the Bank of England and the Chancellor of the Exchequer. Although the Bank may have disagreed with Treasury policy, it always carried it out. With the election of the Labour government in 1997, however, the Bank of England was given independence to decide the course of monetary policy. In particular, this meant that the Bank of England and not the government would now decide interest rates.

Another example of an independent central bank is the European Central Bank, which operates monetary policy for the euro-zone countries. Similarly, the Fed is independent of both President and Congress, and its chairman is generally regarded as having great power in determining the country's economic policy. Although the degree of independence of central banks from government varies considerably around the world, there has nevertheless been a general trend to make central banks more independent.

If the UK adopts the euro, there will be a much reduced role for the Bank of England. At present, however, within its two broad roles, it has a number of different functions. Although we will consider the case of the Bank of England, the same principles apply to other central banks.

It issues notes

The Bank of England is the sole issuer of banknotes in England and Wales (in Scotland and Northern Ireland, retail banks issue banknotes). The amount of banknotes issued by the Bank of England depends largely on the demand for notes from the general public. If people draw more cash from their bank accounts, the banks will have to draw more cash from their balances in the Bank of England.

It acts as a bank

To the government.   It keeps the two major government accounts: 'The Exchequer' and the 'National Loans Fund'. Taxation and government spending pass through the Exchequer. Government borrowing and lending pass through the National Loans Fund. The government tends to keep its deposits in the Bank of England to a minimum. If the deposits begin to build up (from taxation), the government will probably spend it on paying back government debt. If, on the other hand, it runs short of money, it will simply borrow more.

To the recognised banks.   All recognised banks hold operational balances in the Bank of England. As we have seen, these are used for clearing purposes between the banks and to provide them with a source of liquidity.

To overseas central banks.   The Bank of England holds deposits of sterling (or euros in the case of the ECB) made by the authorities of other countries as part of their official reserves and/or for purposes of intervening in the foreign exchange market in order to influence the exchange rate of their currency. We will examine exchange rates in Chapter 12.

Definition

Recognised banks Banks licensed by the Bank of England. All financial institutions using the word 'bank' in their title have to be recognised by the Bank of England. This requires them to have paid-up capital of at least £5 million and to meet other requirements about their asset structure and range of services.

It oversees the activities of banks and other financial institutions

It advises banks on good banking practice. It discusses government policy with them and reports back to the government. It requires all recognised banks to maintain adequate liquidity: this is called prudential control. Since May 1997, the Bank of England has ceased to be responsible for the detailed supervision of banks' activities. This responsibility has passed to the Financial Services Authority (FSA).

It provides liquidity, as necessary, to banks

It ensures that there is always an adequate supply of liquidity to meet the legitimate demands of depositors in recognised banks. As we shall see below, it does this through the discount and gilt repo markets.

It operates the government's monetary and exchange rate policy

Monetary policy.   The Bank of England's Monetary Policy Committee (MPC) sets interest rates (the rate on gilt repos) at its monthly meetings. This nine-member committee consists of four experts appointed by the Chancellor of the Exchequer and four senior members of the Bank of England, plus the Governor in the chair. By careful management of the issue and repurchasing of gilts and Treasury bills, the Bank of England then keeps interest rates at the level decided by the MPC. It also, in the process, influences the size of the money supply. This is explained in Section 9.6.

Exchange rate policy.   The Bank of England manages the country's gold and foreign currency reserves on behalf of the Treasury. This is done through the exchange equalisation account. As we shall see in Chapter 12, by buying and selling foreign currencies on the foreign exchange market, the Bank of England can affect the exchange rate.

The role of the London money market

It is through the London money market that the Bank of England exercises its control of the economy. The market deals in short-term lending and borrowing. It is normally divided into the 'discount' and 'repo' markets and the 'parallel' or 'complementary' markets.

The discount and repo markets

The markets for bills of exchange (the discount market) and for repos play a crucial role in ensuring that banks have sufficient liquidity to meet all their needs.

Assume that bank customers start drawing out more cash. As a result, banks find themselves short of liquid assets. What can they do? The answer is that they borrow from the Bank of England. There are two ways in which this can be done.

The first is to enter a repo agreement, whereby the Bank of England buys gilts from the banks (thereby supplying them with money) on the condition that the banks buy the gilts back at a fixed price and on a fixed date, typically two weeks later. The repurchase price will be above the sale price. The difference is the equivalent of the interest that the banks are being charged for having what amounts to a loan from the Bank of England. The repurchase price (and hence the 'repo rate') is set by the Bank of England to reflect the rate chosen by the MPC (see Section 9.6).

The second method is to sell Treasury bills back to the Bank of England before they have reached maturity (i.e. before the three months are up). This process is known as rediscounting. The Bank of England will pay a price below the face value, thus effectively charging interest to the banks. Again, the price is set so that the 'rediscount rate' reflects the interest rate set by the MPC.

In being prepared to rediscount bills or provide money through gilt repos, the Bank of England is thus the ultimate guarantor of sufficient liquidity in the monetary system and is known as lender of last resort.

The need for banks to acquire liquidity in this way is not uncommon: the 'last resort' occurs on most days! It is generally a deliberate policy of the Bank of England to create a shortage of liquidity in the economy to force banks to obtain liquidity from it. But why should the Bank of England do this? It does it as a means of controlling interest rates. If the banks are forced to obtain liquidity from the Bank of England, they will be borrowing at the Bank of England's *chosen rate* (i.e. the repo rate). The banks will then have to gear their other rates to it, and other institutions will gear their rates to those of the banks.

The way in which the Bank of England creates a shortage of liquidity and the way in which it forces through changes in interest rates are examined in Section 9.6 and Box 9.3.

The parallel money markets

The parallel money markets include the following:

- The inter-bank market (wholesale loans from one bank to another, from one day to up to several months).
- The market for certificates of deposit.
- The inter-companies deposit market (short-term loans from one company to another arranged through the market).
- The foreign currencies market (dealings in foreign currencies deposited short term in London).
- The building society market (wholesale borrowing by the building societies).
- The commercial paper market (borrowing in sterling by companies, banks and other financial institutions by the issue of short-term (less than one year) 'promissory notes'. These, like bills of exchange, are sold at a discount and redeemed at their face value, but in the interim can be traded on the market at any time).

The parallel markets have grown in size and importance in recent years. The main reasons for this have been (a) the opening-up of markets to international dealing, given the abolition of exchange controls in 1979, (b) the deregulation of banking and money market dealing and (c) the volatility of interest rates and exchange rates, and thus the desire of banks to keep funds in a form that can be readily switched from one form of deposit to another, or from one currency to another. The main areas of growth have been in inter-bank deposits, certificates of deposit and the foreign currency markets.

Definitions

Rediscounting bills of exchange
Buying bills before they reach maturity.

Lender of last resort
The role of the Bank of England as the guarantor of sufficient liquidity in the monetary system.

Recap

1. Banks' liabilities include both sight and time deposits. They also include certificates of deposit and repos. Their assets include: notes and coin, balances with the Bank of England, market loans, bills of exchange, advances to customers (the biggest item, including overdrafts, personal loans and mortgages) and investments (government bonds and inter-bank investments).

2. Banks aim to make profits, but they must also maintain sufficient liquidity. Liquid assets, however, tend to be relatively unprofitable, and profitable assets tend to be relatively illiquid. Banks therefore need to keep a balance of profitability and liquidity in their range of assets.

3. The Bank of England is the UK's central bank. It issues notes; it acts as banker to the government, to the commercial banks and to various overseas central banks; it manages the government's borrowing programme; it ensures sufficient liquidity for banks; it operates monetary and exchange rate policy.

4. The money market is the market in short-term deposits and loans. It consists of the discount and repo markets and the parallel money markets.

5. The Bank of England operates in discount and repo markets. By buying (rediscounting) bills and through gilt repos, it provides liquidity to the banks at the rate of interest chosen by the Monetary Policy Committee.

6. The parallel money markets consist of various markets in short-term finance between various financial institutions.

9.3   The supply of money

How is it measured and what determines its size?

If money supply is to be monitored and possibly controlled, it is obviously necessary to measure it. But what should be included in the measure? Here we need to distinguish between the *monetary base* and *broad money*.

The monetary base (or 'high-powered money') consists of cash (notes and coin) in circulation outside the central bank. Thus, in the euro zone, the monetary base is given by cash (euros) in circulation outside the ECB.

In the UK, it is sometimes referred to as the 'narrow monetary base' to distinguish it from the wide monetary base, which also includes banks' balances with the central bank. In the UK, the wide monetary base is known as M0.

But the monetary base gives us a very poor indication of the effective money supply, since it excludes the most important source of liquidity for spending: namely, bank deposits. The problem is which deposits to include. We need to answer three questions:

■ Should we include just sight deposits, or time deposits as well?
■ Should we include just retail deposits, or wholesale deposits as well?
■ Should we include just bank deposits, or building society (savings institution) deposits as well?

In the past there has been a whole range of measures, each including different combinations of these accounts. However, financial deregulation, the abolition of foreign exchange controls and the development of computer technology have

Definitions

Monetary base
Notes and coin outside the central bank.

Wide monetary base (M0)
Notes and coin outside the central bank plus banks' operational deposits with the central bank.

led to huge changes in the financial sector throughout the world. This has led to a blurring of the distinctions between different types of account. It has also made it very easy to switch deposits from one type of account to another. For these reasons, the most usual measure that countries use for money supply is broad money, which in most cases includes both time and sight deposits, retail and wholesale deposits, and bank and building society (savings institution) deposits.

In the UK, this measure of broad money is known as M4. In most other European countries and the USA, it is known as M3. There are, however, minor differences between countries in what is included. (Official UK and euro-zone measures of money supply are given in Box 9.2.)

As we have seen, bank deposits of one form or another constitute by far the largest component of (broad) money supply. To understand how money supply expands and contracts, and how it can be controlled, it is thus necessary to understand what determines the size of bank deposits. Banks can themselves expand the amount of bank deposits, and hence the money supply, by a process known as 'credit creation'.

> **Definition**
>
> **Broad money**
> Cash in circulation plus retail and wholesale bank and building society deposits.

The creation of credit

To illustrate this process in its simplest form, assume that banks have just one type of liability – deposits – and two types of asset – balances with the central bank (to achieve liquidity) and advances to customers (to earn profit).

Banks want to achieve profitability while maintaining sufficient liquidity. Assume that they believe that sufficient liquidity will be achieved if 10 per cent of their assets are held as balances with the central bank. The remaining 90 per cent will then be in advances to customers. In other words, the banks operate a 10 per cent liquidity ratio.

Assume initially that the combined balance sheet of the banks is as shown in Table 9.2. Total deposits are £100 billion, of which £10 billion (10 per cent) are kept in balances with the central bank. The remaining £90 billion (90 per cent) are lent to customers.

Now assume that the government spends more money – £10 billion, say, on roads or education. It pays for this with cheques drawn on its account with the central bank. The people receiving the cheques deposit them in their banks. Banks return these cheques to the central bank and their balances correspondingly increase by £10 billion. The combined banks' balance sheet now is shown in Table 9.3.

But this is not the end of the story. Banks now have surplus liquidity. With their balances in the central bank having increased to £20 billion, they now have a liquidity ratio of 20/110, or 18.2 per cent. If they are to return to a 10 per cent liquidity ratio, they need only retain £11 billion as balances at the central bank

Liabilities	£bn	Assets	£bn
Deposits	100	Balances with the central bank	10
		Advances	90
Total	100	Total	100

Table 9.2
Banks' original balance sheet

Box 9.2

UK monetary aggregates

How long is a piece of string?

UK measures

In the recent past, measures of 'money supply' in the UK have included M0, non-interest-bearing M1, M1, M2, M3, M3H, M3c, M4, M4c, M5. This confusing array of measures reflected the many different types of deposit that might be considered to be part of money.

In the 1980s, the business of banks and building societies became more and more similar, as banks increasingly became a source of mortgages, and building societies offered cheque-book accounts and cash machines. Those measures of money supply, which included bank deposits, but not building society deposits, therefore ceased to provide a useful measure of liquidity in the economy and were dropped.

Today, there are just two official UK measures: M0 and M4. M0 is referred to as the 'wide monetary base' and M4 is referred to as 'broad money' or simply as 'the money supply'. The definitions of the two UK aggregates are as follows:

M0: Cash in circulation with the public and held by banks and building societies, plus banks' operational balances with the Bank of England.

M4: Cash in circulation with the public (but not in banks and building societies), plus private-sector *retail* sterling deposits in banks and building societies, plus private-sector *wholesale* sterling deposits in banks and building societies, plus sterling certificates of deposit.

Table (a) gives the figures for these aggregates for February 2003.

? Why is cash in banks and building societies included in M0, but not in M4?

Euro-zone measures

Although the ECB uses three measures of the money supply, they are different from those used by the Bank of England. The narrowest definition (M1) includes overnight deposits (i.e. call money) as well as cash, and is thus much broader than the UK's M0 measure. The broadest euro-zone measure (M3) is again broader than the UK's broadest measure (M4), since the euro-zone measure includes various other moderately liquid assets. The definitions of the three euro-zone aggregates are:

M1: Cash in circulation with the public, plus overnight deposits.

M2: M1, plus deposits with agreed maturity up to two years, plus deposits redeemable at up to three months' notice.

M3: M2, plus repos, plus money market funds and paper, plus debt securities with residual maturity up to two years.

? What are the benefits of including these additional items in the broad measure of money supply?

Table 9.3

The initial effect of an additional deposit of £10 billion

Liabilities	£bn	Assets	£bn
Deposits (old)	100	Balances with the central bank (old)	10
Deposits (new)	10	Balances with the central bank (new)	10
		Advances	90
Total	110	Total	110

(£11 billion/£110 billion = 10 per cent). The remaining £9 billion they can lend to customers.

Assume now that customers spend this £9 billion in shops and the shopkeepers deposit the cheques in their bank accounts. When the cheques are cleared, the

(a) UK monetary aggregates: end February 2003

		£ million
	Cash outside Bank of England	36 861
+	Banks' operational deposits with Bank of England	91
= M0		**36 952**
	Cash outside banks (i.e. in circulation with the public and non-bank firms)	30 630
+	Private-sector retail bank and building society deposits	676 969
=	**Retail deposits and cash in M4** (previously known as M2)	**707 599**
+	Private-sector wholesale bank and building society deposits + CDs	295 996
= M4		1 003 595

Source: *Monetary and Financial Statistics* (Bank of England).

(b) UK money supply using ECB measures: end February 2003

		£ million
	Currency in circulation	31 351
+	Overnight deposits	513 292
= M1	(estimate of EMU aggregate for the UK)	**544 643**
+	Deposits with agreed maturity up to 2 years	81 696
+	Deposits redeemable at up to 3 months' notice	296 518
= M2	(estimate of EMU aggregate for the UK)	**922 857**
+	Repos	88 978
+	Money market funds and paper	57 496
+	Debt securities with residual maturity up to 2 years	..
= M3	(estimate of EMU aggregate for the UK)	1 069 331

Source: *Monetary and Financial Statistics* (Bank of England).
Note: Holdings of debt securities are not collected by maturity and it is not considered possible to even estimate those with a maturity of less than or equal to two years. These are assumed to be zero. Most of the columns referring to maturity splits are estimated.

balances in the central bank of the customers' banks will duly be debited by £9 billion, but the balances in the central bank of the shopkeepers' banks will be credited by £9 billion: leaving *overall balances in the central bank unaltered*. There is still a surplus of £9 billion over what is required to maintain the 10 per cent liquidity ratio. The new deposits of £9 billion in the shopkeepers' banks, backed by balances in the central bank, can thus be used as the basis for *further* loans. Ten per cent (i.e. £0.9 billion) must be kept back in the central bank, but the remaining 90 per cent (i.e. £8.1 billion) can be lent out again. When the money is spent and the cheques are cleared, this £8.1 billion will still remain as surplus balances in the central bank and can therefore be used as the basis for yet more loans. Again, 10 per cent must be retained and the remaining 90 per cent can be lent out. This process goes on and on until eventually the position is as shown in Table 9.4.

Table 9.4
The full effect of an additional deposit of £10 billion

Liabilities		£bn	Assets	£bn
Deposits (old)		100	Balances with the central bank (old)	10
Deposits (new: initial)		10	Balances with the central bank (new)	10
	(new: subsequent)	90	Advances (old)	90
			Advances (new)	90
Total		200	Total	200

Key Idea 28 p29?

Pause for thought

If banks choose to operate with a 5 per cent liquidity ratio and receive an extra £100 million of cash deposits: (a) What is the size of the bank deposits multiplier? (b) How much will total deposits have expanded after the multiplier has worked through? (c) How much will total credit have expanded?

The initial increase in balances with the central bank of £10 billion has allowed banks to create new advances (and hence deposits) of £90 billion, making a total increase in money supply of £100 billion.

This effect is known as the bank deposits multiplier. In this simple example, with a liquidity ratio of $^1/_{10}$ (i.e. 10 per cent), the bank deposits multiplier is 10. An initial increase in deposits of £10 billion allowed total deposits to rise by £100 billion. In this simple world, therefore, the bank deposits multiplier is the inverse of the liquidity ratio (L).

$$\text{Bank deposits multiplier} = {}^1/_L$$

The creation of credit: the real world

In practice, the creation of credit is not as simple as this. There are three major complications.

Banks' liquidity ratio may vary

Banks may choose a different liquidity ratio. At certain times, banks may decide that it is prudent to hold a larger proportion of liquid assets. If Christmas or the summer holidays are approaching and people are likely to make bigger cash withdrawals, banks may decide to hold more liquid assets. They may also do so if they anticipate that their liquid assets may soon be squeezed by government monetary policy.

On the other hand, there may be an upsurge in consumer demand for credit. Banks may be very keen to grant additional loans and thus make more profits, even though they have acquired no additional assets. They may simply go ahead and expand credit, and accept a lower liquidity ratio.

Customers may not want to take up the credit on offer. Banks may wish to make additional loans, but customers may not want to borrow. There may be insufficient demand. But will the banks not then lower their interest rates, thus encouraging people to borrow? Possibly; but if they lower the rate they charge to borrowers, they must also lower the rate they pay to depositors. But then depositors may switch to other institutions such as building societies.

Banks may not operate a simple liquidity ratio

The fact that banks hold a number of fairly liquid assets, such as money at call, bills of exchange and certificates of deposit, makes it difficult to identify a simple

Definition

Banks deposits multiplier
The number of times greater the expansion of bank deposits is than the additional liquidity in banks that causes it: I/L (the inverse of the liquidity ratio).

liquidity ratio. If the banks use extra cash to buy such liquid assets, can they then use *these* assets as the basis for creating credit? It is largely up to banks' judgements on their overall liquidity position.

Some of the extra cash may be withdrawn from the banks

If extra cash comes into the banking system, and as a result extra deposits are created, part of them may be held by the public as cash *outside* the banks. In other words, some of the extra cash leaks out of the banking system. This will result in an overall money multiplier effect that is smaller than the full bank multiplier.

What causes money supply to rise?

There are three sets of circumstances in which the money supply can rise.

Banks choose to hold a lower liquidity ratio

If banks collectively choose to hold a lower liquidity ratio, they will have surplus liquidity. The banks have tended to choose a lower liquidity ratio over time because of the increasing use of direct debits, cheques and debit-card and credit-card transactions. Surplus liquidity can be used to expand advances, which will lead to a multiplied rise in the money supply.

An important trend in recent years has been the growth in *inter-bank lending*. These wholesale loans are often short term and are thus a liquid asset to the bank making them. Short-term loans to other banks and CDs are now the two largest elements in banks' liquid assets. Being liquid, these assets may be used by a bank as the basis for expanding loans and thereby starting a chain of credit creation. But although these assets are liquid to an *individual* bank, they do not add to the liquidity of the banking system *as a whole*. Thus by using them as the basis for credit creation, the banking system is operating with a lower *overall* liquidity ratio.

An inflow of funds from abroad

Sometimes the Bank of England will choose to build up the foreign currency reserves. To do this it will buy foreign currencies on the foreign exchange market using sterling. When the recipients of this extra sterling deposit it in UK banks, or spend it on UK exports and the exporters deposit in UK banks, credit will be created on the basis of it, leading to a *multiplied* increase in money supply.

A public-sector deficit

The public-sector net cash requirement (PSNCR) is the difference between public-sector expenditure and public-sector receipts. To meet this deficit the government has to borrow money by selling interest-bearing securities (Treasury bills and gilts). In general, the bigger the PSNCR, the greater will be the growth in the money supply. Just how the money supply will be affected, however, depends on who buys the securities.

Such securities could be sold to the Bank of England. In this case the Bank of England credits the government's account to the value of the securities it has purchased. When the government spends the money, it pays with cheques drawn on its account with the Bank of England. When the recipients of these cheques pay

> **Definition**
>
> **Money multiplier**
> The number of times greater the expansion of money supply is than the expansion of the monetary base that caused it: $\Delta M4/\Delta M0$

them into their bank accounts, the banks will present the cheques to the Bank of England and their balances at the Bank will be duly credited. These additional balances will then become the basis for credit creation. There will be a multiplied expansion of the money supply.

Similarly, if the government borrows through additional Treasury bills, and if these are purchased by the banking sector, there will be a multiplied expansion of the money supply. The reason is that, although banks' balances at the Bank of England will go down when the banks purchase the bills, they will go up again when the government spends the money. In addition, the banks will now have additional liquid assets (bills), which can be used as the basis for credit creation.

If, however, the government securities are purchased by the 'non-bank private sector' (i.e. the general public and non-bank firms), then the money supply will remain unchanged. When people buy the bonds or bills, they will draw money from their banks. When the government spends the money, it will be re-deposited in banks. There is no increase in money supply. It is just a case of existing money changing hands.

> **Pause for thought**   ⫼⫼
>
> *Identify the various factors that could cause a fall in the money supply.*

The government could attempt to minimise the boost to money supply by financing the PSNCR through the sale of gilts rather than Treasury bills.

We can now summarise the components of any increase in money supply (M4). $\Delta M4 = $ (1) PSNCR less any purchases of public-sector debt by the *non*-bank private sector, plus (2) increased lending by banks, plus (3) net inflows of funds from abroad.

The relationship between money supply and the rate of interest

Simple monetary theory often assumes that the supply of money is totally independent of interest rates. The money supply is exogenous. This is illustrated in Figure 9.1(a). The supply of money is assumed to be determined by the government or central bank ('the authorities'): what the authorities choose it to be, or what they allow it to be by their choice of the level and method of financing the PSNCR.

Some economists, however, argue that money supply is endogenous, with higher interest rates leading to increases in the supply of money. This is illustrated in Figure 9.1(b). The argument is that the supply of money is responding to the

> **Definitions**
>
> **Exogenous money supply**
> Money supply that does not depend on the demand for money but is set by the authorities (i.e. the central bank or the government).
>
> **Endogenous money supply**
> Money supply that is determined (at least in part) by the demand for money.

Figure 9.1
The supply of money curve

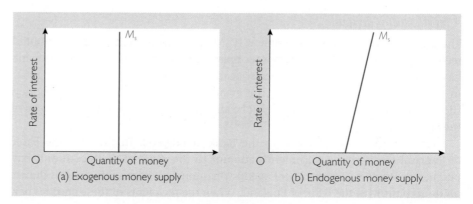

(a) Exogenous money supply   (b) Endogenous money supply

demand for money. If people start borrowing more money, the resulting shortage of money in the banks will drive up interest rates. But if banks have surplus liquidity or are prepared to operate with a lower liquidity ratio, they will create extra credit in response to the increased demand and higher interest rates: money supply will expand.

Recap

1. Money supply can be defined in a number of different ways, depending on what items are included. A useful distinction is between narrow money and broad money. Narrow money includes just cash and possibly banks' balances at the central bank. Broad money also includes deposits in banks and possibly various other short-term deposits in the money market. In the UK, M4 is the preferred measure of broad money. In the euro zone it is M3.

2. Bank deposits expand through a process of credit creation. If banks' liquid assets increase, they can be used as a base for increasing loans. When the loans are redeposited in banks, they form the base for yet more loans, and thus takes place a process of multiple credit expansion. The ratio of the increase of money to an expansion of the liquidity base is called the 'bank deposits multiplier'. It is the inverse of the liquidity ratio.

3. In practice, it is difficult to predict the precise amount by which money supply will expand if there is an increase in banks' liquidity. The reasons are that banks may choose to hold a different liquidity ratio; customers may not take up all the credit on offer; there may be no simple liquidity ratio, given the range of near money assets; and some of the extra cash may leak away into extra cash holdings by the general public.

4. Money supply will rise if (a) banks choose to hold a lower liquidity ratio and thus create more credit for an existing amount of liquidity; (b) there is an inflow of funds from abroad; (c) the government runs a deficit and finances it by borrowing from the banking sector or from abroad.

5. Simple monetary theory assumes that the supply of money is independent of interest rates. In practice, a rise in demand for money and hence a rise in interest rates will often lead to an increase in money supply.

The demand for money   9.4

How much money do we want to hold at any one time?

The demand for money refers to the desire to *hold* money: to keep your wealth in the form of money, rather than spending it on goods and services or using it to purchase financial assets such as bonds or shares. It is usual to distinguish three reasons why people want to hold their assets in the form of money:

The transactions motive.   Since money is a medium of exchange, it is required for conducting transactions. But since people only receive money at intervals (e.g. weekly or monthly) and not continuously, they require to hold balances of money in cash or in current accounts.

The precautionary motive.   Unforeseen circumstances can arise, such as a car breakdown. Thus individuals often hold some additional money as a precaution. Firms too keep precautionary balances because of uncertainties about the timing of their receipts and payments. If a large customer is late in making payment, a firm may be unable to pay its suppliers unless it has spare liquidity.

The assets or speculative motive.   Money is not just a medium of exchange, it is also a means of storing wealth (see page 331). Keeping some or all of your wealth as money in a bank account has the advantage of carrying no risk. It earns a relatively small, but safe rate of return. Some assets, such as company shares or bonds, may earn you more on average, but there is a chance that their price will fall. In other words, they are risky.

What determines the size of the demand for money?

What would cause the demand for money to rise? We now turn to examine the various determinants of the size of the demand for money (M_D). In particular, we will look at the role of the rate of interest. First, however, let us identify the other determinants of the demand for money.

Money national income.   The more money people earn, the greater will be their expenditure and hence the greater the transactions demand for money. A rise in money ('nominal') incomes in a country can be caused either by a rise in real GDP (i.e. real output) or by a rise in prices, or by some combination of the two.

The frequency with which people are paid.   The less frequently people are paid, the greater the level of money balances that will be required to tide them over until the next payment.

Financial innovations.   The increased use of credit cards, debit cards and cash machines, plus the advent of interest-paying current accounts, have resulted in changes in the demand for money. The use of credit cards reduces both the transactions and precautionary demands. Paying once a month for goods requires less money on average than paying separately for each item purchased. Moreover, the possession of a credit card reduces or even eliminates the need to hold precautionary balances for many people. On the other hand, the increased availability of cash machines, the convenience of debit cards and the ability to earn interest on current accounts have all encouraged people to hold more money in bank accounts. The net effect has been an increase in the demand for money.

Speculation about future returns on assets.   The assets motive for holding money depends on people's expectations. If they believe that share prices are about to fall on the stock market, they will sell shares and hold larger balances of money in the meantime. The assets demand, therefore, can be quite high when the price of securities is considered certain to fall. Some clever (or lucky) individuals anticipated the 2000–3 stock market decline. They sold shares and 'went liquid'.

Generally, the more risky such alternatives to money become, the more will people want to hold their assets as money balances in a bank or building society.

People also speculate about changes in the exchange rate. If businesses believe that the exchange rate is about to appreciate (rise), they will hold greater balances of domestic currency in the meantime, hoping to buy foreign currencies with them when the rate has risen (since they will then get more foreign currency for their money).

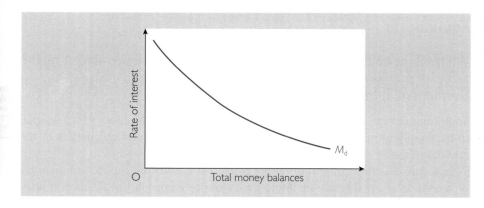

Figure 9.2
The demand for money

The rate of interest. In terms of the operation of money markets, this is the most important determinant. It is related to the opportunity cost of holding money. The opportunity cost is the interest forgone by not holding higher interest-bearing assets, such as shares, bills or bonds. With most bank accounts today paying interest, this opportunity cost is less than in the past and thus the demand for money for assets purposes has increased.

But what is the relationship between money demand and the rate of interest? Generally, if rates of interest rise, they will rise more on shares, bills and bonds than on bank accounts. The demand for money will thus fall. The demand for money is thus inversely related to the rate of interest.

The demand for money curve

The demand for money curve with respect to interest rates is shown in Figure 9.2. It is downward sloping, showing that lower interest rates will encourage people to hold additional money balances.

A change in interest rates is shown by a movement along the demand for money curve. A change in any other determinant of the demand for money (such as national income or expectations about exchange rate movements) will cause the whole curve to shift: a rightward shift representing an increase in demand; a leftward shift representing a decrease.

> **Pause for thought**
>
> Which way is the demand for money curve likely to shift in each of the following cases? (a) Prices rise, but real incomes stay the same. (b) Interest rates abroad rise relative to domestic interest rates. (c) People anticipate that share prices are likely to fall in the near future.

Recap

1. The three motives for holding money are the transactions, precautionary and assets (or speculative) motives.

2. The demand for money will be higher, (a) the higher the level of money national income (i.e. the higher the level of real national income and the higher the price level), (b) the less frequently people are paid, (c) the greater the advantages of holding money in bank accounts, such as the existence of cash machines and the use of debit cards, (d) the more risky alternative assets become and the more likely they are to fall in value, and the more likely the exchange rate is to rise, and (e) the lower the opportunity cost of holding money in terms of interest forgone on alternative assets.

3. The demand for money curve with respect to interest rates is downward sloping.

9.5 Equilibrium

What effect do the demand and supply of money have on interest rates?

Equilibrium in the money market

Equilibrium in the money market occurs when the demand for money (M_d) is equal to the supply of money (M_s). This equilibrium is achieved through changes in the rate of interest.

In Figure 9.3 the equilibrium rate of interest is r_e and the equilibrium quantity of money is M_e. If the rate of interest were above r_e, people would have money balances surplus to their needs. They would use these to buy shares, bonds and other assets. This would drive up the price of these assets. But the price of assets is inversely related to interest rates. The higher the price of an asset (such as a government bond), the less any given interest payment will be as a percentage of its price (e.g. £10 as a percentage of £100 is 10 per cent, but as a percentage of £200 is only 5 per cent). Thus a higher price of assets will correspond to lower interest rates.

As the rate of interest fell, so there would be a contraction of the money supply (a movement down along the M_s curve) and an increase in the demand for money balances, especially speculative balances (a movement down along the M_d curve). The interest rate would go on falling until it reached r_e. Equilibrium would then be achieved.

Similarly, if the rate of interest were below r_e, people would have insufficient money balances. They would sell securities, thus lowering their prices and raising the rate of interest until it reached r_e.

A shift in either the M_s or the M_d curve will lead to a new equilibrium quantity of money and rate of interest at the new intersection of the curves. For example, a rise in the supply of money will cause the rate of interest to fall, whereas a rise in the demand for money will cause the rate of interest to rise.

Equilibrium in the foreign exchange market

Exchange rates are determined by the demand and supply of currencies. (We will examine this in detail in Chapter 12.) If the supply of sterling on the foreign

Figure 9.3

Equilibrium in the money market

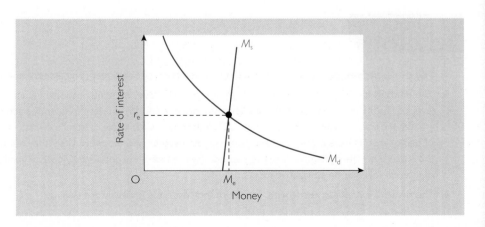

exchange market (e.g. from importers in the UK wishing to buy foreign currencies in order to buy foreign goods) exceeds the demand (e.g. from foreign companies wishing to obtain sterling to buy UK exports), the exchange rate will fall ('depreciate'). For example, the pound might depreciate from $1.65 to $1.50, or from €1.60 to €1.46. Conversely, if the demand for sterling exceeds the supply, the exchange rate will rise ('appreciate').

Changes in the money supply will not only affect interest rates, they will also affect the demand and supply of the currency and thus have an effect on exchange rates. Assume, for example, that the money supply increases. This has three direct effects:

- *Part* of the excess money balances will be used to purchase foreign assets. This will therefore lead to an increase in the supply of domestic currency coming on to the foreign exchange markets.
- The excess supply of money in the domestic money market will push down the rate of interest. This will reduce the return on domestic assets below that on foreign assets. This, like the first effect, will lead to an increased demand for foreign assets and thus an increased supply of domestic currency on the foreign exchange market. It will also reduce the demand for domestic assets by those outside the country, and thus reduce the demand for the domestic currency.
- Speculators will anticipate that the higher supply of domestic currency will cause the exchange rate to depreciate. They will therefore sell domestic currency and buy foreign currencies now, before the depreciation takes place.

The effect of all three is to cause the exchange rate to depreciate.

The full effect of changes in the money supply

The effect of changes in the money supply on interest rates and exchange rates will in turn affect the level of economic activity in the economy. Assume that there is a rise in UK money supply. The sequence of events is as follows:

- A rise in money supply will lead to a fall in the rate of interest: this is necessary to restore equilibrium in the money market.
- The fall in the rate of interest will lead to a rise in investment and other forms of borrowing. (Since borrowing money will be cheaper, investment will cost less.)
- The fall in the domestic rate of interest and the resulting outflow of money from the country, plus the increased demand for foreign assets resulting from the increased money supply, will cause the exchange rate to depreciate.
- The fall in the exchange rate will mean that people abroad have to pay less for a pound. This will make UK exports cheaper and hence more will be sold. People in the UK will get less foreign currency for a pound. This will make imports more expensive and hence less will be purchased.
- The rise in investment and exports will mean increased injections into the circular flow of income (see Section 7.2), and the fall in imports will mean reduced withdrawals from it. The effect will be a rise in aggregate demand and a resulting rise in national income and output, and possibly a rise in inflation too.

> **Pause for thought**
>
> *What determines the amount that real output rises as a result of a rise in the money supply?*

Recap

1. Equilibrium in the money market is where the supply of money is equal to the demand. Equilibrium is achieved through changes in the interest rate and the exchange rate.

2. The interest rate mechanism works as follows: a rise in money supply causes money supply to exceed money demand; interest rates fall; this causes investment to rise; this causes a multiplied rise in national income.

3. The exchange rate mechanism works as follows: a rise in money supply causes interest rates to fall; the rise in money supply plus the fall in interest rates causes an increased supply of domestic currency to come on to the foreign exchange market; this causes the exchange rate to depreciate; this will cause increased exports and reduced imports and hence a multiplied rise in national income.

9.6 Monetary policy

How can the supply of money and interest rates be controlled?

Each month the Bank of England's Monetary Policy Committee meets to set interest rates. The event gets considerable media coverage. Pundits, for two or three days before the meeting, try to predict what the MPC will do and economists give their 'considered' opinions about what the MPC *ought* to do.

The fact is that changes in interest rates have gained a central significance in macroeconomic policy. And it is not just in the UK. Whether it is the European Central Bank setting interest rates for the euro-zone countries, or the Federal Reserve Bank setting US interest rates, or any other central bank around the world choosing what the level of interest rates should be, monetary policy is seen as having a major influence on a whole range of macroeconomic indicators.

But is monetary policy simply the setting of interest rates? In reality, it involves the central bank intervening in the money market to ensure that the interest rate that has been announced is also the *equilibrium* interest rate.

The policy setting

In framing its monetary policy, the government must decide on what the goals of the policy are. Is the aim simply to control inflation, or does the government wish also to affect output and employment, or does it want to control the exchange rate?

The government must also decide where monetary policy fits into the total package of macroeconomic policies. Is it seen as the major or even sole macroeconomic policy instrument, or is it merely one of several?

A decision also has to be made about who is to carry out the policy. There are three possible approaches here.

In the first, the government both sets the policy and decides the measures necessary to achieve it. Here the government would set the interest rate, with the central bank simply influencing money markets to achieve this rate. This first approach was used in the UK before 1997.

The second approach is for the government to set the policy *targets*, but for the central bank to be given independence in deciding interest rates. This is the approach adopted in the UK today. The government has set a target rate of inflation of 2 per cent, but then the MPC is free to choose the rate of interest.

The third approach is for the central bank to be given independence not only in carrying out policy, but in setting the policy targets themselves. The ECB, within the statutory objective of maintaining price stability over the medium term, decides on (a) the target rate of inflation – currently that inflation for the euro zone should be kept close to 2 per cent, and (b) the target rate of growth in money supply. It then sets interest rates to meet these targets.

Finally, there is the question of whether the government or central bank should take a long-term or short-term perspective. Should it adopt a target for money supply growth or inflation and stick to it come what may? Or should it adjust its policy as circumstances change and attempt to 'fine tune' the economy?

We will be looking primarily at *short-term* monetary policy: that is, policy used to keep to a set target for inflation or money supply growth, or policy used to smooth out fluctuations in the business cycle. It is important first, however, to take a longer-term perspective. Governments will generally want to prevent an excessive growth in the money supply over the longer term. If money supply does grow rapidly, then inflation is likely to be high.

Control of the money supply over the medium and long term

One of the major sources of monetary growth is government borrowing. If the government wishes to prevent excessive growth in the money supply over the longer term, therefore, it will have to be careful not to have an excessively high PSNCR (see page 345).

The precise effect of government borrowing on the money supply will depend on how the PSNCR is financed. If it is financed by borrowing from the Bank of England or by the sale of Treasury bills to the banking sector, the money supply will increase. If, however, it is financed by selling bills or gilts outside the banking sector or by selling gilts to the banks, the money supply will not increase (see page 346).

If there is no increase in money supply, however, the increased demand for loans by the government will 'crowd out' lending to the private sector. To attract money the government will have to offer higher interest rates on gilts. This will force up private-sector interest rates and reduce private-sector borrowing and investment. This is known as financial crowding out.

If governments wish to reduce monetary growth and yet avoid financial crowding out, they must therefore reduce the level of the PSNCR.

Short-term monetary measures

Monetary policy may be off target. Alternatively, the government (or central bank) may wish to alter its monetary policy. What can it do? Various techniques could be used. These can be grouped into three categories: (a) altering the money supply; (b) altering interest rates; (c) rationing credit. These are illustrated in Figure 9.4,

Definition

Financial crowding out Where an increase in government borrowing diverts money away from the private sector.

Figure 9.4

The demand for and supply of money

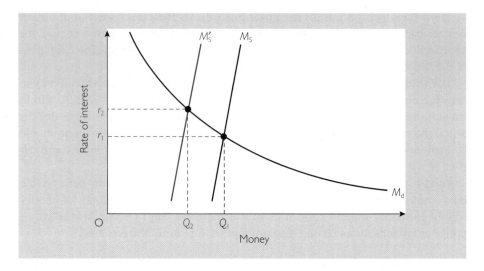

which shows the demand for and supply of money. The equilibrium quantity of money is initially Q_1 and the equilibrium interest rate is r_1.

Assume that the central bank wants to tighten monetary policy in order to reduce inflation. It could (a) seek to shift the supply of money curve to the left: e.g. from M_S to M_S' (resulting in the equilibrium rate of interest rising from r_1 to r_2), (b) raise the interest rate directly from r_1 to r_2, and then manipulate the money supply to reduce it to Q_2, or (c) keep interest rates at r_1, but reduce money supply to Q_2 by rationing the amount of credit granted by banks and other institutions.

Techniques to control the money supply

There are four possible techniques that a central bank could use to control money supply. They have one major feature in common: they involve manipulating the liquid assets of the banking system. The aim is to influence the total money supply by affecting the amount of credit that banks can create.

Open-market operations.   Open-market operations are the most widely used of the four techniques around the world. They involve the sale or purchase by the central bank of government securities (bonds or bills) in the open market. These sales or purchases are *not* in response to changes in the PSNCR, and are thus best understood in the context of an unchanged PSNCR.

If the central bank wishes to *reduce* the money supply, it will sell more securities. When people buy these securities, they pay for them with cheques drawn on banks. Thus banks' balances with the central bank are reduced. If this brings bank reserves below their prudent ratio, banks will reduce advances. There will be a multiple contraction of credit and hence of money supply.

Reduced central bank lending to the banks.   The central bank in most countries is prepared to provide extra money to banks (through gilt repos, rediscounting bills or straight loans). In some countries, it is the policy of the central bank to keep its

---

Definition

Open-market operations
The sale (or purchase) by the authorities of government securities in the open market in order to reduce (or increase) money supply.

Pause for thought

Explain how open-market operations could be used to increase the money supply.

Ke
Ide

5
p2

interest rate to banks *below* market rates, thereby encouraging banks to borrow (or sell back securities) whenever such facilities are available. By cutting back the amount it is willing to provide, the central bank can reduce banks' liquid assets and hence the amount of credit they can create.

In other countries, such as the UK and the euro-zone countries, it is not so much the amount of money made available that is controlled, but rather the rate of interest (or discount). The higher this rate is relative to other market rates, the less will banks be willing to borrow, and the lower, therefore, will be the monetary base. Raising this rate, therefore, has the effect of reducing the money supply.

Funding.   Rather than focusing on controlling the monetary base (as in the case of the above two techniques), an alternative is for the central bank to alter the overall liquidity position of the banks. An example of this approach is a change, by the central bank, in the balance of funding government debt. To reduce money supply the central bank issues more bonds and fewer bills. Banks' balances with the central bank will be little affected, but to the extent that banks hold fewer bills, there will be a reduction in their liquidity and hence a reduction in the amount of credit created. Funding is thus the conversion of one type of government debt (liquid) into another (illiquid).

Variable minimum reserve ratios.   In some countries (such as the USA), banks are required to hold a certain proportion of their assets in liquid form. The assets that count as liquid are known as 'reserve assets'. These include assets such as balances in the central bank, bills of exchange, certificates of deposit and money market loans. The ratio of such assets to total liabilities is known as the minimum reserve ratio. If the central bank raises this ratio (in other words, requires the banks to hold a higher proportion of liquid assets), then banks will have to reduce the amount of credit. The money supply will fall.

Techniques to control interest rates

The approach to monetary control today in most countries is to focus directly on interest rates. Normally an interest rate change will be announced, and then open-market operations will be conducted by the central bank to ensure that the money supply is adjusted so as to make the announced interest rate the *equilibrium* one. Let us assume that the central bank decides to raise interest rates. What does it do?

In general, it will seek to keep banks short of liquidity. This will happen automatically on any day when tax payments by banks' customers exceed the money they receive from government expenditure. This excess is effectively withdrawn from banks and ends up in the government's account at the central bank. Even when this does not occur, sales of bills by the central bank will effectively keep the banking system short of liquidity.

This 'shortage' can then be used as a way of forcing through interest rate changes. Banks will obtain the necessary liquidity from the central bank through repos or by selling it back bills. The central bank can *choose the rate of interest to charge* (i.e. the repo rate or the bill rediscount rate). This will then have a knock-on effect on other interest rates throughout the banking system. (See Box 9.3 for more details on just how the Bank of England manipulates interest rates on a day-to-day basis.)

Definitions

Funding
Where the authorities alter the balance of bills and bonds for any given level of government borrowing.

Minimum reserve ratio
A minimum ratio of specified liquid assets to deposits (either total or selected) that the central bank requires banks to hold.

Box 9.3 Case Studies and Applications

The daily operation of monetary policy

What goes on at Threadneedle Street?

The Bank of England does not attempt to control money supply directly. Instead it seeks to control short-term interest rates by conducting open-market operations in the gilt repo and discount markets. These operations, as we shall see, determine short-term interest rates, which will then have a knock-on effect on longer-term rates, as returns on different forms of assets must remain competitive with each other.

Let us assume that the Monetary Policy Committee of the Bank of England is worried that inflation is set to rise, perhaps because there is excessive growth in the money supply. It thus decides to raise interest rates. What does the Bank of England do?

The first thing is that it will *announce* a rise in interest rates. But it must do more than this. It must back up the announcement by using open-market operations to ensure that its announced interest rate is the *equilibrium rate*. In fact, it has to conduct open-market operations every day to keep interest rates at the level it chooses.

How do these open-market operations work? In general, the Bank of England seeks to keep banks short of liquidity. It achieves this through its weekly sales of Treasury bills to the banks and other financial institutions (collectively known as the Bank's 'counterparties').

The counterparties thus have to borrow from the Bank of England. They do this by entering into sale and repurchase agreements (repos). This entails them selling gilts to the Bank, with an agreement that they will repurchase them from the Bank at a fixed date in the future (typically two weeks). The difference between the sale and repurchase prices will be set by the Bank of England to reflect its chosen rate of interest. By the Bank determining the repo rate in this way, there will then be a knock-on effect on other interest rates throughout the banking system.

Each morning at 9.45 the Bank of England forecasts that day's liquidity shortage. Unless the shortage is too small to necessitate action, it then provides liquidity through open-market operations: i.e. through repos or the repurchasing of bills. The rate charged is that set by the MPC. At 2.30, the Bank revises its forecasts of the market's liquidity shortage, and if necessary undertakes a further round of open-market operations.

Then, at 3.30, it publishes a final update for the day's liquidity shortage, and if necessary makes a further repo facility available, normally on an overnight basis and normally at 1 per cent above the rate set by the MPC. The rate is higher because the Bank expects its counterparties to obtain liquidity at the 9.45 and 2.30 rounds. The 3.30 round is designed to cater for any unforeseen late shortage.

Finally, at 4.20, after the market has closed, banks may apply for additional overnight liquidity through repos to allow the process of clearing to be completed. The Bank will charge them anything from the MPC's agreed repo rate to $1\frac{1}{2}$ per cent above that rate.

Although there is usually a shortage of liquidity in the banking system, on some days there may be a *surplus*. To prevent this driving market interest rates down, the Bank will invite its counterparties to bid for outright purchase of short-dated Treasury bills (i.e. ones part-way through their life) at prices set by the Bank to reflect its current (above equilibrium) interest rate: i.e. at prices lower than the market would otherwise set. At such prices, the Bank has no difficulty in selling them and hence in 'mopping up' the surplus liquidity.

? Assume that the Bank of England wants to reduce interest rates. Trace through the process during the day by which it achieves this.

Techniques to ration credit

In the past, and particularly in the late 1960s, governments attempted to keep interest rates low so as not to discourage investment. This frequently meant that the demand for money exceeded the supply of money that the authorities were prepared to permit.

Faced with this excess demand, the authorities had to ration credit. There were two main ways in which credit was rationed. First, the Bank of England could ask banks to restrict their total lending to a certain amount, or to reduce lending to more risky customers or for non-essential purchases. The Bank of England had the power to order banks to obey, but in practice it always relied on persuasion. This was known as *suggestion and request* (or 'moral persuasion'). Second, the authorities could restrict *hire-purchase credit*, by specifying minimum deposits or maximum repayment periods.

The use of credit rationing has been abandoned by most countries in recent years. The reason is that the open nature of world financial markets makes it very difficult for individual central banks to control credit. Banks and their customers are likely to be able to find ways of getting round the controls.

Recap

1. Control over the growth in the money supply over the longer term will normally involve governments attempting to restrict the size of the budget deficit.

2. In the short term, the government or central bank can use monetary policy to restrict the growth in aggregate demand in one of three ways: (a) reducing money supply directly; (b) reducing the demand for money by raising interest rates; (c) rationing credit.

3. The money supply can be reduced directly by using open-market operations. This involves the central bank selling more government securities and thereby reducing banks' reserves when their customers pay for the securities from their bank accounts. Alternatively, the central bank could reduce the amount it is prepared to lend to banks (other than as a last-resort measure). Or it could use funding, by increasing the sale of bonds relative to bills, thereby reducing banks' liquid assets. Finally it could operate a system of variable minimum reserve ratios. Increasing these would force banks to cut back on the amount of credit they create.

4. The current method of control in the UK and many other countries involves the central bank influencing interest rates by its operations in the discount and repo markets. The central bank keeps banks short of liquidity, and then supplies them with liquidity, largely through repos, at its chosen interest rate (repo rate). This then has a knock-on effect on interest rates throughout the economy.

5. Credit rationing has not been used in the UK and most other countries in recent years.

Box 9.4

Monetary policy in the euro zone

The role of the ECB

The European Central Bank (ECB) is based in Frankfurt and is charged with operating the monetary policy of those EU countries that have adopted the euro. Although it has the overall responsibility for the euro zone's monetary policy, the central banks of the individual countries, such as the Bank of France and the Bundesbank, have not been abolished. They are responsible for distributing euros and for carrying out the ECB's policy with respect to institutions in their own countries. The whole system of the ECB and the national central banks is known as the European System of Central Banks (ESCB).

In operating the monetary policy of a 'euro economy' roughly the size of the USA, and in being independent from national governments, the ECB's power is enormous. So what is the structure of this giant on the European stage, and how does it operate?

The structure of the ECB

The ECB has two major decision-making bodies: the Governing Council and the Executive Board.

■ The Governing Council consists of the members of the Executive Board and the governors of the central banks of each of the euro-zone countries. The Council's role is to set the main targets of monetary policy and to oversee the success (or otherwise) of that policy.

■ The Executive Board consists of a president, a vice-president and four other members. Each serves for an eight-year, non-renewable term. The Executive Board is responsible for implementing the decisions of the Governing Council and for preparing policies for the Council's consideration. Each member of the Executive Board has a responsibility for some particular aspect of monetary policy.

The ECB is one of the most independent central banks in the world. It has very little formal accountability to elected politicians. Although its president can be called before the European Parliament, the Parliament has virtually no powers to influence the ECB's actions. Also its deliberations are secret. Unlike meetings of the Bank of England's Monetary Policy Committee, the minutes of the Council meetings are not published.

The targets of monetary policy

The overall responsibility of the ECB is to achieve price stability in the euro zone. The target set at the launch of the euro in 1999 was a rate of inflation below 2 per cent. In 2003 it was changed to a target 'close to 2 per cent'. The target is a weighted *average* rate for all 12 members, not a rate that has to be met by every member individually.

9.7   The effectiveness of monetary policy

Is monetary policy a reliable means of controlling the economy?

Controlling the money supply over the medium and long term

A government committed to a sustained reduction in the growth of the money supply over a number of years will find this very difficult unless it restricts the size of the public-sector deficit. The Thatcher government in the 1980s recognised this and

The ECB also sets a target for the growth of M3, the broad measure of the money supply (see Box 9.2). The target set at the launch of the euro was $4\frac{1}{2}$ per cent. This too was still the target in 2003. The target for M3 is only an *intermediate* target, seen as a means of achieving the target rate of inflation. If the M3 target turns out to be too high or too low to achieve the target rate of inflation (perhaps because money circulates faster or slower than originally thought: see Section 10.1) then the M3 target is altered. It is reviewed each year in December.

On the basis of its inflation and money supply targets, the ECB then sets the rates of interest. It sets three rates: a rate for 'refinancing operations' of the ESCB (i.e. the rate of interest charged by the ESCB for liquidity on offer to banks, largely through repos); a (higher) 'last resort rate'; and a (lower) 'deposit rate' (the rate paid to banks for depositing surplus liquidity with the ESCB). In April 2003, these rates were 2.5, 3.5 and 1.5 per cent respectively.

Interest rates are set by the Governing Council by simple majority. In the event of a tie, the president has the casting vote.

The operation of monetary policy

The ECB sets a minimum reserve ratio. It argues that this gives greater stability to the system and reduces the need for day-to-day intervention by the ECB. The ECB argues that if there were no minimum reserves, with banks free to use as much of their reserves with the ESCB as they choose, then they will do so if there is an upsurge in demand from customers. After all, the banks know that they can always *borrow* from the ESCB to meet any liquidity requirements. In such a situation, the ECB would be forced to rely much more on open-market operations to prevent excessive lending by banks to their customers, and hence excessive borrowing from the ESCB, and this would mean much greater fluctuations in interest rates.

The minimum reserve ratio is not designed to be used to make *changes* in monetary policy. In other words, it is not used as a *variable* minimum reserves ratio, and for this reason is set at a low level of 2 per cent.

The main instrument for keeping the ECB's desired interest rate as the equilibrium rate is open-market operations in government bonds and other recognised assets, mainly in the form of repos. These repo operations are conducted by the national central banks, which must ensure that the repo rate does not rise above the last resort rate or below the deposit rate.

? What are the arguments for and against publishing the minutes of the meetings of the ECB's Governing Council and Executive Board?

---

made reducing the PSNCR (then known as the PSBR – the public-sector borrowing requirement) the central feature of its 'medium-term financial strategy'. There are serious problems, however, in attempting to reduce the public-sector deficit if it is currently high, principal among which is the difficulty in cutting government expenditure.

Cuts in government expenditure are politically unpopular. The Thatcher government as soon as it came into office met considerable opposition to 'cuts', in Parliament, from public opinion, from local authorities and from various pressure groups. What is more, much of government expenditure is committed a long time in advance and cannot easily be cut. As a result the government may find itself forced into refusing to sanction *new* expenditure. But this will mean a decline in capital projects such as roads, housing, schools and sewers, with the net result that there is a decline in the country's infrastructure and long-term damage to the economy.

The less successful a government is in controlling the public-sector deficit, the more it will have to borrow through bond issue, to prevent money supply growing too fast. This will mean high interest rates and the problem of crowding out, and a growing burden of public-sector debt with interest on it that has to be paid from taxation, from further cuts in government expenditure, or from further borrowing.

It is for reasons such as these that in 1998 the UK Chancellor adopted his 'golden rule' of fiscal policy (see Box 8.5). This is a pledge that over the course of the business cycle, the government will borrow only to invest. In other words, leaving investment aside, there is a target for the PSNCR of zero.

Similarly, under the EU Stability and Growth Pact (again, see Box 8.5), euro-zone countries are required to aim for a zero government deficit over the business cycle, so that in times of economic slowdown the deficit will not exceed 3 per cent – the limit set for deficits under the Pact. A problem with this rule is that if a recession or slowdown persists, the deficit is likely to breach the 3 per cent limit (as happened in France, Germany and some other EU countries in 2003). There then may have to be deflationary cuts in expenditure or rises in taxation, just at a time when a boost to aggregate demand is called for.

Short-term monetary measures

Problems with attempting to control the money supply

Targets for the growth in broad money were an important part of UK monetary policy from 1976 to 1985. Money targets were then abandoned and have not been used since. The European Central Bank targets the growth of M3 (see Box 9.4), but this is a subsidiary policy to that of setting interest rates in order to keep inflation under control. If, however, a central bank did choose to target money supply as its main monetary policy, how would the policy work?

Assume that money supply is above target and that the central bank wishes to reduce it. It would probably use open-market operations: i.e. it would sell more bonds or bills. The purchasers of the bonds or bills would draw liquidity from the banks. Banks would then supposedly be forced to cut down on the credit they create. But is it as simple as this?

The problem is that banks will normally be unwilling to cut down on loans if people want to borrow – after all, borrowing by customers earns profits for the banks. Banks can always 'top up' their liquidity by borrowing from the central bank and then carry on lending. True, they will have to pay the interest rate charged by the central bank, but they can pass on any rise in the rate to their customers.

The point is that as long as people *want* to borrow, banks and other financial institutions will normally try to find ways of meeting the demand. In other words, in the short run at least, the supply of money is to a large extent demand determined. It is for this reason that central banks prefer to control the *demand* for money by controlling interest rates.

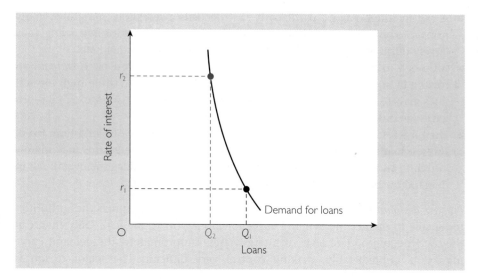

Figure 9.5

An inelastic demand for loans

The effectiveness of changes in interest rates

Even though this is the current preferred method of monetary control, it is not without its difficulties. The problems centre on the nature of the demand for loans. If this demand is (a) unresponsive to interest rate changes or (b) unstable because it is significantly affected by other determinants (such as anticipated income or foreign interest rates), then it will be very difficult to control by controlling the rate of interest.

Problem of an inelastic demand for loans.   If the demand for loans is inelastic, as in Figure 9.5, any attempt to reduce demand (e.g. from Q_1 to Q_2) will involve large rises in interest rates (r_1 to r_2). The problem will be compounded if the demand shifts to the right, due, say, to a consumer spending boom. High interest rates lead to the following problems:

- They may discourage investment and hence long-term growth.
- They add to the costs of production, to the costs of house purchase and generally to the cost of living. They are thus cost inflationary.
- They are politically unpopular, since the general public do not like paying higher interest rates on overdrafts, credit cards and mortgages.
- The necessary bond issue to restrain liquidity will commit the government to paying high rates on these bonds for the next 20 years or so.
- High interest rates encourage inflows of money from abroad. This drives up the exchange rate. (We examine this in Section 12.2.) A higher exchange rate makes domestic goods expensive relative to goods made abroad. This can be very damaging for export industries and industries competing with imports. Many firms in the UK suffered badly in the period 1999–2002, when a higher interest rate in the UK than in the euro zone caused a high exchange rate of sterling against the euro.

Evidence suggests that the demand for loans may indeed be quite inelastic. The reasons include the following:

■ A rise in interest rates, particularly if it deepens a recession, may force many firms into borrowing merely to survive. This increase in 'distress borrowing' may largely offset any decline in borrowing by other firms or individuals.

■ Although investment *plans* may be curtailed by high interest rates, *current* borrowing by many firms cannot easily be curtailed. Similarly, while high interest rates may discourage householders from taking on *new* mortgages, existing mortgages are unlikely to be reduced.

■ High interest rates may discourage many firms from taking out long-term fixed-interest loans. But instead of reducing total borrowing, some firms may merely switch to shorter-term variable-interest loans. This will reduce the overall fall in demand for bank loans, thus making the demand less elastic.

Problem of an unstable demand.   Accurate monetary control requires the authorities to be able to predict the demand curve for money (in Figure 9.4). Only then can they set the appropriate level of interest rates. Unfortunately, the demand curve may shift unpredictably, making control very difficult. The major reason is *speculation*:

■ If people think interest rates will rise and bond prices fall, in the meantime they will demand to hold their assets in liquid form. The demand for money will rise.
■ If people think exchange rates will rise, they will hold the domestic currency while it is still relatively cheap. The demand for money will rise.
■ If people think inflation will rise, the transactions demand for money may rise. People plan to spend more while prices are still relatively low.
■ If people think the economy is going to grow faster, the demand for loans will increase as firms seek to increase their investment.

It is very difficult for the authorities to predict what people's expectations will be. Speculation depends considerably on world political events, rumour and 'random shocks'.

If the demand curve shifts very much, and if it is inelastic, then monetary control will be very difficult. Furthermore, the authorities will have to make frequent and sizeable adjustments to interest rates. These fluctuations can be very damaging to business confidence and may discourage long-term investment.

> **Pause for thought**
>
> Assume that the central bank announces a rise in interest rates and backs this up with open-market operations. What determines the size of the resulting fall in aggregate demand?

The net result of an inelastic and unstable demand for money is that substantial interest rate changes may be necessary to bring about the required change in aggregate demand. An example occurred in 2001 when the US Federal Reserve, seeing the economy moving rapidly into recession, had to cut interest rates several times. At the beginning of 2001, the US 'federal funds rate' was 6 per cent. By the end of the year it had been reduced to 1.75 per cent.

Using monetary policy

It is impossible to use monetary policy as a precise means of controlling aggregate demand. It is especially weak when it is pulling against the expectations of firms and consumers, and when it is implemented too late. However, if the authorities operate a tight monetary policy firmly enough and long enough, they should eventually be able to reduce lending and hence aggregate demand, and with it, inflation. But there will inevitably be time lags and imprecision in the process.

An expansionary monetary policy is even less reliable. If the economy is in recession, no matter how low interest rates are driven, people cannot be forced to borrow if they do not wish to. Firms will not borrow to invest if they predict a continuing recession.

Despite these problems, changing interest rates can be quite effective. After all, they can be changed very rapidly. There are not the time lags of implementation that there are with fiscal policy. Indeed, since the early 1990s, most governments or central banks in OECD countries have used interest rate changes as the major means of keeping aggregate demand and inflation under control.

In the UK, the euro zone and many other countries, a target is set for the rate of inflation. As we have seen, in the UK and the euro zone the target is 2 per cent. If forecasts suggest that inflation is going to be above the target rate, the government or central bank raises interest rates. The advantage of this is that it sends a very clear message to people that inflation *will* be kept under control. People will therefore be more likely to adjust their expectations accordingly and keep their borrowing in check.

Recap

1. It is difficult to control the growth of the money supply over the longer term without controlling the growth of the public-sector deficit. This will be difficult to do in a period of recession.

2. All forms of short-term monetary policy involve problems. The money supply is difficult to control precisely, and even if the government is successful in controlling the money supply, there then arises the problem of severe fluctuations in interest rates if the demand for money fluctuates and is relatively inelastic.

3. The form of monetary policy that has been favoured in recent years is the control of interest rates. Higher interest rates, by reducing the demand for money, effectively also reduce the supply. Nevertheless there are problems with this approach too. With an inelastic demand for loans, interest rates may have to rise to very high levels in order to bring the required reduction in monetary growth.

4. Controlling aggregate demand through controlling interest rates is made even more difficult as a result of *fluctuations* in the demand for money. These fluctuations are made more severe by speculation against changes in interest rates, exchange rates, the rate of inflation, etc.

5. Nevertheless, controlling interest rates is a way of responding rapidly to changing forecasts, and it can be an important signal to markets that inflation will be kept under control – especially when, as in the UK and the euro zone, there is a firm target for the rate of inflation.

Questions

1. How well could each of these fulfil the functions of money? Grain, strawberries, strawberry jam, gold, diamonds, luncheon vouchers, BP share certificates, a savings account requiring one month's notice of withdrawal.

2. What is meant by the terms 'narrow money' and 'broad money'? Does broad money fulfil all the functions of money?

3. Which, if any, of the following count as (broad) money? (a) A credit card. (b) A debit card. (c) A cheque book. (d) A bank deposit account pass book. (e) A building society pass book.

4. If a bank has a surplus of cash, why might it choose to make a market loan with it rather than giving extra personal loans or mortgages to its customers?

5. Why do banks hold a range of assets of varying degrees of liquidity and profitability?

6. If a bank buys a £50 000 Treasury bill at the start of its 91-day life for £48 000, at roughly what price could it sell it to another financial institution after 45 days? Why is it not possible to predict that precise price when the bill is first purchased?

7. Why should Bank of England intervention to influence rates of interest in the discount and repo markets also influence rates of interest in the parallel markets?

8. Would it be possible for an economy to function without a central bank?

9. Imagine that the banking system receives additional deposits of £100 million and that all the individual banks wish to retain their current liquidity ratio of 20 per cent.

   (a) How much of the £100 million will banks choose to lend out initially?
   (b) What will happen to banks' liabilities when the money that is lent out is spent and the recipients of it deposit it in their bank accounts?
   (c) How much of these latest deposits will be lent out by the banks?
   (d) By how much will total deposits (liabilities) eventually have risen, assuming that none of the additional liquidity is held outside the banking sector?

   (e) How much of these extra total deposits are matched by (i) liquid assets; (ii) illiquid assets?
   (f) What is the size of the bank multiplier?
   (g) If one-half of any additional liquidity is held outside the banking sector, by how much less will deposits have risen compared with (d) above?

10. If banks choose to operate a 20 per cent liquidity ratio and receive extra cash deposits of £10 million, assuming that the general public does not wish to hold a larger total amount of cash balances outside the banks:

    (a) How much credit will ultimately be created?
    (b) By how much will total deposits have expanded?
    (c) What is the size of the bank deposits multiplier?

11. Would the demand for securities be low if their price was high, but was expected to go on rising?

12. Why might the relationship between the demand for money and the rate of interest be an unstable one?

13. What effects will the following have on the equilibrium rate of interest? (You should consider which way the demand and/or supply curves of money shift.)

    (a) Banks find that they have a higher liquidity ratio than they need.
    (b) A rise in incomes.
    (c) A growing belief that interest rates will rise from their current level.

14. Trace through the effect of a fall in the supply of money on aggregate demand. What will determine the size of the effect?

15. If the government reduces the size of its public-sector deficit, why might the money supply nevertheless increase more rapidly?

16. If the government ran a public-sector surplus, could the money supply grow?

17. If the government borrows but does not spend the proceeds, what effect will this have on the money supply if it borrows from (a) the banking sector and (b) the non-bank private sector?

18. If the government buys back £1 million of maturing bonds from the general public and

then, keeping the total amount of its borrowing the same, raises £1 million by selling bills to banks, what will happen to the money supply?

19. Assume that a bank has the simplified balance sheet shown in the table below, and is operating at its desired liquidity ratio. Now assume that the central bank repurchases £5 million of government bonds on the open market. Assume that the people who sell the bonds all have their accounts with this bank.

    (a) Draw up the new balance sheet directly after the purchase of the bonds.
    (b) Now draw up the eventual balance sheet after all credit creation has taken place.
    (c) Would there be a similar effect if the central bank rediscounted £5 billion of bills?
    (d) How would such open-market operations affect the rate of interest?

20. What effect would a substantial increase in the sale of government bonds and bills have on interest rates?

21. Why would it be difficult for a central bank to predict the precise effect on money supply of open-market operations?

22. What are the mechanics whereby interest rates are raised?

23. Why does an unstable demand for money make it difficult to control the supply of money?

24. How does the Bank of England attempt to achieve the target rate of inflation of $2\frac{1}{2}$ per cent? What determines its likelihood of success in meeting the target?

Liabilities	£m	Assets	£m
Deposits	100	Balances with central bank	10
		Advances	90
	100		100

Additional case studies on the *Essentials of Economics* website (www.booksites.net/sloman)

9.1 The attributes of money. What makes something, such as metal, paper or electronic records, suitable as money?

9.2 From coins to bank deposit money. This case traces the evolution of modern money.

9.3 Are the days of cash numbered? Does the increased use of credit and debit cards and direct debits mean that cash will become obsolete?

9.4 Secondary marketing. This looks at one of the ways of increasing liquidity without sacrificing profitability. It involves selling an asset to someone else before the asset matures.

9.5 German banking. This case compares the tradition of German banks with that of UK retail banks. Although the banks have become more similar in recent years, German banks have a much closer relationship with industry.

9.6 Making money grow. A light-hearted illustration of the process of credit creation.

9.7 Goodhart's Law. An examination of the difficulty of controlling aggregate demand by setting targets for the money supply. We will explore Goodhart's Law in Section 10.6. It is also a key idea on page 390.

9.8 Central banking and monetary policy in the USA. This case examines how the Fed conducts monetary policy.

9.9 Monetary policy in the euro zone. This is a more detailed examination of the role of monetary policy and the ECB than that contained in Box 9.4.

9.10 Effective monetary policy versus banking efficiency and stability. This case examines potential conflicts between banking stability, efficiency and the effective operation of monetary policy.

9.11 Should central banks be independent of government? An examination of the arguments for and against independent central banks.

Sections of chapter covered in
WinEcon – Sloman, *Essentials of Economics*

Essentials of Economics section	*WinEcon* section
9.1	9.1
9.2	9.2
9.3	9.3
9.4	9.4
9.5	9.5
9.6	9.6
9.7	–

Websites relevant to this chapter

Numbers and sections refer to websites listed in the Web Appendix and hotlinked from this book's website at
www.booksites.net/sloman

- For news articles relevant to this chapter, see the *Economics News Articles* link from the book's website.

- For general news on money, banking and monetary policy, see websites in section A, and particularly A1–5, 7–9, 20–22, 25, 26, 31, 36. See also links to economic and financial news in A42.

- For monetary and financial data (including data for money supply and interest rates), see section F and particularly F2. Note that you can link to central banks worldwide from site F17. See also the links in B1 or 2.

- For monetary policy in the UK, see F1 and E30. For monetary policy in the euro zone, see F6 and 5. For monetary policy in the USA, see F8. For monetary policy in other countries, see the respective central bank site in section F.

- For links to sites on money and monetary policy, see the *Financial Economics* sections in I4, 7, 11, 17.

- For student resources relevant to this chapter, see sites C1–7, 9, 10, 12, 13, 19. See also '2nd floor – economic policy' in site D1.

CHAPTER MAP

CHAPTER TEN

Unemployment, inflation and growth

Now that we have looked at money and interest rates, we are in a position to give a more complete explanation of the relationship between inflation and unemployment, and how it varies with the course of the business cycle. We will also examine how the relationship differs between the short run and the long run. In doing so, we will see that consumer and business expectations play an absolutely key role.

Economists differ somewhat in their analysis of the relationship between inflation, unemployment and the business cycle. We will look at some of the different views: in particular, those of new classical and Keynesian economists. Despite these differences, there is still a large measure of agreement among most economists over these issues.

In the second half of the chapter, we focus on macroeconomic policy to tackle inflation and unemployment, and to achieve higher and more stable rates of economic growth. We will look at policies to control aggregate demand (fiscal and monetary policies) and policies to increase aggregate supply by making the economy more productive. In other words, we will look at both demand-side and supply-side policies.

We start, however, by linking back to the previous chapter and asking: what is the relationship between *money* and the economy? If money supply rises, does this lead to higher output, or does it just lead to higher prices? Is the answer to controlling inflation merely to restrict the growth of the money supply (by raising interest rates), or will doing so lead to a recession?

10.1 The link between money, expenditure, prices and output

Will a rise in money supply cause output and employment to rise, or will it simply cause prices to rise?

In the 1970s and 1980s, many economists were 'monetarists'. The most famous monetarist is Milton Friedman, who argues that inflation can be attributed entirely to increases in the money supply. The faster money supply expands, the higher will be the rate of inflation. New classical economists of today take a similar view. Excessive expansion of the money supply will lead simply to inflation. Keynesians, by contrast, see a much looser association between money and prices.

The debate can best be understood in terms of the quantity theory of money. The theory is simply that the level of prices in the economy depends on the quantity of money: the greater the supply of money, the higher will be the level of prices.

A development of the quantity theory is the *equation of exchange*. Focusing on this equation is the best way of understanding the debate over the relationship between money and prices.

The equation of exchange

The equation of exchange shows the relationship between national expenditure and national income. This identity may be expressed as follows:

$$MV = PY$$

M is the supply of money in the economy. V is its velocity of circulation. This is the number of times per year that money is spent on buying goods and services that have been produced in the economy that year (national output). P is the level of prices, expressed as an index, where the index is 1 in a chosen base year (e.g. 1990). Thus if prices today are double those in the base year, P is 2. Y is *real* national income (real GDP): in other words, the quantity of national output produced in that year measured in base-year prices.

PY is thus nominal national income: i.e. GDP measured at current prices (see the appendix to Chapter 7). For example, if national income at base-year prices is £40 billion and the price index is 2, then national income at current prices is £80 billion.

MV is the total spending on national output. For example, if money supply is £20 billion, and money, as it passes from one person to another, is spent on average four times a year on national output, then total spending (MV) is £80 billion a year. But this too *must* equal GDP at current prices. The reason is that what is spent on output (by consumers, by firms on investment, by the government or by people abroad on exports) must equal the value of goods produced (PY).

The equation of exchange (or 'quantity equation') is true by definition. MV is *necessarily* equal to PY because of the way the terms are defined. Thus a rise in MV *must* be accompanied by a rise in PY. What a change in M alone does to P alone, however, is a matter of debate. The controversy centres on whether and how V and

Definitions

Quantity theory of money
The price level (P) is directly related to the quantity of money in the economy (M).

Equation of exchange
$MV = PY$. The total level of spending on GDP (MV) equals the total value of goods and services produced (PY) that go to make up GDP.

Velocity of circulation
The number of times annually that money on average is spent on goods and services that made up GDP.

Pause for thought

If the money supply is cut by 10 per cent, what must happen to the velocity of circulation if there is no change in GDP at current prices?

Y are affected by changes in the money supply (M). The way in which a change in M affects V and Y will determine what happens to P.

How will a change in money supply affect aggregate demand? Assumptions about the velocity of circulation (V)

The short run

In the short run (up to about two years), V tends to vary inversely with M (i.e. as one rises, the other falls). A rise in money supply will lead to a fall in interest rates and an increased holding of money balances (see pages 350–1), and hence a fall in the average speed at which money circulates (V). A rise in money supply might, therefore, have only a limited effect on total spending (MV and PQ). The effect is also rather unpredictable.

To understand this, let us restate from the last chapter how an increase in money supply affects aggregate demand (see page 351 above):

1. A rise in money supply will lead to a fall in the rate of interest.
2. The fall in the rate of interest will lead to a rise in investment and other forms of borrowing. It will also lead to a fall in the exchange rate and hence a rise in exports and a fall in imports.
3. The rise in investment, and the rise in exports and fall in imports, will mean a rise in aggregate demand and a resulting rise in national income and output.

However, stages 1 and 2 are unreliable, and often weak.

Problems with stage 1: the money–interest rate link. The demand for money for assets purposes can be large and highly responsive to changes in interest rates on alternative assets. Indeed, large sums of money move around the money market as firms and financial institutions respond to and anticipate changes in interest rates. Thus, with an increase in money supply, only a relatively *small* fall in interest rates on bonds and other assets may be necessary to persuade people to hold all the extra money in bank accounts, thereby greatly slowing down the average speed at which money circulates. The fall in V may virtually offset the rise in M.

A more serious criticism is that the demand for money is *unstable*. People hold speculative balances of money when they anticipate that the prices of other assets, such as shares, bonds and bills, will fall (and hence the rate of return or interest on these assets will rise). There are many factors that could affect such expectations, such as changes in foreign interest rates, changes in exchange rates, statements of government intentions on economic policy, good or bad industrial news, or newly published figures on inflation or money supply. With an unstable demand for money, it is difficult to predict the effect on interest rates of a change in money supply.

Problems with stage 2: the interest rate–investment, exports and imports link. The problem here is that investment may be insensitive to changes in interest rates. Businesses are more likely to be influenced in their decision to invest by predictions of the future buoyancy of markets. Interest rates do have some effect on businesses' investment decisions, but the effect is unpredictable, depending on the confidence of investors. Where interest rates are likely to have a stronger effect on spending is via mortgages. If interest rates go up, and mortgage rates follow suit, people will suddenly be faced with higher monthly repayments and will therefore have to cut down their expenditure on goods and services.

Also the amount that the exchange rate will depreciate is uncertain, since exchange rate movements, as we shall see in Chapter 12, depend crucially on expectations about trade prospects and about future world interest rate movements. Thus the effects on imports and exports are also uncertain.

To summarise: the effects on total spending of a change in the money supply *might* be quite strong, but they could be weak. In other words, the effects are highly unpredictable.

$$M \uparrow \rightarrow V \downarrow (?) \rightarrow MV?$$

Keynesians use these arguments to criticise the use of monetary policy as a means of managing aggregate demand.

The long run

In the long run, there will be a stronger link between money supply and aggregate demand. In fact, monetarists claim that in the long run V is determined *totally independently* of the money supply (M). Thus an increase in M will leave V unaffected and hence will directly increase expenditure (MV):

$$M \uparrow \rightarrow M\bar{V} \uparrow$$

where the bar over the V term means that it is exogenously determined: i.e. determined *independently* of M. But why do they claim this?

If money supply increases over the longer term, people will have more money than they require to hold. They will spend this surplus. Much of this spending will go on goods and services, thereby directly increasing aggregate demand.

The theoretical underpinning for this is given by the *theory of portfolio balance*. People have a number of ways of holding their wealth. They can hold it as money, or as financial assets such as bills, bonds and shares, or as physical assets such as houses, cars and televisions. In other words, people hold a whole portfolio of assets of varying degrees of liquidity – from cash to central heating.

If money supply expands, people will find themselves holding more money than they require: their portfolios are 'unnecessarily liquid'. Some of this money will be used to purchase financial assets and some, possibly after a period of time, to purchase *goods and services*. As more assets are purchased, this will drive up their price. This will effectively reduce their 'yield'. For bonds and other *financial* assets, this means a reduction in their rate of interest. For goods and services, it means an increase in their price relative to their usefulness. The process will stop when a balance has been restored in people's portfolios. In the meantime, there will have been extra consumption and hence an increase in aggregate demand.

> **Definition**
>
> **Exogenous variable**
> A variable whose value is determined independently of the model of which it is part.

How will a change in aggregate demand affect output and prices? Assumptions about Y

If there is a rise in aggregate demand (i.e. in *MV*), what will be the result? Will there simply be a rise in prices (*P*)? This is the new classical and monetarist position (at

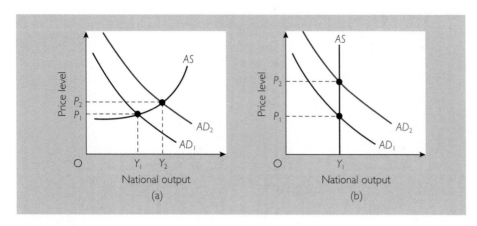

Figure 10.1
Different aggregate supply curves

least in the long run). Or might it also (or even solely) result in a rise in national output (Y)? This is the Keynesian position. The argument here can best be understood in terms of the nature of the aggregate supply (AS) curve. We will start with the short-run AS curve and then look at the long-run curve.

The short-run aggregate supply curve

Most economists argue that aggregate supply is relatively elastic in the short run, except when full employment is approached (see Figure 10.1(a)). In other words, national output (Y) (i.e. real GDP) is variable with respect to changes in aggregate demand. A rise in nominal aggregate demand (i.e. a rise in MV) will lead to a rise in Y. Conversely, a policy of restricting aggregate demand is likely to reduce Y as well as P, especially when there is resistance from monopolistic firms and unions to price and wage cuts. The result will be a rise in unemployment.

There are two main reasons why the AS curve is relatively elastic in the short run.

'Stickiness' of wages and prices.   Wage rates are frequently determined by a process of collective bargaining and, once agreed, will typically be set for a whole year, if not two. Even if they are not determined by collective bargaining, wage rates often change relatively infrequently. So too with prices: except in perfect, or near perfect markets (such as commodity markets, or the markets for fresh fruit and vegetables), or at sale times or when there are special offers, firms tend to change their prices relatively infrequently. They do not immediately raise them when there is an increase in demand or lower them when demand falls. Thus there is a stickiness in both wage rates and prices.

When, therefore, there is an increase in aggregate demand, firms' marginal cost curves are unlikely to shift upwards (as they would do if wage rates rose or input prices rose). It will thus be profitable for them to produce more in response to the rise in demand. This is illustrated in Figure 10.2, where the AR and MR curves have shifted to the right (to AR_2 and MR_2). Thus the profit-maximising position, where the MC and new MR curves intersect, is now at the higher level of output, Q_2. Conversely, a decline in aggregate demand, and hence a leftward shift in firms' AR and MR curves, will lead to a fall in the profit-maximising level of output and employment.

Figure 10.2

Short-run response of a profit-maximising firm to a rise in demand

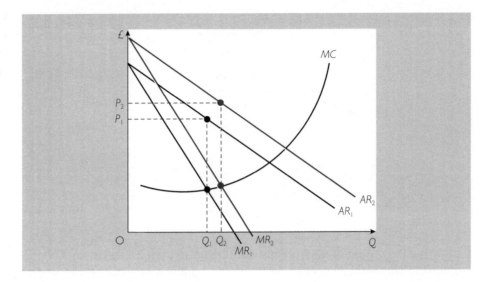

Confidence.   A rise in aggregate demand may encourage firms to produce more in the confidence that they will sell the higher output. A fall in aggregate demand, however, may lead to a decline in confidence. Rather than continuing with current levels of production in the hope that demand will pick up, firms may reduce output and lay off workers.

The long-run aggregate supply curve

Some, indeed many, economists argue that the long-run *AS* curve is *vertical*, as in Figure 10.1(b). New classical and monetarist economists, and some moderate Keynesian economists (the 'new Keynesians') take this position. Any rise in nominal aggregate demand (*MV*) would lead simply to a rise in prices and no long-term increase in output at all. Long-term increases in output could occur only through rightward shifts in this vertical *AS* curve. To achieve this, governments should focus on supply-side policy.

But why do these economists argue that the curve is vertical? They justify this by focusing on the *interdependence of markets*. A rise in aggregate demand will initially lead firms to raise both prices and output, for the reasons we gave above: the short-run aggregate supply curve is upward sloping. There is a movement from point *a* to point *b* in Figure 10.3. However, as raw material and intermediate goods producers raise their prices, so this will raise the costs of production further up the line. A rise in the price of steel will raise the costs of producing cars and washing machines. At the same time, workers, seeing the prices of goods rising, will demand higher wages. Firms will be relatively willing to grant these wage demands, given that they are experiencing a buoyant demand from their customers.

The effect of all this is to raise firms' *costs*, and hence their prices. As prices rise for any given level of output, so the short-run *AS* curve will shift upward. This is shown by a move to $AS_{1(short\ run)}$ in Figure 10.3. The economy moves from point *b* to point *c*.

The long-run effect, therefore, of a rise in aggregate demand from *AD* to AD_1 is a movement from point *a* to point *c*. The long-run aggregate supply curve passes through these two points. It is vertical. A rise in aggregate demand will therefore

Key Idea 7 p41

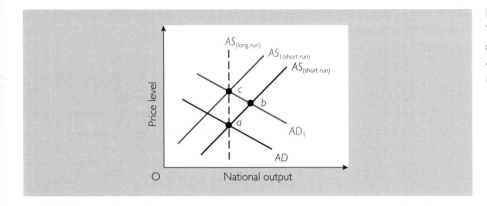

Figure 10.3
The long-run
aggregate supply
curve when firms are
interdependent

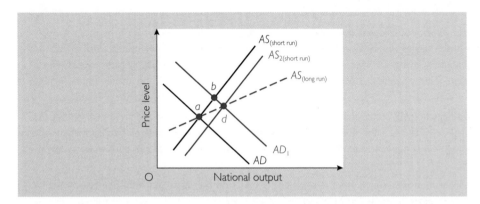

Figure 10.4
Effect of investment
on the long-run
aggregate supply
curve

have no long-run effect on output. The entire effect will be felt in terms of higher prices.

New classical economists go one step further. They assume that markets are very flexible, and that therefore the effects of higher costs will be passed through into higher prices virtually instantly. What is more, firms will anticipate this and hence take it into account *now*. For them, therefore, the *short*-run aggregate supply curve is vertical also.

Some economists, including many Keynesians, argue that the long-run *AS* curve is upward sloping, not vertical. Indeed, it may be even shallower than the short-run curve. The argument hinges on the role of *investment*. With a rise in demand, firms may be encouraged to invest in new plant and machinery (the accelerator effect). In so doing they may well be able to increase output significantly in the long run with little or no increase in their prices. Their long-run *MC* curves are much flatter than their short-run *MC* curves.

In Figure 10.4 the short-run *AS* curve shifts to the right. Equilibrium moves from point *a* to *b* to *d*. In this case, the long-run *AS* curve joining points *a* and *d* is more elastic than the short-run curve. There is a relatively large increase in output and a relatively small increase in price.

The long-run *AS* curve will be flatter still and possibly even downward sloping if the investment involves the introduction of new cost-reducing technology. It will be

> **Pause for thought** ⅢⅢ
>
> *If a shift in the aggregate demand curve from AD to AD₁ in Figure 10.4 causes a movement from point a to point d in the long run, will a shift in the aggregate demand curve from AD₁ to AD cause a movement from point d back to point a in the long run?*

steeper if the extra investment causes significant shortages of materials, machinery or labour. This is more likely when the economy is already operating near its full potential.

One very important element in the analysis of aggregate supply, inflation and unemployment is the role of *expectations*. In order to see the effect of expectations on both inflation *and* unemployment, the analysis is best conducted in terms of the Phillips curve (see page 303 above). We do this in the next section.

Key
Idea
10
p68

Recap

1. The quantity equation $MV = PY$ can be used to analyse the possible relationships between money and prices.

2. In the short run, the velocity of circulation (V) may vary inversely, but unpredictably, with the money supply (M). The reason is that changes in money supply will have unpredictable and possibly rather weak effects on interest rates, and similarly changes in interest rates will have unpredictable and probably rather weak effects on aggregate demand. Thus spending (MV) will change by possibly only a small and rather unpredictable amount.

3. If nominal aggregate demand (MV) does change, then in the short run it is likely to affect national output (Y) according to the degree of slack in the economy. The aggregate supply curve tends to be relatively elastic (except as full employment is approached). This is because both wage rates and prices tend to be relatively sticky.

4 In the long run, changes in money supply have a more direct effect on aggregate demand. The reason is that that if people have an increase in money in their portfolios, they will attempt to restore portfolio balance by purchasing assets, including goods. Thus the velocity of circulation (V) does not vary substantially with change in money supply.

5. In the long run, according to many economists, the aggregate supply curve is vertical because price increases from any rise in aggregate demand tend to be passed on from one firm to another and feed into wage increases. If, however, a sustained increase in demand leads to increased investment, this can have the effect of shifting the short-run aggregate supply curve to the right and making the long-run curve upward sloping, not vertical.

10.2 The relationship between inflation and unemployment: introducing expectations

What happens when people come to expect inflation?

A major contribution to the theory of unemployment and inflation was made by Milton Friedman and others in the late 1960s. They incorporated people's expectations about the future level of prices into the Phillips curve (see pages 303–5 for a reminder about the Phillips curve). This can then be used to derive a *vertical* long-run Phillips curve. In other words, it can be used to explain the contention by many economists that there is *no* trade-off between inflation and unemployment in the long run, and that therefore government policy to expand aggregate demand will not create more jobs (except perhaps in the very short term).

This theory of the vertical long-run Phillips curve is known as the *accelerationist theory*.

The expectations–augmented Phillips curve

In its simplest form, the expectations-augmented Phillips curve is given by the following:

$$\dot{P} = f(1/U) + \dot{P}^e$$

What this states is that inflation ($\dot{P}$) depends on two things:

- The inverse of unemployment ($1/U$). This is simply the normal Phillips curve relationship. The higher the rate of (demand-deficient) unemployment, the lower the rate of inflation.
- The expected rate of inflation ($\dot{P}^e$). The higher the rate of inflation that people expect, the higher will be the level of wage demands and the more willing will firms be to raise prices. Thus the higher will be the actual rate of inflation and thus the vertically higher will be the whole Phillips curve.

Let us assume, for simplicity, that the rate of inflation people expect this year ($\dot{P}^e_t$) (where t represents the current time period: i.e. this year) is the same rate that inflation actually was last year ($\dot{P}_{t-1}$).

$$\dot{P}^e_t = \dot{P}_{t-1}$$

Thus if unemployment is such as to push up prices by 4 per cent ($f(1/U) = 4\%$) and if last year's inflation was 6 per cent, then inflation this year will be 4 per cent + 6 per cent = 10 per cent.

The accelerationist theory

Let us trace the course of inflation and expectations over a number of years in an imaginary economy. To keep the analysis simple, assume there is no growth in the economy.

Year 1.   Assume that at the outset, in year 1, there is no inflation at all; that none is expected; that $AD = AS$; and that equilibrium unemployment is 8 per cent. The economy will be at point *a* in Figure 10.5 and Table 10.1.

Year 2.   Now assume that the government expands aggregate demand in order to reduce unemployment. Unemployment falls to 6 per cent. The economy moves to point *b* along curve I. Inflation has risen to 4 per cent, but people, basing their expectations of inflation on year 1, still expect zero inflation. There is therefore no shift as yet in the Phillips curve. Curve I corresponds to an expected rate of inflation of zero.

Year 3.   People now revise their expectations of inflation to the level of year 2. The Phillips curve shifts up by 4 percentage points to position II. If *nominal* aggregate demand (i.e. demand purely in money terms, irrespective of the level of prices) continues to rise at the same rate, the whole of the increase will now be absorbed in higher prices. *Real* aggregate demand (i.e. in terms of what it can buy) will fall back to its previous level and the economy will move to point *c*. Unemployment will

Key Idea

10
p68

Figure 10.5

The accelerationist theory of inflation and inflationary expectations

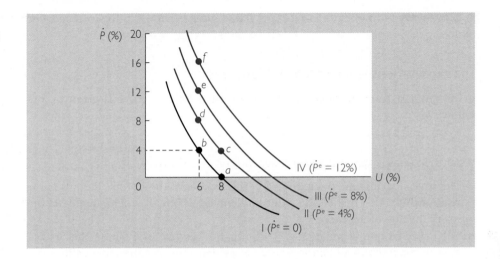

Table 10.1

The accelerationist theory of inflation and inflationary expectations

Year	Point on graph	$\dot{P}$	=	$f(1/U)$	+	$\dot{P}^e$
1	a	0	=	0	+	0
2	b	4	=	4	+	0
3	c	4	=	0	+	4
4	d	8	=	4	+	4
5	e	12	=	4	+	8
6	f	16	=	4	+	12

return to 8 per cent. There is no *demand-pull* inflation now, ($f(1/U) = 0$), but inflation is still 4 per cent due to expectations, ($\dot{P}^e = 4\%$).

Year 4. Assume now that the government expands *real* aggregate demand again so as to reduce unemployment once more to 6 per cent. This time it must expand *nominal* aggregate demand *more* than it did in year 2, because this time, as well as reducing unemployment, it also has to validate the 4 per cent expected inflation. The economy moves to point *d* along curve II. Inflation is now 8 per cent.

Year 5. *Expected* inflation is now 8 per cent (the level of actual inflation in year 4). The Phillips curve shifts up to position III. If at the same time the government tries to keep unemployment at 6 per cent, it must expand nominal aggregate demand 4 per cent faster in order to validate the 8 per cent expected inflation. The economy moves to point *e* along curve III. Inflation is now 12 per cent.

Year 6 onwards. To keep unemployment at 6 per cent, the government must continue to increase nominal aggregate demand by 4 per cent more than the previous year. As the expected inflation rate goes on rising, the Phillips curve will go on shifting up each year.

Definition

Accelerationist theory
The theory that unemployment can only be reduced below the natural rate at the cost of accelerating inflation.

Thus in order to keep unemployment below the initial equilibrium rate, inflation must go on *accelerating* each year. For this reason, this theory of the Phillips curve is sometimes known as the accelerationist theory.

Pause for thought

What determines how rapidly the short-run Phillips curves in Figure 10.5 shift upwards?

This theory of the vertical long-run Phillips curve is known as the *accelerationist theory*.

The expectations–augmented Phillips curve

In its simplest form, the expectations-augmented Phillips curve is given by the following:

$$\dot{P} = f(1/U) + \dot{P}^\text{e}$$

What this states is that inflation ($\dot{P}$) depends on two things:

Definition

Expectations-augmented Phillips curve
A (short-run) Phillips curve whose position depends on the expected rate of inflation.

■ The inverse of unemployment ($1/U$). This is simply the normal Phillips curve relationship. The higher the rate of (demand-deficient) unemployment, the lower the rate of inflation.

■ The expected rate of inflation ($\dot{P}^\text{e}$). The higher the rate of inflation that people expect, the higher will be the level of wage demands and the more willing will firms be to raise prices. Thus the higher will be the actual rate of inflation and thus the vertically higher will be the whole Phillips curve.

Let us assume, for simplicity, that the rate of inflation people expect this year ($\dot{P}_t^\text{e}$) (where t represents the current time period: i.e. this year) is the same rate that inflation actually was last year ($\dot{P}_{t-1}$).

$$\dot{P}_t^\text{e} = \dot{P}_{t-1}$$

Thus if unemployment is such as to push up prices by 4 per cent ($f(1/U) = 4\%$) and if last year's inflation was 6 per cent, then inflation this year will be 4 per cent + 6 per cent = 10 per cent.

The accelerationist theory

Let us trace the course of inflation and expectations over a number of years in an imaginary economy. To keep the analysis simple, assume there is no growth in the economy.

Year 1.   Assume that at the outset, in year 1, there is no inflation at all; that none is expected; that $AD = AS$; and that equilibrium unemployment is 8 per cent. The economy will be at point *a* in Figure 10.5 and Table 10.1.

Year 2.   Now assume that the government expands aggregate demand in order to reduce unemployment. Unemployment falls to 6 per cent. The economy moves to point *b* along curve I. Inflation has risen to 4 per cent, but people, basing their expectations of inflation on year 1, still expect zero inflation. There is therefore no shift as yet in the Phillips curve. Curve I corresponds to an expected rate of inflation of zero.

Year 3.   People now revise their expectations of inflation to the level of year 2. The Phillips curve shifts up by 4 percentage points to position II. If *nominal* aggregate demand (i.e. demand purely in money terms, irrespective of the level of prices) continues to rise at the same rate, the whole of the increase will now be absorbed in higher prices. *Real* aggregate demand (i.e. in terms of what it can buy) will fall back to its previous level and the economy will move to point *c*. Unemployment will

Figure 10.5
The accelerationist theory of inflation and inflationary expectations

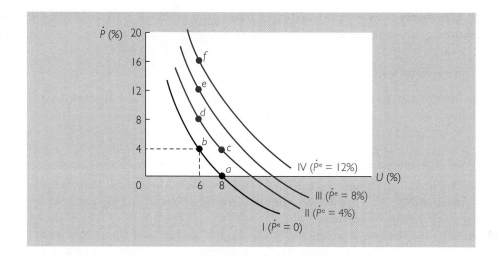

Table 10.1
The accelerationist theory of inflation and inflationary expectations

Year	Point on graph	$\dot{P}$	=	$f(1/U)$	+	$\dot{P}^e$
1	a	0	=	0	+	0
2	b	4	=	4	+	0
3	c	4	=	0	+	4
4	d	8	=	4	+	4
5	e	12	=	4	+	8
6	f	16	=	4	+	12

return to 8 per cent. There is no *demand-pull* inflation now, $(f(1/U) = 0)$, but inflation is still 4 per cent due to expectations, $(\dot{P}^e = 4\%)$.

Year 4. Assume now that the government expands *real* aggregate demand again so as to reduce unemployment once more to 6 per cent. This time it must expand *nominal* aggregate demand *more* than it did in year 2, because this time, as well as reducing unemployment, it also has to validate the 4 per cent expected inflation. The economy moves to point *d* along curve II. Inflation is now 8 per cent.

Year 5. *Expected* inflation is now 8 per cent (the level of actual inflation in year 4). The Phillips curve shifts up to position III. If at the same time the government tries to keep unemployment at 6 per cent, it must expand nominal aggregate demand 4 per cent faster in order to validate the 8 per cent expected inflation. The economy moves to point *e* along curve III. Inflation is now 12 per cent.

Year 6 onwards. To keep unemployment at 6 per cent, the government must continue to increase nominal aggregate demand by 4 per cent more than the previous year. As the expected inflation rate goes on rising, the Phillips curve will go on shifting up each year.

Thus in order to keep unemployment below the initial equilibrium rate, inflation must go on *accelerating* each year. For this reason, this theory of the Phillips curve is sometimes known as the accelerationist theory.

Definition

Accelerationist theory
The theory that unemployment can only be reduced below the natural rate at the cost of accelerating inflation.

Pause for thought

What determines how rapidly the short-run Phillips curves in Figure 10.5 shift upwards?

Box 10.1 Exploring Economics

The political business cycle

The art of looping the loop

The accelerationist theory can be used to analyse the so-called political business cycle. This is where governments manipulate aggregate demand so that, by the time of the next general election, the economy will be growing nicely, with falling unemployment, but with inflation still relatively low.

Imagine that a politically naïve government has been fulfilling election promises to cure unemployment, cut taxes and increase welfare spending. In the diagram, this is shown by a move from point *a* to *b* to *c*.

To its dismay, by the time the next election comes, inflation is accelerating and unemployment is rising again. The economy is moving from point *d* to *e* to *f*. You would hardly be surprised to learn that it loses the election!

But now suppose a much more politically adroit government is elected. What does it do? The answer is that it does politically unpopular things first, so that before the next election it can do nice things and curry favour with the electorate.

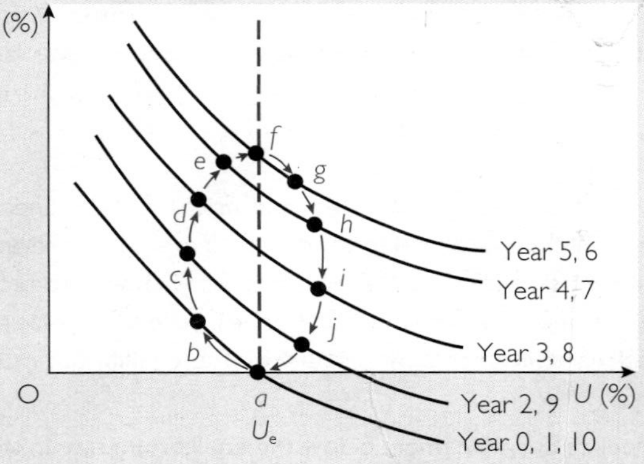

$\dot{P}$ (%)
O
e
f
g
d
h
c
i
j
b
a
U_e
U (%)
Year 5, 6
Year 4, 7
Year 3, 8
Year 2, 9
Year 0, 1, 10

Clockwise Phillips loops

The first thing it does is to have a tough Budget and to raise interest rates. 'We are having to clear up the economic mess left by the last government.' It thus engineers a recession and begins to squeeze down inflationary expectations. The economy moves from point *f* to *g* to *h*. In the meantime, unemployment has risen above the equilibrium rate (U_e).

But people have very short memories (despite opposition attempts to remind them). After a couple of years of misery, the government announces that the economy has 'begun to turn the corner'. Things are looking up. Inflation has fallen and unemployment has stopped rising. The economy has moved from point *h* to *i* to *j*.

'Thanks to prudent management of the economy,' claims the Chancellor, 'I am now in a position to reduce taxes and to allow modest increases in government expenditure.' Unemployment falls rapidly; the economy grows rapidly; the economy moves from point *j* to *a* to *b*.

The government's popularity soars; the pre-election 'give-away' Budget is swallowed by the electorate, who trustingly believe that similar ones will follow if the government is returned to office. The government wins the election.

Then comes the nasty medicine again. But who will be blamed this time?

?

1. Why might a government sometimes 'get it wrong' and find itself at the wrong part of the Phillips 'loop' at the time of an election?
2. Has the political business cycle become impossible in the UK, given the independence of the Bank of England and the Chancellor's 'golden rule' of fiscal policy?

The more the government reduces unemployment, the greater the rise in inflation that year, and the more the rise in expectations the following year and each subsequent year; and hence the more rapidly will price rises accelerate. Thus the true longer-term trade-off is between unemployment and the rate of *increase* in inflation.

The long-run Phillips curve and the equilibrium rate of unemployment

As long as there are demand-pull pressures ($f(1/U) > 0$), inflation will accelerate as the expected rate of inflation ($\dot{P}^e$) rises. In the long run, therefore, the Phillips curve will be vertical at the rate of unemployment where *real* aggregate demand equals *real* aggregate supply. This is the *equilibrium* rate of unemployment (see page 268). Monetarists refer to it as the natural rate (U_n). It sometimes also known as the non-accelerating-inflation rate of unemployment (NAIRU). In Figure 10.5 the equilibrium rate of unemployment is 8 per cent.

The implication for government policy is that expansionary monetary and fiscal policy can only reduce unemployment below the equilibrium rate in the *short run*. In the long run, the effect will be purely inflationary. On the other hand, a policy of restraining the growth in the money supply will *not* in the long run lead to higher unemployment: it will simply lead to lower inflation at the equilibrium rate of unemployment. The implication is that governments should make it a priority to control money supply and thereby nominal aggregate demand and inflation.

Definition

Natural rate of unemployment or non-accelerating-inflation rate of unemployment (NAIRU)
The rate of unemployment consistent with a constant rate of inflation: the rate of unemployment at which the vertical long-run Phillips curve cuts the horizontal axis.

Recap

1. Expectations can be incorporated into the analysis of the Phillips curve. The effect is to give a vertical long-run curve at the equilibrium rate of unemployment.

2. The simplest analysis of expectations is that the expected rate of inflation this year is what it actually was last year:

$$\dot{P}_t^e = \dot{P}_{t-1}$$

3. If there is excess demand in the economy, producing upward pressure on wages and prices, initially unemployment will fall. The reason is that workers and firms will believe that wage and price increases represent *real* wage and price increases. Thus workers are prepared to take jobs more readily and firms choose to produce more. But as people's expectations adapt upwards to these higher wages and prices, so ever-increasing rises in nominal aggregate demand will be necessary to maintain unemployment below the equilibrium rate. Price and wage rises will accelerate: i.e. inflation will rise.

4. Thus a policy of expanding aggregate demand can only reduce unemployment below the equilibrium rate in the short run. On the other hand, according to the theory, a policy of restraining the growth in the money supply in order to reduce inflation will not lead to unemployment higher than the equilibrium rate in the long run.

10.3

The relationship between inflation and unemployment: new classical views

Can expanding aggregate demand have any effect on output and employment at all?

New classical economists go further than the monetarist theory described above. They argue that even the short-run Phillips curve is vertical: that there is *no* trade-off between unemployment and inflation, even in the short run. They base their arguments on two key assumptions:

- Prices and wage rates are flexible and thus markets clear very rapidly. This means that there will be no disequilibrium unemployment. All unemployment will be equilibrium unemployment, or 'voluntary unemployment' as new classical economists prefer to call it.
- Expectations are 'rational', but are based on imperfect information.

Rational expectations

Key Idea 10 p68

In the accelerationist theory, expectations are based on *past* information and thus take a time to catch up with changes in aggregate demand. Thus for a short time a rise in nominal aggregate demand will raise output, and reduce unemployment below the equilibrium level, while prices and wages are still relatively low.

The new classical analysis is based on rational expectations. Rational expectations are not based on past rates of inflation. Instead they are based on the current state of the economy and the current policies being pursued by the government. Workers and firms look at the information available to them – at the various forecasts that are published, at various economic indicators and the assessments of them by various commentators, at government pronouncements, and so on. From this information they predict the rate of inflation as well as they can. It is in this sense that the expectations are 'rational': people use their reason to assess the future on the basis of current information.

But forecasters frequently get it wrong, and so do economic commentators! And the government does not always do what it says it will. Thus workers and firms will be basing expectations on *imperfect information*. The crucial point about the rational expectations theory, however, is that these errors in prediction are *random*. People's predictions of inflation are just as likely to be too high as too low.

If the government raises aggregate demand in an attempt to reduce unemployment, people will anticipate that this will lead to higher prices and wages, and that there will be *no* effect on output and employment. If their expectations of higher inflation are correct, this will *fully* absorb the increase in nominal aggregate demand, such that there will have been no increase in *real* aggregate demand at all. Firms will not produce any more output or employ any more people: after all, why should they? If they anticipate that people will spend 10 per cent more money, but that prices will rise by 10 per cent, their *volume* of sales will remain the same.

Output and employment will only rise, therefore, if people make an error in their predictions (i.e. if they underpredict the rate of inflation and interpret an increase in money spent as an increase in *real* demand). But they are as likely to

> ### Definition
>
> **Rational expectations** Expectations based on the *current* situation. These expectations are based on the information people have to hand. While this information may be imperfect and therefore people will make errors, these errors will be random.

*over*predict the rate of inflation, in which case output and employment will fall! Thus there is no systematic trade-off between inflation and unemployment, even in the short run.

Real business cycles

If unemployment and output fluctuate only *randomly* from the natural level, and then only in the short run, how can the new classical economists explain booms and recessions? How can they explain the business cycle? Their answer, unlike Keynesians, lies not in fluctuations in aggregate demand, but rather in shifts in aggregate *supply*. In a recession, the vertical short- and long-run aggregate supply curves will shift to the left (output falls) and the vertical short- and long-run Phillips curves will shift to the right (unemployment rises). The reverse happens in a boom. Since the new classical theory of cyclical fluctuations focuses on supply, it is known as real business cycle theory.

But what makes aggregate supply shift in the first place, and why, after an initial shift, will the aggregate supply curve *go on* shifting, causing a recession or boom to continue?

The initial shift in aggregate supply could come from a structural change: say, a shift in demand from older manufacturing industries to new service industries. Because of the immobility of labour, not all those laid off in the older industries will find work in the new industries. Structural unemployment (part of equilibrium unemployment) rises and output falls.

Alternatively, the initial shift in aggregate supply could come from a change in technology. For example, a technological breakthrough in telecommunications could shift aggregate supply to the right. Or it could come from an oil price increase, shifting aggregate supply to the left.

But why, when a shift occurs, does the effect persist? Why is there not a single rise or fall in aggregate supply? There are two main reasons. The first is that several changes may take months to complete. For example, a decline in demand for certain older industries, perhaps caused by growing competition from abroad, does not take place overnight. Likewise, a technological breakthrough does not affect all industries simultaneously.

The second reason is that these changes affect the profitability of investment. If investment rises, this will increase firms' capacity and aggregate supply will shift to the right. If investment falls (as a result, say, of the election of a government less sympathetic to industry), aggregate supply will shift to the left. In other words, investment is causing changes in output not through its effect on aggregate *demand* (through the multiplier), but rather through its effect on aggregate *supply*.

So far we have seen how the theory of real business cycles explains persistent rises or falls in aggregate supply. But how does it explain *turning points*? Why do recessions and booms come to an end? The most likely explanation is that, once a shock has worked its way through, aggregate supply will stop shifting. If there is then any shock in the other direction, aggregate supply will start moving back again. For example, after a period of recession, an eventual rise in business confidence will cause investment to rise and hence aggregate supply to shift back to the right. Since these 'reverse shocks' are likely to occur at irregular intervals, they can help to explain why real-world business cycles are themselves irregular.

Definition

Real business cycle theory The new classical theory which explains cyclical fluctuations in terms of shifts in aggregate supply, rather than aggregate demand.

Recap

1. The new classical theory assumes flexible prices and wages in the short run as well as in the long run. It also assumes that people base their expectations of inflation on a rational assessment of the *current* situation.

2. People may predict wrongly, but they are equally likely to underpredict or to overpredict. On average over the years they will predict correctly.

3. The rational expectations theory implies that not only the long-run but also the short-run AS and Phillips curves will be vertical. If people correctly predict the rate of inflation, they will correctly predict that any increase in nominal aggregate demand will simply be reflected in higher prices. Total output and employment will remain the same: at the equilibrium level.

4. With a vertical aggregate supply curve, cyclical fluctuations must arise from shifts in aggregate supply, not shifts in aggregate demand. Real business cycle theory thus focuses on aggregate supply shocks, which then persist for a period of time. Eventually their effect will peter out, and supply shocks in the other direction can lead to turning points in the cycle.

The relationship between inflation and unemployment: Keynesian views   10.4

What will be the effect of expanding demand on business confidence and investment?

Keynesians today accept that the original analysis of the Phillips curve was an over-simplification and that expectations have to be taken into account. Nevertheless, Keynesians still maintain that output and employment depend on the level of aggregate demand, and that *excessive* expansion of aggregate demand will lead to inflation: in other words, that there is a trade-off between inflation and unemployment, even in the long run.

How is it then that both inflation *and* unemployment were generally worse in the 1970s, 1980s and early 1990s than in the 1950s, 1960s, late 1990s and early 2000s? Keynesians argue that there still is a Phillips curve, but that it has shifted: first to the right, then back to the left. They give a number of explanations for this.

Changes in equilibrium unemployment

Structural unemployment

Most Keynesians include growth in equilibrium unemployment (NAIRU) as part of the explanation of a rightward shift in the Phillips curve in the 1970s and 1980s. In particular, Keynesians highlight the considerable structural rigidities in the economy in a period of rapid industrial change. The changes included the following:

■ Dramatic changes in technology. The microchip revolution, for example, had led to many traditional jobs becoming obsolete.

- Competition from abroad. The introduction of new products from abroad, often of superior quality to domestic goods, or produced at lower costs, had led to the decline of many older industries: e.g. the textile industry.
- Shifts in demand away from the products of older labour-intensive industries to new 'high-tech' capital-intensive products.

Keynesians argue that the free market simply could not cope with these changes without a large rise in structural/technological unemployment. Labour is not sufficiently mobile – either geographically or occupationally – to move to industries where there are labour shortages or into jobs where there are skill shortages. A particular problem here is the lack of investment in education and training, with the result that the labour force is not sufficiently flexible to respond to changes in demand for labour.

Hysteresis

If a recession causes a rise in unemployment which is not then fully reversed when the economy recovers, there is a problem of hysteresis. This term, used in physics, refers to the lagging or persistence of an effect, even when the initial cause has been removed. In our context it refers to the persistence of unemployment even when the initial demand deficiency no longer exists.

The recessions of the early 1980s and early 1990s created a growing number of people who were both deskilled and demotivated. Many in their forties and fifties who had lost their jobs were seen as too old by prospective employers. Many young people, unable to obtain jobs, became resigned to 'life on social security' or to doing no more than casual work. What is more, many firms, in an attempt to cut costs, cut down on training programmes. In these circumstances, a rise in aggregate demand will not simply enable the long-term unemployed to be employed again. The effect was a rightward shift in the Phillips curve: a rise in the NAIRU. To reverse this, argue Keynesians, the government should embark on a radical programme of retraining.

Recessions also cause a lack of investment. The reduction in their capital stock means that many firms cannot respond to a recovery in demand by making significant increases in output and taking on many more workers. Instead they are more likely to raise prices. Unemployment may thus fall only modestly and yet inflation may rise substantially. The NAIRU has increased: the Phillips curve has shifted to the right.

If the economy achieves sustained expansion, with no recession, as occurred after 1992, then gradually these effects can be reversed. In other words, the hysteresis is not permanent. As firms increase their investment, the capital stock will expand; firms will engage in more training; the number of long-term unemployed will fall. The Phillips curve will shift back to the left again and the NAIRU will fall.

The persistence of demand–deficient unemployment

If there is demand-deficient unemployment, why will there not be a long-run fall in real wage rates so as eliminate the surplus labour (see Figure 7.5 on page 268)?

Keynesians give two major explanations for the persistence of real wage rates above equilibrium.

Efficiency wages

The argument here is that wage rates fulfil two functions. The first is the traditional one of balancing the demand and supply of labour. To this Keynesians add the function of motivating workers. If real wage rates are reduced when there is a surplus of labour (demand-deficient unemployment), then those workers already in employment may become dispirited and work less hard. If, on the other hand, firms keep wage rates up, then by maintaining a well-motivated workforce, by cutting down on labour turnover and by finding it easier to attract well-qualified labour, firms may find their costs are reduced: a higher real wage is thus more profitable for them. The maximum-profit real wage rate (the efficiency wage rate) is likely to be above the market-clearing real wage rate (see page 179). Demand-deficient unemployment is likely to persist.

Insider power

If those still in employment (the insiders) are members of unions while those out of work (the outsiders) are not, or if the insiders have special skills or knowledge that give them bargaining power with employers while the outsiders have no influence, then there is no mechanism whereby the surplus labour – the outsiders – can drive down the real wage rate and eliminate the demand-deficient unemployment.

These two features help to explain why real wage rates did not fall during the recessions of the early 1980s and early 1990s.

> **Definition**
>
> **Efficiency wage rate**
> The profit-maximising wage rate for the firm after taking into account the effects of wage rates on worker motivation, turnover and recruitment.

The incorporation of expectations

Keynesians criticise the monetarist/new classical approach of focusing exclusively on price expectations. Expectations, argue Keynesians, influence *output* and *employment* decisions, not just pricing decisions.

Unless the economy is at full employment or very close to it, Keynesians argue that an expansion of demand *will* lead to an increase in output and employment, even in the long run after expectations have fully adjusted. If there is a gradual but sustained expansion of aggregate demand, firms, seeing the economy expanding and seeing their orders growing, will start to invest more and make longer-term plans for expanding their labour force. People will generally *expect* a higher level of output, and this optimism will cause that higher level of output to be produced. In other words, expectations will affect output and employment as well as prices.

Graphically, the increased output and employment from the recovery in investment will shift the *AS* curve to the right and the Phillips curve to the left, offsetting (partially, wholly or more than wholly) the upward shift from higher inflationary expectations.

The lesson here for governments is that a sustained, but moderate, increase in aggregate demand can lead to a sustained growth in aggregate supply. What should be avoided is an excessive and unsustainable expansion of aggregate demand, as occurred in the late 1980s. This will lead to a boom, only to be followed by a 'bust' and a consequent recession.

The Keynesian criticism of non-intervention

Keynesians are therefore highly critical of the monetarist/new classical conclusion that governments should not intervene other than to restrain the growth of money supply. High unemployment may persist for many years and become deeply entrenched in the economy without a deliberate government policy of creating a steady expansion of aggregate demand.

Ke
Ide
8
p4£

Pause for thought

Why is it important in the Keynesian analysis for there to be a steady expansion of aggregate demand?

Recap

1. Modern Keynesians argue that the Phillips curve shifted to the right in the 1970s and 1980s, but more recently has shifted back to the left. They give various reasons for this.

2. There was a growth in equilibrium unemployment. This was the result of rapid changes in technology, greater competition from abroad and more rapid changes in demand patterns. It was also the result of the persistence of unemployment beyond the recessions of the early 1980s and early 1990s, because of a deskilling of labour during the recessions (an example of hysteresis).

3. Demand-deficient unemployment may persist because real wage rates may be sticky downwards, even into the longer term. This stickiness may be the result of efficiency real wage rates being above market-clearing real wage rates and/or outsiders not being able to influence wage bargains struck between employers and insiders.

4. If people expect a rise in aggregate demand to be sustained, firms will invest more, thereby reducing unemployment in the long run and not just increasing the rate of inflation. The (short-run) Phillips curve will shift to the left.

5. Keynesians argue that it is important for governments to ensure that there is a sufficient level of aggregate demand.

10.5   Common ground between economists?

Is there an emerging macroeconomic consensus?

We have seen that there is some disagreement between economists over the nature of the aggregate supply and Phillips curves, and hence over the effects of changes in aggregate demand. Nevertheless, there is quite a lot of common ground between the majority of economists over many of the issues we have examined so far in this chapter. Here are three major areas of agreement.

In the short run, changes in aggregate demand will have a major effect on output and employment

With the exception of extreme new classical economists, who argue that markets clear instantly and that expectations are formed rationally, all other economists would accept that the short-run aggregate supply curve is upward sloping, albeit getting steeper as potential output is approached. Similarly they would argue that the short-run Phillips curve is downward sloping. There are two major implications of this analysis.

■ Reductions in aggregate demand can cause reductions in output and increases in unemployment. In other words, too little spending will cause a recession.

■ An expansion of aggregate demand by the government (whether achieved by fiscal or monetary policy, or both) will help to pull an economy out of a recession. There may be considerable time lags, however, before the economy fully responds to such expansionary policies.

In the long run, changes in aggregate demand will have much less effect on output and employment and much more effect on prices

As we have seen, new classical economists and others argue that both the long-run aggregate supply curve and the long-run Phillips curve are vertical. Some Keynesian economists agree, but argue that the long run might be quite a long time. Others, while arguing that these curves are not vertical, would still see them as less elastic than the short-run curves. Nevertheless, some Keynesians argue that changes in aggregate demand *will* have substantial effects on long-term output and employment via changes in investment and hence in potential output (see Figure 10.4 on page 375).

Expectations have important effects on the economy

Virtually all economists argue that expectations are crucial in determining the success of government policy on unemployment and inflation. Whatever people expect to happen, their actions will tend to make it happen.

If people believe that an expansion of money supply will merely lead to inflation (the monetarist and new classical position), then it will. Firms and workers will adjust their prices and wage rates upwards. Firms will make no plans to expand output and will not take on any more labour. If, however, people believe that an expansion of demand will lead to higher output and employment (the Keynesian position), then, via the accelerator mechanism, it will.

Similarly, just how successful a deflationary policy is in curing inflation depends in large measure on people's expectations. If people believe that a deflationary policy will cause a recession, then firms will stop investing and will cut their workforce. If they believe that it will cure inflation and restore firms' competitiveness abroad, firms may increase investment.

To manage the economy successfully, therefore, the government must convince people that its policies will work. This is as much a job of public relations as of pulling the right economic levers. It is one of the reasons for making central banks independent. If people believe that the central bank will not be swayed from its task of keeping inflation on target, either by public opinion or by political pressure, then people will come to expect low inflation and the policy will succeed.

Recap

1. There is a large measure of agreement between macroeconomists on how economies work and on the effects of various policies.

2. The areas of agreement include the following: (a) in the short run, changes in aggregate demand will have an effect on output and employment; (b) in the long run, changes in aggregate demand will have a smaller or even no effect on output and employment; instead, there will be a significant effect on prices; (c) expectations play a major role in determining the outcome of government policy changes.

10.6   Demand-side policy

What will be the effect of attempts by the government to control the level of spending in the economy?

Attitudes towards demand management

The debate over the management of demand has shifted ground somewhat in recent years. There is less debate today over the relative merits of fiscal and monetary policy. There is general agreement now that a *combination* of fiscal and monetary policies will have a more powerful effect on demand than just relying on one of the two policies. For example, a policy of cutting the size of the public-sector deficit by reducing government expenditure and/or increasing taxes (fiscal policy) will enable the central bank much more easily to restrain the growth of the money supply (monetary policy), which in turn will help to reinforce the fiscal policy.

The debate today is much more concerned with whether the government ought to pursue an active ('discretionary') demand management policy at all, or whether it ought merely to adhere to a set of policy rules.

The case for rules

The case against discretionary policy centres on the problem of time lags. Both fiscal and monetary policies can involve long and variable time lags, which can make the policy at best ineffective and at worst destabilising. Taking the measures *before* the problem arises, and thus lessening the problem of lags, is no answer since forecasting tends to be unreliable.

By setting and sticking to rules, however, and then not interfering further, the government can provide a sound monetary framework in which firms are not cushioned from market forces, and are therefore encouraged to be efficient. By the government or central bank setting a clear target either for the growth of money supply, or for the rate of inflation, and then resolutely sticking to it, people's expectations of inflation will be reduced, thereby making the target easier to achieve.

This sound and stable monetary environment, with no likelihood of sudden expansionary or contractionary policy, will encourage firms to take a longer-term perspective, and plan ahead. This could then lead to increased capital investment and long-term growth.

The optimum situation is for all the major countries to adhere to mutually consistent rules, so that their economies do not get out of line. This will create more stable exchange rates and provide the climate for world growth.

Advocates of this point of view in the 1970s and 1980s were monetarists, but in recent years support for the setting of targets has become widespread. As we have seen, in both the UK and the euro-zone countries, targets are set for both inflation and public-sector deficits.

The case for discretion

Keynesians reject the argument that rules provide the environment for high and stable growth. Demand, argue Keynesians, is subject to many and sometimes violent shocks: e.g. changes in expectations, domestic political events (such as an impending election), world economic factors (such as the world economic slowdown of 2001–3) or world political events (such as a war). The resulting shifts in injections or withdrawals cause the economy to deviate from a stable full-employment growth path.

Any change in injections or withdrawals will lead to a cumulative effect on national income via the multiplier and accelerator and via changing expectations. These effects take time and interact with each other, and so a process of expansion or contraction can last many months before a turning point is eventually reached.

Since shocks to demand occur at irregular intervals and are of different magnitudes, the economy is likely to experience cycles of irregular duration and of varying intensity.

Given that the economy is inherently unstable and is buffeted around by various shocks, Keynesians argue that the government needs actively to intervene to stabilise the economy. Otherwise, the uncertainty caused by unpredictable fluctuations will be very damaging to investment and hence to long-term economic growth (quite apart from the short-term effects of recessions on output and employment).

If demand fluctuates in the way Keynesians claim, and if the policy of having a money supply or inflation rule is adhered to, interest rates must fluctuate. But excessive fluctuations in interest rates will discourage long-term business planning and investment.

Difficulties with choice of target

Assume that the government or central bank sets an inflation target. Should it then stick to that rate, come what may? Might not an extended period of relatively low inflation warrant a lower inflation target? The government must at least have the discretion to *change* the rules, even if only occasionally.

Then there is the question of whether success in achieving the target will bring success in achieving other macroeconomic objectives, such as low unemployment and stable economic growth. The problem is that something called Goodhart's Law is likely to apply. The law, named after Charles Goodhart, formerly of the Bank of England, states that attempts to control an *indicator* of a problem may, as a result, make it cease to be a good indicator of the problem.

> **Definition**
>
> **Goodhart's Law**
> Controlling a symptom of a problem, or only part of the problem, will not cure the problem: it will simply mean that the part that is being controlled now becomes a poor indicator of the problem.

> **Goodhart's Law.** Controlling a symptom (i.e. an indicator) of a problem will not cure the problem. Instead, the indicator will merely cease to be a good indicator of the problem.
>
> **Key Idea 29**

Targeting inflation may make it become a poor indicator of the state of the economy. If people believe that the central bank will be successful in achieving its inflation target, then those expectations will feed into their inflationary expectations, and not surprisingly the target will be met. But that target rate of inflation may now be consistent with both a buoyant and a depressed economy. In other words, the Phillips curve may become *horizontal*. Achieving the inflation target has not tackled the much more serious problem of creating stable economic growth and an environment that will therefore encourage long-term investment.

Use of a Taylor rule.   For this reason, many economists have advocated the use of a Taylor rule,[1] rather than a simple inflation target. A Taylor rule takes *two* objectives into account – (1) inflation and (2) either real national income or unemployment – and seeks to get the optimum degree of stability of the two. The degree of importance attached to each of the two objectives can be decided by the government or central bank. The central bank adjusts interest rates when either the rate of inflation diverges from its target or the level of real national income (or unemployment) diverges from its sustainable (or equilibrium) level.

Take the case where inflation is above its target level. The central bank following a Taylor rule will raise the rate of interest. It knows, however, that this will reduce real national income. This, therefore, limits the amount that the central bank is prepared to raise the rate of interest. The more weight it attaches to stabilising inflation, the more it will raise the rate of interest. The more weight it attaches to stabilising real national income, the less it will raise the rate of interest.

Thus the central bank has to trade off inflation stability against real income stability.

Current demand–side policy in the UK

Fiscal policy

Since 1998, the government has set targets for government expenditure, not for just one year, but for a three-year period. Does this mean, therefore, that fiscal policy as a means of adjusting aggregate demand has been abandoned? In one sense, this is the case. The government is now committed to following its 'golden rule', whereby public-sector receipts should cover all current spending, averaged over the course of the business cycle (see Box 8.5). In fact, in supporting sticking to the golden rule, the Chancellor explicitly rejected Keynesian fine tuning:

> In today's deregulated, liberalised financial markets, the Keynesian fine tuning of the past, which worked in relatively sheltered, closed national economies and which

---

Definition

Taylor rule
A rule adopted by a central bank for setting the rate of interest. It will raise the interest rate if (a) inflation is above target or (b) real national income is above the sustainable level (or unemployment is below the equilibrium rate). The rule states how much interest rates will be changed in each case.

[1] Named after John Taylor, from Stanford University, who proposed that for every 1 per cent that GDP rises above sustainable GDP, real interest rates should be raised by 0.5 percentage points and for every 1 per cent that inflation rises above its target level, real interest rates should be raised by 0.5 percentage points (i.e. nominal rates should be raised by 1.5 percentage points).

tried to exploit a supposed long-term trade-off between inflation and unemployment, will simply not work.[2]

But despite this apparent rejection of short-term discretionary fiscal adjustments, there is still a role for *automatic* fiscal stabilisers: with deficits rising in a recession and falling in a boom. There is also still the possibility, within the golden rule, of financing additional *investment* by borrowing, thereby providing a stimulus to a sluggish economy.

The golden rule also permits increased government expenditure (or tax cuts) if there is a budget surplus. Thus in the 2001 Budget the Chancellor announced spending increases of 3.7 per cent per year for three years. The effect was to provide a stimulus to the economy just at a time when the world economy was slowing down. This helped to make the slowdown in economic growth in the period 2001–3 much less severe in the UK than in many other countries.

Monetary policy

Since 1992, both Conservative and Labour governments have used monetary policy to achieve a target rate of inflation. The Conservative government chose both the target (to be within a range of 1 to 4 per cent) and also the rate of interest felt necessary to achieve that target. The interest rate, however, was chosen in consultation with the Governor of the Bank of England and was based on forecasts of the rate of inflation. The Chancellor met monthly with the Governor to discuss interest rates and the minutes of the meetings were published six weeks later, in order to give transparency to the process.

In 1997, the incoming Labour government set a target for inflation of $2\frac{1}{2}$ per cent, which has remained unchanged. Unlike its predecessor, however, it decided to make the Bank of England independent. Indeed, this was the first action taken by the Chancellor when the government came to power.

But why did the government give up its right to set interest rates? First, there is the political advantage of taking 'blame' away from the government if interest rates need to be raised in order to prevent inflation rising above its target. Second, an independent central bank, free to set interest rates in order to achieve a clear target, is more likely to be consistent in pursuit of this objective than a government concerned about its popularity. Then there is the question of transparency in decision making.

> If inflation is more than 1 percentage point higher or lower than the target, an open letter will be sent by the Governor to the Chancellor so that the public is fully informed as to why the divergence has occurred; the policy action being taken to deal with it; the period within which inflation is expected to return to the target; and how this approach meets the government's monetary policy objectives. Monetary policy decision-making is now among the most transparent and accountable in the world.[3]

Transparency is enhanced by the publication of the minutes of the monthly meetings of the Bank of England's Monetary Policy Committee at which interest rates are set. One of the main purposes of transparency is to convince people of the

---

[2] Extract from the Chancellor's Mansion House speech, 11 June 1998.

[3] *The Government's Overall Economic Strategy* (http://www.hm-treasury.gov.uk/pub/html/ e_info/overview/1_goes.html).

Box 10.2

Inflation targeting

The fashion of the age

More and more countries are turning to inflation targeting as their main macroeconomic policy. The diagram shows that in a survey by the Bank of England of 91 countries, 55 of them targeted inflation in 1998. Only nine of them targeted inflation in 1990. But why is it becoming so fashionable?

Part of the reason is the apparent failure of discretionary macroeconomic policies. Discretionary fiscal and monetary policies suffer from time lags, from being used for short-term political purposes and from failing to straighten out the business cycle. But if discretionary policies have seemed not to work, why choose an inflation target rather than a target for the money supply or the exchange rate?

Money supply targets were adopted by many countries in the 1980s, including the UK, and this policy too was largely a failure. Money supply targets proved very difficult to achieve. As we have seen, money supply depends on the amount of credit banks create and this is not easy for the authorities to control. Then, even if money supply is controlled, this does not necessarily mean that aggregate demand will be controlled: the velocity of circulation may change. Nevertheless, many countries do still target the money supply, although in most cases it is not the main target. For example, as we saw in Box 9.4, the ECB targets money supply as well as inflation. In the diagram, 31 of the 55 countries targeting inflation also targeted the money supply.

Exchange-rate targets, as we shall see in Chapter 12, may have serious disadvantages if the equilibrium exchange rate is not the one that is being targeted. The main instrument for keeping the exchange rate on target is the rate of interest. For example, if the exchange rate target were £1 = $1.50, and the exchange rate were currently £1 = $1.40, then interest rates would be raised. This would cause an inflow of money into the economy and hence push up the exchange rate. But if the rate of interest is being used to achieve an exchange rate target, it cannot be used for other purposes, such as controlling aggregate demand or inflation. Raising interest rates to achieve an exchange rate target may lead to a recession.

Inflation targets have proved relatively easy to achieve. There may be problems at first, if the actual rate of inflation is way above the target level. The high rates of interest necessary to bring inflation down may cause a recession. But once inflation has been brought

seriousness with which the Bank will adhere to its targets. This, it is hoped, will keep people's *expectations* of inflation low: the lower expected inflation is, the lower will be the actual rate of inflation.

With monetary policy geared to an inflation target and fiscal policy geared to following the golden rule, there seems to be virtually no scope for discretionary demand management policy. Rules appear to have replaced discretion.

When there are ever more rapid financial flows across the world that are unpredictable and uncertain, the answer is to ensure stability through establishing the right long-term policy objectives and to build credibility in the policy through well-understood procedural rules that are followed for fiscal and monetary policy.[4]

> **Pause for thought** |||
>
> *Do you agree that 'ever more rapid financial flows across the world that are unpredictable and uncertain' make Keynesian discretionary fiscal (and monetary) policy less suitable? Explain.*

There is, however, a new form of fine tuning: the frequent adjustment of interest rates, not to smooth out the business cycle, but to make sure that the inflation rule is adhered to.

---

[4] Extract from the Chancellor's Mansion House speech, 11 June 1998.

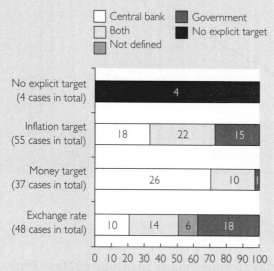

Central bank | Government
Both | No explicit target
Not defined

No explicit target
(4 cases in total) — 4

Inflation target
(55 cases in total) — 18 | 22 | 15

Money target
(37 cases in total) — 26 | 10

Exchange rate
(48 cases in total) — 10 | 14 | 6 | 18

0 10 20 30 40 50 60 70 80 90 100

Source: Gabriel Sterne, *The Use of Explicit Targets for Monetary Policy: Practical experiences of 91 economies in the 1990s* Bank of England Quarterly Bulletin, August 1999. *Monetary Policy Frameworks in a Global Context* (Mahadeva and Sterne, 2000).

Who sets explicit targets and monitoring ranges for the exchange rate, money and inflation?

down and the objective is then simply to maintain it at the target level, most countries have been relatively successful. And the more successful they are, the more people will expect this success to be maintained, which in turn will help to ensure this success.

So, are there any problems with inflation targeting? Ironically, one of the main problems lies in its success. With worldwide inflation having fallen, and with global trade and competition helping to keep prices down, there is now less of a link between inflation and the business cycle. Booms no longer seem to generate the inflation they once did. Gearing interest-rate policy to maintaining low inflation could still see economies experiencing unsustainable booms, followed by recessions. Inflation may be controlled, but the business cycle may not be.

More details of the Bank of England study and of the relative merits of different targets are given in Web case 10.7.

? Why may there be problems in targeting (a) both inflation and money supply; (b) both inflation and the exchange rate?

Key Idea

29
p390

Recap

1. The case against discretionary policy is that it involves unpredictable time lags, which can make the policy destabilising. The government may as a result overcorrect. Also the government may ignore the long-run adverse consequences of policies designed for short-run political gain.

2. The case in favour of rules is that they help to reduce inflationary expectations and thus create a stable environment for investment and growth.

3. The case against sticking to money supply or inflation rules is that they may cause severe fluctuations in interest rates and thus create a less stable economic environment for business planning. Also, given the changing economic environment in which we live, rules adopted in the past may no longer be suitable for the present. Keynesians thus argue that the government must have the discretion to change its policy as circumstances demand.

4. Since 1992, both Conservative and Labour governments in the UK have pursued a largely rules-based demand-side policy.

5. Fiscal policy is geared to achieving a balanced budget over the course of the business cycle. The only exception to this is borrowing for public *investment*. Monetary policy is geared to achieving a target rate of inflation of 2 per cent. The Bank of England adjusts interest rates in order to keep to this target.

Figure 10.6
UK GDP at market
prices (1995 = 100)

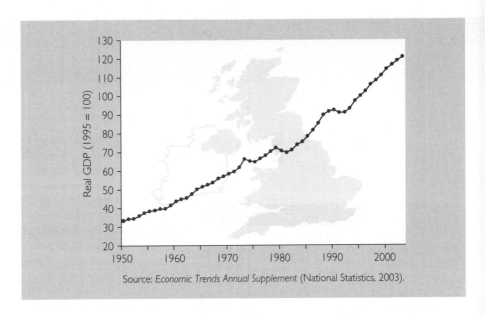

Source: *Economic Trends Annual Supplement* (National Statistics, 2003).

10.7

Long-term economic growth

Why is income per head today so much higher than a generation ago?

Growth over the decades

Quite naturally, governments and individuals are concerned with the ups and downs of the business cycle. How does this year's economic performance compare with last year's? Are the various macroeconomic indicators, such as growth, unemployment and inflation, getting better or worse?

When we step back, however, and look at the longer span of history, these short-term fluctuations take on less significance. What we see is that economies tend to experience long-term economic growth, not long-term economic decline. Measured in terms of income per head (after adjusting for inflation), all developed nations are richer today than they were 50 years ago. Figure 10.6 shows UK GDP from 1950 to 2003. As you can see, the fluctuations in output appear minor compared with its long-term growth.

The causes of economic growth

The sources of economic growth can be grouped into two broad categories:

■ An increase in the *quantity* of factors. Here we would include an increase in the workforce or the average number of hours that people work, an increase in raw materials (e.g. discoveries of oil) and an increase in capital. Of these, for most countries it is an increase in the capital stock, brought about by investment, that is the most important source of growth.

■ An increase in the *productivity* of factors. Here we would include an increase in the skills of workers, a more efficient organisation of inputs by management and more productive capital equipment. Most significant here is technological progress. Developments of computer technology, of new techniques in engineering, of lighter, stronger and cheaper materials, of digital technology in communications and of more efficient motors have all contributed to a massive increase in the productivity of capital. Machines today can produce much more output than machines in the past that cost the same to manufacture.

In this section, we will examine these two sources of growth, focusing first on capital accumulation (an increase in the *quantity* of capital) and then on technological progress (an increase in the *productivity* of factors).

Capital accumulation

An increase in capital per worker will generally increase output. In other words, the more equipment that is used by people at work, the more they are likely to produce. But to increase capital requires investment, and that investment requires resources – resources that could have been used for producing consumer goods. Thus more investment over the longer term requires more saving.

A simple model of economic growth

Figure 10.7 shows a simple model of growth. Assuming that the size of the workforce is constant, any increase in the capital stock means an increase in the average amount of capital per worker. The size of the capital stock (K) is measured on the horizontal axis; the level of national output (Y) is measured on the vertical axis.

As the capital stock increases, so output increases. This is shown by the Y curve. Output increases, however, at a diminishing rate (the curve gets less and less steep). The reason for this is the law of diminishing returns: in this case, diminishing returns to capital. For example, if, in an office, you start equipping workers with PCs, at first output will increase very rapidly. But as more and more workers have their own PC rather than having to share, so the rate of increase in output slows

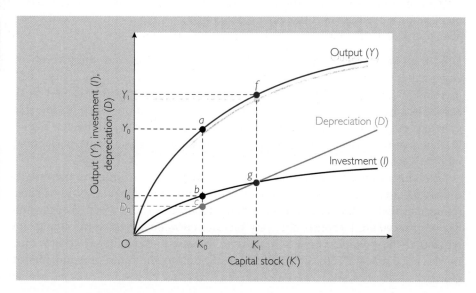

Figure 10.7
Steady-state output

Figure 10.8

Effect of an increase
in the rate of saving
and investment

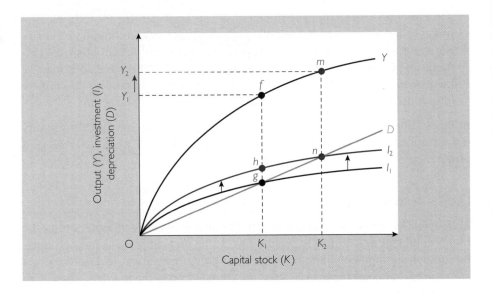

down. When everyone has their own, output is likely to be at a maximum. Any additional PCs (of the same specification) will remain unused.

Increased output will mean increased saving and hence increased investment. This is shown by the investment curve (I). The higher the rate of investment, the steeper will be this line.

The depreciation (D) line shows the amount of depreciation of capital that takes place, and hence the amount of replacement investment required. The bigger the capital stock, the larger the amount of replacement investment required.

Assume initially that the size of the capital stock is K_0. This will generate an output of Y_0 (point a). This output, in turn, will generate saving and investment of I_0, but of this, D_0 will have to be used for replacement purposes. The difference ($b - c$) will be available to increase the size of the capital stock. The capital stock will thus increase up to K_1 (point g). At this point, all investment will be required for replacement purposes. Output will therefore cease growing. Y_1 represents the steady-state level of national income.

Definition

**Steady-state
national income**

The long-run
equilibrium level of
national income. The
level at which all
investment is used to
maintain the existing
capital stock at its
current level.

Effect of an increase in the saving rate.   If the saving rate increases, the investment curve will shift upwards. This is shown by a shift from I_1 to I_2 in Figure 10.8. Investment is now above that which is necessary to maintain the capital stock at K_1. The capital stock will grow, therefore, and so will national income. But this growth is only temporary. Once the capital stock has risen to K_2, all the new higher level of investment will be absorbed in replacing capital ($I = D$ at point n). National income stops rising. Y_2 represents the new steady-state national income.

Does this mean, therefore, that there is no long-term gain from an increase in the saving rate? There *is* a gain, to the extent that income per worker is now higher (remember that we are assuming a constant labour force), and this higher income will be received not just once, but every year from now on as long as the saving rate remains at the new higher level. There is no increase in the long-term *growth rate*, however. To achieve that, we would have to look to the other determinants of growth.

What should be clear from the above analysis is that, without technological progress or some other means of increasing output from a given quantity of inputs, long-term growth cannot be sustained.

Technological progress

The effect of technological progress on output

Technological progress has the effect of increasing the output from a given amount of investment. This is shown in Figure 10.9. Initial investment and income curves are I_1 and Y_1; steady-state income is at a level of Y_1 (point f). A technological advance has the effect of shifting the Y line upwards, say to Y_2. The higher income curve leads to a higher investment curve (for a given rate of saving). This is shown by curve I_2. The new long-term equilibrium capital stock is thus K_2, and the new steady-state level of income is Y_2 (point p).

If there is a 'one-off' technological advance, the effect is the one we have just illustrated. National income rises to a higher level, but does not go on rising once the new steady-state level has been reached. But technological progress marches on over time. New inventions are made; new processes are discovered; old ones are improved. In terms of Figure 10.9, the Y curve *goes on* shifting upwards over time. The faster the rate of technological progress, the faster will the Y curve shift upwards and the higher will be the rate of economic growth.

Endogenous growth theory

It should be clear from what we have argued that an increase in technological progress is essential if a country wants to achieve faster rates of growth in the long term. But is this purely in the lap of the scientists and engineers? Or can scientific breakthroughs and developments be stimulated? Can anything be done to speed up the rate of innovation? Many economists argue that the rate of technological

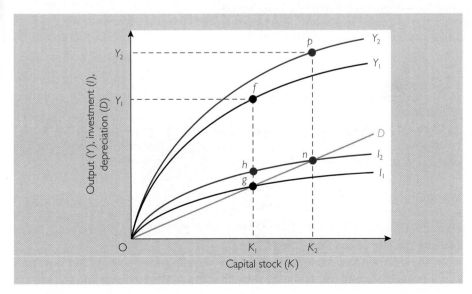

Figure 10.9
Effect of a technological advance

Key
Idea

12
p84

Box 10.3

Productivity and economic growth

The key to a better standard of living?

A country's potential output depends on the productivity of its factors of production. There are three common ways of measuring productivity. The first is output per worker. This is the most straightforward measure to calculate. All that is required is a measure of total output and employment.

The second measure is output per hour worked. This has the advantage that it is not influenced by the *number* of hours worked. So for an economy like the UK, with a very high percentage of part-time workers on the one hand, and long average hours worked by full-time employees on the other, such a measure would be more accurate in gauging worker efficiency.

The first two measures focus solely on the productivity of labour. In order to account directly for the productivity of capital we need to consider the growth in *total* factor productivity (TFP). This third measure gives output relative to the amount of factors used. Changes in total factor productivity over time provide a good indicator of technical progress.

The chart shows comparative productivity levels of four countries using the first two measures.

The importance of productivity

The faster the growth in productivity, the faster is likely to be the country's rate of economic growth.

Any government seeking to raise the long-term growth rate, therefore, must find ways of stimulating productivity growth.

On what does the growth of productivity depend? There are seven main determinants:

■ Private investment in new physical capital (machinery and buildings) and in research and development (R&D).
■ Public investment in education, R&D and infrastructure.

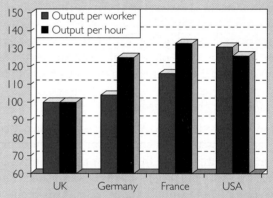

Source: *Budget 2003, Economic and Fiscal Strategy Report* (HM Treasury, 2003).

Productivity in selected countries, 2001 (UK = 100)

Definition

Endogenous growth theory
A theory that the rate of economic growth depends on the rate of technological progress and diffusion, both of which depend on institutions, incentives and the role of government.

progress *can* be increased if more resources are devoted to research and development and to education and training, and if people are given appropriate incentives to innovate.

Once a discovery is made, its effects will depend on how widely the knowledge is dispersed. The more people can use the new technology and replicate and develop it, the greater will be the resulting increase in output.

What endogenous growth theory argues is that the rate of invention and technological development and the rate of diffusion of new technology depend on economic institutions, incentives and the role of government. All this suggests that appropriate policies can increase the rate of technological progress and hence increase the rate of economic growth.

In the next section, we look at the range of supply-side policies and how they can influence not only economic growth, but also unemployment and inflation.

■ Training and the development of labour skills.

■ Innovation and the application of new technology.

■ The organisation and management of factors of production.

■ The rate of entry of new firms into markets: generally such firms will have higher productivity than existing firms.

■ The business environment in which firms operate. Is there competition over the quality and design of products? Is there competitive pressure to reduce costs?

? 1. Identify some policies a government could pursue to stimulate productivity growth through each of the above means.

But what are the mechanisms whereby productivity growth feeds through into growth of the economy?

■ The capacity of the economy to grow will increase as productivity improvements extend potential output.

■ Productivity improvements will drive prices downwards, stimulating demand and actual growth.

■ With high returns from their investment, investors might be prepared to embark upon new projects

and enterprises, stimulating yet further productivity growth and higher output.

■ As labour productivity rises, so wages are likely to rise. The higher wages will lead to higher consumption, and hence, via the multiplier and accelerator, to higher output and higher investment, thereby stimulating further advances in productivity.

■ In the longer term, businesses experiencing higher productivity growth would expect their lower costs, and hence enhanced competitiveness, to allow them to gain greater market share. This will encourage further investment and productivity growth.

It is clear that the prosperity of a nation rests upon its ability to improve its productivity. The more successful it is in doing this, the greater will be its rate of economic growth.

For decades the UK has invested a smaller proportion of its national income than most other industrialised nations. This has resulted in relatively low productivity growth and a comparatively low level of labour productivity. This is illustrated in the chart.

? 2. What could explain the differences in productivity between the four countries in the chart, and why do the differences vary according to which of the two measures is used?

Recap

1. The determinants of economic growth in the long run lie primarily on the supply side. They can be put into two broad categories: an increase in the quantity of factors and an increase in the productivity of factors.

2. An increased saving rate will lead to higher investment and hence to an increase in the capital stock. This, in turn, will lead to a higher level of national income. A larger capital stock, however, will require a higher level of replacement investment. Once this has risen to absorb all the extra investment, national income will stop rising: growth will cease. An increased saving rate will therefore lead only to a rise in output, not to a long-term rise in the rate of growth.

3. A higher long-term rate of growth will normally require a faster rate of technological progress. Endogenous growth theory argues that the rate of technological progress and its rate of diffusion depend on economic institutions and incentives. Supply-side policy could be used to alter these.

10.8   Supply–side policy

How might the government attempt to control the level of output and employment directly?

Supply-side policies, as the name suggests, focus on aggregate supply. If successful, they will shift the aggregate supply curve to the right, thus increasing output for any given level of prices (or reducing the price level for any given level of output). They may also shift the Phillips curve to the left, reducing the rate of unemployment for any given rate of inflation.

Key Idea 8 p45

Unemployment and supply-side policies

Equilibrium unemployment – frictional, structural, etc. – is caused by various rigidities or imperfections in the market. There is a mismatching of aggregate supply and demand, and vacancies are not filled despite the existence of unemployment. Perhaps workers have the wrong qualifications, or are poorly motivated, or are living a long way away from the job, or are simply unaware of the jobs that are vacant. Generally, the problem is that labour is not sufficiently mobile, either occupationally or geographically, to respond to changes in the job market. Labour supply for particular jobs is too inelastic.

Supply-side policies aim to influence labour supply. They aim to make workers more responsive to changes in job opportunities. Alternatively, they may aim to make employers more adaptable and willing to operate within existing labour constraints.

Key Idea 4 p26

Inflation and supply-side policies

If inflation is caused by cost-push pressures, supply-side policy can help to reduce these cost pressures in two ways:

■ By reducing the power of unions and/or firms (e.g. by anti-monopoly legislation) and thereby encouraging more competition in the supply of labour and/or goods.
■ By encouraging increases in productivity through the retraining of labour, or by investment grants to firms, or by tax incentives, etc.

Growth and supply-side policies

Supply-side economics focuses on *potential* income. Supply-side policies aim to increase the total quantity of factors of production (e.g. policies designed to encourage the building of new factories) or they can be used to encourage greater productivity of factors of production (e.g. policies to encourage the training of labour, or incentives for people to work harder). Box 10.3 examines the link between productivity and economic growth.

Supply-side policies can take various forms. They can be *market orientated* and focus on ways of 'freeing up' the market, such as encouraging private enterprise, risk taking and competition: policies that provide incentives and reward initiative, hard work and productivity. Alternatively, they can be *interventionist* in nature and focus

Key Idea 4 p26

on means of counteracting the deficiencies of the free market. Thus supply-side policies are advocated across the political and economic spectrum.

First we will examine market-orientated policies. Then we will turn to interventionist policies.

Market–orientated supply–side policies

Radical market-orientated supply-side policies were first adopted in the early 1980s by the Thatcher government in the UK and the Reagan administration in the USA. The essence of these policies was to encourage and reward individual enterprise and initiative, and to reduce the role of government; to put more reliance on market forces and competition, and less on government intervention and regulation. The policies were associated with the following:

- Reducing government expenditure so as to release more resources for the private sector.
- Reducing taxes so as to increase incentives.
- Reducing the monopoly power of trade unions so as to encourage greater flexibility in both wages and working practices, and to allow labour markets to clear.
- Reducing the automatic entitlement to certain welfare benefits so as to encourage greater self-reliance.
- Reducing red tape and other impediments to investment and risk taking.
- Encouraging competition through policies of deregulation and privatisation.
- Abolishing exchange controls and other impediments to the free movement of capital.

Such policies were increasingly copied by other governments around the world. Today most countries have adopted some or all of the above measures.

Reducing government expenditure

The desire by many governments to cut government expenditure is not just to reduce the PSNCR and hence reduce the growth of money supply; it is also an essential ingredient of their supply-side strategy.

In most countries the size of the public sector, relative to national income, grew substantially up until the mid-1980s (see Table 10.2). A major aim of Conservative governments throughout the world has been to reverse this trend. The public sector is portrayed as more bureaucratic and less efficient than the private sector. What

	1961–70	1971–80	1981–85	1986–90	1991–95	1996–2000	2001–03
Belgium	33.7	50.6	61.5	55.3	54.1	50.9	49.7
Germany	37.0	45.3	48.2	46.0	48.2	48.6	48.6
France	38.3	42.4	51.5	50.2	53.0	54.1	53.4
Japan	–	26.8	33.2	31.5	33.2	39.1	39.9
Netherlands	39.9	49.3	59.5	55.0	53.0	47.5	47.0
Sweden	–	52.8	65.0	58.5	65.6	61.4	58.2
UK	36.5	41.2	44.6	39.8	42.3	40.0	40.8
USA	29.1	33.1	36.5	34.9	35.9	33.1	34.6

Table 10.2

General government expenditure as a percentage of GDP

Source: *European Economy* (Commission of the European Union).

is more, it is claimed that a growing proportion of public money has been spent on administration and other 'non-productive' activities, rather than on the direct provision of goods and services.

Two things are needed, it is argued: (a) a more efficient use of resources within the public sector and (b) a reduction in the size of the public sector. This would allow private investment to increase with no overall rise in aggregate demand. Thus the supply-side benefits of higher investment could be achieved without the demand-side costs of higher inflation.

In practice, governments have found it very difficult to cut their expenditure without cutting services and the provision of infrastructure.

Tax cuts: the effects on labour supply and employment

Cutting the marginal rate of income tax was a major objective of the Thatcher and Major governments (1979–97). In 1979, the standard rate of income tax in the UK was 33 per cent and the top rate was 83 per cent. By 1997 the standard rate was only 23 per cent (with a starting rate of just 20 per cent), and the top rate was only 40 per cent. The Blair government continued with this policy. In 2004 the standard rate was 22 per cent and the starting rate was only 10 per cent. Cuts in the marginal rate of income tax are claimed to have many beneficial effects: for example, people work longer hours; more people wish to work; people work more enthusiastically; unemployment falls; employment rises. The evidence regarding the truth of these claims, however, is less than certain.

For example, do more people wish to work? This applies largely to second income earners in a family, mainly women. A rise in after-tax wages may encourage more women to look for jobs. It may now be worth the cost in terms of transport, child minders, family disruption, etc. However, the effect of a 1 or 2 per cent cut in income tax rates is likely to be negligible. A more significant effect may be achieved by raising tax allowances: the amount of income that can be earned before taxes are paid. Part-time workers, especially, could end up paying no taxes.

Whether people will be prepared to work longer hours is also questionable. On the one hand, each hour worked will be more valuable in terms of take-home pay, and thus people may be encouraged to work more and have less leisure time (a substitution effect – see pages 193–4). On the other hand, a cut in income tax will make people better off, and therefore they may feel less need to do overtime than before (an income effect). The evidence on these two effects suggests that they just about cancel each other out. Anyway, for many people there is no such choice in the short run. There is no chance of doing overtime or working a shorter week. In the long run, there may be some flexibility in that people can change jobs.

One of the main arguments is that tax cuts, especially at the lower end (by having a low starting rate of tax, or high personal allowances), will help to reduce unemployment. If income taxes are cut (especially if unemployment benefits are also cut), there will be a bigger difference between after-tax wage rates and unemployment benefit. More people will be motivated to take jobs rather than remain unemployed.

Despite the cuts in marginal rates of income tax, there have been significant tax *increases* elsewhere. In particular, VAT stood at only 8 per cent in 1979; in 2004 it was $17\frac{1}{2}$ per cent. The marginal rate of national insurance contributions was $6\frac{1}{2}$ per cent in 1979; in 2004 it was 11 per cent. The net effect was that taxes as a proportion of national income rose from 34.2 per cent in 1979 to 36.8 per cent in 2004.

To the extent that tax cuts do succeed in increasing take-home pay, there is a danger of 'sucking in' imports. In the UK, there is a high income elasticity of demand for imports. Extra consumer incomes may be spent on Japanese videos and hi-fi, foreign cars, holidays abroad, and so on. Tax cuts can therefore have a serious effect on the balance of trade.

> **Pause for thought**
>
> If taxes as a proportion of national income have risen since 1979, does this mean that there can have been no positive incentive effects of the various tax measures taken by first the Conservative and then the Labour governments?

Tax cuts for business and other investment incentives

Key Idea 4 p26

A number of financial incentives can be given to encourage investment. Market-orientated policies seek to reduce the general level of taxation on profits, or to give greater tax relief to investment.

A cut in corporation tax (the tax on business profits) will increase after-tax profits. This will leave more funds for ploughing back into investment. Also the higher after-tax return on investment will encourage more investment to take place. In 1983 the main rate of corporation tax in the UK stood at 52 per cent. A series of reductions have taken place since then, and by 2004 the rate was 30 per cent for large companies and 19 per cent for small ones.

Reducing the power of labour

The argument here is that, if labour costs to employers are reduced, their profits will probably rise. This could encourage and enable more investment and hence economic growth. If the monopoly power of labour is reduced, then cost-push inflation will also be reduced.

The Thatcher government took a number of measures to weaken the power of labour. These included restrictions on union closed shops, restrictions on secondary picketing and enforced secret ballots on strike proposals (see pages 178–9). It set a lead in resisting strikes in the public sector. Unlike previous Labour governments, it did not consult with union leaders over questions of economic policy. It was publicly very critical of trade union militancy and blamed the unions for many of the UK's economic ills. As a result, unions lost a lot of political standing and influence.

As labour markets have become more flexible, with increased part-time working and short-term contracts, so this has further eroded the power of labour in many sectors of the economy (see Box 5.2 on page 180).

Reducing welfare

New classical economists claim that a major cause of unemployment is the small difference between the welfare benefits of the unemployed and the take-home pay of the employed. This causes voluntary unemployment (i.e. frictional unemployment). People are caught in a 'poverty trap': if they take a job, they lose their benefits (see page 180).

A dramatic solution to this problem would be to cut unemployment benefits. In the early 1980s the gap between take-home pay and welfare benefits to the unemployed did indeed widen. However, over the same period unemployment rose dramatically. This suggests that too high benefits were not a significant cause of growing unemployment over this period. Nevertheless, the claim that there was too little incentive for people to work was still a major part of the Thatcher government's explanation of growing unemployment.

A major problem is that with changing requirements for labour skills, many of the redundant workers from the older industries are simply not qualified for new jobs that are created. What is more, the longer people are unemployed, the more demoralised they become. Employers would probably be prepared to pay only very low wages to such workers. To persuade these unemployed people to take low-paid jobs, the welfare benefits would have to be slashed. A 'market' solution to the problem, therefore, may be a very cruel solution. A fairer solution would be an interventionist policy: a policy of retraining labour.

Another alternative is to make the payment of unemployment benefits conditional on the recipient making a concerted effort to find a job. In the jobseeker's allowance introduced in 1996, claimants must be available for and actively seeking work, and must complete a jobseeker's agreement, which sets out the types of work the person is willing to do, and the plan to find work. Payment can be refused if the claimant refuses to accept the offer of a job.

Key Idea 17 p192

Key Idea 4 p26

Policies to encourage competition

If the government can encourage more competition, this should have the effect of increasing national output and reducing inflation. Five major types of policy have been pursued under this heading.

Privatisation. If privatisation simply involves the transfer of a natural monopoly to private hands (e.g. the water companies), the scope for increased competition is limited. However, where there is genuine scope for increased competition (e.g. in the supply of gas and electricity), privatisation can lead to increased efficiency, more consumer choice and lower prices (see Box 6.2 on page 224).

Alternatively, privatisation can involve the introduction of private services into the public sector (e.g. private contractors providing cleaning services in hospitals, or refuse collection for local authorities). Private contractors may compete against each other for the franchise. This may well lower the cost of provision of these services, but the quality of provision may also suffer unless closely monitored. The effects on unemployment are uncertain. Private contractors may offer lower wages and thus may use more labour. But if they are trying to supply the service at minimum cost, they may employ less labour.

Deregulation. This involves the removal of monopoly rights: again, largely in the public sector. The deregulation of the bus industry, opening it up to private operators, is a good example of this initiative. An example in the private sector was the so-called Big Bang on the Stock Exchange in 1986. Under this, the monopoly power of 'jobbers' to deal in stocks and shares on the Stock Exchange was abolished. In addition, stockbrokers now compete with each other in the commission rates they charge.

Introducing market relationships into the public sector. This is where the government tries to get different departments or elements within a particular part of the public sector to 'trade' with each other, so as to encourage competition and efficiency. The best-known examples are within health and education.

The process often involves 'devolved budgeting'. For example, under the locally managed schools scheme (LMS), schools have become self-financing. Rather than the local authority meeting the bill for teachers' salaries, the schools have to manage their own budgets. The objective is to encourage them to cut costs, thereby reducing the burden on council tax payers. However, one result is that schools have tended to appoint inexperienced (and hence cheaper) teachers rather than those who can bring the benefits of their years of teaching.

Perhaps the most radical example of devolved budgeting was the introduction by the Thatcher government of an 'internal market' into the national health service. General practitioners were offered the opportunity to control their own budget. The size of the budget was determined by the number of patients and by their age and health profiles. GP fundholders purchased services directly from hospitals and had to cover their drugs bill. The suppliers of treatment, the hospitals, depended for much of their income on attracting the business of GP purchasers. They were thus put in competition with other hospitals.

Advocates of the internal market in the NHS argued that it created greater efficiency through competition. Critics, however, claimed that it led to growing inequalities of service between practices and between hospitals, and increased the administrative costs of the NHS.

The Private Finance Initiative. In 1993 the government introduced its Private Finance Initiative (PFI). This became the new way in which public projects were to be financed and run. Instead of the government or local authority planning, building and then running a public project (such as a new toll bridge, a maintenance depot, a prison, a records office or a block of inner-city workshops), it merely decides in broad terms the service it requires, and then seeks tenders from the private sector for designing, building, financing and running such projects. The capital costs are borne by the private sector, but then, if the provision of the service is not self-financing, the public sector pays the private-sector firm for providing it. Thus instead of the public sector being a provider, it is merely an enabler, buying services from the private sector.

The aim of these 'public–private partnerships' (PPPs) is to introduce competition (through the tendering process) and private-sector expertise into the provision of public services. It is hoped that the extra burden to the taxpayer of the private-sector profits will be more than offset by gains in efficiency. Critics, however, claim that PPPs have resulted in poorer quality of provision and that cost control has often been poor too, resulting in a higher burden for the taxpayer in the long term.

Free trade and capital movements. The opening-up of international trade and investment is central to a market-orientated supply-side policy. One of the first measures of the Thatcher government (in October 1979) was to remove all exchange controls, thereby permitting the free inflow and outflow of capital, both long term and short term. Most other industrialised countries also removed or relaxed exchange controls during the 1980s and early 1990s.

The Single European Act of 1986, which came into force in 1993, was another example of international liberalisation. As we shall see in Section 11.5, it created a 'single market' in the EU: a market without barriers to the movement of goods, services, capital and labour.

Interventionist supply-side policies

The basis of the case for government intervention is that the free market is likely to provide too little research and development, training and investment.

There are potentially large external benefits from research and development (see page 208). Firms investing in developing and improving products, and especially firms engaged in more general scientific research, may produce results that provide benefits to many other firms. Thus the *social* rate of return on investment may be much higher than the private rate of return. Investment that is privately unprofitable for a firm may therefore still be economically desirable for the nation.

Similarly, investment in training may continue yielding benefits to society that are lost to the firms providing the training when the workers leave.

Investment often involves risks. Firms may be unwilling to take those risks, since the costs of possible failure may be too high. When looked at nationally, however, the benefits of investment might well have substantially outweighed the costs, and thus it would have been socially desirable for firms to have taken the risk. Successes would have outweighed failures.

Even when firms do wish to make such investments, they may find difficulties in raising finance. Banks may be unwilling to lend. Alternatively, if firms rely on raising finance by the issue of new shares, this makes them very dependent on the stock market performance of their shares. This depends largely on current profitability and expected profitability in the near future, not on *long-term* profitability.

Types of interventionist supply-side policy

Direct provision.   Improvements in infrastructure, such as a better motorway system, can be of direct benefit to industry. Alternatively, the government could provide factories or equipment to specific firms.

Research and development.   The government may sponsor research and development in certain industries (e.g. aerospace) or in specific fields (e.g. microprocessors). The amount of government support in this field has been very small in the UK compared with Japan, France and the USA. What is more, that amount of support declined between the mid-1980s and the late 1990s. In 1999, however, the Labour government introduced a system of tax credits for small firms that invest in research and development. Then, in 2002, tax relief of 20 per cent of R & D expenditure by large firms was introduced.

Training and education.   The government may set up training schemes, or encourage educational institutions to make their courses more vocationally relevant, or introduce new vocational qualifications (such as the GNVQs and NVQs in the UK). Alternatively, the government can provide grants or tax relief to firms which themselves provide training schemes. The UK invests little in training programmes compared with most of its industrial competitors.

Pause for thought

How might a new classical economist criticise these various forms of interventionist supply-side policy?

Assistance to small firms.   UK governments in recent years have recognised the importance of small firms to the economy and have introduced various forms of advisory services,

Box 10.4 Case Studies and Applications

A new approach to industrial policy

As with many other areas of economic policy, industrial policy throughout most of the world has undergone a radical reorientation in recent years. The government's role has shifted from one of direct intervention in the form of subsidies and protecting industry from competition, to one of focusing upon the external business environment and the conditions that influence its competitiveness.

The reasons for such a change are both philosophical and structural:

■ The 1980s saw the efficacy of government intervention questioned, and the re-emergence of the belief that, where possible, the productive potential of an economy ought to be developed by free-market forces.

■ Growing government debt and a desire to curb public expenditure acted as a key incentive to reduce the state's role in industrial affairs. This is argued to have been one of the driving forces behind the European privatisation process since the 1980s.

■ Industry, during the 1980s, became progressively more global in its outlook. As such, its investment decisions were increasingly being determined by external environmental factors, such as comparative labour costs in different countries and countries' transport and communication links. Old-style industrial policy, which focuses on the national economy in isolation and on distinct sectors within it, has become increasingly less effective and relevant in meeting the needs of national economies operating in an open trading environment, where business investment and strategy are assessed in global terms.

The new approach to industrial policy, being widely adopted by many advanced countries, is to focus on improving those factors that shape a nation's competitiveness. This involves shifting away from particular sectors to targeting what are referred to as 'framework conditions for industry'.

Such 'conditions' have been the subject of a series of reviews by the OECD, which found that the following initiatives are forming the basis of a new industrial competitiveness policy:

■ The promotion of investment in physical and human capital. Human capital in particular, and the existence of a sound skills base, are seen as crucial for attracting global business and ensuring long-run economic growth.

■ A reduction in non-wage employment costs, such as employers' social security and pension contributions. Many governments see these costs as too high and as a severe limitation on competitiveness and employment creation.

■ The promotion of innovation and the encouragement of greater levels of R & D.

■ Support for small and medium-sized enterprises (SMEs). SMEs have received particular attention due to their crucial role in enhancing innovation, creating employment and contributing to skills development, especially in high-tech areas.

■ The improvement of infrastructure. This includes both physical transport, such as roads and railways, as well as information highways.

■ The protection of intellectual property by more effective use of patents and copyright. By reinforcing the law in these areas it is hoped to encourage firms to develop new products and commit themselves to research.

These initiatives, if they are to be truly effective, are likely to require co-ordination and integration, since they represent a radical departure from established industrial policy.

1. In what senses could these new policies be described as (a) non-interventionist; (b) interventionist?
2. Does globalisation, and in particular the global perspective of multinational corporations, make industrial policy in the form of selective subsidies and tax relief more or less likely?

Box 10.5

Alternative approaches to training and education

It is generally recognised by economists and politicians alike that improvements in training and education can yield significant supply-side gains. Indeed, the UK's failure to invest as much in training as many of its major competitors is seen as a key explanation for the country's poor economic performance since the early 1970s.

Training and economic performance are linked in three main ways:

■ *Labour productivity*. In various studies comparing the productivity of UK and German industry, education and training was seen as the principal reason for the productivity gap between the two countries (see diagram in Box 10.3).
■ *Innovation and change*. A key factor in shaping a firm's willingness to introduce new products or processes is the adaptability and skills of its workforce. If the firm has to spend a lot of money on retraining, or on attracting skilled workers away from other firms, the costs may prove prohibitive.
■ *Costs of production*. A shortage of skilled workers will quickly create labour bottlenecks and cause production costs to increase. This will stifle economic growth.

If training is left to the employer, the benefits will become an externality if the workers leave to work elsewhere. Society has benefited from the training, but the firm has not. The free market, therefore, will provide a less than optimal amount of training. The more mobile the labour force, and the more 'transferable' the skills acquired from training, the more likely it is that workers will leave, and the less willing firms will be to invest in training.

In the UK, there is a high level of labour turnover. What is more, wage differentials between skilled and unskilled workers are narrower than in many other countries, and so there is less incentive for workers to train.

How can increased training be achieved? There are three broad approaches:

■ Workers could be encouraged to stay with their employer so that employers would be more willing to invest in training. Externalities would be reduced.
■ The government could provide subsidies for training. Alternatively, the government or some other agency could provide education and training directly.
■ Firms could co-operate to prevent 'poaching' and set up industry-wide training programmes, perhaps in partnership with the government and unions.

Approaches to training in various countries

As far as the first approach is concerned, most countries have seen a movement towards *greater* labour mobility. The rise in the 'flexible firm' (see Box 5.2) has involved the employment of fewer permanent workers and more part-time and temporary workers. Some countries, such as Japan and Germany, however, have a generally lower rate of labour turnover than most. In Japan, in particular, it has been common for workers to stay with one employer throughout their career. There the relationship between employer and employee has traditionally extended well beyond a simple short-term economic arrangement. Workers give loyalty and commitment to their employer, which in return virtually guarantees long-term employment and provides various fringe benefits (such as housing, child care, holiday schemes and health care). It is not surprising that Japanese firms invest highly in training.

In the USA, labour turnover is very high and yet there is little in the way of industry-wide training. Instead, the US government hopes, by having a high percentage of young people in further and higher education, that sufficient numbers and quality of workers are available for industry. Approximately 45 per cent of the US population enters higher education with 33 per cent of the population graduating, and only just over 0.2 per cent of GDP is spent on training.

In Germany the proportion entering higher education is considerably lower (some 28 per cent, with just over 19 per cent of the population graduating), but expenditure on training accounts for nearly 1.6 per cent of GDP. Most young people who do not enter higher education embark on some form of apprenticeship. They attend school for part of the week, and receive work-based training for the rest. The state, unions and employers' associations work closely in determining training provision, and they have developed a set of vocational qualifications based around the apprenticeship system. Given that virtually all firms are involved in training, the 'free-rider' problem of firms poaching labour without themselves paying for training is virtually eliminated. The result is that the German workforce is highly skilled. Many of the skills, however, are highly specific. This is a problem when the demand for particular skills declines.

The UK approach

In the UK, the Conservative government's attitude towards training was initially influenced by its free-market approach to supply-side policy. Training was to be left largely to employers. However, with growing worries over the UK's 'productivity gap', the government set up Training and Enterprise Councils (TECs) in 1988. The TECs identified regional skills needs, organised training and financed work-based training schemes.

The TECs were replaced in 2001 by the Learning and Skills Council (LSC). This has a budget of some £6 billion and is responsible for planning and funding sixth forms, further education colleges, work-based training for young people aged 16–24 ('Modern Apprenticeships'), adult and community learning, the provision of information, advice and guidance for adults and developing links between education and business. Through its 'Connexions' service, it offers training and employment advice and support for young people between the ages of 13 and 19.

In 1991, the National Vocational Qualification (NVQ) was launched. Students work for an employer, and receive on-the-job training. They also attend college on an occasional basis. The NVQ is awarded when they have achieved sufficient experience. In addition the government launched General National Vocational Qualifications (GNVQs). These further-education qualifications were intended to bridge the gap between education and work, by ensuring that education was more work relevant.

The GNVQ system was modelled on that in France, where a clear vocational educational route is seen as the key to reducing skills shortages. At the age of 14, French students can choose to pursue academic or vocational education routes. The vocational route provides high-level, broad-based skills (unlike in Germany, where skills tend to be more job specific).

Another approach adopted by the Labour government in the UK has been to encourage 'lifelong learning'. Measures include:

- A University of Industry, which through its 'Learndirect' brand offers online courses in a range of business, technical and IT subjects.
- Some 700 information and communication technology (ICT) learning centres, which provide basic IT, literacy and numeracy skills.
- 'Work-based Learning for Adults' in England and Wales and 'Training for Work' in Scotland: two schemes to provide work-based training for people aged 25 and over who have been out of work for six months or more, with grants paid to employers.

Another measure, launched in England in 2001, was the introduction of two-year foundation degrees. These are offered by universities or higher education colleges. They are designed in conjunction with employers to meet various skill shortages. They are taken at the university or an associated college, normally on a part-time basis, and often include work-based study with local employers.

Critics of the UK strategy have argued that employers still face the threat of having newly trained labour poached; that the regional activities of the LSC fail to account for national, long-term training issues; and that NVQs often provide too narrow forms of training. Most importantly, the funding devoted to training is still low compared with most other industrialised countries. They claim that the UK system has the worst features of both the US and the German systems: too little training and too specific training.

?

1. Governments and educationalists generally regard it as desirable that trainees acquire transferable skills. Why may many employers disagree?
2. There are externalities (benefits) when employers provide training. What externalities are there from the undergoing of training by the individual? Do they imply that individuals will choose to receive more or less than the socially optimal amount of training?

grants and tax concessions. For example, small firms pay a 19 per cent rate of corporation tax compared with 30 per cent for larger companies. In addition, small firms are subject to fewer planning and other bureaucratic controls than large companies.

Advice and persuasion. The government may engage in discussions with private firms in order to find ways to improve efficiency and innovation. It may bring firms together to exchange information, so as to co-ordinate their decisions and create a climate of greater certainty. It may bring firms and unions together to try to create greater industrial harmony.

Information. The government may provide various information services to firms: technical assistance, the results of public research, information on markets, etc.

Recap

1. Market-orientated supply-side policies aim to increase the rate of growth of aggregate supply and reduce the rate of unemployment by encouraging private enterprise and the freer play of market forces.

2. Reducing government expenditure as a proportion of GDP is a major element of such policies. This involves measures such as the use of cash limits on government departments and local authorities, reducing grants and subsidies, reducing the number of public employees, resisting pay increases in the public sector, and reorganising public-sector industries and departments in order to achieve greater efficiency.

3. Tax cuts can be used to encourage more people to take up jobs, to work longer hours and to work more enthusiastically. The effects of tax cuts will depend on how people respond to incentives.

4. Reducing the power of trade unions and a reduction in welfare benefits, especially those related to unemployment, may force workers to accept jobs at lower wage rates, thereby decreasing equilibrium unemployment.

5. Other examples of market-orientated supply-side policy include privatisation, competitive tendering for public-sector contracts, deregulation, the Private Finance Initiative and free trade and capital movements.

6. Interventionist supply-side policy can take the form of grants for investment and research and development, advice and persuasion, the provision of information, the direct provision of infrastructure and the provision, funding or encouragement of various training schemes.

Questions

1. If V is constant, will (a) a £10 million rise in M give a £10 million rise in MV and (b) a 10 per cent rise in M give a 10 per cent rise in MV? (Test your answer by fitting some numbers to the terms.)

2. If both V and Y are constant, will (a) a £10 million rise in M lead to a £10 million rise in P and (b) a 10 per cent rise in M lead to a 10 per cent rise in P? (Again, try fitting some numbers to the terms.)

3. What would be the implications of different assumptions about the V and Y terms in the quantity equation $MV = PY$ for the effectiveness of monetary policy to control inflation?

4. Assume that inflation depends on two things: the level of aggregate demand, indicated by the inverse of unemployment ($1/U$), and the expected rate of inflation ($\dot{P}_t^e$). Assume that the rate of inflation ($\dot{P}_t$) is given by the equation:

$$\dot{P}_t = (48/U - 6) + \dot{P}_t^e$$

Assume initially (year 0) that the actual and expected rate of inflation is zero.

   (a) Now assume in year 1 that the government wishes to reduce unemployment to 4 per cent and continues to expand aggregate demand by as much as is necessary to achieve this. Fill in the rows for years 0 to 4 in the table below. It is assumed for simplicity that the expected rate of inflation in a given year ($\dot{P}_t^e$) is equal to the actual rate of inflation in the previous year ($\dot{P}_{t-1}$).
   (b) Now assume in year 5 that the government, worried about rising inflation, reduces aggregate demand sufficiently to reduce inflation by 3 per cent in that year. What must the rate of unemployment be raised to in that year?
   (c) Assuming that unemployment stays at this high level, continue the table for years 5 to 7.

5. In the accelerationist model, if the government tries to maintain unemployment below the natural rate, what will determine the speed at which inflation accelerates?

6. For what reasons may the NAIRU (the equilibrium rate of unemployment) increase?

7. Given the Keynesian explanation for the persistence of high levels of unemployment after the recession of the 1980s, what policies would you advocate to reduce unemployment in such circumstances?

8. Taking first a new classical viewpoint and then a Keynesian one, explain each of the following:

   (a) Why there were simultaneously higher levels of inflation *and* unemployment in the 1970s and 1980s than in the 1950s and 1960s.
   (b) Why there were simultaneously lower levels of inflation *and* unemployment in the late 1990s and early 2000s than in the 1970s and 1980s?

9. For what reasons might the long-run aggregate supply curve be (a) vertical; (b) upward sloping?

Year	U	$48/U - 6$	+	$\dot{P}^e$	=	$\dot{P}$
0	...	...	+	...	=	...
1	...	...	+	...	=	...
2	...	...	+	...	=	...
3	...	...	+	...	=	...
4	...	...	+	...	=	...
5	...	...	+	...	=	...
6	...	...	+	...	=	...
7	...	...	+	...	=	...

10. What implications would a vertical short-run aggregate supply curve have for the effects of demand management policy?

11. (a) In the extreme Keynesian model with a horizontal *AS* curve, is there any point in supply-side policies?
    (b) In the model with a vertical *AS* curve, is there any point in using supply-side policies as a weapon against inflation?

12. Describe the effect of a contractionary monetary policy on national income from (a) a Keynesian perspective; (b) a new classical perspective.

13. Imagine you were called in by the government to advise on whether it should adopt a policy of targeting the money supply. What advice would you give and how would you justify the advice?

14. Imagine you were called in by the government to advise on whether it should attempt to prevent cyclical fluctuations by the use of fiscal policy. What advice would you give and how would you justify the advice?

15. Is there a compromise between purely discretionary policy and adhering to strict targets?

16. Under what circumstances would adherence to inflation targets lead to (a) more stable interest rates, (b) less stable interest rates than pursuing discretionary demand management policy?

17. What are the determinants of long-run economic growth? Is long-run economic growth sustainable without technological progress?

18. Why might market-orientated supply-side policies have undesirable side-effects on aggregate demand?

19. If supply-side measures led to a 'shake-out' of labour and a resulting reduction in overstaffing, but also a resulting rightward shift in the Phillips curve, would you judge the policy a success?

20. What types of tax cut are likely to create the greatest (a) incentives, (b) disincentives to effort?

21. In what ways can interventionist supply-side policy work *with* the market, rather than against it? What are the arguments for and against such policy?

Additional case studies on the *Essentials of Economics* website (www.booksites.net/sloman)

10.1 **Money and inflation in ancient Rome.** A very early case study of the quantity theory of money: how the minting of extra coins by the Romans caused prices to rise.

10.2 **The equation of exchange.** This examines two more versions that are commonly used: the Fisher version and the Cambridge version.

10.3 **Explaining the shape of the short-run Phillips curve.** This shows how money illusion on the part of workers can explain why the Phillips curve is downward sloping.

10.4 **The quantity theory of money restated.** An examination of how the vertical long-run *AS* curve in the adaptive expectations model can be used to justify the quantity theory of money.

10.5 **Milton Friedman (1912–).** A profile of the most influential of the monetarist economists.

10.6   The rational expectations revolution. A profile of two of the most famous economists of the new classical rational expectations school.

10.7   Monetary targeting: its use around the world. An expanded version of Box 10.2.

10.8   Managing the macroeconomy. This considers whether there have been conflicts of objectives in recent UK macroeconomic policy.

10.9   Managing the US economy. The use of expansionary fiscal and monetary policy in 2001/2 to stave off recession in the USA.

10.10 Productivity performance and the UK economy. A detailed examination of how the UK's productivity compares with that in other countries.

10.11 The USA: is it a 'new economy'? An examination of whether US productivity increases are likely to be sustained.

10.12 Technology and economic change. How to get the benefits from technological advance.

10.13 Controlling inflation in the past. This case study looks at the history of prices and incomes policies in the UK.

10.14 UK industrial performance. This examines why the UK has had a poorer investment record than many other industrial countries and why it has suffered a process of 'deindustrialisation'.

10.15 The new economy. Does globalisation bring economic success?

10.16 Assistance to small firms in the UK. An examination of current government measures to assist small firms.

10.17 Small-firm policy in the EU. This looks at the range of support available to small and medium-sized firms in the EU.

10.18 Welfare to work. An examination of the policy of the UK Labour government whereby welfare payments are designed to encourage people into employment.

Sections of chapter covered in
WinEcon – Sloman, *Essentials of Economics*

Essentials of Economics section	*WinEcon* section
10.1	10.1
10.2	10.2
10.3	10.3
10.4	10.4
10.5	–
10.6	–
10.7	–
10.8	–

Websites relevant to this chapter

Numbers and sections refer to websites listed in the Web Appendix and hotlinked from this book's website at www.booksites.net/sloman

- For news articles relevant to this chapter, see the *Economics News Articles* link from the book's website.

- For general news on unemployment, inflation, economic growth and supply-side policy, see websites in section A, and particularly A1–5. See also links to newspapers worldwide in A38 and 39, and the news search feature in Google at A41. See also links to economics news in A42.

- For data on unemployment, inflation and growth, see links in B1 or 2; see also B4 and 12. For UK data, see B3 and 34. For EU data, see G1 > *The Statistical Annex*. For US data, see *Current economic indicators* in B5 and the *Data* section of B17. For international data, see B15, 21, 24, 31, 33. For links to data sets, see B28; I14.

- For specific data on UK unemployment, see B1, *1. National Statistics* > the fourth link > *Labour Market* > *Labour Market Trends*. For international data on unemployment, see G1; H3 and 5.

- For information on the development of ideas, including information on classical, Keynesian, monetarist, new classical and new Keynesian thought, see C12, 18; see also links under *Methodology and History of Economic Thought* in C14, and links to economists in I4 and I7. See also sites I7 and I1 > *Economic Systems and Theories* > *History of Economic Thought*.

- For demand-side policy in the UK, see the latest Budget Report (e.g. the section on maintaining macroeconomic stability) at site E30.

- For inflation targeting in the UK and the euro zone, see sites F1 and 6.

- For the current approach to UK supply-side policy, see the latest Budget Report (e.g. the sections on productivity and training) at site E30. See also sites E5 and 9.

- For information on training in the UK and Europe, see sites D7; E5; G5, 14.

- For support for a market-orientated approach to supply-side policy, see C17 and E34.

- For student resources relevant to this chapter, see sites C1–7, 9, 10, 19. See also the *Labour market reforms* simulation in D3.

Part C International Economics

CHAPTER ELEVEN

International trade

Trade between nations has the potential to benefit all participating countries (albeit to differing extents). This chapter explains why.

Totally free trade, however, may bring problems to countries or to groups of people within those countries. Many people argue strongly for restrictions on trade. Textile workers see their jobs threatened by cheap imported cloth. Car manufacturers worry about falling sales as customers switch to Japanese models or other east Asian ones. But are people justified in fearing international competition, or are they merely trying to protect some vested interest at the expense of everyone else? Section 11.2 examines the arguments for restricting trade.

If there are conflicting views as to whether we should have more or less trade, what has been happening on the world stage? Section 11.3 looks at the various moves towards making trade freer and at the obstacles that have been met.

A step on the road to freer trade is for countries to enter free-trade agreements with just a limited number of other countries. Examples include the EU and the North American Free Trade Association, NAFTA (the USA, Canada and Mexico). We consider such 'preferential trading systems' in Section 11.4. Then, in Section 11.5, we look at probably the world's most famous preferential trading system, the European Union, and, in particular, at the development of a 'single European market'.

Finally we turn to examine the role of trade for developing countries. Does trade with the rich world help them to develop, or does it merely result in them being dominated by rich countries and giant multinational companies?

11.1   The gains from trade

Can international trade make all countries better off?

Specialisation as the basis for trade

Why do countries trade with each other and what do they gain out of it? The
reasons for international trade are really only an extension of the reasons for trade
within a nation. Rather than people trying to be self-sufficient and do everything for
themselves, it makes sense to specialise.

Firms specialise in producing certain types of goods. This allows them to gain
economies of scale and to exploit their entrepreneurial and management skills and
the skills of their labour force. It also allows them to benefit from their particular
location and from the ownership of any particular capital equipment or other assets
they might possess. With the revenues that firms earn, they buy in the inputs that
they need from other firms and the labour they require. Firms thus trade with each
other.

Countries also specialise. They produce more than they need of certain goods.
What is not consumed domestically is exported. The revenues earned from the
exports are used to import goods that are not produced in sufficient amounts at
home.

But which goods should a country specialise in? What should it export and what
should it import? The answer is that it should specialise in those goods in which it
has a *comparative advantage*. Let us examine what this means.

The law of comparative advantage

Countries have different endowments of factors of production. They differ in population density, labour skills, climate, raw materials, capital equipment, etc. These
differences tend to persist because factors are relatively immobile between countries. Obviously land and climate are totally immobile, but even with labour and
capital there tend to be more restrictions (physical, social, cultural or legal) on their
international movement than on their movement within countries. Thus the
ability to supply goods differs between countries.

What this means is that the relative costs of producing goods will vary from
country to country. For example, one country may be able to produce 1 fridge for
the same cost as 6 tonnes of wheat or 3 compact disc players, whereas another
country may be able to produce 1 fridge for the same cost as only 3 tonnes of wheat
but 4 CD players. It is these differences in relative costs that form the basis of
trade.

At this stage we need to distinguish between *absolute advantage* and *comparative
advantage*.

Absolute advantage

When one country can produce a good with less resources than another country it
is said to have an absolute advantage in that good. If France can produce wine with
less resources than the UK, and the UK can produce gin with less resources than
France, then France has an absolute advantage in wine and the UK an absolute

Definition

**Absolute
advantage**
A country has an
absolute advantage
over another in the
production of a good if
it can produce it with
less resources than the
other country.

		Kilos of wheat		Metres of cloth
Less developed country	Either	2	or	I
Developed country	Either	4	or	8

Table 11.1
Production possibilities for two countries

advantage in gin. Production of both wine and gin will be maximised by each country specialising and then trading with the other country. Both will gain.

Comparative advantage

The above seems obvious, but trade between two countries can still be beneficial even if one country could produce all goods with less resources than the other, providing the *relative* efficiency with which goods can be produced differs between the two countries.

Take the case of a developed country that is absolutely more efficient than a less developed country at producing both wheat and cloth. Assume that with a given amount of resources (labour, land and capital) the alternatives shown in Table 11.1 can be produced in each country.

Despite the developed country having an absolute advantage in both wheat and cloth, the less developed country (LDC) has a *comparative* advantage in wheat, and the developed country has a *comparative* advantage in cloth. This is because wheat is relatively cheaper in terms of cloth in the LDC: only 1 metre of cloth has to be sacrificed to produce 2 kilos of wheat, whereas 8 metres of cloth would have to be sacrificed in the developed country to produce 4 kilos of wheat. In other words, the opportunity cost of wheat is 4 times higher in the developed country (8/4 compared with 1/2).

On the other hand, cloth is relatively cheaper in the developed country. Here the opportunity cost of producing 8 metres of cloth is only 4 kilos of wheat, whereas in the LDC 1 metre of cloth costs 2 kilos of wheat. Thus the opportunity cost of cloth is 4 times higher in the LDC (2/1 compared with 4/8).

To summarise: countries have a comparative advantage in those goods that can be produced at a lower opportunity cost than in other countries.

If countries are to gain from trade, they should export those goods in which they have a comparative advantage and import those goods in which they have a comparative disadvantage. Given this we can state a law of comparative advantage.

> **Definitions**
>
> **Comparative advantage**
> A country has a comparative advantage over another in the production of a good if it can produce it at a lower opportunity cost: i.e. if it has to forgo less of other goods in order to produce it.
>
> **The law of comparative advantage**
> Trade can benefit all countries if they specialise in the goods in which they have a comparative advantage.

> **Pause for thought**
>
> Draw up a table similar to Table 11.1, only this time assume that the figures are: LDC 6 wheat or 2 cloth; DC 8 wheat or 20 cloth. What are the opportunity cost ratios now?

> **The law of comparative advantage.** Provided opportunity costs of various goods differ in two countries, both of them can gain from mutual trade if they specialise in producing (and exporting) those goods that have relatively low opportunity costs compared with the other country.
>
> **Key Idea 30**

But why do they gain if they specialise according to this law? And just what will that gain be? We will consider these questions next.

The gains from trade based on comparative advantage

Before trade, unless markets are very imperfect, the prices of the two goods are likely to reflect their opportunity costs. For example, in Table 11.1, since the less developed country can produce 2 kilos of wheat for 1 metre of cloth, the *price* of 2 kilos of wheat will roughly equal 1 metre of cloth.

Assume, then, that the pre-trade exchange ratios of wheat for cloth are as follows:

LDC: 2 wheat for 1 cloth
Developed country: 1 wheat for 2 cloth (i.e. 4 for 8)

Both countries will now gain from trade, provided the exchange ratio is somewhere between 2:1 and 1:2. Assume, for the sake of argument, that it is 1:1: that 1 wheat trades internationally for 1 cloth. How will each country gain?

The LDC gains by exporting wheat and importing cloth. At an exchange ratio of 1:1, it now only has to give up 1 kilo of wheat to obtain a metre of cloth, whereas before trade it had to give up 2 kilos of wheat.

The developed country gains by exporting cloth and importing wheat. Again at an exchange ratio of 1:1, it now only has to give up 1 metre of cloth to obtain a kilo of wheat, whereas before it had to give up 2 metres of cloth.

Thus both countries have gained from trade.

The actual exchange ratios will depend on the relative prices of wheat and cloth after trade takes place. These prices will depend on total demand for and supply of the two goods. It may be that the trade exchange ratio is nearer to the pre-trade exchange ratio of one country than the other. Thus the gains to the two countries need not be equal.

The limits to specialisation and trade

Does the law of comparative advantage suggest that countries will completely specialise in just a few products? In practice, countries are likely to experience *increasing* opportunity costs. The reason for this is that, as a country increasingly specialises in one good, it will have to use resources that are less and less suited to its production and which were more suited to other goods. Thus ever-increasing amounts of the other goods will have to be sacrificed. For example, as a country specialises more and more in grain production, it will have to use land that is less and less suited to growing grain.

These increasing costs as a country becomes more and more specialised will lead to the disappearance of its comparative cost advantage. When this happens, there will be no point in further specialisation. Thus whereas a country like Germany has a comparative advantage in capital-intensive manufactures, it does not produce only manufactures. It would make no sense not to use its fertile lands to produce food or its forests to produce timber. The opportunity costs of diverting all agricultural labour to industry would be very high.

The terms of trade

What price will our exports fetch abroad? What will we have to pay for imports? The answer to these questions is given by the terms of trade. The terms of trade are defined as:

Definition

Terms of trade
The price index of exports divided by the price index of imports and then expressed as a percentage. This means that the terms of trade will be 100 in the base year.

$$\frac{\text{The average price of exports}}{\text{The average price of imports}}$$

expressed as an index, where prices are measured against a base year in which the terms of trade are assumed to be 100. Thus if the average price of exports relative to the average price of imports has risen by 20 per cent since the base year, the terms of trade will now be 120.

If the terms of trade rise (export prices rising relative to import prices), they are said to have 'improved', since fewer exports now have to be sold to purchase any given quantity of imports. Changes in the terms of trade are caused by changes in the demand and supply of imports and exports and by changes in the exchange rate.

Other reasons for gains from trade

Decreasing costs. Even if there are no initial comparative cost differences between two countries, it will still benefit both to specialise in industries where economies of scale can be gained, and then to trade. Once the economies of scale begin to appear, comparative cost differences will also appear, and thus the countries will have gained a comparative advantage in these industries.

This reason for trade is particularly relevant for small countries where the domestic market is not large enough to support large-scale industries. Thus exports form a much higher percentage of GDP in small countries such as Singapore than in large countries such as the USA.

Differences in demand. Even with no comparative cost differences and no potential economies of scale, trade can benefit both countries if demand conditions differ.

If people in country A like beef more than lamb, and people in country B like lamb more than beef, then rather than A using resources better suited for lamb to produce beef, and B using resources better suited for producing beef to produce lamb, it will benefit both to produce beef *and* lamb and to export the one they like less in return for the one they like more.

Increased competition. If a country trades, the competition from imports may stimulate greater efficiency at home. This extra competition may prevent domestic monopolies/oligopolies from charging high prices. It may stimulate greater research and development and the more rapid adoption of new technology. It may lead to a greater variety of products being made available to consumers.

Trade as an 'engine of growth'. In a growing world economy, the demand for a country's exports is likely to grow over time, especially when these exports have a high income elasticity of demand. This will provide a stimulus to growth in the exporting country.

Non-economic advantages. There may be political, social and cultural advantages to be gained by fostering trading links between countries.

Recap

1. Countries can gain from trade if they specialise in producing those goods in which they have a comparative advantage: i.e. those goods that can be produced at relatively low opportunity costs. This is merely an extension of the argument that gains can be made from the specialisation and division of labour.

2. If two countries trade, then, provided that the trade price ratio of exports and imports is somewhere between the pre-trade price ratios of these goods in the two countries, both countries can gain.

3. With increasing opportunity costs there will be a limit to specialisation and trade. As a country increasingly specialises, its (marginal) comparative advantage will eventually disappear.

4. The terms of trade give the price of exports relative to the price of imports expressed as an index, where the base year is 100.

5. Gains from trade also arise from decreasing costs (economies of scale), differences in demand between countries, increased competition from trade and the transmission of growth from one country to another. There may also be non-economic advantages from trade.

11.2   Arguments for restricting trade

If trade can benefit everyone, then why do countries attempt to limit trade?

We have seen how trade can bring benefits to all countries. But when we look around the world we often see countries erecting barriers to trade. Their politicians know that trade involves costs as well as benefits.

In looking at the costs and benefits of trade, the choice is not the stark one of whether to have free trade or no trade at all. Although countries may sometimes contemplate having completely free trade, typically countries limit their trade. However, they certainly do not ban it altogether.

Before we look at the arguments for restricting trade, we must first see what types of restriction governments can employ.

Methods of restricting trade

Definition

Ad valorem tariffs
Tariffs levied as a percentage of the price of the import.

Tariffs (customs duties).   These are taxes on imports and are usually ad valorem tariffs: i.e. a percentage of the price of the import. Tariffs used to restrict imports are most effective if demand is elastic (e.g. when there are close domestically produced substitutes). Tariffs can also be used as a means of raising revenue. Here they will be more effective if demand is inelastic. They can also be used to raise the price of imported goods to prevent 'unfair' competition for domestic producers.

Quotas.   These are limits imposed on the quantity of a good that can be imported. Quotas can be imposed by the government, or negotiated with other countries that agree 'voluntarily' to restrict the amount of exports to the first country.

Exchange controls.   These include limits on the amount of foreign exchange made available to importers (financial quotas), or to citizens travelling abroad, or for

Box 11.1 Exploring Economics

Do we exploit foreign workers by buying cheap foreign imports?

People sometimes question the morality of buying imports from countries where workers are paid 'pittance' wages. 'Is it right', they ask, 'for us to support a system where workers are so exploited?' As is often the case with emotive issues, there is some truth and some misunderstanding in a point of view like this.

First the truth. If a country like the UK trades with a regime that denies human rights and treats its workers very badly, then we may thereby be helping to sustain a corrupt system. We might also be seen to be lending it moral support. In this sense, therefore, trade may not help the cause of the workers in these countries. Arguments like these were used to support the imposition of trade sanctions against South Africa in the days of apartheid.

Now the misunderstanding. If we buy goods from countries that pay low wages, we are *not* as a result contributing to their low-wage problem. Quite the reverse. If countries like India export textiles to the West, this will help to *increase* the wages of Indian workers. If India has a comparative advantage in labour-intensive goods, these goods will earn a better price by being exported than by being sold entirely in the domestic Indian market. Provided *some* of the extra revenues go to the workers (as opposed to their bosses), they will gain from trade.

? Under what circumstances would a gain in revenues by exporting firms *not* lead to an increase in wage rates?

---

investment. Alternatively, they can be in the form of charges for the purchase of foreign currencies.

Import licensing.   The imposition of exchange controls or quotas will often involve importers obtaining licences so that the government can better enforce its restrictions.

Embargoes.   This is where the government completely bans certain imports (e.g. drugs) or exports to certain countries (e.g. to enemies during war).

Export taxes.   These can be used to increase the price of exports when the country has monopoly power in their supply.

Subsidies.   These can be given to domestic producers to prevent competition from otherwise lower-priced imports. They can also be applied to exports in a process known as dumping. The goods are 'dumped' at artificially low prices in the foreign market. (This, of course, is a means of artificially increasing exports, rather than reducing imports.)

Administrative barriers.   Regulations may be designed to exclude imports. For example, all lagers that do not meet certain rigid purity standards could be banned. The Germans effectively excluded foreign brands by such measures. Other administrative barriers include taxes that favour locally produced products or ingredients.

Procurement policies.   This is where governments favour domestic producers when purchasing equipment (e.g. defence equipment).

Definition

Dumping
Where exports are sold at prices below marginal cost – often as a result of government subsidy.

Arguments in favour of restricting trade

Arguments having some general validity

The infant industry argument. Some industries in a country may be in their infancy but have a potential comparative advantage. This is particularly likely in developing countries. Such industries are too small yet to have gained economies of scale; their workers are inexperienced; there is a lack of back-up facilities – communications networks, specialist research and development, specialist suppliers, etc. – and they may have only limited access to finance for expansion. Without protection, these infant industries will not survive competition from abroad.

Protection from foreign competition, however, will allow them to expand and become more efficient. Once they have achieved a comparative advantage, the protection can then be removed to enable them to compete internationally.

Similar to the infant industry argument is the *senile industry* argument. This is where industries with a potential comparative advantage have been allowed to run down and can no longer compete effectively. They may have considerable potential, but be simply unable to make enough profit to afford the necessary investment without some temporary protection from foreign competition. This argument has been used to justify the use of special protection for the automobile and steel industries in the USA.

To reduce reliance on goods with little dynamic potential. Many developing countries have traditionally exported primaries: foodstuffs and raw materials. The world demand for these, however, is fairly income inelastic, and thus grows relatively slowly (see Section 11.6). In such cases, free trade is not an engine of growth. Instead, if it encourages countries' economies to become locked in to a pattern of primary production, it may prevent them from expanding in sectors like manufacturing which have a higher income elasticity of demand. There may thus be a valid argument for protecting or promoting manufacturing industry.

To prevent 'dumping' and other unfair trade practices. A country may engage in dumping by subsidising its exports. Alternatively, firms may practise price discrimination by selling at a higher price in home markets and a lower price in foreign markets in order to increase their profits. Either way, prices may no longer reflect comparative costs. Thus the world would benefit from tariffs being imposed by importers to counteract the subsidy.

It can also be argued that there is a case for retaliating against countries which impose restrictions on your exports. In the short run, both countries are likely to be made worse off by a contraction in trade. But if the retaliation persuades the other country to remove its restrictions, it may have a longer-term benefit. In some cases, the mere threat of retaliation may be enough to get another country to remove its protection.

To prevent the establishment of a foreign-based monopoly. Competition from abroad could drive domestic producers out of business. The foreign company, now having a monopoly of the market, could charge high prices with a resulting misallocation of resources. The problem could be tackled either by restricting imports or by subsidising the domestic producer(s).

Definition

Infant industry
An industry that has a potential comparative advantage, but which is as yet too underdeveloped to be able to realise this potential.

All of the above arguments suggest that governments should adopt a 'strategic' approach to trade. Strategic trade theory argues that protecting certain industries allows a net gain in the *long* run from increased competition in the market. This argument has been used to justify the huge financial support given to the aircraft manufacturer Airbus, a consortium based in four European countries. The subsidies have allowed it to compete with Boeing, which would otherwise have a monopoly in many types of passenger aircraft. Airlines and their passengers worldwide, it is argued, have benefited from the increased competition.

To spread the risks of fluctuating markets. A highly specialised economy – Zambia with copper, Cuba with sugar – will be highly susceptible to world market fluctuations. Greater diversity and greater self-sufficiency, although maybe leading to less efficiency, can reduce these risks.

To reduce the influence of trade on consumer tastes. The assumption of fixed consumer tastes dictating the pattern of production through trade is false. Multinational companies through their advertising and other forms of sales promotion may influence consumer tastes. Thus some restriction on trade may be justified in order to reduce this 'producer sovereignty'.

To prevent the importation of harmful goods. A country may want to ban or severely curtail the importation of things such as drugs, pornographic literature and live animals.

To take account of externalities. Free trade will tend to reflect private costs. Both imports and exports, however, can involve externalities. The mining of many minerals for export may adversely affect the health of miners; the production of chemicals for export may involve pollution; the importation of juggernaut lorries may lead to structural damage to houses.

Arguments having some validity for specific groups or countries

The arguments considered so far are of general validity: restricting trade for such reasons could be of net benefit to the world. There are other arguments, however, that are used by individual governments for restricting trade, where their country will gain, but at the expense of other countries, such that there will be a net loss to the world. Such arguments include the following.

The exploitation of monopoly power. If a country, or a group of countries, has monopsony power in the purchase of imports (i.e. they are individually or collectively a very large economy, such as the USA or the EU), then they could gain by restricting imports so as to drive down their price. Similarly, if countries have monopoly power in the sale of some export (e.g. OPEC countries with oil), then they could gain by restricting exports, thereby forcing up the price (see Box 4.4).

To protect declining industries. The human costs of sudden industrial closures can be very high. In such circumstances, temporary protection may be warranted to allow the industry to decline more slowly, thus avoiding excessive structural unemployment. Such policies will be at the expense of the consumer, however, who will be denied access to cheaper foreign imports.

> **Definition**
>
> **Strategic trade theory**
> The theory that protecting/supporting certain industries can enable them to compete more effectively with large monopolistic rivals abroad. The effect of the protection is to increase long-run competition and may enable the protected firms to exploit a comparative advantage that they could not have done otherwise.

'Non-economic' arguments for restricting trade. A country may be prepared to forgo the direct economic advantages of free trade in order to achieve objectives that are often described as 'non-economic':

■ It may wish to maintain a degree of self-sufficiency in case trade is cut off in times of war. This may apply particularly to the production of food and armaments.
■ It may decide not to trade with certain countries with which it disagrees politically.
■ It may wish to preserve traditional ways of life. Rural communities or communities built round old traditional industries may be destroyed by foreign competition.
■ It may prefer to retain as diverse a society as possible, rather than one too narrowly based on certain industries.

Pursuing such objectives, however, will involve costs. Preserving a traditional way of life, for example, may mean that consumers are denied access to cheaper goods from abroad. Society must therefore weigh up the benefits against the costs of such policies.

Problems with protection

Tariffs and other forms of protection impose a cost on society. This is illustrated in Figure 11.1. It illustrates the case of a good that is partly home produced and partly imported. Domestic demand and supply are given by D_{dom} and S_{dom}. It is assumed that firms in the country produce under perfect competition and that therefore the supply curve is the sum of the firms' marginal cost curves.

Let us assume that the country is too small to affect world prices: it is a price taker. The world price is given, at P_{w}. At P_{w}, Q_2 is demanded, Q_1 is supplied by domestic suppliers and hence $Q_2 - Q_1$ is imported.

Now a tariff is imposed. This increases the price to consumers by the amount of the tariff. Price rises to $P_{\text{w}} + t$. Domestic production increases to Q_3, consumption falls to Q_4, and hence imports fall to $Q_4 - Q_3$.

What are the costs of this tariff to the country? Consumers are having to pay a higher price, and hence consumer surplus falls from area *ABC* to *ADE* (see pages 212–13 if you are unsure about consumer surplus). The cost to consumers in lost consumer surplus is thus *EDBC* (i.e. areas 1 + 2 + 3 + 4). *Part* of this cost, however, is redistributed as a *benefit* to other sections in society. *Firms* get a higher price, and thus gain extra profits (area 1): where profit is given by the area between the price and the *MC* curve. The *government* receives extra revenue from the tariff payments (area 3): i.e. $Q_4 - Q_3 \times$ tariff. These revenues can be used, for example, to reduce taxes.

But *part* of this cost is not recouped elsewhere. It is a net cost to society (areas 2 and 4).

Area 2 represents the extra costs of producing $Q_3 - Q_1$ at home, rather than importing it. If $Q_3 - Q_1$ were still imported, the country would only be paying P_{w}. By producing it at home, however, the costs are given by the domestic supply curve (= *MC*). The difference between *MC* and P_{w} (area 2) is thus the efficiency loss on the production side.

Area 4 represents the loss of consumer surplus by the reduction in consumption from Q_2 to Q_4. Consumers have saved area FBQ_2Q_4 of expenditure, but have sacrificed area DBQ_2Q_4 of utility in so doing – a net loss of area 4.

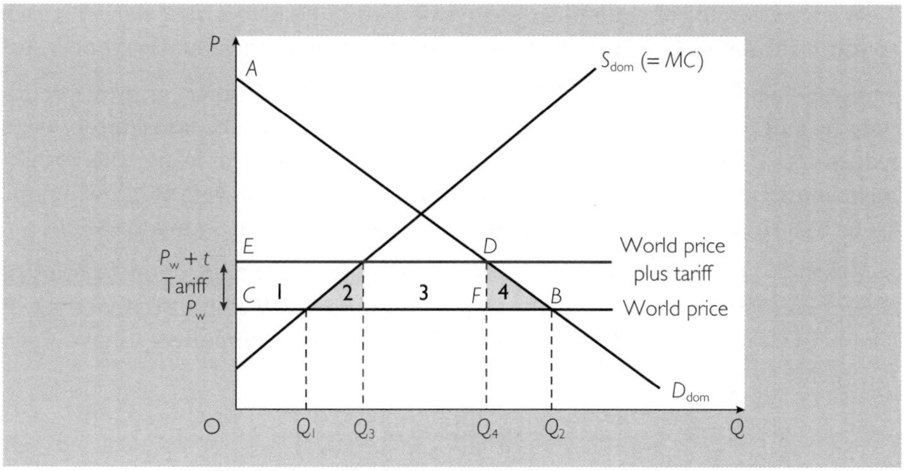

Figure 11.1

The cost of protection

The government should ideally weigh up such costs against any benefits that are gained from protection.

Apart from these direct costs to the consumer, there are several other problems with protection. Some are a direct effect of the protection; others follow from the reactions of other nations.

Protection as 'second-best'. Many of the arguments for protection amount merely to arguments for some type of government intervention in the economy. Protection, however, may not be the best way of dealing with the problem, since protection may have undesirable side-effects. There may be a more direct form of intervention that has no side-effects. In such a case, protection will be no more than a *second-best* solution.

For example, using tariffs to protect old inefficient industries from foreign competition may help prevent unemployment in those parts of the economy, but the consumer will suffer from higher prices. A better solution would be to subsidise retraining and investment in those areas of the country in *new efficient industries* – industries with a comparative advantage. In this way, unemployment is avoided, but the consumer does not suffer.

> **Pause for thought**
>
> (a) Protection to allow the exploitation of monopoly/monopsony power can be seen as a 'first-best' policy for the country concerned. Similarly, the use of tariffs to counteract externalities directly involved in the trade process (e.g. the environmental costs of an oil tanker disaster) could be seen to be a first-best policy. Explain why.
>
> (b) All the other arguments for tariffs or other forms of protection that we have considered can really be seen as arguments for intervention, with protection being no more than a second-best form of intervention. Go through each of the arguments and consider what would be a 'first-best' form of intervention.

World multiplier effects. If the UK imposes tariffs or other restrictions, imports will be reduced. But these imports are other countries' exports. A reduction in their exports will reduce the level of injections into the 'rest-of-the-world' economy, and thus lead to a multiplied fall in rest-of-the-world income. This in turn will lead to a reduction in demand for UK exports. This, therefore, tends to undo the benefits of the tariffs.

Retaliation. If the USA imposes restrictions on, say, imports from the EU, then the EU may impose restrictions on imports from the USA. Any gain to US firms competing with EU imports is offset by a loss to US exporters. What is more, US consumers suffer, since the benefits from comparative advantage have been lost.

The increased use of tariffs and other restrictions can lead to a trade war, with each country cutting back on imports from other countries. In the end, everyone loses.

Protection may allow firms to remain inefficient.   Tariffs and other forms of protection, by removing or reducing foreign competition, may reduce firms' incentive to reduce costs. Thus if protection is being given to an infant industry, the government must ensure that the lack of competition does not prevent it 'growing up'. Protection should not be excessive and should be removed as soon as possible.

Bureaucracy.   If a government is to avoid giving excessive protection to firms, it should examine each case carefully. This can lead to large administrative costs. It could also lead to corrupt officials accepting bribes from importers to give them favourable treatment.

Recap

1. Countries use various methods to restrict trade, including tariffs, quotas, exchange controls, import licensing, export taxes, and legal and administrative barriers. Countries may also promote their own industries by subsidies.

2. Reasons for restricting trade that have some validity in a world context include the infant industry argument, the problems of relying on exporting goods whose market is growing slowly or even declining, dumping and other unfair trade practices, the danger of the establishment of a foreign-based monopoly, the need to spread the risks of fluctuating export prices, and the problems that free trade may adversely affect consumer tastes, that it may allow the importation of harmful goods and not take account of externalities.

3. Countries may also have other objectives in restricting trade, such as remaining self-sufficient in certain strategic products, not trading with certain countries of which it disapproves, protecting traditional ways of life or simply retaining a non-specialised economy.

4. Protection in the form of tariffs results in higher prices. The resulting loss in consumer surplus is not fully offset by the gain in profits to domestic firms and the tariff revenue for the government. Even if government intervention to protect certain parts of the economy is desirable, restricting trade is unlikely to be a first-best solution to the problem, since it involves side-effect costs. What is more, restricting trade may have adverse world multiplier effects; it may encourage retaliation; it may allow inefficient firms to remain inefficient; it may involve considerable bureaucracy and possibly even corruption.

11.3   World attitudes towards trade and protection

Is trade becoming freer or less free?

History of protectionism

After the Wall Street crash of 1929 (when prices on the US stock exchange plummeted), the world plunged into the Great Depression (see Box 8.1). Countries found their exports falling dramatically and many suffered severe balance of payments difficulties. The response of many countries was to restrict imports by the use of tariffs and quotas. Of course, this reduced other countries' exports, which encouraged them to resort to even greater protectionism. The net effect of the Depression and the rise in protectionism was a dramatic fall in world trade. The volume of world trade in manufactures fell by more than a third in the three years following the Wall Street crash. Clearly there was a net economic loss to the world from this decline in trade.

Post-war reduction in protectionism and the role of GATT

After the Second World War there was a general desire to reduce trade restrictions, so that all countries could gain the maximum benefits from trade. There was no desire to return to the beggar-my-neighbour policies of the 1930s.

In 1947, 23 countries got together and signed the General Agreement on Tariffs and Trade (GATT). By 2003 there were 146 members of its successor organisation, the World Trade Organisation, which was formed in 1995. Between them, the members of the WTO account for 93 per cent of world trade. The aims of GATT, and now the WTO, have been to liberalise trade. Periodically, member countries have met to negotiate reductions in tariffs and other trade restrictions. There have been nine 'rounds' of such negotiations since 1947. The four major ones have been the Kennedy round (1964–7), the Tokyo round (1973–9), the Uruguay round (1986–93) and, beginning in 2001, the Doha round (the 'Doha Development Agenda', see Box 11.2). On completion of the Uruguay round, the average tariff on manufactured products was 4 per cent and falling. In 1947 the figure was nearly 40 per cent.

Since 1947, world trade has consistently grown faster than world output. In 2003, world merchandise exports were worth over $6 trillion. In real terms, that represents a 21-fold increase since 1950, compared with a 7-fold increase in world real GDP. In 1950, only 8 per cent of countries' output of goods and services was sold abroad; today the figure is 26 per cent. An illustration of the growth of trade is given by Figure 11.2. It shows that the growth in world exports since 1960 has been substantially higher than the growth in GDP, but has fluctuated more.

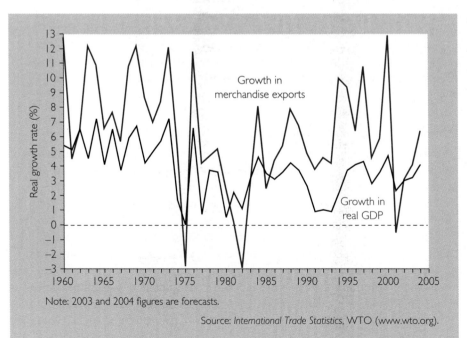

Figure 11.2
Growth in world
real GDP and world
merchandise exports

Note: 2003 and 2004 figures are forecasts.

Source: *International Trade Statistics*, WTO (www.wto.org).

Box 11.2

The Doha Development Agenda

A new direction for the WTO?

Globalisation, based on the free play of comparative advantage, economies of scale and innovation, has produced a genuinely radical force, in the true sense of the word. It essentially amplifies and reinforces the strengths, but also the weaknesses, of market capitalism: its efficiency, its instability, and its inequality. If we want globalisation not only to be efficiency-boosting but also fair, we need more international rules and stronger multilateral institutions.[1]

In November 1999, the members of the World Trade Organisation met in Seattle in the USA. What ensued became known as the 'battle of Seattle' (see Web case 11.7). Anti-globalisation protesters fought with police; the world's developing economies fell out with the world's developed economies; and the very future of the WTO was called into question. The WTO was accused of being a free trader's charter, in which the objective of free trade was allowed to ride rough-shod over anything that might stand in its way. Whatever the issue – the environment, the plight of developing

countries, the dominance of trade by multinationals – free trade was king.

At Seattle, both the protesters and developing countries argued that things had gone far enough. The WTO must redefine its role, they argued, to respect *all* stakeholders. More radical voices called for the organisation to be scrapped. As Pascal Lamy, the EU Trade Commissioner, made clear in the quote above, rules had to be strengthened, and the WTO had to ensure that the gains from trade were fairer and more sustainable.

The rebuilding process of the WTO began in Doha, Qatar, in November 2001. The meeting between the then 142 members of the WTO concluded with the decision to launch a new round of WTO trade talks, to be called the 'Doha Development Agenda'. The talks are designed to increase the liberalisation of trade. However, such a goal is to be tempered by a policy of strengthening assistance to developing economies.

The Doha Development Agenda moves the WTO into a new era: one which allows the organisation to play a fuller role in the pursuit of economic growth, employment and poverty reduction, in

[1] 'Global policy without democracy' (speech by Pascal Lamy, EU Trade Commissioner, given in 2001).

The re-emergence of protectionist sentiments in the 1980s

The balance of payments problems that many countries experienced after the oil crisis of 1973 and the recession of the early 1980s led many politicians around the world to call for trade restrictions. Although a tariff war was averted, there was a gradual increase in non-tariff barriers, such as subsidies on domestic products, the prohibition of imports that do not meet precise safety or other specifications, administrative delays in customs clearance, limits on investment by foreign companies, and governments favouring domestic firms when purchasing supplies.

Quotas were increasingly used, especially against Japanese imports. In most cases these were 'voluntary' agreements. Japan, on a number of occasions, agreed to restrict the number of cars it exported to the USA and various European countries. Similar restrictions applied to Japanese televisions and videos. Over 200 voluntary export restraints (VERs) were in force around the world in the early 1990s.

Definition

Voluntary export restraints (VERs) Where one country agrees to limit its imports to another to a particular quota.

global governance, and in the promotion of sustainable development, while maintaining its key function of increasing and improving the conditions for worldwide trade and investment.[2]

The talks are due to start in January 2005, and will last for three years.

At Doha it was agreed that the new trade talks would address questions such as:

■ Sustainable development and the environment. In the past, international trade agreements always seemed to take precedence over international environmental agreements, even though they are legally equivalent. In the new Doha round, this relationship is to be clarified. The hope is to achieve greater coherence between various areas of international policy making.

■ Trade and development. The Doha round will attempt to address a number of issues of concern to developing countries as they become more integrated into the world's trading system. For

example, it will seek to extend special provisions to developing economies to improve their access to markets in developed countries. It will also attempt to strengthen the current special treatment that developing countries receive, such as the ability to maintain higher rates of tariff protection.

Other areas identified for discussion include: greater liberalisation of agriculture; rules to govern foreign direct investment; the co-ordination of countries' competition policies; the use and abuse of patents on medicines and the needs of developing countries.

The proof of the pudding is in the eating. Only time will show whether the rhetoric of the Doha Development Agenda is transformed into fundamental improvements for the world's poorest countries, and whether the outcome will reduce the fears of those who feel that the global economy is increasingly beyond their influence.

[2] EU summary of Doha Ministerial Conference, http://trade-info.cec.eu.int/europa/2001newround/compas.htm

?
Outline the advantages and drawbacks of adopting a free trade strategy for developing economies. How might the Doha Development Agenda go some way to reducing these drawbacks?

The Uruguay round

The problem of increasing protectionism was recognised in the Uruguay round of GATT negotiations.[1] This was much more comprehensive than previous rounds. Unlike the others, it included negotiations on tariff reductions in agricultural products and in services (as well as in industrial products), and reductions in non-tariff barriers. Despite fears that an agreement would never be reached, negotiations were completed in December 1993 and a deal was signed in April 1994. This involved a programme of phasing in substantial reductions in tariffs and other restrictions up to the year 2002.

[1] Although the initial meeting was in Uruguay, subsequent meetings were in different locations around the world.

The World Trade Organisation

The Uruguay round deal also led to the setting up of the World Trade Organisation (WTO) in 1995 as the successor to GATT. The WTO adopted and strengthened most of the GATT rules governing trade. These include the following:

- Non-discrimination. Under the 'most favoured nations clause', any trade concession that a country makes to one member must be granted to *all* signatories.
- Reciprocity. Any nation benefiting from a tariff reduction made by another country must reciprocate by making similar tariff reductions itself.
- The general prohibition of quotas.
- Fair competition. If unfair barriers are erected against a particular country, the WTO can sanction retaliatory action by that country. The country is not allowed, however, to take such action without permission.
- Binding tariffs. Countries cannot raise existing tariffs without negotiating with their trading partners.

Unlike GATT, the WTO has the power to impose sanctions on countries breaking trade agreements. If there are disputes between member nations, these will be settled by the WTO, although there is provision for appeals and the parties can agree to go to arbitration. However, countries then found to be in the wrong must abide by the ruling or face sanctions.

The greater power of the WTO has persuaded many countries to bring their disputes to it. In the first nine years of its existence it had dealt with over 300 disputes (compared with 300 by GATT over the whole of its 48 years). The WTO has also carried on from the Uruguay round and has completed several new international agreements, for example to lower trade barriers in telecommunications and information technology.

Recap

1. Most countries of the world are members of the WTO and in theory are in favour of moves towards freer trade.
2. The Uruguay round brought significant reductions in trade restrictions, both tariff and non-tariff.
3. In practice, however, countries have been very unwilling to abandon restrictions if they believe that they can gain from them, even though it might be at the expense of other countries.
4. The WTO is more powerful than its predecessor, GATT. It has a disputes procedure and can enforce its rulings.

11.4 Trading blocs

Why do some countries get together and trade more freely between themselves?

The world economy seems to have been increasingly forming into a series of trade blocs, based upon regional groupings of countries: a European region centred on the European Union, an Asian region on Japan, and a North American region on the United States. Although such trade blocs clearly encourage trade between their members, many countries outside these blocs complain that they benefit the members at the expense of the rest of the world. For many developing economies, in need of access to the most prosperous nations in the world, this represents a significant check on their ability to grow and develop.

Types of preferential trading arrangement

If a group of countries wish to become more open and trade more freely with each other, but do not want the vulnerability of facing unbridled global competition, they might attempt to remove trade restrictions between themselves, but maintain them with the rest of the world.

Such preferential trading arrangements might take three possible forms.

Free trade areas

A free trade area is where member countries remove tariffs and quotas between themselves, but retain whatever restrictions *each member chooses* with non-member countries. Some provision will have to be made to prevent imports from outside coming into the area via the country with the lowest external tariff.

Customs unions

A customs union is like a free trade area, but in addition members must adopt *common* external tariffs and quotas with non-member countries.

Common markets

A common market is where member countries operate as a *single* market. Like a customs union there are no tariffs and quotas between member countries and there are common external tariffs and quotas. But a common market goes further than this. A full common market includes the following features.

- *A common system of taxation.* In the case of a *perfect* common market, this will involve identical rates of tax in all member countries.
- *A common system of laws and regulations governing production, employment and trade.* For example, in a perfect common market there would be a *single* set of laws governing issues such as product specification (e.g. permissible artificial additives to foods, or levels of exhaust emissions from cars), the employment and dismissal of labour, mergers and takeovers, and monopolies and restrictive practices.
- *Free movement of labour, capital and materials, and of goods and services.* In a perfect common market, this will involve a total absence of border controls between member states, the freedom of workers to work in any member country, and the freedom of firms to expand into any member state.
- *The absence of special treatment by member governments of their own domestic industries.* Governments are large purchasers of goods and services. In a perfect common market, they should buy from whichever companies within the market offer the most competitive deal and not show favouritism towards domestic suppliers: they should operate a *common procurement policy*.

The definition of a common market is sometimes extended to include the following two features of *economic and monetary union*.

- *A fixed exchange rate between the member countries' currencies.* In the extreme case, this would involve a single currency for the whole market.
- *Common macroeconomic policies.* To some extent this must follow from a fixed exchange rate, but in the extreme case it will involve a single macroeconomic management of the whole market, and hence the abolition of separate fiscal or monetary intervention by individual member states.

We will examine European economic and monetary union in Section 12.6.

The direct effects of a customs union: trade creation and trade diversion

By joining a customs union (or free trade area), a country will find that its trade patterns change. Two such changes can be distinguished: trade creation and trade diversion.

Trade creation

Trade creation is where consumption shifts from a high-cost producer to a low-cost producer. The removal of trade barriers allows greater specialisation according to comparative advantage. Instead of consumers having to pay high prices for domestically produced goods in which the country has a comparative disadvantage, the goods can now be obtained more cheaply from other members of the customs union. In return, the country can export to them goods in which it has a comparative advantage.

Trade diversion

Trade diversion is where consumption shifts from a lower-cost producer outside the customs union to a higher-cost producer within the union.

Assume that the most efficient producer in the world of a particular good is New Zealand – outside the EU. Assume that before membership, the UK paid a similar tariff on this good from any country, and thus imported the product from New Zealand rather than from the EU.

After joining the EU, however, the removal of the tariff made the EU product cheaper, since the tariff remained on the New Zealand product. Consumption thus switched to a higher-cost producer. There was thus a net loss in world efficiency. As far as the UK was concerned, consumers still gained, since they were paying a lower price than before. There was a loss, however, to domestic producers (from the reduction in protection, and hence reduced prices and profits) and to the government (from reduced tariff revenue). These losses may have been smaller or larger than the gain to consumers: in other words, there may still have been a net gain to the UK, but there could have been a net loss, depending on the circumstances.

Long-term effects of a customs union

Over the longer term, there may be other gains and losses from being a member of a customs union.

Definitions

Trade creation
Where a customs union leads to greater specialisation according to comparative advantage and thus a shift in production from higher-cost to lower-cost sources.

Trade diversion
Where a customs union diverts consumption from goods produced at a lower cost outside the union to goods produced at a higher cost (but tariff free) within the union.

Pause for thought

Is joining a customs union more likely to lead to trade creation or trade diversion in each of the following cases? (a) The union has a very high external tariff. (b) Cost differences are very great between the country and members of the union.

Longer-term advantages

■ Increased market size may allow a country's firms to exploit (*internal*) *economies of scale*. This argument is more important for small countries, which have therefore more to gain from an enlargement of their markets.

■ *External economies of scale.* Increased trade may lead to improvements in the infrastructure of the members of the customs union (better roads, railways, financial services, etc.). This in turn could bring bigger long-term benefits from trade between members, and from external trade too, by making the transport and handling of imports and exports cheaper.

■ The bargaining power of the whole customs union with the rest of the world may allow member countries to gain *better terms of trade*. This, of course, will necessarily involve a degree of political co-operation between the members.

■ *Increased competition* between member countries may stimulate efficiency, encourage investment and reduce monopoly power. Of course, a similar advantage could be gained by the simple removal of tariffs with any competing country.

■ Integration may encourage a *more rapid spread of technology*.

Longer-term disadvantages

■ Resources may flow from the country to more efficient members of the customs union, or to the geographical centre of the union (so as to minimise transport costs). This can be a major problem for a *common market* (where there is free movement of labour and capital). The country could become a depressed 'region' of the community.

■ If integration encourages greater co-operation between firms in member countries, it may also encourage *greater oligopolistic collusion*, thus keeping prices higher to the consumer. It may also encourage mergers and takeovers that would increase monopoly power.

■ *Diseconomies of scale.* If the union leads to the development of very large companies, they may become bureaucratic and inefficient.

■ The *costs of administering* the customs union may be high. This problem is likely to be worse, the more intervention there is in the affairs of individual members.

Preferential trading in practice

Preferential trading has the greatest potential to benefit countries whose domestic market is too small, taken on its own, to enable them to benefit from economies of scale, and where they face substantial barriers to their exports. Most developing countries fall into this category and as a result many have attempted to form preferential trading arrangements.

Examples in Latin America and the Caribbean include the Latin American Integration Association (LAIA), the Andean Community, the Central American Common Market (CACM) and the Caribbean Community (CARICOM). A Southern Common Market (MerCoSur) was formed in 1991, consisting of Argentina, Brazil, Paraguay and Uruguay. It has a common external tariff and most of its internal trade is free of tariffs.

In 1993, the six ASEAN nations (Brunei, Indonesia, Malaysia, the Philippines, Singapore and Thailand) agreed to work towards an ASEAN Free Trade Area (AFTA).

ASEAN (the Association of South-East Asian Nations) now has ten members (the new ones being Laos, Myanmar, Vietnam and Cambodia) and is dedicated to increased economic co-operation within the region. What progress has been made in achieving AFTA? By 2002 the original six members had reduced internal tariffs to a maximum of 5 per cent on most products. Plans are to eliminate all tariffs between these six by 2010 and for the remaining countries by 2015.

In Africa the Economic Community of West African States (ECOWAS) has been attempting to create a common market between its 16 members and plans to move to the adoption of a single currency for most of its members in July 2005.

North American Free Trade Association (NAFTA)

Along with the EU, NAFTA is one of the two most powerful trading blocs in the world. It was formed in 1993 and consists of the USA, Canada and Mexico. These three countries have agreed to abolish tariffs between themselves in the hope that increased trade and co-operation will follow. Tariffs between the USA and Canada were phased out by 1999 and tariffs between Mexico and the other two countries will be by 2009. New non-tariff restrictions will not be permitted either, but many existing ones can remain in force, thus preventing the development of true free trade between the members. Indeed, some industries, such as textiles and agriculture, will continue to have major non-tariff restrictions.

NAFTA members hope that, with a market similar in size to the EU (a combined GDP of $12.5 trillion and a population of over 420 million), they will able to rival the EU's economic power in world trade. Other countries may join in the future, so NAFTA may eventually develop into a western hemisphere free trade association.

NAFTA is, however, at most only a free trade area and not a common market. Unlike the EU, it does not seek to harmonise laws and regulations, except in very specific areas such as environmental management and labour standards. Member countries are permitted total legal independence, subject to the one proviso that they must treat firms of other member countries equally with their own firms. Nevertheless, NAFTA has encouraged a growth in trade between its members, most of which is trade creation rather than trade diversion.

Asia–Pacific Economic Co-operation Forum (APEC)

The most significant move towards establishing a more widespread regional economic organisation in east Asia appeared with the creation of the Asia–Pacific Economic Co-operation Forum (APEC). APEC links the economies of the Pacific rim, including Asian, Australasian and North and South American countries (19 countries, plus Hong Kong and Taiwan). These countries account for some 62 per cent of the world's total output and 47 per cent of world trade. At the 1994 meeting of APEC leaders, it was resolved to create a free trade area across the Pacific by 2010 for the developed industrial countries, and by 2020 for the rest.

Unlike the EU and NAFTA, APEC is likely to remain solely a free trade area and not to develop into a customs union, let alone a common market. Within the region there exists a wide disparity in GDP per capita, ranging from Japan and the USA at over $34 000 to Vietnam at a mere $400. Such disparities create a wide range of national interests and goals. Countries are unlikely to share common economic problems or concerns. In addition, political differences and conflicts within the region are widespread, reducing the likelihood that any organisational agreement beyond a simple economic one would succeed. However, the economic benefits from free trade, and the resulting closer regional ties, could be immense.

In the next section we consider the longest and most comprehensive preferential trading arrangement: the European Union.

Recap

1. Countries may make a partial movement towards free trade by the adoption of a preferential trading system. This involves free trade between the members, but restrictions on trade with the rest of the world. Such a system can be either a simple free trade area, or a customs union (where there are common restrictions with the rest of the world) or a common market (where in addition there is free movement of capital and labour, and common taxes and trade laws).

2. A preferential trading area can lead to trade creation, where production shifts to low-cost producers within the area, or to trade diversion, where trade shifts away from lower-cost producers outside the area to higher-cost producers within the area.

3. Preferential trading may bring longer-term advantages of increased economies of scale (both internal and external), improved terms of trade from increased bargaining power with the rest of the world, increased efficiency from greater competition between member countries and a more rapid spread of technology. On the other hand, it can lead to increased regional problems for members, greater oligopolistic collusion and various diseconomies of scale. There may also be large costs of administering the system.

4. There have been several attempts around the world to form preferential trading systems.

The European Union   11.5

What have been the effects of the creation of a 'single market' in the EU?

The European Economic Community (EEC) was formed by the signing of the Treaty of Rome in 1957 and came into operation on 1 January 1958.

The original six member countries of the EEC (Belgium, France, Italy, Luxembourg, Netherlands and West Germany) had already made a move towards integration with the formation of the European Coal and Steel Community in 1952. This had removed all restrictions on trade in coal, steel and iron ore between the six countries. The aim had been to gain economies of scale and allow more effective competition with the USA and other foreign producers.

The EEC extended this principle and aimed eventually to be a full common market with completely free trade between members in all products, and with completely free movement of labour, enterprise and capital. By uniting many of the countries of western Europe, it was hoped too that the conflicts of the two world wars would never be repeated, and that acting together the countries of the EEC could be an effective political and economic force in a world dominated by political giants such as the USA and the USSR, and economic giants such as the USA (and later Japan).

All internal tariffs between the six members had been abolished and common external tariffs established by 1968. But this still only made the EEC a *customs union*, since a number of restrictions on internal trade remained (legal, administrative, fiscal, etc.). Nevertheless the aim was eventually to create a full common market.

In 1973 the UK, Denmark and Ireland joined the EEC. Greece joined in 1981, Spain and Portugal in 1986, Sweden, Austria and Finland in 1995, and Hungary, Poland, the Czech Republic, Slovakia, Slovenia, Estonia, Lithuania, Latvia, Cyprus and Malta in 2004.

From customs union to common market

The European Union (as it is now known) is clearly a customs union. It has common external tariffs and no internal tariffs. But is it also a common market?

For many years there have been *certain* common economic policies.

Common Agricultural Policy (CAP).   The Union sets common high prices for farm products. This involves charging variable import duties to bring foreign food imports up to EU prices and intervention to buy up surpluses of food produced within the EU at these above-equilibrium prices (see Box 2.4).

Regional policy.   EU regional policy provides grants to firms and local authorities in depressed regions of the Union.

Monopoly and restrictive practice policy.   EU policy here has applied primarily to companies operating in more than one member state. For example, Article 81 of the Amsterdam Treaty prohibits agreements between firms (e.g. over pricing or sharing out markets) which adversely affect competition in trade between member states.

Harmonisation of taxation.   VAT is the standard form of indirect tax throughout the EU. There are, however, substantial differences in VAT rates between member states, as there are with other tax rates (see Box 11.3).

Social policy.   Articles 117–28 of the Treaty of Rome refer to social policy, and include calls for collaboration between member states on laws relating to employment, health and safety at work and collective bargaining rights, and equal pay for women and men for doing the same work.

In 1989 the European Commission presented a *social charter* to the EU heads of state. This spelt out a series of worker and social rights that should apply in all member states. These rights were grouped under 12 headings covering areas such as the guarantee of decent levels of income for both the employed and the non-employed, freedom of movement of labour between EU countries, freedom to belong to a trade union and equal treatment of women and men in the labour market. The social charter was only a recommendation and each element had to be approved separately by the European Council of Ministers.

The social chapter of the Maastricht Treaty (1991) attempted to move the Community forward in implementing the details of the social charter in areas such as maximum hours, minimum working conditions, health and safety protection, information and consultation of workers, and equal opportunities.

The UK Conservative government refused to sign this part of the Maastricht Treaty. It maintained that such measures would increase costs of production and would, therefore, make EU goods less competitive in world trade and increase unemployment. Critics of the UK position argued that the refusal to adopt minimum working conditions (and also a minimum wage rate) would help to make the UK the 'cheap labour sweat-shop' of Europe. One of the first acts of the incoming Labour government in 1997 was to sign up to the social chapter.

Despite these various common policies, in other respects the Community of the 1970s and 1980s was far from a true common market: there were all sorts of non-tariff barriers such as high taxes on wine by non-wine producing countries, special regulations designed to favour domestic producers, governments giving contracts to domestic producers (e.g. for defence equipment), and so on. The Single European Act of 1986, however, sought to remove these barriers and to form a genuine common market by the end of 1992 (see Box 11.3).

The benefits and costs of the single market

It is difficult to quantify the benefits and costs of the single market, given that many occur over a long period, and that it is difficult to know to what extent the changes that are taking place are the direct result of the single market. Nevertheless it is possible to identify the *types* of benefit and cost that have resulted. The benefits have included the following.

Trade creation.   Costs and prices have fallen as a result of a greater exploitation of comparative advantage. Member countries can now specialise further in those goods and services that they can produce at a comparatively low opportunity cost.

Reduction in the direct costs of barriers.   This category includes administrative costs, border delays and technical regulations. Their abolition or harmonisation has led to substantial cost savings.

Economies of scale.   With industries based on a Europe-wide scale, many firms can now be large enough, and their plants large enough, to gain the full potential economies of scale. Yet the whole European market is large enough for there still to be adequate competition. Such gains vary from industry to industry, depending on the minimum efficient scale of a plant or firm.

Greater competition.   More effective competition from other EU countries has (a) squeezed profit margins and thus brought prices more in line with costs, and (b) encouraged more efficient use of resources and thus reduced costs. In the long run, greater competition can stimulate greater innovation, the greater flow of technical information and the rationalisation of production.

Despite these gains, the single market has not received a universal welcome within the EU. Its critics argue that, in a Europe of oligopolies, unequal ownership of resources, rapidly changing technologies and industrial practices, and factor immobility, the removal of internal barriers to trade has merely exaggerated the problems of inequality and economic power. More specifically, the following criticisms are made.

Radical economic change is costly.   Substantial economic change is necessary to achieve the full economies of scale and efficiency gains from a single European market. These changes necessarily involve redundancies – from bankruptcies,

Box 11.3

Features of the single market

Since 1 January 1993 trade within the EU has oper-ated very much like trade within a country. In theory it should be no more difficult for a firm in Birmingham to sell its goods in Paris than in London. At the same time, the single market allows free movement of labour and involves the use of common technical standards.

The features of the single market are summed up in two European Commission publications:[1]

- Elimination of border controls on goods within the EU: no more long waits.
- Free movement of people across borders.
- Common security arrangements.
- No import taxes on goods bought in other mem-ber states for personal use.
- The right for everyone to live in another member state.
- Recognition of vocational qualifications in other member states: engineers, accountants, medical practitioners, teachers and other professionals able to practise throughout Europe.

[1] *A Single Market for Goods* (Commission of the European Communities, 1993); *10 Key Points about the Single Euro-pean Market* (Commission of the European Communities, 1992).

VAT rates (%) in the EU: 1988 and 2003

	1988		2003
	Standard rate	High rates	Standard rate
Austria			20
Belgium	19	25, 33	21
Denmark	22	–	25
Finland			22
France	18.6	33.3	19.6
Germany	14	–	16
Greece	18	36	18
Ireland	25	–	21
Italy	18	38	20
Luxembourg	12	–	15
Netherlands	20	–	19
Portugal	16	30	17
Spain	12	33	16
Sweden			25
UK	15	–	17.5

- Technical standards brought into line, and product tests and certification agreed across the whole EU.
- Common commercial laws – making it attractive to form Europe-wide companies and to start joint ventures.
- Public contracts to supply equipment and services to state organisations now open to tenders across the EU.

takeovers, rationalisation and the introduction of new technology. The severity of this 'structural' and 'technological' unemployment (see Section 7.4) depends on (a) the pace of economic change and (b) the mobility of labour – both occupa-tional and geographical. Clearly, the more integrated markets become across the EU, the less the costs of future change.

Adverse regional effects.   Firms are likely to locate as near as possible to the 'centre of gravity' of their markets and sources of supply. If, before barriers are removed, a firm's prime market was the UK, it might well have located in the Midlands or the north of England. If, however, with barriers now removed, its market has become Europe as a whole, it may choose to locate in the south of England or in France, Germany or the Benelux countries instead. The creation of a single European mar-ket thus tends to attract capital and jobs away from the edges of the Union and towards its geographical centre.

Key Idea

28
p293

Case Studies and Applications

So what does the single market mean for individuals and for businesses?

Individuals

Before 1993, if you were travelling in Europe, you had a 'duty-free allowance'. This meant that you could only take goods up to the value of €600 across borders within the EU without having to pay VAT in the country into which you were importing them. Now you can take as many goods as you like from one EU country to another, provided they are for your own consumption. But to prevent fraud, member states may ask for evidence that the goods have been purchased for the traveller's own consumption if they exceed specified amounts (e.g. 800 cigarettes, 10 litres of spirits, 90 litres of wine, 110 litres of beer).

Individuals have the right to live and work in any other member state. Qualifications obtained in one member state must be recognised by other member states.

Firms

Before 1993 all goods traded in the EU were subject to VAT at every internal border. This involved some 60 million customs clearance documents at a cost of some €70 per consignment.[2]

This has all now disappeared. Goods can cross from one member state to another without any border controls: in fact the concepts of 'importing' and 'exporting' within the EU no longer officially exist. All goods sent from one EU country to another are charged VAT only in the country of destination. They are exempt from VAT in the country where they are produced.

One of the important requirements for fair competition in the single market is the convergence of tax rates. Although income tax rates, corporate tax rates and excise duties still differ between member states, there has been some narrowing in the range of VAT rates. There is now a lower limit of 15 per cent on the standard rate of VAT. What is more, the member states have agreed to abolish higher rates of VAT on luxury goods, and to have no more than two lower rates on 'socially necessary' goods, such as food and water supply. The table shows VAT rates in 1988 and 2003.

> In what ways would competition be 'unfair' if VAT rates differed widely between member states?

[2] See *A Single Market for Goods* (Commission of the European Communities, 1993).

In an ideal market situation, areas like the south of Italy and Portugal should attract resources from other parts of the Union. Being relatively depressed areas, wage rates and land prices are lower. The resulting lower industrial costs should encourage firms to move into the areas. In practice, however, as capital and labour (and especially young and skilled workers) leave the extremities of the Union, so these regions are likely to become more depressed. If, as a result, their infrastructure is neglected, they then become even less attractive to new investment.

The development of monopoly/oligopoly power. The free movement of capital can encourage the development of giant 'Euro-firms' with substantial economic power. Indeed, recent years have seen some very large European mergers. This can lead to higher, not lower prices, and less choice for the consumer. It all depends on just how effective competition is, and how effective EU competition policy is in preventing monopolistic and collusive practices.

Key
Idea
14
p118

Trade diversion. Just as increased trade creation has been a potential advantage of completing the internal market, so trade diversion has been a possibility too. This is more likely if *external* barriers remain high (or are even increased) and internal barriers are *completely* abolished.

Perhaps the biggest objection raised against the single European market is a political one: the loss of national sovereignty. Governments find it much more difficult to intervene at a microeconomic level in their own economies.

Recent developments

By the mid-1990s it was becoming clear from the evidence that the single market was bringing substantial benefits.

- The elimination of border controls for goods had reduced costs, shortened delivery times and resulted in a larger choice of suppliers.
- The simplification of VAT arrangements had reduced costs.
- Substantial trade creation had taken place.
- Increased competition between firms had led to lower costs, lower prices and a wider range of products available to consumers. This was particularly so in the newly liberalised service sectors such as transport, financial services, telecommunications and broadcasting.
- Mergers and other forms of industrial restructuring had resulted in economies of scale and lower prices.

The economic evidence was backed up by the perceptions of business. Firms from across the range of industries felt that the single market project had removed a series of obstacles to trade within the EU and had increased market opportunities.

Nevertheless, the internal market was still not 'complete'. In other words, various barriers to trade between member states still remained. Thus, in June 1997, an Action Plan was adopted by the European Council. Its aim was to ensure that all barriers were dismantled by the launch of the euro in January 1999.

The Action Plan was largely, but not totally successful. In 1997, individual member countries had on average failed to transpose into their national law 35 per cent of over 1300 measures identified as being necessary to complete the internal market. By 1999, this 'transposition deficit' was less than 10 per cent. By 2002, the figure was just 2.1 per cent, with a target of 1.5 per cent by April 2003.

Despite this success, national governments have continued to introduce *new* technical standards, several of which have had the effect of erecting new barriers to trade. Also, infringements of single market rules by governments have not always been dealt with. The net result is that, although trade is much freer today than in the early 1990s, especially given the transparency of pricing with the euro, there still exist various barriers, especially to the free movement of goods.

Every six months, the EU publishes an 'Internal Market Scoreboard' to show progress towards the total abandonment of all forms of internal trade restrictions. In addition to giving each country's implementation deficit, the scoreboard identifies the number of infringements of the internal market that have taken place. The hope is that the 'naming and shaming' of countries will encourage them to make more rapid progress towards totally free trade within the EU.

The future

In future years, with the euro being used by at least 12 of the member states, trade within the EU is likely to continue to grow as a proportion of GDP. We examine the benefits and costs of the single currency and the whole process of economic and monetary union in the EU in Section 12.6.

A major issue is the question of the impact of the new members of the Union. With ten new members joining in 2004, there are new pressures on the EU and calls upon its budget. The larger the EU becomes, the more difficult will be political union and full monetary union, and the more likely it is that the European Union will remain primarily a single market.

> **Pause for thought**
>
> Why may the new members of the EU have the most to gain from the single market, but also the most to lose?

To examine the arguments about full monetary union, we need first to look at the whole question of exchange rate determination and alternative exchange rate systems. This is the subject of the next chapter.

Recap

1. The European Union is a customs union, in that it has common external tariffs and no internal ones. But virtually from the outset it has also had elements of a common market, particularly in the areas of agricultural policy, regional policy, monopoly and restrictive practice policy, and to some extent in the areas of tax harmonisation and social policy.

2. Nevertheless, there were substantial non-tariff barriers to trade within the EU: e.g. different tax rates, various regulations over product quality, licensing, state procurement policies, educational qualification requirements, and subsidies or tax relief to domestic producers.

3. The Single European Act of 1986 sought to sweep away these restrictions and to establish a genuine free market within the EU: to establish a full common market. Benefits from completing the internal market have included trade creation, cost savings from no longer having to administer barriers, economies of scale for firms now able to operate on a Europe-wide scale, and greater competition leading to reduced costs and prices, greater flows of technical information and more innovation.

4. Critics of the single market point to the costs of radical changes in industrial structure, the attraction of capital away from the periphery of the EU to its geographical centre, possible problems of market power with the development of giant 'Euro-firms', and the possibilities of trade diversion.

5. The actual costs and benefits of EU membership to the various countries vary with their particular economic circumstances. These costs and benefits in the future will depend on just how completely the barriers to trade are removed, on the extent of monetary union and on the effects of enlarging the Union.

Trade and developing countries   11.6

The importance of international trade to developing countries

The role of international trade is one of the most contentious for developing countries. Should they adopt an open trading policy with few if any barriers to imports? Should they go further and actively promote trade by subsidising their export sector? Or should they restrict trade and pursue a policy of greater self-sufficiency? These are issues we shall be examining in this section.

Whether it is desirable that developing countries should adopt policies of more trade or less, trade is still vital. Certain raw materials, capital equipment and intermediate products that are necessary for development can be obtained only from abroad. Others *could* be produced domestically but only at much higher cost.

Trade strategies

As they develop, countries' policies towards trade typically go through various stages.

Primary outward-looking stage.   Traditionally, developing countries have exported primaries – minerals such as copper, cash crops such as coffee, and non-foodstuffs such as cotton – in exchange for manufactured consumer goods. In their early phase of development, countries have little in the way of an industrial base and thus if they want to consume manufactured goods they have to import them.

Secondary inward-looking stage.   In seeking rapid economic development, most developing countries drew lessons from the experience of the advanced countries. The main conclusion was that industrialisation was the key to economic success.

But industrialisation required foreign exchange to purchase capital equipment. This led to a policy of import-substituting industrialisation, which involved cutting back on non-essential imports and thereby releasing foreign exchange. Tariffs and other restrictions were imposed on those imports for which a domestic substitute existed or which were regarded as unimportant.

Secondary outward-looking stage.   Once an industry had satisfied domestic demand, it had to seek markets abroad if expansion was to continue. What is more, as we shall see, import substitution brought a number of serious problems for developing countries. The answer seemed to be to look outward again, this time to the export of manufactured goods. Many of the most economically successful developing countries (especially Hong Kong, Singapore, South Korea and Taiwan) owed their high growth rates to a rapid expansion of manufactured exports.

We will now examine the three stages in more detail.

Approach 1: Exporting primaries – exploiting comparative advantage

The justification for exporting primaries

Despite moves towards import substitution and secondary export promotion, many developing countries still rely heavily on primary exports. Three major arguments have been traditionally used for pursuing a policy of exporting primaries. In each case the arguments have also been used to justify a policy of free or virtually free trade.

Exporting primaries exploits comparative advantage.   Traditional trade theory implies that countries should specialise in producing those items in which they have a comparative advantage: i.e. those goods that can be produced at relatively low

> **Definition**
>
> Import-
> substituting
> industrialisation
> (ISI)
> A strategy of
> restricting imports of
> manufactured goods
> and using the foreign
> exchange saved to
> build up domestic
> industries.

opportunity costs. For most developing countries this means that a large proportion of their exports should be primaries.

Exporting primaries provides a 'vent for surplus'. Trade offers a vent for surplus: i.e. a means of putting to use resources that would otherwise not be used. These surpluses occur where the domestic market is simply not big enough to consume all the available output of a particular good. There is far too little demand within Zambia to consume its potential output of copper. The same applies to Namibian uranium and Peruvian tin.

Exporting primaries provides an 'engine for economic growth'. According to this argument, developing countries benefit from the growth of the economies of the developed world. As industrial expansion takes place in the rich North, this will create additional demand for primaries from the poor South.

Traditional trade theory in the context of development

There are several reasons for questioning whether the above arguments justify a policy of relying on primary exports as the means to development.

Comparative costs change over time. Over time, with the acquisition of new skills and an increase in the capital stock, a developing country that once had a comparative advantage in primaries may find that it now has a comparative advantage in certain *manufactured* products, especially those which are more labour intensive and use raw materials of which the country has a plentiful supply. The market, however, cannot necessarily be relied upon to bring about a smooth transition to producing such products.

Concentrating on primary production may hinder growth. A country may gain in the short run by exporting primaries and using the money earned to buy imports. But primary production may have little potential for expansion and thus growth may be slower.

The benefits from trade may not accrue to the nationals of the country. If a mine or plantation is owned by a foreign company, it will be the foreign shareholders who get the profits from the sale of exports. In addition, these companies may bring in their own capital and skilled labour from abroad. The benefits gained by the local people will probably be confined to the additional wages they earn. With these companies being in a position of monopsony power, these wages are often very low.

Trade may lead to greater inequality. Trade shifts income distribution in favour of those factors of production employed intensively in the export sector. If exports are labour intensive, greater equality will tend to result. But if they are land or raw material intensive then trade will redistribute income in favour of large landowners or mine owners.

Exporting primary exports may involve external costs. Mining can lead to huge external costs, such as the despoiling of the countryside and damage to the health of miners. Mines and plantations can lead to the destruction of traditional communities and their values.

These arguments cast doubt on whether a policy of relying on free trade in primary exports is the best way of achieving economic development. Various trends in the international economy have also worked against primary exporters.

Problems for primary exporters: long term

Long-term trends in international trade have caused problems for primary exporting countries in a number of ways.

Low income elasticity of demand for primary products.   As world incomes grow, so a smaller proportion of these incomes is spent on primaries. But why? Since food is a necessity of life, consumers, especially in rich countries, already consume virtually all they require. A rise in incomes, therefore, tends to be spent more on luxury goods and services, and only slightly more on basic foodstuffs.

Agricultural protection in advanced countries.   Faced with the problem of a slowly growing demand for food produced by their own farmers, advanced countries increasingly imposed restrictions on imported food. This was one of the major issues considered at the Uruguay round of GATT negotiations and at subsequent WTO meetings (see pages 430–1).

Technological developments.   Synthetic substitutes have in many cases replaced primaries in the making of consumer durables (such as furniture and household appliances), clothing and industrial equipment. Also, the process of miniaturisation, as microchips have replaced machines, has meant that less and less raw materials have been required to produce any given amount of output.

Rapid growth in imports.   There tends to be a high income elasticity of demand for imported manufactures. This is the result partly of the better-off in developing countries increasingly being able to afford luxury goods, and partly of the development of new tastes as people are exposed to the products of the developed world – products such as Coca-Cola, Levi jeans and Sony Walkmans. In fact, the whole process has been dubbed 'Coca-Colanisation'.

The terms of trade.   The slow growth in demand for primaries has led to a fall in their prices relative to those of manufactured goods. Between 1980 and 2000, non-fuel primary product prices halved. This long-term decline in the terms of trade for primary exporters has meant that they are having to export more and more in order to buy any given quantity of imports. Tables 11.2 and 11.3 show how the terms of trade have moved against developing countries over the years.

Table 11.2

Average annual change in prices of various products

	1985–94	1995–2004
Non-oil primary product exports of developing countries	1.2	−1.4
Non-oil primary product exports of heavily indebted poor countries	−0.4	−1.6
Oil prices	−5.7	4.6
Manufactured exports of advanced economies	5.0	−0.1

Source: *World Economic Outlook*, based on Table 23 (IMF, 2003).

	1960	1970	1980	1990	2000
Agricultural commodities	208	182	192	100	87
Metals and minerals	137	161	131	100	82
All non-fuel commodities	187	175	174	100	86
Oil	34	21	224	100	122

Table 11.3
World primary
commodity prices
(1990 = 100)

Source: *World Development Indicators*, extracts from Table 6.4 (World Bank).

Approach 2: Import–substituting industrialisation (ISI)

Dissatisfaction with relying on primary exporting has led most countries to embark on a process of industrialisation. The newly industrialised countries (NICs), such as Malaysia and Brazil, are already well advanced along the industrialisation road. Other developing countries have not yet progressed very far, especially the poorest African countries.

The most obvious way for countries to industrialise was to cut back on the import of manufactures and substitute them with home-produced manufactures. This could not be done overnight: it had to be done in stages, beginning with assembly, then making some of the components, and finally making all, or nearly all, of the inputs into production. Most developing countries have at least started on the first stage. Several of the more advanced developing countries have component manufacturing industries. Only a few of the larger NICs, such as India, Brazil and South Korea, have built extensive capital goods industries.

The method most favoured by policy makers is tariff escalation. Here tariff rates (or other restrictions) increase as one moves from the raw materials to the intermediate product to the finished product stage. Thus finished goods have higher tariffs than intermediate products. This encourages assembly plants, which are protected by high tariffs from imported finished products, and are able to obtain components at a lower tariff rate.

One of the problems with ISI is that countries are desperately short of resources to invest in industry. As a result, a policy of ISI has usually involved encouraging investment by multinational companies (see Box 11.4). But even without specific 'perks' (e.g. tax concessions, cheap sites, the cutting of red tape), multinationals will still probably be attracted by the protection afforded by the tariffs or quotas.

Definition

Tariff escalation
The system whereby tariff rates increase the closer a product is to the finished stage of production.

Adverse effects of import substitution

Some countries, such as South Korea and Taiwan, pursued an inward-looking ISI policy for only a few years. For them it was merely a stage in development, rapidly to be followed by a secondary outward-looking policy. Infant industries were initially given protection, but when they had achieved sufficient economies of scale, the barriers to imports were gradually removed.

The countries that have continued to pursue protectionist ISI policies have generally had a poorer growth record. They have also tended to suffer from other problems, such as a deepening of inequality. The development of the modern industrial sector has often been to the detriment of the traditional sectors and also to the export sector.

Box 11.4

Multinational corporations and developing economies

A partnership of equals?

The poorest countries of the world are most in need of investment and yet are most vulnerable to exploitation by multinational corporations (MNCs) and have the least power to resist it. There tends, therefore, to be a love–hate relationship between the peoples of the developing world and the giant corporations that are seen to be increasingly dominating their lives: from the spread of agri-business into the countryside through the ownership and control of plantations, to international mining corporations despoiling vast tracts of land, to industrial giants dominating manufacturing, to international banks controlling the flow of finance, to international tour operators and hotels bringing the socially disruptive effects of affluent tourists from North America, Japan, Europe and Australasia, to the products of the rich industrialised countries fashioning consumer tastes and eroding traditional culture.

Although MNCs employ only a small proportion of the total labour force in developing countries, they have a powerful effect on these countries' economies, often dominating the import and export sectors. They also often exert considerable power and influence over political leaders and their policies and over civil servants, and are frequently accused of 'meddling' in politics.

It is easy to see the harmful social, environmental and economic effects of multinationals on developing countries, and yet governments in these countries are so eager to attract overseas investment that they are frequently prepared to offer considerable perks to MNCs and to turn a blind eye to many of their excesses.

The scale of multinational investment in developing countries

The developing countries that receive the most multinational investment are those perceived to have the highest growth potential. They are generally what is known as 'newly-industrialised countries', and include Asian countries such as China, Singapore, Hong Kong, Malaysia and Thailand, and Latin American countries such as Mexico, Brazil and Argentina. The ten biggest recipients of foreign direct investment (FDI) receive over 90 per cent of the total, while all the African countries put together receive only around 5 per cent. The poorest 50 countries of the world between them receive less than 2 per cent.

Originally, most MNC investment in developing countries was in mines and plantations. Today, mining accounts for only about 7 per cent, with manufacturing and services accounting for half and oil for one-third of the total.

The value of total MNC investment worldwide is about $1 trillion ($1 000 000 000 000) per year, of which approximately one-quarter is in the developing world. Given the low levels of income of developing countries and their powerless position in world trade, this proportion is very large and shows the dominance of MNCs over their economies.

Does MNC investment aid development?

Whether investment by multinationals in developing countries is seen to be a net benefit or a net cost to these countries depends on what are perceived to be their development goals. If maximising the growth in national income is the goal, then MNC investment has probably made a positive contribution. If, however, the objectives of development are seen as more wide reaching, and include goals such as greater equality, the relief of poverty, a growth in the provision of basic needs (such as food, health care, housing, sanitation) and a general growth in the freedom and sense of wellbeing of the mass of the population, then the net effect of multinational investment could be argued to be anti-developmental.

Advantages to the host country. In order for countries to achieve economic growth there must be investment. In general, the higher the rate of investment, the higher will be the rate of economic growth. The need for economic growth tends to be more pressing in developing countries than in advanced countries. One obvious reason is their lower level of income. If they are ever to aspire to the living standards of the rich North, then income per head will have to grow at a considerably faster rate than in rich countries and for many years. Another reason is the higher rates of population growth in developing countries – often some 2 per cent higher than in the rich countries. This means that for income per head to grow at merely the *same* rate as in rich countries, developing countries will have to achieve growth rates 2 per cent higher.

Investment requires finance. But developing countries are generally acutely short of funds: FDI can help to make up the shortfall.

MNCs also bring management expertise and often provide training programmes for local labour. The capital that flows into the developing countries with MNC investment often embodies the latest technology, access to which the developing country would otherwise be denied.

Disadvantages to the host country.   MNCs may use their power in the markets of developing countries to drive domestic producers out of business, thereby lowering domestic profits and domestic investment. Also, they may buy few, if any, of their components from domestic firms, but import them instead: perhaps from one of their subsidiaries.

The bulk of their profits may simply be repatriated to shareholders in the rich countries, with little, if any, reinvested in the developing country. If the developing countries try to tax these profits, the MNCs may take their investment elsewhere, or transfer their profits to countries charging them lower rates of profit tax. They can do this by choosing what price to charge themselves for semi-finished products trans-

ferred from their factories in one country to those in another. If they charge themselves a high 'transfer price', then the profits will be largely made in the first country (the one selling the semi-finished product). If they charge themselves a low price, then the profits will be made in the second country (the one purchasing the semi-finished product and using it to produce a finished product). Governments of developing countries are effectively put in competition with each other, each trying to undercut the others' tax rates.

Similarly, governments of developing countries compete with each other to offer the most favourable terms to MNCs (e.g. government grants, government contracts, tax concessions and rent-free sites). The more favourable the terms, the less the gain for developing countries as a whole.

In addition to these problems, MNCs can alter the whole course of development in ways that many would argue are undesirable. By locating in cities, they tend to attract floods of migrants from the countryside looking for work, but of whom only a small fraction will find employment in these industries. The rest swell the ranks of the urban unemployed, often dwelling in squatter settlements on the outskirts of cities and living in appalling conditions.

More fundamentally, they are accused of distorting the whole pattern of development and of worsening the gap between the rich and poor. Their technology is capital intensive (compared with indigenous technology). The result is too few job opportunities. Those who are employed, however, receive relatively high wages, and are able to buy their products. These are the products consumed in affluent countries – from cars, to luxury foodstuffs to household appliances – products that the MNCs often advertise heavily, and where they have considerable monopoly/oligopoly power. This creates wants for the mass of people, but wants that they have no means of satisfying.

Key
Idea
17
p192

Key
Idea
14
p118

ey
ea
4
118

ey
ea
17
192

What can developing countries do?

Can developing countries gain the benefits of FDI while avoiding the effects of growing inequality and inappropriate products and technologies? If a developing country is large and is seen as an important market for the multinational, if it would be costly for the multinational to relocate, and if the government is well informed about the multinational's costs, then the country's bargaining position will be relatively strong. It may be able to get away with relatively high taxes on the MNC's profits and tight regulation of its behaviour (e.g. its employment practices and its care for the environment). If, however, the country is economically weak and the MNC is footloose, then the deal it can negotiate is unlikely to be very favourable.

The bargaining position of developing countries would be enhanced if they could act jointly in imposing conditions on multinational investment and behaviour. Such agreement is unlikely, however, given the diverse nature of developing countries' governments and economies. In the pro free-market, deregulated world of the twenty-first century, such agreements seem to be becoming even less likely.

? What other ways are there for a developing country to finance a higher level of investment? Are there any drawbacks in the methods you have identified?

The criticisms of ISI are numerous, and include the following.

It has run directly counter to the principle of comparative advantage. Rather than confining ISI to genuine infant industries and then gradually removing the protection, ISI has been applied indiscriminately to a whole range of industries. Countries are producing goods in which they have a comparative *disadvantage*.

It has cushioned inefficient practices and encouraged the establishment of monopolies. Without the competition from imports, many of the industries are highly inefficient and wasteful of resources. What is more, in all but the largest or most developed of the developing countries the domestic market for manufactures is small. If a newly established industry is to be large enough to gain the full potential economies of scale, it will necessarily be large relative to the market. This means that it will have considerable monopoly power.

It has involved artificially low real interest rates. In order to encourage capital investment in the import-substituting industries, governments have often intervened to keep interest rates low. This has encouraged the use of capital-intensive technology with a consequent lack of jobs. It has also starved other sectors (such as agriculture) of much needed finance, and it has discouraged saving.

It has led to urban wages above the market-clearing level. Wages in the industrial sector, although still low compared with advanced countries, are often considerably higher than in the traditional sectors.

- They are pushed up by firms seeking to retain labour in which they have invested training.
- Governments, seeking to appease the politically powerful urban industrial working class, have often passed minimum wage laws.
- Trade unions, although less widespread in developing than in advanced countries, are mainly confined to the new industries.

Higher industrial wages again encourage firms to use capital-intensive techniques.

It has involved overvalued exchange rates.   Restricting imports tends to lead to an appreciation of the exchange rate. This makes non-restricted imports cheaper, which then discourages the production of domestic goods, such as food and component parts, which compete with those imports. Also, a higher exchange rate discourages exports. Exports tend to be priced in dollars. If the exchange rate appreciates, domestic currency will buy more dollars; or put another way, a dollar will exchange for less domestic currency. Thus exporters will earn less domestic currency as the exchange rate appreciates.

It does not necessarily save on foreign exchange.   Many of the new industries are highly dependent on the importation of raw materials, capital equipment and component parts. Foreign inputs, unlike foreign finished goods, are often supplied by a single firm, which can thus charge monopoly prices. What is more, a large proportion of the extra incomes generated by these industries tends to be spent on imports by the new urban elites.

Protection has not been applied evenly.   Many different tariff rates are often used in one country: in fact, a policy of tariff escalation demands this. In addition, governments often use a whole range of other protectionist instruments – such as the licensing of importers, physical and value quotas and foreign exchange rationing. These are often applied in a haphazard way. The result is that protection is highly uneven.

Income distribution is made less equal.   Additional incomes generated by the modern sector tend to be spent on modern-sector goods and imported goods. Thus there is a multiplier effect *within* the modern sector, but virtually none between the modern sector and the traditional sectors. Also as we saw above, an overvalued exchange rate leads to a bias against agriculture and thus further deepens the divide between rich and poor. Finally, the relatively high wages of the modern sector encourage workers to migrate to the towns, where many, failing to get a job, live in dire poverty.

Social, cultural and environmental problems.   A policy of ISI often involves imposing an alien set of values. Urban life can be harsh, competitive and materialistic. Moreover, the drive for industrialisation may involve major costs to the environment, as a result of waste products from new industries, often with low environmental standards.

Finally, import substitution is necessarily limited by the size of the domestic market. Once that is saturated, ISI can come to an abrupt halt. At that stage, further expansion can only come from exporting; but if these industries have been overprotected, they will be unable to compete in world markets.

Approach 3: Exporting manufactures – a possible way forward?

The countries with the highest rates of economic growth have been those that have successfully made the transition to being exporters of manufactures. Table 11.4 gives some examples.

Table 11.4
Growth rates and export performance of selected secondary outward-looking countries

	Average annual growth in real GDP (%) 1965–2001	Share of manufactures in merchandise exports (%)		Annual average growth rate of exports (%) 1965–2001
		1970	2001	
Brazil	4.4	15	53	8.4
Malaysia	6.9	8	80	9.6
South Korea	8.0	76	90	15.3
Singapore	8.1	31	84	9.4
Hong Kong	7.2	96	95	11.5
All developing countries	4.1	27	65	5.7

Sources: *World Bank, IMF, WTO*, compiled from various publications.

The transition from inward-looking to outward-looking industrialisation

How is a country to move from import substituting to being outward looking? One approach is to take it industry by industry. When an industry has saturated the home market and there is no further scope for import substitution, it should then be encouraged to seek markets overseas. The trouble with this approach is that if the country is still protecting other industries, there will probably still be an overvalued exchange rate. Thus specific subsidies, tax concessions or other 'perks' would have to be given to this industry to enable it to compete. The country would still be highly interventionist, with all the distortions and misallocation of resources this tends to bring.

The alternative is to wean the whole economy off protection. Three major things will need doing. There will need to be a devaluation of the currency (see Section 12.4) in order to restore the potential profitability of the export sector. There will also need to be a dismantling of the various protective measures that had biased production towards the home market. Finally there will probably need to be a removal or relaxing of price controls. But these are things that cannot be done 'at a stroke'. Firms may have to be introduced gradually to the greater forces of competition that an outward-looking trade policy brings. Otherwise there may be massive bankruptcies and a corresponding massive rise in unemployment.

The benefits from a secondary outward-looking policy

The advocates of outward-looking industrialisation make a number of points in its favour.

It conforms more closely to comparative advantage.   Countries pursuing an open trade regime will only be able to export goods in which they have a comparative advantage. The resources used in earning a unit of foreign exchange from exports will be less than those used in saving a unit of foreign exchange by replacing imports with home-produced goods. In other words, resources will be used more efficiently.

Economies of scale.   If the home market is too small to allow a firm to gain all the potential economies of scale, these can be gained by expanding into the export market.

Increased competition.   By having to compete with foreign companies, exporters will be under a greater competitive pressure than industries sheltering behind protective barriers. This will encourage (a) resource saving in the short run through reductions in inefficiency, and (b) innovation and investment, as firms attempt to adopt the latest technology, often obtained from developed countries.

Increased investment.   To the extent that outward-looking policies lead to a greater potential for economic growth, they may attract more foreign capital. To the extent that they involve an increase in interest rates, they will tend to encourage saving. To the extent that they lead to increased incomes, additional saving will be generated, especially given that the *marginal* propensity to save may be quite high. The extra savings can be used to finance extra investment.

It can lead to more employment and a more equal distribution of income.   The manufactured goods in which a country has a comparative advantage will be those produced by labour-intensive techniques (since wage rates are comparatively low in developing countries). Export expansion will thus increase the demand for labour relative to capital and thus create more employment. The increased demand for labour will tend to lead to a rise in wages relative to profits.

It removes many of the costs associated with ISI.   Under a policy of ISI, managers may spend a lot of their time lobbying politicians and officials, seeking licences (and sometimes paying bribes to obtain them), adhering to norms and regulations or trying to find ways round them. If an outward-looking policy involves removing all this, managers can turn their attention to producing goods more efficiently.

Drawbacks of an export-orientated industrialisation strategy

The export of manufactures is seen by many developed countries as very threatening to their own industries. Their response has often been to erect trade barriers. These barriers have tended to be highest in the very industries (such as textiles, footwear and processed food) where developing countries have the greatest comparative advantage. Even if the barriers are *currently* low, developing countries may feel that it is too risky to expand their exports of these products for fear of a future rise in barriers. Recognising this problem, the WTO is very keen to ensure fair access for developing countries to the markets of the rich world.

The success of developing countries such as Malaysia and South Korea in exporting manufactures does not imply that other developing countries will have similar success. As additional developing countries attempt to export their manufactures, they will be facing more and more competition from each other.

Another problem is that, if a more open trade policy involves removing or reducing exchange and capital controls, the country may become more vulnerable to speculative attack. This was one of the major factors contributing to the east Asian crisis of the late 1990s. Gripped by currency and stock market speculation, and by banking and company insolvency, many countries of the region found that economic growth had turned into a major recession. The 'miracle' seemed to be over. Nevertheless, the countries with the least distortions fared the best during the crisis. Thus Singapore and Taiwan, which are open and relatively flexible, experienced only a slowdown, rather than a recession.

Exporting manufactures can be a very risky strategy for developing countries. Perhaps the best hope for the future for the poorer nations lies in increased

Pause for thought

Why may small developing countries have more to gain than large ones from a policy of becoming exporters of manufactured products?

manufacturing trade *between* themselves. That way they can gain the benefits of specialisation and economies of scale that trade brings, while at the same time producing for a growing market. The feasibility of this approach depends on whether developing countries can agree to free trade areas or even customs unions (see page 433).

Recap

1. Trade is of vital importance for the vast majority of developing countries, and yet most developing countries suffer from chronic balance of trade deficits.

2. Developing countries have traditionally been primary exporters. This has allowed them to exploit their comparative advantage in labour-intensive goods and has provided a market for certain goods that would otherwise have no market at home. It has also provided a means whereby growth can be transmitted from the advanced countries.

3. There are reasons for questioning the wisdom of relying on traditional primary exports, however. With a low world income elasticity of demand for primary products, with the development of synthetic substitutes for minerals and with the protection of agriculture in developed countries, the demand for primary exports from the developing world has grown only slowly. At the same time, the demand for manufactured imports into developing countries has grown rapidly. The result has been a decline in the terms of trade. In addition to these problems, there is also the danger that comparative costs may change over time; that most of the benefits from primary exports may accrue to foreign owners of mines and plantations, or to wealthy elites in the domestic population; and that mines and plantations can involve substantial environmental and other external costs.

4. Import-substituting industrialisation was seen to be the answer to these problems. This was normally achieved in stages, beginning with the finished goods stage and then working back towards the capital goods stage. ISI, it was hoped, would allow countries to benefit from the various long-term advantages associated with manufacturing.

5. For many countries, however, ISI brought as many, if not more, problems than it solved. It often led to the establishment of inefficient industries, protected from foreign competition and facing little or no competition at home either. It led to considerable market distortions, with tariffs and other forms of protection haphazardly applied; to overvalued exchange rates, with a resulting bias against exports and the agricultural sector generally; to a deepening of inequalities and to large-scale social problems as the cities expanded, as poverty and unemployment grew and as traditional values were undermined; and to growing environmental problems. Finally, the problem that ISI was supposed to ease – the balance of payments constraint – was in many cases made worse as the new industries became increasingly dependent on imported inputs and as growing urbanisation caused a growing demand for imported consumer goods.

6. The most rapidly growing of the developing countries are those that have pursued a policy of export-orientated industrialisation. This has allowed them to achieve the benefits of economies of scale and foreign competition, and to specialise in goods in which they have a comparative advantage (i.e. labour-intensive goods) and yet which have a relatively high income elasticity of demand. Whether countries that have pursued ISI can successfully turn to an open, export-orientated approach will depend to a large extent on the degree of competition they face not only from advanced countries but also from other developing countries.

Questions

1. Referring to Table 11.1, show how each country could gain from trade if the LDC could produce (before trade) 3 wheat for 1 cloth and the developed country could produce (before trade) 2 wheat for 5 cloth, and if the exchange ratio (with trade) was 1 wheat for 2 cloth. Would they both still gain if the exchange ratio was (a) 1 wheat for 1 cloth and (b) 1 wheat for 3 cloth?

2. Imagine that two countries, Richland and Poorland, can produce just two goods, computers and coal. Assume that for a given amount of land and capital, the output of these two products requires the following constant amounts of labour:

	Richland	Poorland
I computer	2	4
I00 tonnes of coal	4	5

Assume that each country has 20 million workers.

(a) If there is no trade, and in each country 12 million workers produce computers and 8 million workers produce coal, how many computers and tonnes of coal will each country produce? What will be the total production of each product?

(b) What is the opportunity cost of a computer in (i) Richland; (ii) Poorland?

(c) What is the opportunity cost of 100 tonnes of coal in (i) Richland; (ii) Poorland?

(d) Which country has a comparative advantage in which product?

(e) Assuming that price equals marginal cost, which of the following would represent possible exchange ratios? (i) 1 computer for 40 tonnes of coal; (ii) 2 computers for 140 tonnes of coal; (iii) 1 computer for 100 tonnes of coal; (iv) 1 computer for 60 tonnes of coal; (v) 4 computers for 360 tonnes of coal.

(f) Assume that trade now takes place and that 1 computer exchanges for 65 tonnes of coal. Both countries specialise completely in the product in which they have a comparative advantage. How much does each country produce of its respective product?

(g) The country producing computers sells 6 million domestically. How many does it export to the other country?

(h) How much coal does the other country consume?

3. Why doesn't the USA specialise as much as General Motors or Texaco? Why doesn't the UK specialise as much as Unilever? Is the answer to these questions similar to the answer to the questions, 'Why doesn't the USA specialise as much as Luxembourg?' and 'Why doesn't Unilever specialise as much as the local florist?'

4. To what extent are the arguments for countries specialising and then trading with each other the same as those for individuals specialising in doing the jobs to which they are relatively well suited?

5. The following are four items that are traded internationally: wheat; computers; textiles; insurance. In which one of the four is each of the following most likely to have a comparative advantage: India; the UK; Canada; Japan? Give reasons for your answer.

6. Would it be possible for a country with a comparative disadvantage in a given product at *pre*-trade levels of output to obtain a comparative advantage in it by specialising in its production and exporting it?

7. Go through each of the arguments for restricting trade and provide a counter-argument for not restricting trade.

8. It is often argued that if the market fails to develop infant industries, then this is an argument for government intervention, but not necessarily in the form of restricting imports. What *other* ways could infant industries be given government support?

9. How would you set about judging whether an industry had a genuine case for infant/senile industry protection?

10. Does the consumer in the importing country gain or lose from dumping? (Consider both the short run and the long run.)

11. What is fallacious about the following two arguments? Is there any truth in either?

    (a) 'Imports should be reduced because money is going abroad which would be better spent at home.'
    (b) 'We should protect our industries from being undercut by imports produced using cheap labour.'

12. Make out a case for restricting trade between the UK and Japan. Are there any arguments here that could not equally apply to a case for restricting trade between Scotland and England or between Liverpool and Manchester?

13. In what ways may free trade result in harmful environmental effects? Is the best solution to these problems to impose restrictions on trade?

14. If countries are so keen to reduce the barriers to trade, why do many countries frequently attempt to erect barriers?

15. What factors will determine whether a country's joining a customs union will lead to trade creation or trade diversion?

16. How would you set about assessing whether or not a country had made a net dynamic gain by joining a customs union? What sort of evidence would you look for?

17. What would be the economic effects of (a) different rates of VAT; (b) different rates of personal income tax; (c) different rates of company taxation between member states, if in all other respects there were no barriers to trade or factor movements between the members of a customs union?

18. Is trade diversion in the EU more likely or less likely in the following cases?

    (a) European producers gain monopoly power in world trade.
    (b) Modern developments in technology and communications reduce the differences in production costs associated with different locations.

    (c) The development of the internal market produces substantial economies of scale in many industries.

19. Why is it difficult to estimate the magnitude of the benefits of completing the internal market of the EU?

20. Look through the costs and benefits that we identified from the single European market. Do the same costs and benefits arise from a substantially enlarged EU?

21. If there have been clear benefits from the single market programme, why do individual member governments still try to erect barriers, such as new technical standards?

22. If a developing country has a comparative advantage in primary products, should the government allow market forces to dictate the pattern of trade?

23. Why will a high exchange rate harm the agricultural sector in a developing country?

24. In what ways may free trade have harmful cultural effects on a developing country?

25. If a developing country has a comparative advantage in the production of wheat, should it specialise as much as possible in the production of wheat and export what is not consumed domestically?

26. What are the advantages and disadvantages for a developing country of pursuing a policy of ISI?

27. Will the production of labour-intensive manufactures for export lead to more or less inequality in a developing country?

28. Would the use of import controls help or hinder a policy of export-orientated industrialisation?

29. Should all developing countries aim over the long term to become *exporters* of manufactured products?

Additional case studies on the *Essentials of Economics* website (www.booksites.net/sloman)

11.1 **David Ricardo and the law of comparative advantage.** The first clear statement of the law of comparative advantage (in 1817).

11.2 **Fallacious arguments for restricting trade.** Some of the more common mistaken arguments for protection.

11.3 **Strategic trade theory.** The case of Airbus is used to illustrate the arguments that trade restrictions can be to the strategic advantage of countries in developing certain industries and preventing the establishment of foreign monopolies.

11.4 **The Uruguay round.** An examination of the negotiations that led to substantial cuts in trade barriers.

11.5 **The World Trade Organisation.** This looks at the various opportunities and threats posed by this major international organisation.

11.6 **Looking after the US steel industry.** This case considers the US administration's imposition of tariffs on imported steel in 2002, and the reactions of other countries to these tariffs.

11.7 **The Battle of Seattle.** This looks at the protests against the WTO at Seattle in November 1999 and considers the arguments for and against the free trade policies of the WTO.

11.8 **Assessing NAFTA.** Who are the winners and losers from NAFTA?

11.9 **High oil prices.** What is their effect on the world economy?

11.10 **Free trade and the environment.** Do whales, the rainforests and the atmosphere gain from free trade?

11.11 **The social dimension of the EU.** The principles of the Social Charter.

11.12 **The benefits of the single market.** Evidence of achievements and the Single Market Action Plan of 1997.

11.13 **The Internal Market Scoreboard.** Keeping a tally on progress to a true single market.

11.14 **A miracle gone wrong.** Lessons from east Asia.

11.15 **Ethical business.** An examination of the likelihood of success of companies that trade fairly with developing countries.

Sections of chapter covered in
WinEcon – Sloman, *Essentials of Economics*

Essentials of Economics section	*WinEcon* section
11.1	–
11.2	11.2
11.3	–
11.4	–
11.5	–
11.6	11.6

Websites relevant to this chapter

Numbers and sections refer to websites listed in the Web Appendix and hotlinked from this book's website at www.booksites.net/sloman

■ For news articles relevant to this chapter, see the *Economics News Articles* link from the book's website.

■ For general news on international trade, see websites in section A, and particularly A1–5, 7–9, 24, 25, 31. For articles on various aspects of trade and developing countries, see A27, 28; I9. See also links to newspapers worldwide in A38 and 39, and the news search feature in Google at A41. See also links to economics news in A42.

■ For international data on imports and exports, see site H16 > *Resources* > *Trade statistics*. See also *World Economic Outlook* in H4 and trade data in B23. See also the trade topic in I14.

■ For details of individual countries' structure of imports and exports, see B32.

■ For UK data, see B1, *1. National Statistics* > the fourth link > *Compendia and Reference* > *Annual Abstract* > *External trade and investment*. See also B3 and 34. For EU data, see G1 > *The Statistical Annex* > *Foreign trade and current balance*.

■ For discussion papers on trade, see H4 and 7.

■ For trade disputes, see H16.

■ For various pressure groups critical of the effects of free trade and globalisation, see H12–14.

■ For information on various preferential trading arrangements, see H20–22.

■ For EU sites, see G1, 3, 7–14, 16–18.

■ For information on trade and developing countries, see H4, 7, 9, 10, 16, 17. See also links to development sites in I9.

■ Sites I7 and 11 contain links to various topics in *International Economics* (*International trade*, *International agreements*, *Economic co-operation* and *EU Economics*) and to *Trade and trade policy* in *Economic Development*. Site I4 has links to *International economics*, *Development economics* and *Economic development*. Site I17 has links to *International economics*, *Trade policy* and *Development economics*.

■ For student resources relevant to this chapter, see sites C1–7, 9, 10, 19.

CHAPTER TWELVE

Balance of payments and exchange rates

In this chapter we will first explain what is meant by the balance of payments. In doing so we will see just how the various monetary transactions between the domestic economy and the rest of the world are recorded.

Then (in Sections 12.2 and 12.3) we will examine how rates of exchange are determined, and how they are related to the balance of payments. We will see what causes exchange rate fluctuations, and how the government can attempt to prevent these fluctuations.

A government could decide to leave its country's exchange rates entirely to market forces (a free-floating exchange rate). Alternatively, it could attempt to fix its currency's exchange rate to some other currency (e.g. the US dollar). Or it could simply try to reduce the degree to which its currency fluctuates. In Section 12.4, we look at the relative merits of different degrees of government intervention in the foreign exchange market: of different 'exchange rate regimes'.

We then turn to look at attempts to achieve greater currency stability between the members of the EU. Section 12.5 looks at the European exchange rate mechanism, which sought in the 1980s and 1990s to limit the amount that member currencies were allowed to fluctuate against each other. Then Section 12.6 examines the euro. Has the adoption of a single currency by twelve EU countries been of benefit to them? Would it benefit the UK to join?

We then take a global perspective. We ask whether an expansion of global trade and a closer integration of the economies of the world has led to greater or less stability. Finally, as with Chapter 11, we look at the position of developing countries, and in particular focus on the issue of debt. Why are so many developing countries facing severe debt problems and what can be done about it?

| 12.1 | The balance of payments account |

What is meant by a balance of payments deficit or surplus?

In Chapter 7 we identified balance of payments deficits as one of the main macro-economic problems that governments face. But what precisely do we mean by 'balance of payments deficits' (or surpluses), and what is their significance?

A country's balance of payments account records all the flows of money between residents of that country and the rest of the world. *Receipts* of money from abroad are regarded as credits and are entered in the accounts with a positive sign. *Outflows* of money from the country are regarded as debits and are entered with a negative sign.

There are three main parts of the balance of payments account: the *current account*, the *capital account* and the *financial account*. Each part is then subdivided. We shall look at each part in turn, and take the UK as an example. Table 12.1 gives a summary of the UK balance of payments for 2002.

The current account

The current account records payments for imports and exports of goods and services, plus incomes flowing into and out of the country, plus net transfers of money into and out of the country. It is normally divided into four subdivisions.

The trade in goods account. This records imports and exports of physical goods (previously known as 'visibles'). Exports result in an inflow of money and are therefore a credit item. Imports result in an outflow of money and are therefore a debit item. The balance of these is called the balance on trade in goods or balance of visible trade or merchandise balance. A *surplus* is when exports exceed imports. A deficit is when imports exceed exports.

The trade in services account. This records imports and exports of services (such as transport, tourism and insurance). Thus the purchase of a foreign holiday would be a debit, since it represents an outflow of money, whereas the purchase by an overseas resident of a UK insurance policy would be a credit to the UK services account. The balance of these is called the services balance.

The balance of both the goods and services accounts together is known as the balance on trade in goods and services or simply the balance of trade.

Income flows. These consist of wages, interest and profits flowing into and out of the country. For example, dividends earned by a foreign resident from shares in a UK company would be an outflow of money (a debit item).

Current transfers of money. These include government contributions to and receipts from the EU and international organisations, and international transfers of money by private individuals and firms. Transfers out of the country are debits. Transfers into the country (e.g. money sent from Greece to a Greek student studying in the UK) would be a credit item.

Definitions

Current account of the balance of payments
The record of a country's imports and exports of goods and services, plus incomes and transfers of money to and from abroad.

Balance on trade in goods or balance of visible trade or merchandise balance
Exports of goods minus imports of goods.

Services balance
Exports of services minus imports of services.

Balance on trade in goods and services or balance of trade
Exports of goods and services minus imports of goods and services.

	£ million	
Current account		
1. Trade in goods		
(a) Exports of goods	+185 848	
(b) Imports of goods	−220 242	
Balance on trade in goods	−34 394	
2. Trade in services		
(a) Exports of services	+83 348	
(b) Imports of services	−67 826	
Balance on trade in services	+15 522	
Balance on trade in goods and services		−18 872
3. Net income flows (wages and investment income)		+19 233
4. Net current transfers (government and private)		−9 047
Current account balance		**−8 686**
Capital account		
5. Net capital transfers, etc:		+1 082
Capital account balance		**+1 082**
Financial account		
6. Investment (direct and portfolio)		
(a) Net investment in UK from abroad	+78 084	
(b) Net UK investment abroad	−27 127	
Balance of direct and portfolio investment		+50 957
7. Other financial flows (mainly short-term)		
(a) Net deposits in UK from abroad and borrowing from abroad by UK residents	+86 376	
(b) Net deposits abroad by UK residents and UK lending to overseas residents	−115 032	
Balance of other financial flows		−28 656
8. Reserves (drawing on + adding to −)		+459
Financial account balance		**+22 760**
Total of all three accounts		**+15 156**
9. Net errors and omissions		−15 156
		0

Table 12.1
UK balance of payments: 2002

Source: *UK Economic Accounts* (National Statistics).

The current account balance is the overall balance of all the above four subdivisions. A *current account surplus* is where credits exceed debits. A *current account deficit* is where debits exceed credits. Figure 12.1 shows the current account balances of the UK, the USA and Japan as a proportion of their GDP (national output).

The capital account

The capital account records the flows of funds, into the country (credits) and out of the country (debits), associated with the acquisition or disposal of fixed assets (e.g. land), the transfer of funds by migrants, and the payment of grants by the government for overseas projects and the receipt of EU money for capital projects (e.g. from the Agricultural Guidance Fund).

Definitions

Balance of payments on current account
The balance on trade in goods and services plus net income flows and current transfers.

Capital account of the balance of payments
The record of transfers of capital to and from abroad.

Figure 12.1

Current account balance as a percentage of GDP in selected countries: 1970–2003

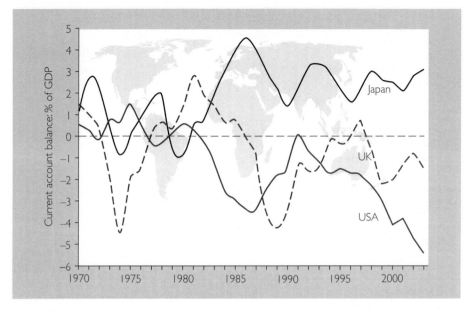

The financial account[1]

Definition

Financial account of the balance of payments
The record of the flows of money into and out of the country for the purpose of investment or as deposits in banks and other financial institutions.

The financial account of the balance of payments records cross-border changes in the holding of shares, property, bank deposits and loans, government securities, etc. In other words, unlike the current account, which is concerned with money incomes, the financial account is concerned with the purchase and sale of assets.

Investment (direct and portfolio). This account covers primarily long-term investment.

■ Direct investment. If a foreign company invests money from abroad in one of its branches or associated companies in the UK, this represents an inflow of money when the investment is made and is thus a credit item. (Any subsequent profit from this investment that flows abroad will be recorded as an *investment income outflow* on the current account.) Investment abroad by UK companies represents an outflow of money when the investment is made. It is thus a debit item.

Note that what we are talking about here is the acquisition or sale of assets: e.g. a factory or farm, or the takeover of a whole firm, not the imports or exports of equipment.

■ Portfolio investment. This is changes in the holding of paper assets, such as company shares. Thus if a UK resident buys shares in an overseas company, this is an outflow of funds and is hence a debit item.

Other financial flows. These consist primarily of various types of short-term monetary movement between the UK and the rest of the world. Deposits by overseas

---

[1] Prior to October 1998, this account was called the 'capital account'. The account that is *now* called the capital account used to be included in the transfers section of the current account. This potentially confusing change of names was adopted in order to bring the UK accounts in line with the system used by the International Monetary Fund (IMF), the EU and most individual countries.

residents in banks in the UK and loans to the UK from abroad are credit items, since they represent an inflow of money. Deposits by UK residents in overseas banks and loans by UK banks to overseas residents are debit items. They represent an outflow of money.

Short-term monetary flows are common between international financial centres to take advantage of differences in countries' interest rates and changes in exchange rates.

> **Pause for thought**
>
> Where would interest payments on short-term foreign deposits in UK banks be entered on the balance of payments account?

Flows to and from the reserves. The UK, like all other countries, holds reserves of gold and foreign currencies. From time to time the Bank of England (acting as the government's agent) will sell some of these reserves to purchase sterling on the foreign exchange market. It does this normally as a means of supporting the rate of exchange (as we shall see below). Drawing on reserves represents a *credit* item in the balance of payments accounts: money drawn from the reserves represents an *inflow* to the balance of payments (albeit an outflow from the reserves account). The reserves can thus be used to support a deficit elsewhere in the balance of payments.

Conversely, if there is a surplus elsewhere in the balance of payments, the Bank of England can use it to build up the reserves. Building up the reserves counts as a debit item in the balance of payments, since it represents an outflow from it (to the reserves).

When all the components of the balance of payments account are taken together, the balance of payments should exactly balance: credits should equal debits. As we shall see below, if they were not equal, the rate of exchange would have to adjust until they were, or the government would have to intervene to make them equal.

When the statistics are compiled, however, a number of errors are likely to occur. As a result there will not be a balance. To 'correct' for this, a net errors and omissions item is included in the accounts. This ensures that there will be an exact balance. The main reason for the errors is that the statistics are obtained from a number of sources, and there are often delays before items are recorded and sometimes omissions too.

> **Definition**
>
> **Net errors and omissions item** A statistical adjustment to ensure that the two sides of the balance of payments account balance. It is necessary because of errors in compiling the statistics.

Recap

1. The balance of payments account records all payments to and receipts from foreign countries.
2. The current account records payments for the imports and exports of goods and services, plus incomes and transfers of money to and from abroad.
3. The capital account records all transfers of capital to and from abroad.
4. The financial account records inflows and outflows of money for investment and as deposits in banks and other financial institutions. It also includes dealings in the country's foreign exchange reserves.
5. The whole account must balance, but surpluses or deficits can be recorded on any specific part of the account. Thus the current account could be in deficit, but it would have to be matched by an equal and opposite capital plus financial account surplus.

12.2 Exchange rates

What causes exchange rates to change?

An exchange rate is the rate at which one currency trades for another on the foreign exchange market.

If you want to go abroad, you will need to exchange your pounds into euros, dollars, Swiss francs or whatever. To do this you will go to a bank. The bank will quote you that day's exchange rates: for example, €1.45 to the pound, or $1.50 to the pound. It is similar for firms. If an importer wants to buy, say, some machinery from Japan, it will require yen to pay the Japanese supplier. It will thus ask the foreign exchange section of a bank to quote it a rate of exchange of the pound into yen. Similarly, if you want to buy some foreign stocks and shares, or if companies based in the UK want to invest abroad, sterling will have to be exchanged into the appropriate foreign currency.

Likewise, if Americans want to come on holiday to the UK or to buy UK assets, or American firms want to import UK goods or to invest in the UK, they will require sterling. They will be quoted an exchange rate for the pound in the USA: say, £1 = $1.54. This means that they will have to pay $1.54 to obtain £1 worth of UK goods or assets.

Exchange rates are quoted between each of the major currencies of the world. These exchange rates are constantly changing. Minute by minute, dealers in the foreign exchange dealing rooms of the banks are adjusting the rates of exchange. They charge commission when they exchange currencies. It is important for them, therefore, to ensure that they are not left with a large amount of any currency unsold. What they need to do is to balance the supply and demand of each currency: to balance the amount they purchase to the amount they sell. To do this they will need to adjust the price of each currency – namely, the exchange rate – in line with changes in supply and demand.

One of the problems in assessing what is happening to a particular currency is that its rate of exchange may rise against some currencies (weak currencies) and fall against others (strong currencies). In order to gain an overall picture of its fluctuations, therefore, it is best to look at a weighted average exchange rate against all other currencies. This is known as the exchange rate index. The weight given to each currency in the index depends on the proportion of transactions done with that country. Table 12.2 shows exchange rates between the pound and various currencies and the sterling exchange rate index from 1980 to 2003.

Determination of the rate of exchange in a free market

In a free foreign exchange market, the rate of exchange is determined by demand and supply. This is known as a floating exchange rate, and is illustrated in Figure 12.2.

For simplicity, assume that there are just two countries: the UK and the USA. When UK importers wish to buy goods from the USA, or when UK residents wish to invest in the USA, they *supply* pounds on the foreign exchange market in order

---

Definitions

Exchange rate index
A weighted average exchange rate expressed as an index, where the value of the index is 100 in a given base year. The weights of the different currencies in the index add up to 1.

Floating exchange rate
When the government does not intervene in the foreign exchange markets, but simply allows the exchange rate to be freely determined by demand and supply.

Pause for thought

How did the pound 'fare' compared with the dollar, the (former) lira and the yen from 1980 to 2001? What conclusions can be drawn about the relative movements of these three currencies?

	US dollar	Japanese yen	French franc	German mark	Italian lira	Euro	Sterling exchange rate index (1990 = 100)
1980	2.33	526	9.83	4.23	1992		124.4
1981	2.03	445	10.94	4.56	2287		127.9
1982	1.75	435	11.48	4.24	2364		123.2
1983	1.52	360	11.55	3.87	2302		115.6
1984	1.34	307	11.63	3.79	2339		111.4
1985	1.30	247	11.55	3.78	2453		111.3
1986	1.47	237	10.16	3.18	2186		101.4
1987	1.64	228	9.84	2.94	2123		99.3
1988	1.78	226	10.60	3.12	2315		105.4
1989	1.64	257	10.45	3.08	2247		102.3
1990	1.79	257	9.69	2.88	2133		100.0
1991	1.77	238	9.95	2.93	2187		100.8
1992	1.77	224	9.32	2.75	2163		96.9
1993	1.50	167	8.51	2.48	2360		88.9
1994	1.53	156	8.49	2.48	2467		89.2
1995	1.58	148	7.87	2.26	2571		84.8
1996	1.56	170	7.99	2.35	2408		86.3
1997	1.64	198	9.56	2.84	2789		100.6
1998	1.66	217	9.77	2.91	2876		103.9
1999	1.62	184	(9.96)	(2.97)	(2941)	1.52	103.8
2000	1.52	163	(10.77)	(3.21)	(3180)	1.64	107.5
2001	1.44	175	(10.55)	(3.15)	(3115)	1.61	105.8
2002	1.50	188	–	–	–	1.59	106.0
2003 Q2	1.62	192	–	–	–	1.43	99.1

Table 12.2

Sterling exchange rates: 1980–2003

Source: *Datastream.*

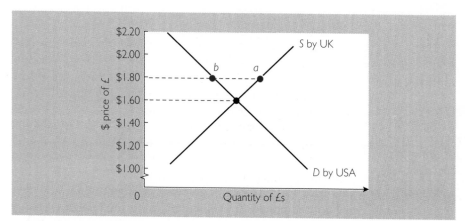

Figure 12.2

Determination of the rate of exchange

to obtain dollars. In other words, they go to banks or other foreign exchange dealers to buy dollars in exchange for pounds. The higher the exchange rate, the more dollars they obtain for their pounds. This effectively makes American goods cheaper to buy, and investment more profitable. Thus the *higher* the exchange rate, the *more* pounds are supplied. The supply curve of pounds therefore typically slopes upwards.

The sterling index

What goes into the basket?

The UK's *effective* exchange rate measures the value of the pound against a group or 'basket' of other currencies. Each currency's exchange rate with the pound enters with a weight somewhere between 0 and 1. The size of each currency's weight depends on the relative importance of that country as a trading partner with the UK. The more important it is, the bigger its weight. All the weights must add up to 1.

The effective exchange rate is expressed as an index with the base year equal to 100. The effective increase or decrease in the value of the pound can thus be expressed in terms of the percentage increase or decrease in this index.

The current official sterling index was introduced in February 1995. It is a weighted average of the sterling exchange rates with the currencies of twenty other countries. The weights are chosen to reflect the importance of UK trade with the various countries. The table shows the current and previous weights. The changes in these weights reflect the changing pattern of the UK's international trade and are based on 1989–91 trade flows.

? What are the current and previous total weights of the EU countries? Comment.

The weights of the currencies of various countries in the sterling exchange rate index

	Previous	Current		Previous	Current
Euro	–	0.6513			
(Germany)	0.2001	0.2249	(Ireland)	0.0242	0.0308
USA	0.2044	0.1649	(Finland)	0.0145	0.0141
(France)	0.1175	0.1259	Canada	0.0190	0.0138
(Italy)	0.0766	0.0827	Denmark	0.0145	0.0138
Japan	0.0883	0.0700	Norway	0.0131	0.0119
(Netherlands)	0.0500	0.0571	(Austria)	0.0124	0.0119
(Belgium)	0.0525	0.0539	(Portugal)	–	0.0084
(Spain)	0.0202	0.0385	Australia	–	0.0048
Sweden	0.0379	0.0345	(Greece)	–	0.0031
Switzerland	0.0548	0.0327	New Zealand	–	0.0021

When US residents wish to purchase UK goods or to invest in the UK, they require pounds. They *demand* pounds by selling dollars on the foreign exchange market. In other words, they go to banks or other foreign exchange dealers to buy pounds in exchange for dollars. The lower the dollar price of the pound (the exchange rate), the cheaper it is for them to obtain UK goods and assets, and hence the more pounds they are likely to demand. The demand curve for pounds, therefore, typically slopes downwards.

The equilibrium exchange rate is where the demand for pounds equals the supply. In Figure 12.2 this is at an exchange rate of £1 = $1.60. But what is the mechanism that equates demand and supply?

Key
Idea

7
p41

If the current exchange rate were above the equilibrium, the supply of pounds being offered to the banks would exceed the demand. For example, in Figure 12.2 if the exchange rate were $1.80, there would be an excess supply of pounds of $a - b$. Banks would not have enough dollars to exchange for all these pounds. But the banks make money by *exchanging* currency, not by holding on to it. They would thus lower the exchange rate in order to encourage a greater demand for pounds and reduce the excessive supply. They would continue lowering the rate until demand equalled supply.

Similarly, if the rate were below the equilibrium, say at $1.40, there would be a shortage of pounds. The banks would find themselves with too few pounds to meet all the demand. At the same time they would have an excess supply of dollars. The banks would thus raise the exchange rate until demand equalled supply.

In practice, the process of reaching equilibrium is extremely rapid. The foreign exchange dealers in the banks are continually adjusting the rate as new customers make new demands for currencies. What is more, the banks have to watch closely what each other is doing. They are constantly in competition with each other and thus have to keep their rates in line. The dealers receive minute-by-minute updates on their computer screens of the rates being offered round the world.

Shifts in the currency demand and supply curves

Key Idea

5
p27

Any shift in the demand or supply curves will cause the exchange rate to change. This is illustrated in Figure 12.3, which this time shows the euro/sterling exchange rate. If the demand and supply curves shift from D_1 and S_1 to D_2 and S_2 respectively, the exchange rate will fall from €1.40 to €1.20. A fall in the exchange rate is called a depreciation. A rise in the exchange rate is called an appreciation.

But why should the demand and supply curves shift? The following are the major possible causes of a depreciation:

■ *A fall in domestic interest rates*. UK rates would now be less competitive for savers and other depositors. More UK residents would be likely to deposit their money abroad (the supply of sterling would rise), and fewer people abroad would deposit their money in the UK (the demand for sterling would fall).

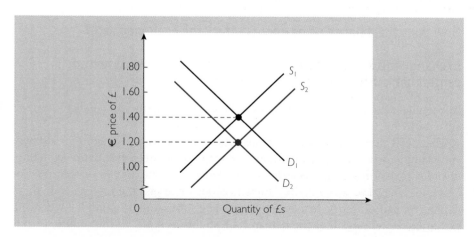

Figure 12.3
Floating exchange rates: movement to a new equilibrium

- *Higher inflation in the domestic economy than abroad.* UK exports will become less competitive. The demand for sterling will fall. At the same time, imports will become relatively cheaper for UK consumers. The supply of sterling will rise.
- *A rise in domestic incomes relative to incomes abroad.* If UK incomes rise, the demand for imports, and hence the supply of sterling, will rise. If incomes in other countries fall, the demand for UK exports, and hence the demand for sterling will fall.
- *Relative investment prospects improving abroad.* If investment prospects become brighter abroad than in the UK, perhaps because of better incentives abroad, or because of worries about an impending recession in the UK, again the demand for sterling will fall and the supply of sterling will rise.
- *Speculation that the exchange rate will fall.* If businesses involved in importing and exporting, and also banks and other foreign exchange dealers, think that the exchange rate is about to fall, they will sell pounds now before the rate does fall. The supply of sterling will thus rise.

> **Pause for thought**
>
> Go through each of the above reasons for shifts in the demand for and supply of sterling and consider what would cause an appreciation of the pound.

Key Idea
10
p68

Recap

1. The rate of exchange is the rate at which one currency exchanges for another. Rates of exchange are determined by demand and supply in the foreign exchange market. Demand for the domestic currency consists of all the credit items in the balance of payments account. Supply consists of all the debit items.

2. The exchange rate will depreciate (fall) if the demand for the domestic currency falls or the supply increases. These shifts can be caused by a fall in the domestic interest rates, higher inflation in the domestic economy than abroad, a rise in domestic incomes relative to incomes abroad, relative investment prospects improving abroad or the belief by speculators that the exchange rate will fall.

3. The opposite in each case would cause an appreciation (rise).

12.3   Exchange rates and the balance of payments

How does the balance of payments affect the exchange rate?

Exchange rates and the balance of payments: no government or central bank intervention

In a free foreign exchange market, the balance of payments will *automatically* balance. But why?

Key Idea
5
p27

The credit side of the balance of payments constitutes the demand for sterling. For example, when people abroad buy UK exports or assets they demand sterling in order to pay for them. The debit side constitutes the supply of sterling. For example, when UK residents buy foreign goods or assets, the importers of them require foreign currency to pay for them. They thus supply pounds. A floating exchange rate ensures that the demand for pounds is equal to the supply. It thus

Box 12.2 Case Studies and Applications

Dealing in foreign currencies

A daily juggling act

Imagine that a large car importer in the UK wants to import 5000 cars from Japan costing ¥15 billion. What does it do?

It will probably contact a number of banks' foreign exchange dealing rooms in London and ask them for exchange rate quotes. It thus puts all the banks in competition with each other. Each bank will want to get the business and thereby obtain the commission on the deal. To do this it must offer a higher rate than the other banks, since the higher the ¥/£ exchange rate, the more yen the firm will get for its money. (For an importer a rate of, say, ¥200 to £1 is better than a rate of, say, ¥180.)

Now it is highly unlikely that any of the banks will have a spare ¥15 billion. But a bank cannot say to the importer 'Sorry, you will have to wait before we can agree to sell them to you.' Instead the bank will offer a deal and then, if the firm agrees, the bank will have to set about obtaining the ¥15 billion. To do this it must offer Japanese who are supplying yen to obtain

pounds at a sufficiently *low* ¥/£ exchange rate. (The lower the ¥/£ exchange rate, the fewer yen the Japanese will have to pay to obtain pounds.)

The banks' dealers thus find themselves in the delicate position of wanting to offer a *high* enough exchange rate to the car importer in order to gain its business, but a *low* enough exchange rate in order to obtain the required amount of yen. The dealers are thus constantly having to adjust the rates of exchange in order to balance the demand and supply of each currency.

In general, the more of any foreign currency that dealers are asked to supply (by being offered sterling), the lower will be the exchange rate they will offer. In other words, a higher supply of sterling pushes down the foreign currency price of sterling.

 Assume that an American firm wants to import Scotch whisky from the UK. Describe how foreign exchange dealers will respond.

also ensures that the credits on the balance of payments are equal to the debits: that the balance of payments balances.

This does not mean that each part of the balance of payments account separately balances, but simply that any current account deficit must be matched by a capital plus financial account surplus and vice versa.

For example, suppose initially that each part of the balance of payments *did* separately balance. Then let us assume that interest rates rise. This encourages larger short-term financial inflows as people abroad are attracted to deposit money in the UK: the demand for sterling would shift to the right (e.g. from D_2 to D_1 in Figure 12.3). It will also cause smaller short-term financial outflows as UK residents keep more of their money in the country: the supply of sterling shifts to the left (e.g. from S_2 to S_1 in Figure 12.3). The financial account will go into surplus. The exchange rate will appreciate.

As the exchange rate rises, this will cause imports to be cheaper and exports to be more expensive. The current account will move into deficit. There is a movement up along the new demand and supply curves until a new equilibrium is reached. At this point, any financial account surplus is matched by an equal current (plus capital) account deficit.

Exchange rates and the balance of payments: with government or central bank intervention

The government may be unwilling to let the country's currency float freely. Frequent shifts in the demand and supply curves would cause frequent changes in the exchange rate. This, in turn, might cause uncertainty for businesses, which might curtail their trade and investment.

The government may thus intervene in the foreign exchange market. But what can it do? The answer to this depends on its objectives. It may simply want to reduce the day-to-day fluctuations in the exchange rate, or it may want to prevent longer-term, more fundamental shifts in the rate.

Reducing short-term fluctuations

Assume that the government believes that an exchange rate of €1.40 to the pound is approximately the long-term equilibrium rate. Short-term leftward shifts in the demand for sterling and rightward shifts in the supply, however, are causing the exchange rate to fall below this level (see Figure 12.3). What can the government do to keep the rate at €1.40?

Using reserves. The Bank of England can sell gold and foreign currencies from the reserves to buy pounds. This will shift the demand for sterling back to the right.

Borrowing from abroad. The government can negotiate a foreign currency loan from other countries or from an international agency such as the International Monetary Fund. It can then use these moneys to buy pounds on the foreign exchange market, thus again shifting the demand for sterling back to the right.

Raising interest rates. If the government raises interest rates, it will encourage people to deposit money in the UK and encourage UK residents to keep their money in the country. The demand for sterling will increase and the supply of sterling will decrease.

Maintaining a fixed rate of exchange over the longer term

Governments may choose to maintain a fixed rate over a number of months or even years. The following are possible methods it can use to achieve this (we are assuming that there are downward pressures on the exchange rate: e.g. as a result of higher aggregate demand and higher inflation).

Deflation. This is where the government deliberately curtails aggregate demand by either *fiscal policy or monetary policy* or both.

Deflationary fiscal policy involves raising taxes and/or reducing government expenditure. Deflationary monetary policy involves reducing the supply of money and raising interest rates. Note that in this case we are talking about not just the temporary raising of interest rates to prevent a short-term outflow of money from the country, but the use of higher interest rates to reduce borrowing and hence dampen aggregate demand.

A reduction in aggregate demand works in two ways:

- It reduces the level of consumer spending. This directly cuts imports, since there will be reduced spending on Japanese videos, German cars, Spanish holidays and so on. The supply of sterling coming on to the foreign exchange market thus decreases.

- It reduces the rate of inflation. This makes UK goods more competitive abroad, thus increasing the demand for sterling. It will also cut back on imports as UK consumers switch to the now more competitive home-produced goods. The supply of sterling falls.

Supply-side policies. This is where the government attempts to increase the long-term competitiveness of UK goods by encouraging reductions in the costs of production and/or improvements in the quality of UK goods. For example, the government may attempt to improve the quantity and quality of training and research and development (see Section 10.8).

Controls on imports and/or foreign exchange dealing. This is where the government restricts the outflow of money, either by restricting people's access to foreign exchange, or by the use of tariffs (customs duties) and quotas.

> **Pause for thought**
>
> What problems might arise if the government were to adopt this third method of maintaining a fixed exchange rate?

Recap

1. In a free foreign exchange market, the balance of payments will automatically balance, since changes in the exchange rate will balance the demand for the currency (credits on the balance of payments) with the supply (debits on the balance of payments).

2. There is no guarantee, however, that there will be a balance on each of the separate parts of the balance of payments account.

3. The government can attempt to prevent the rate of exchange falling by central bank purchases of the domestic currency in the foreign exchange market, either by selling foreign currency reserves or by using foreign loans. Alternatively, the government can raise interest rates. The reverse actions can be taken if it wants to prevent the rate from rising.

4. In the longer term, it can attempt to prevent the rate from falling by pursuing deflationary policies, protectionist policies or supply-side policies to increase the competitiveness of the country's exports.

Fixed versus floating exchange rates | 12.4

Should exchange rates be 'left to the market'?

Are exchange rates best left free to fluctuate and be determined purely by market forces, or should the government or central bank intervene to fix exchange rates, either rigidly or within bands? Unfortunately, the answer is not clear cut. Both floating and fixed exchange rates have their advantages and disadvantages.

Advantages of fixed exchange rates

Surveys reveal that most business people prefer relatively rigid exchange rates: if not totally fixed, then at least pegged for periods of time. The following arguments are used to justify this preference.

Certainty. With fixed exchange rates, international trade and investment become much less risky, since profits are not affected by movements in the exchange rate.

Assume that a firm correctly forecasts that its product will sell in the USA for $1.50. It costs 80p to produce. If the rate of exchange is fixed at £1 = $1.50, each unit will earn £1 and hence make a 20p profit. If, however, the rate of exchange were not fixed, exchange fluctuations could wipe out this profit. If, say, the rate appreciated to £1 = $2, and if units continued to sell for $1.50, they would now earn only 75p each, and hence make a 5p loss.

Little or no speculation. Provided the rate is *absolutely* fixed – and people believe that it will remain so – there is no point in speculating. For example, between 1999 and 2001, when the old currencies of the euro-zone countries were still used, but were totally fixed to the euro, there was no speculation that the German mark, say, would change in value against the French franc or the Dutch guilder.

Prevents governments pursuing 'irresponsible' macroeconomic policies. If a government deliberately and excessively expands aggregate demand – perhaps in an attempt to gain short-term popularity with the electorate – the resulting balance of payments deficit will force it to constrain demand again (unless it resorts to import controls).

Governments cannot allow their economies to have a persistently higher inflation rate than competitor countries without running into balance of payments crises, and hence a depletion of reserves. Fixed rates thus force governments (in the absence of trade restrictions) to keep the rate of inflation roughly to world levels.

Disadvantages of fixed exchange rates

Exchange rate policy may conflict with the interests of domestic business and the economy as a whole. A balance of payments deficit can occur even if the economy is not 'overheating'. For example, there can be a fall in the demand for the country's exports as a result of an external shock (such as a recession in other countries) or because of increased foreign competition. If protectionism is to be avoided, and if supply-side policies work only over the long run, the government will be forced to raise interest rates. This is likely to have two adverse effects on the domestic economy:

■ Higher interest rates may discourage long-term business investment. This in turn will lower firms' profits in the long term and reduce the country's long-term rate of economic growth. The country's capacity to produce will be restricted and businesses are likely to fall behind in the competitive race with their international rivals to develop new products and improve existing ones.

■ Higher interest rates will have a deflationary effect on the economy by making borrowing more expensive and thereby cutting back on both consumer demand and investment. This can result in a recession with rising unemployment. It will, however, improve the balance of payments. There will be an improvement not only on the financial account, as money flows into the country to take advantage of the higher rates of interest, but also on the current account. The recession will lead to reduced demand for imports, and lower inflation is likely to make exports more competitive and imports relatively more expensive.

The problem is that, with fixed exchange rates, domestic policy is entirely constrained by the balance of payments. Any attempt to reflate and cure unemployment will simply lead to a balance of payments deficit and thus force governments to deflate again.

Competitive deflations leading to world depression. If deficit countries deflated, but surplus countries *reflated*, there would be no overall world deflation or reflation. Countries may be quite happy, however, to run a balance of payments surplus and build up reserves. Countries may thus competitively deflate – all trying to achieve a balance of payments surplus. But this is beggar-my-neighbour policy. Not all countries can have a surplus! Overall the world must be in balance. The result of these policies is to lead to general world deflation and a restriction in growth.

Problems of international liquidity. If trade is to expand, there must be an expansion in the supply of currencies acceptable for world trade (dollars, euros, pounds, gold, etc.): there must be adequate international liquidity. Countries' reserves of these currencies must grow if they are to be sufficient to maintain a fixed rate at times of balance of payments disequilibrium. Conversely, there must not be excessive international liquidity. Otherwise the extra demand that would result would lead to world inflation. It is important under fixed exchange rates, therefore, to avoid too much or too little international liquidity. The problem is whether there is adequate control of international liquidity. The supply of dollars, for example, depends largely on US policy, which may be dominated by its internal economic situation rather than by a concern for the wellbeing of the international community.

Inability to adjust to shocks. With sticky prices and wage rates, there is no swift mechanism for dealing with sudden balance of payments crises – like that caused by a sudden increase in oil prices. In the short run, countries will need huge reserves or loan facilities to support their currencies. There may be insufficient international liquidity to permit this. In the longer run, countries may be forced into a depression by having to deflate. The alternative may be to resort to protectionism, or to abandon the fixed rate and devalue.

Speculation. If speculators believe that a fixed rate simply cannot be maintained, speculation is likely to be massive. If, for example, there is a large balance of payments deficit, speculative selling will worsen the deficit and may itself force a devaluation.

Advantages of a free-floating exchange rate

The advantages and disadvantages of free-floating rates are to a large extent the opposite of fixed rates.

Definitions

International liquidity
The supply of currencies in the world acceptable for financing international trade and investment.

Devaluation
Where the government refixes the exchange rate at a lower level.

Automatic correction. The government simply lets the exchange rate move freely to the equilibrium. In this way, balance of payments disequilibria are automatically and instantaneously corrected without the need for specific government policies.

No problem of international liquidity and reserves. Since there is no central bank intervention in the foreign exchange market, there is no need to hold reserves. A currency is automatically convertible at the current market exchange rate.

Insulation from external economic events. A country is not tied to a possibly un-acceptably high world inflation rate, as it could be under a fixed exchange rate. It is also to some extent protected against world economic fluctuations and shocks.

Governments are free to choose their domestic policy. Under a floating rate the gov-ernment can choose whatever level of domestic demand it considers appropriate, and simply leave exchange rate movements to take care of any balance of payments effect. Similarly, the central bank can choose whatever rate of interest is necessary to meet domestic objectives, such as achieving a target rate of inflation. The exchange rate will simply adjust to the new rate of interest – a rise in interest rates causing an appreciation, a fall causing a depreciation. This freedom for the gov-ernment and central bank is a major advantage, especially when the effectiveness of deflation under fixed exchange rates is reduced by downward wage and price rigidity, and when competitive deflation between countries may end up causing a world recession.

Disadvantages of a free–floating exchange rate

Despite these advantages there are still a number of serious problems with free-floating exchange rates.

Unstable exchange rates. The less elastic are the demand and supply curves for the currency in Figure 12.3, the greater the change in exchange rate that will be neces-sary to restore equilibrium following a shift in either demand or supply. In the long run, in a competitive world with domestic substitutes for imports and foreign sub-stitutes for exports, demand and supply curves are relatively elastic. Nevertheless, in the short run, given that many firms have contracts with specific overseas sup-pliers or distributors, the demands for imports and exports are less elastic.

Speculation. In an uncertain world, where there are few restrictions on currency speculation, where the fortunes and policies of governments can change rapidly, and where large amounts of short-term deposits are internationally 'footloose', speculation can be highly destabilising in the short run. If people think that the exchange rate will fall, then they will sell the currency, and this will cause the exchange rate to fall even further, perhaps overshooting the eventual equilibrium. At times of international currency turmoil (see Box 12.4), such speculation can be enormous. Worldwide, over a tril-lion dollars on average passes daily across the foreign exchanges: greatly in excess of countries' foreign exchange reserves!

> **Pause for thought**
>
> If speculators on average gain from their speculation, who loses?

Uncertainty for traders and investors. The uncertainty caused by currency fluctu-ations can discourage international trade and investment. To some extent the

Box 12.3 Exploring Economics

The importance of international financial movements

How a current account deficit can coincide with an appreciating exchange rate

Since the early 1970s, most of the major economies of the world have operated with floating exchange rates. The opportunities that this gives for speculative gain has led to a huge increase in short-term international financial movements. Vast amounts of moneys transfer from country to country in search of higher interest rates or a currency that is likely to appreciate. This can have a bizarre effect on exchange rates.

If a country pursues an expansionary fiscal policy, the current account will tend to go into deficit as extra imports are 'sucked in'. What effect will this have on exchange rates? You might think that the answer is obvious: the higher demand for imports will create an extra supply of domestic currency on the foreign exchange market and hence drive down the exchange rate.

In fact the opposite is likely. The higher interest rates resulting from the higher domestic demand can lead to a massive inflow of short-term finance. The financial account can thus move sharply into surplus. This is likely to outweigh the current account deficit and cause an *appreciation* of the exchange rate.

Exchange rate movements, especially in the short term, are largely brought about by changes on the financial rather than the current account.

? Why do high international financial mobility and an absence of exchange controls severely limit a country's ability to choose its interest rate?

---

problem can be overcome by using the forward exchange market. Here traders agree with a bank *today* the rate of exchange for some point in the *future* (say, six months' time). This allows traders to plan future purchases of imports or sales of exports at a known rate of exchange. Of course, banks charge for this service, since they are taking on the risks themselves of adverse exchange rate fluctuations.

But dealing in the futures market only takes care of short-run uncertainty. Banks will not be prepared to take on the risks of offering forward contracts for several years hence. Thus firms simply have to live with the uncertainty over exchange rates in future years. This will discourage long-term investment. For example, the possibility of exchange rate appreciation may well discourage firms from investing abroad, since a higher exchange rate means that foreign exchange earnings will be worth less in the domestic currency.

Figure 12.4 on page 480 shows the fluctuations in the dollar/pound exchange rate and the exchange rate index from 1976 to 2003. As you can see, there have been large changes in exchange rates. Such changes do not only make it difficult for exporters. Importers too will be hesitant about making long-term deals. For example, a UK manufacturing firm signing a contract to buy US components in 1980, when $2.40 worth of components could be purchased for £1, would find a struggle to make a profit some four years later when only just over $1.00 worth of US components could be purchased for £1!

Definition

Forward exchange market Where contracts are made today for the price at which a currency will be exchanged at some specified future date.

Box 12.4

Currency turmoil

Unleashing the power of speculation

For periods of time, world currency markets can be quite peaceful, with only modest changes in exchange rates. But with the ability to move vast sums of money very rapidly from one part of the world to another and from one currency to another, speculators can suddenly turn this relatively peaceful world into one of extreme turmoil. In this box we examine three periods over just eight years when such turmoil occurred.

1995

The problem started towards the end of 1994 with an economic crisis in Mexico. To help its neighbour, the USA quickly arranged a $20 billion aid package. But speculators saw trouble for the dollar. A decline in US sales to Mexico was likely to damage the USA's export recovery. On top of this, market analysts were predicting that US interest rates, which had previously been rising, would now fall as US economic growth slowed. In contrast, interest rates in Germany looked set to rise, as the German authorities faced growing inflationary pressures. Faced by all this, many investors moved out of dollars and into the more stable German mark.

By March 1995 the dollar had reached post-war lows against the German mark and the Japanese yen. The fall in value against the yen represented a 32 per cent depreciation since 1992.

In Europe, the knock-on effect of the strong mark was felt in some measure by all the currencies, especially those within the ERM (see Section 12.5). The Spanish peseta, under pressure prior to the mark's rise, was devalued by 7 per cent, and the Portuguese escudo by 3.5 per cent. Both the French and Swedish governments, with their currencies reaching record lows against the mark, were forced to put up interest rates to prevent further depreciation.

The high yen and mark proved to be equally problematic for Japan and Germany, which found their competitive positions significantly eroded: exports were falling and domestic firms found it very difficult to compete with cheap imports.

The US Federal Reserve seemed unconcerned about the falling dollar and took no steps to support it. This expression of total indifference led speculators to believe that the dollar's fall was not yet over, encouraging yet further selling of dollar balances.

1997

In the summer of 1997, the Thai baht collapsed. It had been pegged to the US dollar and, with strong economic growth, this had encouraged large-scale inward investment. But with a slowing economy in 1997 and a widening trade deficit, investors began to question whether the pegged rate could be maintained. There was massive speculative selling of the currency, and hence the collapse.

The massive depreciation of the baht acted as a catalyst, plunging the whole of south-east Asia into financial turmoil. The shock waves, as one currency after another came under speculative attack, spread outwards from the region. Brazil, Argentina, Mexico, Russia and the Ukraine all saw their currencies come under speculative pressure. All were forced to raise interest rates in an attempt to prevent further depreciation of their exchange rates.

As short-term financial flows increase and currency markets become freer, as the growth in information technology and the process of globalisation make the world's financial markets more integrated, and as fear and rumour seem increasingly able to spread like a bush fire around the world's financial capitals, so the greater is the potential for financial volatility and economic crisis.

1999–2003

On 1 January 1999, the euro was launched and exchanged for $1.16. By October 2000 the euro had fallen to $0.85. What was the cause of this 27 per cent depreciation? The main cause was the growing fear that inflationary pressures were increasing in the

USA and that, therefore, the Federal Reserve Bank would have to raise interest rates. At the same time, the euro-zone economy was growing only slowly and inflation was well below the 2 per cent ceiling set by the European Central Bank. There was thus pressure on the ECB to cut interest rates.

The speculators were not wrong. As the diagram shows, US interest rates rose, and ECB interest rates initially fell, and when eventually they did rise (in October 1999), the gap between US and ECB interest rates soon widened again.

In addition to the differences in interest rates, a lack of confidence in the recovery of the euro-zone economy and a continuing confidence in the US economy encouraged investment to flow to the USA. This inflow of finance (and lack of inflow to the euro zone) further pushed up the dollar relative to the euro.

The low value of the euro meant a high value of the pound relative to the euro. This made it very difficult for UK companies exporting to euro-zone countries and also for those competing with imports from the euro zone (which had been made cheaper by the fall in the euro).

The position completely changed in 2001. With the US economy slowing rapidly and fears of an impending recession, the Federal Reserve Bank reduced interest rates 11 times during the year: from 6 per cent at the beginning of the year to 1.25 per cent at the end. Although the ECB also cut interest rates, the cuts were relatively modest: from 4.75 at the beginning of the year to 3.25 at the end. With euro-zone interest rates now considerably above US rates, the euro began to rise. This rise was substantial throughout 2002 and into 2003, so that by May 2003 the exchange rate had risen to $1.18: a 39 per cent appreciation since June 2001.

These massive currency fluctuations are a major disincentive to US and euro-zone companies thinking of trading with each other or investing in each other's country/region.

? If in 1995 the Japanese yen was already above its long-term equilibrium exchange rate, and was therefore likely to depreciate some time in the future, why did speculators still continue to buy yen? Similarly, why did people sell euros in 1999/2000?

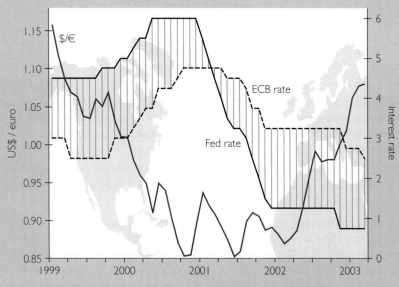

Fluctuations between the euro and the dollar

Figure 12.4
Dollar/sterling
exchange rate and
sterling exchange
rate index:
1976–2003

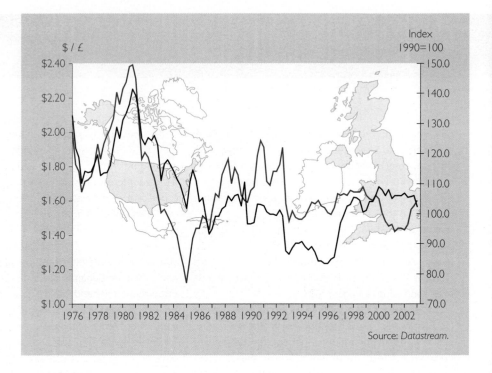

Source: *Datastream.*

Lack of discipline on the domestic economy.   Governments may pursue irresponsibly inflationary policies (for short-term political gain, say). This will have adverse effects over the longer term as the government will at some point have to deflate the economy again, with a resulting fall in output and rise in unemployment.

Recap

1. Completely fixed exchange rates bring the advantage of certainty for the business community, which encourages trade and foreign investment. They also help to prevent governments from pursuing irresponsible macroeconomic policies.

2. However, with fixed rates domestic policy is entirely constrained by the balance of payments. What is more, they can lead to competitive deflation worldwide; there may be problems of excessive or insufficient international liquidity; there may be difficulty in adjusting to external shocks; and speculation could be very severe if people came to believe that a fixed rate was about to break down.

3. The advantages of free-floating exchange rates are that they automatically correct balance of payments disequilibria; they eliminate the need for reserves; and they give governments a greater independence to pursue their chosen domestic policy.

4. On the other hand, a completely free exchange rate can be highly unstable, especially when the elasticities of demand for imports and exports are low and there are shifts in currency demand and supply; in addition, speculation may be destabilising. This may discourage firms from trading and investing abroad. What is more, a flexible exchange rate, by removing the balance of payments constraint on domestic policy, may encourage governments to pursue irresponsible domestic policies for short-term political gain.

The origins of the euro

How did the majority of the EU countries arrive at a single currency?

There have been many attempts to regulate exchange rates since 1945. By far the most successful was the Bretton Woods system, which was adopted worldwide from the end of the Second World War until 1971. This was a form of adjustable peg exchange rate, where countries pegged (i.e. fixed) their exchange rate to the US dollar, but could re-peg it at a lower or higher level ('devalue' or 'revalue' their exchange rate) if there was a persistent and substantial balance of payments deficit or surplus.

With growing world inflation and instability from the mid-1960s, it became more and more difficult to maintain fixed exchange rates, and the growing likelihood of devaluations and revaluations fuelled speculation. The system was abandoned in the early 1970s. What followed was a period of exchange rate management known as managed floating. Under this system, exchange rates were not pegged but allowed to float. However, central banks intervened from time to time to prevent excessive exchange rate fluctuations. This system largely continues to this day.

However, on a regional basis, especially within Europe, there were attempts to create greater exchange rate stability. The European system involved establishing exchange rate bands: upper and lower limits within which exchange rates were allowed to fluctuate. The name given to the EU system was the exchange rate mechanism (ERM).

The ERM

The ERM came into existence in March 1979 and the majority of the EU countries were members. The UK, however, chose not to join. When Greece joined the EU in 1984, it too stayed outside the ERM. Spain joined in 1989, the UK in 1990 and Portugal in April 1992. Then in September 1992, the UK and Italy indefinitely suspended their membership of the ERM, but Italy rejoined in November 1996 as part of its bid to join the single European currency (see Section 12.6). Austria joined in 1995, Finland in 1996 and Greece in 1998. By the time the ERM was replaced by the single currency in 1999, only Sweden and the UK were outside the ERM.

Any of the ten new members that have joined the EU in 2004 that also wish to join the euro must first be a member of an ERM version 2 for two years, with their exchange rates pegged to the euro. So too must the UK, Denmark or Sweden, if they choose to join.

Features of the ERM

Under the system, each currency was given a central exchange rate with each of the other ERM currencies in a grid. However, fluctuations were allowed from the central rate within specified bands. For most countries these bands were set at $\pm 2^1/_4$ per cent. The central rates could be adjusted from time to time by agreement, thus making the ERM an 'adjustable peg' system. All the currencies floated jointly with currencies outside the ERM.

Definitions

Adjustable peg
A system whereby exchange rates are fixed for a period of time, but may be devalued (or revalued) if a deficit (or surplus) becomes substantial.

Managed floating
A system of flexible exchange rates, but where the government intervenes to prevent excessive fluctuations or even to achieve an unofficial target exchange rate.

The exchange rate mechanism (ERM)
A semi-fixed system whereby participating EU countries allow fluctuations against each other's currencies only within agreed bands. Collectively they float freely against all other currencies.

If a currency approached the upper or lower limit against *any* other ERM currency, the two countries had to intervene to maintain their currencies within the band. This could take the form of their central banks selling the stronger currency and buying the weaker one, or reducing interest rates in the case of the strong currency and raising interest rates in the case of the weak currency.

The ERM in practice

In a system of pegged exchange rates, countries should harmonise their policies to avoid excessive currency misalignments and hence the need for large devaluations or revaluations. There should be a convergence of their economies: they should be at a similar point on the business cycle and have similar inflation rates and interest rates.

The ERM in the 1980s.   In the early 1980s, however, French and Italian inflation rates were persistently higher than German rates. This meant that there had to be several realignments (devaluations and revaluations). After 1983 realignments became less frequent, and then from 1987 to 1992 they ceased altogether. This was due to a growing convergence of members' internal policies.

By the time the UK joined the ERM in 1990, it was generally seen by its existing members as being a great success. It had created a zone of currency stability in a world of highly unstable exchange rates, and had provided the necessary environment for the establishment of a truly common market by the end of 1992.

Crisis in the ERM.   Shortly after the UK joined the ERM, strains began to show. The reunification of Germany involved considerable reconstruction in the eastern part of the country. Financing this reconstruction was causing a growing budget deficit. The Bundesbank (the German central bank) thus felt obliged to maintain high interest rates in order to keep inflation in check. At the same time, the UK was experiencing a massive current account deficit (partly the result of entering the ERM at what many commentators argued was too high an exchange rate). It was thus obliged to raise interest rates in order to protect the pound, despite the fact that the economy was sliding rapidly into recession. The French franc and Italian lira were also perceived to be overvalued, and there were the first signs of worries as to whether their exchange rates within the ERM could be retained.

At the same time, the US economy was moving into recession and, as a result, US interest rates were cut. This led to a large outflow of capital from the USA. With high German interest rates, much of this capital flowed to Germany. This pushed up the value of the German mark and with it the other ERM currencies. In September 1992, things reached crisis point. First the lira was devalued. Then two days later, on 'Black Wednesday' (16 September), the UK and Italy were forced to suspend their membership of the ERM: the pound and the lira were floated. At the same time, the Spanish peseta was devalued by 5 per cent.

> **Pause for thought**
>
> Under what circumstances may a currency bloc like the ERM (a) help to prevent speculation; (b) aggravate the problem of speculation?

Turmoil returned in the summer of 1993. The French economy was moving into recession and there were calls for cuts in French interest rates. But this was only possible if Germany was prepared to cut its rates too, and it was not. Speculators began to sell francs and it became obvious that the existing franc/mark parity could not be maintained. In an attempt to rescue the ERM, the EU finance ministers agreed to adopt wide ±15 per cent bands. The result was that the franc and the Danish krone depreciated against the mark.

A return of calm. The old ERM appeared to be at an end. The new ±15 per cent bands hardly seemed like a 'pegged' system at all. However, the ERM did not die. Within months, the members were again managing to keep fluctuations within a very narrow range (for most of the time, within ±2$^{1}/_{4}$ per cent!). The scene was being set for the abandonment of separate currencies and the adoption of a single currency: the euro.

The Maastricht Treaty and the road to the single currency

The ERM was conceived as a stage on the road to complete economic and monetary union (EMU) of member states. Details of the path towards EMU were finalised in the Maastricht Treaty, which was signed in February 1992. The timetable for EMU involved the adoption of a single currency by 1999 at the latest.

One of the first moves was to establish a European Monetary Institute (EMI). Its role was to co-ordinate monetary policy and encourage greater co-operation between EU central banks. It also monitored the operation of the ERM and prepared the ground for the establishment of a European central bank in time for the launch of the single currency.

Before they could join the single currency, member states were obliged to achieve convergence of their economies. Each country had to meet five convergence criteria:

- Inflation: should be no more than 1$^{1}/_{2}$ per cent above the average inflation rate of the three countries in the EU with the lowest inflation.
- Interest rates: the rate on long-term government bonds should be no more than 2 per cent above the average of the three countries with the lowest inflation.
- Budget deficit: should be no more than 3 per cent of GDP.
- National debt: should be no more than 60 per cent of GDP.
- Exchange rates: the currency should have been within the normal ERM bands for at least two years with no realignments or excessive intervention.

Before the launch of the single currency, the Council of Ministers had to decide which countries had met the convergence criteria and would thus be eligible to form a currency union by fixing their currencies permanently to the euro. Their national currencies would effectively disappear.

At the same time a European System of Central Banks (ESCB) would be created, consisting of a European Central Bank (ECB) and the central banks of the participating member states. The ECB would be independent, both from governments and from EU political institutions. It would operate the monetary policy on behalf of the countries that had adopted the single currency.

Definition

Currency union A group of countries (or regions) using a common currency.

Recap

1. One means of achieving greater currency stability is for a group of countries to peg their internal exchange rates and yet float jointly with the rest of the world. The exchange rate mechanism of the EU (ERM) was an example. Members' currencies were allowed to fluctuate against other member currencies within a band. The band was $\pm 2\frac{1}{4}$ per cent for the majority of the ERM countries until 1993.

2. The need for realignments seemed to have diminished in the late 1980s as greater convergence was achieved between the members' economies. However, growing strains in the system in the early 1990s led to a crisis in September 1992. The UK and Italy left the ERM. There was a further crisis in July 1993 and the bands were widened to ± 15 per cent.

3. Thereafter, as convergence of the economies of ERM members increased, fluctuations decreased and remained largely within $\pm 2\frac{1}{4}$ per cent.

4. The ERM was seen as an important first stage on the road to complete economic and monetary union (EMU) in the EU.

5. The Maastricht Treaty set out a timetable for achieving EMU. This would culminate in the creation of a currency union: a single European currency with a common monetary policy operated by an independent European Central Bank.

12.6 Economic and monetary union (EMU) in Europe

Do countries benefit from using the euro?

Birth of the euro

In March 1998, the European Commission ruled that 11 of the 15 member states were eligible to proceed to EMU in January 1999. The UK and Denmark were to exercise an opt-out negotiated at Maastricht, and Sweden and Greece failed to meet one or more of the convergence criteria. (Greece joined the euro in 2001.)

All 11 countries unambiguously met the interest rate and inflation criteria, but doubts were expressed by many 'Eurosceptics' as to whether they all genuinely met the other three criteria.

■ Exchange rates. Neither Finland nor Italy had been in the ERM for two years (Finland had joined the ERM in October 1996 and Italy had rejoined in November 1996), and the Irish punt was revalued by 3 per cent on 16 March 1998. However, the Commission regarded these three countries as being sufficiently close to the reference value.

■ Government deficits. All 11 countries met this criterion, but some countries only managed to achieve a deficit of 3 per cent or below by taking one-off measures, such as a special tax in Italy, and counting privatisation receipts in Germany. Yet, under the Stability and Growth Pact, euro-zone countries would be required to keep their deficits within the 3 per cent limit (see Box 8.5). The concern was that countries that only just met this criterion at time of entry would find it difficult to keep within the limit in times of recession or low growth, when tax revenues were not keeping pace with government expenditure. This proved to be the case with Germany and France in 2002/3.

■ Government debt. Only four countries had debts that did not exceed 60 per cent (France, Finland, Luxembourg and the UK). However, the Maastricht Treaty allowed countries to exceed this value as long as the debt was 'sufficiently diminishing and approaching the reference value at a satisfactory pace'. Critics argued that this phrase was interpreted too loosely.

The euro came into being on 1 January 1999, but euro banknotes and coins were not introduced until 1 January 2002. In the meantime, national currencies continued to exist alongside the euro, but at irrevocably fixed rates. The old notes and coins were withdrawn a few weeks after the introduction of euro notes and coins.

How desirable is EMU?

Advantages of the single currency

Elimination of the costs of converting currencies. With separate currencies in each of the EU countries, costs were incurred each time one currency was exchanged into another. The elimination of these costs, however, was probably the least important benefit from the single currency. The European Commission estimated that the effect was to increase the GDP of the countries concerned by an average of only 0.4 per cent. The gains to countries like the UK, which have well-developed financial markets, would be even smaller.

Increased competition and efficiency. Despite the advent of the single market, large price differences remained between member states. Not only has the single currency eliminated the need to convert one currency into another (a barrier to competition), but it has brought more transparency in pricing, and has put greater downward pressure on prices in high-cost firms and countries.

Elimination of exchange-rate uncertainty (between the members). Even with a narrow-banded ERM, realignments might still have occurred from time to time if separate currencies had remained. As the events of 1992 and 1993 showed, this could cause massive speculation if it was believed that currencies were out of line. Removal of this uncertainty has helped to encourage trade between the euro-zone countries. Perhaps more importantly, it has encouraged investment by firms that trade between these countries, given the greater certainty in calculating costs and revenues from such trade.

Increased inward investment. Investment from the rest of the world is attracted to a euro zone of over 300 million inhabitants, where there is no fear of internal currency movements. By contrast, the UK, by not joining, has found that inward investment has been diverted away to countries within the euro zone. From 1990 to 1999, the UK's share of inward investment to the EU was nearly 40 per cent. From 1999 to 2002, it was 24 per cent.

Lower inflation and interest rates. A single monetary policy forces convergence in inflation rates (just as inflation rates are very similar between the different regions *within* a country). Provided the ECB succeeds in remaining independent from short-term political manipulation, this is likely to result in a lower average inflation rate in the euro-zone countries. This, in turn, will help to convince markets that the euro will be strong relative to other currencies. The result will be lower long-term rates of interest. This, in turn, would further encourage investment in the euro-zone countries, both by member states and by the rest of the world.

Opposition to EMU

Monetary union has been bitterly opposed, however, by certain groups. Many Euro-sceptics see within it a surrender of national political and economic sovereignty. The lack of an independent monetary and exchange rate policy is a serious problem, they argue, if an economy is at all out of harmony with the rest of the Union. For example if countries like Italy and Spain have higher endemic rates of inflation (due, say, to greater cost-push pressures), then how are they to make their goods competitive with the rest of the Union? With separate currencies these countries could allow their currencies to depreciate. With a single currency, however, they could become depressed 'regions' of Europe, with rising unemployment and all the other regional problems of depressed regions *within* a country. This may then require significant regional policies – policies that may not be in place or, if they were, would be seen as too interventionist by the political right.

> **Pause for thought** ▕▐▐
>
> *How might multiplier effects (the principle of cumulative causation) lead to prosperous regions becoming more prosperous and less prosperous regions falling even further behind?*

The answer given by proponents of EMU is that it is better to tackle the problem of high inflation in such countries by the disciplines of competition from other EU countries, than merely to feed that inflation by keeping separate currencies and allowing repeated devaluations, with all the uncertainty that that brings. If such countries become depressed, they argue, it is better to have a fully developed *fiscal* policy for the Union which will divert funds into investment in such regions. What is more, the high-inflation countries tend to be the poorer ones with lower wage levels (albeit faster wage *increases*). With the high mobility of labour and capital that will accompany the development of the single market, resources are likely to be attracted to such countries. This could help to narrow the gap between the richer and poorer member states. The critics of EMU argue that labour is relatively immobile, given cultural and language barriers. Thus an unemployed worker in Wales could not easily move to a job in Turin or Helsinki. What the critics are arguing here is that the EU is not an optimal currency area (see Box 12.5).

Perhaps the most serious criticism is that the same rate of interest must apply to all euro-zone countries: the 'one-size-fits-all' problem. The trouble is that while one country might require a lower rate of interest in order to ward off recession (such as Germany in 2003), another might require a higher one to prevent inflation. As convergence between the member economies increases, however, this problem is likely to lessen.

Another problem for members of a single currency occurs in adjusting to a shock when that shock affects members to different degrees. These are known as **asymmetric shocks**. For example, a sudden change in the price of oil would affect an oil-exporting country like the UK differently from oil-importing countries. This problem is more serious, the less the factor mobility between member countries and the less the price flexibility within member countries.

Definitions

Optimal currency area
The optimal size of a currency area is one that maximises the benefits from having a single currency relative to the costs. If the area were to be increased or decreased in size, the costs would rise relative to the benefits.

Asymmetric shocks
Shocks (such as an oil price increase or a recession in another part of the world) that have different-sized effects on different industries, regions or countries.

Box 12.5 Exploring Economics

Optimal currency areas

When it pays to pay in the same currency

Imagine that each town and village used a different currency. Think how inconvenient it would be having to keep exchanging one currency into another, and how difficult it would be working out the relative value of items in different parts of the country.

Clearly there are benefits of using a common currency, not only within a country but across different countries. The benefits include greater transparency in pricing, more open competition, greater certainty for investors and the avoidance of having to pay commission when you change one currency into another. There are also the benefits from having a single monetary policy if that is delivered in a more consistent and effective way than by individual countries.

So why not have a single currency for the whole world? The problem is that the bigger a single-currency area gets, the more likely the conditions are to diverge in the different parts of the area. Some parts may have high unemployment and require reflationary policies. Others may have low unemployment and suffer from inflationary pressures. They may require *deflationary* policies.

What is more, different members of the currency area may experience quite different shocks to their economies, whether from outside the union (e.g. a fall in the price of one of their major exports) or from inside (e.g. a prolonged strike). These 'asymmetric shocks' would imply that different parts of the currency area should adopt different policies. But with a common monetary policy and hence common interest rates, and with no possibility of devaluation/revaluation of the currency of individual members, the scope for separate economic policies is reduced.

The costs of asymmetric shocks (and hence the costs of a single-currency area) will be greater, the less the mobility of labour and capital, the less the flexibility of prices and wage rates, and the fewer the

alternative policies there are that can be turned to (such as fiscal and regional policies).

So is the euro zone an optimal currency area? Certainly strong doubts have been raised by many economists.

- Labour is relatively immobile.
- There are structural differences between the member states.
- The transmission effects of interest rate changes are different between the member countries, given that countries have proportions of borrowing at variable interest rates and different proportions of consumer debt to GDP.
- Exports to countries outside the euro zone account for different proportions of the members' GDP, and thus their economies are affected differently by a change in the rate of exchange of the euro against other currencies.
- Wage rates are relatively inflexible.
- Under the Stability and Growth Pact (see Box 8.5), the scope for using discretionary fiscal policy is curtailed.

This does not necessarily mean, however, that the costs of having a single European currency outweigh the benefits. Also, the problems outlined above should decline over time as the single market develops. Finally, the problem of asymmetric shocks can be exaggerated. European economies are highly diversified; there are often more differences *within* economies than between them. Thus shocks are more likely to affect different industries or localities than whole countries. Changing the exchange rate, if that were still possible, would hardly be an appropriate policy in these circumstances.

? Why is a single currency area likely to move towards becoming an optimal currency area over time?

This problem, however, should not be overstated. The divergences between economies are often the result of a lack of harmony between countries in their demand-management policies: something that is impossible in the case of monetary policy, and more difficult in the case of fiscal policy, for countries in the euro zone. Also, many of the shocks that face economies today are global and have similar (albeit not identical) effects on all countries. Adjustment to such shocks would often be better with a single co-ordinated policy – something that would be much easier with a single currency and a single central bank.

Even when shocks are uniformly felt in the member states, however, there is still the problem that policies adopted centrally will have different impacts on each country. For example, in the UK, a large proportion of borrowing is at variable interest rates. In Germany, by contrast, much is at fixed rates. Thus if the ECB were to raise interest rates, the deflationary effects would be felt disproportionately in the UK. Of course, were this balance to change – and there is some evidence that types of borrowing are becoming more uniform across the EU – this problem would diminish.

The problem for economists is that the issue of monetary union is a very emotive one. 'Europhiles' often see monetary union as a vital element in their vision of a united Europe. Many Eurosceptics, however, see EMU as a surrender of sovereignty and a threat to nationhood. In such an environment, a calm assessment of the arguments and evidence is very difficult.

Recap

1. The euro was born on 1 January 1999. Twelve countries adopted it, having at least nominally met the Maastricht convergence criteria. Euro notes and coins were introduced on 1 January 2002, with the notes and coins of the old currencies withdrawn a few weeks later.

2. The advantages claimed for EMU are that it eliminates the costs of converting currencies and the uncertainties associated with possible changes in inter-EU exchange rates. This encourages more investment, both inward and by domestic firms. What is more, a common central bank, independent from domestic governments, provides the stable monetary environment necessary for a convergence of the EU economies and the encouragement of investment and inter-Union trade.

3. Critics claim, however, that it might make adjustment to domestic economic problems more difficult. The loss of independence in policy making is seen by such people to be a major issue, not only because of the loss of political sovereignty, but also because domestic economic concerns may be at variance with those of the Union as a whole. A single monetary policy is claimed to be inappropriate for dealing with asymmetric shocks. What is more, countries and regions at the periphery of the Union may become depressed unless there is an effective regional policy.

Globalisation and the problem of instability   12.7

Can governments do anything to create greater harmony in the world economy?

We live in an interdependent world. Countries are affected by the economic health of other countries and by their governments' policies. Problems in one part of the world can spread like a contagion to other parts, with perhaps no country immune.

There are two major ways in which this process of 'globalisation' affects individual economies. The first is through trade. The second is through financial markets.

Interdependence through trade

So long as nations trade with one another, the domestic economic actions of one nation will have implications for those which trade with it. For example, if the US administration feels that the US economy is growing too fast, it might adopt various deflationary fiscal and monetary measures, such as higher tax rates or interest rates. US consumers will not only consume fewer domestically produced goods but also reduce their consumption of imported products. But US imports are other countries' exports. A fall in these other countries' exports will lead to a multiplier effect in these countries. Output and employment will fall.

Changes in aggregate demand in one country thus send ripples throughout the global economy. The process whereby changes in imports into (or exports from) one country affect national income in other countries is known as the international trade multiplier.

The more open an economy, the more vulnerable it will be to changes in the level of economic activity in the rest of the world. This problem will be particularly acute if a nation is heavily dependent on trade with one other nation (e.g. Canada on the USA) or one other region (e.g. Switzerland on the EU).

As we saw in Figure 11.2 (see page 429), international trade has been growing as a proportion of countries' national income for many years. With most nations committed to freer trade, and with the WTO overseeing the dismantling of trade barriers, so international trade is likely to continue growing as a proportion of world GDP. This will increase countries' interdependence and their vulnerability to world trade fluctuations.

Financial interdependence

International trade has grown rapidly over the past 30 years, but international financial flows have grown much more rapidly. The value of banks' holdings of liabilities to foreign residents (individuals and institutions) has been increasing by an average of some 15 per cent per year over the past 25 years. The value of cross-border transactions in bonds and equities has increased by nearly 30 per cent per

Key Idea

28
293

> **Definition**
>
> **International trade multiplier** The effect on national income in country B of a change in exports (or imports) of country A.

year over the same period. Even after taking inflation into account, this is still a very large real rate of increase.

Each day, over $1 trillion of assets are traded across the foreign exchanges. Many of the transactions are short-term financial flows, moving to where interest rates are most favourable or to currencies where the exchange rate is likely to appreciate. This again makes countries interdependent.

Assume that the Federal Reserve Bank (the Fed) in the USA, worried about rising inflation, decides to raise interest rates. These higher interest rates will attract an inflow of funds from other countries. This will cause the dollar to appreciate. Knowing that this will happen, speculators will seek to buy dollars quickly before the exchange rate has finished appreciating. They may well buy dollars *before* the Fed raises interest rates, in anticipation that it will do so.

The inflow of funds to the USA represents an outflow from other countries and will thus have a knock-on effect on their interest rates (pushing them up). And just as the dollar has appreciated against other currencies, so these other currencies have depreciated against the dollar. The larger the financial flows, the more will interest rate changes in one country affect the economies of other countries: the greater will be the financial interdependence.

> ### Pause for thought
>
> What will be the effect on the UK economy if the European Central Bank cuts interest rates?

The need for international policy co-ordination

There is an old saying: 'If America sneezes, the rest of the world catches a cold.' Viruses of a similar nature regularly infect the world economy. A dramatic example was the 'Asian contagion' of 1997–8. Economic crises spread rapidly around southeast and east Asia and then to Russia and then to Brazil. World leaders were seriously worried that the whole world would plunge into recession. What was needed was a co-ordinated policy response.

For many years now the leaders of the seven major industrial countries – the USA, Japan, Germany, France, the UK, Italy and Canada – have met once a year at an economic summit conference (and more frequently if felt necessary). Top of the agenda in most of these 'Group of Seven' (G7) meetings has been how to generate world economic growth without major currency fluctuations. But to achieve this it is important that there is a harmonisation of economic policies between nations. In other words, it is important that all the major countries are pursuing consistent policies aiming at common international goals.

But how can policy harmonisation be achieved? As long as there are significant domestic differences between the major economies, there is likely to be conflict not harmony. For example, if one country, say the USA, is worried about the size of its budget deficit, it may be unwilling to respond to world demands for a stimulus to aggregate demand to pull the world economy out of recession. What is more, speculators, seeing differences between countries, are likely to exaggerate them by their actions, causing large changes in exchange rates. The G7 countries have therefore sought to achieve greater convergence of their economies. However, although convergence may be a goal of policy, in practice it has proved illusive.

Because of a lack of convergence, there are serious difficulties in achieving international policy harmonisation:

> ### Definitions
>
> **International harmonisation of economic policies** Where countries attempt to co-ordinate their macroeconomic policies so as to achieve common goals.
>
> **Convergence of economies** When countries achieve similar rates of growth, inflation, budget deficits as a percentage of GDP, balance of payments, etc. and when they are at a similar point in the business cycle.

■ Countries' budget deficits and national debt differ substantially as a proportion of their national income. This puts very different pressures on the interest rates necessary to service these debts.

■ Harmonising rates of monetary growth or inflation targets would involve letting interest rates fluctuate with the demand for money. Without convergence in the demand for money, interest rate fluctuations could be severe.

■ Harmonising interest rates would involve abandoning monetary, inflation and exchange rate targets (unless interest rate 'harmonisation' meant adjusting interest rates so as to maintain monetary or inflation targets or a fixed exchange rate).

■ Countries have different internal structural relationships. A lack of convergence here means that countries with higher endemic *cost* inflation would require higher interest rates and higher unemployment if international inflation rates were to be harmonised, or higher inflation if interest rates were to be harmonised.

■ Countries have different rates of productivity increase, product development, investment and market penetration. A lack of convergence here means that the growth in exports (relative to imports) will differ for any given level of inflation or growth.

■ Countries may be very unwilling to change their domestic policies to fall in line with other countries. They may prefer the other countries to fall in line with them!

If any one of the four – interest rates, growth rates, inflation rates or current account balance of payments – could be harmonised across countries, it is likely that the other three would then not be harmonised.

Total convergence and thus total harmonisation may not be possible. Nevertheless most governments favour some movement in that direction: some is better than none.

Recap

1. Changes in aggregate demand in one country will affect the amount of imports purchased and thus the amount of exports sold by other countries and hence their national income. There is thus an international trade multiplier effect.

2. Changes in interest rates in one country will affect financial flows to and from other countries, and hence their exchange rates, interest rates and national income.

3. To prevent problems in one country spilling over to other countries and to stabilise the international business cycle will require co-ordinated policies between nations.

4. Leaders of the G7 countries meet regularly to discuss ways of harmonising their policies. Usually, however, domestic issues are more important to the leaders than international ones, and frequently they pursue policies that are not in the interests of the other countries.

Table 12.3 Debt ratios: average of all developing countries, selected years

	1974	1980	1982	1984	1986	1990	1993	1995	1998	2000	2002
Ratio of debt to GNY (%)	15	18	31	34	36	31	39	43	44	41	41
Ratio of debt to exports (%)	80	85	124	147	213	171	176	151	153	119	113
Ratio of debt service to exports (%)	12	13	20	22	27	18	18	23	27	22	19

12.8   Debt and developing countries

Can their debt burden be lifted?

Perhaps the most serious of all balance of payments problems in the world today is that faced by some of the poorest developing countries. Many of them experience massive financial outflows year after year as a result of having to 'service' debts that they have incurred in their attempts to finance development (see Table 12.3). This debt problem has its origins back in the 1970s.

The oil shocks of the 1970s

In 1973–4, oil prices quadrupled and the world went into recession. Oil imports cost more and export demand was sluggish. The current account deficit of oil-importing developing countries rose from 1.1 per cent of GDP in 1973 to 4.3 per cent in 1975.

It was not difficult to finance these deficits, however. The oil surpluses deposited in commercial banks in the industrialised world provided an important additional source of finance. The banks, flush with money and faced with slack demand in the industrialised world, were very willing to lend to developing countries to help them finance continued expansion. The world recession was short lived, and with a recovery in the demand for their exports and with their debts being eroded by high world inflation, developing countries found it relatively easy to service these increased debts (i.e. pay interest and make the necessary capital repayments).

In 1979/80 world oil prices rose again (from $15 to $38 per barrel). This second oil shock, like the first one, caused a large increase in the import bills of developing countries. But the full effects on their economies this time were very much worse, given the debts that had been accumulated in the 1970s and given the policies adopted by the industrialised world after 1979. But why were things so much worse this time?

■ The world recession was deeper and lasted longer (1980–3) and, when recovery came, it came very slowly. Developing countries' current account balance of payments deteriorated sharply. This was due both to a marked slowing down in the growth of their exports and to a fall in their export prices.

■ The tight monetary policies pursued by the industrialised countries led to a sharp increase in interest rates. This greatly increased developing countries' costs of servicing their debts. It also led to a sharp fall in inflation, which meant that the debts were not being eroded so rapidly.

■ The problem was made worse by the growing proportion of debt that was at variable interest rates. This was largely due to the increasing proportion of debt that was in the form of loans from commercial banks.

After 1979, many developing countries found it increasingly difficult to service their debts. Then in 1982 Mexico, followed by several other countries such as Brazil, Bolivia, Zaire and Sudan, declared that it would have to suspend payments. There was now a debt crisis, which threatened not only the debtor countries, but also the world banking system.

Coping with debt: rescheduling

There are two dimensions to dealing with debt problems of developing countries. The first is to cope with difficulties in servicing their debt. This usually involves some form of rescheduling of the repayments. The second dimension is to deal with the underlying causes of the problem. Here we will focus on rescheduling.

Rescheduling official loans

Official loans are renegotiated through the 'Paris Club'. Industrialised countries are members of the club, which arranges terms for the rescheduling of their loans to developing countries. Agreements normally involve delaying the date for repayment of loans currently maturing, or spreading the repayments over a longer period of time. Paris Club agreements are often made in consultation with the International Monetary Fund, which works out a programme for the debtor country to tackle its underlying economic problems.

Several attempts have been made since the mid-1980s to make rescheduling terms more generous, with longer periods before repayments start, longer to repay when they do start, and lower interest rates. In return, the developing countries have had to undertake various 'structural adjustment programmes' supervised by the IMF (see below).

But despite apparent advances made by the Paris Club in making its terms more generous, the majority of low-income countries failed to meet the required IMF conditions, and thus failed to have their debts reduced. What is more, individual Paris Club members were often reluctant to reduce debts unless they were first convinced that other members were 'paying their share'. Nevertheless some creditor countries have unilaterally introduced more generous terms and even cancelled some debts.

Rescheduling commercial bank loans

After the declarations by Mexico and other countries of their inability to service their debts, there was fear of an imminent collapse of the world banking system. Banks realised that disaster could only be averted by collective action of the banks to reschedule debts. Banks were prepared to reschedule some of the debts and to provide some additional loans in return for debtor countries undertaking structural adjustment (as described below). Additional loans, however, fell well short of the amount that was needed. Banks were unwilling to supply extra money to deal with current debt-servicing problems when they saw the problem as a long-term one of countries' inability to pay. Nevertheless, banks were increasingly setting aside funds to cover bad debt, and thus the crisis for the banks began to recede.

As banks felt less exposed to default, so they became less worried about it and less concerned to negotiate deals with debtor countries. Many of the more severely indebted countries, however, found their position still deteriorating rapidly. What is more, many of them were finding that the IMF adjustment programmes were too painful (often involving deep cuts in government expenditure) and were therefore abandoning them. Thus in 1989 US Treasury Secretary Nicholas Brady proposed measures to *reduce* debt.

The *Brady Plan* involved the IMF and the World Bank lending funds to debtor countries to enable them to repay debts to banks. In return for this instant source of liquidity, the banks would have to be prepared to accept repayment of less than the full sum (i.e. they would sell the debt back to the country at a discount). To benefit from such deals, the debtor countries would have to agree to structural adjustment programmes.

> **Pause for thought**
>
> *What are the relative advantages and disadvantages to a developing country of rescheduling its debts compared with simply defaulting on them (either temporarily or permanently)?*

Dealing with the debt

Structural reforms

The severe structural adjustment programmes frequently demanded by the IMF before it is prepared to sanction the rescheduling of debts include:

- Tight fiscal and monetary policies to reduce government deficits and reduce inflation.
- Supply-side reforms to encourage greater use of the market mechanism and greater incentives for investment.
- A more open trade policy and devaluation of the currency in order to encourage more exports and more competition.

These policies, however, can bring extreme hardship as countries are forced to deflate. Unemployment and poverty increase and growth slows down or becomes negative. Even though in the long run developing countries may emerge as more efficient and better able to compete in international trade, in the short run the suffering may be too great to bear. Popular unrest and resentment against the IMF and the country's government may lead to riots and the breakdown of law and order, and even to the overthrow of the government.

A more 'complete' structural adjustment would extend beyond simple market liberalisation and tough monetary policies to much more open access to the markets of the rich countries, to more aid and debt relief being channelled into health and education, and to greater research and development in areas that will benefit the poor (e.g. into efficient labour-intensive technology).

Debt forgiveness

By the end of the 1990s, the debt burden of many of the poorest countries had become intolerable. Despite portions of their debt being written off under Paris Club terms, the debts of many countries were still rising. Between 1980 and 2000, the debt of sub-Saharan Africa had quadrupled from $61 billion to nearly $250 billion. Some countries, such as Ethiopia and Mozambique, were spending nearly half their export earnings on merely servicing their debt.

Even with substantial debt rescheduling and some debt cancellation, highly indebted countries have been forced to make savage cuts in government expenditure, much of it on health, education and transport. The consequence has been a growth in poverty, hunger, disease and illiteracy. African countries on average were paying four times more to rich countries in debt servicing than they were spending on health and education: it was like a patient giving a blood transfusion to a doctor! The majority of these countries had no chance of 'growing their way out of debt'. The only solution for them was for a more substantial proportion of their debt to be written off.

The heavily indebted poor countries (HIPC) initiative.   In 1996 the World Bank and the IMF launched the HIPC initiative. A total of 42 countries, mainly in Africa, have been identified as being in need of substantial debt relief. The object of the initiative was to reduce the debts of such countries to 'sustainable' levels by cancelling debts above 200–250 per cent of GDP (this was reduced to 150 per cent in 1999 and to a lower level for five countries).

The HIPC process involves countries passing through two stages. In the first stage, eligible countries must demonstrate a three-year track record of 'good performance'. This means that they must satisfy the IMF, World Bank and Paris Club that they are undertaking adjustment measures, such as cutting government expenditure and liberalising their markets. It also involves the countries preparing a Poverty Reduction Strategy Paper (PRSP) to show how they will use debt relief to tackle poverty, and especially how they will improve health and education.

During this first stage, some rescheduling of debt takes place and at the end of the stage – the 'decision point' – further relief is given by creditor countries, companies and multilateral agencies, such as the World Bank.

If this debt relief is insufficient for the country to achieve sustainable debt (as defined above), the country enters stage 2. During this stage the country must establish a 'sound track record' by implementing policies established at the decision point and based on the PRSP. The length of this stage depends on how long it takes the country to implement the policies. The end of this stage is thus known as the 'floating completion point'. In the meantime, some interim debt relief is provided. At the end of the stage, debts are cancelled by the various creditors, on a pro rata basis, to bring the debt to the sustainable threshold.

Despite the initial welcome given to the HIPC initiative, it has been heavily criticised:

■ The thresholds have been set too high, with the resulting reduction in debt servicing being quite modest, or in many cases zero. Although, when complete, it will reduce the qualifying countries' debt stock by about 50 per cent, much of this debt was not being serviced and thus the deal resulted in only a modest reduction (less than one-third) in the crippling interest payments that most of these countries were paying. These savings amount to only 1.2 per cent of the HIPCs' GDP.

■ The qualifying period is too long. By January 2003, only six countries had reached the completion point, with another 20 having reached the decision point. In four cases, debt was considered sustainable, and therefore no HIPC relief was available. Despite having a previous 'good track record' many countries still had to adhere to the full two-stage process, which could be very lengthy.

■ Countries in arrears to multilateral agencies, such as the World Bank and the IMF, have first to make the back payments due. For some of the poorest countries, particularly those which have suffered civil wars (such as the Republic of Congo), such a requirement is virtually impossible to meet. Individual donor countries have sometimes agreed to partial forgiveness of arrears, but this has generally been insufficient to allow enough funds to be diverted to clear arrears with multilateral agencies.

■ The IMF reform programmes have been too harsh. The required reductions in government expenditure lead to deep cuts in basic health and education, and deflationary policies lead to reductions in investment. What is more, past experience shows that two-thirds of IMF programmes in the poorest countries break down within three years. If such experience were repeated, most countries would never receive HIPC relief.

According to many charities, such as Oxfam, a much better approach would be to target debt relief directly at poverty reduction, with the resources released being used for investment in fields such as health, education, rural development and basic infrastructure. The IMF argues that HIPC relief has indeed allowed increased expenditure on such 'social programmes'. For the 26 countries that had reached the decision or completion points by 2003, the ratio of social expenditure to debt service had risen from 1.9 to 4.0.

Nevertheless, many commentators argue that the rich world could do much more to help developing countries, particularly those ravaged by war, drought or AIDS. The United Nations has for many years called on wealthy countries to give 0.7 per cent of their GDP in aid. In practice, they give only a little over 0.2 per cent.

> **Pause for thought**
>
> Should rich countries cancel all debts owed to them by developing countries?

Recap

1. After the 1973 oil crisis, many developing countries borrowed heavily in order to finance their balance of trade deficits and to maintain a programme of investment. After the 1979 oil price rises, the debt problem became much more serious. There was a world recession and real interest rates were much higher. Debt increased dramatically, and much of it at variable interest rates.

2. Rescheduling can help developing countries cope with increased debt in the short run and various schemes have been adopted by creditor countries and the banks.

3. If the problem of developing countries' debt is to be tackled then simple rescheduling is not enough. The IMF favours harsh structural adjustment programmes, involving deflation and market-orientated supply-side policies. A more 'complete' structural adjustment, however, would involve more open access to the markets of the rich countries, more aid and debt relief being channelled into health and education, and greater research and development in areas that will benefit the poor.

4. In 1996 the World Bank and the IMF launched the HIPC initiative to help reduce the debts of heavily indebted poor countries to sustainable levels. HIPC relief has been criticised, however, for being made conditional on the debtor countries pursuing excessively tough IMF adjustment programmes, for being too modest in the amount of debts cancelled, for having an excessively long qualifying period and for delays in its implementation. A better approach might be to target debt relief directly at programmes to help the poor.

Questions

1. Which of the following items are credits on the UK balance of payments and which are debits?

   (a) The expenditure by UK tourists on holidays in Greece.
   (b) The payment of dividends by foreign companies to investors resident in the UK.
   (c) Foreign residents taking out insurance policies with UK companies.
   (d) Drawing on reserves.
   (e) Investment by UK companies overseas.

2. The table below shows the items in the UK's 2001 balance of payments. Calculate the following: (a) the balance on trade in goods; (b) the balance on trade in goods and services; (c) the balance of payments on current account; (d) the financial account balance; (e) the total current plus capital plus financial account balance; (f) net errors and omissions.

	£ billions
Exports of goods	191.2
Imports of goods	224.3
Exports of services	77.1
Imports of services	65.4
Net income flows	+11.2
Net current transfers	−7.2
Net capital transfers	+1.4
Net investment in UK from abroad (direct and portfolio)	75.5
Net UK investment abroad (direct and portfolio)	116.7
Other financial inflows	219.1
Other financial outflows	161.1
Reserves	+3.1

3. Explain how the current account of the balance of payments is likely to vary with the course of the business cycle.

4. Is it a 'bad thing' to have a deficit on the direct and portfolio investment part of the financial account?

5. Why may credits on a country's short-term financial account create problems for its economy in the future?

6. List some factors that could cause an increase in the credit items of the balance of payments and a decrease in the debit items. What would be the effect on the exchange rate (assuming that it is freely floating)? What effect would these exchange rate movements have on the balance of payments?

7. What policy measures could the government adopt to prevent the exchange rate movements in question 6?

8. What are the major advantages and disadvantages of fixing the exchange rate with a majority currency such as the US dollar?

9. What adverse effects on the domestic economy may follow from (a) a depreciation of the exchange rate and (b) an appreciation of the exchange rate?

10. What will be the effects on the domestic economy under free-floating exchange rates if there is a rapid expansion in world economic activity? What will determine the size of these effects?

11. Why would banks not be prepared to offer a forward exchange rate to a firm for, say, five years' time?

12. Under what circumstances would the demand for imports be likely to be inelastic? How would an inelastic demand for imports affect the magnitude of fluctuations in the exchange rate?

13. Why are the price elasticities of demand for imports and exports likely to be lower in the short run than in the long run?

14. Assume that the government pursued an expansionary fiscal policy and that the resulting budget deficit led to higher interest rates. What would happen to (a) the current account and (b) the financial account of the balance of payments? What would be the likely effect on the exchange rate, given a high degree of international financial mobility?

15. Consider the argument that in the modern world of large-scale short-term international financial movements, the ability of individual countries to affect their exchange rate is very limited.

16. Why does high international financial mobility and an absence of exchange controls severely limit a country's ability to choose its interest rate?

17. What practical problems are there in achieving a general harmonisation of economic policies between (a) EU countries; (b) the major industrialised countries?

18. What are the causes of exchange rate volatility? Have these problems become greater or lesser in the past ten years? Explain why.

19. Why did the ERM with narrow bands collapse in 1993? Could this have been avoided?

20. Did the exchange rate difficulties experienced by countries under the ERM strengthen or weaken the arguments for progressing to a single European currency?

21. Under what circumstances may a pegged exchange rate system like the ERM (a) help to prevent speculation; (b) aggravate the problem of speculation?

22. By what means would a depressed country in an Economic Union with a single currency be able to recover? Would the market provide a satisfactory solution or would (Union) government intervention be necessary, and if so, what form would the intervention take?

23. Assume that just some of the members of a common market like the EU adopt full economic and monetary union, including a common currency. What are the advantages and disadvantages to those members joining the full EMU and to those not joining?

24. Is the euro zone likely to be an optimal currency area? Is it more or less likely to be so over time? Explain your answer.

25. It is often argued that international convergence of economic indicators is a desirable objective. Does this mean that countries should seek to achieve the same rate of economic growth, monetary growth, interest rates, budget deficits as a percentage of their GDP, etc?

26. Why is it difficult to achieve international harmonisation of economic policies?

27. To what extent was the debt crisis of the early 1980s caused by inappropriate policies that had been pursued by the debtor countries?

28. Imagine that you are an ambassador of a developing country at an international conference. What would you try to persuade the rich countries to do in order to help you and other poor countries overcome the debt problem? How would you set about persuading them that it was in their own interests to help you?

Additional case studies on the *Essentials of Economics* website (www.booksites.net/sloman)

12.1 The UK's balance of payments deficit. An examination of the UK's persistent trade and current account deficits.

12.2 The Gold Standard. A historical example of fixed exchange rates.

12.3 A high exchange rate. This case looks at whether a high exchange rate is necessarily bad news for exporters.

12.4 The sterling crisis of early 1985. When the pound fell almost to $1.00.

12.5 Currency turmoil in the mid-1990s. A crisis in Mexico; a rising yen and German mark; a falling US dollar – why did this all happen? (An expansion of the material in the first part of Box 12.4.)

12.6 The 1997/8 crisis in Asia. The role played by the IMF.

12.7 Argentina in crisis. An examination of the collapse of the Argentinian economy in 2001/2.

12.8 Attempts at harmonisation. A look at the meetings of the G7 economies, where they attempt to come to agreement on means of achieving stable and sustained worldwide economic growth.

12.9 The Tobin tax. An examination of the possible use of small taxes on foreign exchange transactions. The purpose is to reduce currency fluctuations.

12.10 The euro, the US dollar and world currency markets. An analysis of the relationship between the euro and the dollar.

12.11 Using interest rates to control both aggregate demand and the exchange rate. A problem of one instrument and two targets.

12.12 The UK Labour government's convergence criteria for euro membership. An examination of the five tests set by the UK government that would have to be passed before the question of euro membership would be put to the electorate in a referendum.

12.13 Debt and the environment. How high levels of debt can encourage developing countries to damage their environment in an attempt to increase export earnings.

12.14 The great escape. This case examines the problem of capital flight from developing countries to rich countries.

12.15 Swapping debt. Schemes to convert a developing country's debt into other forms, such as shares in its industries.

12.16 Economic aid. Does aid provide a solution to the debt problem?

Sections of chapter covered in
WinEcon – Sloman, *Essentials of Economics*

Essentials of Economics section	*WinEcon* section
12.1	12.1
12.2	12.2
12.3	12.3
12.4	–
12.5	–
12.6	–
12.7	–
12.8	12.8

See also, *WinEcon* Chapter 13 on Basic Maths for Economics.

Websites relevant to this chapter

Numbers and sections refer to websites listed in the Web Appendix and hotlinked from this book's website at
www.booksites.net/sloman

- For news articles relevant to this chapter, see the *Economics News Articles* link from the book's website.

- For general news on countries' balance of payments and exchange rates, see websites in section A, and particularly A1–5, 7–9, 20–25, 31. For articles on various aspects of economic development, see A27, 28; I9. See also links to newspapers worldwide in A38 and 39, and the news search feature in Google at A41. See also links to economics news in A42.

- For international data on balance of payments and exchange rates, see *World Economic Outlook* in H4 and *OECD Economic Outlook* in B21 (also in section 6 of B1). See also the trade topic in I14.

- For details of individual countries' balance of payments, see B32.

- For UK data on balance of payments, see B1, *1. National Statistics* > the fourth link > *Economy* > *United Kingdom Balance of Payments – the Pink Book*. See also B3, 34; F2. For EU data, see G1 > *The Statistical Annex* > *Foreign trade and current balance*.

- For exchange rates, see A3; B34; F2, 6, 8.

- For data on debt and development, see B24 (*Global Development Finance*) and B31. Also see the debt section in I14.

- For discussion papers on the balance of payments and exchange rates, see H4 and 7.

- For information on debt and developing countries, see H4, 7, 9, 10, 12–14, 17–19. See also links to development sites in I9.

- Sites I7 and I11 contain links to *Balance of payments and exchange rates* in *International economics* and to *Capital flows and aid* in *Economic Development*.

- For student resources relevant to this chapter, see sites C1–7, 9, 10, 19. See also *Virtual Developing Country* in *Virtual Worlds* in site C2.

Answers to odd-numbered end-of-chapter questions

Introduction

1. For most people it would certainly be eased! But it would not be solved. As the old saying goes, money can't buy everything. Many things would still be scarce. For example, you would still have only a finite amount of time to enjoy what the money could buy: there are only 24 hours in a day, and we do not live for ever. Then, for many lottery winners, happiness has proved elusive. Friendships and family relationships may become strained or even be destroyed and it may be very difficult to trust people's motives. Do they really want to be my friend, or are they merely after my money?

3. If people specialise in jobs in which they are relatively able, total production (and hence consumption) in the economy will be larger than if everyone tried to do a little of everything. Part of the reason is that people would be spending much of their time doing things in which they had little or no ability; part is that a lot of time would be wasted in moving from job to job; part is that concentrating on just one job allows people to develop skills. It is the same for countries: total world production and consumption can be higher if countries specialise in producing those goods at which they are relatively efficient and then trading with other countries (see the 'law of comparative advantage' in Section 11.1).

5. For the parent thinking of taking the job, the opportunity cost would include lost leisure time, and time spent with other family members (e.g. with the children) and the possible unpleasantness of the job.

   For the family as a whole, the opportunity costs would include all the adverse effects on the family: such as stress, reduced time for each other, reduced time available for household tasks, and increased burdens on the other family members.

Whether these will all be taken into account depends on how carefully the decision is made, and how much the parent thinking of taking the job cares for the other family members.

Giving values to the opportunity costs is very difficult and it is unlikely that the process would be a mechanical one. Most families, trying to come to a 'rational' decision, would simply attempt to use their judgement as to whether the extra income (plus any other benefits from the job) would be worth the sacrifices: a decision that could well turn out to be wrong, once the imagined sacrifices had become reality.

7. You should weigh up whether the extra pay (benefit) from the better-paid job is worth the extra hardship (cost) involved in doing it.

9. (a) When there are constant opportunity costs. This will occur when resources are equally suited to producing either good. This might possibly occur in our highly simplified world of just two goods. In the real world it is unlikely.
   (b) When there are decreasing opportunity costs. This will occur when increased specialisation in one good allows the country to become more efficient in its production. It gains 'economies of scale' sufficient to offset having to use less suitable resources. We look at economies of scale in Chapter 3, Section 3.2. Economies of scale are common in the real world.

Chapter 1

1. (a) See Figure A1.1(a).
   (b) See Figure A1.1(b).

3. You would try to reduce the price of each item as little as was necessary to get rid of the remaining

Figure A1.1

The price mechanism

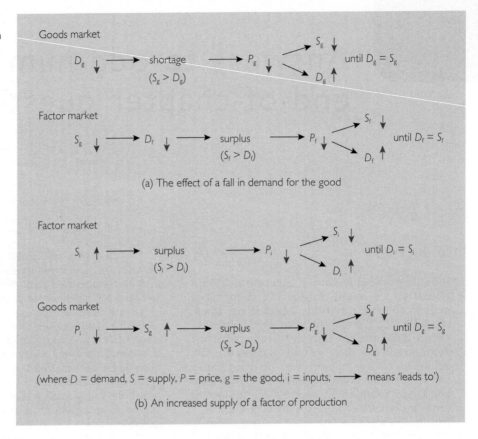

(a) The effect of a fall in demand for the good

(where D = demand, S = supply, P = price, g = the good, i = inputs, ⟶ means 'leads to')

(b) An increased supply of a factor of production

stock. The problem for shop owners is that they do not have enough information about consumer demand to make precise calculations here. Many shops try a fairly cautious approach first, and then, if that is not enough to sell all the stock, they make further 'end of sale' reductions later.

5. The reduction in supply will cause a shortage of oil at current prices. This will cause the price of oil to rise. This will then have a twin effect: it will reduce demand and it will also make it profitable to use more expensive extraction methods, thereby increasing supply. The effect of the higher price, therefore, will be to eliminate the shortage.

7. (a) Equilibrium is where quantity demanded equals quantity supplied: $P = £5$; $Q = 12$ million.
   (b) The schedules are shown in the following table:

Price (£)	8	7	6	5	4	3	2	1
Quantity demanded	10	12	14	16	18	20	22	24
Quantity supplied	18	16	14	12	10	8	6	4

Equilibrium price and quantity are now as follows: $P = £6$; $Q = 14$ million.

Demand has risen by 4 million but equilibrium quantity has only risen by 2 million (from 12 million to 14 million). The reason why quantity sold has risen by less than demand is that price has risen. This has choked off some of the extra demand (i.e. 2 of the 4 million).

(c) See Figure A1.2.

9. ■ A rise in the price of air travel (supply).
   ■ A fall in the exchange rate, giving less foreign currency for the pound (supply – tour operators' costs abroad rise when measured in pounds).
   ■ The economy booms (demand – more people can afford to go on holiday; supply – inflation raises tour operators' costs).
   ■ The price of domestic holidays increases (demand – a rise in the price of a substitute).
   ■ Certain tour operators go out of business or cut down on the number of holidays on offer (supply).
   ■ Poor weather at home (demand – more people decide to take their holidays abroad).

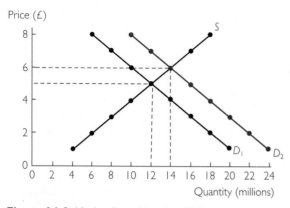

Figure A1.2 Market for t-shirts (weekly)

11. (a) Price rises, quantity rises (demand shifts to the right: butter and margarine are substitutes).
    (b) Price falls, quantity rises (supply shifts to the right: butter and yoghurt are in joint supply).
    (c) Price falls, quantity falls (demand shifts to the left: bread and butter are complementary goods).
    (d) Price rises, quantity rises (demand shifts to the right: bread and butter are complementary goods).
    (e) Price rises, quantity rises or falls depending on relative sizes of the shifts in demand and supply (demand shifts to the right as people buy now before the price rises; supply shifts to the left as producers hold back stocks until the price does rise).
    (f) Price rises, quantity falls (supply shifts to the left).
    (g) Price rises, quantity rises or falls depending on the relative size of the shifts in demand and supply (demand shifts to the right as more health-conscious people start buying butter; supply shifts to the left as a result of the increased cost of production).

Chapter 2

1. With the flatter of the two supply curves, the price will rise less and the quantity rise more than in the case of the steeper supply curve.

3. Because there has been a *rightward shift* in the demand curve for oil. This is likely to be the result of rising incomes. Car ownership and use increase as incomes increase. Also tastes may have changed so that people want to drive more. There may also have been a decline in substitute modes of transport, such as rail transport and buses.

Finally, people may travel longer distances to work as a result of a general move to the suburbs.

5. As long as demand remains inelastic, the firm should go on raising its price if it wants to increase revenue. Eventually consumers will stop buying the good: even if there is no close substitute, the income effect will become large – people will simply not be able to afford to buy the good. This illustrates the fact that a demand curve is likely to have different elasticities along its length.

7. Two brands of coffee, because they are closer substitutes than coffee and tea.

9. Generally, stabilising speculation will benefit both consumers and firms, as it will create a more stable market environment in which it is easier to plan purchases, production or investment. Generally people prefer certainty to uncertainty. Destabilising speculation, on the other hand, by exaggerating the upswings and downswings in markets, will make it more difficult to plan – something that will be unpopular with consumers and producers alike.

   Of course, to the extent that the consumers or producers are themselves taking part in the speculation, they will gain from it, whether it is stabilising or destabilising, provided that they predict correctly. For example, if you are thinking of buying a house and, correctly, predict that house prices will rise in the near future, then you will gain by buying now before they do.

11. (a) Equilibrium is where quantity demanded equals quantity supplied: where $P = £2.00$ per kilo; $Q = 50\,000$ kilos.
    (b) (i) There will be a surplus of 22 000 kilos (i.e. 62 000 – 40 000).
        (ii) No effect. The equilibrium price of £2.00 is above the minimum.
    (c) (i) With the £1.00 subsidy, producers will supply at each price the amount that they were previously willing to supply for £1.00 more. The schedules will now be as follows:

Price (£ per kilo)	4.00	3.50	3.00	2.50	2.00	1.50	1.00	0.50	0.00
Q_d (000 kilos)	30	35	40	45	50	55	60		
Q_s (000 kilos)			80	68	62	55	50	45	38

       (ii) The new equilibrium price will be £1.50 (where quantity demanded and the new quantity supplied are equal).
       (iii) The cost will be £1 × 55 000 = £55 000.

(d) (i) At a price of £2.50, (original) supply exceeds demand by 10 000 kilos. The government would therefore have to buy this amount in order to ensure that all the tomatoes produced were sold.
(ii) £2.50 × 10 000 = £25 000
(e) (i) It would have purchased 55 000. To dispose of all these, price would have to fall to £1.50.
(ii) The cost of this course of action would be (£2.50 – £1.50) × 55 000 = £55 000.

13. Two examples are:
   ■ Rent controls. Advantages: makes cheap housing available to those who would otherwise have difficulty in affording reasonable accommodation. Disadvantages: causes a reduction in the supply of private rented accommodation; causes demand to exceed supply and thus some people will be unable to find accommodation.
   ■ Tickets for a concert. Advantages: allows the price to be advertised in advance and guarantees a full house; makes seats available to those who could not afford the free-market price. Disadvantages: causes queuing or seats being available only to those booking well in advance.

Chapter 3

1. (a) Two or three days: the time necessary to acquire new equipment or DJs.
   (b) Two or more years: the time taken to plan and build a new power station.
   (c) Several weeks: the time taken to acquire additional premises.
   (d) One or two years: the time taken to plan and build a new store.

3. (a) Variable.
   (b) Fixed (unless the fee negotiated depends on the success of the campaign).
   (c) Variable (the more that is produced, the more the wear and tear).
   (d) Fixed.
   (e) Fixed if the factory will be heated and lit to the same extent irrespective of output, but variable if the amount of heating and lighting depends on the amount of the factory in operation, which in turn depends on output.
   (f) Variable.
   (g) Variable (although the basic wage is fixed per worker, the cost will still be variable because the total cost will increase with output if the number of workers is increased).

(h) Variable.
(i) Fixed (because it does not depend on output).

5. Because economies of scale, given that most arise from increasing returns to scale, will be fully realised after a certain level of output (see Box 3.4 on page 100), whereas diseconomies of scale, given that they largely arise from the managerial problems of running large organisations, are only likely to set in beyond a certain level of output.

7. Diagram (a): The long-run marginal cost curve would be falling (and below the LRAC curve) and thus the long-run total cost would be rising less and less steeply.
Diagram (b): The long-run marginal cost curve would be rising (and above the LRAC curve) and thus the long-run total cost curve would be rising more and more steeply.
Diagram (c): The long-run marginal cost curve would be horizontal and (equal to the LRAC curve) and thus the long-run total cost curve would be rising at a constant rate: i.e. it would be a straight line up from the origin.

9. The diagram should look something like Figure 3.8. The table should be set out like Table 3.5. Total revenue (TR) is simply P × Q and marginal revenue (MR) is the rise in TR per 1 unit rise in Q. (The MR figures are plotted between the values for Q: i.e. between 1 and 2, 2 and 3, 3 and 4, etc.) The figures for MR should then be simply read off the table and plotted on your diagram.

11. The slopes are the same. Given that the slope of the total curve gives the respective marginal, this means that marginal revenue will be equal to marginal cost.

13. Normal profit is the opportunity cost of capital for owners. It is the return they could have earned on their capital elsewhere, and is thus the minimum profit they must make to persuade them to continue producing in the long run and not to close down and move into some alternative business.

15. Its fixed costs have already been incurred. Provided, therefore, that it can cover its variable costs, anything over can be used to help pay off these fixed costs. Once the fixed costs come up for renewal, however (and thus cease to be fixed costs), the firm will close down if it cannot cover these also. It will thus be willing to make a loss only as long as the fixed costs have been paid (or committed).

17. (a) See the following table:

Output	1		2		3		4		5		6		7		8		9		10
AC (£)	7.00		5.00		4.00		3.30		3.00		3.10		3.50		4.20		5.00		6.00
TC (£)	7.00		10.00		12.00		13.20		15.00		18.60		24.50		33.60		45.00		60.00
MC (£)		3.00		2.00		1.20		1.80		3.60		5.90		9.10		11.40		15.00	
AR (£)	10.00		9.50		9.00		8.50		8.00		7.50		7.00		6.50		6.00		5.50
TR (£)	10.00		19.00		27.00		34.00		40.00		45.00		49.00		52.00		54.00		55.00
MR (£)		9.00		8.00		7.00		6.00		5.00		4.00		3.00		2.00		1.00	

(b) Profit is maximised where $MC = MR$: at an output of 6.

(c) Total profit equals $TR - TC$.
At an output of 5, total profit is
£40.00 – £15.00 = £25.00.
At an output of 6, total profit is
£45.00 – £18.60 = £26.40.
At an output of 7, total profit is
£49.00 – £24.50 = £24.50.
Profit rises up to 6 units of output and then falls. Profit is thus maximised at 6 units: it is £26.40 per period of time.

(d) See Figure A3.1.

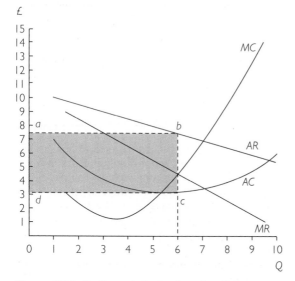

£

Figure A3.1 Profit maximisation for a firm facing a downward-sloping demand curve

(e) See Figure A3.1. Profit is maximised where $MC = MR$, at an output of 6. At this output, $AR = £7.50$ (point a); $AC = £3.10$ (point d).

(f) This area is shown by the rectangle $abcd$ in Figure A3.1.

Chapter 4

1. (a)

Output	0	1	2	3	4	5	6	7	8
TC (£)	10	18	24	30	38	50	66	91	120
AC (£)	–	18	12	10	9½	10	11	13	15
MC (£)		8	6	6	8	12	16	25	29

(b) See Figure A4.1.

(c) Profit is maximised where $MC = MR$ (point b): i.e. at an output of 5.

(d) £20
Profit per unit is given by $AR - AC$.
$AR (= MR)$ is constant at £14; AC at an output of 5 units is £10.
Thus profit per unit = 14 – 10 = 4.
Total profit is then found by multiplying this by the number of units sold:
i.e. £4 × 5 = £20.
This is shown by the area $abcd$.

(e) Supernormal profit would encourage new firms to enter the industry. This would cause price to fall until it was equal to the minimum point of the *long-run* average cost curve (at that point, there would be no supernormal

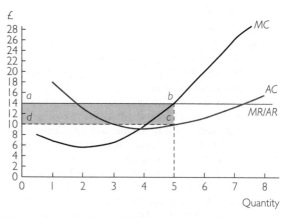

£

Figure A4.1 Profit maximisation under perfect competition

Figure A4.2

Long run under
perfect competition

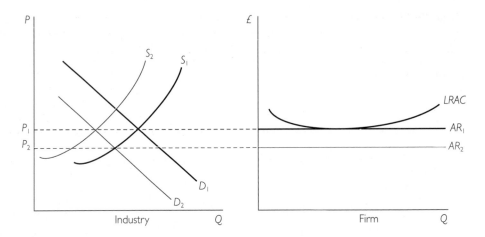

profit remaining and hence firms would stop
entering and the price would stop falling).

3. This is illustrated in Figure A4.2. The long-run
equilibrium is shown where the *AR* curve is tangential to the *LRAC* curve (and where, therefore,
there is no supernormal profit). If the demand
curve now shifts from D_1 to D_2, the equilibrium
price will fall to P_2. Less than normal profit will
now be made. Firms will therefore leave the
industry. As they do, so the industry supply curve
will shift to the left, causing the price to rise
again. Once the supply curve has reached S_2 and
price has risen back to P_1, long-run equilibrium
will have been restored, with the remaining firms
making normal profit again.

5. The criticism should really be directed at the
market system as a whole: that where significant
economies of scale exist, markets are bound to
be imperfect. Of course, there may be significant
benefits to consumers and society generally from
such imperfect markets (see pages 129–31): there
are advantages as well as disadvantages of imperfect markets. What is more, if the market is highly
contestable, many of the advantages of perfect
competition may be achieved even though the
industry is actually a monopoly (or oligopoly).

7. Demand is elastic at the point where $MR = MC$.
The reason is that *MC* must be positive and therefore *MR* must also be positive. But if *MR* is positive, demand must be elastic. Nevertheless, at any
given price a monopoly will face a less elastic
demand curve than a firm producing the same
good under monopolistic competition or oligopoly. This enables it to raise price further before
demand becomes elastic (and before the point is
reached where $MR = MC$).

9. (a) High. The plant cannot be used for other
purposes.

(b) Relatively low. The industry is not very
capital intensive, and the various tools and
equipment could be sold or transferred to
producing other crops.

(c) Very high. The plant cannot be used for other
purposes and decommissioning costs are very
high.

(d) Low. The capital costs are low and offices can
be sold.

(e) Relatively low. The plant and machinery can
probably be adapted to producing other toys.

(f) Low to moderate. It is likely that a pharmaceutical company can relatively easily switch
to producing alternative drugs. Substantial
exit costs are only likely to arise if the company is committed to a long-term research
and development programme or if equipment
is not transferable to producing alternative
drugs.

(g) Low to moderate. Exit costs from one particular client are likely to be low if the firm can
easily transfer to supplying alternative clients.
Costs will be higher if there are penalties for
breaking contracts, or if the firm wishes to
exit from catering altogether. In this latter
case the costs will depend on the second-hand
value of its equipment.

(h) Low to moderate. The exit costs again will
depend on the second-hand value of the
equipment.

(i) Relatively low if the ships can be transferred
to other routes. Much higher if the company
wishes to move out of shipping entirely and if
the market for second-hand ships is depressed.

11. You will see when you think about this question
that it is often difficult to identify the boundaries
of a market. Take a product like chocolate. If the
product is defined as bars of chocolate, then there
are probably about three or four different makes

available, but maybe only one or two in any one shop. If, however, the product is defined to include filled chocolate bars, then there are many more varieties available, but, of course, several made by each individual company (such as Cadbury's, Mars, Nestlé, etc). You will also notice for many products that there are one or two large producers, and many small producers, making the market a hybrid form of oligopoly if the large producers dominate the market.

The sorts of competition to look out for are: price competition, advertising, product specification, product availability, after-sales service, etc.

13. The first type of customer will have a lower price-elasticity of demand, since they will not have the time to shop around, and will thus be prepared to pay a higher price than at the supermarket. It is this type of customer that the small shop relies on. The other type of customer will probably simply wait until they next visit the supermarket. For such customers, the supermarket provides a substitute service.

15. No. Demand would become less elastic and the lack of competition may enable remaining petrol stations to make supernormal profits in the long run as well as the short run. If, with a reduced number of firms, there was still sufficient competition to allow profits to be kept at a normal level, cost conditions would have to change so that the *LRAC* would now continue sloping downward for longer (so that the point of tangency is at a higher output): this would require changes in technology such as new computerised systems that allow one cashier to handle a larger number of customers.

17. In all cases collusion is quite likely: check out the factors favouring collusion on page 147. In some cases it is more likely than others: for example, in the case of cement, where there is little product differentiation and a limited number of producers, collusion is more likely than in the case of carpets, where there is much more product differentiation.

19. (a) and (c) are examples of effective counter-vailing power, because the individual purchasing firms are large relative to the total market for the product.

21. Examples include: a firm charging different prices for the same product in different countries; a supermarket chain charging higher prices in more affluent areas; airlines charging different prices for the same flight with the same booking conditions through different tour operators; cheaper travel for particular categories of person (children, students, elderly people).

Generally consumers gain if they buy in the low-price market and lose if they buy in the high-price market. If the discrimination were first degree, however, no one would gain, since everyone would be charged the highest price they were prepared to pay. The use of price discrimination, by enabling the firm to make higher profits, may also enable it to compete more effectively with its rivals. This could help consumers if competition thereby increased (e.g. if a firm used price discrimination to enable it to compete more effectively against a powerful rival), but could be against consumers' interests if firms used it to drive rivals out of business.

In order to form a judgement, it is necessary to know the extent of the gains and losses to consumers. It is also important to know to what extent differences in prices are the result of genuine price discrimination, rather than merely a reflection of the different costs that firms incur in different markets, or a reflection of a *different* service. For example, it is not price discrimination to charge a higher price for a better seat at a concert: the price difference is, at least in part, a reflection of the *quality* of the seat.

Chapter 5

1. In the first case (skilled workers), the supply curve is less elastic. A rightward shift in demand would mean that the firm would have to give a substantial rise in wages (the second policy) in order to attract sufficient workers from outside. Thus it may be profitable for the firm itself to undertake the expense of training to avoid having to pay these high wages. There is a danger, however, that once it has trained its workers they could now get a higher wage elsewhere. The effect would be a vertical shift in the supply curve, and the firm may end up having to pay the higher wages anyway.

In the second case (unskilled workers), supply is more elastic: workers can readily transfer from and to other jobs. Thus a rightward shift in demand will lead to only a relatively small rise in wages.

If it used the second policy (of offering a wage rise) in the first case (that of a shortage of *skilled* workers), the wage rise is likely to have to be substantial in order to recruit the necessary extra labour. The less elastic the supply of labour, the higher the rise in wages will have to be.

3. Because they require fewer qualifications, and thus there is a plentiful supply of labour available to do them.

5.

Number of workers (1)	Wage rate (£) (2)	Total cost of labour (£) (3)	Marginal cost of labour (£) (4)	Marginal revenue product (£) (5)
1	100	100		
			110	230
2	105	210		
			120	240
3	110	330		
			130	240
4	115	460		
			140	230
5	120	600		
			150	210
6	125	750		
			160	190
7	130	910		
			170	170
8	135	1080		
			180	150
9	140	1260		
			190	130
10	145	1450		

The figures have been added in the above table. The firm should employ workers up to the point where $MC_L = MRP_L$: it should employ seven or eight workers.

7. You would need to look at the following factors: (a) differences in the productivity of workers in each group; (b) whether the demand for each type of worker is expanding or contracting, and in that context, the elasticity of supply of labour (since the less elastic the supply, the bigger will be the change in the wage rate for any shift in the demand for labour); (c) the price of the good that they produce (which will determine the workers' marginal *revenue* product); (d) whether the workers are members of unions and, if so, how strong are the unions; (e) whether their employers have monopsony power; (f) whether there are any other factors, such as custom and practice or discrimination, that determine their wage rate.

9. See the reasons given in Box 5.3: 'Equal Pay for Equal Work?'

11. See page 192 in the text.
A progressive tax is defined as one whose *average* rate with respect to income rises as income rises. It is possible for this to happen even when the marginal rate is constant. For example, if people can earn a certain proportion of their income tax-free, and above that pay at a constant marginal rate, then the average rate will go on rising as income rises because the tax-free element will account for a smaller and smaller proportion of the total.

13. An example will illustrate why. Assume that before tax one person earns £20 000 and the other earns £10 000: the first person's income is twice that of the second. Now assume that a 50 per cent income tax is imposed on every pound (a proportional tax). The first person now has a disposable (after tax) income of £10 000, and the second of £5000. The distribution is unaffected: the first person's income is still twice that of the second.

15. A person on low income. There would be little income effect to offset the substitution effect. With a person on high income, however, a cut in income tax rates would lead to a substantial windfall income. The income effect is therefore likely to be large and may outweigh the substitution effect (causing the rich person to work less).
In the case of people on very low incomes, who are below the tax threshold, a cut in income tax will have no effect at all. If personal allowances were zero, however, this would not apply. The substitution effect would outweigh the income effect.

17. This is when poor people have little or no incentive to get a job, because the combined effect of paying taxes and losing benefits would make them virtually no better off than before (or even worse off).
Universal benefits would help because, not being means tested, they would not be lost as a person's income increased: the marginal tax-plus-lost-benefit rate would be lower. The problem is that they are less narrowly targeted, and therefore are paid to people who are less needy. This means that it costs the taxpayer a lot more to help the poor through universal benefits than through means-tested ones. The result would be either less help for the poor or higher taxes (which could themselves act as a disincentive).

Chapter 6

1. (a) 7 units (where marginal revenue (= P) equals marginal cost).
   (b) 5 units (where marginal social benefit (= P) equals marginal social cost.
   (c) Because the environment becomes ever less able to cope with additional amounts of pollution.

3. (a) External costs of production ($MSC > MC$)
   The pollution of rivers and streams by slurry and nitrate run-off from farms; road congestion near a factory.
   (b) External benefits of production ($MSC < MC$)
   Beneficial spin-offs from the development of new products (for example, the various space programmes in the USA, the former Soviet Union and Europe have contributed to advances in medicine, materials technology, etc.); where the opening of a new environmentally friendly factory results in less output from factories that pollute.

(c) External costs of consumption ($MSB < MB$) The effect of CFC aerosols on the ozone layer; the unpleasant sight of satellite dishes.

(d) External benefits of consumption ($MSB > MB$) People decorating the outside of their houses or making their gardens look attractive benefits neighbours and passers-by; people insulating their houses reduces fuel consumption and the pollution associated with it.

5. *Publicly provided goods* are merely goods that the government or some other public agency provides, whether or not they could be provided by the market.

   Public goods are the much narrower category of goods that the market would fail to provide because of their characteristics of non-rivalry and non-excludability. Thus a local government might provide both street lighting and public libraries: they are both publicly provided goods, but only street lighting is a public good.

   A *merit good* is either publicly provided or subsidised. It is one that the government feels that people would otherwise underconsume (e.g. health care). It is not normally a public good, however, because it *would* be provided by the market: it is just that people would consume too little of it.

7. Roads where there are relatively few access points and where therefore it would be practical to charge tolls. Charges could be regarded as a useful means of restricting use of the roads in question, or, by charging more at peak times, of encouraging people to travel at off-peak times. Such a system, however, could be regarded as unfair by those using the toll roads, and might merely divert congestion on to the non-toll roads.

9. (a) (i) or (ii) (e.g. *Which?* magazine);
   (b) (iii) (by asking people currently doing the job) or (iv);
   (c) (iii) (by obtaining estimates);
   (d) (iii) (albeit imperfect, by inspecting other work that the different builders have done) or (iv);
   (e) as (d);
   (f) (iii);
   (g) (iii);
   (h) (i) or (ii) (as in (a)) or (iii) by experimenting.
   All could involve the non-monetary costs of the time involved in finding out.

   If the information is purely factual (as in (c) above), and you can trust the source of your information, there is no problem. If you cannot trust the source, or if the information is subjective (such as other people's experiences in (b) above), then you will only have imperfect information of the costs and/or benefits until you actually experience them.

11. Virtually all the categories of market failure (except public goods) apply to a free-market system of educational provision.
   ■ In any given area there may be oligopolistic collusion to keep fees high.
   ■ There are positive externalities from education: for example, the benefits to other members of society from a well-educated workforce. Thus too few resources would be allocated to education.
   ■ Education can be seen as a merit good: something that the government feels that people are entitled to and should not depend on ability to pay.
   ■ Access to education would depend on parents' income: this could be argued to be unfair.
   ■ Children would also be dependent on their parents' *willingness* to pay. Parents differ in the amount that they care for their children's welfare.
   ■ Parents and potential students may be ignorant of the precise benefits of particular courses – something that an unscrupulous educational establishment might exploit, by pushing the 'merits' of their establishment.

13. Assuming that the external benefit was in production, the MSC curve in Figure 6.5 would be *below* the MC curve. The optimum subsidy would be equal to the gap between MSC and MC at the point where the MSC curve crossed the $D = MSB$ line.

15. (a) This would be very difficult given that large numbers of people are affected by the pollution. One possible answer would be to legislate such that if specific health problems could be traced to atmospheric pollution, then those affected would have rights to sue.
   (b) If tracts of the river were privately owned, then as relatively few owners would be involved, it would be relatively easy to pursue polluters through the courts, provided they could be clearly identified (i.e. it would be easier to pursue factories for specific toxic emissions than individuals for dumping litter).
   (c) Again if the dumpers could be identified and the dumping were on private ground, then the owners could use the courts to prevent it. The problem here is that the owners may be quite happy to charge the company for dumping, not caring about the effects on other people of polluting, say, the water table.
   (d) This is more difficult, given that the ugly buildings are on land owned by owners of the

buildings! The law would have to give people the right to sue for *visual* pollution. This could be difficult to prove, as it involves aesthetic judgments.

(e) There would have to be laws prohibiting noise above a certain level within the hearing of residents. Then it would be a relatively simple case of the affected residents demonstrating to the satisfaction of the courts that a noise offence had been committed. It would be easier if the summons could be brought by an environmental inspectorate.

It should be clear from these answers that the boundaries between legal controls and exercising property rights are rather blurred. The ability of people to exercise property rights depends on the laws of property.

17. (a) Very suitable, provided that periodic tests and possibly spot checks are carried out.

(b) Good in certain cases: e.g. one-way systems, banning lorries of a certain size from city centres during certain parts of the day, bus lanes.

(c) Not very, given that the main problem is excessive profits, which would be difficult to define legally and relatively easy to evade even if they were defined. Various types of unsafe or shoddy goods (which are possibly more likely to be produced by firms not facing competition) could be made illegal, however.

(d) Good. The law could give the government or some other body the right to ban any merger it considered not to be in the public interest. (See Section 6.5.)

(e) Not. It would require an army of inspectors to identify marginal costs, or to check that a firm's reported marginal costs were what it claimed. The scope for evasion and ambiguity would be immense.

19. (a) This increases the marginal cost of motoring and thus does discourage people from using their cars. But it affects everyone, including those driving their cars on uncongested roads.

(b) This is not very effective at all, since it is not a marginal charge related to congestion. You do not pay more, the more you use your car: the marginal cost is zero. In fact it may even have the perverse effect of encouraging people to use their cars more. After all, if they are paying a large annual fee, they may feel that they want to get 'full value for money' by using their cars as much as possible. The only positive effect is that it may discourage people from owning a car or a second car, and for that reason may encourage the increased use of public transport.

(c) This is a version of 'road pricing' and is an example of a system most favoured by economists, since the charge is directly related to the level of congestion. It is quite expensive, however, to install and operate the system.

(d) This is a somewhat less sophisticated system of road pricing than that in (c), since the charge is fixed during the designated hours irrespective of the amount of congestion. It can also lead to a build-up of congestion outside the zone. It is generally cheaper to install, however, than that in (c).

(e) This is quite effective, especially if the tolls can vary according to the amount of congestion. They have the disadvantage, however, of causing possible tailbacks from the booths. There is also the problem that traffic may simply be diverted on to other roads where there are no tolls, thus worsening the problem of congestion elsewhere.

(f) These may encourage the use of bicycles and buses, but they can increase the level of congestion for cars, as they are forced into one lane.

(g) This can be effective, provided that public transport is fast, efficient, frequent and clean. They are especially useful when applied to city centre transport, or transport from park-and-ride car parks to city centres.

21. Fixing prices

(a) (i)   to enable those on low incomes to be able to afford the good.

   (ii) to prevent firms with market power from exploiting their position.

   (iii) to help in the fight against inflation.

(b) (i)   to protect the incomes of producers (e.g. farmers).

   (ii) to increase profits and thereby encourage investment.

   (iii) (in the case of wages) to protect workers' incomes.

   (iv) to create a surplus in times of glut which can be stored in preparation for possible future shortages.

Alternatives to fixing prices

(a) (i)   cash benefits and benefits in kind; subsidising the good.

   (ii) anti-monopoly legislation; lump-sum taxes.

   (iii) fiscal, monetary and supply-side policies (see Part B).

(b) (i)   subsidies and tax relief.

   (ii) subsidies and tax relief.

   (iii) benefits and progressive taxation.

   (iv) state acting as purchaser or seller on the open market.

Table A7.1

	1996	1997	1998	1999	2000	2001	2002	2003
USA	3.60	4.34	4.35	3.81	3.84	0.27	2.66	1.60
Japan	3.50	1.84	−1.14	0.19	2.78	0.47	0.28	0.19
Germany	0.80	1.39	2.05	1.92	3.10	0.64	0.27	0.09
France	1.10	1.88	3.50	3.19	4.18	1.83	1.20	0.93
UK	2.60	3.41	3.02	2.38	3.13	1.99	1.61	1.17

Chapter 7

1. (a) See Table A7.1.
   In each case the growth rate (G) is found by using the following formula:
   $$G = (Y_t - Y_{t-1})/Y_{t-1} \times 100$$
   (b) See Figure A7.1.
   The USA, the UK and France generally had a higher growth rate than Japan and Germany. Japan had negative growth in 2001. All five countries experienced relatively high growth in 2000 and relatively low growth in 2001.

3. (a) Neither, there is merely a redistribution of factor payments on the left-hand side of the inner flow. (The only exception to this would be if a smaller proportion of wages were saved than of profits. In this case there would be a net reduction in withdrawals.)
   (b) Increase in injections (investment).
   (c) Decrease in withdrawals (taxes).
   (d) Increase in withdrawals (saving). Note that 'investing' in building societies is really *saving* not investment.
   (e) Fall in withdrawals (a reduction in net outflow abroad from the household sector).

(f) Neither. The inner flow is unaffected. If, however, this were financed from higher taxes, it would result in an increase in withdrawals.
(g) Neither. The inner flow is unaffected. The consumption of domestically produced goods and services remains the same.
(h) Decrease in withdrawals (saving).
(i) Neither. An increase in government expenditure (or decrease in taxes, or both) is offset by an increase in saving (i.e. people buying government securities).
(j) Net injections. An increase in government expenditure (or decrease in taxes, or both) is not offset by changes elsewhere. Extra money is printed to finance the net injection.

5. The curve would still slope upwards during phase 4, but its slope would be less than in the other phases. Its slope would also be less than that of the potential output curve, with the result that the gap between actual and potential output would widen.

7. Look back over the last few years and see what pattern emerges. What predictions are currently being made for output growth over the next two years in the press by various forecasting organisations and commentators?

9. On the surface it would seem desirable that nobody would be suffering from being unemployed. But for an economy to be able to absorb everyone looking for a job, one of three conditions would have to hold, each of which brings serious problems. First, the economy would have to be suffering from such a huge shortage of labour that firms were providing all sorts of inducements to keep

Figure A7.1

Growth rates of selected industrial countries 1996–2003

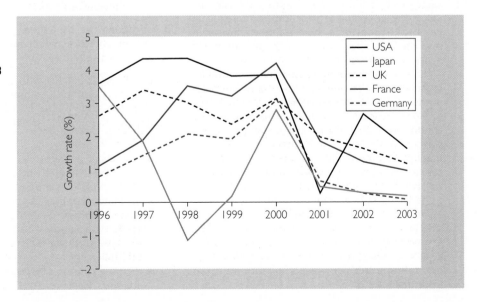

labour. The shortage of labour could be a serious constraint on some firms' ability to expand and it would probably lead to considerable inflation, which itself brings problems. Alternatively, un-employment benefits would have to be so low (or non-existent) that people would be forced to accept work at pittance wages. Alternatively, the government would have to provide work for everyone who would otherwise be unemployed: such schemes, unless carefully devised and man-aged, could prove an expensive way of reducing unemployment, might not be seen as 'real work' and could be demoralising to those involved.

11. First you will need to see to what extent changes in employment in your area reflect national trends. If they do, then the causes may be cyclical fluctuations in demand or longer-term changes in the labour market (such as changes in trade union power or patterns of part-time working), or in the competitiveness of the national economy, or in work practices or in unemployment benefits. Then you will need to see whether there are any factors in your area that cause unemployment to be different from the national average: e.g. certain industries that are concentrated in your area either declining or expanding.

13. Generally economists argue that an economic problem should be tackled at source: i.e. that it is better to tackle the root of a problem than merely treating its symptoms. This means that if unem-ployment is caused by a deficiency of aggregate demand, then the most appropriate policy would be to ensure that demand is sufficient. Econom-ists disagree, however (as we shall see in later chapters), as to whether it is better to manage aggregate demand over the short term (say, by increasing government expenditure or reducing taxes) or to provide a more stable environment over the longer term in which the economy will be less subject to recessions.

If unemployment is caused by structural or technological change, or by too many 'frictions' in the economy, the best approach is to make the economy adapt more rapidly to these changing conditions. This involves what are called 'supply-side policies'. These could involve 'freeing up' markets to remove impediments to labour and capital mobility (e.g. deregulation or reducing the power of trade unions). Such policies tend to be favoured by the political right. The altern-ative would be to have interventionist supply-side policy. For example, the government could invest in education and training in order to create a more flexible workforce, or provide better job information, or invest in the transport infrastructure.

15. Most of the costs of inflation would disappear, but menu costs would still remain. Investment, balance of payments and speculation costs would only disappear if everyone correctly anticipated *future* inflation.

Chapter 8

1. (a) In equilibrium, income (Y) = expenditure (E)
   $$E = C + I + G + X - M$$
   $$= £60\text{bn} + £5\text{bn} + £8\text{bn} + £7\text{bn} - £10\text{bn}$$
   $$= £70\text{bn}$$

   (b) $J = I + G + X$
   $$= £5\text{bn} + £8\text{bn} + £7\text{bn}$$
   $$= £20\text{bn}$$

   (c) In equilibrium, $W = J$. As this economy is in equilibrium, withdrawals will equal current injections.
   $$W = £20\text{bn}$$

   (d) $W = S + T + M$
   $$= S + £7\text{bn} + £10\text{bn}$$
   $$\therefore S = £20\text{bn} - £7\text{bn} - £10\text{bn}$$
   $$= £3\text{bn}$$

   (e) $C_d = C - M = £50\text{bn}$
   $$mpc_d = \Delta C_d / \Delta Y = (£58\text{bn} - £50\text{bn})/(£80\text{bn} - £70\text{bn})$$
   $$= £8\text{bn}/£10\text{bn}$$
   $$= 0.8 \text{ or } 4/5$$

   (f) Multiplier $= 1/(1 - mpc_d)$
   $$= 1/^1/_5$$
   $$= 5$$

   (g) Injections have risen by £4bn + £1bn − £2bn
   $$= £3\text{bn}$$
   $\therefore$ national income will rise by 5 times this amount
   = increase of £15bn

3. Injections rise by £100m + (£200m − £50m) = £250m. Therefore, with a multiplier of 3, national income will rise by £750m.

5. The E line is parallel with the C_d line (assuming that the J 'curve' is a horizontal straight line). Thus the slope of the E line is the same as the slope of the C_d line, which is given by the mpc_d ($\Delta C_d / \Delta Y$).

7. ■ The lower a country's national income, the higher will tend to be its *mpc* and thus the higher will be its multiplier.
   ■ In some countries there is much more of a 'savings culture' and thus the *mps* is higher. Those with less of a savings culture will tend to have a lower *mps* and hence a higher multiplier.
   ■ In some countries, especially large ones, trade accounts for a relatively small proportion of

national income. In such countries the *mpm* will be lower and hence the multiplier will be higher than in countries with a higher proportion of trade relative to national income.

■ The marginal tax rate, the *mpt*, differs from one country to another. The lower the *mpt*, the higher the multiplier.

9. (a) For each £20 billion rise in *Y* there is a £15 billion rise in *E*.
   ∴ $mpc_d = {}^3/4$
   ∴ multiplier = $1/(1 - {}^3/4) = 4$

   (b) The current equilibrium national income is £160 billion (where *Y* = *E*).
   Thus national income is £40 billion below the full-employment national income.
   With a multiplier of 4, there is a deflationary gap of £10 billion.

   (c) It would have to be increased by £10 billion.

11. Because demand for the output of these industries (which are 'investment' goods industries) fluctuates much more – the accelerator effect.

13. Multiplier
   The proportion of a rise in income that people spend on domestic goods (*mpc_d*) will vary in ways that are difficult to predict. It depends on:
   ■ Exchange rates, since these determine the proportion of a rise in income that will go on imports.
   ■ Consumer expectations about price rises. If consumers think that prices will rise in the near future, they are likely to increase their spending now, in order to beat the price increases.
   ■ Consumer confidence about future incomes and employment prospects. The more 'upbeat' consumers are, the more they are likely to spend out of any given rise in income.
   ■ Changes in interest rates, since these determine the cost of credit and the attractiveness of saving.
   Accelerator
   ■ Many firms may have spare capacity and/or carry stocks. This will enable them to meet extra demand without having to invest.
   ■ The willingness of firms to invest will depend on their confidence in *future* demand. Firms will only respond to a rise in demand by investing if they think that the rise in demand will persist.
   ■ Firms may make their investment plans a long time in advance and may be unable to change them quickly.
   ■ Even if firms do decide to invest more, the producer goods industries may not have the capacity to meet a sudden surge in demand for machines.

■ Machines do not as a rule suddenly wear out. A firm could thus delay replacing machines and keep the old ones for a bit longer if it was uncertain about its future level of demand.

15. (a) Assuming that the government does not alter tax or benefit rates, the budget deficit is likely to increase as the economy moves into recession. Tax revenues will fall because people are earning and spending less. The payment of benefits, on the other hand, is likely to increase as more people claim unemployment benefit. In a boom, the budget deficit is likely to decrease and there may even be a budget surplus.

   (b) Since the budget deficit tends to increase in a recession, the size of the national debt will increase more rapidly, as government debts are built up more rapidly. In a boom, the national debt will rise more slowly as the budget deficit falls. If there is a budget surplus, the national debt will fall.

17. A rise in income tax has an income and a substitution effect. Higher taxes reduce people's incomes: this is the income effect. Being poorer, they have to work more to make up for some of their lost income. The income effect, therefore, makes income tax increases an incentive to work more. Higher taxes, however, also mean that work is worth less than before, and therefore people might well substitute leisure for work: there is no point in working so much if you bring home less. This is the substitution effect, and makes income tax increases a disincentive.

   (i) If the substitution effect is bigger than the income effect, then a rise in income tax will act as a net disincentive to work. As is shown on page 194, this is likely for those people with few commitments and for second income earners in families where the second income is not relied on for 'essential consumption'. It is also likely for those who are only currently paying a small amount of tax, and for whom, therefore, the income effect is likely to be small; and also for those just in a higher tax bracket when that higher tax rate is raised.

   (ii) If the income effect is bigger than the substitution effect, a rise in tax will act as a net incentive. This is most likely for those currently paying a large amount of tax and who would suddenly be faced with a substantial increase in their tax bill. It is also likely if the tax increase takes the form of a cut in tax allowances. Except for those having to pay tax for the first time, or those pushed into a higher tax band, cutting allowances has no substitution effect since it does not alter the marginal rate.

19. ■ A rise in government expenditure on research and development or training may make firms feel less need to invest in these areas themselves.

■ A rise in taxes may make people feel less able to save such a large proportion of their income.

■ A rise in exports may stimulate firms to invest more in the export sector.

Chapter 9

1. ■ Acceptability: most are not currently acceptable as a medium of exchange, with the possible exception of gold under certain circumstances. Most, however, could be acceptable, if society chose. Strawberries would be a clear exception! Clearly the degree of acceptability would depend on the extent to which the item met the other six requirements.

■ Durability: gold, diamonds and a savings account have almost perfect durability; luncheon vouchers and share certificates have moderately high durability; grain and strawberry jam have moderate durability; strawberries clearly have very low durability (unless frozen).

■ Convenience: luncheon vouchers and share certificates would be very convenient; gold and diamonds would be moderately convenient for large transactions; again, strawberries would be very inconvenient.

■ Divisibility: a savings account scores highest here (assuming that any amount can be withdrawn or transferred); share certificates and luncheon vouchers also score highly (especially if they come in different 'denominations'); gold and diamonds are divisible down to moderately low levels; strawberries are also good in this respect (mind you, it's about the only one!); strawberry jam would be quite good, if it came in small-sized jars as well as normal-sized ones; grain is virtually perfectly divisible.

■ Uniformity: the paper assets are the best in this respect; the others are only suitable here if there is a means of identifying quality.

■ Hard for individuals to produce themselves: in the case of the commodities, there would be no problem here providing that their value as money was no higher than their market value as a commodity; as far as the other assets are concerned, a savings account would also be good, providing it was not possible for people to get unauthorised access to the account; the suitability of share certificates and luncheon

vouchers would depend on how easy they were to forge.

■ Stability of value: a savings account is as good as the currency in which it is denominated; luncheon vouchers could be good, but only if their supply were tightly controlled; share certificates are bad, given that share prices fluctuate with the fortunes of the company; diamonds and gold are good, as their supply is relatively constant; grain and especially strawberries are bad, given that their supply fluctuates with the harvest; strawberry jam is not very good either, given that its cost of production also fluctuates – with the price of strawberries.

3. None. They are all means of obtaining access to the money held in accounts, but they are not the money itself.

5. So that they can balance the two objectives of liquidity and profitability and also spread their risks, given that the relative profitability and security of different types of asset may change. For reasons of profitability the banks will want to minimise their holdings of cash; but to avoid the risks of insufficient liquidity, they hold a whole range of other liquid assets (such as money at call), which, although they are highly liquid, do, nevertheless, earn some interest for the bank.

7. Because market forces will ensure that interest rates in the two markets will move together: otherwise deposits would flow to the higher interest rate market and loans would be sought in the lower interest rate market. The higher interest rate market would thus have a glut of funds and the lower interest rate market would have a shortage of funds. These shortages and surpluses would act to eliminate the interest rate differential.

9. (a) £80 million (retaining £20 million as reserves). In other words, banks retain $1/5$ and lend out the remaining $4/5$.

(b) Increase by a further £80 million.

(c) £64 million (i.e. $4/5$ of £80 million).

(d) £500 million (given a bank multiplier of $5 = 1/L = 1/^1/5$).

(e) (i) £100 million; (ii) £400 million.

(f) 5.

(g) £250 million, since initial new deposits (and hence extra liquid assets) in the banking sector will have only been £50 million.

11. No. The demand would be high. People would want to hold the securities, so that they could benefit from the anticipated capital gain.

13. (a) They will increase credit and hence the money supply. M_s will shift to the right. The equilibrium rate of interest will therefore fall.

(b) Higher incomes will increase the transactions demand for money. The demand for money curve will shift to the right, causing the equilibrium rate of interest to rise.

(c) If people believe that interest rates will rise, the assets demand for money will rise. Again, the demand for money curve will shift to the right, causing the equilibrium rate of interest to rise.

15. Because one of the other determinants of money supply may cause it to grow more rapidly even though the reduction in the public-sector deficit, other things being equal, is causing the growth in the money supply to slow down. For example, if the economy is experiencing a boom, the growth in national income will increase the level of tax receipts and reduce the amount paid out in government benefits, thereby reducing the public-sector deficit. At the same time, however, the buoyant demand for bank loans is likely to increase bank lending.

17. (a) Little or no effect, if it simply replaces one liquid asset by another; but reduce it, if it involves reducing the liquidity of the banking sector (e.g. by the sale of bonds).

(b) Reduce it. The liquidity of the banking sector will be reduced (when people pay for the securities with cash withdrawn from the banks, or cheques drawn on the banks).

19. (a) Balance sheet directly after purchase of bonds

Liabilities	(£m)	Assets	(£m)
Old deposits	100	Old balances with central bank	10
New deposits	5	New balances with central bank	5
		Advances	90
	105		105

(b) Eventual balance sheet after credit creation has taken place (assuming a 10% liquidity ratio)

Liabilities	(£m)	Assets	(£m)
Old deposits	100	Old balances with central bank	10
New deposits	5	New balances with central bank	5
Further deposits	45	Old advances	90
		Further advances	45
	150		150

(c) No. To the extent that the holding of Treasury bills by the banking sector was reduced, this would reduce the size of the increase in banks' liquidity and hence reduce the size of the increase in advances. Only if all the bills purchased by the central bank came from *outside* the banking sector would the effect be the

same as in (b) above. If *all* the bills came from the banking sector, there would be little or no increase in liquidity, and hence little or no increase in advances.

(d) The extra demand for bills by the central bank would increase their price and hence reduce their rate of rediscount. The effect would be to drive down interest rates.

21. ■ Banks may vary their liquidity ratio.
■ It is difficult to predict how much the holding of Treasury bills by the banks will vary, and how much the banks will take this into account when deciding how much credit to grant.

23. Because the supply of money depends in part on the demand for money.

Chapter 10

1. (a) No (unless $V = 1$).
(b) Yes.

3. If both V and Y are exogenously (independently) determined (at least over the longer term) and relatively stable, then changes in money supply (M) have a direct effect on prices (P). This makes control of the growth in the money supply essential for controlling inflation.

Keynesians argue that both V and Y are endogenously determined (i.e. dependent on M), but subject to exogenous shocks). This means that changes in M will affect both V and Y. A rise in money supply, by leading to lower interest rates, is likely to increase speculative balances and therefore reduce the velocity of circulation (V). On the other hand, to the extent that a rise in money supply does affect MV and hence aggregate demand, then it could be output (Y) that is affected, rather than prices. The effects on both V and Y, however, are rather unpredictable. This makes monetary policy a very unreliable weapon for controlling inflation, especially over the short term.

5. The amount that unemployment is held below the natural rate. The lower level of unemployment that the government tries to maintain, the faster must it increase the level of aggregate demand and thus the faster will inflation accelerate.

7. A careful management of demand so as to avoid recessions, and thus encouraging more investment and more training and preventing people being forced into long-term unemployment (and thereby becoming de-skilled); supply-side policies, involving increased government expenditure on training and education and improved infrastructure.

9. (a) (i) Markets are highly interdependent, such that a rise in costs in one firm is passed on in full to those firms which it supplies; (ii) long-run equilibrium can only be at the natural rate of unemployment (i.e. there can be no long-run deficiency of demand); (iii) perfectly flexible wages and prices in the long run; (iv) no increase in capacity as a result of investment stimulated by a rise in demand, or decrease in capacity caused by lack of investment during a recession.

(b) If the above, and especially (iv), do not hold.

11. (a) Yes. Successful supply-side policies, by increasing potential output, will shift the vertical portion of the AS curve to the right. As a result, expansionary demand management policies could now increase output to a higher level than before.

(b) No. Demand-side policy must be used to control inflation. Supply-side policy will be the policy to use to reduce unemployment. If successful, it will shift the (vertical) AS curve to the right, and shift the (vertical) Phillips curve to the left by reducing the equilibrium level of unemployment.

13. Targeting the money supply could involve large changes in interest rates, given the unstable and interest-inelastic nature of the demand for money. This, in turn, could be very damaging to investment and reduce long-term growth. It is therefore better to avoid targeting the money supply. Instead, a discretionary approach should be adopted, with policies changed according to the changing nature of the real economy.

15. Yes. Targets could be set, but reassessed periodically in the light of the evidence of the success of policy and of changing circumstances. Alternatively, loose targets for a number of different objectives could be set, and then the government could seek to achieve the best compromise between them if there were any apparent conflict.

17. These can be put into two broad categories: an increase in the quantity of factors of production and an increase in their productivity. The *quantity* of factors can be increased largely through increasing the stock of capital. Higher saving will allow higher investment, a higher stock of capital and a higher level of national income. But growth will cease once this higher level of national income has been reached. To achieve sustained economic growth, therefore, the *productivity* of factors must increase over time. This will be brought about largely through technological progress.

19. Clearly there are costs and benefits. The benefits are an increase in efficiency and an increase in potential output in the economy. The costs are the increase in unemployment and the wastes associated with it. An important question is whether the government (or the market) can eventually reduce the equilibrium level of unemployment again, and thereby shift the Phillips curve back to the left. This could be done, for example, by policies of retraining and improved information on job opportunities.

21. By providing various forms of modern infrastructure (roads, railways, telecommunications, etc.) to help private-sector firms operate more effectively; by subsidising or giving tax relief for private-sector investment and training.

By relying on such measures, rather than on regulation, the government is still allowing the market to continue providing the incentives to firms to innovate and invest, and at the same time the government can use the policy to correct for various market failures (such as externalities). However, when there is a serious problem of the abuse of monopoly power or serious externalities, regulation or direct government provision (e.g. educational establishments) may be more appropriate (see the arguments developed in Sections 6.5 and 6.6).

Chapter 11

1. The LDC still gains by exporting wheat and importing cloth. At an exchange ratio of 1:2, it now only has to give up 1 kilo of wheat to obtain 2 metres of cloth, whereas without trade it would have to give up 3 kilos of wheat to obtain just 1 metre of cloth.

The developed country still gains by importing wheat and exporting cloth. At an exchange ratio of 1:2, it can now import 1 kilo of wheat for only 2 metres of cloth, whereas without trade it would have to give up 5 metres of cloth for 2 of wheat (i.e. $2^1/_2$ of cloth for 1 of wheat).

(a) Yes. (This ratio is between their two pre-trade ratios.)

(b) No. The LDC would gain, but the DC would lose. It would now have to give 3 metres of cloth for 1 kilo of wheat, whereas before trade it only had to give $2^1/_2$ metres of cloth for 1 kilo of wheat. Thus the developed country would choose not to trade at this ratio.

3. There are two elements to the answer. One concerns costs, one concerns demand and revenue.

In terms of costs, as a firm or country specialises and increases production, so the opportunity costs of production are likely to fall at first, due to economies of scale, and then rise as resources become increasingly scarce. The local florist may not have reached the point of rising long-run opportunity costs. Also it is too small to push up the price of inputs as it increases its production. It is a price taker. Unilever and Texaco, however, probably will have reached the point of rising opportunity costs. Countries certainly would have if they specialised in only one product. Thus the larger the organisation or country, the more diversified they are likely to be.

Turning to the demand side: the local florist supplies a relatively small market and faces a relatively elastic demand. It is therefore likely to find that complete specialisation in just one type of product is unlikely to lead to market saturation and a highly depressed price. Large companies, however, may find that complete specialisation in one product restricts their ability to expand. The market simply is not big enough. Countries would certainly find this. The USA could hardly just produce one product! The world market would be nowhere near big enough for it. The general point is that overspecialisation would push the price of the product down and reduce profits.

5. India: textiles
   UK: insurance
   Canada: wheat
   Japan: computers
   The reason in each case is that the products are intensive in factors that are relatively abundant in that country (e.g. Canada has an abundance of land that is suited to growing wheat; India has an abundance of labour and land suited to growing cotton).

7. *The infant industry argument.* Infants may never 'grow up': the support may allow them to remain inefficient; not all those industries claiming and receiving infant-industry protection are genuine infants (i.e. those which have a potential comparative advantage); infants may be better promoted through subsidies or other support, rather than by restricting trade – imposing tariffs, by raising prices, cuts down on the consumption not only of imported substitutes, but also of the goods produced by the infant itself.

Changing comparative advantage and the inflexibility of markets. Factor immobility is better tackled directly, rather than by protecting industries that have growth potential in export markets. Examples of schemes to encourage greater factor mobility are: retraining schemes, investment grants, tax relief for companies' relocation expenses and government advice on exporting.

To prevent dumping and other unfair trade practices. In the short run, consumers will *gain* from cheap imports. Even if the country loses in the long run from the dumping, the use of protection to stop the dumping may contribute to growing worldwide protectionism. It would be better to try to negotiate an end to the dumping, perhaps through the auspices of the World Trade Organisation.

To prevent the establishment of a foreign-based monopoly. There might be *international* competition to prevent individual foreign companies gaining monopoly power. Also, in practice it would be very difficult to decide when protection is warranted, given that many domestic companies would want to make a case for protection for themselves.

To reduce reliance on goods with little dynamic potential. In many cases, world market conditions change relatively slowly, and thus most firms will be able to adjust to new opportunities and declining old ones without the need for intervention.

To spread the risks of fluctuating markets. If countries are vulnerable to fluctuations in international markets, then individual companies trading in such markets will also be vulnerable, and therefore may themselves decide to diversify.

To reduce the influence of trade on consumer tastes. Given the global nature of mass communication, it is very difficult in practice to prevent people's tastes being influenced by the products and marketing of multinational companies.

To prevent the importation of harmful goods. If it is agreed that the goods are harmful (e.g. certain drugs), then attempting to stop imports may well be desirable, but should probably be part of a much broader strategy to stop the production, sale and consumption of such products.

To take account of externalities. If the externalities are within the country, then they are better dealt with by tackling them at source: e.g. taxing production or consumption that involves negative externalities and subsidising production or consumption that involves positive externalities.

To improve a country's terms of trade by exploiting its market power. Although the export monopoly argument is valid in a static context for certain products, it is likely that export taxes will erode the country's monopoly power over the longer term. By driving up the price of exports in which the country has monopoly power, other firms in other countries are likely to break into the international market. In practice there are few goods in which individual countries do have significant monopoly power (except for a few raw materials). There are even fewer where countries have significant monopsony power in importing: with a growing process of globalisation, companies have many alternative markets in which to sell.

To protect declining industries. There are various ways of helping individuals cope with the adjustment costs of economic change that are not as drastic as cutting down on trade. For example, retraining and special redundancy settlements could help workers who lose their jobs in declining industries.

To improve the balance of payments. In virtually all cases, there are other methods of dealing with balance of payments problems, both short term and long term.

9. Whether it can be demonstrated that, with appropriate investment, costs can be reduced sufficiently to make the industry internationally competitive.

11. (a) Imports are consumed and thus add directly to consumer welfare. Also, provided they are matched by exports there is no net outflow of money. Trade, because of the law of comparative advantage, allows countries to increase their standard of living: to import products that could only have been produced relatively inefficiently at home.

    (b) Importing cheap goods from, say, Hong Kong, allows more goods to be consumed. The UK uses less resources by buying these goods through the production and sale of exports, than by producing them at home. However, there will be a cost to *certain* UK workers whose jobs are lost through foreign competition. Policy makers must weigh up the benefits of trade to consumers and export industries against the costs to specific workers.

13. Countries may have a comparative advantage in products whose production causes pollution. Comparative advantage is based on *private* costs, not social costs. Thus Brazil exports hardwood from the rainforests, but cutting down the trees contributes towards global warming. As countries such as Brazil, China and India take an increasingly large share of world exports of industrial products, so these problems are likely to grow. All these countries have much lower environmental protection standards than in Europe and North America.

    There is no simple answer to the question of whether restrictions should be imposed on trade in those products whose production or consumption has harmful environmental effects. In terms of social efficiency, trade should take place as long as the marginal social benefit is greater than the marginal social cost (where environmental costs are included in marginal social costs). The problem with this approach is in identifying and measuring such benefits and costs. Then there is the problem of whether a social efficiency approach towards sustainability is the appropriate one (see Box 6.3). For example, should trade in hardwoods from the rainforests be simply banned? Then there is the issue of the response by countries to the restrictions. Will they respond by introducing cleaner technology? This may prove difficult to predict.

15. ■ The size of the external tariff. The higher the external tariff, the more likely it is that trade diversion will take place.
    ■ The difference in costs of production between countries inside and outside the union. The smaller the cost differences, the more likely it is that trade diversion will take place.

17. (a) Consumers would buy items in those countries that charged the lower rates of VAT. This would push up the prices in these countries and thus have the effect of equalising the tax-inclusive prices between member countries. This effect will be greater with expensive items (such as a car), where it would be worthwhile for the consumer to incur the costs of travelling to another country to purchase it.

    (b) Workers would move to countries with lower income taxes, thus depressing gross wage rates there and equalising after-tax wages. This effect would be greater, the greater is the mobility of labour between member countries.

    (c) Capital would move to countries with lower rates of company tax, thus depressing the rate of profit in the low-tax countries and equalising the after-tax rate of profit. This effect will be greater, the greater is the mobility of capital between member countries.

    In these last two cases, there will be an opposite effect caused by the multiplier. Workers or capital moving into a country will generate incomes there and hence increase the demand for factors and push up wages and profits.

19. ■ Removing barriers to trade creates opportunities. The degree to which firms and individuals will take advantage of those opportunities is uncertain.
    ■ It depends on whether any barriers remain (e.g. administrative barriers), and on which countries choose to join the single currency.
    ■ It depends on the rate of economic growth and other macroeconomic factors. The macroeconomy is difficult to forecast more than a few months ahead.

- It is difficult to predict the degree to which the increased competition in the single market will stimulate increased technical progress and the increased spread of skills and information.

21. Because barriers sometimes enable them to gain at the expense of other member countries, or because barriers benefit an individual pressure group (such as sheep farmers, or the car industry).

23. With a high exchange rate, the domestic currency will exchange for more dollars (i.e. a dollar will exchange for less domestic currency). But on international markets, agricultural commodities are priced in dollars. Thus farmers will earn less domestic currency from their agricultural exports. Also, a high exchange rate reduces the domestic price of imported foodstuffs. This forces down the price of domestically produced foodstuffs and thus reduces the profits for domestic farmers.

25. Even though a country may have an initial comparative advantage in wheat, the gains from specialising in its production and exporting it may be offset by other disadvantages – disadvantages that build over time. With a low world income elasticity of demand for wheat and with the protection of agriculture in developed countries, the demand for primary exports from developing countries has grown only slowly. At the same time, the demand for manufactured imports into developing countries has grown rapidly. The result has been a worsening balance of trade problem; and with a *price*-inelastic demand for both imports and exports, the terms of trade have worsened too. In addition, comparative advantage changes over time. There may be more potential for the country to diversify into labour-intensive manufactured products.

27. If a country specialises in labour-intensive products, this will increase the demand for labour and hence push up wage rates in those industries. This could result in greater equality. It might not, however, if the amount of investment varied significantly from one sector of the economy to another. If it did, then those working in sectors with new efficient labour-intensive technology would gain, while the poor, the dispossessed and those working in old inefficient industries would not. Income distribution could become less equal.

29. Not necessarily: it depends on each country's resource endowments – both present and potential future; on the nature of the manufactured products, their income elasticity of demand and their resource requirements; and on the world trading environment – whether countries would face barriers to the export of such products, either from countries or from multinationals controlling distribution channels. If countries do seek to become exporters of manufactures, they should normally specialise in labour-intensive manufactures or manufactures that use local materials, especially if such materials are costly to transport.

Chapter 12

1. (a) debit; (b) credit; (c) credit; (d) credit; (e) debit.

3. During the boom, the current account will tend to deteriorate. There are two reasons. The first is the direct result of higher incomes. Part of the extra incomes will be spent on imports. The second is the result of higher inflation. Higher prices of domestic goods and services relative to foreign ones will lead to both an increase in imports and a decrease in exports.

   The opposite effects are likely to occur during a recession. Lower incomes and relative prices of domestic goods and services will cause a fall in imports and a rise in exports: the current account will improve.

   In both cases we are assuming that other countries are not at the same time experiencing similar effects. If other countries were at the same phase of their business cycle, the above effects could be neutralised. For example, any fall in demand for imports by country A from country B could be offset by a fall in demand for imports by country B from country A. Imports and exports of both countries would fall (but not necessarily by the same amount).

5. Inward investment in the country (a credit on the financial account when it is made) will yield profits for the overseas investors in the future. This will enter as a *debit* on the investment income part of the current account.

7. Reduction in interest rates; the central bank buying in foreign currencies into the reserves by selling domestic currency on the foreign exchange market; lending abroad or paying back loans from abroad by the government/central bank; reflationary fiscal and monetary policy; lifting or reducing controls on imports or access to foreign exchange.

9. (a) It may fuel inflation by increasing the price of imported goods and reducing the need for export industries to restrain cost increases.
   (b) It may damage export industries and domestic import-competing industries, which would now find it more difficult to remain competitive.

11. It would involve too much risk. The longer the time period, the greater the scope for movements in the exchange rate and the more unpredictable they become. (Look at Figure 12.4 on page 480 of the text and see what happened to the exchange rate over the five-year period from 1980 to 1985!)

13. Both consumers and firms (when buying inputs) may take a time to change their consumption patterns. Thus the shorter the time period, the less will be the response to a change in the prices of imports and exports, and therefore the less price elastic will be their demand.

15. It depends on the effect of government policy on the views of speculators. The point is that the power of speculation to influence the exchange rate is likely to exceed the power of governments. The exchange rate is dependent on the demand for and supply of the domestic currency on the foreign exchange market. If there are very large-scale short-term international financial movements, these will be the major short-term determinant of the rate of exchange – far more important than central bank intervention from the reserves. If speculators believe that the government is not going to be able to maintain the current exchange rate at such a high level, no matter how much it intervenes on the foreign exchange market or raises interest rates, then their actions will virtually ensure that the government will fail. This is why the UK was forced out of the ERM in September 1992.

17. In both cases the following problems are likely to arise:
    ■ Countries' budget deficits and national debt differ substantially as a proportion of their national income. This puts very different pressures on the interest rates necessary to service these debts.
    ■ Harmonising rates of monetary growth would involve letting interest rates fluctuate with the demand for money. Such fluctuations could be severe.
    ■ Harmonising interest rates would involve abandoning both monetary targets and exchange rate targets (unless interest rate 'harmonisation' meant adjusting interest rates so as to maintain monetary targets or a fixed exchange rate).
    ■ Countries have different internal structural relationships. A lack of convergence here means that countries with higher endemic *cost* inflation would require higher interest rates and higher unemployment if international inflation rates were to be harmonised, or higher inflation if interest rates were to be harmonised.

■ Countries have different rates of productivity increase, product development, investment and market penetration. A lack of convergence here means that the growth in exports (relative to imports) will differ for any given level of inflation or growth.
■ Countries may be very unwilling to change their domestic policies to fall in line with other countries.

19. Because there was too much divergence in the economic conditions of the member countries. Greater convergence would clearly have helped. Achieving such convergence, however, would have been difficult at the time, given the pressures arising from German reunification.

21. (a) By its persuading speculators that the combined strength of the countries' reserves and their combined monetary policies would guarantee that rate of exchange could be maintained within their bands. Under these circumstances, speculation would be pointless.
    (b) If exchange rates were being maintained at clearly disequilibrium levels. The longer devaluation/revaluation were put off, and the more inevitable speculators believed the devaluation to be, the more would speculation take place.

23. Trade is likely to be attracted to those countries that have joined and they may have greater influence in determining future EU policy. Those that did not join are in principle able to take advantage of exchange rate movements to deal with any economic shocks that have a different effect on them from other members. They are vulnerable, however, to speculative international financial movements between their currency and others, including the euro: movements that are not merely a reflection of their *trade* account divergences. In the UK, however, exchange rate movements have *not* been used as a means of dealing with shocks and maintaining competitiveness. Instead, interest rates have been used as a means of keeping to the inflation target of $2^1/2$ per cent. This has generally meant that the pound has been kept high relative to the euro, much to the consternation of UK exporters.

25. Given the differences between countries, it is unlikely that the same *levels* of these indicators could all be achieved simultaneously: achieving the same level of one indicator may mean divergence of another. What is more important is that countries' economies should be progressing together with the *minimum* degree of divergence of the various indicators. This will normally mean

that countries need to be at the same phase of their business cycles and should be pursuing complementary policies.

27. Several of the causes of the crisis were outside the control of developing countries and could not therefore be blamed on them: for example, the world recession of the early 1980s and the much higher real interest rates that accompanied it. Nevertheless, it is easy with hindsight to put some of the blame on the policies of import-substituting industrialisation that many developing countries were pursuing: policies that involved large-scale borrowing to finance investment, with much of the borrowing at variable rates of interest. Although real rates of interest were low in the 1970s, there was still the *risk* that they might subsequently rise, making it difficult for the developing countries to service their debts.

Web appendix

All the following websites can be accessed from this book's own website (http://www.booksites.net/sloman). When you enter the site, click on *Student Resources* and then click on *Hot Links* in the left-hand panel. You will find all the following sites listed. Click on the one you want and the 'hot link' will take you straight to it.

The sections and numbers below refer to the ones used in the Web references at the end of each chapter of the text. Thus if the reference were to number A21, this would refer to the Money World site.

A   General news sources

As the title of this section implies, websites here can be used for finding material on current news issues or tapping into news archives. Most archives are offered free of charge. However, some do require you to register. As well as key UK and American sources, you will also notice some slightly different places from where you can get your news, such as the St Petersburg Times and Kyodo News (from Japan). Check out sites number 38, My Virtual Newspaper; 39, Newspapers on World Wide Web; and 43, Guardian World News Guide for links to newspapers across the world. Try searching for an article on a particular topic by using site number 41, Google News Search.

1. BBC news
2. The Economist
3. The Financial Times
4. The Guardian
5. The Independent
6. ITN
7. The Observer
8. The Telegraph
9. The Times, Sunday Times
10. The New York Times
11. Fortune
12. Time Magazine
13. The Washington Post
14. Moscow Times (English)
15. St Petersburg Times (English)
16. Straits Times
17. New Straits Times
18. The Scotsman
19. The Herald
20. Euromoney
21. Money World
22. Market News International
23. BusinessWeek online
24. Ananova

25. CNN Financial Net
26. Wall Street Journal
27. Asia related news
28. allAfrica.com
29. Greek News Sources (English)
30. Kyodo News: Japan (English)
31. RFE/RL NewsLine
32. The Australian
33. Sydney Morning Herald
34. Japan Times
35. Reuters
36. Bloomberg
37. David Smith's Economics UK.com
38. My Virtual Newspaper (links to a whole range of news sources)
39. Newspapers on World Wide Web
40. Economics in the News from Gametheory.net
41. Google News Search
42. Moreover
43. Guardian World News Guide

Sources of economic and business data B

Using websites to find up-to-date data is of immense value to the economist. The data sources below offer you a range of specialist and non-specialist data information. Universities have free access to the MIMAS site, which is a huge database of statistics. The last site in this set, the Treasury Pocket Data Bank, is a very useful source of key UK and world statistics, and is updated monthly. It downloads as an Excel file.

1. Economics LTSN gateway to economic data
2. Biz/ed Gateway to economic and company data
3. National Statistics
4. Data Archive (Essex)
5. Econ Links
6. Economic Resources (About)
7. Nationwide House Prices
8. House Web (data on housing market)
9. Incomes Data Services
10. Keynote Publications Ltd.
11. Land Registry (house prices, etc.)
12. Manchester Information and Associated Services (MIMAS)
13. Global Financial Data
14. PACIFIC International trade and business reference page
15. Economagic
16. Groningen Growth and Development Centre
17. Resources for economists on the Internet
18. Joseph Rowntree Foundation
19. Social Science Information Gateway (SOSIG)
20. Slavic and East European Resources
21. OECD statistics
22. CIA world statistics site
23. UN Millennium Country Profiles
24. World Bank statistics
25. Japanese Economic Foundation
26. Ministry of International Trade and Industry (Japan)
27. Nomura Research Institute (Japan)
28. Nanyang Technological University, Singapore: Statistical Data Locators
29. Richard Tucker's Data Resources
30. Oanda Currency Converter
31. World Economic Outlook Database (IMF)
32. Economist Country Briefings
33. OFFSTATS links to data sets
34. Treasury Pocket Data Bank (source of UK and world economic data)

Sites for students and teachers of economics C

The following websites offer useful ideas and resources to those who are studying or teaching economics. It is worth browsing through some just to see what is on offer. Try out the first four sites, for starters. The Internet Economist is a very helpful tutorial for economics students on using the Internet.

1. Economics Subject Centre of the UK, Learning and Teaching Support Network (LTSN)
2. Biz/ed
3. Ecedweb
4. Econ Links: student resources
5. Economics and Business Education Association
6. Tutor2U
7. Economics America
8. The Internet Economist (tutorial on using the Web)
9. Oxford School of Learning
10. Teaching resources for economists
11. Resources for University Teachers of Economics (University of Melbourne)
12. Federal Reserve Bank of San Francisco: Economics Education
13. Federal Reserve Bank of Minneapolis Economic Education
14. WebEc resources
15. BibEc papers
16. Online Opinion (Economics)
17. The Idea Channel
18. History of Economic Thought
19. Resources For Economists on the Internet (RFE)
20. Classroom Expernomics
21. VCE Economics (Economics teaching resources – Australian)
22. Paul Krugman Website
23. JokEc: economics jokes!

D   Economic models and simulations

Economic modelling is an important aspect of economic analysis. There are a number of sites that offer access to a model for you to use, e.g. Virtual economy (where you can play being Chancellor of the Exchequer). Using such models can be a useful way of finding out how economic theory works within an environment that claims to reflect reality.

1. Virtual economy
2. Virtual factory
3. Virtual Learning Arcade
4. About.com Economics
5. Estima (statistical analysis)
6. SPSS (statistical analysis)
7. National Institute of Economic and Social Research
8. Software available on Economics LTSN site
9. RFE Software

E   UK government and UK organisations' sites

If you want to see what a government department is up to, then look no further than the list below. Government departments' websites are an excellent source of information and data. They are particularly good at offering information on current legislation and policy initiatives.

1. Gateway site (UK Online)
2. Office of the Deputy Prime Minister
3. Central Office of Information
4. Competition Commission
5. Department for Education and Skills
6. Department for International Development
7. Department for Transport
8. Department of Health
9. Department for Work and Pensions
10. Department of Trade and Industry (DTI)
11. Environment Agency
12. UK euro information site
13. Low Pay Commission
14. Department for Environment, Food and Rural Affairs (DEFRA)
15. Office of Communications (Ofcom)

16. Office of Gas and Electricity Markets (Ofgem)
17. Official Documents OnLine
18. Office of Fair Trading (OFT)
19. Office of the Rail Regulator (ORR)
20. The Takeover Panel
21. Oftel
22. OFWAT
23. National Statistics (NS)
24. National Statistics Time Series Data
25. Strategic Rail Authority (SRA)
26. Patent Office
27. Parliament website
28. Scottish Executive
29. Scottish Environment Protection Agency
30. Treasury
31. Equal Opportunities Commission
32. Trades Union Congress (TUC)
33. Confederation of British Industry
34. Adam Smith Institute
35. Royal Institute of International Affairs
36. Institute of Fiscal Studies
37. Advertising Standards Authority

Sources of monetary and financial data   F

As the title suggests, here are listed useful websites for finding information on financial matters. You will see that the list comprises mainly central banks, both within Europe and further afield.

1. Bank of England
2. Bank of England Monetary and Financial Statistics
3. Banque de France
4. Bundesbank (German central bank)
5. Central Bank of Ireland
6. European Central Bank
7. Eurostat
8. US Federal Reserve Bank
9. Netherlands Central Bank
10. Bank of Japan
11. Reserve Bank of Austalia
12. Bank Negara Malaysia (English)
13. Monetary Authority of Singapore
14. National Bank of Canada
15. National Bank of Denmark (English)
16. Reserve Bank of India
17. Links to central bank websites from the Bank for International Settlements
18. The London Stock Exchange

European Union and related sources   G

For information on European issues, the following is a wide range of useful sites. The sites maintained by the European Union are an excellent source of information and are provided free of charge.

1. Economic and Financial Affairs: (EC DG)
2. European Central Bank
3. EU official website
4. Eurostat
5. Employment and Social Affairs (EC DG)
6. Site for information on the euro and EMU
7. Enterprise: (EC DG)
8. Competition: (EC DG)
9. Agriculture: (EC DG)
10. Energy and Transport: (EC DG)
11. Environment: (EC DG)
12. Regional Policy: (EC DG)
13. Taxation and Customs Union: (EC DG)
14. Education and training: (EC DG)
15. European Patent Office
16. European Commission
17. European Parliament
18. European Council

H   International organisations

This section casts its net beyond Europe and lists the Web addresses of the main international organisations in the global economy. You will notice that some sites are run by pressure groups, such as Jubilee Research, while others represent organisations set up to manage international affairs, such as the International Monetary Fund and the United Nations.

1. Food and Agriculture Organisation
2. International Air Transport Association (IATA)
3. International Labour Organisation (ILO)
4. International Monetary Fund (IMF)
5. Organisation for Economic Co-operation and Development (OECD)
6. OPEC
7. World Bank
8. World Health Organisation
9. United Nations
10. United Nations Industrial Development Organisation
11. Friends of the Earth
12. Jubilee Research
13. Oxfam
14. Christian Aid (reports on development issues)
15. European Bank for Reconstruction and Development (EBRD)
16. World Trade Organisation (WTO)
17. United Nations Development Program
18. UNICEF
19. EURODAD – European Network on Debt and Development
20. NAFTA
21. South American free trade areas
22. ASEAN
23. APEC

I   Economics search and link sites

If you are having difficulty finding what you want from the list of sites above, the following sites offer links to other sites and are a very useful resource when you are looking for something a little bit more specialist. Once again, it is worth having a look at what these sites have to offer in order to judge their usefulness.

1. Gateway for UK official sites
2. Alta Plana
3. Data Archive Search
4. Inomics (search engine for economics information)
5. International Digital Electronic Access Library
6. Links to economics resources sites
7. Social Science Information Gateway (SOSIG)
8. WebEc
9. One World (link to economic development sites)
10. Economic development sites (list)
11. Biz/ed Internet catalogue
12. Web links for economists from the Economics LTSN Subject Centre
13. Yahoo's links to economic data
14. OFFSTATS links to data sets
15. UniGuide academic guide to the Internet (Economics)
16. Internet Resources for Economists
17. Google Web Directory: Economics
18. Resources for Economists on the Internet

Internet search engines

The following search engines have been found to be useful.

1. Google
2. Altavista
3. Overture
4. Excite
5. Infoseek

6. Search.com
7. MSN
8. UK Plus
9. Yahoo!

Glossary and key ideas

Key Ideas

1. **Scarcity** is the excess of human wants over what can actually be produced. Because of scarcity, various choices have to be made between alternatives (page 5).

2. **Opportunity cost.** The cost of something measured in terms of what you give up to get it/do it. The best alternative forgone (page 8).

3. **Rational decision making** involves weighing up the marginal benefit and marginal cost of any activity. If the marginal benefit exceeds the marginal cost, it is rational to do the activity (or to do more of it). If the marginal cost exceeds the marginal benefit, it is rational not to do it (or to do less of it) (page 10).

4. **People respond to incentives.** It is important, therefore, that incentives are appropriate and have the desired effect (page 26).

5. **Changes in demand or supply cause markets to adjust.** Whenever such changes occur, the resulting 'disequilibrium' will bring an automatic change in prices, thereby restoring equilibrium (i.e. a balance of demand and supply) (page 27).

6. **The principle of diminishing marginal utility.** The more of a product a person consumes over a given period of time, the less will be the additional utility gained from one more unit (page 34).

7. **Equilibrium is the point where conflicting interests are balanced.** Only at this point is the amount that demanders are willing to purchase the same as the amount that suppliers are willing to supply. It is a point that will be automatically reached in a free market through the operation of the price mechanism (page 41).

8. **Government intervention may be able to rectify various failings of the market.** Government intervention in the market can be used to achieve various economic objectives which may not be best achieved by the market. Governments, however, are not perfect and their actions may bring adverse as well as beneficial consequences (page 45).

9. **Elasticity.** The responsiveness of one variable (e.g. demand) to a change in another (e.g. price). This concept is fundamental to understanding how markets work. The more elastic variables are, the more responsive is the market to changing circumstances (page 64).

10. **People's actions are influenced by their expectations.** People respond not just to what is happening now (such as a change in price), but to what they anticipate will happen in the future (page 68).

11. **People's actions are influenced by their attitudes towards risk.** Many decisions are taken under conditions of risk or uncertainty. Generally, the lower the probability of (or the more uncertain) the desired outcome of an action, the less likely it is that people will undertake the action (page 71).

12. **Output depends on the amount of resources and how they are used.** Different amounts and combinations of inputs will lead to different amounts of output. If output is to be produced efficiently, then inputs should be combined in the optimum proportions (page 84).

13. **The law of diminishing marginal returns.** When increasing amounts of a variable factor are used with a given amount of a fixed factor, there will come a point when each extra unit of the variable factor will produce less extra output than the previous unit (page 85).

14. **Market power benefits the powerful at the expense of others.** When firms have market power over prices, they can use this to raise prices and profits above the perfectly competitive level. Other things being equal, the firm will gain at the expense of the consumer. Similarly, if consumers or workers have market power, they can use this to their own benefit (page 118).

15. **Economic efficiency** is achieved when each good is produced at the minimum cost and where consumers get maximum benefit from their income (page 126).

16. **People often think and behave strategically.** How you think others will respond to your actions is likely to influence your own behaviour. Firms, for example, when considering a price or product change will often take into account the likely reactions of their rivals (page 142).

17. **Equity** is where income is distributed in a way that is considered to be fair or just. Note that an equitable distribution is not the same as a totally equal distribution and that different people have different views on what is equitable (page 192).

18. **Allocative efficiency in any activity is achieved where any reallocation would lead to a decline in net benefit.** It is achieved where marginal benefit equals marginal cost. Private efficiency is achieved where marginal private benefit equals marginal private cost ($MB = MC$). Social efficiency is achieved where marginal social benefit equals marginal social cost ($MSB = MSC$) (page 206).

19. **Markets generally fail to achieve social efficiency.** There are various types of market failure. Market failures provide one of the major justifications for government intervention in the economy (page 207).

20. **Externalities are spillover costs or benefits.** Where these exist, even an otherwise perfect market will fail to achieve social efficiency (page 207).

21. **The free-rider problem.** People are often unwilling to pay for things if they can make use of things other people have bought. This problem can lead to people not purchasing things which would be to the benefit of themselves and other members of society to have (page 210).

22. **The problem of time lags.** Many economic actions can take a long time to take effect. This can cause problems of instability and an inability of the economy to achieve social efficiency (page 214).

23. **The principal–agent problem.** Where people (principals), as a result of a lack of knowledge, cannot ensure that their best interests are served by their agents. Agents may take advantage of this situation to the disadvantage of the principals (page 216).

24. **Societies face trade-offs between economic objectives.** For example, the goal of faster growth may conflict with that of greater equality; the goal of lower unemployment may conflict with that of lower inflation (at least in the short run). This is an example of opportunity cost: the cost of achieving more of one objective may be achieving less of another. The existence of trade-offs means that policy-makers must make choices (page 217).

25. **Economies suffer from inherent instability.** As a result, economic growth and other macroeconomic indicators tend to fluctuate (page 250).

26. **Living standards are limited by a country's ability to produce.** Potential national output depends on the country's resources, technology and productivity (page 257).

27. **The distinction between nominal and real figures.** Nominal figures are those using current prices, interest rates, etc. Real figures are figures corrected for inflation (page 275).

28. **The principle of cumulative causation.** An initial event can cause an ultimate effect that is much larger (page 293).

29. **Goodhart's Law.** Controlling a symptom (i.e. an indicator) of a problem will not cure the problem. Instead, the indicator will merely cease to be a good indicator of the problem (page 390).

30. **The law of comparative advantage.** Provided opportunity costs of various goods differ in two countries, both of them can gain from mutual trade if they specialise in producing (and exporting) those goods that have relatively low opportunity costs compared with the other country (page 419).

Absolute advantage A country has an absolute advantage over another in the production of a good if it can produce it with less resources than the other country can.

Accelerationist theory The theory that unemployment can only be reduced below the natural level at the cost of accelerating inflation.

Accelerator theory The *level* of investment depends on the *rate of change* of national income, and as a result tends to be subject to substantial fluctuations.

Active balances Money held for transactions and precautionary purposes.

Actual growth The percentage annual increase in national output actually produced.

Ad valorem tariffs Tariffs levied as a percentage of the price of the import.

Ad valorem tax A tax on a good levied as a percentage of its value. It can be a single-stage tax or a multi-stage tax (such as VAT).

Adaptive expectations hypothesis The theory that people base their expectations of inflation on past inflation rates.

Adjustable peg A system whereby exchange rates are fixed for a period of time, but may be devalued (or revalued) if a deficit (or surplus) becomes substantial.

Aggregate demand Total spending on goods and services made in the economy. It consists of four elements, consumer spending (C), investment (I), government spending (G) and the expenditure on exports (X), less any expenditure on imports of goods and services (M): $AD = C + I + G + X - M$.

Aggregate demand for labour curve A curve showing the total demand for labour in the economy at different levels of real wage rates.

Aggregate supply The total amount of output in the economy.

Aggregate supply of labour curve A curve showing the total number of people willing and able to work at different average real wage rates.

Allocative efficiency A situation where the current combination of goods produced and sold gives the maximum satisfaction for each consumer at their current levels of income. Note that a redistribution of income would lead to a different combination of goods that was allocatively efficient.

Appreciation A rise in the free-market exchange rate of the domestic currency with foreign currencies.

Arc elasticity The measurement of elasticity between two points on a curve.

Assets Possessions, or claims held on others.

Asymmetric information Where one party in an economic relationship (e.g. an agent) has more information than another (e.g. the principal).

Asymmetric shocks Shocks (such as an oil price increase or a recession in another part of the world) that have different-sized effects on different industries, regions or countries.

Automatic fiscal stabilisers Tax revenues that rise and government expenditure that falls as national income rises. The more they change with income, the bigger the stabilising effect on national income.

Average (total) cost Total cost (fixed plus variable) per unit of output: $AC = TC/Q = AFC + AVC$.

Average cost pricing or **mark-up pricing** Where firms set the price by adding a profit mark-up to average cost.

Average fixed cost Total fixed cost per unit of output: $AFC = TFC/Q$.

Average physical product Total output (TPP) per unit of the variable factor in question: $APP = TPP/Q_v$.

Average rate of income tax Income taxes as a proportion of a person's total (gross) income: T/Y.

Average revenue Total revenue per unit of output. When all output is sold at the same price, average revenue will be the same as price: $AR = TR/Q = P$.

Average variable cost Total variable cost per unit of output: $AVC = TVC/Q$.

Balance of payments account A record of the country's transactions with the rest of the world. It shows the country's payments to or deposits in other countries (debits) and its receipts or deposits from other countries (credits). It also shows the balance between these debits and credits under various headings.

Balance of payments on current account The balance on trade in goods and services plus net investment income and current transfers.

Balance on trade in goods Exports of goods minus imports of goods.

Balance on trade in goods and services (or balance of trade) Exports of goods and services minus imports of goods and services.

Balance on trade in services Exports of services minus imports of services.

Balancing item (in the balance of payments) A statistical adjustment to ensure that the two sides of the balance of payments account balance. It is necessary because of errors in compiling the statistics.

Bank bills Bills that have been accepted by another institution and hence insured against default.

Bank (or deposits) multiplier The number of times greater the expansion of bank deposits is than the additional liquidity in banks that causes it: $1/L$ (the inverse of the liquidity ratio).

Barometric firm price leadership Where the price leader is the one whose prices are believed to reflect market conditions in the most satisfactory way.

Barriers to entry Anything that prevents or impedes the entry of firms into an industry and thereby limits the amount of competition faced by existing firms.

Barter economy An economy where people exchange goods and services directly with one another without any payment of money. Workers would be paid with bundles of goods.

Base year (for index numbers) The year whose index number is set at 100.

Basic rate of tax The main marginal rate of tax, applying to most people's incomes.

Benefits in kind Goods or services which the state provides directly to the recipient at no charge or at a subsidised price. Alternatively, the state can subsidise the private sector to provide them.

Bilateral monopoly Where a monopsony buyer faces a monopoly seller.

Bill of exchange A certificate promising to repay a stated amount on a certain date, typically three months from the issue of the bill. Bills pay no interest as such, but are sold at a discount and redeemed at face value, thereby earning a rate of discount for the purchaser.

Bretton Woods system An adjustable peg system whereby currencies were pegged to the US dollar. The USA maintained convertibility of the dollar into gold at the rate of $35 to an ounce.

Broad definitions of money Items in narrow definitions plus other items that can be readily converted into cash.

Broad money in UK (M4) Cash in circulation plus retail and wholesale bank and building society deposits.

Budget deficit The excess of central government's spending over its tax receipts.

Budget surplus The excess of central government's tax receipts over its spending.

Business cycle or trade cycle The periodic fluctuations of national output round its long-term trend.

Capital All inputs into production that have themselves been produced: e.g. factories, machines and tools.

Capital account of the balance of payments The record of the transfers of capital to and from abroad.

Cartel A formal collusive agreement.

Central bank Banker to the banks and the government.

Centrally planned or command economy An economy where all economic decisions are taken by the central authorities.

Certificates of deposit (CDs) Certificates issued by banks for fixed-term interest-bearing deposits. They can be resold by the owner to another party.

Ceteris paribus Latin for 'other things being equal'. This assumption has to be made when making deductions from theories.

Change in demand This is the term used for a shift in the demand curve. It occurs when a determinant of demand *other* than price changes.

Change in supply The term used for a shift in the supply curve. It occurs when a determinant *other* than price changes.

Change in the quantity demanded The term used for a movement along the demand curve to a new point. It occurs when there is a change in price.

Change in the quantity supplied The term used for a movement along the supply curve to a new point. It occurs when there is a change in price.

Claimant unemployment Those in receipt of unemployment-related benefits.

Clearing system A system whereby inter-bank debts are settled.

Closed shop Where a firm agrees to employ only union members.

Collusive oligopoly Where oligopolists agree (formally or informally) to limit competition between themselves. They may set output quotas, fix prices, limit product promotion or development, or agree not to 'poach' each other's markets.

Collusive tendering Where two or more firms secretly agree on the prices they will tender for a contract. These prices will be above those which would be put in under a genuinely competitive tendering process.

Command-and-control (CAC) systems The use of laws or regulations backed up by inspections and penalties (such as fines) for non-compliance.

Commercial bills Bills of exchange issued by firms.

Common market A customs union where the member countries act as a single market with free movement of labour and capital, common taxes and common trade laws.

Comparative advantage A country has a comparative advantage over another in the production of a good if it can produce it at a lower opportunity cost: i.e. if it has to forgo less of other goods in order to produce it.

Competition for corporate control The competition for the control of companies through takeovers.

Complementary goods A pair of goods consumed together. As the price of one goes up, the demand for both goods will fall.

Compounding The process of adding interest each year to an initial capital sum.

Compromise strategy One whose worst outcome is better than the maximax strategy and whose best outcome is better than the maximin strategy.

Conglomerate merger When two firms in different industries merge.

Consumer durable A consumer good that lasts a period of time, during which the consumer can continue gaining utility from it.

Consumer sovereignty A situation where firms respond to changes in consumer demand without being in a position in the long run to charge a price above average cost.

Consumer surplus The excess of what a person would have been prepared to pay for a good (i.e. the utility) over what that person actually pays.

Consumption The act of using goods and services to satisfy wants. This will normally involve purchasing the goods and services.

Consumption function The relationship between consumption and national income. It can be expressed algebraically or graphically.

Consumption of domestically produced goods and services (C_d) The direct flow of money payments from households to firms.

Convergence of economies When countries achieve similar levels of growth, inflation, budget deficits as a percentage of GDP, balance of payments, etc.

Core workers Workers, normally with specific skills, who are employed on a permanent or long-term basis.

Cost–benefit analysis The identification, measurement and weighing up of the costs and benefits of a project in order to decide whether or not it should go ahead.

Cost-plus pricing (full-cost pricing) When firms price their product by adding a certain profit 'mark-up' to average cost.

Cost-push inflation Inflation caused by persistent rises in costs of production (independently of demand).

Countervailing power When the power of a monopolistic/oligopolistic seller is offset by powerful buyers who can prevent the price from being pushed up.

Credible threat (or promise) One that is believable to rivals because it is in the threatener's interests to carry it out.

Cross-price elasticity of demand The percentage (or proportionate) change in quantity demanded of one good divided by the percentage (or proportionate) change in the price of another.

Cross-price elasticity of demand (arc formula) ΔQ_{Da}/average $Q_{Da} \div \Delta P_b$/average P_b.

Cross-subsidise To use profits in one market to subsidise prices in another.

Crowding out Where increased public expenditure diverts money or resources away from the private sector.

Currency union A group of countries (or regions) using a common currency.

Current account balance of payments Exports of goods and services minus imports of goods and services plus net incomes and current transfers from abroad. If inflows of money (from the sale of exports, etc.) exceed outflows of money (from the purchase of imports, etc.), there is a 'current account surplus' (a positive figure). If outflows exceed inflows, there is a 'current account deficit' (a negative figure).

Customs union A free trade area with common external tariffs and quotas.

Cyclical or demand-deficient unemployment Disequilibrium unemployment caused by a fall in aggregate demand with no corresponding fall in the real wage rate.

Deadweight loss of an indirect tax The loss of consumer plus producer surplus from the imposition of an indirect tax.

Deadweight welfare loss The loss of consumer plus producer surplus in imperfect markets (when compared with perfect competition).

Debit card A card that has the same use as a cheque. Its use directly debits the person's current account.

Debt servicing Paying the interest and capital repayments on debt.

Decision tree (or game tree) A diagram showing the sequence of possible decisions by competitor firms and the outcome of each combination of decisions.

Deflationary gap The shortfall of national expenditure below national income (and injections below withdrawals) at the full-employment level of national income.

Deflationary policy Fiscal or monetary policy designed to reduce the rate of growth of aggregate demand.

Demand curve A graph showing the relationship between the price of a good and the quantity of the good demanded over a given time period. Price is measured on the vertical axis; quantity demanded is measured on the horizontal axis. A demand curve can be for an individual consumer or group of consumers, or more usually for the whole market.

Demand management policies Demand-side policies (fiscal and/or monetary) designed to smooth out the fluctuations in the business cycle.

Demand schedule for an individual A table showing the different quantities of a good that a person is willing and able to buy at various prices over a given period of time.

Demand schedule (market) A table showing the different total quantities of a good that consumers are willing and able to buy at various prices over a given period of time.

Demand-deficient or cyclical unemployment Disequilibrium unemployment caused by a fall in aggregate demand with no corresponding fall in the real wage rate.

Demand-pull inflation Inflation caused by persistent rises in aggregate demand.

Demand-side policies Policies designed to affect aggregate demand: fiscal policy and monetary policy.

Dependency Where the development of a developing country is hampered by its relationships with the industrialised world.

Depreciation (of capital) The decline in value of capital equipment due to age, or wear and tear.

Depreciation (of a currency) A fall in the free-market exchange rate of the domestic currency with foreign currencies.

Deregulation Where the government removes official barriers to competition (e.g. licences and minimum quality standards).

Derived demand The demand for a factor of production depends on the demand for the good that uses it.

Destabilising speculation Where the actions of speculators tend to make price movements larger.

Devaluation Where the government re-pegs the exchange rate at a lower level.

Diminishing marginal utility As more units of a good are consumed, additional units will provide less additional satisfaction than previous units.

Diminishing marginal utility of income Where each additional pound earned yields less additional utility.

Direct taxes Taxes on income and wealth. Paid directly to the tax authorities on that income or wealth.

Discounting The process of reducing the value of future flows to give them a present valuation.

Discretionary fiscal policy Deliberate changes in tax rates or the level of government expenditure in order to influence the level of aggregate demand.

Diseconomies of scale Where costs per unit of output increase as the scale of production increases.

Disequilibrium unemployment Unemployment resulting from real wage rates in the economy being above the equilibrium level.

Disguised unemployment Where the same work could be done by fewer people.

Disposable income Household income after the deduction of taxes and the addition of benefits.

Diversification Where a firm expands into new types of business.

Dominant firm price leadership When firms (the followers) choose the same price as that set by a dominant firm in the industry (the leader).

Dominant strategy game Where the *same* policy is suggested by different strategies.

Dumping When exports are sold at prices below marginal cost – often as a result of government subsidy.

Economic efficiency A situation where each good is produced at the minimum cost and where individual people and firms get the maximum benefit from their resources.

Economic model A formal presentation of an economic theory.

Economies of scale When increasing the scale of production leads to a lower cost per unit of output.

Economies of scope When increasing the range of products produced by a firm reduces the cost of producing each one.

ECU (European Currency Unit) The predecessor to the euro: a weighted average of EU currencies. It was used as a reserve currency and for the operation of the exchange rate mechanism (ERM).

Efficiency wage rate The profit-maximising wage rate for the firm after taking into account the effects of wage rates on worker motivation, turnover and recruitment.

Elastic demand (with respect to price) Where quantity demanded changes by a larger percentage than price. Ignoring the negative sign, it will have a value greater than 1.

Elasticity A measure of the responsiveness of a variable (e.g. quantity demanded or quantity supplied) to a change in one of its determinants (e.g. price or income).

Endogenous money supply Money supply that is determined (at least in part) by the demand for money.

Entrepreneurship The initiating and organising of the production of new goods, or the introduction of new techniques, and the risk taking associated with it.

Envelope curve A long-run average cost curve drawn as the tangency points of a series of short-run average cost curves.

Environmental charges Charges for using natural resources (e.g. water or national parks), or for using the environment as a dump for waste (e.g. factory emissions or sewage).

Equation of exchange $MV = PQ$. The total level of spending on GDP (MV) equals the total value of goods and services produced (PQ) that go to make up GDP.

Equilibrium A position of balance. A position from which there is no inherent tendency to move away.

Equilibrium price The price where the quantity demanded equals the quantity supplied: the price where there is no shortage or surplus.

Equilibrium unemployment ('natural') unemployment The difference between those who would like employment at the current wage rate and those willing and able to take a job.

Equities Company shares. Holders of equities are owners of the company and share in its profits by receiving dividends.

Equity A distribution of income that is considered to be fair or just. Note that an equitable distribution is not the same as an equal distribution and that different people have different views on what is equitable.

ERM (the exchange rate mechanism) A system of semi-fixed exchange rates used by most of the EU countries prior to adoption of the euro. Members' currencies were allowed to fluctuate against each other only within agreed bands. Collectively they floated against all other currencies.

Excess capacity (under monopolistic competition) In the long run, firms under monopolistic competition will produce at an output below their minimum-cost point.

Exchange equalisation account The gold and foreign exchange reserves account in the Bank of England.

Exchange rate The rate at which one national currency exchanges for another. The rate is expressed as the amount of one currency that is necessary to purchase *one unit* of another currency (e.g. $1.60 = £1).

Exchange rate band Where a currency is allowed to float between an upper and lower exchange rate, but is not allowed to move outside this band.

Exchange rate index A weighted average exchange rate expressed as an index where the value of the index is 100 in a given base year. The weights of the different currencies in the index add up to 1.

Exchange rate overshooting Where a fall (or rise) in the long-run equilibrium exchange rate causes the actual exchange rate to fall (or rise) by a greater amount before eventually moving back to the new long-run equilibrium level.

Exchange rate regime The system under which the government allows the exchange rate to be determined.

Exogenous money supply Money supply that does not depend on the demand for money but is set by the authorities.

Exogenous variable A variable whose value is determined independently of the model of which it is part.

Expectations-augmented Phillips curve A (short-run) Phillips curve whose position depends on the expected rate of inflation.

Explicit costs The payments to outside suppliers of inputs.

External benefits Benefits from production (or consumption) experienced by people *other* than the producer (or consumer).

External costs Costs of production (or consumption) borne by people *other* than the producer (or consumer).

External diseconomies of scale Where a firm's costs per unit of output increase as the size of the whole industry increases.

External economies of scale Where a firm's costs per unit of output decrease as the size of the whole *industry* grows.

Externalities Costs or benefits of production or consumption experienced by society but not by the producers or consumers themselves. Sometimes referred to as 'spillover' or 'third-party' costs or benefits.

Factors of production (or resources) The inputs into the production of goods and services: labour, land and raw materials, and capital.

Financial account of the balance of payments The record of the flows of money into and out of the country for the purposes of investment or as deposits in banks and other financial institutions.

Financial crowding out When an increase in government borrowing diverts money away from the private sector.

Financial deregulation The removal of or reduction in legal rules and regulations governing the activities of financial institutions.

Financial flexibility Where employers can vary their wage costs by changing the composition of their workforce or the terms on which workers are employed.

Financial intermediaries The general name for financial institutions (banks, building societies, etc.) which act as a means of channelling funds from depositors to borrowers.

Fine tuning The use of demand management policy (fiscal or monetary) to smooth out cyclical fluctuations in the economy.

First-mover advantage When a firm gains from being the first one to take action.

Fiscal drag The tendency of automatic fiscal stabilisers to reduce the recovery of an economy from recession.

Fiscal policy Policy to affect aggregate demand by altering the balance between government expenditure and taxation.

Fiscal stance How deflationary or reflationary the Budget is.

Fixed costs Total costs that do not vary with the amount of output produced.

Fixed exchange rate (totally) Where the government takes whatever measures are necessary to maintain the exchange rate at some stated level.

Fixed factor An input that cannot be increased in supply within a given time period.

Flexible firm A firm that has the flexibility to respond to changing market conditions by changing the composition of its workforce.

Floating exchange rate When the government does not intervene in the foreign exchange markets, but simply allows the exchange rate to be freely determined by demand and supply.

Forward exchange market Where contracts are made today for the price at which currency will be exchanged at some specified future date.

Franchising Where a firm is given the licence to operate a given part of an industry for a specified length of time.

Free trade area A group of countries with no trade barriers between them.

Freely floating exchange rate Where the exchange rate is determined entirely by the forces of demand and supply in the foreign exchange market with no government intervention whatsoever.

Free-market economy An economy where all economic decisions are taken by individual households and firms and with no government intervention.

Free-rider problem When it is not possible to exclude other people from consuming a good that someone has bought.

Frictional (search) unemployment Unemployment that occurs as a result of imperfect information in the labour market. It often takes time for workers to find jobs (even though there are vacancies) and in the meantime they are unemployed.

Full-employment level of national income The level of national income at which there is no deficiency of demand.

Functional flexibility Where employers can switch workers from job to job as requirements change.

Funding Where the authorities alter the balance of bills and bonds for any given level of government borrowing.

Future price A price agreed today at which an item (e.g. commodities) will be exchanged at some set date in the future.

Futures or forward market A market in which contracts are made to buy or sell at some future date at a price agreed today.

Gaia philosophy The respect for the rights of the environment to remain unharmed by human activity. Humans should live in harmony with the planet and other species. We have a duty to be stewards of the natural environment, so that it can continue to be a self-maintaining and self-regulating system.

Game theory (or the theory of games) The study of alternative strategies oligopolists may choose to adopt, depending on their assumptions about their rivals' behaviour.

GDP (gross domestic product at market prices) The value of output (or income or expenditure) in terms of the prices actually paid. GDP = GVA + taxes on products − subsidies on products.

General equilibrium A situation where all the millions of markets throughout the economy are in a simultaneous state of equilibrium.

General government debt The combined accumulated debt of central and local government.

General government deficit (or surplus) The combined deficit (or surplus) of central and local government.

Geographical immobility The lack of ability or willingness of people to move to jobs in other parts of the country.

GNY (gross national income) GDP plus net income from abroad.

Goodhart's Law Controlling a symptom of a problem, or only part of the problem, will not cure the problem: it will simply mean that the part that is being controlled now becomes a poor indicator of the problem.

Government bonds or 'gilt-edged securities' A government security paying a fixed sum of money each year. It is redeemed by the government on its maturity date at its face value.

Government surplus (from a tax on a good) The total tax revenue earned by the government from sales of a good.

Green tax A tax on output designed to charge for the adverse effects of production on the environment. The socially efficient level of a green tax is equal to the marginal environmental cost of production.

Gross domestic product (GDP) The value of output produced within the country over a 12-month period.

Gross national income (GNY) GDP plus net income from abroad.

Gross value added at basic prices (GVA) The sum of all the values added by all industries in the economy over a year. The figures exclude taxes on products (such as VAT) and include subsidies on products.

Historic costs The original amount a firm paid for factors it now owns.

Hit-and-run competition When a firm enters an industry to take advantage of temporarily high profits and then leaves again as soon as the high profits have been exhausted.

Horizontal merger When two firms in the same industry at the same stage in the production process merge.

Households' disposable income The income available for households to spend: i.e. personal incomes after deducting taxes on incomes and adding benefits.

Human capital The qualifications, skills and expertise that contribute to a worker's productivity.

Human Development Index (HDI) A composite index made up of three elements: an index for life expectancy, an index for school enrolment and adult literacy, and an index for GDP per capita (in PPP$).

Hysteresis The persistence of an effect even when the initial cause has ceased to operate. In economics, it refers to the persistence of unemployment even when the demand deficiency that caused it no longer exists.

Idle balances Money held for speculative purposes: money held in anticipation of a fall in asset prices.

Imperfect competition The collective name for monopolistic competition and oligopoly.

Implicit costs Costs which do not involve a direct payment of money to a third party, but which nevertheless involve a sacrifice of some alternative.

Import-substituting industrialisation (ISI) A strategy of restricting imports of manufactured goods and using the foreign exchange saved to build up domestic substitute industries.

Income effect (of a price change) The effect of a change in price on quantity demanded arising from the consumer becoming better or worse off as a result of the price change.

Income effect of a rise in wage rates Workers get a higher income for a given number of hours worked and may thus feel they need to work *fewer* hours as wage rates rise.

Income effect of a tax rise Tax increases reduce people's incomes and thus encourage people to work more.

Income elasticity of demand The percentage (or proportionate) change in quantity demanded divided by the percentage (or proportionate) change in income.

Income elasticity of demand (arc formula) $\Delta Q_D/\text{average } Q_D \div \Delta Y/\text{average } Y$.

Increasing opportunity costs of production When additional production of one good involves ever-increasing sacrifices of another.

Independence (of firms in a market) Where the decisions of one firm in a market will not have any significant effect on the demand curves of its rivals.

Independent risks Where two risky events are unconnected. The occurrence of one will not affect the likelihood of the occurrence of the other.

Index number The value of a variable expressed as 100 plus or minus its percentage deviation from a base year.

Indirect taxes Taxes on expenditure (e.g. VAT). Paid to the tax authorities, not by the consumer, but indirectly by the suppliers of the goods or services.

Indivisibilities The impossibility of dividing a factor into smaller units.

Induced investment Investment that firms make to enable them to meet extra consumer demand.

Industrial policies Policies to encourage industrial investment and greater industrial efficiency.

Inelastic demand Where quantity demanded changes by a smaller percentage than price. Ignoring the negative sign, it will have a value less than 1.

Infant industry An industry that has a potential comparative advantage, but which is as yet too underdeveloped to be able to realise this potential.

Inferior goods Goods whose demand *decreases* as consumer incomes increase. Such goods have a negative income elasticity of demand.

Inflationary gap The excess of national expenditure over income (and injections over withdrawals) at the full-employment level of national income.

Infrastructure (industry's) The network of supply agents, communications, skills, training facilities, distribution channels, specialised financial services, etc. that supports a particular industry.

Injections (J) Expenditure on the production of domestic firms coming from outside the inner flow of the circular flow of income. Injections equal investment (*I*) plus government expenditure (*G*) plus expenditure on exports (*X*).

Input–output analysis This involves dividing the economy into sectors where each sector is a user of inputs from and a supplier of outputs to other sectors. The technique examines how these inputs and outputs can be matched to the total resources available in the economy.

Insiders Those in employment who can use their privileged position (either as members of unions or because of specific skills) to secure pay rises despite an excess supply of labour (unemployment).

Interdependence (under oligopoly) One of the two key features of oligopoly. Each firm will be affected by its rivals' decisions. Likewise its decisions will affect its rivals. Firms recognise this interdependence. This recognition will affect their decisions.

International harmonisation of economic policies Where countries attempt to co-ordinate their macroeconomic policies so as to achieve common goals.

International liquidity The supply of currencies in the world acceptable for financing international trade and investment.

International trade multiplier The effect on national income in country B of a change in exports (or imports) of country A.

Intervention price (in the CAP) The price at which the EU is prepared to buy a foodstuff if the market price were to be below it.

Interventionist supply-side policies Policies to increase aggregate supply by government intervention to counteract the deficiencies of the market.

Investment The production of items that are not for immediate consumption.

Joint float Where a group of currencies pegged to each other jointly float against other currencies.

Joint supply Where the production of more of one good leads to the production of more of another.

Kinked demand theory The theory that oligopolists face a demand curve that is kinked at the current price, demand being significantly more elastic above the current price than below. The effect of this is to create a situation of price stability.

Labour All forms of human input, both physical and mental, into current production.

Labour force The number employed plus the number unemployed.

Land (and raw materials) Inputs into production that are provided by nature: e.g. unimproved land and mineral deposits in the ground.

Law of comparative advantage Trade can benefit all countries if they specialise in the goods in which they have a comparative advantage.

Law of demand The quantity of a good demanded per period of time will fall as price rises and will rise as price falls, other things being equal (*ceteris paribus*).

Law of diminishing (marginal) returns When one or more factors are held fixed, there will come a point beyond which the extra output from additional units of the variable factor will diminish.

Lender of last resort The role of the Bank of England as the guarantor of sufficient liquidity in the monetary system.

Liabilities All legal claims for payment that outsiders have on an institution.

Liquidity The ease with which an asset can be converted into cash without loss.

Liquidity preference The demand for holding assets in the form of money.

Liquidity ratio The proportion of a bank's total assets held in liquid form.

Lock-outs Union members are temporarily laid off until they are prepared to agree to the firm's conditions.

Long run The period of time long enough for *all* factors to be varied.

Long run under perfect competition The period of time that is long enough for new firms to enter the industry.

Long-run average cost curve A curve that shows how average cost varies with output on the assumption that *all* factors are variable. (It is assumed that the least-cost method of production will be chosen for each output.)

Long-run marginal cost The extra cost of producing one more unit of output assuming that all factors are variable. (It is assumed that the least-cost method of production will be chosen for this extra output.)

Long-run profit maximisation An alternative theory of the firm which assumes that managers aim to shift cost and revenue curves so as to maximise profits over some longer time period.

Long-run shut-down point This is where the AR curve is tangential to the $LRAC$ curve. The firm can just make normal profits. Any fall in revenue below this level will cause a profit-maximising firm to shut down once all costs have become variable.

Lorenz curve A curve showing the proportion of national income earned by any given percentage of the population (measured from the poorest upwards).

Macroeconomics The branch of economics that studies economic aggregates (grand totals): e.g. the overall level of prices, output and employment in the economy.

Managed floating A system of flexible exchange rates but where the government intervenes to prevent excessive fluctuations or even to achieve an unofficial target exchange rate.

Marginal benefit The additional benefit of doing a little bit more (or 1 unit more if a unit can be measured) of an activity.

Marginal consumer surplus The excess of utility from the consumption of one more unit of a good (MU) over the price paid: $MCS = MU - P$.

Marginal cost (of an activity) The additional cost of doing a little bit more (or 1 unit more if a unit can be measured) of an activity.

Marginal cost (of production) The cost of producing one more unit of output: $MC = \Delta TC/\Delta Q$.

Marginal disutility of work The extra sacrifice/hardship to a worker of working an extra unit of time in any given time period (e.g. an extra hour per day).

Marginal physical product The extra output gained by the employment of one more unit of the variable factor: $MPP = \Delta TPP/\Delta Q_v$.

Marginal productivity theory The theory that the demand for a factor depends on its marginal revenue product.

Marginal propensity to consume The proportion of a rise in national income that goes on consumption: $mpc = \Delta C/\Delta Y$.

Marginal propensity to import The proportion of an increase in national income that is spent on imports: $mpm = \Delta M/\Delta Y$.

Marginal propensity to save The proportion of an increase in national income saved: $mps = \Delta S/\Delta Y$.

Marginal propensity to withdraw The proportion of an increase in national income that is withdrawn from the circular flow: $mpw = \Delta W/\Delta Y$, where $mpw = mps + mpt + mpm$.

Marginal rate of income tax The income tax rate. The rate paid on each *additional* pound earned: $\Delta T/\Delta Y$.

Marginal revenue The extra revenue gained by selling one more unit per time period: $MR = \Delta TR/\Delta Q$.

Marginal revenue product (of a factor) The extra revenue a firm earns from employing one more unit of a variable factor: $MRP_{factor} = MPP_{factor} \times MR_{good}$.

Marginal tax propensity The proportion of an increase in national income paid in tax: $mpt = \Delta T/\Delta Y$.

Marginal utility The extra satisfaction gained from consuming one extra unit of a good within a given time period.

Market The interaction between buyers and sellers.

Market clearing A market clears when supply matches demand, leaving no shortage or surplus.

Market for loanable funds The market for loans from and deposits into the banking system.

Market loans Short-term loans (e.g. money at call and short notice).

Market-orientated supply-side policies Policies to increase aggregate supply by freeing up the market.

Mark-up A profit margin added to average cost to arrive at price.

Maximax The strategy of choosing the policy that has the best possible outcome.

Maximin The strategy of choosing the policy whose worst possible outcome is the least bad.

Maximum price A price ceiling set by the government or some other agency. The price is not allowed to rise above this level (although it is allowed to fall below it).

Mean (or arithmetic mean) The sum of the values of each of the members of the sample divided by the total number in the sample.

Means-tested benefits Benefits whose amount depends on the recipient's income or assets.

Median The value of the middle member of the sample.

Medium of exchange Something that is acceptable in exchange for goods and services.

Menu costs of inflation The costs associated with having to adjust price lists or labels.

Merit goods Goods which the government feels that people will underconsume and which therefore ought to be subsidised or provided free.

Microeconomics The branch of economics that studies individual units: e.g. households, firms and industries. It studies the interrelationships between these units in determining the pattern of production and distribution of goods and services.

Minimum price A price floor set by the government or some other agency. The price is not allowed to fall below this level (although it is allowed to rise above it).

Minimum reserve ratio A minimum ratio of cash (or other specified liquid assets) to deposits (either total or selected) that the central bank requires banks to hold.

Mixed economy An economy where economic decisions are made partly by the government and partly through the market.

Mixed market economy A market economy where there is some government intervention.

Monetarists Those who attribute inflation solely to rises in money supply.

Monetary base Notes and coin outside the central bank.

Monetary policy Policy to affect aggregate demand by altering the supply or cost of money (rate of interest).

Money illusion When people believe that a money wage or price increase represents a *real* increase: in other words, they ignore or underestimate inflation.

Money market The market for short-term loans and deposits.

Money multiplier The number of times greater the expansion of money supply is than the expansion of the monetary base that caused it: $\Delta Ms/\Delta Mb$.

Monopolistic competition A market structure where, like perfect competition, there are many firms and freedom of entry into the industry, but where each firm produces a differentiated product and thus has some control over its price.

Monopoly A market structure where there is only one firm in the industry.

Monopsony A market with a single buyer or employer.

Multiplier (injections multiplier) The number of times a rise in income exceeds the rise in injections that caused it: $k = \Delta Y/\Delta J$.

Multiplier effect An initial increase in aggregate demand of £xm leads to an eventual rise in national income that is greater than £xm.

Multiplier formula (injections multiplier) The formula for the multiplier is $k = 1/mpw$ or $1/(1 - mpc_d)$.

Narrow definitions of money Items of money that can be spent directly (cash and money in cheque-book/debit-card accounts).

Nash equilibrium The position resulting from everyone making their optimal decision based on their assumptions about their rivals' decisions. Without collusion, there is no incentive for any firm to move from this position.

National debt The accumulated budget deficits (less surpluses) over the years: the total amount of government borrowing.

National expenditure on domestic product (E) Aggregate demand in the Keynesian model: i.e. $C_d + J$.

Nationalised industries State-owned industries that produce goods or services that are sold in the market.

Natural level of output The level of output in monetarist analysis where the vertical long-run aggregate supply curve cuts the horizontal axis.

Natural level of unemployment The level of equilibrium unemployment in monetarist analysis measured as the difference between the (vertical) long-run gross labour supply curve (N) and the (vertical) long-run effective labour supply curve (AS_L).

Natural monopoly A situation where long-run average costs would be lower if an industry were under monopoly than if it were shared between two or more competitors.

Natural rate of unemployment The rate of unemployment at which there is no excess or deficiency of demand for labour.

Natural wastage When a firm wishing to reduce its workforce does so by not replacing those who leave or retire.

Near money Highly liquid assets (other than cash).

Negative income tax A combined system of tax and benefits. As people earn more, they gradually lose their benefits until beyond a certain level they begin paying taxes.

Net errors and omissions A statistical adjustment to ensure that the two sides of the balance of payments account balance. It is necessary because of errors in compiling the statistics.

Net investment Total investment minus depreciation.

Net national product (NNY) GNY minus depreciation.

New classical school The school of economists which believes that markets clear virtually instantaneously and that expectations are formed 'rationally'.

New Keynesians Economists who seek to explain the downward stickiness of real wages and the resulting persistence of unemployment.

Nominal national income National income measured at current prices.

Nominal values Money values measured at *current* prices.

Non-accelerating-inflation rate of unemployment (NAIRU) The rate of unemployment consistent with a constant rate of inflation. (In monetarist analysis, this is the same as the natural rate of unemployment: the rate of unemployment at which the vertical long-run Phillips curve cuts the horizontal axis.)

Non-collusive oligopoly Where oligopolists have no agreement between themselves, either formal, informal or tacit.

Non-excludability Where it is not possible to provide a good or service to one person without it thereby being available for others to enjoy.

Non-price competition Competition in terms of product promotion (advertising, packaging, etc.) or product development.

Non-rivalry Where the consumption of a good or service by one person will not prevent others from enjoying it.

Normal goods Goods whose demand increases as consumer incomes increase. They have a positive income elasticity of demand. Luxury goods will have a higher income elasticity of demand than more basic goods.

Normal profit The opportunity cost of being in business: the profit that could have been earned in the next best alternative business. It is counted as a cost of production.

Normal rate of return The rate of return (after taking risks into account) that could be earned elsewhere.

Normative statement A value judgement.

Numerical flexibility Where employers can change the size of their workforce as their labour requirements change.

Occupational immobility The lack of ability or willingness of people to move to other jobs irrespective of location.

Oligopoly A market structure where there are few enough firms to enable barriers to be erected against the entry of new firms.

Oligopsony A market with just a few buyers or employers.

Open economy One that trades with and has financial dealings with other countries.

Open-market operations The sale (or purchase) by the authorities of government securities in the open market in order to reduce (or increase) money supply or influence interest rates.

Opportunity cost Cost measured in terms of the best alternative forgone.

Optimal currency area The optimal size of a currency area is the one that maximises the benefits from having a single currency relative to the costs. If the area were increased or decreased in size, the costs would rise relative to the benefits.

Outsiders Those out of work or employed on a casual, part-time or short-term basis, who have little or no power to influence wages or employment.

Overheads Costs arising from the general running of an organisation, and only indirectly related to the level of output.

Participation rate The percentage of the working-age population that is part of the workforce.

Perfect competition A market structure where there are many firms; where there is freedom of entry into the industry; where all firms produce an identical product; and where all firms are price takers.

Perfectly contestable market A market where there is free and costless entry and exit.

Phillips curve A curve showing the relationship between (price) inflation and unemployment. The original Phillips curve plotted *wage* inflation against unemployment for the years 1861–1957.

Picketing When people on strike gather at the entrance to the firm and attempt to persuade workers or delivery vehicles from entering.

Plant economies of scale Economies of scale that arise because of the large size of the factory.

Poll tax A lump-sum tax per head of the population. Since it is a fixed *amount*, it has a marginal rate of zero with respect to both income and wealth.

Portfolio balance The balance of assets, according to their liquidity, that people choose to hold in their portfolios.

Positive statement A value-free statement that can be tested by an appeal to the facts.

Potential growth The percentage annual increase in the capacity of the economy to produce.

Potential output The output that could be produced in the economy if there were a full employment of resources (including labour).

Poverty trap Where poor people are discouraged from working or getting a better job because any extra income they earn will be largely taken away in taxes and lost benefits.

Predatory pricing Where a firm sets its prices below average cost in order to drive competitors out of business.

Preferential trading arrangements A trade agreement whereby trade between the signatories is freer than trade with the rest of the world.

Price benchmark A price that is typically used. Firms, when raising prices, will usually raise them from one benchmark to another.

Price discrimination Where a firm sells the same product at different prices in different markets or different parts of the market or to different customers.

Price elasticity of demand ($P\varepsilon_D$) The percentage (or proportionate) change in quantity demanded divided by the percentage (or proportionate) change in price: $\%\Delta Q_D \div \%\Delta P$.

Price elasticity of demand (arc formula) $\Delta Q/$average $Q \div \Delta P/$average P. The average in each case is the average between the two points being measured.

Price elasticity of supply The percentage (or proportionate) change in quantity supplied divided by the percentage (or proportionate) change in price: $\%\Delta Q_S \div \%\Delta P$.

Price elasticity of supply (arc formula) $\Delta Q_S/$average $Q_S \div \Delta P/$average P.

Price mechanism The system in a market economy whereby changes in price in response to changes in demand and supply have the effect of making demand equal to supply.

Price taker A person or firm with no power to be able to influence the market price.

Primary labour market The market for permanent full-time core workers.

Principal–agent problem Where people (principals), as a result of lack of knowledge, cannot ensure that their best interests are served by their agents.

Prisoners' dilemma Where two or more firms (or people), by attempting independently to choose the best strategy for whatever the other(s) are likely to do, end up in a worse position than if they had co-operated in the first place.

Private efficiency Where a person's marginal benefit from a given activity equals the marginal cost.

Private limited company A company owned by its shareholders. Shareholders' liability is limited to the value of their shares. Shares can only be bought and sold privately.

Product differentiation When one firm's product is sufficiently different from its rivals' to allow it to raise the price of the product without customers all switching to the rivals' products. A situation where a firm faces a downward-sloping demand curve.

Production The transformation of inputs into outputs by firms in order to earn profit (or meet some other objective).

Production possibility curve A curve showing all the possible combinations of two goods that a country can produce within a specified time period with all its resources fully and efficiently employed.

Productive efficiency A situation where firms are producing the maximum output for a given amount of inputs, or producing a given output at the least cost.

Productivity deal When, in return for a wage increase, a union agrees to changes in working practices that will increase output per worker.

Profit (rate of) Total profit ($T\Pi$) as a proportion of the total capital employed (K): $r = T\Pi/K$.

Profit-maximising rule Profit is maximised where marginal revenue equals marginal cost.

Progressive tax A tax whose average rate with respect to income rises as income rises.

Proportional tax A tax whose average rate with respect to income stays the same as income rises.

Public good A good or service that has the features of non-rivalry and non-excludability and as a result would not be provided by the free market.

Public limited company A company owned by its shareholders. Shareholders' liability is limited to the value of their shares. Shares may be bought and sold publicly – on the Stock Exchange.

Public-sector borrowing requirement The old name for the public-sector net cash requirement.

Public-sector debt repayment (PSDR) or **Public-sector surplus** The old name for a negative public-sector net cash requirement. The (annual) surplus of the public sector, and thus the amount of debt that can be repaid.

Public-sector net cash requirement The (annual) deficit of the public sector (central government, local government and public corporations), and thus the amount that the public sector must borrow.

Purchasing-power parity exchange rate The rate of exchange of a country's currency into the US dollar that would allow a given amount of that currency to buy the same amount of goods in the USA as within the country concerned.

Pure fiscal policy Fiscal policy that does not involve any change in money supply.

Quantity demanded The amount of a good a consumer is willing and able to buy at a given price over a given period of time.

Quantity theory of money The price level (P) is directly related to the quantity of money in the economy (M).

Quota (set by a cartel) The output that a given member of a cartel is allowed to produce (production quota) or sell (sales quota).

Rate of economic growth The percentage increase in output over a 12-month period.

Rate of inflation The percentage increase in the level of prices over a 12-month period.

Rate of profit Total profit ($T\Pi$) as a proportion of the capital employed (K): $r = T\Pi/K$.

Rational choices Choices that involve weighing up the benefit of any activity against its opportunity cost.

Rational consumer A person who weighs up the costs and benefits to him or her of each additional unit of a good purchased.

Rational consumer behaviour The attempt to maximise total consumer surplus.

Rational economic behaviour Doing more of activities whose marginal benefit exceeds their marginal cost and doing less of those activities whose marginal cost exceeds their marginal benefit.

Rational expectations Expectations based on the *current* situation. These expectations are based on the information people have to hand. Whilst this information may be imperfect and therefore people will make errors, these errors will be random.

Rational producer behaviour When a firm weighs up the costs and benefits of alternative courses of action and then seeks to maximise its net benefit.

Rationalisation The reorganising of production (often after a merger) so as to cut out waste and duplication and generally to reduce costs.

Rationing Where the government restricts the amount of a good that people are allowed to buy.

Real business cycle theory The new classical theory that explains cyclical fluctuations in terms of shifts in aggregate supply, rather than aggregate demand.

Real growth values Values of the rate of growth of GDP or any other variable after taking inflation into account. The real value of the growth in a variable equals its growth in money (or 'nominal') value minus the rate of inflation.

Real income Income measured in terms of how much it can buy. If your *money* income rises by 10 per cent, but prices rise by 8 per cent, you can only buy 2 per cent more goods than before. Your *real* income has risen by 2 per cent.

Real national income National income after allowing for inflation: i.e. national income measured in constant prices: i.e. in terms of the prices ruling in some base year.

Real values Money values corrected for inflation.

Real-wage unemployment Disequilibrium unemployment caused by real wages being driven up above the market-clearing level.

Recession A period where national output falls for six months or more.

Recognised banks Banks licensed by the Bank of England. All financial institutions using the word 'bank' in their title have to be recognised by the Bank of England. This requires them to have paid-up capital of at least £5 million and to meet other requirements about their asset structure and range of services.

Rediscounting bills of exchange Buying bills before they reach maturity.

Reflationary policy Fiscal or monetary policy designed to increase the rate of growth of aggregate demand.

Regional multiplier effects When a change in injections into or withdrawals from a particular region causes a multiplied change in income in that region.

Regional unemployment Structural unemployment occurring in specific regions of the country.

Regressive tax A tax whose average rate with respect to income falls as income rises.

Relative price The price of one good compared with another (e.g. good X is twice the price of good Y).

Repos Sale and repurchase agreements. An agreement between two financial institutions whereby one in effect borrows from another by selling it assets, agreeing to buy them back (repurchase them) at a fixed price and on a fixed date.

Restrictive practice Where two or more firms agree to adopt common practices to restrict competition.

Retail banks 'High street banks'. Banks operating extensive branch networks and dealing directly with the general public, with published interest rates and charges.

Retail deposits and loans Deposits and loans made through bank/building society branches at published interest rates.

Retail price index (RPI) An index of the prices of goods bought by a typical household.

Revaluation Where the government re-pegs the exchange rate at a higher level.

Reverse repos When gilts or other assets are *purchased* under a sale and repurchase agreement. They become an asset to the purchaser.

Risk When an outcome may or may not occur, but its probability of occurring is known.

Sale and repurchase agreement (repos) An agreement between two financial institutions whereby one in effect borrows from another by selling it assets, agreeing to buy them back (repurchase them) at a fixed price and on a fixed date.

Scarcity The excess of human wants over what can actually be produced to fulfil these wants.

Search theory This examines people's behaviour under conditions of ignorance where it takes time to search for information.

Seasonal unemployment Unemployment associated with industries or regions where the demand for labour is lower at certain times of the year.

Secondary action Industrial action taken against a company not directly involved in a dispute (e.g. a supplier of raw materials to a firm whose employees are on strike).

Secondary labour market The market for peripheral workers, usually employed on a temporary or part-time basis, or a less secure 'permanent' basis.

Self-fulfilling speculation The actions of speculators tend to cause the very effect that they had anticipated.

Set-aside A system in the EU of paying farmers not to use a certain proportion of their land.

Short run (in production) The period of time over which at least one factor is fixed.

Short-run shut-down point This is where the *AR* curve is tangential to the *AVC* curve. The firm can only just cover its variable costs. Any fall in revenue below this level will cause a profit-maximising firm to shut down immediately.

Short run under perfect competition The period during which there is too little time for new firms to enter the industry.

Sight deposits Deposits that can be withdrawn on demand without penalty.

Social benefit Private benefit plus externalities in consumption.

Social cost Private cost plus externalities in production.

Social efficiency Production and consumption at the point where marginal social benefit equals marginal social cost ($MSB = MSC$).

Special deposits A system used up to 1980. Deposits that the banks could be required to make in the Bank of England. They remained frozen there until the Bank of England chose to release them.

Specialisation and division of labour Where production is broken down into a number of simpler, more specialised tasks, thus allowing workers to acquire a high degree of efficiency.

Specific tax A tax on a good levied at a fixed amount per unit of the good, irrespective of the price of that unit.

Speculation Where people make buying or selling decisions based on their anticipations of future prices.

Speculators People who buy (or sell) commodities or financial assets with the intention of profiting by selling them (or buying them back) at a later date at a higher (lower) price.

Spot price The current market price.

Stabilising speculation Where the actions of speculators tend to reduce price fluctuations.

Stakeholders (in a company) People who are affected by a company's activities and/or performance (customers, employees, owners, creditors, people living in the neighbourhood, etc.). They may or may not be in a position to take decisions, or influence decision taking, in the firm.

Standardised unemployment rate The measure of the unemployment rate used by the ILO and OECD. The unemployed are defined as persons of working age who are without work, available to start work within two weeks and either have

actively looked for work in the last four weeks or are waiting to take up an appointment.

Structural unemployment Unemployment that arises from changes in the pattern of demand or supply in the economy. People made redundant in one part of the economy cannot immediately take up jobs in other parts (even though there are vacancies).

Substitute goods A pair of goods that are considered by consumers to be alternatives to each other. As the price of one goes up, the demand for the other rises.

Substitutes in supply These are two goods where an increased production of one means diverting resources away from producing the other.

Substitution effect of a price change The effect of a change in price on quantity demanded arising from the consumer switching to or from alternative (substitute) products.

Substitution effect of a rise in wage rates Workers will tend to substitute income for leisure as leisure now has a higher opportunity cost. This effect leads to *more* hours being worked as wage rates rise.

Substitution effect of a tax rise Tax increases reduce the opportunity cost of leisure and thus encourage people to work less.

Sunk costs Costs that cannot be recouped (e.g. by transferring assets to other uses).

Supernormal profit (also known as **pure profit**, **economic profit**, **abnormal profit**, or simply **profit**) The excess of total profit above normal profit.

Supply curve A graph showing the relationship between the price of a good and the quantity of the good supplied over a given period of time.

Supply schedule A table showing the different quantities of a good that producers are willing and able to supply at various prices over a given time period. A supply schedule can be for an individual producer or group of producers, or for all producers (the market supply schedule).

Supply-side economics An approach that focuses directly on aggregate supply and how to shift the aggregate supply curve outwards.

Supply-side policy Government policy that attempts to alter the level of aggregate supply directly (rather than through changes in aggregate demand).

Sustainability (environmental) The ability of the environment to survive its use for economic activity.

Sustainable output The level of national output corresponding to no excess or deficiency of aggregate demand.

Tacit collusion Where oligopolists take care not to engage in price cutting, excessive advertising or other forms of competition. There may be unwritten 'rules' of collusive behaviour such as price leadership.

Tariff escalation The system whereby tariff rates increase the closer a product is to the finished stage of production.

Tariffs (or import levies) Taxes on imported products: i.e. customs duties.

Tax allowance An amount of income that can be earned tax-free. Tax allowances vary according to a person's circumstances.

Taylor rule A rule adopted by a central bank for setting the rate of interest. It will raise the interest rate if (a) inflation is above target or (b) real national income is above the sustainable level (or unemployment is below the equilibrium rate). The rule states how much interest rates will be changed in each case.

Technological unemployment Structural unemployment that occurs as a result of the introduction of labour-saving technology.

Terms of trade The price index of exports divided by the price index of imports and then expressed as a percentage. This means that the terms of trade will be 100 in the base year.

Third-degree price discrimination When a firm divides consumers into different groups and charges a different price to consumers in different groups, but the same price to all the consumers within a group.

Time deposits Deposits that require notice of withdrawal or where a penalty is charged for withdrawals on demand.

Total consumer expenditure on a product (*TE*) (per period of time) The price of the product multiplied by the quantity purchased: $TE = P \times Q$.

Total consumer surplus The excess of a person's total utility from the consumption of a good (*TU*) over the amount that person spends on it (*TE*): $TCS = TU - TE$.

Total cost The sum of total fixed costs and total variable costs: $TC = TFC + TVC$.

Total physical product The total output of a product per period of time that is obtained from a given amount of inputs.

Total (private) surplus Total consumer surplus (*TU – TE*) plus total producer surplus (*TR – TVC*).

Total producer surplus (*TPS*) Total revenue minus total variable cost (*TR – TVC*): in other words, total profit plus total fixed cost (*TΠ + TFC*).

Total revenue (*TR*) (per period of time) The total amount received by firms from the sale of a product, before the deduction of taxes or any other costs. The price multiplied by the quantity sold: $TR = P \times Q$.

Total social surplus Total benefits to society from consuming a good minus total costs to society from producing it. In the absence of externalities, total social surplus is the same as total (private) surplus.

Total utility The total satisfaction a consumer gets from the consumption of all the units of a good consumed within a given time period.

Tradable permits Each firm is given a permit to produce a given level of pollution. If less than the permitted amount is produced, the firm is given a credit. This can then be sold to another firm, allowing it to exceed its original limit.

Trade creation Where a customs union leads to greater specialisation according to comparative advantage and thus a shift in production from higher-cost to lower-cost sources.

Trade cycle or business cycle The periodic fluctuations of national output round its long-term trend.

Trade diversion Where a customs union diverts consumption from goods produced at a lower cost outside the union to goods produced at a higher cost (but tariff free) within the union.

Traditional theory of the firm The analysis of pricing and output decisions of the firm under various market conditions, assuming that the firm wishes to maximise profit.

Transfer payments Moneys transferred from one person or group to another (e.g. from the government to individuals) without production taking place.

Treasury bills Bills of exchange issued by the Bank of England on behalf of the government. They are a means whereby the government raises short-term finance.

Uncertainty When an outcome may or may not occur and its probability of occurring is not known.

Underemployment Where people who want full-time work are only able to find part-time work.

Unemployment The number of people who are actively looking for work but are currently without a job. (Note that there is much debate as to who should officially be counted as unemployed.)

Unemployment rate The number unemployed expressed as a percentage of the labour force.

Unit elastic demand Where quantity demanded changes by the same percentage as price. Ignoring the negative sign, it will have a value equal to 1.

Universal benefits Benefits paid to everyone in a certain category irrespective of their income or assets.

Value added tax (VAT) A tax on goods and services, charged at each stage of production as a percentage of the value added at that stage.

Variable costs Total costs that vary with the amount of output produced.

Variable factor An input that can be increased in supply within a given time period.

Velocity of circulation The number of times annually that money on average is spent on goods and services that make up GDP.

Vent for surplus When international trade enables a country to exploit resources that would otherwise be unused.

Wage–price spiral Wages and prices chasing each other as the aggregate demand curve continually shifts to the right and the aggregate supply curve continually shifts upwards.

Weighted average The average of several items, where each item is ascribed a weight according to its importance. The weights must add up to 1.

Wholesale banks Banks specialising in large-scale deposits and loans and dealing mainly with companies.

Wholesale deposits and loans Large-scale deposits and loans made by and to firms at negotiated interest rates.

Wide monetary base (M0) Notes and coin outside the central bank plus banks' operational deposits with the central bank.

Withdrawals (W) (or leakages) Incomes of households or firms that are not passed on round the inner flow. Withdrawals equal net saving (S) plus net taxes (T) plus expenditure on imports (M): $W = S + T + M$.

Working to rule Workers do the bare minimum they have to, as set out in their job descriptions.

Index

Note: Page numbers in red indicate definitions.